PUBLIC PROCUREMENT AND AID EFFECTIVENESS

This edited collection fills a significant gap in the literature by gathering contributions from the most prominent academics and practioners of aid and procurement. It explores the economic, political and legal relationship between procurement and aid effectiveness in developing countries, and takes stock of current debates in the field. More specifically, the contributions analyse the failures and successes of current initiatives to foster effectiveness and streamline the aid procurement process, and address current themes emerging in the literature related to development, procurement and aid success.

A pivotal and timely publication, *Public Procurement and Aid Effectiveness* will be of interest to a varied and multicultural international audience and a wide range of actors working on aid effectiveness, development, procurement and good governance initiatives in both donor and beneficiary countries.

'Alice: Would you tell me, please, which way I ought to go from here?
The Cheshire Cat: That depends a good deal on where you want to get to.
Alice: I don't much care where.
The Cheshire Cat: Then it doesn't much matter which way you go.
Alice: … So long as I get somewhere.
The Cheshire Cat: Oh, you're sure to do that, if only you walk long enough.'

Lewis Carroll
Alice's Adventures in Wonderland

Public Procurement and Aid Effectiveness

A Roadmap under Construction

Edited by
Annamaria La Chimia
and
Peter Trepte

•HART•
OXFORD • LONDON • NEW YORK • NEW DELHI • SYDNEY

HART PUBLISHING

Bloomsbury Publishing Plc

Kemp House, Chawley Park, Cumnor Hill, Oxford, OX2 9PH, UK

HART PUBLISHING, the Hart/Stag logo, BLOOMSBURY and the Diana logo are trademarks of Bloomsbury Publishing Plc

First published in Great Britain 2019

A catalogue record for this book is available from the British Library.

A catalogue record for this book is available from the Library of Congress

ISBN: HB: 978-1-50992-243-7
ePDF: 978-1-50992-244-4
ePub: 978-1-50992-245-1

Typeset by Compuscript Ltd, Shannon
Printed and bound in Great Britain by CPI Group (UK) Ltd, Croydon CR0 4YY

MIX
Paper from responsible sources
FSC® C013604
www.fsc.org

To find out more about our authors and books visit www.hartpublishing.co.uk. Here you will find extracts, author information, details of forthcoming events and the option to sign up for our newsletters.

To our respective children

James & Daniel
Santí, Almaia & Kalisha

lest they start believing in fairy tales …

PREFACE

According to the Organisation for Economic Cooperation and Development (OECD), financial flows from developed to developing countries are defined as 'Official Development Assistance' (ODA) or, more commonly as aid, when they promote and specifically target 'the economic development and welfare of developing countries'.[1] In order to be classified as ODA, financial flows need also to be provided by official agencies (including State and local governments, or by their executive agencies) and need to be concessional in character, with a minimum grant element of 25 per cent. Private flows and other financial flows with an exclusive economic character or purpose, such as export credits, are excluded from this classification. This definition of ODA dates back to 1969 and, though outdated, it remains the only definition of development aid officially available; it will be the definition of development aid used in this book. The book does not, therefore, look at private flows, private and blended financing, although we recognise and acknowledge the growing importance of these types of financing in the development context,[2] especially since the endorsement of the Sustainable Development Goals and the recognition, through the Addis Ababa Agenda for Action, of the growing importance of mobilising, often through aid, private flows for development.[3] The OECD is currently working on a new definition of aid and blended finance which is giving rise to much debate within the development community.[4] An agreement, however, has not yet been reached.

The first use of aid resources is usually traced back to the Marshall Plan and the USA's efforts to help Europe after the Second World War in its post-war reconstruction efforts. Since then, aid programmes have been a permanent feature, generally maintaining the same official political expedient of eradicating poverty, but with changing geographical focus, depending on the political, economic or even historical motivations that really lie behind the reasons why aid is granted (eg during the 'Cold War', as a result of the 'War on Terror', with a view to enhancing trade relations, to former colonies etc). Donors tend be more or less vocal in disclosing these 'other' reasons for donating aid depending on the historical/political context. More recently, for example,

[1] OECD, 'What is ODA', April 2018, available at www.oecd.org/dac/stats/What-is-ODA.pdf.

[2] See also the references to the growing importance of non-aid financing recognised at the Busan High-Level Forum and discussed in ch 3.

[3] https://sustainabledevelopment.un.org/hlpf.

[4] For a definition of blended finance, see J Pereira, 'Blended Finance: What it is, how it works and how it is used', Research Report (Oxfam/Eurodad, February 2017), available at https://eurodad.org/files/pdf/58a1e294657ab.pdf. For the controversy surrounding the new definition of ODA, see JB Atwwo, R Manning and H Riegler, 'Don't undermine the basic architecture of OECD/DAC statistics: a letter of warning', 21 December 2018, available at www.brookings.edu/blog/future-development/2018/12/21/dont-undermine-the-basic-architecture-of-oecd-dac-statistics-a-letter-of-warning/.

Ms Priti Patel, at the time UK foreign secretary for international development, had no qualms in saying that aid is a soft power to be used tactically by Britain. Similarly, the US President, Donald J Trump, has openly said that aid will be given only to America's allies and that aid will be withdrawn from those who vote against American interests at the UN.

Against this background, talking about aid effectiveness becomes, at the very least, difficult if not hypocritical: the real causes of aid effectiveness and ineffectiveness have long ago been identified by many critics of aid donation such as Alesina and Dollar, Williamson, Easterly and many more.[5] Such causes can often be traced back to the very way in which aid is allocated and to the donors' political and economic rationales for granting aid which often result in the countries that need aid the most not receiving that aid.[6]

Aid is a very controversial instrument for development. Critics of development aid are quick to point out that, despite over a trillion US dollars having been disbursed as foreign aid over the past 60 years, poverty is far from being eradicated. Aid is accused of being costly and ineffective, when not useless and damaging for aid recipients. Yet, as it is often argued, many countries and many people would struggle without donors' aid and one cannot ignore the fact that aid has also done a lot of good. The criticism levelled against development aid has called into question the sustainability of aid projects as we have come to know them today. Nonetheless, aid is still and will continue to be granted, at least for the foreseeable future. Indeed, aid continues to be regarded as a key tool for the success of the newly agreed Sustainable Development Goals,[7] while donors will continue to allocate aid on the basis of various rationales that often compromise any chance the aid has to be successful. As explained in this book, a series of initiatives has taken place over the past two decades to improve the way aid is allocated, managed and spent, even if the results may be questionable.

From an international law perspective, aid is also regarded as one of the means through which the international community can fulfil its duty of cooperation and assistance towards countries in need, as recognised by various international legal instruments, for example, by the UN Charter (art 52 and 56), by the International Covenant on Economic, Social and Cultural Rights (art 2), by the Convention on the

[5] Cited in the various chapters of this book.

[6] D Dollar and V Levin, 'Sowing and Reaping: Institutional Quality and Project Outcomes in Developing Countries', World Bank Policy Research Working Paper 3524 (Washington DC, World Bank, 2005); L Dudley and C Montmarquette, 'A Model of the Supply of Bilateral Foreign Aid' (1976) 64 *American Economic Review* 132; CR Williamson, 'Exploring the Failure of Foreign Aid' (2010) 23 *Review of Austrian Economics* 17. Also S Andersson and PM Heywood, 'The Politics of Perception: Use and Abuse of Transparency International's Approach to Measuring Corruption' (2009) 57 *Political Studies* 746; C Kenny, *Results not Receipts: Counting the Right Things in Aid and Corruption* (Washington DC, Center for Global Development, 2017); D Moyo, *Dead Aid: Why Aid Is Not Working and How There Is a Better Way for Africa* (New York, Farrar, Straus and Giroux, 2009); W Easterly, *The White Man's Burden: Why the West's Efforts to Aid the Rest Have Done So Much Ill and So Little Good* (New York, Penguin Press, 2006). A large part of the literature on foreign aid shows that the neediest countries do not receive the most aid and that a large portion of foreign aid is wasted and only increases unproductive public consumption. The literature is divided on the development value and impact of aid; the harshest critics have called for the abolition of aid altogether. See also *The Economist*, 'Leaders: Missing the Point', 14 March 2002.

[7] Addis Ababa, 3rd Financing for Development Conference (2015). Referred to in the website at n 3.

rights of the Child etc. While the existence of a legal obligation to provide aid is still controversial,[8] an official recognition, albeit one that is not legally binding, of the role aid can play for development came, more recently, in Monterrey in 2002 at the International Conference on Financing for Development where donors have been exhorted to provide more and more effective aid to developing and least developed countries.

Addressing the problems linked to donors' aid has catalysed the attention of the international community for the past 15 years; and donors, aid recipients, international organisations and academics have focused attention on how to make aid more effective. Donors have acknowledged (at least in theory) the weaknesses of a system of aid governance that does not place aid recipients at the centre of the development discourse. Hence the quest, emphasised in recent years, to align donors' policies to recipient countries' national development strategies; to guarantee true partnership between donors and recipients when aid is disbursed; and to ensure ownership by the recipients of the aid donated.

In this book we use the metaphor of a journey to refer to the process started in Monterrey in 2002 at the International Conference of Financing for Development to make aid more effective. In Monterrey, the international community of donors, of recipient countries and of international organisations recognised that ODA plays an 'essential role as a complement to other sources of financing for development';[9] and agreed that more and more effective aid is needed by developing and Least Developed Countries. The emphasis on aid effectiveness was staunch, with recipient and donor countries (as well as international institutions) called upon to 'strive to make ODA more effective'[10].

Since Monterrey, many other initiatives dedicated to aid effectiveness have taken place, notably the four High-Level Fora on Aid effectiveness, in Rome (2003), Paris (2005), Accra (2008) and Busan (2011),[11] respectively which have paved the way for a recognition (at least as a matter of principle towards which the international community aspired) that 'business as usual' was no longer acceptable.[12]

From Monterrey to Busan, the actors involved in the aid effectiveness initiatives were driven by the common assumption that aid had to become more effective if poverty is to be eradicated. Crucially, and differently from previous initiatives, the aid effectiveness agenda, consolidated in Paris through the Paris Declaration on Aid Effectiveness, lays down key principles and measurable targets to steer donors' and recipients' actions, namely ownership, alignment, harmonisation, results and mutual accountability. As Riddell argues, these initiatives are the result of many years of debate over aid and how to improve aid effectiveness and none of these principles are new; but for the first time, the Paris Declaration importantly sets targets and clear indicators to monitor progress

[8] Even when that obligation is recognised its contours are so feeble and unclear as to make the existence of such obligation of little relevance in practical terms.

[9] UN, Monterrey Consensus of the International Conference on Financing for Development point 39, available at www.un.org/en/development/desa/population/migration/generalassembly/docs/globalcompact/A_CONF.198_11.pdf.

[10] ibid point 43. Those who call for an end to foreign aid include the famous D Moyo.

[11] Further information is available at www.oecd.org/dac/effectiveness/thehighlevelforaonaideffectivenessa-history.htm.

[12] RC Riddell, 'Does foreign aid really work? An updated assessment', Development Policy Centre Discussion Paper 33 (Crawford School of Public Policy, The Australian National University, Canberra, 2014).

towards the implementation and achievement of such principles and is, for this reason, often hailed as the most important stop in the aid effectiveness roadmap. Further, the Paris Declaration achieved wide consensus, with 138 countries – donors and recipients – 28 international organisations, numerous NGOs and civil society networks signing the declaration; and it is, up to now, seen as the most important of the aid effectiveness initiatives.[13]

The 2005 Paris Declaration on Aid Effectiveness (the Paris Declaration) not only recognises that aid 'could and should provide better impacts' but also lays down the first international plan of action (or 'roadmap') to ensure that development assistance is well-spent. The Paris Declaration also establishes the first ever monitoring system to assess progress towards the achievement of its targets and 'to ensure that donors and recipients hold each other accountable'. These principles were further expanded and strengthened in subsequent meetings resulting in the Accra Agenda for Action (AAA) in 2008 and the Busan Partnership Agreement for Effective Development Co-operation in 2011.

After Busan the aid effectiveness agenda has been pursued by the Global Partnership for Development. However, new actors are now involved, including the private sector and civil society, prompting commentators to question whether the Global Partnership for Development is to be distinguished from the previous aid effectiveness initiatives linked to the High-Level Fora and whether the new trajectory taken by the Global Partnership effectively signals the end of the aid effectiveness crusade.

Within the 'aid effectiveness' debate, great attention has been paid to the role that efficient and effective procurement systems, in both donor and beneficiary countries, could play in enhancing aid success. Given that an overwhelming proportion of aid is delivered through the public contracting process, improving the efficiency of the procurement process and strengthening the capacities of procurement agents has been seen as leading to greater value for the aid money and ultimately better use of aid resources. It is clear that procurement linked to development aid (ie development aid procurement) is at a critical juncture.

This book explores the links between procurement and aid effectiveness and it examines the various initiatives that have been undertaken by the international community to make aid more effective. In particular, it looks at how and why procurement and aid effectiveness have been interlinked, examining why improving the procurement practices linked to development aid has been regarded as crucial to aid effectiveness and what actions and initiatives have been put in place to this effect.

It does so first by tracing, in part I of the book, the history of the aid effectiveness agenda, explaining its broader economic and political context, together with an investigation of the links between procurement and aid effectiveness. The chapters that follow in parts II, III and IV will analyse in detail the issues that emerge out of the aid effectiveness agenda presented in the initial discussion in part I and that are the reasons that prompted us to work on this edited collection.

[13] N Gulrajani, 'Organising for Donor Effectiveness: An Analytical Framework for Improving Aid Effectiveness Policies' (2014) 32 *Development Policy Review* 89.

We believe the link between procurement and aid effectiveness is key to understanding what is happening with the aid effectiveness agenda. The nexus between procurement and aid effectiveness has been overlooked by the development community and needs to be rediscovered to understand where the aid effectiveness agenda is heading, if anywhere at all (is the agenda dead as some experts claim?). This book explores exactly that.

Development aid procurement has been subject to an intense reform process, which now involves both donors' and beneficiaries' practices and systems. After ten years of talks, agreements and negotiations between donors (bilateral and multilateral) and aid recipients in an attempt substantially to reform development aid procurement, little progress appears to have been made to build a comprehensive strategy and implement a framework for enhancing the efficiency of the procurement process when spending aid money. What is worse, after the initial enthusiasm for the initiatives undertaken under the umbrella of the Paris Declaration, academics and practitioners are paying little attention to the on-going reform process. The failure of some of the pioneering initiatives falling within this umbrella, such as the World Bank's piloting scheme for the use of country systems, has prompted a hasty retreat from the initial grandiose intentions and attracted little scrutiny by either academics or practitioners, of the programme for future reforms.

While the on-going international reform process for development aid procurement will shape the future success of development aid, little is known about the shape, form, governance and power imbalances that underpin it. Reforms tend to be piecemeal and respond to isolated problems. The absence of a broader academic debate has resulted in a limited framework and restricted parameters with which to address the problems raised analytically.

This is the gap in the literature that this volume seeks to fill. Going further than any current work on procurement and development aid, the book will use current debates on aid effectiveness and procurement to explore the economic, political and legal relationship between procurement and aid effectiveness. After analysing the failures and successes of current initiatives to foster the effectiveness and streamline the aid procurement process, it will address current themes emerging in the sparse literature related to development, procurement and aid success. The purpose of the volume is to provide a framework for future discussion and prompt some debate on where we have reached and where we need to go in achieving effectiveness in development aid procurement. Despite the fact that some important initiatives were set in motion in the aftermath of the adoption of the Paris Declaration, the road to effective aid procurement is paved with 'work under construction' signs. Alice's question to the Cheshire cat is curiously apposite to the effectiveness of development aid procurement. Which way ought we to go from here?

The book starts with three chapters providing an assessment of the international initiatives aimed at fostering effective public expenditure as a means of enhancing aid success and looks at both the economic, legal and political rationales which lie behind the aid effectiveness and procurement discourse. This first part of the book starts with a chapter by Marco Zupi, which looks at the issue of aid effectiveness more broadly from both an economic and a socio-political perspective, providing an account of the theories and methods used for assessing aid effectiveness, and an account of the economic rationale behind the aid effectiveness and procurement link, in chapter 2, by Oliver Morrissey. This first part will also provide, in chapter 3, an account of the link between procurement and aid effectiveness, explaining why procurement is relevant, where the problems lay, and what has led to the failure of some of the initiatives undertaken.

Chapter 3 returns to the issue of procurement in the international context and explains how improving both the recipients' procurement systems and the system linked to the spending of aid money have been top priorities in the aid effectiveness discourse. This chapter explains that, via the Paris, Accra and Busan initiatives, donors and beneficiaries have endorsed a series of commitments to foster beneficiaries' ownership of aid projects and ultimately improve the efficiency of the aid procurement process. In particular, donors have committed to provide aid as budget support and make use 'to the maximum extent possible' of beneficiary countries' systems when these are deemed 'adequate' as per mutually agreed standards. Other 'procurement-related' targets included an end to tying aid (ie aid provided on condition that goods and services for the financed project will be purchased from the donor country or a selected list of countries), simplifying donors' aid systems and procurement requirements, and coordinating their aid efforts by, for example, reducing the number of project implementation units external to the government services. For their part, beneficiaries have committed to fighting corruption and implementing procurement reforms to promote, amongst other things, efficiency-related objectives and the use of their systems by donors. The chapter also looks at the new Global Partnership for Effective Development Cooperation and draws a parallel between the aid effectiveness initiatives and the procurement-specific initiatives undertaken in the past 15 years. The chapter will show how and explains why 'aid effectiveness' is the common tread to all these initiatives.

The book then turns to the issues of harmonisation which has been a key question of the reform agenda. Laurence Folliot-Lalliot and Joshua Schwartz look respectively in chapters 4 and 5 at the issues of harmonisation and alignment in developing countries and at post-modern harmonisation of procurement rules. Folliot-Lalliot argues that despite efforts to harmonise the rules of the development partners and the increasing convergence of international norms (EU, UNCITRAL and GPA[14], for example), potential conflicts persist with more recent efforts to ensure that country context is taken into account in procurement reforms and the implication that there is no 'one-size-fits-all' solution to improving procurement outcomes at the developing country level. Schwartz instead considers harmonisation at an international level and looks at harmonisation as a way of addressing key problems identified in part I, namely fragmentation and lack of coordination. By harmonising donor rules, there is a chance to overcome fragmentation. By harmonising procurement systems (eg UNCITRAL, GPA, EU etc), it may be possible to identify a common goal which is measurable. Donor rules and systems have gradually been harmonised over the last two decades but this may be changing, especially in light of recent protectionist trends and the return to nationalism.

Some of the themes touched on in the first and second part are then further analysed in the third part of the book. Chapters 6-8 continue by providing an assessment of major

[14] The European Union, the United Nations Commission on International Trade Law and the Government Procurement Agreement of the World Trade Organization.

issues linked to development aid procurement such as tied aid, corruption and, a new entry, sustainable procurement. In chapter 6, La Chimia describes how the revival of protectionism is favouring a return to tied aid practices which risks overturning the successes of over ten years of progressive policies on aid untying. This return, La Chimia argues, has been facilitated by the lack of binding rules and commitments on the untying of aid. In chapter 7, Trepte deals with one of the most controversial issues in the aid effectiveness debate, namely corruption. Trepte challenges common approaches to procurement and corruption and explains why the anti-corruption efforts might have failed, suggesting that fighting corruption is not the 'be all and end all' of ensuring effective procurement. In chapter 8, Roberto Caranta and Carol Carvero consider the course of development objectives from the original economic goals to the newer UN's millennium development goals (MDGs) and sustainable development goals (SDGs) and show how these are and can be applied in procurement through the application of environmental and social policies (development, labour, human rights, SMEs etc). Is this how aid effectiveness is now to be measured? The chapter also provides a brief history of how sustainable procurement has developed over the years and will provide an account of the role it can play in a development context.

The fourth part of the book is dedicated to initiatives aimed at strengthening recipients' procurement systems. Chapter 9 by Diesing and Magina describes the history of the evolution of the Methodology for Assessing Procurement Systems (MAPS), describing how the process has evolved from the Baseline Indicator System through MAPS to MAPS II and how the conceptual framework, aims and objectives of the methodology have changed over the years. Rightly or wrongly, MAPS was used as a diagnostic and benchmark tool to assess national procurement systems in an effort to strengthen and to increase the use of country systems. However, as this chapter explains, MAPS was never conceptualised as a fiduciary tool or a compliance tool to facilitate use of country systems policy. Instead, the main driver behind the creation of the MAPS was to develop a diagnostic tool to support country reforms. This chapter, after retracing the origins of the tool, and explaining how it was subsequently used, provides an account of the revision that this tool is currently undergoing and the opportunities it offers to strengthen procurement systems. Chapter 10 by La Chimia and Williams-Elegbe on the use of country systems discusses how alignment of national systems, based on a shared understanding of procurement, was supposed to lead to reliance on national systems rather than donors' systems, thus eliminating fragmentation, improving coordination, enhancing ownership and building capacity. However, the degree of donors' reliance on recipients' country systems has been disappointing and the first experiment was unsuccessful. This chapter then focuses on the World Bank's new initiative in this area, namely the use of Alternative Procurement Arrangements. This part is concluded in chapter 11 by an account by Meyer on the MCC's Maturity Model, piloted in Indonesia, and how this novel model has been used to strengthen recipient countries' systems.

The fifth part of the book continues by examining donors' approaches to aid procurement and by evaluating the most recent initiatives to reform the procurement system of the MDBs as key drivers of reforms at present including but not limited to the World Bank (chapter 12 by Yukins and Williams-Elegbe) and other development Banks (chapter 13 by Trepte), and some major bilateral donors, such as USAID (chapter 14 by Jin and Wietecha).

The book's concluding section contains a chapter by Gutman on new developments and perspectives on procurement reforms, looking at outcomes as the only viable way to improve effectiveness through a holistic approach to procurement. Finally, there is a concluding chapter by the editors, reviewing various mooted approaches to procurement reform and offering some reflections on whether and how aid systems have changed almost 15 years since the Paris Declaration, whether aid effectiveness has been fostered as a result of these initiatives and whether the system of aid procurement (in both donor and recipient countries) has changed in any substantial way.

This book is the result of our own journey into the world of public procurement and aid effectiveness. Having jointly taught a module on public procurement and development at our University's Executive LLM in Public Procurement Law and Policy for a number of years, we have long been of the opinion that insufficient attention has been placed on this particular area of study and that, despite some isolated books, papers and articles which consider the issues either tangentially or for very specific and often self-serving purposes, there has been no attempt to look at the questions raised by this interaction of public procurement and development in any systematic way. We have long believed that what was needed was a framework for academic discussion which would enable serious thought to be given to both academic and practical topics in this area in a meaningful way so that, rather than coming across discrete pieces of the jigsaw by chance in disparate places, there could be a semblance of a bigger picture where there might be a chance of seeing where those pieces of the jigsaw would fit.

This idea took shape during discussions with our students and with speakers who were (deliberately) invited to speak on these issues at the series of 'Public Procurement: Global Revolution' conferences held bi-annually by the University's Public Procurement Research Group in Nottingham. These speakers, both academics and practitioners, are among the most prominent experts on 'aid and procurement' and we extend our immense thanks to those of them that kindly agreed to contribute to this edited collection as a means of realising that idea and thus providing us with a framework for future debate and discussion on this important area of public procurement. We would also like to extend our thanks to our two very able editorial assistants, Dr Serban Filipon and Ashraf-Ul-Bari Nobel, whose help during the home stretch was invaluable. We thank also our respective partners for their forbearance.

Annamaria La Chimia & Peter Trepte
Public Procurement Research Group
University of Nottingham

TABLE OF CONTENTS

PART IV
STRENGTHENING DEVELOPING COUNTRIES' SYSTEMS: TURNING THE TIDE?

PART V
THE PATH OF DONORS' REFORMS

PART VI
THE ROAD AHEAD

LIST OF CONTRIBUTORS

Roberto Caranta is a full Professor with the Law Department of the University of Turin (Italy).

Carol Cravero is a PhD student at the University of Turin and the University of Paris Nanterre.

Lena Diesing is Policy Analyst for Public Procurement at the OECD Directorate for Public Governance.

Laurence Folliot Lalliot is Professor of Public Law at the University of Paris Nanterre, where she is the Director of the Centre of Research on Public Law and Co-Director of the Masters Degree in Law and Economics.

Jeffrey Gutman is a non-resident Senior Fellow in the Global Economy and Development program of the Brookings Institution.

S Jun Jin is the Assistant General Counsel for Acquisition and Assistance in the USAID Office of the General Counsel.

Annamaria La Chimia is Professor of Law and Development, School of Law University of Nottingham and Research Fellow, African Procurement Law Unit, Department of Mercantile Law, Stellenbosch University.

Paolo Magina is Director at Public Procurement Unit in the Public Sector Integrity Division, Directorate for Public Governance, Organisation for Economic Co-operation and Development (OECD).

Jeanmarie Meyer is Senior Director and Project Lead for the Procurement Modernization Project, Millennium Challenge Corporation.

Oliver Morrissey is a Professor at the School of Economics and Director of the Centre for Research in Economic Development and International Trade (CREDIT), University of Nottingham.

Joshua Schwartz is the E.K. Gubin Professor of Government Contracts Law at the George Washington University Law School.

Peter Trepte is a barrister and Senior Research Fellow, School of Law, University of Nottingham.

Ronald O Wietecha is a Resident Legal Officer for USAID currently serving in the West Africa Mission in Accra, Ghana

Sope Williams-Elegbe is Professor and head of the Department of Mercantile Law and the Deputy Director of the African Procurement Law Unit, Stellenbosch University, South Africa.

Christopher Yukins is the Lynn David Research Professor in Government Procurement Law at the George Washington University Law School, in Washington, DC. He regularly works and lectures on issues in procurement and development, in countries around the world.

Marco Zupi is Scientific Director of Centro studi di politica internazionale and Professor of Development Studies at Bac Ha International University.

PART I

The Roadmap

1

The Political Economy of Aid: Foreign Aid Effectiveness, Theories, Methods and the Challenges that Lie Ahead

MARCO ZUPI

I. The Ambiguous Nature of Foreign Aid

Seventy years ago, the US President Harry Truman's inauguration speech on 20 January 1949 marked the beginning of a new 'developmental' era.[1] The previous colonial period, characterised by the asymmetrical relations between the European mainland (the colonisers) and the colonised countries, was replaced by a new asymmetrical relationship between the rich OECD donors and the poor developing countries in the South of the world. The poor countries became the recipients of foreign aid, technically defined as Official Development Assistance (ODA) that consisted of grants, soft loans and technical assistance.[2]

The main objective of foreign aid was to assist poor nations in their development and fight against mass poverty, so as to approach the status of rich countries.

At the same time, foreign aid was part of a wider approach to foreign policy oriented to forge new alliances in the international chess match, based on the prevailing goal of national security in a period dominated by bi-polarism, through defence alliances such as NATO and the Warsaw Pact.

In practice, the world quickly discovered a gap between the rhetoric around the fight against poverty through foreign aid and the reality of the security priority during the Cold War. For the USA and the Western bloc, the war on poverty in developing countries had to be fought in order to limit the Soviet influence; the Eastern bloc tried

[1] G Rist, *The History of Development: From Western Origins to Global Faith*, 4th edn (London, Zed Books, 2014) trans P Camiller. In French as *Le développement. Histoire d'une croyance occidentale*, 2nd edn (Presses de Sciences Po, Paris, 1996, 2001).

[2] See www.oecd.org/dac/effectiveness/aideffectivenessglossary.htm.

to offer financial and military support to poor countries so that they would choose the Communist road to progress.

Thus, even though it is held that the term foreign aid is applicable if the capital transfer is for developmental and not military purposes, foreign aid has rarely been just based on disinterested motivations. Foreign aid has always been linked, to a considerable extent, to the national political interests of the donors: firstly security, peace and trade, including the goal to secure energy and resources supply.

II. The Proliferation of Goals

Even assuming that foreign aid was just driven by the altruistic ideals of solidarity to assist the poor and promote development, the conceptualisation of development after the Second World War paved the way for a patchwork of different aims, approaches and instruments rather than a coherent plan of financial and budgetary provisions for operational practice.

In practical terms, the juxtaposition of different priorities and financial instruments has caused the interaction of competing, confused and contradictory focuses and actions.

Sketchily summarising some of the main strands of development theory and aid policies that emerged in the past decades, the main rationale of foreign aid in the 1950s and 1960s was to provide the necessary capital resource transfer to allow poor countries to achieve a high enough savings rate to propel them into growth, with just an indirect attention to development issues (trickle-down).[3] Thereafter, gradually a greater focus went to investing in human capital and raising the standard of living of the poor through increased employment opportunities. In the 1970s, a greater foreign aid focus on poverty meant more emphasis on direct interventions to benefit the poor – projects in agriculture, rural development and social services including housing, education and health – as instruments directly targeted to promote people's development in general and in its multidimensional nature.[4] In the late 1970s and early 1980s the situation changed dramatically and the global ascendancy of the 'Washington Consensus' dominated aid policy during the 1980s and the first half of the 1990s.[5] The term denoted a neo-liberal macroeconomic manifesto, summed up by the three keywords of liberalisation, deregulation and privatisation and by the so-called market-friendly approach to development.[6] In the context of the new pro-market and anti-state rhetoric, foreign aid went back to represent – as in the early 1950s and 1960s – a basic inflow to fill financial gaps (and allow poor countries to service their external debt), but also to support the

[3] M Akinci, 'Inequality and Economic Growth: Trickle-down Effect Revisited' (2018) 36:S1 *Development Policy Review* O1.

[4] E Thorbecke, 'The Evolution of the Development Doctrine and the Role of Foreign Aid, 1950–2000' in F Tarp (ed), *Foreign Aid and Development. Lessons Learnt and Directions for the Future* (London, Routledge, 2000) 17–47.

[5] H-J Chang, *Globalisation, Economic Development and the Role of the State* (London, Zed Books, 2003).

[6] J Williamson, 'What Washington Means by Policy Reform' in J Williamson (ed), *Latin American Adjustment: How much has Happened?* (Washington DC, Institute for International Economics, 1989) 7–20.

implementation of structural transformation and adjustment of the economies through conditionalities, with an increased recourse to the private sector and NGOs in an effort to privatise aid.[7]

At the turn of the Millennium, the international political consensus on the development agenda led to the signature of the eight UN Millennium Development Goals (with 18 targets and 48 indicators that later became 60), strictly focused on social dimensions to address the dramatic situation of poverty.[8]

Subsequently, in 2015 a new consensus landed in a new pact, with a more complex and ambitious system of 17 goals, 169 targets and 232 indicators, the UN Sustainable Development Goals (SDGs) meant to address the three pillars of development (social, economic and environmental) and eradicate poverty.[9]

Thus, through the past decades the inspiring vision of economic development and capital accumulation has never changed, though only partial progress has been made with the global development agenda: poverty has not been eradicated and indeed, income inequality has increased between as well as within North and South, and environmental degradation and ecological imbalance has worsened. Above all, some additional and heterogeneous dimensions of capital have been included in the process of capital accumulation in order to better conceptualise the process of economic development. This vision has been used to prove the necessity of foreign aid for poor countries. Figure 1 provides a graphical representation of this vision. Capital accumulation has been considered the key to prosperity, and this comes about through industrialisation, based on a combination of increased savings (domestic and international savings, through foreign aid, external debt, foreign direct investment (FDI) and workers' remittances) to be transformed into productive investment. Growth – conceived as the main development engine and based on a financial injection to support productive investments in physical and infrastructure capital[10] – was additionally helped by investment (through financial support) in the following:

- Human capital (education, health, research and development as a way to increase skills, improve labour productivity and induce technological innovations).
- Social capital (institutions, social norms of trust and reciprocity among different actors, formal and informal relational goods, which can create a favourable environment to make investment more productive and efficient through direct support to the private sector and NGOs).
- Knowledge capital (in particular information and communication technology and the need to become – as mentioned in the EU Lisbon strategy adopted in 2000 by the European Council – a dynamic and competitive knowledge-based economy).[11]

[7] Thorbecke, 'The Evolution of the Development Doctrine and the Role of Foreign Aid, 1950–2000' (n 4).

[8] M Fehling, DN Brett and S Venkatapuram, 'Limitations of the Millennium Development Goals: a Literature Review' (2013) 8 *Global Public Health* 1109.

[9] UN, *The Sustainable Development Goals Report 2017* (New York, UN, 2017).

[10] W Yu, 'Human Capital, Social Capital and Economic Growth' (2015) 2 *Athens Journal of Social Sciences* 161.

[11] European Commission, *Facing the Challenge. The Lisbon Strategy for Growth and Employment. Report from the High Level Group Chaired by Wim Kok* (Luxembourg, Office for Official Publications of the European Communities, 2004).

- Institutional capital (taking for granted that institutions do matter a lot, the purpose is to promote the democratisation process, the rule of law, fight against corruption, decentralisation of political power and administration, high quality and managerial skills of organisations and public administration, capacity- and institution-building).
- Natural capital (assuming environment as a cross-cutting dimension or a mainstream in the development process, which can be adequately assessed only in the inter-generational perspective of the so-called sustainable development, as described in the UN Commission Report on sustainable development chaired by Gro Harlem Brundtland in 1987, during the Rio Summit in 1992 and the Rio+20 in 2012 and, finally, in the SDGs).

Figure 1 The Role of ODA in the Process of Capital Accumulation

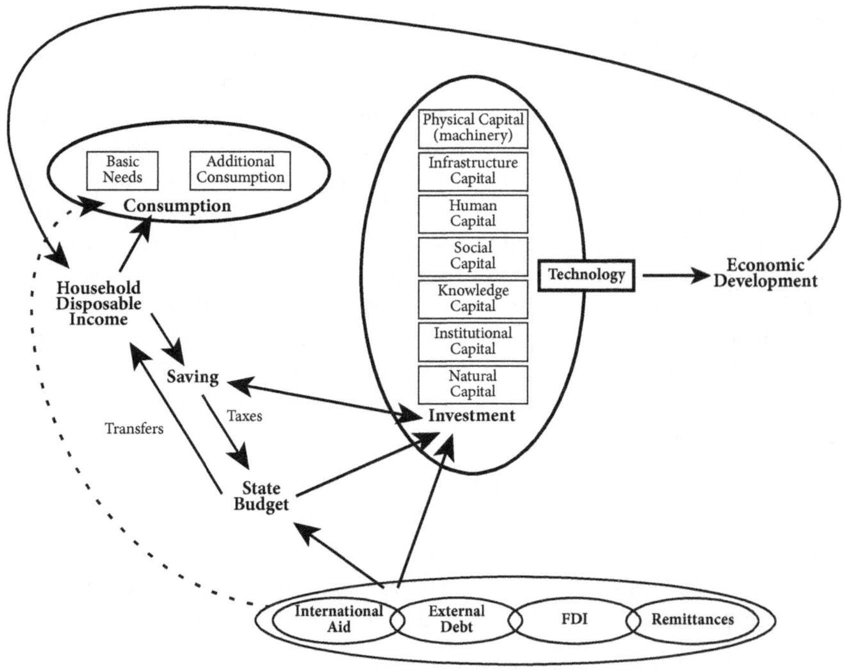

III. The Process of Conditionality Accumulation

During the last 70 years, foreign aid has been funding infrastructure projects, social expenditures (particularly basic health and education), training activities (with technical assistance), private sector development, good governance and sustainable development projects. At the same time, there has been evolution for each of these components. In particular, increasing attention was paid to good governance so as to prevent an ineffective waste of money through aid and its negative impact on the local political context; however the elusive nature of this concept led to different interpretations amongst the actors involved in aid community. According to the UN discourse good governance means participation, ensuring the rule of law, democracy, transparency and capacity in public administration, by making governmental institutions, private sectors and civil society organisations accountable to the public and institutional stakeholders.[12] According to a more restricted and technical view adopted by the World Bank, good governance is to be intended as the capacity of governments to formulate policies and have them effectively implemented and has to be translated into an effective public sector management of national resources. Since the 1980s, the World Bank has adopted a new framework to govern lending and debt relief programmes, by emphasising the need to make public sector management more effective in terms of budgeting, prioritisation, delivery, monitoring and strengthening of the civil service capacity. Translated into practical terms, good governance appeared just as a processing task, with public procurement policies, procedures and processes confined to the application of rules for government purchase of goods, services and works.[13] This view was in conflict with the stated commitment to transparency and participation and induced a reconsideration of procurement as a critical management activity to support accountability and participation, with a more political relevance. In other terms, good governance is linked to the democratic process, and means the capacity of states to factor the common interest into 'inclusive' policies. Clearly, this approach based on multiple and evolving components has represented a flexible and indirect pro-poor strategy based on a trickle-down effect, rather than a policy directly focused on addressing just some specific needs identified by a narrow focus on poverty.

No specific instrument or purpose of foreign aid was completely substituted by new instruments and aims. Rather, a proliferation of objectives emerged as a structural characteristic of foreign aid together with a lot of different instruments and different approaches (sometimes representing different visions of development). Project aid and programme aid, commodity aid and balance of payments support, technical assistance, NGOs' activities, sector programme and sector-wide approach, budget aid and decentralised co-operation coexist with difficulties and problems of coherence, because they can represent different visions and they are not simple instruments.

This cumulative approach to foreign aid as a sum of different, often rival but never contradictory dimensions of capital to be funded internationally in order to create a favourable context to address the needs of the poor, is confirmed by looking at the evolution of conditionality, a specific aid 'instrument' designed to improve the effectiveness and impact of aid.

Due to the fact that a grant given for one purpose can end up financing something else because, in the absence of foreign aid, the government itself financed the project (the so-called aid fungibility),[14] donors – both governments and international financial institutions – have tried to induce recipient/partner countries to adopt some specific measures through the so-called conditionality.

As concerns this instrument there has been a cumulative approach as well.

[12] UNESCAP, 'What is Good Governance?' (2009) (mimeo), available at www.unescap.org/resources/what-good-governance. See also www.un.org/ruleoflaw.

[13] African Development Bank, 'Governance in Public Procurement. Comprehensive Review of AFDB's Procurement Policy and Procedures. Summary of Literature on Governance in Public Procurement' (Abidjan, African Development Bank, 2014).

[14] S Leiderer, 'Fungibility and the Choice of Aid Modalities: The Red Herring Revisited', Working Paper No 2012/68 (Helsinki, UNU-WIDER, 2012).

Table 1 Five Generations of Conditionalities

Why *(Focus)*	**When** *(Start up)*	**Why** *(Goal)*
Macroeconomic policy reforms (*First generation*)	1980s	Growth
Favourable political and governance context (*Second generation*)	1990s	Democracy
National Poverty Reduction Strategies (*Third generation*)	2000s	Poverty Reduction
War on terrorism (*Fourth generation*)		Global Security
Migration management (*Fifth generation*)	2010s	Human Rights & National Security

In the 1980s, after (and thanks to the opportunity offered by) the outbreak of the external debt crisis, the IMF and the World Bank, in accordance with the main Western donor countries, introduced the first generation of conditionality. These rules/guidelines urged the recipient governments to adopt market-friendly structural reforms and integration into the world economy as the best way to promote growth.

In the 1990s, after the collapse of the Soviet bloc, the community of international donors introduced a second generation of conditionality. The idea was that a favourable environment for making development effective is a mixture of sound macroeconomic policies and complementary political and institutional reforms in terms of good governance (in the more limited sense of better public sector management and accountability), rule of law, consolidation of democracy and respect for human rights. This occurred in the case of the EU during the renewal process of the Cotonou Agreement with the African, Caribbean and Pacific Group of States (ACP), with the inclusion of the political conditionality on good governance as a key component of the agreement.[15]

In the new Millennium, after the implementation of the enhanced heavily indebted poor countries initiative[16] to reduce external debt, and in accordance with Western donor countries, the IMF and the World Bank introduced a third generation of conditionality. For the first time the so-called Poverty Reduction Strategies (PRS) introduced a direct poor-oriented conditionality focused on health, education, and water and food security, which represents the new framework to govern the lending, foreign aid and debt relief programmes as social policies in pro-poor terms.[17]

[15] S Koch, 'A Typology of Political Conditionality Beyond Aid: Conceptual Horizons Based on Lessons from the European Union' (2015) 75 *World Development*, 97.

[16] Due to rising evidence that the development prospects of many of the SSA countries suffered from unsustainable debt, the member governments of the International Monetary Fund and the World Bank agreed in the autumn of 1996 the initiative for 'Heavily Indebted Poor Countries' (HIPC). In November 1999, the Paris Club creditor countries decided, after of the G-7 Cologne Summit, to raise the level of cancellation for the poorest countries if necessary in the framework of the HIPC initiative and the initiative became the Enhanced HIPC.

[17] J Gould, *The New Conditionality: The Politics of Poverty Reduction Strategies* (London, Zed Books, 2005).

At the beginning of the 2000s the new rationale for foreign aid emerged as the result of a number of consequences of globalisation and its cross-border and global externalities. There are a lot of spill-overs from the lack of development in poor countries on the well-being of donor countries, and these spill-overs (terrorism, crime, wars and refugees, migrations, environmental problems, diseases) have become important elements for redefining the rationale for foreign aid in recent years. After the attacks of 11 September 2001 and the emerging new security priorities on the international agenda set up by the US-led coalition for the war on terrorism, foreign aid has redefined its role and mandate. This process seemed to open up new opportunities for foreign aid to conquer new and stronger political commitment, since for the first time after the collapse of the Soviet bloc a new strong rationale (again security/strategic, as during the Cold War) could impose its interests and priorities. First, there was an increased international focus on post-conflict situations and the so-called 'complex emergencies', translated into higher percentages of financial flows to fund short-term emergency interventions rather than long-term development ones. Then, a border contamination of foreign aid actions with military conflict-prevention, peace-keeping and peace-enforcing initiatives occurred, the so-called securitisation of foreign aid, with uncertain implications in terms of international law (starting from the idea of restoring State legitimacy through military intervention).[18] The war on terrorism has also boosted directly foreign aid flows. Between 2001 and 2003, net foreign aid to Afghanistan from all sources rose from USD 0.4 billion to USD 1.5 billion and aid to Iraq increased from USD 0.1 billion to USD 2.3 billion. Foreign aid to Pakistan has remained between USD 2 billion and USD 3 billion in gross terms in each of the three years.

Finally, a fifth generation of conditionality has emerged in recent years. It is related to the issue of regulation and management of the flows of migrant and asylum seekers, and it is at the heart of the political agenda of many OECD countries, in particular the EU.[19] Differently from the goals of the previous conditionalities, the complex inter-linkages between migration and the development nexus implies a combination of different objectives (economic, social, political, legal, humanitarian, security-related as well as individual, national, regional and global ones). This further complicates the scenario because of the inherent tension and trade-offs between different and not necessarily convergent interests embedded in the same general goal. According to the OECD, in 2016 10.8 per cent of the total net ODA went to hosting refugees inside donor countries and to dealing with the impact of the refugee crisis, up from 9.2 per cent in 2015 and

[18] K Aning, 'Security, the War on Terror, and Official Development Assistance' (2010) 3 *Critical Studies on Terrorism* 7.

[19] European Union Global Strategy, *Shared Vision, Common Action: A Stronger Europe. A Global Strategy for the European Union's Foreign And Security Policy* (European Union, June 2016) available at europa.eu/globalstrategy/en/shared-vision-common-action-stronger-europe; European Commission, *Communication from the Commission to the European Parliament, the European Council, the Council and the European Investment Bank on Establishing a New Partnership Framework with Third Countries under the European Agenda on Migration* (Strasbourg, 7 June 2016, COM [2016] 385 final); European Commission, *Report from the Commission to the European Parliament, The European Council and the Council: Fourth Progress Report on the Partnership Framework with third countries under the European Agenda on Migration* (Strasbourg, 13.6.2016 COM [2017] 350 final); European Commission, *The New European Consensus on Development 'Our World, Our Dignity, Our Future': Joint Statement by the Council and the Representatives of the Governments of the Member States Meeting within the Council, the European Parliament and the European Commission* (Brussels, 2017) available at ec.europa.eu/europeaid/policies/european-development-policy/european-consensus-development_en.

4.8 per cent in 2014.[20] This distortion is criticised by many NGOs, among others, because the importance of 'Development benefits of migration and addressing root causes of irregular migration and forced displacement', 'Legal migration and mobility' and 'Protection and asylum' is marginalised compared to 'Prevention of and fight against irregular migration, migrant smuggling and trafficking in human beings' and 'Return, readmission and reintegration'.[21]

In general, the idea of combining various conditionalities is to induce recipient governments to commit themselves seriously to these objectives in a comprehensive way and to make foreign aid a more flexible tool available for foreign policy priorities. Obviously, this implies higher goals and broadens scope for foreign aid (which means a diluted focus, since the last conditionality is not substituting the previous ones), with an increasing risk of competing and contradictory objectives and over-proliferation of instruments with limited resources.

IV. More of the Same without a Proportionate Increase of Resources

Looking back on the past 60 years, it is obvious that 'business-as-usual' is no longer an option for aid policies.

Aid policy has had as its primary objective the reduction and, in the long term, the eradication of poverty. At the same time, however, the new SDGs agenda proposes an over-proliferation of sectoral and separate objectives in social, economic, political and environmental dimensions, without emphasising their intertwined nature and mutual linkages.

With specific reference to aid policies the attempt to adopt a wider agenda, not strictly focused on the social dimension of poverty as in the past, combines with emergency pressures from the donor countries. Today the scale and complexity of the refugee crisis affecting Europe is making migration a key challenge for foreign aid policies.

Multiple instruments, approaches and conditionalities thus continue to suffer from insufficient coherence, because they can represent different visions and they are not simple components of a shared vision.

Moreover, the rationale of foreign aid is that it should support national strategies, to guarantee ownership of development processes. Therefore, the balance between the (long- or short-term) priorities of donor and recipient countries should tend to favour the latter.

The key point is that a country's macroeconomic, structural and social policies must be consistent with the objectives of poverty reduction and social development, as well as those of environmental sustainability (in the context of the '2030 Agenda for Sustainable Development'[22]). As clearly stated in the aid effectiveness agenda (especially

[20] OECD, *Development Co-operation Report 2017: Data for Development* (Paris, OECD Publishing, 2017).

[21] These terms are a quotation of the five pillars of the Joint Valletta Action Plan of the Valletta Summit on migration of November 2015. See Concord Italia, *Partenariato o condizionalità dell'aiuto?* (Rome, November 2017) available at www.concorditalia.org/blog/2017/11/23/partenariato-o-condizionalita-dellaiuto-nuovo-rapporto-sul-fondo-fiduciario-dellunione-europea-di-emergenza-per-lafrica/.

[22] In 2015, 193 countries of the UN General Assembly adopted the 2030 Agenda for Sustainable Development and its 17 Sustainable Development Goals, which were developed to succeed the Millennium Development Goals (MDGs) which ended in 2015. See UN General Assembly, 'Transforming our world: the 2030 Agenda

in the 2005 Paris Declaration) developing countries must exercise effective leadership over their development policies, whereas donors are responsible for supporting and enabling developing countries' ownership by respecting their policies and helping strengthen their capacity to implement them.

Within this framework, aid and correlated public procurement effectiveness are not just technical matters related to procedures but are elements hampering aid effectiveness.

Jan Tinbergen, a Dutch economist and 1969 Nobel laureate, argued that a separate (and effective) policy instrument is needed in order to achieve each individual economic objective without having to face undesirable side effects. Two goals cannot be achieved effectively with the same policy instrument.[23] When applied to the field of foreign aid, the Tinbergen rule suggests that a separate instrument is needed for each particular objective if one wants to pursue successfully a variety of different goals. Not only does ODA violate the famous Tinbergen rule of economic policy and risks being ineffective – since foreign aid is guided by many different self-interested and moral motivations, which benefit recipient and/or donor countries, and are only partially and indirectly related to poverty reduction – but ODA is also severely affected by financial constraints. This is a paradox: at a time of still increasing objectives and instruments (and conditionalities), and despite the fact that since 1969, through the Report of the UN Commission on International Development, the international community of donors committed itself to reaching flows of foreign aid net disbursements equal to 0.7 per cent of their Gross national product (GNP) now Gross National Income (GNI), within ten years,[24] on average donors have never been on target for this objective. In 2016, total foreign aid – combining bilateral and multilateral aid – averaged 0.32 per cent of GNI and amounted to USD 172 billion, constant prices.[25]

Graph 1 Official Development Assistance over the past 57 Years (USD billion)

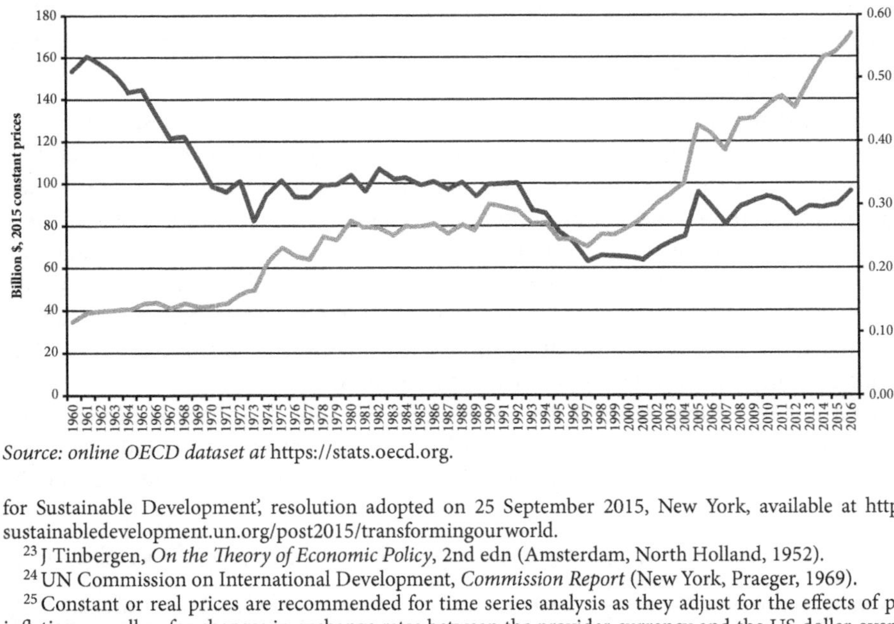

Source: online OECD dataset at https://stats.oecd.org.

for Sustainable Development', resolution adopted on 25 September 2015, New York, available at https://sustainabledevelopment.un.org/post2015/transformingourworld.

[23] J Tinbergen, *On the Theory of Economic Policy*, 2nd edn (Amsterdam, North Holland, 1952).

[24] UN Commission on International Development, *Commission Report* (New York, Praeger, 1969).

[25] Constant or real prices are recommended for time series analysis as they adjust for the effects of price inflation as well as for changes in exchange rates between the provider currency and the US dollar over the same period to get the so-called deflated amounts.

Graph 1 shows that, despite the reiterated commitment to provide 0.7 per cent of GNI in foreign aid to developing countries, including the SDGs Agenda, there has been no return of foreign aid as percentage of GNI to the levels prior to the fall of the Berlin Wall.

Whilst it is true that rich economies have not taken concrete steps towards scaling up their foreign aid contributions in terms of relative efforts (ie ODA/GNI), it must be emphasised that foreign aid flows have been increasing steadily in absolute terms.

Even though the increase of the total amount of financial resources is not proportional to the proliferation of foreign aid goals, conditionalities and instruments, the thorny question of aid effectiveness is unescapable. Whether one considers foreign aid resources commensurate or not with the challenges to be met, the fact remains that USD 4733 billion were devoted to foreign aid over the past 57 years. Was that money properly used for the development purposes for which it was assigned or was it a waste of money?

V. The Challenge of Foreign Aid Effectiveness

Quite aside from the fact that they are few or many, foreign aid resources should be judged based on whether and to what extent they concretely contribute to meet core purposes of foreign aid policy.

The key questions to orient the evaluation process aimed at assessing foreign aid effectiveness and impact are the following:

1. Have the planned results of intervention been effectively achieved? Why yes or why not?
2. To what extent has foreign aid contributed to its longer term goals? What are the effects, including unanticipated and unintended ones, caused by its results on the development process?

Two main and intertwined reasons should make clear the importance of these questions.

On one side, the accountability aim implies the need to demonstrate the level of responsibility for using the taxpayers' resources in the most cost-efficient way in order to get 'value for money'. This motivation is very critical in the current tight fiscal environment in many donor countries and mainstream literature abounds on the value for money conceptualisation.[26] The New Zealand aid program (2011) defines value for money as 'achieving the best possible development outcomes over the life of an activity relative to the total cost of managing and resourcing that activity and ensuring that resources are used effectively, economically, and without waste'.[27]

What this definition shows is that the concept of value for money is expressed in terms of cost-effectiveness through a ratio between the relative costs and outcomes (effects) associated with the given activity. This way a logical chain of events is implicitly

[26] H Jakupec and M Kelly (eds), *Assessing the Impact of Foreign Aid. Value for Money and Aid for Trade* (London, Academic Press – Elsevier, 2016).

[27] A Banke-Thomas et al, 'Assessing Value-for-money in Maternal and Newborn Health' (2017) 2(2) *BMJ Global Health* doi:10.1136/bmjgh-2017-000310.

assumed, combining an efficient implementation of activities by minimising the cost of resources to be used and the achievement of expected results by maximising outcomes.

Figure 2 The Linear Inputs-Results Process of Foreign Aid Initiatives

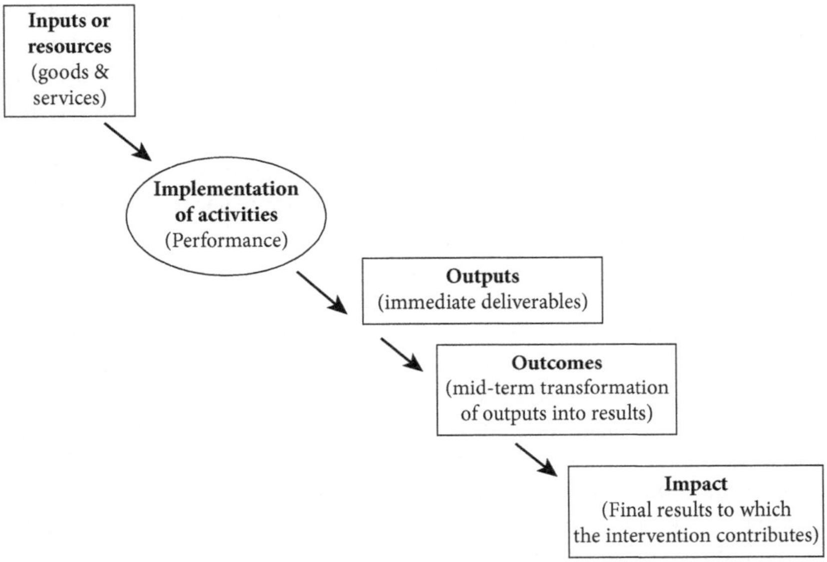

The emphasis on the importance of demonstrating good allocation of resources, transparency and credibility of foreign aid policies to taxpayers means that special attention is paid to the link between the implementation of activities (focusing on financial and performance information) and the direct results of interventions. This also requires an effort in terms of communicating results to the constituencies in a meaningful manner and a clarification about the profile of the real constituencies or audiences of interest, because taxpayers are different from the foreign aid self-referential community of experts and funding agencies. Therefore, a correct balance between proper demonstration and effective communication and dissemination of results is indeed important, being aware of the risks of making communication the prevailing and leading component with demonstration playing just a functional role sired to it.

On another side, the second reason why foreign aid effectiveness and the impact issue are so important is the adoption of the overarching framework of foreign aid policy, with clearly defined objectives, for 2015 and post-2015.

With the advent of the eight MDGs in 2000, it was therefore obvious that 'business-as-usual' was no longer an option for foreign aid policy.

However, the MDGs did not represent a new narrative with their focus on poverty reduction and social dimensions. In 1973, Robert McNamara, then President of the World Bank, in a speech delivered during the Bank's Annual Meetings held in Nairobi called for an eradication of absolute poverty by 2000.[28] In 2000, this objective was not

[28] PA Sharma, *Robert McNamara's Other War: The World Bank and International Development* (Philadelphia, University of Pennsylvania Press, 2017).

accomplished and it was reformulated under the MDGs narrative to reduce the rate of extreme poverty by half by 2015 compared to its 1990 level, in order to eradicate poverty (in its absolute sense) by 2025.

The MDGs confirmed a new foreign aid trend: since the late 1990s, the fight against poverty has become the core mission of international aid, and the MDGs framework helped to galvanise development efforts and set global and national goals and priorities.

Within the MDGs framework and its focus on the outcomes of policy, a new results-based agenda of foreign aid was set up to make development cooperation more effective over the projection horizon of 15 years.

The High-Level Fora on Aid Effectiveness in Rome (2003), Paris (2005), Accra (2008) and Busan (2011) laid the foundations and formulated the principles of an ambitious effective foreign aid policy.

In 2012, the Working Party on Aid Effectiveness gave way to a new Global Partnership for Effective Development Cooperation, jointly supported by the OECD and UNDP, to forge stronger partnerships for effective foreign aid policy. An inclusive partnership on aid effectiveness was conceived as a necessary condition for ensuring the achievement of the ambitious targets set by the MDGs.

The MDGs were a particularly attractive tool for development policies because of their inherent clarity and associated simplicity. The MDGs were clear about what recipient countries and donors' support were trying to achieve, namely a few social goals: fight against poverty and hunger, equal opportunity – with equality associated to gender issues – and human development. They were clear also about how all these should have been achieved: specific targets and a monitoring and evaluation (M&E) system with measurable indicators put in place.

The principles of the 2005 Paris Declaration on Aid Effectiveness were a turning point on the aid effectiveness agenda, with a single set of concise pillars for improving aid.

Figure 3 The Five Principles of the Paris Declaration (Result-based Pyramid)

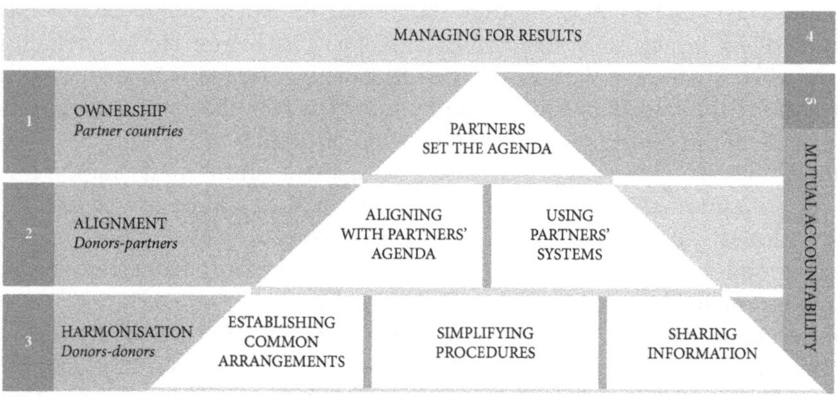

Source: OECD, *Aid Effectiveness 2011: Progress in Implementing the Paris Declaration. Better Aid* (Paris, OECD Publishing, 2012).

To improve the quality of foreign aid and its impact on development, developing countries (ie partners) must exercise effective leadership over their development policies and strategies and coordinate development efforts (ownership principle). Donor countries must align behind these objectives and use local systems (alignment principle) and they must coordinate, simplify procedures and share information to avoid duplication (harmonisation principle). Therefore, donors and partner countries must shift focus to development results, which must be measured (results-based principle), and they are accountable for development results (mutual accountability principle).

In 2015, the much wider and ambitious SDGs agenda renewed the crucial commitment to improve development effectiveness and impact.

This may seem obvious, but it verges on a Copernican Revolution in comparison with what was the origin of foreign aid policies in the 1950s, when the foreign aid approach was led by benevolent giving (or charity) from donors to support 'recipient' countries by providing them with outputs. From such an inputs-driven approach in order to get outputs, a total shake-up of the framework approach occurred and the MDGs and SDGSs frameworks imposed a complete reversal of the logical chain embedded into a results-driven approach: from Results-Based Management, Management through Results, or Management through Objectives to a more recent concept of Managing for Development Results (MfDR)[29] indicating a management modality focused on the achievement of development objectives and on the short-, medium- and long-term sustainable improvements of a country.

The implementation of the Busan 2011 Commitments on effective development co-operation has been focused on four principles:

1. focus on results,
2. country ownership,
3. inclusive partnerships for development, and
4. transparency and mutual accountability.

Based on its 2016 monitoring round, the Global Partnership, which was mandated to support the regular monitoring of progress in implementation of the Busan commitments, analysed information about 12 key indicators on foreign aid effectiveness to use the information on results to learn and support decision-making. This analysis shows that results frameworks are taking place in donors and partners. Encouraging results occur in terms of planning, with a clearer definition of priorities, targets and indicators, at national level, with donors aligning to them. Differently, results appear less successful in terms of managing, where budgeting, M&E processes still need to be improved and strengthened.[30]

The recent improvements made in parallel by donors and partners in planning and, less clearly, in managing development policies must not mean forgetting that donors and partners have different roles to play. The new SDGs agenda has the ambition to be a universal framework; differently from the MDGs agenda, which focused on development cooperation goals to improve the conditions in developing countries, the SDGs agenda should represent a transformative tool for developed and developing countries.

[29] The World Bank, *MfDR Capacity Scan: A Toolkit for the Assessment of Country Capacity in MfDR. Sourcebook* (Washington DC, The World Bank, 2008).

[30] OECD and UNDP, *Making Development Co-operation More Effective. 2016 Progress Report* (Paris, OECD, 2016).

In practice, the SDGs agenda should orient both development policies (of donors and partners in their own countries) and development cooperation policies (of donors in partners' countries). In a foreign aid context, long-term development results have to be set up by partner countries, whereas donors should contextualise and correlate development cooperation results to development results. Looking at the long linear chain from inputs to impact of foreign aid initiatives (Figure 2), the long-term link between outcomes and impact means development change at national and global level to which foreign aid is aimed to contribute, but this is an area that relates to development results. The mid-term link between outputs and outcomes is the consequence of a proper operational, financial and organisational performance of foreign aid initiatives and it is the area of foreign aid competence and attribution.[31]

Figure 4 The Foreign Aid and Development Results Chain

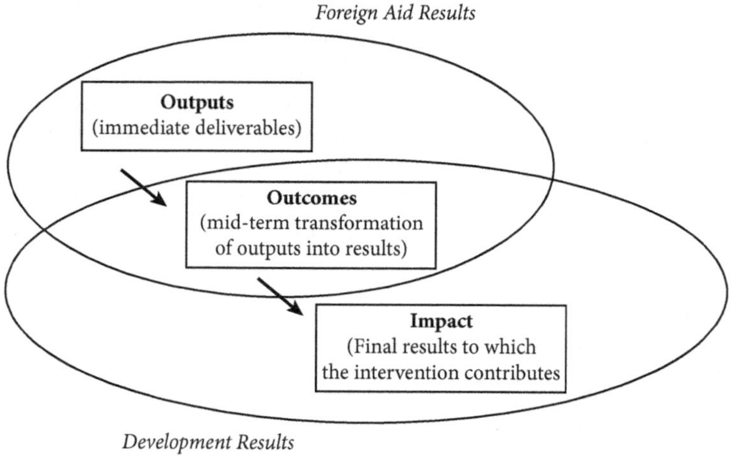

Foreign aid should not be detached from impact implications and adequate and reliable indicators to measure immediate outputs and mid-term outcomes are useful for impact assessment. At the same time, we cannot hide the distinction and the presence of an inherent tension and potential clash between accountability needs and the urgency of delivering evidence-based information on the results from one side, and the realisation of outcomes and impact which take a long time to obtain from another side.

Based on these considerations, we can summarise the complementarity between effectiveness and impact as currently conceived.

Effectiveness means the measurement of change in the observed outcomes, by attributing this change to the foreign aid intervention, judging the value of the intervention by using comparisons such as targets, benchmarks, similar interventions and/or the assessments of involved stakeholders.[32] In cases of inexistent or poorly defined

[31] R Zwart, 'Strengthening the results chain: Synthesis of case studies of results-based management by providers' Policy paper 7 (Paris, OECD, 2017).

[32] The abuse of rhetoric on multi-stakeholders' involvement should not disguise that development strategies should mainly respond to the right-holders, who do not experience full rights, rather than the stakeholders,

objectives, of unrealistic and/or conflicting objectives, of a lack of targets or measures of success, measuring effectiveness becomes very challenging.

Impact means to decide what effects or consequences on development to select for consideration, and the challenge is significant. In dealing with complex adaptive systems[33] such as societies, rather than assuming the linear inputs-results process of foreign aid initiatives, there is a preliminary decision in terms of delimiting the area of interest. Once the decision on what results are to be considered has been taken, there is also the challenge of measuring direct attribution (to determine what caused the observed results) as well as contribution (what helped and was part of what caused the observed results). The importance of contribution is due to the fact that change is seldom attributable to a simple factor in presence of many influencing determinants.

Indeed, we must not forget that a clear distinction between effectiveness and impact as well as between foreign aid and development results is a convenient way of addressing the complexity of causality, especially taking into account the presence of a shared zone of outcomes, of both foreign aid and development competence.

VI. Theories Addressing Aid Effectiveness Issue in Comparison

As Dick Hebdige wrote, 'The struggle between different discourses, different definitions and meanings within ideology is always, at the same time, a struggle within signification.'[34]

Unlike the past, now four apparently opposing discourses dominate the political debate and literature on foreign aid effectiveness. All of them reject the temptations of great narratives to explore the deep and intricate dynamics of history and prefer to follow the practical discourse of aid effectiveness.

The first approach is represented by Jeffrey Sachs.[35] Quoting George Bernard Shaw, who wrote that '[t]he greatest of evils and the worst of crimes is poverty',[36] Sachs passionately offered a tragic run-down of the tragedy in developing countries. Thousands of children die every day from extreme poverty – for example from diarrhoea that could be prevented with 10-cent doses of oral rehydration therapy – despite the concrete opportunity to spread the benefits of technology and finance to all parts of the world. However, there is hope from a big plan: success in ending the poverty trap will

who are typically associated with civil society organisations and the private sector, to protect the public space. The so-called rights-based approach to development is an approach to development promoted to achieve a positive transformation of power relations by empowering the rights-holders. This approach conflicts with a tendency for donors to consider democratisation and human rights as a series of formal rules, procedures and norms demanding assistance and protection, rather than empowering processes. See J Degnbol-Martinussen and P Engberg-Pedersen, *Aid: Understanding International Development Cooperation* (London, Zed Books, 2003).

[33] JH Holland, *Hidden Order: How Adaptation Builds Complexity* (Boston, Addison-Wesley, 1996).

[34] D Hebdige, *Subculture. The Meaning of Style* (London, Routledge, 1979) 17.

[35] JD Sachs, *The End of Poverty: Economic Possibilities for Our Time* (New York, Penguin Books, 2006); JD Sachs, *The Age of Sustainable Development* (New York, Columbia University Press, 2015).

[36] GB Shaw, 'Preface' to *John Bull's Other Island and Major Barbara* (New York, Brentano's, 1907).

be much easier than it appears, as there is a lot of evidence about effective foreign aid: broad-based technical support and large-scale public investments in health, education, agriculture, infrastructure and environmental management can provide high-quality aid. A commitment to the 'big push' requires just will and more funds for appropriate foreign aid.

The second approach is led by a much more pessimistic William Easterly, who criticised the influence of planners who want to achieve the ambitious MDGs and SDGs with the help of planning. The planners set goals and they think they already know exactly what to do and where to go, considering poverty as a technical engineering problem that their answers will solve.[37] Easterly advocated a key role for a more modest researchers' attitude, those who do not pretend to know exactly what and how everything works in advance of the implementation of the plan. Poverty is a complicated tangle of political, social, historical, institutional and technological factors, and researchers hope to find answers to individual problems only by trial and error experimentation. Easterly endorses the claims about the tragedy of poverty, but also says that there is a second tragedy, as the donors' community prepares big plans and spend trillions of dollars on aid over decades and babies with diarrhoea are still not getting the 10-cent doses of oral rehydration therapy, because money did not reach the poor. This demonstrates the failure of foreign aid's big plans implying that all foreign aid donors and partners are collectively and globally responsible for meeting the multiple MDGs and SDGs, even though that also depends on lots of other things besides the governments. In the end, nobody is individually responsible for any result in the absence of individual accountability related to very specific outcomes, and unanticipated and unintended effects of foreign aid can make aid harmful more than unnecessary.

Another economist, Paul Collier,[38] now symbolises the third approach. He avoids a complete opposition like the one between Sachs and Easterly and seriously questions the role of foreign aid. Rather than discussing whether aid policy needs big plans or not, Collier links foreign aid effectiveness to the nature of the poverty trap. If Sachs' assumption is based on saving, poverty and population traps, with poor health, poor education and poor infrastructure reinforcing one another, Collier emphasises other prevailing traps. Conflicts, dependency on natural resources, weaknesses of landlocked small countries and bad governance and institutional traps represent the key critical determinants of poverty. Therefore, foreign aid is not automatically useful and effective in addressing the prevailing traps in a given country. Free trade, military actions, new norms can be more useful in some cases; foreign aid may even be detrimental under different circumstances, since aid can fuel insecurity and conflict in a very fragmented post-conflict context. Collier recommends a combination of different policies and continuous use of conditionalities, but implicitly he also suggests that the ambiguous combination of short-term humanitarian and long-term developmental approaches cannot harbour any illusions about going together without tension and in

[37] W Easterly, *The White Man's Burden: Why the West's Efforts to Aid the Rest Have Done So Much Ill and So Little Good* (New York, The Penguin Press, 2006); W Easterly, *The Tyranny of Experts: Economists, Dictators, and the Forgotten Rights of the Poor* (New York, Basic Books, 2014).

[38] P Collier, *The Bottom Billion: Why the Poorest Countries Are Failing and What Can Be Done About It* (Oxford, Oxford University Press, 2007).

an effective way. Foreign aid cannot be conceived as just one solution which is suited to all situations: the quality of institutions and governance affects aid effectiveness; very strong governments or very weak States require appropriate policies, not necessarily foreign aid. He also addresses the aid effectiveness issue in somewhat provocative terms by underlining a real concern: a result-oriented culture is likely to lead to the paradox of encouraging the adoption of the easiest solution and the most experienced approaches, promoting risk aversion and discouraging error experimentation, open search, uncertain but innovative paths. This is due to the obsession of demonstrating concrete and immediate positive results of any initiative rather than investing in innovation, vision and long-term structural transformation. Collier and Betts[39] have recently criticised the international top-down refugee regime created in the aftermath of the Second World War to protect people fleeing persecution and still in force by inertia, which is clearly inadequate to a changing world. There is a need for error experimentation, as Easterly emphasised, and the results-based management may induce excessive prudence by being so afraid of failure.

A fourth economist, the only woman in the group, to propose an alternative approach to address the effectiveness of foreign aid is Esther Duflo.[40] Radically avoiding any generalisation about development, she insists on the lack of adjustment and change of policies due to the prevailing inertia by the implementer; she also criticises the power of ideology driving many policies, with actors pretending to have the right solution without considering any possible alternative. However, differently from the previous approaches, she mentions a third trap preventing policies from being effective, which is ignorance. No one knows exactly what is happening and how the poor behave; therefore, ineffectiveness of aid is due to an inadequate understanding of poverty. The key ingredient to promote aid effectiveness is to become much more rigorous in applying correct methods to learn by using an evidence-based approach through the so-called randomised control trials, together with a real willingness to learn and to change strategies.

VII. From Theories to Methods and Techniques to Assess Aid Effectiveness

The transformation of theoretical hypotheses into empirical research operations demands exploration of methods, methodologies and both qualitative and quantitative techniques.

In all cases, the most important challenge is the connection between effects or impact (in terms of attribution or contribution), and context (the delimitation of the area of interest, affected by various externalities and spill-overs, varying with the delimited context of interest).

[39] P Collier and A Betts, *Refuge. Rethinking Refugee Policy in a Changing World* (Oxford, Oxford University Press, 2017).

[40] AV Banerjee and E Duflo, *Poor Economics: A Radical Rethinking of the Way to Fight Global Poverty* (New York, PublicAffairs, 2012).

In this context, it is important to emphasise that management improvement in delivering aid and own democratic governance – not only in technical terms – contributes to the net improvement of aid performance, in terms of its main objective, that is sustainable development. Public procurement itself becomes relevant in terms of creating an enabling environment for development and, particularly during a critical phase of aid fatigue, results-based aid or 'ex post conditionality' to link disbursements to progress achieved towards targets agreed *ex ante*, which clearly provides strong incentives for recipient governments to get as close as possible to pre-set targets and to citizens to assess the relevance of aid policies and projects.

For reasons of space, we can summarise the alternative methodological approaches to assess aid effectiveness based on epistemological inspiration, by distinguishing between (neo-) positivism and hermeneutics, and also between different types of mainstream approaches.

Figure 5 A Tentative Map of Alternative Methodological Approaches to Aid Effectiveness

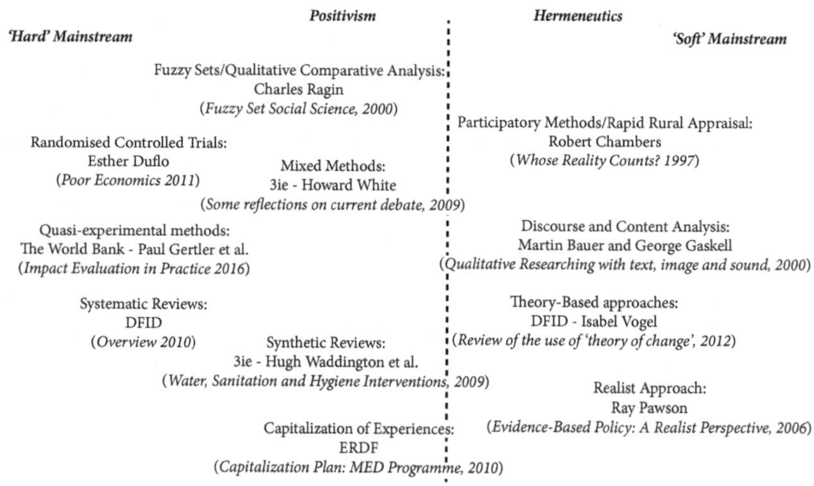

This map is intended to be just illustrative and not limiting or an accurate representation of different views. This subjective representation includes the names of some authors who are linked to various methods and techniques.

We also distinguish between 'hard' and 'soft' mainstream approaches. The former, such as the randomised control trials, quasi-experimental methods and systematic reviews, are based on econometric and statistic methods and techniques to conduct a counter-factual evaluation and attribute causality.[41] On the opposite side, we define as 'soft' mainstream approaches those approaches – such as theory-based and

[41] PJ Gertler et al, *Impact Evaluation in Practice*, 2nd edn (Washington, DC, Inter-American Development Bank and World Bank, 2016); DFID, *Systematic Reviews and Evidence-Informed Policy: Overview* (London, DFID, 2010).

realist approaches, participatory methods and discourse and content analysis[42] – that are much more focused on the mechanisms through which changes should occur (based on the so-called theory of change), on expectations and voices of different stakeholders, and on setting the context and boundaries of interest. These interpretative approaches are associated to other disciplines than statistics and econometrics: sociology, anthropology, geography, psychology and other social sciences.

In-between we find those approaches that are trying to combine different approaches: the mixed method (trying to promote a triangulation of approaches and techniques using both qualitative and quantitative methods), but also 'fuzzy sets' and 'qualitative comparative analysis' (to systematically compare a limited number of cases or observations: a serious weakness for statistic and econometric techniques), synthetic reviews and capitalisation of experiences.[43] Implicitly, the intermediate nature of these approaches is an attempt to combine variable-oriented (or generalising) techniques and case-oriented (or particularising) ones.

A mutual distrust between disciplines and correlated approaches prevails and our definition of 'hard' and 'soft' mainstreams simply reflects the social sciences hierarchy defined by the market approval, placing statistics and economics at the heart and implicitly assigning to experimental methods the 'gold standard', in the name of methodological uniformity.[44] A corporatist disciplinary attitude reinforces the distance between approaches rather than fertilising a terrain for potential exchange.

At the same time, the temptation to link the epistemological distinction between positivism and hermeneutics to the disciplinary approaches is misleading. Within each discipline we can find again orthodox and heterodox views, inspired by positivism or hermeneutics. In economics there are authors like Paul Davidson, who insist on the non-ergodic nature of the world: that is, we cannot project the future from past data

[42] R Chambers, *Whose Reality Counts? Putting the First Last* (Rugby, Practical Action Publishing, 1997); MW Bauer and G Gaskell (eds), *Qualitative Researching with Text, Image and Sound: A Practical Handbook for Social Research* (London, Sage, 2000); I Vogel, *Review of the Use of 'Theory of Change' in International Development* (London, DFID, 2012); R Pawson, *Evidence-Based Policy: A Realist Perspective* (London, Sage, 2006).

[43] H White, 'Some Reflections on Current Debate in Impact Evaluation', International Initiative for Impact Evaluation (3ie) Working Paper 1 (New Delhi, International Initiative for Impact Evaluation, 2009) available at www.3ieimpact.org/evidence-hub/publications/working-papers/some-reflections-current-debates-impact-evaluation; C Ragin, *Fuzzy-Set Social Science* (Chicago, The University of Chicago Press, 2000); H Waddington et al, 'Water, sanitation and hygiene interventions to combat childhood diarrhoea in developing countries', International Initiative for Impact Evaluation (3ie) Synthetic Review 001 (New Delhi, International Initiative for Impact Evaluation, 2009) available at http://3ieimpact.org/evidence-hub/systematic-review-repository/water-sanitation-and-hygiene-interventions-combat; ERDF, *Capitalization Plan MED Programme 2007–2013. Managing Authority: Provence Alpes Côte d'Azur Region – Working Document*, March 2010 (mimeo, In this context, it is important to emphasise that management improvement in delivering aid and own democratic governance – not only in technical terms – contributes to the net improvement of aid performance, in terms of its main objective, that is sustainable development. Public procurement itself becomes relevant in terms of creating an enabling environment for development and, particularly during a critical phase of aid fatigue, results-based aid or 'ex post conditionality', to link disbursements to progress achieved towards targets agreed *ex ante*, which clearly provides strong incentives for recipient governments to get as close as possible to pre-set targets and to citizens to assess the relevance of aid policies and projects; available at www.programmemed.eu/fileadmin/PROG_MED/Capitalisation/MED_CAPITALISATION_PLAN_EN.pdf.

[44] N Stame, 'What Doesn't Work? Three Failures, Many Answers' (2010) 16 *Evaluation* 371.

modelled in a statistical or econometric fashion,[45] which can be seen as a strong critique to the dominance of economic positivism. In statistics and econometrics, there are Nobel Laureates such as James Heckman and Christopher Sims, who are not supporters of the 'gold standard' idea.

VIII. Some Epistemological Considerations Beyond Theories. The Challenges that Lie Ahead

Somehow, the four apparently opposing discourses dominating the political debate and literature on foreign aid effectiveness share a profound critique of ideology: ideology against aid and State (Sachs) or market (Easterly), ideology against innovation (Collier), flexibility and micro-foundation of strategies (Duflo).

However, developing a critical approach to development and foreign aid making requires, first of all, recognising the central importance of ideology in contemporary development culture. The universality of development discourse is tautologically unfounded and unfoundable: it is the universal that is the specific way to perceiving the reality and 'truth' according to the Western metaphysical rationalist and empiricist traditions.

The assumption of an external validity of such a universal specificity extended to the world as a whole, which is what Paul Feyerabend would have called the 'Western myth or superstition',[46] and considering it as liberation through hiding its intrinsic imposition represents a typical example of what Jürgen Habermas defined as ideology.[47]

The traditional dichotomous dialectic between public and private sector, with the new synthesis represented by the so-called – Private Partnership (PPP), by reconciling their common truths and forming a new thesis, or foreign aid paradigm, is just another way of conceptualising development in a simple and potentially harmonious way.[48]

Nevertheless, the reality is that development or foreign aid is an amoeba word, taking many shapes, meaning different things to different people and the idea of a consensus on it is false by definition. Broadly speaking, development and foreign aid can be interpreted as dynamics of complex, institutionally-embedded, path-dependent and evolving systems, with intertwined objectives and processes.

Foreign aid standardised practice carries risks of routinising, institutionalising and depoliticising transformations that should be an active empowering process to enable people's involvement in the self-determined development of their lives and environment, rather than a co-opting practice of making people participate in the project to achieve pre-determined national or global development goals.

[45] P Davidson, 'Reality and Economic Theory' (1996) 18 *Journal of Post Keynesian Economics* 479.

[46] PK Feyerabend, *Knowledge, Science and Relativism* (Cambridge, Cambridge University Press, 1999).

[47] FG Lawrence (tr), J Habermas, *Philosophical Discourse of Modernity: Twelve Lectures* (Massachusetts, MIT Press, 1990).

[48] Current emphasis on Public-Private Partnerships (PPP) runs the risk of promoting the involvement of an undistinguished and homogeneous private sector as a driver of poverty reduction, even if there is no evidence about the effectiveness of these solutions. Equally, the emphasis on private sector mobilisation and involvement relegates the need for binding rules to reorient the current business model dominated by transnational corporations to second place.

Given that premise, the key starting question on effectiveness should be: whose logic model, and for whom? Is the SDGs call for governments to 'leave no one behind' in development just a slogan or a political paradigm change?[49]

Foreign aid is a field where many gaps exist between and within:

1. policymakers who define development strategies;
2. those temporarily established organisations who actively participate in funding, planning and implementation of aid initiatives;
3. the partners of recipient countries involved in implementing and monitoring initiatives;
4. the final beneficiaries who receive and use aid;
5. those who are not directly reached by the intervention in the recipient countries; and
6. the right-holders in general.

Those who decide the goals and the amount of aid and those who supply funds and manage the administrative process play an important mediation role. Their role is crucial in terms of direct and indirect influence over planning and effectiveness of aid. Aid initiatives are expected to satisfy their expectations, and use their grammar and language. This creates problems to some implementing transformative actors that may have clear strategies and visions but are obliged to divide artificially complex problems into small parts (ie limited projects) suitable for aid financing.

Language is never simply a neutral instrument to convey meaning, but rather a culturally subjective system reflecting peoples' worldview and is populated – overpopulated – with the intentions of others, as Mikhail Bakhtin said.[50] The consequence is that an initiative supposedly conceived to support changes in the life of final beneficiaries of aid is planned using the professional language of funders in aid interaction, and funders are quite distant and different (culturally, not just physically) from final users on the basis of their asymmetrical relationships. This situation creates external incentives and pressures, for those who submit proposals to be financed, to adopt the forms and logic of the funders; this is the practice of 'isomorphic mimicry',[51] the camouflage strategy consistent with funders' expectations.

The foreign aid discourse is intrinsically based on mimicry, because it adopts a 'rigorous' language of academic science by mimicking empiricist and positivist methods, coining some scientific key terms such as aid effectiveness, money for value, impact evaluation, result-based management, poverty reduction and sustainability.

A second consideration is that logic models are subjective. 'Since the measuring device has been constructed by the observer, we have to remember that what

[49] If the combination of inequality and inclusion becomes an essential component for the SDGs agenda implementation, it would be a dramatic change for conventional foreign aid, strictly focused on assisting the poor, rather than looking simultaneously at prosperity and poverty, privileged and the poor as very closely connected, with agency at the core.

[50] MM Bakhtin, *The Dialogic Imagination: Four Essays* (Austin, University of Texas Press, 1981).

[51] L Pritchett, M Woolcock, and M Andrews, 'Capability Traps? The Mechanisms of Persistent Implementation Failure', Center for Global Development Working Paper 234 (Washington DC, Center for Global Development, 2010) available at www.cgdev.org/sites/default/files/1424651_file_Pritchett_Capability_FINAL.pdf.

we observe is not nature itself but nature exposed to our method of questioning' as Werner Heisenberg said.[52] And '[w]e see things not as they are, but as we are …' added Anais Nin.[53]

The main risk of imposing an external logic through foreign aid initiatives has always been a main concern, and the technicisation of foreign aid policy and measurement of aid effectiveness renders it less publicly accountable.

We always interpret effectiveness and impact through a set of lenses or a veil to match such elusive 'reality'. Self-critical epistemological awareness, questioning how we come to know what we think we know, is always recommendable.

There is an inescapable gap between foreign aid projects and development, and such inherent tension must be managed. Development is embedded into life and change; it cannot be constrained into boundaries of aid projects.[54]

This implies a gap between a project and the real processes associated to it, as well as between reality and evaluation, so that the ambition should be to lend wings to the project, that is, to consider it wider beyond its own boundaries.

In an epistemological perspective, this line of thought can be summarised in the importance of uncertainty about the future, determined by the overarching role of external and unpredictable events as well as the constant and non-linear interaction of a complex set of factors on the final results of choices and situations. Uncertainty dominates everywhere and one cannot escape from it by means of the tunnel vision of linear inputs-results logic.

The mainstream argument, adopted as a principle and assumption – that foreign aid and the development results chain are associated with time's arrow, and that impact on development requires a long term, whereas outcomes are direct effects of foreign aid that find their fulfilment in the mid-term – is comforting but questionable. A permanent and significant effect on development may occur simultaneously with the implementation phase or together with the immediate delivery of outputs. To avoid complications linked to complexity,[55] the conventional approach to aid effectiveness and impact is in danger of overlooking an area of great importance, the prevalence of feedback effects and mutual reinforcements, as well as the acceptance of a structural component of unpredictability in every change as well as in history. Gunnar Myrdal elaborated theories on path dependence and non-linear processes of cumulative and circular causation, clarifying the subjective nature of social phenomena evaluation;[56] Albert Hirschman developed these arguments,[57] and from a philosophical view Martha Nussbaum analysed the problem of human vulnerability to factors outside a person's control.[58]

[52] W Heisenberg, *Physics and Philosophy: The Revolution in Modern Science* (New York, Harper and Row, 1958).

[53] A Nin, *The Seduction of the Minotaur* (Denver, Alan Swallow, 1961).

[54] R Millett, S Dodson and C Phillips, *Application of Logic Modelling Processes to Explore Theory of Change from Diverse Cultural Perspectives* (American Evaluation Association, mimeo, 2000). [Paper not published.]

[55] MM Waldrop, *Complexity: The Emerging Science at the Edge of Order and Chaos* (London, Viking, 1992).

[56] G Myrdal, *Value in Social Theory. A Selection of Essays on Methodology by Gunnar Myrdal* (London, Routledge & K Paul, 1958).

[57] AO Hirschman, 'Political Economics and Possibilism' in AO Hirschman, *A Bias for Hope: Essays on Development in Latin America* (Yale, Yale University Press, 1971) 1–34.

[58] MC Nussbaum, *The Fragility of Goodness: Luck and Ethics in Greek Tragedy and Philosophy*, 2nd edn (Cambridge, Cambridge University Press, 2001).

Using the categories adopted by Glouberman and Zimmerman,[59] based on the ground-breaking studies on complexity during the 1970s,[60] systems can be understood as being simple, complicated, complex or chaotic. Simple and complicated systems or processes (or projects/plans) are related to separate entities or discrete activities (there is a linear dynamics and the sum of individual components generates an outcome corresponding to their combination). Complex systems are based on relationships, and their properties of self-organisation, interconnectedness and evolution prevail, through non-predictable and non-linear dynamics in which the whole is greater than the sum of the known and knowable parts.

The tunnel vision of the linear inputs-results logic was imagined 50 years ago and applied since then to simple or complicated evidence-based projects around defined diagnoses with discrete interventions. Nowadays development is theorised as a complex adaptive system embedded in a multi-dimensional web of interconnections between and within contexts and specificities, through historical, social and ecological connections. This new conceptualisation of development implies the interconnecting principles of (eco-system and social-system) resilience, adaptation, equity, access, transformative empowerment, community self-determination and inter-sectoral collaboration, by encompassing the environmental, social, economic, political and cultural dimensions.[61]

Yet there are not standardised mainstreaming approaches in aid effectiveness, and impact analyses that replace traditional approaches to simple or complicated projects are used to address the complexity domain in practice. The problem is, to cite Albert-László Barabási, that: 'Complexity is the science of the 21st century. The catch is that we may have to wait decades to see it applied'.[62]

Additionally, during the last 40 years, there have been various heterodox contributions to treat social, economic, political and environmental dimensions in a holistic approach.[63] If the idea of complex systems demonstrates that they cannot be understood solely by simple or complicated approaches to evidence, then also the so-called micro-macro paradox of aid[64] may be misleading. The Keynesian concerns with the fact that uncertainty drives an epistemological gap between individual (micro) behaviour and developmental (macro) outcomes, because everything and everyone is dependent and embedded into the context, should suggest using caution to avoid the risk of

[59] S Glouberman and B Zimmerman, 'Complicated and Complex Systems: What Would Successful Reform of Medicare Look Like?' Commission on the Future of Health Care in Canada, Discussion Paper No 8 (2002) available at www.alnap.org/system/files/content/resource/files/main/complicatedandcomplexsystems-zimmermanreport-medicare-reform.pdf.

[60] H Atlan, *L'organisation biologique et la théorie de l'information* (Paris, Hermann, 1972).

[61] CM Martin and JP Sturmberg, 'General Practice: Chaos, Complexity and Innovation' (2005) 183 *The Medical Journal of Australia* 106.

[62] AL Barabási, *Linked: How Everything Is Connected to Everything Else and What It Means for Business, Science and Everyday Life* (New York, Plume, 2003).

[63] For a recent proposal, see K Raworth, *Doughnut Economics. Seven Ways to Think Like a 21st-Century Economist* (London, Cornerstone, 2017).

[64] At a micro level, all donors report the success of most of their projects and programmes, but – due to the aid fungibility and the leakage of the aid into unproductive expenditure in the public sector – there is no impact at macro level so that it is impossible to establish any significant correlation between aid and growth rate of GNI in developing countries. See P Mosley, 'Aid-effectiveness: The Micro-Macro Paradox' (1986) 17(2) *IDS Bulletin* 22.

committing the so-called fallacy of composition (or atomistic fallacy).[65] Simply, the individual project level cannot be generalised and equated to the collective level of systemic and complex development.

Finally, by drawing eclectic inspiration from Roy Bhaskar[66] and Tony Lawson's[67] realist perspective, 'reality' does neither merely consist of a puzzle where the pieces are known in advance nor does it exist independently of observations and interpretations. The nature of social reality (its ontology) is both open and indeterminate, and it determines the type of knowledge that can be acquired. Moreover, according to critical realism, the knowledge of reality is mediated by our perceptions and beliefs.[68]

Institutions are crucial and intertwined parts of our complex social reality in the form of formal power relationships (legislative action), formal/informal agreements (eg negotiations) and the organisation of the social arena (such as markets).

Figure 6 Ontological Dimensions or Levels of Observable Reality

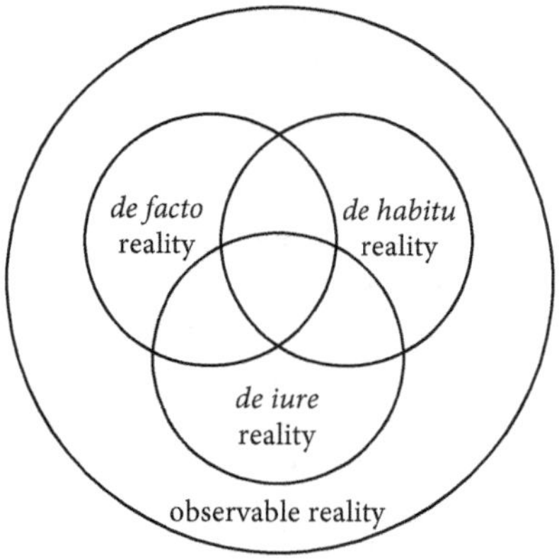

Our knowledge of reality can be depicted in stratified form, by considering three different levels of cognitive data organised. The so-called 'deep stratum' of reality, beyond the empirical and factual strata, is not directly observable as it is associated to causal mechanisms, power structures and institutional relations to be investigated. At analytical level, the epistemological approach we propose to face the complexity of effectiveness and aid measurement is as follows:

1. the constitutional discourse of the rule of law (*de iure* reality);
2. empirical 'objective' facts and practices (*de facto* reality); and
3. subjective perceptions, opinions and attitudes (*de habitu* reality).

[65] J Jespersen, *Macroeconomic Methodology: Post-Keynesian Perspective* (Cheltenham, Edward Elgar Publishing, 2009).

[66] R Bhaskar, *A Realist Theory of Science*, 2nd edn (Hassocks Sussex, Harvester Press, 1978).

[67] T Lawson, *Economics and Reality* (Routledge, London, 1997); T Lawson *Reorienting Economics* (London, Routledge, 2003).

[68] M Zupi, *Measuring Women's Empowerment and Discriminatory Social Institutions in Senegal. Definition, Conceptualization & Measurement* (Dakar, ONU-Femmes et CeSPI, 2015, -mimeo unpublished but available document).

They are three different levels of reality; they are all important, they interact but are not the same.[69] Each of them can be translated into numerical 'facts' or products, always embedded in the social and political structure of the time and place where they are made.

Therefore, a permanent combination of information on narratives (the rule of law discourse), stylised facts ('objective' facts) and perceptions (opinions and attitudes) is recommended to look at foreign aid policies and institutions.

Looking at things from different points of view is a method to translate critical realism into action, to overcome the limitation of a single theory, a single discipline, a single dataset, a single method of data analysis. Essentially, it is an invitation to become more aware of the complexity of policies effectiveness and impact on development.

[69] M Zupi, *Una proposta teorico-metodologica per la valutazione strategica delle iniziative di sviluppo* (Rome, CeSPI, 2011, mimeo); M Zupi (ed), *Manuel méthodologique sur la mesure de l'autonomisation des femmes. Le cas du Sénégal* (Dakar, ONU-Femmes et CeSPI, 2016).

2

Public Procurement, Investment and Aid Effectiveness

OLIVER MORRISSEY

I. Introduction

Procurement is at the core of purchase management and as such is a vital function in all businesses, including the public sector, in securing value for money and monitoring the performance of suppliers. While this is true at all levels it is especially important for large contracts in public infrastructure projects (the concern of this chapter). The quality and integrity of the procurement process is fundamental to ensuring that contracts are awarded competitively and fairly, implemented effectively, and monitored to reduce fiduciary risk. It follows that better procurement ensures better and more effective projects, financially and in terms of ensuring the project delivers the expected outcome, and a better return on public spending. This chapter is largely concerned with low-income countries where two features are salient: government procurement systems are often weak and public infrastructure projects are typically financed (largely or fully) by aid (grants or concessional loans from bilateral or multilateral aid agencies).

This chapter considers the role of public procurement in aid from the perspective of the economics literature on aid. The importance of procurement for aid-financed projects is obvious, to the extent that better processes ensure better projects. The relevance of aid, and specifically donors, for procurement is equally important but less often considered. Donors are concerned with monitoring how their aid is spent as they aim to ensure that the aid is fully spent on the intended projects or sectors and that the investment delivers the desired benefits, and therefore take a strong interest in the procurement process. If donors are not fully satisfied with the government systems, often the case in low-income countries, they will aim to use their own process. As there are multiple donors, an implication is that multiple procurement processes may be in place in any country. This raises issues of coordination and more generally how donors can, ideally acting together, help to improve procurement systems in recipient countries.

The economics literature on aid does not address procurement. Although there is clear recognition that a vital function of aid is to finance physical investment (especially public infrastructure) and the productivity of (or return on) such investment determines the contribution of aid to the economy, the focus is on the overall effect on growth. Aid effectiveness, interpreted as the effect of aid on growth, has attracted considerable research attention that appears to have generated more heat than light. There is no consensus view: it is not unusual for different researchers using essentially the same data and econometric approach to arrive at dramatically different conclusions because of apparently minor changes to the sample or specific modelling choice (typically the researcher faces a number of alternative specification or estimation choices where none is definitively favoured over others). The consequence is that the empirical literature is characterised by disagreement; econometric results are not robust and are often conflicting. This is unfortunate because aid is an important issue politically and in terms of economic research. The current state of the literature is unsatisfactory because it is not capable of shifting priors: those who believe aid is ineffective can cite studies in support of that view while those who want to claim that aid is effective can also point to supporting evidence.

A fundamental determinant of the effect of aid on growth is the effect on public investment, both the level and efficiency, because aid is an important source of finance for investment; indeed, this is one of the primary economic motivations for aid. The theme in this chapter is to explore three dimensions of public investment in the context of aid. The first relates to the inconsistent treatment of investment in studies of aid effectiveness. The second relates to how donors can influence government decisions, in particular the allocation of spending (as a general indicator of choice of investment projects). If donors are able to monitor the use of aid they are better able to ensure that investment is allocated efficiently; the issue here relates to selecting which projects or sectors are financed (and by which donors or combination of donors). The final issue is that, once investment projects have been chosen, improving the process by which contracts are awarded and implemented is essential. Procurement processes are at the heart of this latter issue.

Corruption is a serious problem in low-income countries. Evidence shows a high positive correlation between high corruption, weak economic performance and poor institutions. Even if causality is difficult to establish, it is reasonable to accept that corruption undermines investment and growth. Indeed, the extent of corruption is a good indicator of the weakness of political and economic (regulatory) institutions. However, given its inherently opaque nature, corruption is difficult to capture and incorporate in terms of quantitative effects. In the context of aid effectiveness the most common argument is that corruption encourages the misuse of aid, in particular that the money is not actually spent on providing the public goods and services for which it is allocated. Improved tracking and monitoring can mitigate such misuse. A more specific concern is that corruption reduces 'value for money' or quality of investment projects. Again monitoring, and specifically transparent procurement, can mitigate adverse effects. These issues are addressed throughout the chapter.

Section II argues that three particular features of how aid effectiveness has been addressed help to explain why cross-country growth regressions are inconclusive. The first is that it is not clear how to measure aid to capture how it may affect growth, especially fully accounting for the effect through investment. At an aggregate country level, the amount that donors record as allocated to a recipient is greater than the amount the recipient records as received (especially for the amount delivered through the government). The amount itself may not be the most important factor, as how the aid is implemented and associated policy reforms (conditionality and the donor-recipient relationship) are significant determinants of the effects of aid.

The second is endogeneity, given that aid and growth are inter-related: economic performance influences the amount of aid received, whilst aid influences performance, and these two-way effects are likely to be persistent. Consequently, identifying the effect of aid on performance is extremely difficult if not strictly impossible (ie one cannot show definitively that aid was the cause of observed growth, but likewise one cannot be certain that aid did not support growth). The countries that are major recipients are by definition poor and have low growth for a variety of reasons that are inter-related with the impact of aid and donor-related policy reforms.

The third is that heterogeneity is fundamental and pervasive; the environments in aid recipient countries are very different and multiple political and economic, internal and external, factors are interacting in complex dynamic ways. The way in which aid is implemented also varies considerably as donors differ in the types of aid and procedures employed (and recipients receive many forms of aid from numerous donors). Analysing this variation across recipients is complicated by differences in the performance of aid projects within country – some will perform better than others (and procurement plays a role).

Section III turns attention to conditionality, the ability of donors to attach conditions to aid to enhance its effectiveness. Often these conditions are concerned with aid-related policy reforms, but conditions on monitoring the use of aid are of equal if not greater importance. The theoretical literature generally argues that conditionality is ineffective because unwilling recipients can circumvent any requirements, but this assumes weak monitoring. The empirical evidence is more encouraging. Significant improvements in aid monitoring and public financial management over the past 20 years have enhanced the ability of donors to demonstrate that aid is spent in the way they intended. Section IV concludes by considering the role of procurement processes in the allocation of aid to investment projects and the monitoring of projects to ensure 'value for money' and enhance returns. Although there is very limited economic research on procurement, in general or specifically for aid, good practice will improve the effectiveness of investment projects.

II. Aid and Growth: The Nature of the Disagreements

Although the issue of aid effectiveness, the impact of aid on growth, has attracted considerable research attention there is no consensus view. It is not unusual for different researchers using the same data and econometric approach to arrive at dramatically different conclusions by altering a specific modelling choice. For example, Rajan and Subramanian posit that aid impacts growth by adding to physical capital (they assume aid has no effect on productivity) and recognise that not all aid goes to investment so the anticipated effect if there is one will be modest.[1] In the empirical analysis, they find no evidence that aid has any effect on growth. Using the same data sample, but with some

[1] R Rajan and A Subramanian, 'Aid and Growth: what does the Cross-country Evidence really Show?' (2008) 90 *The Review of Economics and Statistics* 643.

adjustment to the econometric method, Arndt, Jones and Tarp find that aid is effective with a significant coefficient of about 0.2 in most regressions (interestingly, this is often the value in studies that find a positive effect of aid), although their preferred estimate is 0.1,[2] which happens to be the null hypothesis suggested by Rajan and Subramanian (2008).[3] The implication is that, on average, a 10 per cent increase in aid-financed physical capital increases the growth rate by one per cent.

The example above is just one example of two very similar studies yielding completely different conclusions – aid does not affect growth versus aid increases growth. The economics literature on aid and growth is characterised by such disagreements because econometric results tend not to be robust. This arises from three specific limitations of cross-country growth regressions in the aid context: measuring aid so as to capture the ways in which it can affect growth; challenges in addressing simultaneity and endogeneity; and the heterogeneity that characterises the data.

The empirical cross-country evidence is based on a rather strict criterion of aid effectiveness, namely that the amount of aid received impacts on economic growth within a relatively short period (typically about five years). The aid measurement challenge arises because not all aid is spent in a way that would be expected to have a medium-term observable impact on growth. Aid that finances physical capital investment should promote growth in the medium term, although given the long gestation period for many infrastructure projects this may require longer than five years. Furthermore, the effect depends on the productivity of investment, itself determined by the recipient environment of which corruption is one element (this is an important reason why corruption reduces growth, because it undermines the productivity of investment). Another problem is that investment is not consistently incorporated, or is omitted, in aid effectiveness studies, an issue we return to below.

This investment measure of aid used in most studies overstates the volume of aid that could influence growth in the medium term because no more than a third of aid finances physical investment. About a third of aid finances human capital, such as health and education services, or technical assistance and this could only affect growth in the fairly long term. In many recipients, a significant amount of aid is given to support consumption, such as food aid, humanitarian assistance or emergency relief. Such aid may not affect growth at all, or at least indirectly, and is often associated with crises in the country (which would be associated with lower growth). Thus, simply due to the way aid is measured there are good reasons to expect it will be difficult to find a positive effect of aid on growth in cross-country regression analysis. Studies that attempt to construct a measure capturing aid for investment tend to find an effect on growth.[4]

As the policies associated with aid (conditionality and the donor-recipient relationship) affect the recipient environment, the amount of aid alone is a weak proxy

[2] C Arndt, S Jones and F Tarp, 'Aid, Growth and Development: Have We Come Full Circle?'(2010) 1(2) *Journal of Globalization and Development* 1.

[3] Rajan and A Subramanian, 'Aid and Growth: what does the Cross-country Evidence really Show?' (n 1).

[4] K Gomanee, S Girma and O Morrissey, 'Aid and Growth in sub-Saharan Africa: Accounting for Transmission Mechanisms' (2005) 17 *Journal of International Development* 1055; MA Clemens at al, 'Counting Chickens when they Hatch: Timing and the Effects of Aid on Growth' (2012) 122 *The Economic Journal* 590.

for the potential of aid to affect growth. Aid serves a purpose in providing finance but also influencing policy. Both are relevant to investment and procurement; when aid funding is involved there will be greater monitoring of expenditure, as donors audit to be accountable, and support for improved public finance management and tackling corruption in the recipient. Obviously, donor encouragement and support does not eliminate corruption, and corrupt practices undermine the effectiveness of aid investments. Nevertheless, the extent of corruption can be reduced through more careful monitoring of aid-financed projects and through quality procurement systems.

In a seminal paper, Burnside and Dollar[5] argued that aid was only effective in recipients with good policies, as captured in an index combining three policy indicators – the Sachs-Warner measure of openness, the budget surplus or deficit as a share of Gross Domestic Product (GDP), and inflation. Their argument is based on the assumption that aid (or donors) did not affect the measure of policy. This is unlikely to be a credible assumption. Most aid recipients followed donor advice in implementing trade, exchange rate and economic liberalisation since the 1980s, so there is a donor policy effect on the openness measure (tending to reduce tariffs, black market premia and state control of tradable sectors). The other two indicators (which capture outcomes rather than policy inputs) are likely to be affected by aid and by donors. To the extent that aid finances government spending and donor advice supported improved fiscal management (see section III), more aid will tend to be associated with lower deficits net of aid.[6] As aid reduces the need for seigniorage (government printing of money to pay for deficits) and donor advice supported improved macroeconomic management, more aid will tend to be associated with lower inflation *ceteris paribus*. Furthermore, Burnside and Dollar omitted investment from their model, with the assumption that (all) aid financed (all) investment.[7] Given that only some (probably no more than a third of) aid finances physical public investment, this generates a downward bias on the aid coefficient. Gomanee, Girma and Morrissey allow for the relationship between aid and investment and find a positive effect of aid on growth for a sample of sub-Saharan African (SSA) countries.[8] They conclude that a major issue in SSA is not that aid is ineffective but that the return on investment is very low (although not discussed in the paper, corruption may be one reason for this).

A paper by Hansen and Tarp[9] was the first to demonstrate that the results of Burnside and Dollar[10] were not robust; indeed, they found evidence of aid effectiveness. Many subsequent studies showed that results tend not to be robust to changes in the sample or specification.[11] However, in models where Hansen and Tarp included

[5] C Burnside and D Dollar, 'Aid, Policies, and Growth' (2000) 90 *American Economic Review* 847.

[6] This is not the precise measure used; although recognising that (some) aid is included in revenue they assume incorrectly that 'aid-financed projects [are] included in expenditures, so that there is no necessary relationship between aid and this measure' (Burnside and Dollar (n 5) 849–50). As discussed in O Morrissey, 'Aid and Government Fiscal Behaviour: What Does the Evidence Say?' (2015) 69 *World Development* 98, aid is incompletely captured in revenue and expenditure so this may not be correct.

[7] Burnside and Dollar, 'Aid, Policies, and Growth' (n 5).

[8] Gomanee, Girma and Morrissey, 'Aid and Growth in sub-Saharan Africa' (n 4).

[9] H Hansen and F Tarp, 'Aid and Growth Regressions' (2001) 64 *Journal of Development Economics* 547.

[10] Burnside and Dollar (n 5).

[11] D Roodman, 'The Anarchy of Numbers: Aid, Development and Cross-Country Empirics' (2007) 21 *World Bank Economic Review* 255.

investment, the coefficient was positive and significant (the coefficient on aid was only sometimes significant).[12] In general, and unsurprisingly, investment is a more important determinant of growth than aid itself. The amount of aid is not as important in determining the effect as how the aid is used, and specifically the productivity of investments financed by the aid.

In an approach that is explicit on the relationship between aid and investment, Herzer and Morrissey posit that the effect of aid on GDP depends on a country-specific combination of two effects.[13] The first is the direct effect through financing investment, which is expected to be positive, although it may not be significant and may be modest as it depends on the productivity of investment. The aid effectiveness literature essentially only considers this direct effect. The second is an indirect effect through aggregate productivity; the argument is that aid is mediated by, may affect and interacts with various factors that represent the recipient's economic environment, such as determinants of the productivity of investment and corruption. The indirect effect can be negative if aid is given to countries that exhibit severe growth-retarding factors, such as poor governance or macroeconomic instability (that may reflect poor policy). The indirect effect can be positive if the economic environment is relatively good. There is no presumption that aid affects the environment, but policies associated with aid/donors can do so (the estimation strategy does not capture this); rather, the presumption is that the environment conditions how aid affects growth.

Herzer and Morrissey use data for 59 developing countries over 1971–2003 to derive country-specific time series estimates of the long-run association between aid and output (the indirect effect), and between investment and output (the direct effect).[14] The aid-output coefficients are, on average, negative: for 25 countries the negative coefficient is significant; in about a third of cases the coefficient is positive (but only significant in nine cases); and for 25 countries the estimate is insignificant. The aid-output coefficients are generally smaller than the positive investment-output coefficients (positive in 44 cases, 26 of which are significant, and only negative and significant in four countries). Insofar as aid is used to finance investment, the overall effect on output is likely to be positive. The results may not be robust (many country estimates are insignificant) but the purpose is to demonstrate differences in the country-specific environment that influence aid effectiveness. Country differences in factors influencing aggregate productivity influence the effect of aid in the country; of 20 variables considered, the most important are found to be law and order (for quality of institutions), religious tensions (political stability) and government size. Although corruption was not itself among the significant determinants of aid effectiveness, it was significantly associated with the law and order variable: higher corruption is associated with lower quality institutions, which in turn reduce aggregate productivity (so aid is less effective).

Some recent studies address the related issue of the return on aid; rather than relating aid to a measure of growth the focus is on the productivity of aid-financed investment. Arndt, Jones and Tarp, using simulation methods, find that the average

[12] Hansen and Tarp, 'Aid and Growth Regressions' (n 9).

[13] D Herzer and O Morrissey, 'Aid and Domestic Output in the Long Run' (2013) 149 *Review of World Economics* 723.

[14] ibid.

internal rate of return is about 10 per cent,[15] which corresponds to estimates reported above using different methods. Dalgaard and Hansen estimate the aggregate return on aid-financed investment, the marginal productivity of aid capital, and compare this to returns on private investment projects.[16] They estimate that the return on aid capital of 20 per cent is similar to the return on public capital but higher than the return on private capital. What the studies reviewed here that address investment show is that, notwithstanding difficulties in establishing an effect of aid on growth, aid-financed investment generates rates of return at least comparable to other investments in developing countries.

The basic problem of the aid effectiveness literature is that endogeneity and heterogeneity combine to limit how informative cross-country regressions can be because there are multiple factors that affect and may be affected by growth and by aid in different ways in different countries. Consider corruption, especially where the measure is based on survey responses by private sector investors, to illustrate the argument. Corruption would generally be accepted as a good indicator of the recipient economic environment such that higher corruption is expected to be associated with lower productivity of investment, hence lower aid effectiveness via investment (and perhaps also via government spending). However, whether aid affects corruption is a separate question, and one that is not easy to address. As availability of money is likely to attract corrupt activity, one may posit an association between aid and corruption (separate from the tendency of poor countries to attract more aid and have higher corruption). However, it is reasonable to posit that corrupt individuals are most concerned with easy money, ie less transparent transactions are more attractive because the corrupt wish to minimise the possibility of being observed.[17] This suggests that they would rank the attractiveness of money flows according to transparency, suggesting a ranking (in terms of being associated with corruption) of private capital including Foreign Direct Investment (FDI), government spending and finally aid, assuming that monitoring and procurement is more rigorous and transparent for aid.

On this basis, aid is the least attractive simply because it is subject to greater monitoring by donors (the only claim is less, not no, corruption); corruption involving donor funds is more likely to be observed and investigated. To the extent that donor technical support and institutional interventions have improved public sector management (of tax and spending), public financial flows are likely to be monitored more openly than private flows. Aid may be subject to corruption but less so than private capital flows that are less transparent. To the extent that donors are effective in improving the monitoring of aid and public expenditure, more of the corrupt activities may be diverted to private flows. If corruption is measured by surveying private investors it is possible that reductions in corruption due to donors are associated with an increase in measured corruption (pertaining to private flows). Cross-country regressions of effects of aid on corruption or including aid-corruption interaction are likely

[15] C Arndt, S Jones and F Tarp, 'What is the Aggregate Economic Rate of Return to Foreign Aid?' (2016) 30 *World Bank Economic Review* 446.

[16] CJ Dalgaard and H Hansen, 'The Return to Foreign Aid' (2017) 53 *Journal of Development Studies* 7.

[17] O Morrissey, 'Aid and Domestic Resource Mobilisation with a Focus on sub-Saharan Africa' (2015) 31 *Oxford Review of Economic Policy* 447.

to be misleading or uninformative. Measures that reduce or discourage corruption will improve the effectiveness of investment, so improved monitoring and procurement processes have the potential to deliver considerable benefits.

III. Aid, Conditionality and the Public Sector

Arguments that aid is not, or has not been, effective in contributing to economic growth often locate the problem as giving aid to governments that do not make the best use of the aid. Most aid either goes to the government to finance public spending or supports the provision of public goods and services (through donor projects), so may encourage too large a public sector, rather than promoting the private sector (or effectively ensuring that the government supports private sector development). This effect may be exacerbated to the extent that aid alleviates the need for government to impose fiscal and budgetary discipline: the availability of aid is often argued to encourage corruption and allow governments to continue with 'bad' or inferior policies. Underpinning these arguments is a belief that conditionality does not work, ie donor/aid leverage does not ensure that governments implement good policies, or even the policies that donors promote. Conditionality failure is a particular concern to those who accept the Burnside and Dollar argument that aid makes a positive contribution to growth only in those countries with high values for the policy indicator.[18] In this case, if aid/donors cannot improve policy, aid cannot improve growth; in our context, if aid/donors cannot mitigate corruption or inefficiencies in procurement, aid-financed investments will be less effective than intended.

The strength of this critique is moderated to the extent that aid is effective independently of policy (which some studies find) and/or that conditionality influences policy. The latter seems quite likely as most developing countries have, to a greater or lesser extent, implemented the types of policy reforms supported by donors over the last 25 years. It is appropriate to take a long-term view because sustained policy reform is a slow process: the more (politically) challenging the reform the longer it is likely to take. For this reason, and because external shocks undermine the implementation and effect of policy reform, it can be very difficult to identify an effect of reform on performance. Furthermore, it is very difficult to measure policy reform effort or implementation and therefore very difficult to assess the effect of donor conditions.[19] Indeed, at least in a cross-country regression context, it may be futile to attempt to quantify effects of conditionality on reform and performance. Nevertheless, it is evident that in most countries trade and macroeconomic policy is better now than in the 1980s, and much of this attributable to donors working with recipients. There is evidence for this in the case of trade policy reform; taking Africa as an example, since the mid-1980s many countries have implemented the types of reforms advocated by donors.[20]

[18] Burnside and Dollar (n 5).

[19] O Morrissey, 'Conditionality and Aid Effectiveness Re-evaluated' (2004) 27 *The World Economy* 153.

[20] C Jones, O Morrissey and D Nelson, 'Did the World Bank Drive Tariff Reforms in Eastern Africa?' (2011) 39 *World Development* 324.

Conditionality refers to the practice of attaching policy reform requirements to aid to enhance the effectiveness of the aid in promoting growth and poverty reduction. The focus in the conditionality literature is on policy reforms rather than any administrative conditions relating to monitoring the way in which aid money is used and accounted for (in practice, such conditions may be very important). Donors face two particular challenges when engaging with recipients that may not be willing to implement the reforms favoured by donors: identifying recipients that will make good use of the aid; and ensuring incentives or an enforcement mechanism so that the conditions are complied with. The first of these relates to avoiding adverse selection by ensuring there are costs associated with the aid, such as commitments to reform, so unwilling reformers will not accept the aid conditions. The second concerns avoiding moral hazard by providing incentives and mechanisms to encourage effective use of the aid. These two concerns have counterparts in conditions to ensure an aid-financed investment project is implemented effectively, such as transparent procurement and monitoring to minimise exposure to corruption. Donors want to select good projects and ensure they are implemented.

The typical enforcement mechanism is to allocate aid in tranches and monitor compliance at each stage so that the next tranche is only released if there is sufficient compliance. Aid represents a classic principal-agent problem: donors (principals) design an aid contract that is attractive only to 'good' recipients (agents) and provide incentives for recipients to implement the contract.[21] However, once they have decided to finance the project the donors have incentives to disburse the aid.[22] Consequently, donors may be unwilling or unable to stop the project if problems arise, such as suspecting (but being unable to prove) that corruption is undermining the effectiveness of the investment. The implication is that donors should place most emphasis on awarding contracts to good agents because, once awarded, donor leverage is more restricted. The procurement process serves this aim.

While the argument for conditionality failure (recipients do not reform) has some historical merit it is not supported by recent evidence. Donor leverage and aid conditions do influence policy. Since the 1980s, for example, aid recipients have implemented policies liberalising exchange rates, reducing tax distortions (especially tariffs), removing price controls in agriculture, and establishing more stable macroeconomic policy. These have improved the quality of the economic environment so that aid-financed investment can be more productive, noting that in the poorest countries public investment is necessary to establish the physical and human capital infrastructure to crowd in private investment.

There is often a belief that governments misuse aid because it is fungible, arising when recipients do not use aid for the purposes intended by donors (aid adds to the budget envelope available so the government can simply reallocate spending). Thus, for example, USD 10 million given by donors for road construction may not be all spent on roads or, even if it is, may not increase spending on roads by USD 10 million

[21] J-P Azam and J-J Laffont, 'Contracting for Aid' (2003) 70 *Journal of Development Economics* 25.

[22] B Martens et al, *The Institutional Economics of Foreign Aid* (Cambridge, Cambridge University Press, 2002).

(because the recipient reallocates some of their resources that had been earmarked for roads). Even if aid is fungible the evidence suggests it has supported increases in spending on the provision of social (public) services, and increasing social sector spending is a clear intention of donors (and perhaps the most important reason why less than half of aid is allocated to capital investment). Aid recipients are often in a situation where domestic revenue is too low to meet expenditure needs to provide the level of public goods required for growth and development. The low domestic revenue does not imply that tax effort is weak, ie that tax/GDP ratios are particularly low; given the tax base and structure of such economies domestic revenue mobilisation may be as high as is feasible or even desirable, given that poor countries tend to rely on highly distorting taxes on trade.[23] The evidence on tax reform is promising: significant reforms to tax structure have been implemented in many countries, increasing efficiency (of the tax system and collection) and reducing distortions, especially given the reduced dependence on taxes on trade.[24] This is an indication that administrative and institutional reforms associated with aid (conditionality) can have positive impacts on performance, even if these are low in magnitude and only gradually realised.

The possibility that aid is fungible relates to two issues: is the aid all allocated to the particular area of expenditure targeted by donors and does expenditure on that area increase by the amount of the aid (is the aid additional)? Even if all the aid is allocated as intended, domestic resources previously allocated may be redirected so aid is not fully additional. The general argument is that recipients divert aid to government consumption spending rather than using it to finance growth-promoting investment. The evidence for this is weak as consumption (recurrent) spending includes wages and equipment, for example for health and education (necessary for human capital), and costs of maintaining infrastructure, so aid is often intended to support recurrent spending and such spending can contribute to growth.

The counter-argument is that if one analyses the dynamics of expenditure within the context of the evolution of fiscal aggregates (including taxes and borrowing), it is apparent that over time spending increases in the areas targeted by donors and often total spending increases by more than the value of aid.[25] Given the lack of good data over time for many aid recipients on government spending and its composition, there are few major cross-country regression studies of the impact of aid on spending, and no solid evidence on the relationship. There are a number of studies addressing if aid is fungible; here the evidence is mixed and inconclusive, largely resolving around how off-budget aid is treated. There are also a number of country time series studies of the fiscal effects of aid: these demonstrate heterogeneity in the sense that quantitative results differ across countries, although the general pattern is that aid increases aggregate government spending while poor countries have limited ability to alter

[23] P Clist and O Morrissey, 'Aid and Tax Revenue: Signs of a Positive Effect since the 1980s' (2011) 23 *Journal of International Development* 180; O Morrissey and S Torrance, 'Aid and Taxation', ch 31 in BM Arvin and B Lew (eds), *Handbook on the Economics of Foreign Aid* (Cheltenham, Edward Elgar Publishing, 2015) 555–76.

[24] Morrissey, 'Aid and Domestic Resource Mobilisation' (n 17).

[25] M McGillivray and O Morrissey, 'Fiscal Effects of Aid' in T Addison and A Roe (eds), *Fiscal Policy for Development: Poverty, Reconstruction and Growth* (Basingstoke, Palgrave Macmillan/WIDER, 2004).

tax revenue in the short to medium term.[26] What the evidence does show is that aid, and more explicitly the donor-recipient relationship underpinned by aid, can induce improvements in expenditure allocation and monitoring.

Another implication of the literature is that the effect of aid on government fiscal behaviour (including taxation) depends more on technical assistance and policy reforms associated with aid than on the amount of aid. The typical argument for why the amount of aid may reduce tax effort is that because people do not like paying taxes, governments have little incentive to exert administrative and political effort in collecting unpopular taxes. This is one reason why poor countries have often relied on trade taxes, especially on imports. The border is one place where transactions are recorded so administratively is the easiest place to collect taxes. Whilst importers have incentives to evade tariffs, such taxes may not be unpopular: import-competing producers lobby for tariff protection while the public can be persuaded (incorrectly) that foreigners rather than they pay the tariff. Since the 1980s, trade liberalisation and especially tariff reductions has been a major donor-promoted policy (often an aid condition). In some cases, increases in aid were provided to compensate for the revenue loss of reducing tariffs (assumed to be temporary while other taxes are increased to substitute for tariffs, although in practice it can be difficult to make up the lost revenue). In this example, allowing for conditionality, one could observe aid increasing while tax revenue declines.

The argument that aid reduces tax effort assumes that governments are concerned about political costs of taxes, but do not offset these against political costs of aid. This is not consistent with concerns expressed about aid dependence. Governments may be most amenable to aid when they view it as a resource to which they have (personal) access (arguments such as this lie at the root of theoretical papers on aid conditionality failure). Thus, when aid supports corrupt autocratic regimes one would not be surprised if tax collection was relatively low. This is a problem of the particular donor-recipient relationship rather than the effect of an amount of aid on tax effort (in another country the same amount of aid could be used effectively). As noted above, over at least the past 20 years donors have placed more emphasis on improving public finance management and encouraging anti-corruption measures. Even if these initiatives have had only limited success,[27] aid is now more transparent and monitored more carefully than was the case in the past. Governments (politicians and officials) are less likely now to view aid as an easily accessible resource. Furthermore, governments may face greater constraints on how they can use aid than on how they can misuse domestic revenue.

These changes provide a reason to believe that governments face a different type of trade-off between aid and tax because both involve political costs.[28] A government that wants to be less aid dependent will choose more tax effort. This choice will depend on the nature of the aid relationship and the tax options. Countries with access to resource rents have less incentive to increase taxes whatever their willingness to accept aid. Aid is likely to imply the highest costs of accountability; more effort has to be made to account

[26] Morrissey (n 17).

[27] M Andrews, *The Limits of Institutional Reform in Development* (Cambridge, Cambridge University Press, 2013).

[28] Morrissey (n 17).

(to donors) for how aid is used than to account to taxpayers for how taxes are raised or spent. The latter will depend on the nature of the democracy, which is typically weak, at least for accountability, in poor countries. To the extent that resource revenues are the least transparent they incur the lowest accountability costs. As donor agencies have to account to their own government and parliament, and even public, donors place increasing emphasis on measures to monitor the use of aid, minimise fungible use and tackle corruption. The policy reform conditions and technical assistance associated with aid include public financial management and tax administration. Whilst in principle this can improve accountability to taxpayers it also increases the political costs of aid as some control and influence is ceded to donors.

The requirements of accounting to donors and negotiating on conditionality reduce the autonomy of aid recipients by limiting their policy discretion; even limited conditionality is a constraint on policy action (if only because effort has to be expended to avoid or circumvent the conditions). Governments are not likely to want to be dependent on aid if this implies ceding policy influence to donors; they would prefer greater autonomy (being seen as subject to foreign influences can undermine their domestic popularity). A desire for greater autonomy would encourage governments to increase tax effort to reduce aid dependence. Increasing taxes may impose a cost of being more accountable to domestic constituencies but this is unlikely to offset the benefits of autonomy. The accountability costs of aid are likely to be higher than for taxation.

IV. Procurement, Investment and Effective Aid

From an aid and effective investment perspective, the concern with weak procurement systems is that they facilitate or disguise corrupt practices. There is no quantitative evidence on this; given the difficulty in identifying and incorporating measures of corruption, the few economic studies on procurement have tended to focus on how competitive the process appears, from which inferences on corruption can be drawn. For example, the competition effect predicts that as the number of bidders increases the price should fall;[29] if this is not observed to be the case the competitiveness of the process is called into question (collusion among bidders would be one explanation). Another testable prediction is the winner's curse: in order to win, some bidders understate the 'true' cost and successful low bidders cannot profitably deliver the project.[30] This is a commonly observed feature of bidding competitions and does not imply corruption – one needs to observe what happens after the award. One possibility is post-award renegotiation that increases the price upwards, and this may be more likely if local firms win the contract. Larger firms have experience and information to make the most realistic bid but not necessarily the lowest, whereas smaller, less experienced

[29] A Estache and A Iimi, 'Bidder Asymmetry in Infrastructure Procurement: Are There any Fringe Bidders?' (2010) 36 *Review of Industrial Organization* 163.

[30] A Estache and A Iimi, 'Joint Bidding, Governance and Public Procurement Costs: A Case of Road Projects' (2009) 80 *Annals of Public and Cooperative Economics* 393.

firms may make less realistic bids, typically lower. The smaller firms can win where there is a policy intention not to favour larger bidders, either because they are foreign companies (or affiliates of multinationals) or because of a desire to promote smaller local firms.

Taking these factors into consideration, an analysis of competition in procurement contracts would permit inferences about corruption. Of particular interest is where local firms win with the lowest bid in competition against larger, especially foreign, firms and are then able to renegotiate an increased post-award price that is above that of some losing bidders. Evidence for this would suggest corrupt activity. In contrast, if the winning bidder is able to deliver the project with minimal renegotiation it suggests a fair and competitive process. Unfortunately, there is very little empirical evidence on these issues. A partial exception is Galletta, Jametti and Redonda who find, in a study of public works procurement in the Democratic Republic of Congo, that a higher number of bidders is associated with a lower winning contract price.[31] This suggests that competition in the process can encourage efficiency and ultimately improve investment performance. Better procurement supports more competition and facilitates more effective investment projects.

Concerns with misuse and misallocation of funds provide a tangible link from aid to investment (the effectiveness of which is undermined) and the role of procurement (where improved processes reduce the scope for misuse). This is especially true for corruption, which can reduce the return on public investment in a number of ways. Most directly, some of the money is diverted away from the project (used for 'side payments') so that not all of the aid is actually used for investment. Less directly, but as important, contracts may not be awarded to the most efficient bidder; transparent procurement procedures can reduce this by ensuring competition and oversight. Better procurement processes address both of these issues, especially the latter, and increase the effectiveness of aid spending, especially for investment projects. More generally, government decisions on spending allocation may be distorted so that the investment is not directed at the most important or highest return projects so the aggregate return on investment is lower than it would otherwise be. This is not directly related to procurement, although better procurement systems are likely to enhance public spending management and allocation. In these ways, improving procurement contributes to aid effectiveness.

Aid, or more generally donors, can also contribute to improving procurement. This is most obvious where donors provide financial support or technical assistance for procurement reform, in terms of procurement law, rules and regulations; guidance on preparing bidding manuals and documents; and training for officials and regulatory bodies. The mixed success of donor support for institutional reforms has lessons here, the most important of which is perhaps that local buy-in and commitment is essential for even limited effective reforms. Externally designed and promoted reforms that can be perceived as imposed by donors in a top-down manner are rarely successful.[32]

[31] S Galletta, M Jametti and A Redonda, 'Highway to Economic Growth: Competition in Public Works Tenders in the Democratic Republic of Congo' (2015) 83 *South African Journal of Economics* 240.

[32] Andrews, *The Limits of Institutional Reform* (n 27).

The way in which sustained donor support for public financial management reform has delivered improvements is a more promising lesson, highlighting the importance of working with committed officials and accepting that institutional reform is a gradual process.

Donor coordination is also important. The fact that multiple donors operate multiple projects, some of which involve donor consortia, with their own procurement practices, imposes a burden on recipient countries. In practice, procurement officers with their own systems may also have to keep abreast of the different requirements of various donors, a situation which at the least creates inefficiencies and may also confound ability to identify what are the best practices. This also applies at the multilateral level where different bodies are engaged in devising procurement guidelines; even if not actually competing, this can make it more difficult for procurement agencies to decide what is best to adopt.

There is a shared interest, as good procurement improves projects and donors want more effective investment. The aid literature may not give clear messages on how aid contributes to growth, but this is as much a limitation of the literature as of aid. It is not surprising that the aid effectiveness literature is so contentious: aid is a political issue and the determinants of the growth process differ across countries so it is difficult to quantitatively establish the effect of aid. However, it is generally agreed that investment is the major growth driver, and although the productivity of investment varies greatly within and across countries, aid-financed investment is associated with respectable returns. The aid literature is more positive in showing the importance of policy and institutional reform, which can be supported and promoted by financial and technical assistance. There is evidence that conditionality has effects in promoting policy and institutional reforms, and this has to some extent been associated with improved expenditure allocation, monitoring and public financial management. This implies that donor support could be effective in implementing more transparent and competitive procurement processes that in turn would enhance the effectiveness of investment projects.

3

Procurement and Aid Effectiveness: The Journey so far

ANNAMARIA LA CHIMIA AND PETER TREPTE

I. Introduction

In seeking to establish a framework for understanding the role of procurement in the aid effectiveness agenda and for promoting future research and discussion in a coherent and constructive manner, this chapter explores the reasons why development procurement, ie the process for purchasing and ultimately delivering aid-funded goods and services, is important in the context of aid effectiveness and what may be the practices and factors in respect of procurement that could undermine, or contribute to undermining, the effectiveness of aid. The chapter also investigates the links between public procurement and aid effectiveness by looking at the international initiatives that have been undertaken to make aid more effective and provides an initial account of the status and results of these initiatives, arguing that it is not possible to evaluate the success or failure of such initiatives without understanding what is happening in the aid procurement context.

The adoption of the Monterrey Consensus at the 2002 International Conference on Financing for Development marks a turning point in the history of development assistance. The Consensus provided a direct answer to the various criticisms levelled against foreign aid (eg its ineffectiveness, wastage, the damage it causes to recipient countries and to their sovereignty[1]) and marks the start of a new era, of a journey, to make aid

[1] See references in chs 1 and 2 as well as W Easterly, *The White Man's Burden: Why the West's Efforts to Aid the Rest Have Done So Much Ill and So Little Good* (New York, Penguin Press, 2006); P Collier, *The Bottom Billion: Why the Poorest Countries are Failing and What Can Be Done About It* (Oxford, Oxford University Press, 2007); G Mohan, *Structural Adjustment Theory, Practice and Impact* (London, Routledge, 2000); A Alesina and D Dollar, 'Who Gives Foreign Aid to Whom and Why?' (2000) 5 *Journal of Economic Growth* 33, 33–36; L Dudley and C Montmarquette, 'A Model of the Supply of Bilateral Foreign Aid' (1976) 64 *American Economic Review* 132; A Maizels and MK Nissanke, 'Motivations for Aid to Developing Countries' (1984) 12 *World Development* 879; RD MacKinlay and R Little, 'A Foreign Policy Model of US Bilateral Aid Allocations' (1977) 30 *World Politics* 58, cited in HV Milner, 'Why Multilateralism? Foreign Aid and Domestic Principal-Agent Problems' in DG Hawkins et al (eds), *Delegation and Agency in International Organizations* (New York, Cambridge University Press, 2006) 107–39.

more effective. Important pit stops on this journey have been the four High-Level Fora on Aid Effectiveness, held in Rome (2003), Paris (2005), Accra (2008) and Busan (2011), respectively. After Busan, the aid effectiveness journey has continued under the auspices of the Global Partnership for Effective Development Cooperation (GPEDC), which was established by the partners involved at the Busan Forum to support implementation at the political level.[2] It may be noted that, as further explained below, the objectives and the actors involved in this latter initiative differ somewhat from those who have been involved from Monterrey to Busan, prompting some commentators to question whether the trajectory taken by the new Global Partnership effectively signals the end of the aid effectiveness crusade.[3] Given the marked failure of many of the initiatives launched under the aid effectiveness agenda and discussed further in subsequent chapters of this book, this may be a recognition of those failures and the beginning of a new approach. It is perhaps too early to tell, but the previous apparent commitment to some of the key goals of the Paris Declaration (discussed below) has clearly foundered. The explicit change of characterisation of the agenda from 'aid' effectiveness to 'development' effectiveness, originating in Busan with the endorsement of the principles of effective development cooperation, certainly suggests a move away from a narrow assessment of aid effectiveness to a broader assessment of development in more general terms, which may prelude the broadening (or diluting?) of the scope of the new initiatives and signal the decrease of the relevance of aid within the development context in favour of other forms of 'financing for development' such as commercial financing and Public-Private Partnerships[4] and the inclusion of new actors such as civil society and emerging non-traditional donors such as China, India and Brazil.[5]

More or less in parallel with the High-Level Fora meetings, a series of other initiatives took place that were specifically focused on procurement in the development context and linked to the aid effectiveness agenda. These gained momentum with the 2003 OECD-World Bank Procurement Roundtable focused on strengthening procurement capacity in developing countries[6] (the Roundtable included bilateral and multilateral donors and recipient countries.) The Roundtable, which over time grew to include more than 30 partners (multilateral and bilateral donors and recipient countries), later developed other procurement-specific initiatives such as the Joint Venture on Procurement and the Task Force on Procurement, operating under the chapeau of the Working Party on Aid Effectiveness (WP-EFF) and the Global Country Systems Cluster.[7]

[2] See the Outcome Document of the meeting (Busan Partnership): 'Busan Partnership for Effective Development Co-operation, Fourth High Level Forum on Aid Effectiveness, Busan, Republic of Korea, 29 November-1 December 2011', para 3, available at www.oecd.org/dac/effectiveness/49650173.pdf.

[3] E Mawdsley, L Savage and S Kim, '"A Post-aid World"? Paradigm Shift in Foreign Aid and Development Cooperation at the 2011 Busan High Level Forum' (2014) 180 *The Geographical Journal* 27; N Gulrajani, 'Organising for Donor Effectiveness: An Analytical Framework for Improving Aid Effectiveness Policies' (2014) 32 *Development Policy Review* 89.

[4] Mawdsley, Savage and Kim, '"A Post-aid World"?' (n 3).

[5] R Eyben and L Savage, 'Emerging and Submerging Powers: Imagined Geographies in the New Development Partnership at the Busan Fourth High Level Forum' (2013) 49 *Journal of Development Studies* 457.

[6] See World Bank, 'Strengthening Country Procurement Systems: Results and Opportunities – Report for the 4th High Level Forum on Aid Effectiveness' (Washington DC, World Bank, 2011) 3, available at siteresources.worldbank.org/INTALBANIA/Resources/Strengthening_Procurement_Systems.pdf.

[7] P Bigart, K Ejlskov-Jensen and R Roos, 'Strengthening Country Procurement Systems: Results and Opportunities, a report for the OECD/DAC Task Force on Procurement' 2, 8 (file with the author).

The same actors who were behind the aid effectiveness agenda, ie multilateral donors such as the World Bank, international organisations such as the OECD, like-minded donors such as Germany and UK, also lead these procurement initiatives. The main scope of these initiatives was to encourage donors to support, through aid, countries that have in place good development plans and that have implemented effective country systems reforms. These procurement-specific initiatives fed directly into the work of the High-Level Fora. For example, the Roundtable presented a report at the Second High-Level Forum in Paris on how procurement might contribute to the 'development effectiveness agenda' (namely Volume 3 of the DAC Guidelines and Reference Series on Harmonising Donor Practices for Effective Aid Delivery[8]). The procurement-specific initiatives focused on sharing best practices between members to 'discuss issues of common interest and introduce new tools that support the development of capacity and improved procurement systems'.[9] It is perhaps noteworthy that while these procurement initiatives are explicitly linked to the aid effectiveness agenda, they are not referred to in the aid effectiveness agenda itself[10] even though most of the actions taken were in the realm of procurement.

This chapter analyses the links between procurement and aid effectiveness by first explaining why procurement is important for aid effectiveness and what problems might be associated with procurement that undermine the success of aid projects. The chapter then looks at the initiatives within the aid effectiveness agenda that link procurement to aid effectiveness and discusses how these initiatives have changed and transformed over time. The chapter also discusses the differences between the pre- and post-Busan journey to understand whether, if at all, the narrative and the concrete actions that link procurement to aid effectiveness have changed, and if so how. In line with the objectives of the first part of this book, the chapter aims at providing an historical reconstruction of the international initiatives undertaken to use procurement as a tool to make aid more effective from Monterrey to the present day and to show that the aid effectiveness principles are relevant in the context of public procurement. Similarly, that public procurement occupies a central role within the targets and indicators of the aid effectiveness agenda, to the extent that some of the targets and indicators of the aid effectiveness agenda can be met only through addressing problems associated with the procurement process. In order to understand whether the aid effectiveness agenda is successful it is, therefore, critical to look at procurement and the developments that have occurred in the procurement sphere.

This is especially important given that the nexus between procurement and aid effectiveness has in some ways been overlooked by the development community; aid experts have often discussed the outcomes and results of the aid effectiveness agenda without considering the actions linked to the spending (disbursement) of the aid money. The impact that developments in procurement have had on the aid effectiveness agenda do not appear to have been investigated or conceptualised in any meaningful way. This chapter, and more fundamentally this book, seeks to do just that. The community

[8] See World Bank, 'Strengthening Country Procurement Systems: Results and Opportunities' (n 6) 9.
[9] ibid.
[10] Table 1 in the Annex to this chapter shows the landmark meetings of the aid effectiveness agenda and of the procurement initiatives to further highlight their parallel and intertwined development.

of development experts has neglected procurement and has not understood the deep and fundamental links that exist between the aid effectiveness agenda and procurement. Yet, without exploring the link between procurement and aid effectiveness, one cannot really assess if Paris is a comet or a shooting star.

The remaining chapters will analyse in detail the issues that emerge from this initial discussion allowing us to understand the mutual influence that developments in the procurement sector and in the aid effectiveness agenda have had on each other and showing, in particular, how the aid effectiveness agenda has managed to permeate, change and in some cases drive developments in the public procurement sector linked to aid. The influence is such, however, that it sometimes becomes difficult to pinpoint the origin of some of the key principles and whether it is the procurement 'agenda' that has borrowed from the aid agenda or vice versa.

II. Measuring the Unmeasurable?

As is clear from the previous two chapters, aid effectiveness has been an unsatisfactory area for discussion, generating much debate but reaching little in the way of consensus, much less drawing any conclusions. Much of this has to do with the difficulty of identifying what is being measured, something which also plagues other issues related to procurement and discussed in this volume.[11] Historically, the purpose of aid was seen as a means of developing economies and alleviating poverty. Even where these are not the only goals, the core objectives of economic growth and, particularly, poverty reduction have been maintained[12] as is also clear from the Millennium Development Goals (MDGs) and Sustainable Development Goals (SDGs).[13] As a result, economists and others have long focused attention on the effect on growth as the key determinant and measure of aid effectiveness although this has proven difficult to measure for a number of reasons, not least of which is the inability of commentators to agree on how to identify and measure economic growth.[14] Indeed, even the concept of aid has proven elusive. As Morrissey explains,[15] it is not only that aid is not necessarily directed towards growth-promoting initiatives, and often used for humanitarian purposes for example,[16] thus depriving assessors of growth-inducing aid to measure, 'the amount of aid alone is also a weak proxy for the potential of aid to affect growth'. There has thus been a recognition that it is also important to look at the allocation and implementation of aid rather than the amount of aid in order to assess its effectiveness.

From a simple procurement perspective implementation implies at least two things. First, that the money intended for development is actually spent on development so that

[11] See eg the problem of defining corruption discussed in ch 7.

[12] See ch 2.

[13] See sustainabledevelopment.un.org/?menu=1300.

[14] See ch 2.

[15] ibid s II.

[16] RC Riddell, 'Does foreign aid really work? An updated assessment', Development Policy Centre Discussion Paper 33 (Crawford School of Public Policy, The Australian National University, Canberra, 2014), 3, available at papers.ssrn.com/sol3/papers.cfm?abstract_id=2409847, s 2

something that could, in theory, be measurable (eg aid directed at financing physical infrastructure which can provide a return in terms of measurable growth) should, in practice, be implemented in a way that provides such measurability. This has always been the fundamental approach of the multilateral development banks (MDBs) whose fiduciary obligation, notwithstanding changes in articulation,[17] is set out in their Articles of Agreement, namely to 'ensure that the proceeds of any loan are *used only for the purposes for which the loan was granted*, with due attention to considerations of economy and efficiency and without regard to political or other non-economic influences or considerations' (emphasis added).[18] Second, that in terms of implementation, those funds should be spent well; an obligation represented by the second part of the same citation.

Despite the attempt in many MDB concept notes[19] to frame procurement reform as a direct promoter of growth, ie seeking to link procurement directly to the goals of aid (eg poverty reduction) as a means of justifying expenditure, it is usually very difficult to demonstrate a direct causal link between the procurement process (*a fortiori* procurement reform) and the aid objective itself. Notwithstanding the appearance of procurement in the new SDGs, for example in SDG 12, promoting sustainable procurement practices,[20] procurement is the process of delivering the aid; not the purpose of the aid. Delivery can be done well or badly and thus affect the outcome of the aid but that is a question of the quality of the delivery and, whilst delivery may have significant implications for the effectiveness of providing the aid, it is not a measure of the effectiveness of the result of the aid itself. Infrastructure may be procured well but if the infrastructure was not needed[21] and does not promote growth, the efficiency of its delivery does not work alchemy and turn lead into gold. Having said that, it is also true to say that the latest approaches to procurement reform (outside, but informing, the aid effectiveness agenda) are based on improving the quality of outcomes rather than looking at delivery as a simple matter of process, a view which has prevailed for some time and which motivated, at least in part, the procurement perspective of the aid effectiveness agenda. Effectiveness of procurement[22] has become the holy grail of procurement reform and, for the purposes of this current investigation, may be said to have eclipsed the pursuit of the effectiveness of aid.

The quality of delivery (but not necessarily of the outcome) has been a key feature of procurement reforms paralleling the aid effectiveness agenda. The reason is not hard to find. As Morrissey points out in chapter 2, heterogeneity has been one of the key obstacles to measuring growth. The beneficiary environments differ significantly from each other with many home-grown political, economic and social interests at play in addition

[17] ch 12.

[18] Articles of Agreement of the World Bank, art III, s 5(b), reproduced in similar terms in the articles of agreement of the regional banks also.

[19] Documents used internally by the MDBs to initiate loans and justify the need for them.

[20] See sustainabledevelopment.un.org/sdg12.

[21] A particularly egregious example of an economically unnecessary but politically motivated construction, Alaska's 'road to nowhere' even has its own Wikipedia entry at en.wikipedia.org/wiki/Gravina_Island_Bridge.

[22] With 'effectiveness' being defined in a number of ways linked to technical efficiency, value for money and probity etc.

to external forces. Aid is allocated and implemented in myriad ways and donors usually engage in their preferred means of implementation. As Riddell puts it so succinctly,

> [o]fficial aid-giving is thus characterised by an ever-increasing number of donors overseeing a growing number of discrete projects, creating an ever-more complex web of transactions and parallel management systems, many replicating and duplicating each other.[23]

The absence of homogeneity means that there is no single benchmark against which to measure the effectiveness of the aid. Multiple implementation methods (procurement rules) are applied so that there is no consistency in process and, therefore, no consistent method of assessing effectiveness. So, even if it were possible to identify how aid could affect growth and even where it could be shown that the aid did in fact affect growth (and that it was not the result of any other factor – the endogeneity problem also raised by Morrisey[24]), there remains no mechanism for measuring those effects on a like-for-like basis given the multiple contexts within which aid is granted, the allocation decisions of different donors and the differing methods of implementation that such donors employ. We may well be seeking to measure the unmeasurable.

The danger of such a situation to effective procurement (and thus potentially to the ultimate effectiveness of the aid) is not difficult to discern and was explicitly recognised as part of the aid effectiveness agenda. In the context of procurement, two issues in particular have emerged. The first stems from the observation made by Riddell cited in the passage above.[25] It consists in the fragmentation caused by the multiplicity of donors and, more precisely, of procurement implementation methods. In terms of procurement rules, donors have often required adherence to their own procurement rules, whether the procurement is conducted by their own agents or by the beneficiary countries themselves.[26] Given the differences between those rules, this has often led to what has been termed 'capacity erosion', which surfaces where borrowers are required to know and implement a multiplicity of donor rules.[27] The second issue is very much linked to the first and is an example of Morrissey's heterogeneity. If donors apply different procurement rules and thus, presumably, have a different concept of what constitutes effective procurement, how is it possible to measure effective procurement (and the role it plays in ensuring effective aid) in an objective and consistent way? This dilemma has given way to talk of harmonisation, ie a means of bringing together the disparate procurement rules so that they are mutually consistent,[28] although the term conceals two different elements.

[23] Riddell, 'Does foreign aid really work?' (n 16) 27.

[24] See ch 2.

[25] See also S Knack and A Rahman, 'Donor Fragmentation' in W Easterly (ed), *Reinventing Foreign Aid* (Cambridge, MIT Press, 2008) 334.

[26] A La Chimia, 'Donors' Influence on Developing Countries' Procurement Systems, Rules and Markets: a Critical Analysis' in G Quinot and S Arrowsmith (eds), *Public Procurement Regulation in Africa* (Cambridge, Cambridge University Press, 2013) 232 ff.

[27] P Trepte, 'Building Sustainable Capacity in Public Procurement' in S Arrowsmith and R Anderson (eds), *The WTO Regime on Government Procurement: Challenge and Reform* (Cambridge, Cambridge University Press 2011) 377, 381.

[28] This is not intended to be a definition of 'harmonisation' which is another word that defies a unanimously accepted definition.

As we will see in chapters 4 and 5, the term signifies both 'alignment' and 'harmonisation'. Whilst in the general aid context (as articulated in the Paris Declaration) alignment refers to a strengthening of the connection between donor assistance and borrower country strategies and systems, in terms of procurement this has been applied more directly to the alignment of donor rules and country systems. The use of country systems implies, however, the acceptability of that system to the donors, so that the commitment to alignment seems also to imply the bringing of the procurement rules of the donor and the beneficiary countries closer together. One way of doing this, and the one which has held sway for the longest time, is to encourage (or require) beneficiary countries to adapt (or establish) national procurement rules that reflect those of the donors. The technical assistance programmes provided to beneficiaries as part of the donors' loan agreements have done just that by providing assistance to beneficiaries to draft and adopt 'acceptable' procurement legislation. For instance, as discussed in chapter 14, supporting procurement reforms in developing countries has been one of the major objectives of the USAID model; interestingly, as the authors of chapter 14 argue 'the main motivations [for USAID] for providing support to countries on procurement in any given instance are to strengthen governance, accountability and economic growth'[29] and not necessarily to use country systems.

The acceptability of such legislation has frequently been measured against the donors' own procurement rules. As we will see in chapter 9, under one of the key initiatives of the OECD/DAC Roundtable on Strengthening Procurement Capacity, namely the creation of the MAPS tool, MAPS was used (rightly or wrongly) to inject some form of objective benchmark into this process. Conceived as a method for assessing national systems against a benchmark of accepted good practice, it was more frequently used as a benchmark against which the acceptability of national systems was measured in respect of donors' rules. Alignment was thus seen either as having national rules that were close copies of donor rules or meeting the indicators[30] of the MAPS tool which amounted to much the same thing in many cases given the extensive involvement of the donors in the development of the MAPS tool.

MAPS was also, in part, an exercise in harmonisation. Precisely because the donors were involved in its development, it came to be seen as an expression of the most accepted example of good practice which would satisfy all of the participating donors. In this sense, harmonisation consists in the alignment not of the donors' rules with the beneficiaries' rules but of a rapprochement between the rules of the donors themselves. This is a process that has been going on for some time with the procurement guidelines, and the standard bidding documents, of the various multilateral development banks becoming ever more similar. The benefit of this, of course, would be less fragmentation in the sense that beneficiary countries' procurement officers would need to be familiar with fewer sets of procurement rules or, at least, that those procurement rules with which they needed to be familiar became so similar that familiarisation with one set of rules would be sufficient. As explained in chapter 12, the World Bank has recently

[29] see ch 14, n 115.

[30] These were previously assessed by a scoring mechanism but the new MAPS tool, described in ch 9, is far more aspirational in nature and closer to the original conception.

made some bold moves to reform its own procurement rules, in part to make them more effective and deliver better outcomes (see above). Whilst the regional banks and other donors have habitually followed the World Bank's lead, it is evident that this is no longer the case.[31] Despite the assertion of Yukins and Williams-Elegbe in chapter 12, that 'the Bank's new Procurement Framework is likely to shape the procurement policies of the other multilateral development banks', this may yet turn out to be more an expression of optimism than a Delphic prediction. A number of regional banks (for example, the Inter-American Development Bank and the European Bank for Reconstruction and Development) are pointedly not following the example of the World Bank.[32] Others, such as the African Development Bank[33] and the Asian Development Bank, have chosen to be inspired by the World Bank reforms but have taken a slightly different path. The harmonisation process of the last 20 years or so between the MDBs has come to abrupt halt. It may be hoped that a common path may yet be found but the current signs do not augur well.[34]

It was not only the donors that entered into the harmonisation game. As Schwarz points out in chapter 4, it was also a broader phenomenon which brought in the World Trade Organization, the European Union and UNCITRAL, among others. Possibly due to the actors common to all of these initiatives (including MAPS[35]), the procurement instruments of those actors came to resemble each other very closely so that there was little to distinguish them.[36] Similar procurement provisions appeared in other international procurement instruments and proposed instruments, notably the T-TIP.[37] Schwarz, whilst not giving up all hope of continuing convergence, sets out some of the difficulties and obstacles facing what appeared to be an inexorable march. For example, not only are the harmonised provisions of UNCITRAL and the GPA too stringent for lesser developed countries, requiring differential treatment,[38] they appear too open and permissive to politicians whose main concerns are informed by a mercantilist approach to international trade.

Together, the idea of minimising fragmentation through alignment and harmonisation has reinforced one of the other key initiatives of the aid effectiveness agenda, namely country ownership. In terms of procurement, where reliance can be placed on nationally aligned or harmonised procurement rules, the implication is that beneficiaries will not only own the aid objective but also the process used to achieve it. All of the

[31] See ch 13.

[32] A Salazar and M López, 'The Inter-American Development Bank: Reform to Build Up and Increase the Use of National Procurement Systems in Latin America and the Caribbean' (2016) 25 *Public Procurement Law Review* 164; J Jackholt, 'The Procurement Policies and Rules and the Procurement Activities of the European Bank for Reconstruction and Development' (2016) 25 *Public Procurement Law Review* 172.

[33] V Sharma, 'An Update on Procurement Reforms at the African Development Bank' (2016) 25 *Public Procurement Law Review* 151.

[34] see ch 13 in this collection.

[35] Although the EU was late to the MAPS table (which is may be why the European Directives did not comply with all of the earlier MAPS indicators, conceived as they were by the other donors).

[36] Important in the case of the WTO and the EU, eg, where, as a signatory to the WTO's Government Procurement Agreement (GPA), the EU Procurement Directives were required to comply with the provisions of the GPA.

[37] See ch 4.

[38] With the knock-on effect this has on their relationships with the donors who themselves have been heading in the harmonisation direction.

procurement initiatives discussed in this volume go some way to addressing this issue although the difficulties associated with alignment (and what it implies for country systems) and harmonisation are such that this objective is proving very elusive. Country ownership may reach its apogee in terms of procurement when donors rely entirely on beneficiary country procurement systems for the disbursement and delivery of aid. Such a situation is far from being achieved and the most ambitious attempt to do so ended in (silent) failure.[39] The World Bank's recent reforms speak of using Alternative Procurement Arrangements (APA), in part meaning the use of country systems, but the test for doing so is more stringent than that applied to the pilot project that failed.[40] It is not clear why this should bring the stated objective of the aid effectiveness agenda any closer.

This section began by implying that economic growth and alleviation of poverty were not the only goals of aid. From the outset, decisions on the allocation of aid have been motivated by other goals and imperatives. As Zupi points out,[41] foreign aid has been seen as part of the broader foreign policy approach of donors with aid being allocated to those beneficiaries who shared the vision of the donors or who were needed as allies on any number of foreign policy, trade, military and security fronts. From limiting the spread of Soviet influence to the current concern of the Trump administration with promoting national interests in the face of perceived international trade threats,[42] notably from China, the allocation of aid remains a powerful tool to build like-minded coalitions and promote domestic interests. The recent emergence of China as a key player in the aid market[43] is testimony to the power of aid as a tool influence.[44] La Chimia discusses the (resurgent) tied aid modality often used to advance the political or economic agendas of donors in chapter 6. Effectiveness of aid, if measured in such circumstances, is not measured by the yardstick of growth or poverty reduction but must be seen in the context of the less benign objectives sought.

However, even where there is no overtly political or security agenda, the pursuit of development itself has changed and expanded over the years. In the early years, the focus was on capital investment as a means of promoting growth and this gradually developed into investing in human capital and raising the standard of living of the poor more directly.[45] By the mid-1980s, a new vision had emerged in the donor community based on what has become known as the 'Washington Consensus' which focused on the principles of liberalisation, deregulation and privatisation and encouraged market-friendly national policies. This was accompanied by a strong emphasis on *governance* and on

[39] See ch 10; P Trepte, 'All Change at the World Bank? The New Procurement Framework' (2016) 25 *Public Procurement Law Review* 121, 129.

[40] Trepte, ibid 141.

[41] See ch 1.

[42] See also ch 4.

[43] And the potential disruption this causes through the way in which it allocated its funds, forgoing the conditionalities of the MDBs and Western donors.

[44] D Bräutigam, 'Aid "with Chinese Characteristics": Chinese Foreign Aid and Development Finance Meet the OECD-DAC Aid Regime' (2011) 23 *Journal of International Development* 752; P Brant, 'Chinese Aid in the South Pacific: Linked to Resources?' (2013) 37 *Asian Studies Review* 158, available at www.tandfonline.com/doi/abs/10.1080/10357823.2013.767311; M Naím, 'Rogue Aid' (2007) 159 *Foreign Policy* 95, 95–96.

[45] See ch 2, s II.

ensuring that the national institutions in place were sufficiently robust (and compliant with the donors' approach) to allow for the desired development to take place. This is the point at which the use of donor conditionalities became most prevalent, viz the use of conditions attached to loans in an attempt to improve governance and thus make aid more effective. From the procurement perspective, this meant enhancing national procurement systems and bringing them into line with acceptable international practices. This explains the focus described above, on alignment and harmonisation. It also needs to be recognised, however, that the donors' view of governance was probably coloured by their own experiences so that good governance reflected their own structures of governance. As Andersson and Heywood have put it:

> the so-called best practices which underpin [the good governance] approach are in reality unattainable (certainly, no Western political system would fully conform), and it is certainly possible that in many developing societies disrupting socially ingrained ways of getting things done in the interests of 'good management' and 'efficiency' could do real damage… there is no one best way of organising the effective management of states.[46]

The conditionalities imposed to bring about good governance could also be seen as something alien and potentially incompatible with the systems in place in the borrower countries. Far from increasing borrower ownership of the results of aid, the imposition of foreign practices could well be seen as inimical to country ownership since those practices (and procurement processes) are, by definition, imposed. A number of commentators point to this hallmark of traditional donor aid as one of the reasons that the Busan High-Level Forum resulted in such a dramatic change in the approach to aid and development, pointing to a fatigue with post-colonial type patriarchy and a new openness to the emergence of a 'South-South' dialogue.[47]

Another notable feature of this governance agenda, however, was an arguably exaggerated concern with process and of ensuring compliance with accepted practices as a means of improving integrity.[48] It may be that this is the result of the harmonisation process itself which, in the case of donor harmonisation,[49] was brought about by much detailed discussion on the minutiae of the procurement rules and on how these might affect national systems and the use of national systems. Such an approach, where small differences in detail appear to matter very much and are applied with rigour by the various MDBs, was bound to lead to a very prescriptive set of rules. Effectiveness of the procurement process came to be seen primarily as a question of technical efficiency which could be measured through an assessment of compliance with rules. As procurement reform moves in the direction of performance and outcomes, matching

[46] S Andersson and PM Heywood, 'The Politics of Perception: Use and Abuse of Transparency International's Approach to Measuring Corruption' (2009) 57 *Political Studies* 746, 752.

[47] Eyben and Savage, 'Emerging and Submerging Powers' (n 5); Brant, 'Chinese Aid in the South Pacific' (n 44). Brant explains: 'For both domestic and international reasons, and unlike "traditional donors", Chinese foreign aid does not include a focus on democracy, good governance or human rights, which has led to much criticism and concern in the West. It instead stresses the importance of stimulating economic growth and implementing a development model based on each country's specific requirements and circumstances. In this way China seeks to differentiate itself from traditional donor'.

[48] See also ch 7.

[49] See further ch 13.

the strategic objectives of borrower countries, it is arguable that this narrowly defined governance agenda is no longer sustainable given the increasing need to take context more into account and ensure that the procurement methods and strategies adopted are fit for purpose in that given context. Of course, even outcomes-based procurement requires an adequate set of rules of the game but the rigidity and formalism of a one-size-fits-all form of regulation (based on the donors' vision) needs must give way to the flexibility which characterises the strategic approach to procurement. It is perhaps no coincidence that the new MAPS tool, discussed in chapter 9, is no longer a scores-based compliance test but a much more ambitious tool enabling those countries carrying out the assessment to determine their own goals and priorities against a set of broader aspirational benchmarks.

Adding to this mix were developments taking place at the international level that led to the adoption of the United Nations' Millennium Development Goals (MDGs) which arose in 2000 out of the United Nations Millennium Summit where the development agencies and 189 States of the United Nations made a commitment to work towards a world in which the elimination of poverty and sustained development would have the highest priority. With poverty elimination still the core objective, the MDGs established targets and yardsticks for measuring results in achieving eight MDGs which were to guide the efforts of virtually all organisations working in development and which were commonly accepted as a framework for measuring development progress.[50] Donor projects and loans were expected to be the means by which the envisaged activities would achieve or contribute to the achievement of the MDGs.

The target date for the achievement of the MDGs arrived in 2015 and the final MDG Report found that whilst the 15-year effort had produced the most successful anti-poverty movement in history, it also recognised that there was still much to do. At the United Nations Sustainable Development Summit in 2015, world leaders adopted a replacement set of 17 Sustainable Development Goals (SDGs) to end poverty, fight inequality and injustice and tackle climate change by 2030. The new SDGs, and the broader sustainability agenda, aspire to go further than the MDGs, addressing the root causes of poverty and the universal need for development that works for all people.[51] At the level of procurement, discussed further in chapter 8, this has translated into a greater focus on sustainable procurement which takes account of social and environmental considerations and goes beyond the earlier governance driven emphasis on process, linking in with donors' new appetite for improved outcomes and value for money. Rather than focus on process, the mood is now to consider outcomes and seek ways of improving those outcomes. The World Bank has started the process[52] and Gutman, in chapter 15, considers ways of achieving such objectives. Other donors are also investigating ways of achieving these goals.[53]

[50] The eight goals were to eradicate extreme poverty and hunger; achieve universal primary education; promote gender equality and empower women; reduce child mortality; improve maternal health; combat HIV/AIDS, malaria and other diseases; ensure environmental sustainability; and develop a Global Partnership for Development.

[51] See further sustainabledevelopment.un.org/.

[52] See ch 12 and Trepte, 'All Change at the World Bank?' (n 39).

[53] See chs 11 and 14.

Given these developments, there are perhaps two questions that become relevant to the issue of procurement and aid effectiveness. First, and assuming that the core objectives of aid, namely economic growth and poverty reduction, remain valid objectives (notwithstanding other motivations and additional goals), does the way in which procurement is used in delivery of that aid make that aid more effective or, at least, does it not undermine its effectiveness? Second, what effect do the additional political or emerging (sustainability) goals have on the role procurement has to play in aid effectiveness? These are some of the themes underlying the subsequent chapters.

III. The Nexus between Procurement and Aid Effectiveness

In looking at the role of procurement in light of the above, it is clear that public procurement became relevant in the development context, and in the context of aid effectiveness in particular, in two distinct but connected ways.

Firstly, it became relevant because public procurement is directly linked to the spending of the aid money and to the delivery of the goods and services necessary for the realisation of aid projects, a process known as development aid procurement.[54] An overwhelming portion of aid is spent through the public procurement process.[55] Eurodad has estimated that, in 2015 alone, 'donors have spent US$ 55 billion – or more than 44 per cent of Real Official Development Assistance (ODA) – on the procurement of goods and services'.[56] Recent data for individual donors confirm this trend. For example, DFID has spent £1.4 billion of aid money through the public purchasing process in 2017 alone.[57] Given the size of procurement spend, inefficient procurement practices and systems can lead to huge wastage of precious resources and can have a negative impact on development. Mismanagement in procurement affects the quality and quantity of the goods/services purchased, ie how much and how many goods/services can be bought for the aid donated,[58] can lead to fewer goods/services being purchased with the aid money, and can result in worse quality of goods/works etc. As part of a technocratic procurement process, efficiency was traditionally seen by donors as a matter of technical efficiency and the procurement rules they conceived as a result were designed to achieve this. Recently, however, new goals have emerged and good procurement now

[54] For the first definition of this term, see A La Chimia, *Tied Aid within the Framework of EU and WTO Law: the Imperative of change* (Oxford, Hart Publishing, 2013).

[55] OECD, *Harmonising Donor Practices for Effective Aid Delivery: Good Practice Papers – A DAC Reference Document*, DAC Guidelines and Reference Series (Paris, OECD Publications, 2003) available at www.oecd.org/development/effectiveness/20896122.pdf.

[56] P Meeks, 'Development United: Unleashing the Catalytic Power of Official Development Assistance though Renewed Action on Untying (Eurodad, September 2018) available at eurodad.org/files/pdf/5ba3a41be1899.pdf.

[57] Independent Commission for Aid Impact (ICAI), *Achieving value for money through procurement – Part 1: DFID's approach to its supplier market* (Independent Commission for Aid Impact, November 2017) available at icai.independent.gov.uk/wp-content/uploads/ICAI-Procurement-review-DFID%E2%80%99s-approach-to-its-supplier-market.pdf.

[58] Hence, strengthening government procurement practices in the delivery of aid money can drastically increase aid effectiveness. See Department of International Development (DFID), *Procurement Capacity Building: Applying Lessons Learned Elsewhere* (Paris, OECD, 22–23 January 2003) 4. This document was presented at the Joint DAC/World Bank Roundtable on Strengthening Procurement Capacities in Developing Countries.

tends to encompass a broader concept of value for money,[59] obtaining more for what you pay and therefore meaning more for aid. Strengthening the procurement process during the spending of the aid money became very important for donors and this remains the case, even if the content of the rules that govern that process have developed. Not surprisingly, ever more often donors are conducting assessments of their aid procurement practices and of the effectiveness of the procurement process linked with the spending of the aid money. For example, the UK's International Commission on Aid Impact (ICAI) has recently undertaken two studies to monitor the effectiveness of UK aid purchasing practices.[60]

Secondly, in the 1980s, public procurement became relevant within the context of good governance, institutional reforms and capacity-building, issues which were directly linked to the development agenda and connected with the idea pioneered by Dollar and Levin that 'the success of aid-sponsored programmes depends primarily on the quality of institutions in the recipient country'.[61] Strengthening the institutional apparatus within recipient countries was regarded as a key step for development.[62] Over time, public procurement emerged as a key state-building function, central to good governance, to fighting corruption and to building trust in the government.[63] Efficient and effective procurement was seen as an essential element of good governance, which in turn was a 'key driver of economic growth and development'.[64] Ensuring that developing countries had sound procurement systems was seen as important for the functioning and the success of the State and, ultimately, of all aid policies and projects. The discussion in section II above suggests that this donor vision of governance may be flawed or at least in need of refinement and a number of commentators have pointed out the difficulties in applying this approach.[65] Leeson, for example, shows that where

[59] Going beyond the idea of achieving the lowest price. The World Bank's definition refers to 'the effective, efficient, and economic use of resources, which requires an evaluation of relevant costs and benefits, along with an assessment of risks, and non-price attributes and/or life cycle costs, as appropriate. Price alone may not necessarily represent value for money'. See World Bank, *Bank Policy, Procurement in IPF and Other Operational Procurement Matters* (Washington DC, World Bank, 2017) s III.C.1, available at policies.worldbank.org/sites/ppf3/PPFDocuments/a3656cb78847417b886f11fa0235216e.pdf. The MDBs all use similar, but not identical definitions.

[60] See ICAI 'Achieving value for money through procurement – Part 1: DFID's approach to its supplier market' available at https://icai.independent.gov.uk/report/achieving-value-money-procurement-part-1-dfids-approach-supplier-market/ and ICAI' Achieving value for money through procurement Part 2: DFID's approach to value for money through tendering and contract management' available at https://icai.independent.gov.uk/report/procurement2/ retrieved April 2019.

[61] D Dollar and V Levin, *Sowing and Reaping: Institutional Quality and Project Outcomes in Developing Countries*, World Bank Policy Research Working Paper 3524 (Washington DC, World Bank, 2005); see also M Winters, 'Accountability, Participation and Foreign Aid Effectiveness' (2010) 12 *International Studies Review* 218, 227 and 238.

[62] This is a concept that arose in the 1980s as part of the Washington Consensus and that has further been developed in the 1990s and 2000s. The pioneering World Bank Report by D Dollar and L Pritchett, *Assessing Aid: What Works, What Doesn't, and Why* (Washington DC, World Bank, 1998) (available at documents.worldbank.org/curated/en/612481468764422935/Assessing-aid-what-works-what-doesnt-and-why) for instance argues that strong institutions are key to aid success. Similarly, in the literature Riddell argues that aid can have a positive effect on growth when combined with the right policies and the appropriate institutional environment.

[63] See eg the case of Afghanistan in Islamic Republic of Afghanistan, 'Afghanistan National Peace and Development Framework (ANPDF) 2017–2021', available at extwprlegs1.fao.org/docs/pdf/afg148215.pdf.

[64] OECD, 'The Cusco Declaration of the OECD/DAC Task Force on Procurement: "Strong Procurement Systems for Effective States"'.

[65] Andersson and Heywood, 'The Politics of Perception' (n 46).

foreign aid is needed, countries do not have the right institutions and environment to take advantage of it, but that, on the contrary, countries with the appropriate institutions and environment, do not need aid.[66] The results of the Busan High-Level Forum suggest also that a new approach is needed to this concept of governance.[67]

The functioning of recipients' own procurement systems has long been a concern for donors, a concern which has led donors to setting standards and rules to be applied (the UNCITRAL Model Law first, the OECD Recommendation on procurement more recently), devising monitoring mechanisms to check these systems (such as the MDBs' Country Procurement Assessment Reports first, and the MAPS and other similar tools later), and financing – with conspicuous amount of money – the establishment or the reform, depending on the country and the starting point of those systems, of new procurement systems.[68] This approach should not come as a surprise considering that public procurement in developing countries is estimated[69] to represent around 14.5 per cent of GDP or USD 820 billion per year by the World Bank, a considerable part of which is financed through donor aid.[70] 10 to 20 per cent is not uncommon for low-income developing countries.[71] This percentage can reach higher levels; for instance in Nicaragua around 45 per cent and in Haiti as much as 70 per cent of government projects are financed through bilateral assistance.[72] In Ghana, ODA accounts for 42 per cent of the national budget.[73] Hence, as explained above, better procurement systems have a direct impact on the effectiveness of the aid given.

Acceptability of the borrower's systems, has become particularly important with the move away from project lending to budgetary support and investment lending where MDB funds and the government's own funds are fungible, ie indistinguishable in the budget, and cannot be isolated for the purpose of applying procurement or other rules for their use.[74] All the procurement activities are funded by a single budget

[66] PT Leeson, 'Escaping Poverty: Foreign Aid, Private Poverty, and Economic Development' (2008) 23 *Journal of Private Enterprise* 39, 18.

[67] Eyben and Savage (n 5); Brant (n 44).

[68] This has been the case in Afghanistan for example, where a procurement system did not exist before the intervention of the World Bank and of other donors.

[69] OECD 2004, study conducted on 106 non-OECD countries.

[70] As Evenett has noted 'developing countries tend to have a sizeable proportion of their non-defence government budgets funded by aid, loans, or grants'; see SJ Evenett, *Can Developing Countries Benefit from Negotiations on Transparency in Government Procurement in the Doha Round?* Task Force 9 (Open, Rule-Based Trading System) of the United Nations Millennium Project, 2003, available at www.alexandria.unisg.ch/22164/.

[71] See SJ Evenett and BM Hoekman, 'International Cooperation and the Reform of Public Procurement Policies', World Bank Policy Research Working Paper 3720 (Washington DC, World Bank, September 2005) 7, available at openknowledge.worldbank.org/bitstream/handle/10986/8268/wps3720.pdf?sequence=1&isAllowed=y, where Hoekman and Evenett point out that 'Available data on the relative importance of aid flows as a share of government expenditure suggest that aid finances a significant share of total purchases of goods and services by developing country governments. The ratio of official aid flows (bi- and multilateral) to total expenditure was equivalent to 35 percent of total expenditures on goods and services for low-income countries in the early 1990s. For lower middle-income nations, total aid accounted for 16 percent of expenditures; for upper middle-income economies the figure dropped to 6 percent'.

[72] World Bank data in T Mkandawire, 'Aid, Accountability, and Democracy in Africa' (2010) 77 *Social Research: An International Quarterly* 1447–59; in Samoa it is 27%, in Sao Tome and Principe it goes up to 55.9%.

[73] Eurodad, 'For whose gain? Procurement, tied aid and the use of country systems in Ghana' (Eurodad, 2010) available at https://eurodad.org/uploadedfiles/whats_new/reports/for_whose_gain.pdf.

[74] Trepte (n 39) 127.

without it being possible to identify the precise source of the budget funds. It is not possible, therefore, to apply one set of procurement rules to the MDB-funded portion and another set of rules to portions funded by the national budget since the sources of funding are indistinguishable. In such cases, the national system applies and, where that is inadequate, the MDB funds are at risk. Improving that national system reduces that risk, so that strengthening that system becomes an imperative for the MDBs.

It is evident that when the recipient country is also in charge of carrying out the aid procurement process, 'fixing' national procurement systems has allowed donors to combine their own macro- and micro-aspirations of aid success, namely, by addressing structural causes of aid ineffectiveness linked to good governance (or lack thereof), accountability and weak institutions, while also ensuring the realisation of more immediate aid effectiveness concerns, namely ensuring that aid reaches its beneficiaries, ie the hospital/the road being built, the medicines delivered. Furthermore, addressing structural procurement issues linked to the 'macro' aspiration of aid can lead to recipients' self-reliance, something that could remove the need for aid altogether and a motivating factor in the pursuit of using country systems. Addressing the microeconomic goals of aid effectiveness, ie delivering the project for which aid was granted, also allows donors to obtain support for aid policies at home and to strengthen the relationship of donors with the direct beneficiaries of the aid. Fixing procurement is therefore seen as a win-win situation and investing in reforming recipients' systems has been very important for donors because it makes or appears to make their own aid more effective while also addressing the root causes of poverty.[75]

This focus on 'fixing' country systems, with a view ultimately to relying on them, led in part to the culture of conditionality which consisted of requiring adherence to a set of rules that were acceptable to the donors. To the extent that national rules were not acceptable, they would be disapplied or replaced by acceptable rules through the loan agreements which imposed these conditionalities. In addition to the converging rules and standards of the donors as well as international instruments such as the UNCITRAL Model Law, OECD Recommendations and even the WTO's Government Procurement Agreement (as explained in chapter 4), the original MAPS tool was used in practice to provide a common benchmark against which country systems could be measured. As is the way with any common benchmark agreed by a large number of stakeholders, the result is usually reduction to the lowest common denominator acceptable to the participating members. It was in some ways a rather rigid tool and based on the MDBs' combined view of procurement[76] and the box-ticking scoring method inevitably led to a culture of compliance. In line with the donors' own governance agenda, the approach to conditionality became technocratic and based on efficiency and compliance with

[75] It is therefore not surprising that donors have committed to assist developing countries to implement procurement reforms and to providing 'sufficient resources to support and sustain medium and long-term procurement reforms and capacity development'. See Arusha Statement of the OECD/DAC Joint Venture on Procurement, 'To Support the Implementation of the Paris Declaration Principles by Building Reliable Public Procurement Systems' (2008) para 3, points ii and iii, available at www.unpcdc.org/media/4140/global%20jv%20on%20procurement.pdf.

[76] Indeed, the EU Directives, had they been assessed against the tool, would have failed a number of the indicators.

accepted norms and, as mentioned above, the process of reaching consensus on those common rules, may itself be responsible for the prescription that has ensued. There was little room in this prescriptive arena for alternative approaches or creativity in the objectives sought.

However, economic efficiency is only part of the answer and the donor world is waking up to the fact that technical efficiency alone does not necessarily bring better procurement results and thus, arguably, more effective use of aid. The way in which the procurement process is devised, regulated and run, has an impact on the appropriateness of the aid donated and its very capacity to meet the development objectives for which the aid is donated in the first place. Questions linked to *how* goods/services should and will be purchased, ie whether following national/international rules, or from *where* goods/services should be purchased, ie locally, from the donors, from the international market, not only affect the *economic* value of the goods/services purchased (whether aid will be more or less expensive) but it can affect the *nature* of the aid itself, the suitability of the aid goods/services purchased to fulfil the recipients' needs from a cultural, religious, practical and moral perspective. The donor community has also begun to look more closely at the procurement *cycle*, namely planning, buying and project management, rather than focusing solely on the process of purchasing.[77]

The result of these changes in thinking about the content and purpose of procurement rules means that the 'traditional' prescriptive, compliance-based approach championed through the governance agenda also needs to be viewed in a fresh light. This does not mean that procurement rules will disappear but rather that they will need to become more instrumental and responsive to the context (of the country, the sector, the market etc) to meet the stated development objectives in a strategic manner and thus become fit for purpose. This is a journey that has all but started but the experiences and lessons learned to date in the field of procurement reform and reflected in many chapters of this book will be valuable considerations on the road ahead. This evolution in the approach to procurement reform is about making procurement more effective in the sense that it is not only efficient but actually achieves the strategic objectives of the purchaser. It requires a re-assessment of how aid effectiveness is to be assessed, ie it is no longer about only ensuring efficient purchase and delivery and the elimination of waste, it is ultimately about deciding what procurement strategy will produce the most effective result in terms of meeting project objectives, achieving the desired outcomes, extracting the highest performance and obtaining value for money. This is an immediate challenge for those involved in development aid and procurement.

In addition to this challenge, it is also now well understood that sound procurement practices in the delivery of aid projects and in the spending of aid money can be a means of realising social and economic objectives and hence contribute to sustainable development. This is the challenge presented by the SDGs which now feature prominently in aided projects, including those concerned specifically with procurement.

[77] See further ch 12 and Trepte (n 39).

They have found their way also into the new MAPS tool which now provides a basis for sustainable procurement where that is one of the strategic goals of the country, as it frequently now is. Procurement can be used instrumentally to promote a number of desirable sustainability goals such as social and environmental policies, the promotion of human rights, protection of SMEs and measures to boost the economy. Procurement can play a role in addressing inequalities, helping people with disabilities, women and other marginalised groups of society. Importantly, as Meeks correctly points out, the impact of procurement on these groups can be twofold: as consumers, by facilitating (or constraining) access to goods and services, and as suppliers, by 'breaking down the barriers that hold people back as producers'[78] and constrain their capacity to participate to the economy. The importance of the economic activities of the government as purchaser in the market gives it immense power to influence the economy in those sectors in which it is active. Where it is the dominant buyer, such influence may be decisive.[79] As a result, the reach and leverage of the government as purchaser goes way beyond what is being purchased. In developing countries, the spending of aid money can become an opportunity for trade and for boosting the local economy, especially in countries where governments are major outlets for trade. It can be harnessed to pursue sustainable goals which go beyond the traditional pursuit of the lowest price. This is far from being a new phenomenon[80] and much has been written about the instrumental use of procurement in specific contexts.[81] What is perhaps new is that the instrumentality of procurement has entered the international stage and been identified as a vehicle for the pursuit of a broader range of sustainability goals, notably those envisaged by the SDGs.

The following chapters and the continuing trajectory of procurement and aid effectiveness will thus need to be read and assessed against the background of the evolving procurement reform landscape which is moving from efficiency-based technical compliance to world of strategic procurement where value for money is determined not only by price but by the achievement of better outcomes, improved performance and the attainment of sustainability goals. These developments are also being played out to some degree in the High-Level Fora on aid effectiveness to which we will now turn.

[78] Meeks, 'Development United' (n 56).

[79] P Trepte, *Regulating Procurement: Understanding the Ends and Means of Procurement Regulation* (Oxford, Oxford University Press, 2004) 137.

[80] And, as already discussed, procurement has been used with political and security objectives as well as for economic reasons linked to the tying of aid.

[81] See, for comprehensive analyses, S Arrowsmith, 'Public Procurement as an Instrument of Policy and the Impact of Market Liberalisation' (1995) 111 *Law Quarterly Review* 235; F Martín, *The EC Public Procurement Rules: A Critical Analysis* (Oxford, Oxford University Press, 1996) ch 2; C Jeanrenaud, 'Marchés Publics et Politique Economique' in Jeanrenaud (ed), *Regional Impact of Public Procurement* (Saint-Saphorin, Georgi, 1984). See also RB Watermeyer, 'Facilitating Sustainable Development through Public and Donor Procurement Regimes: Tools and Techniques' (2004) 13 *Public Procurement Law Review* 30. For a recent analysis in the context of the EU, see S Arrowsmith and P Kunzlik, 'Public Procurement and Horizonal Policies in EC Law: General Principles' in S Arrowsmith and P Kunzlik (eds), *Social and Environmental Policies in EC Procurement Law* (Cambridge, Cambridge University Press, 2009).

IV. Procurement in the International Initiatives to Enhance Aid Effectiveness

This section provides a brief history of the High-Level Fora (HLF) Initiatives and the Global Partnership for Development, focusing exclusively on the principles, targets and indicators endorsed therewith that are relevant for and link procurement with aid effectiveness. The aim is to identify what solutions these initiatives foresee for the problems linked to development procurement that we have identified above and how they envisage procurement can be improved to foster aid success. This section also looks at the procurement-specific initiatives, such as the Procurement Roundtable, that have been developed in parallel to the mainstream High-Level Fora on aid effectiveness.

These latter important initiatives were specifically focused on procurement and included the OECD/DAC-World Bank Roundtable on Procurement (the Roundtable), followed by the Joint Venture on Procurement (an innovative initiative jointly sponsored by the World Bank and the OECD, acting as a sub-committee of the OECD/DAC Working Party on Aid Effectiveness, strictly linked to the Joint Venture on monitoring the Paris Declaration,[82]) and the OECD/DAC Task Force on Procurement. These initiatives have been overlooked by the development aid community, but they are interlinked with the more mainstream aid initiatives and, as far as procurement is concerned, further develop the aid effectiveness principles. Developments occurring as part of these procurement specific initiatives (ie within the Roundtable first and the Joint Venture and the Task Force later) are worth mentioning because they are important indications of how the aid effectiveness agenda will evolve in regards to procurement and they help understanding why HLF fell short of the commitments undertaken in these other fora.

As mentioned in the preface, the first event highlighting the importance of aid for development and the need to both increase the amount of aid donated and to improve aid effectiveness was the International Conference on Financing for Development held in Monterrey in 2002. Monterrey is often regarded as a landmark event because donors recognised, for the first time, that responsibility for aid's failure was not to be attributed to recipient countries alone and admitted that aid incapacity to eradicate poverty – despite the trillions of dollars spent – was to be attributed to the way aid was granted and managed.[83] With the Monterrey Consensus, donors and recipient countries recognised the need to work together to make aid work for the poor. However, the Monterrey Consensus provides little guidance on how to improve aid effectiveness. Reference is made to 'improving administrative capacity and good governance', and 'increasing ownership and harmonisation of rules' but no clear guidance is provided on what 'ownership', 'harmonisation' 'administrative capacity' and 'good governance; are and how they are to be achieved.

This guidance came later via the High-Level Fora on aid effectiveness, which were championed by the Working Party on Aid Effectiveness (WP-EFF) and hosted by

[82] See B Killen, 'Communications, Aid Effectiveness and Accra' (OECD) available at www.oecd.org/development/pgd/39635615.pdf.

[83] See Riddell (n 16).

the OECD-DAC. The first of these Fora was held in Rome in 2003 where the Rome Declaration on the harmonisation of donors' practices was agreed by Ministers, Heads of Aid Agencies and other Senior Officials representing 28 aid recipient countries and more than 40 multilateral and bilateral development institutions.

The opening statement of the Rome Declaration reaffirms donors' commitment to sustainable development and to eradicating poverty, reinforcing the Monterrey's Consensus. The Rome Declaration, like Monterrey before it, starts with a recognition of donors' responsibilities for aid failure. Importantly for our analysis, the Declaration states:

> the totality and wide variety of donor requirements and processes for preparing, delivering, and monitoring development assistance are generating unproductive transaction costs for, and drawing down the limited capacity of, partner countries. We are also aware of partner country concerns that donors' practices do not always fit well with national development priorities and systems, including their budget, programme, and project planning cycles and *public expenditure* and financial management systems.

By making an explicit reference to public expenditures, the Rome Declaration places procurement – and the process linked to the spending of the aid money – at the forefront of the aid effectiveness debate. Yet the link to procurement here is not very strong and those who were following the initiatives of the Roundtable on procurement might have been disappointed to find so little reference to it. Indeed, it is worth noting that the first meeting of the Roundtable was held in January just before the first HLF in Rome. The Roundtable links procurement to aid effectiveness from the very outset. At the group's first meeting in Paris it was explained that the Roundtable's aims were to 'promote partnership approaches and ownership'[84] and to 'identify and address key procurement capacity building needs and to build procurement systems in developing countries around which donors can harmonise their procedures'.[85] During the opening remarks of the first meeting the co-chairs Chard and Hunja emphasised the importance of the Roundtable work and

> its connections with the wider development agenda – public expenditure management, good governance, new modes of resource transfer such as budget aid, and the Monterrey (e.g. aid effectiveness, donor practices) and Doha (e.g. transparency in government procurement, WTO Government Procurement Agreement) agendas.[86]

The Rome Declaration focuses on harmonisation and is clear in identifying fragmentation and lack of coordination of donors' practices as the major reasons for the lack of aid success. It proposes as solution to these problems, the harmonisation of donors' practices. Harmonisation of donors' practices becomes a leading aid effectiveness principle. However, the Rome Declaration does not indicate specific actions or measures through which such harmonisation will be achieved, although the MDBs entered into

[84] OECD/DAC, 'Strengthening Procurement Capacities in Developing Countries: Summary Report of the OECD/DAC – World Bank Roundtable, Paris, 22–23 January 2003' (Washington DC, World Bank, 2003) available at www.oecd.org/dac/effectiveness/2500769.pdf.

[85] ibid.

[86] ibid 4.

a concerted effort to harmonise both their procurement guidelines and the standard bidding documents that accompanied them. It would be for the Paris Declaration, two years later in 2005, to give precise guidance (through the setting of indicators and targets) as to what actions should be taken to improve aid effectiveness.

Continuing on from the Rome Declaration, the Paris Declaration includes harmonisation as one of its five core principles together with *ownership, alignment, managing for results* and *mutual accountability*. Importantly, the Paris Declaration sets specific indicators and targets to monitor progress towards the realisation of these principles. Some of these indicators and targets link procurement and aid effectiveness explicitly, some others do so indirectly. Furthermore, within the aid effectiveness process linked to the Paris Declaration donors also agreed to be subjected to scrutiny and external monitoring in regard to their progress in implementing the Paris Declaration. Two progress Reports on implementing the Paris Declaration were carried out, one (an interim Report) in 2008[87] and one (final report) in 2011.[88] These Reports are important because they (try to) make donors accountable for the (soft-law) commitments they have endorsed and in so doing they (were supposed to) give the Paris Declaration unprecedented strength. However, as explained below, the negative findings of these Reports (of the second especially) and the absence of any consequence for donors' lack of fulfillment of their commitments and the absence of any remedial measure carried out to address those negative findings ended up significantly undermining the aid effectiveness agenda.

Just before the Paris Declaration the Procurement Roundtable met again in 2004 in Johannesburg where the Johannesburg Declaration on procurement was adopted. The Johannesburg Declaration maintains that improvements in the performance of public procurement systems will facilitate 'harmonisation and aid effectiveness' and effective procurement systems are described as 'a key part of development'. As part of the Johannesburg Declaration the first publication of a public procurement benchmarking methodology (now known as MAPS) was launched. The Johannesburg Declaration concludes the works of the Roundtable.

The principles in the Johannesburg Declaration resonate within the principles of the Paris Declaration. The first principle of the Paris Declaration is *ownership*, defined as the exercise by partner countries of 'effective leadership over their development policies, and strategies and co-ordinate development actions'. (Paris Declaration, points 14 and 15). This is akin to an umbrella principle, a principle relevant to all the other principles, the indicators and targets. Even if procurement is not explicitly mentioned under this principle, its relevance for procurement is clear: as with any other development strategy, the procurement process, the procurement system and the procurement strategies need to be 'owned' by the country that will benefit by the goods and services purchased. This implies that needs have to be set having regard to what the *country* believes is necessary, evaluating all the resources available. Under the aegis of the

[87] See B Wood, D Kabell, F Sagasti and N Muwanga, *Synthesis Report on the First Phase of the Evaluation of the Implementation of the Paris Declaration* (Copenhagen, July 2008) available at assets.publishing.service.gov.uk/government/uploads/system/uploads/attachment_data/file/67753/Paris-Dec-Synthesis-Report.pdf.

[88] B Wood, K Betts, F Etta, J Gayfer, D Kabell, N Ngwira, F Sagasti and M Samaranayake, *The Evaluation of the Paris Declaration, Final Report* (Copenhagen, May 2011) available at pd-website.inforce.dk/content/pdf/PD-EN-web.pdf.

principle of *ownership*, donors committed to: 'respect partner country leadership and help strengthen their capacity to exercise it'. The numerous capacity-building programme implemented over the years in developing (or partner, as there are referred to in the Paris Declaration) countries – including within the procurement sector – can certainly be reconnected to it.

The second principle of the Paris Declaration is alignment, viz the donors' commitment to bring their support into line with 'partner' countries' strategies and use institutions and procedures (ie use of country systems). Procurement is specifically mentioned under this principle of *alignment*, under Indicators 5b and 8, entitled *Strengthen national procurement systems* (5b) and *Untie aid: getting better value for money* (8). Indicator 5b is especially important for the discourse on aid effectiveness because donors commit to 'Progressively rely on partner country systems for procurement when the country has implemented mutually agreed standards and processes' (point 30, linked to Indicator 5b). The targets for this indicator foresee the increase of the percentage of donors that use country system, setting an ambitious 90 per cent to 100 per cent target for aid to the public sector to be granted using country procurement systems and a one-third to two-thirds reduction in the percentage of aid to the public sector not using partner countries' procurement systems.

Indicator 8 identifies untying aid as a way to get better value for money. It explicitly says

> Untying aid generally increases aid effectiveness by reducing transaction costs for partner countries and improving country ownership and alignment. DAC Donors will continue to make progress on untying as encouraged by the 2001 DAC Recommendation on Untying Official Development Assistance to the Least Developed Countries (PD, Indicator 8).

The target for this indicator is not very ambitious and is limited to a commitment to continue progress overtime towards untying. Both the use of country system and aid untying will be the topic of two specific chapters in this collection, chapter 10 and 6 respectively.

Other indicators under the principle of alignment are also relevant for procurement, even if procurement is not expressly mentioned. This is the case for Indicator 2 on 'mutually agreed frameworks that provide reliable assessments of performance, transparency and accountability of country systems (point 19 linked to Indicator 2)'. Indicator 2 sets in motion an intense process to develop assessment tools – used especially in procurement – to assess recipients' systems. As explained above, in the procurement field this process has been initiated with the OECD Methodology for Assessing Procurement Systems (MAPS). Other assessment tools further developed by aid agencies include the World Bank's MAPA and the Maturity Model used by the US Millennium Challenge Corporation. These tools will be analysed in-depth in chapters 9, 10 and 11. It is worth noting that developments in procurement that have originated in the aid procurement sector – and specifically within the aid effectiveness context – have now become of general relevance for procurement in both developed and developing countries. This is the case of the methodology for assessing procurement systems which now is used to assess developed countries' systems.

The third principle reiterates the importance of harmonisation. The indicators and targets set to implement this principle recognise the need for donors to coordinate their actions, simplify procedures and share information to avoid duplication. In particular, donors commit to 'work together to reduce the number of separate, duplicative, missions to the field and diagnostic reviews (Indicator 10); and promote joint training to share lessons learnt and build a community of practice'. They include a commitment to 'a pragmatic approach to the division of labour and burden sharing increases complementarity and can reduce transaction costs'. Again, this principle is important in the area of procurement. Fragmentation and the many and diversified ways and agencies through which donors provide aid is cause of inefficiency and a burden for partner countries. In Uganda, for example, between 1998 and 2008 grant agreements were signed with 58 donors in total, all with their own procurement rules and standards.

The final two principles, namely managing for results and mutual accountability are described as 'managing and implementing aid in a way that focuses on the desired results and uses information to improve decision-making' (paragraph 43) and as a commitment to 'enhance mutual accountability and transparency in the use of development resources. This also helps strengthen public support for national policies and development assistance' (para 47, Paris Declaration). These two principles have, at first, had little resonance in the procurement field.[89] Indeed, as Gutman explains in chapter 15, the attention of policy-makers has often been exclusively focused on the bid and award process, on the transparency of the procurement process, on competition and the time required for processing (further corroborating the idea that procurement is (just) a technical issue.) As Gutman argues, 'nobody seems to ask the obvious question: "how much of the success or failure of the project outcome is attributable to how the procurement was designed and executed?"' As further explained below and in chapter 15, in this principle lies one of the most important innovations of the aid effectiveness process linked to procurement that could potentially change how we approach and implement procurement in general, beyond the links to aid and aid effectiveness.

The principles, indicators and targets of the Paris Declaration were once again reiterated in Accra, in 2008 with the endorsement of the Accra Agenda of Action. Accra came after the publication of the 2008 interim Monitoring Survey on the Implementation of the Paris Declaration,[90] which showed that although the Paris Declaration had 'created powerful momentum to change the way developing countries and donors work together on the ground' progress in implementing the Paris Declaration was slow. Accra offered the opportunity to reiterate the principles of the Paris Declaration and to 'take action to accelerate progress' (point 7 of AAA), to strengthen the terms and renew the political commitments of the Paris Declaration. The principles that relate to procurement acquired even more prominence in Accra. The AAA reiterated the importance of country systems, firmly linking the use of country systems to ownership of development policies and strategies. Donors committed to 'use developing country systems to the maximum extent possible' (point 15 of AAA). Importantly, country systems have to become the first option for donors in support of activities managed by the public

[89] In the broader aid context the principle of results is often regarded as a mere technocratic principle that risks undermining ownership. See M Sjöstedt, 'Aid Effectiveness and the Paris Declaration: A Mismatch between Ownership and Results-Based Management?' (2013) 33(2) *Public Administration and Development* 143.

[90] Wood, Kabell, Sagasti and Muwanga, *Synthesis Report on the First Phase of the Evaluation of the Implementation of the Paris Declaration* (n 87).

sector.[91] 'Building reliable procurement systems' with a view to supporting the implementation of the Paris Declaration is also the major goal of the 2008 Arusha Statement on Procurement Capacity.[92]

The commitment to harmonise donors' aid policies is reiterated in paragraph 17 of the AAA.[93] The principle of delivering and accounting for development results is stronger than in Paris as is the link with transparency and anti-corruption. Donors and recipients commit to be 'more accountable and transparent to our public for results' (point 24 of AAA).

Yet despite these renewed political commitments the 2011 Survey on monitoring the Paris Declaration revealed a grim picture. For example, only 22 per cent of donors' missions were coordinated in the countries participating in the Survey (registering a 2 per cent decrease compared to the levels in 2008.)[94] The percentage of aid using country systems also remained low. The 2011 surveys in particular not only showed a lack of progress in the implementation of the aid effectiveness commitments but it registered some significant steps backwards on some of the most important indicators of the Paris Declaration, such as the use of country systems. Overall, the 2011 survey reveals that donors had not adhered to the Paris Principles as much as it had first been hoped. Just before the final forum, the OECD/DAC Task Force on procurement met and endorsed the 2011 Cusco Declaration where efficient and effective public procurement systems are seen as 'fundamental component of good governance'.

The final High-Level Forum was held in Busan in 2011 and resulted in the endorsement of a new Partnership for Effective Development Co-operation. As mentioned above, in Busan the focus of the high level forum shifted from aid to development, signalling a decrease in importance in the role that aid plays in the development context in favour of the emergence of new forms of cooperation, mainly linked to the private sector.[95] The Partnership 'offers a framework for continued dialogue and efforts to enhance the effectiveness of development co-operation'.[96] The number of actors involved in Busan grew significantly. More than 160 countries and over 50 organisations participated in Busan and agreed on the Busan Partnership Agreement, and there was an especially strong presence from civil society organisations and non-state actors.[97] The Busan Partnership

[91] para 15 of the AAA reads 'Donors agree to use country systems as the first option for aid programmes in support of activities managed by the public sector'. See OECD, 'The Paris Declaration on Aid Effectiveness and the Accra Agenda for Action' (OECD, 2005/2008) available at www.oecd.org/development/effectiveness/34428351.pdf.

[92] Arusha Statement of the OECD/DAC Joint Venture on Procurement (n 75).

[93] para 17 of the AAA (n 92) reads: 'the effectiveness of aid is reduced when there are too many duplicating initiatives, especially at country and sector levels. We will reduce the fragmentation of aid by improving the complementarity of donors' efforts and the division of labour among donors, including through improved allocation of resources within sectors, within countries, and across countries'.

[94] See OECD/DAC, *Aid Effectiveness 2005–10: Progress in implementing the Paris Declaration* (OECD, 2011) available at effectivecooperation.org/wp-content/uploads/2016/03/2011%20Report%20on%20Monitoring%20the%20Paris%20Declaration%20ENGLISH.pdf. 32 countries participated in the 2006, 2008 and 2010 Survey on Monitoring the Paris Declaration. 78 countries participated in the most recent survey. The data reported here refers to the 32 countries who participated in all surveys.

[95] Above n 3

[96] See effectivecooperation.org.

[97] Busan Partnership (n 2) para 7 states 'We commit to modernise, deepen and broaden our co-operation, involving state and non-state actors that wish to shape an agenda that has until recently been dominated by a narrower group of development actors'.

Agreement opens with members' defiant admission that they 'recognise that progress [in meeting the commitments of the Paris Declaration] has been uneven and neither fast nor far-reaching enough'.[98] Busan is often criticised because partners missed the opportunity to agree measures to address the negative findings of the 2011 report on the implementation of the Paris Declaration.[99] As Gulrajani states 'aid effectiveness transformed itself into a pejorative word. As of now, there are no concrete commitments to supplant the Paris targets, leaving the goals and objectives of aid effectiveness in a state of confusion and flux'.[100]

With the move away from aid to development more generally, the commitments endorsed are diluted. There are no targets and no precise indicators (a commitment is made to agree on new indicators and targets in 2012). The original five principles endorsed in Paris (namely ownership, alignment, harmonisation, managing for results and mutual accountability) are reframed in four new principles. Only the principle of ownership remains the same as it was.[101] 'Managing for results' acquired a new prominence and becomes 'a focus on results'. The OECD explains that this now means 'having a sustainable impact' which 'should be the driving force behind investments and efforts in development policy making'.[102]

What under Paris were *Harmonisation* and *Alignment* now become 'Partnerships for development'. When describing this principle the OECD explains 'Development depends on the participation of all actors, and recognises the diversity and complementarity of their functions. A fourth new principle of 'Transparency and shared responsibility' is added. This principle resembles but it does not exactly mirror the principle of 'mutual accountability'. According to this principle 'Development co-operation must be transparent and accountable to all citizens'.[103]

Although the Busan Partnership agreement no longer sets the specific indicators and targets of the Paris Declaration, most commitments endorsed in Paris are confirmed and others are endorsed with a softer and more generic language. As regards procurement the commitment to use country system is reaffirmed and parties agreed to use country systems as 'the default option'. This commitment to use country systems as the default option might seem stronger than in Paris, but the absence of specific targets against which to measure the implementation of such commitments renders it weaker. All the evidence of action on this objective to date does not provide much optimism.

The Busan Partnership also plants the seed for what was to become the new Global Partnership for Effective Development Cooperation (GPEDC). Partners commit to

> establish a new, inclusive and representative Global Partnership for Effective Development Co-operation to support and ensure accountability for the implementation of commitments

[98] ibid para 6.
[99] Gulrajani, 'Organising for Donor Effectiveness' (n 3).
[100] ibid.
[101] In the wording of the OECD Ownership of development priorities by developing countries means 'Countries should define the development model that they want to implement'. OECD 'the Busan partnership for effective development cooperation' July 2012 available at http://www.oecd.org/dac/effectiveness/Busan%20partnership.pdf retrieved April 2019.
[102] ibid.
[103] ibid.

> at the political level. This Partnership will offer an open platform that embraces diversity, providing a forum for the exchange of knowledge and the regular review of progress.[104] (para 36).

The OECD and the UNDP are called to support 'the effective functioning of the Global Partnership'.[105] Interestingly the World Bank seems to no longer play a central role within the Global Partnership and this might very well have had an impact reducing the resonance that the GPEDC has had so far, especially if one compares it to the Paris Declaration.

The Global Partnership builds on the four Busan principles of effective development cooperation, reiterating those principles and proposing a framework for their implementation based on the mutual exchange of information and monitoring tools. Two progress reports have been released so far – in 2014 and 2016[106] – and a series of interactive maps have been developed to check progress on the implementation of the new indicators. Importantly, two of the indicators used in each country to measure progress towards the fulfilment of the partnership commitments, relate to procurement, ie they include the use of country procurement systems and the level of aid which is untied (the results of these two surveys in respect of these two indicators are further analysed in chapter 10 and chapter 6 in this collection).

The post Busan partnership reveals, once again, the continued importance of procurement in the development agenda. Procurement-specific initiatives have also intensified after Busan, but this time they seem much more detached from the aid agenda than before. Details of these meetings are given in chapter 9 where the developments linked to the MAPS II methodology are described.

It is important to note that the procurement-specific initiatives that were mentioned above have developed in *parallel* to the aid effectiveness agenda and while strictly connected to this agenda they remained separate to it. This meant that while they have had the merit of successfully pursuing the objective of mainstreaming the issue of procurement within the aid effectiveness agenda, by having a life of their own they avoided being associated with the failure of that agenda and have been able to continue independently from it. This has allowed up to now a refocus of the objectives, the strategies and the goals of these procurement initiatives beyond and independently from aid effectiveness. This is illustrated well in the case of the revision of the MAPS (now MAPS II) which, as explained in chapter 9, has now moved away from the assumption (voluntary or involuntary) that it is a preliminary assessment for the use of country systems but it is a diagnostic instrument of value to both developed and developing countries alike.

In the concluding remarks of this collection, in chapter 16, we will further reflect on how the aid effectiveness agenda has changed in the procurement context and what opportunities the new partnership might offer.

[104] Busan Partnership (n 2), para 36c: 'Call on the Working Party on Aid Effectiveness (WP-EFF) to convene representatives of all countries and stakeholders endorsing this document with a view to reaching agreement on the working arrangements for the Global Partnership – and the indicators and channels through which global monitoring and accountability will be supported – in preparation for the phasing out of the WP-EFF and its associated structures in June 2012'.

[105] ibid.

[106] See www.oecd.org/dac/effectiveness/monitoring-effectiveness.htm; see also videos at www.youtube.com/watch?v=2OIftTTMNlQ.

Annex

The table below gives details of the various procurement and aid effectiveness initiatives which have taken place in the past two decades. Details of the related policy goals are also included.

Table 1 International Initiatives Linked to Public Procurement and Aid

Aid Effectiveness Initiatives			Procurement-specific Initiatives		
Date	**Aid effectiveness Event**	**Policy Commitment**	**Date**	**Procurement Event**	**Policy Commitment**
March 2002	Monterrey Financing for Development Conference and 'Monterrey Consensus'	Aid Effectiveness			
February 2003	1st High-Level Forum on Aid Effectiveness, Rome, and 'Rome Declaration'		January 2003	Launch of the World Bank/OECD Development Assistance Committee (DAC) Procurement Roundtable	Mainstreaming Public Procurement in aid effectiveness agenda
	Johannesburg Declaration, Conclusion of Roundtable		December 2004	2004, Johannesburg Declaration of December, produced by the World Bank – OECD/DAC Roundtable on Strengthening Procurement Capacity. First publication of a public procurement benchmarking methodology (aka MAPS) as part of the Johannesburg Declaration, Conclusion of Roundtable	Public Procurement

(continued)

Table 1 ***(Continued)***

Aid Effectiveness Initiatives			**Procurement-specific Initiatives**		
Date	**Aid effectiveness Event**	**Policy Commitment**	**Date**	**Procurement Event**	**Policy Commitment**
March 2005	2nd High-Level Forum on Aid Effectiveness, Paris, and 'Paris Declaration'	Aid Effectiveness			
2006	Resolution adopted by the General Assembly 60/193. Implementation of Agenda 21, the Programme for the Further Implementation of Agenda 21				
September 2008	3rd High Level Forum on Aid Effectiveness, Accra, and 'Accra Agenda for Action' (AAA)	Aid Effectiveness	May 2008	Arusha Statement of the OECD DAC Joint Venture on Procurement	Public Procurement
2009	Doha				
November 2011	4th High-Level Forum on Aid Effectiveness, Busan, and the 'Global Partnership for Effective Development Cooperation' (GPEDC)			Cusco Declaration of the OECD DAC Taskforce on Procurement	Aid Effectiveness Public Procurement
			October 2013	Meeting on the Task Force on Procurement, Rabat	Public Procurement

(continued)

Table 1 ***(Continued)***

Aid Effectiveness Initiatives			Procurement-specific Initiatives		
Date	**Aid effectiveness Event**	**Policy Commitment**	**Date**	**Procurement Event**	**Policy Commitment**
			April 2015	Global Public Procurement conference, Manila	Public Procurement
July 2015	3rd International Conference on Financing for Development and the 'Addis Ababa Action Agenda' (AAAA)	Aid Effectiveness	June 2015	First meeting of the Stakeholder Group on the Revision of MAPS	Public Procurement
September 2015	Sustainable Development Goals (SDGs)				General
			2016	Meeting of the Stakeholder Group on the Revision of MAPS	Public Procurement
	Global Partnership				

PART II

Harmonisation: The First Pit Stop

4

A Post-Modern Assessment of Global Harmonisation and Convergence: The Prospects and Challenges Going Forward to Further Global Standardisation of Procurement Regimes

JOSHUA I SCHWARTZ

I. Introduction

A. Looking Backward and Looking Forward

On 15 June 2015, the paper that forms the heart of this chapter was presented at the seventh iteration of the Global Revolution Conference on public procurement law that occurs biennially at the University of Nottingham put on by the Public Procurement Research Group. The United States' election campaign was heating up but the election of Donald Trump was more than a year away in the future, and it was not generally foreseen that he would even get the nomination of the Republican Party. In the UK, the Conservative Party had won the General Election just over a month before the Conference with a manifesto promising of a referendum on what came to be known as Brexit. But that referendum was just over a year away and the victory of the Leave position was not generally anticipated. That is why, as I write this introduction, three years after the Global Revolution VII Conference, that time seems a world far away.

Yet the divisive trends that have dominated the news of the period since the Global Revolution VII Conference were already of concern in June of 2015. Indeed, this chapter reflects the author's strongly rising concern that powerful trends in world political economy were increasingly challenging or even threatening to reverse the progress made in the preceding decades towards harmonisation of public procurement regimes across the face of the world.

Never have I wanted so badly to be proven wrong as when I observed in mid-2015 that 'continuing advancement of … harmonization of systems of public procurement … now seems fraught with challenges and difficulties'.[1] However, as events have turned out, the concerns reflected in my June 2015 paper were not misplaced. It seems worthwhile to capture here just what was apprehended from the perspective of three years ago, before the Brexit referendum outcome and the election of Donald Trump became realities. Thus the paper that forms the heart of this chapter is presented essentially as it was in June of 2015 with modest editing and supplementation of the references. This introductory note is intended primarily to place that paper in the context of the time in which it was delivered, and to make the briefest of observations about the trends that have marked the intervening years. As to what comes next, we hope to address that more fully in a session at the next Global Revolution Conference hereafter, Global Revolution IX, scheduled for June 2019.

It bears emphasis that the paper presented here was by no means entirely pessimistic about the prospects over the medium to long term of further progress towards harmonisation and integration. This author argued then that continued pursuit of a 'measured, selective, iterative and incrementalist' approach to harmonisation would continue to bear fruit – albeit patience would be required before much progress resumed and could not be expected in an 'artificially short time period'.[2] And even in the face of the challenges that the world financial crisis posed to the opening of free trade in the acquisition of government goods and services, it was noted there were also particular developments such as increased attention to the problems of corruption in many national regimes that gave particular hope for progress in the course of harmonisation.[3]

The intervening years have borne out both the prediction of troubled waters ahead and the underlying confidence that the work of harmonisation would not be drastically or permanently reversed. More particularly, the on-going political and economic struggles over increased protectionism in the United States as well as the enormous practical difficulties that have appeared as the UK seeks to actually implement Brexit suggest that pauses and reversals for freer trade in the public procurement sector do not necessarily portend an end to harmonisation. The economic policies associated with the Trump administration, to the extent that any coherent thread emerges, appear to reflect a kind of resurgence of mercantilism, complete with the idea that a sufficiently powerful nation state can successfully 'beggar' its neighbours, forcing disadvantageous trade relationships upon them, and thereby prosper. But as the reader will be aware, both the European Union and China are capable of retaliation and threatened retaliation, and the prospect of trade war scarcely provides assurance that the United States' embrace of this new mercantilism will lead to the promised prosperity. And each passing week brings to light unanticipated consequences and costs associated with implementation of the Brexit policy. Of course the difficulty of implementing Brexit in the context of the border between the Irish Republic – remaining in the EU – and Northern Ireland, departing the EU along with the UK, is frequently noted[4]. But there is a host of other

[1] Quoting this author's language used in s I.B below.

[2] See s VI of this chapter.

[3] See s VI of this chapter.

[4] S Castle, 'U.K. Reaches Brexit Transition Deal with E.U' *New York Times*, 19 March 2018, available at www.nytimes.com/2018/03/19/world/europe/uk-brexit-eu.html. (Stating that, in order to reach a final arrangement for Brexit, the parties would be required to work out, 'Among other issues, … how the two sides intend to avoid a "hard border," one with checkpoints, between Northern Ireland and Ireland. Such a barrier could jeopardize the two-decade-old peace process that largely ended sectarian strife in the north'.)

examples to be noted – some might say, indeed, wherever one looks, the unappreciated costs of Brexit are salient.[5]

Accordingly, one might conclude that both the concern for the short to medium term reflected in this 2015 perspective presented below as well as the patient optimism about the longer-term prognosis for public procurement harmonisation and liberalisation of trade reflected therein were justified. The very fact that Brexit has spawned manifold difficulties of implementation, and that President Trump's new mercantilism has very real costs that its proponents did not acknowledge or appreciate supports this balanced reading as to the lessons of the history that has unfolded since the author's June 2015 cautions were articulated. The reader, and subsequent history, will judge whether this assessment is fair.

It is appropriate to end this introduction with a note of caution: prognosticators and critics far more erudite than this author have from time to time predicted changing historical currents or a reversal of historical trends on a far grander stage – that is, with a much broader sweep than this chapter with its forecast of an at least temporary end to the progress of harmonisation in public procurement policy. Such prognostication is inherently risky. Indeed it appears particularly risky to forecast the end of some longstanding historical moment. Let me offer some examples.

- For instance, in the late 1950s and the start of the 1960s Seymour Martin Lipset and Daniel Bell described an 'End to Ideology', predicting that ideology was becoming irrelevant to those Bell labelled 'sensible' people, and that political controversies would increasingly be decided on technocratic grounds.[6]
- Then in 1989 Francis Fukuyama famously forecast the 'End of History'.[7] He predicted the achievement of a kind of stasis, the culmination of a Hegelian dialectic in which 'liberal democracy' represented the 'endpoint of mankind's ideological evolution'.[8] As Fukuyama refined his far-reaching claim, '[w]hile some present-day countries might fail to achieve stable liberal democracy, and others might lapse back into other, more primitive forms of rule like theocracy or military dictatorship, the *ideal* of liberal democracy could not be improved upon'.[9]
- Similarly, consider the observation that in the world of fiscal policy, 'We are all Keynesians now'.[10]

[5] Examples highlighted by the *New York Times* in the last few months run the gamut from fish processing to classical music companies. See D Segal, 'In Brexit Vote, Town's Nostalgia for Seafaring Past Muddied Its Future' *New York Times*, 23 April 2018) available at www.nytimes.com/2018/04/23/business/grimsby-brexit.html (adverse impact of Brexit on fish processing industry dwarfs impact on small fishing industry); also A Dickson, 'As Brexit Looms, Musicians Brace for the Worst' *New York Times*, 3 August 2018, available at www.nytimes.com/2018/08/03/arts/music/brexit-howard-goodall-classical-music.html (exploring the deleterious impact of a hard Brexit upon the commercial prospects of British cultural institutions, including its highly successful orchestras and musical companies).

[6] D Bell, *The End of Ideology: On the Exhaustion of Political Ideas in the Fifties* (New York, Free Press, 1960); SM Lipset, *Political Man: The Social Bases of Politics* (New York, Doubleday & Co., 1960). See also WW Rostow, *The Stages of Economic Growth: A Non-Communist Manifesto* (Cambridge, Cambridge University Press, 1960); JK Galbraith, *The New Industrial State* (Princeton, Princeton University Press, 1967).

[7] This phrase became the title of his book, F Fukuyama, *The End of History and the Last Man* (New York, Free Press, 1992).

[8] F Fukuyama, *The End of History and The Last Man*, reissue edn (New York, Free Press, 2006) xi.

[9] ibid.

[10] ('Keynesians' refers to the followers of the macroeconomics of John Maynard Keynes.) The provenance of the quoted phrase is complicated. It is generally attributed to economist Milton Friedman, whose embrace of

Predictions of the ends of movements and trends appear increasingly *au courant*. Most recently, we have David Runciman's 'How Democracy Ends'[11] as well as Stephen Levitsky and Daniel Ziblatt's 'How Democracies Die'.[12] While it is almost assuredly too soon to evaluate the accuracy of these versions of what one commentator has recently labelled 'crisisology',[13] one would be foolhardy to fail to take heed that earlier sweeping predictions of change, or of the end of change, have frequently proven either over-wrought or at least somewhat short-sighted and over-simplified.

For instance, Lipset and Bell's confidence that the ideological clashes of the late nineteenth century and first half of the twentieth century appeared over-confident and one-sided before even a decade had passed. In particular, the wars of national liberation of the 1960s appeared to many to be a rebuttal or to require a qualification of the Lipset-Bell claim. With the benefit of our greater hindsight it might be suggested that Bell and Lipset mistook a temporary pause in a historical trend for a true cessation or more permanent transformation. Similarly, for Fukuyama, the era of 9/11 and the 'Clash of Civilisations' hypothesis, appeared to some as a refutation of the unchallenged hegemony of the 'Washington Consensus' (based on free markets, free trade and restrictive monetary policy) that some associated with Fukuyama's thesis.[14] With regard to the claim that a universal acceptance of Keynesian fiscal management had made the clash of economic philosophies obsolete, the time since the financial crises of the last decade makes that claim appear overstated. In particular, the austerity that the EU has imposed on its debtor nations appears to contradict the expectation of Keynesian hegemony.

So perhaps it is common for sharp-eyed commentators to mistake a genuine mid-range trend, or a pause in an on-going trend of development, for a much more open-ended and irreversible shift in politics to the technocratic. Shifting our focus back to our own field, that of public procurement, the analogy between the elusive vision of a technocratic future glimpsed (prematurely?) by the proponents of the political eschatology and the convergence of national public procurement mechanisms on a regime of best practices curated by transnational experts, is worth considering. Perhaps what we are witnessing in operation can best be modelled as a swinging pendulum that oscillates between convergence phases and more exceptionalistic or nationalist phases.[15]

it was actually rather qualified. The attribution to Friedman is usually traced to *Time Magazine* (31 December 1965). Friedman wrote a letter to the editor insisting on the qualification: 'In one sense, we are all Keynesians now; in another, nobody is any longer a Keynesian' in 'Letter: Friedman and Keynes' *Time*, 4 February 1966. The popularisation of the phrase is associated with Richard Nixon's 1971 declaration that 'I am now a Keynesian in Economics' *New York Times*, 4 January 1971, explaining a shift in his economic policies.

[11] D Runciman, *How Democracy Ends* (New York, Basic Books, 2018).

[12] S Levitsky and D Ziblatt, *How Democracies Die* (New York, Crown, 2018).

[13] T Shenk, 'Crisisology: Why so many commentators are forecasting the end of democracy' (September 2018) *The New Republic* 58–63, available on line as 'Is Democracy Really Dying' at newrepublic.com/article/150507/democracy-really-dying?.

[14] S Huntington, *The Clash of Civilizations and the Remaking of the World Order* (New York, Simon & Schuster, 1996). However, the facile opposition between Fukuyama (see nn 7 and 8) and Huntington is oversimplified, if not outright mistaken. Huntington did not discern or forecast a revival of 19th-century ideological conflict as much as identity-based conflicts based on religion or cultural identity.

[15] In describing the evolution of public procurement 'reform' domestically in the United States, the author has portrayed an analogous kind of oscillation between reform aimed at curbing abuses in procurement – reform that tends to heighten regulation – and reform aimed at the excesses of over-regulation, a kind of deregulatory phase in the evolution of public procurement law and policy; JI Schwartz, 'Regulation and

With that caution against reading too much into the evidence of the present and the near past, let us turn to the world of procurement as it appeared to the author in June of 2015. What follows is that presentation, essentially as delivered in June 2015.

B. Looking Forward from June 2015

Perhaps it is presumptuous to try to tie major trends in our specialised field of public procurement law and policy to larger movements on the stage of world affairs. Yet it seems worth the effort. What would actually be strange would be the absence of any such larger pattern of causation, correspondence and reaction. If that is indeed so, intelligent efforts at shaping procurement policy trans-nationally, if they are to meet with reasonable success, can scarcely ignore the underlying connections to larger social, political and economic trends. Hence I offer this exploration of the trends in procurement and its environment, broadly conceived, that have marked the last decades and which challenge us going forward.

The basic claim that I make here is that continuing advancement of a process of convergence and/or progress in efforts at harmonisation of systems of public procurement across the face of the world, which seemed inexorable a decade or so ago, now seems fraught with challenges and difficulties. First let us acknowledge the very real reasons for the optimism. The optimism that has prevailed in this area is reflected in the history of this conference – dating to the late 1990s – and arguably is reflected in its label: 'Global Revolution'.[16] Surely, 'Global Revolution' was never just an assertion that *dramatic changes* affecting public procurement are occurring *in many places* in the world, but tacitly asserts the existence of a common thread and important central tendencies.

The basic convergence proposition was anchored in important social, political and economic realities. The 1990s brought the fall of the Soviet Union and the emergence of a new economy in China that tolerates and even encourages private entrepreneurship. It was not much of an exaggeration to say that every nation state – save perhaps North Korea – has a private sector. And yet all such states still recognise the existence of public needs and public goods. Accordingly, even in mixed economies of disparate types there is a need to secure public goods and to fulfil public needs by patronising the markets of the private sector. Hence the need for a body of public procurement law is universally recognised. For both developing economies and transitional economies – nations that formerly had soviet-style socialist economies – there appeared to be only one model to follow: the procurement model that had developed in the United States, and/or the remarkably similar regime that was evolving in the developing EU. Furthermore, however important the differences between these two dominant regimes, or those between developing nations' economies and transitional economies might appear in

Deregulation in Public Procurement Law Reform in the United States' in G Piga and K Thai, *Advancing Public Procurement: Practices, Innovation and Knowledge-Sharing* (Boca Raton, Florida, PrAcademics Press, 2007) 177–201.

[16] See S Arrowsmith and A Davis (eds), *Public Procurement: Global Revolution* (Alphen aan den Rijn, Netherlands, Kluwer Law International, 1998).

the eyes of procurement specialists or development economists, the strong similarities appeared most salient to 'public procurement newbies'. These include: similar values, desiderata and procedures. Indeed, Western experts were invited to Beijing by the Chinese government and NGOs to help China to begin developing a competitive public procurement regime. And in turn, Chinese experts came to the US and EU to share lessons learned and best practices.[17]

I argue here, however, that today a reasonable prognosticator would be less confident of meaningful continued progress in the near to medium term. The basic reason for this more checkered, 'post-modern' outlook is that the optimism about achieving a socio-political convergence worldwide that flourished after the end of the Cold War – the 'end of ideology' – has been eroded by twin socio-economic and political developments.[18]

In the broadest sense, this more pessimistic prognosis flows from recognition, driven by events too numerous and traumatic to ignore, that our world remains one riven by fundamental conflicts of ideology and resurgent nationalism. Tensions between Russia and the West suggest elements of a new Cold War. At the same time, just a year after the centennial of the inception of World War I, the world appears all too similar, in many respects, to the world of a hundred years ago.

The more procurement-focused reason for the diminishing prospects for convergence is [in 2015] the economic shock and political after-effects of the world-wide financial crisis and 'Great Recession' that began in 2008 and has yet to reach an ending point. The dramatic confrontation, on-going as I write this [in 2015], about Greece's debt to its creditors and future within the Eurozone and the EU, and the political confrontation in the United States between the proponents and opponents of further liberalised trade are but the most vivid evidence of the resistance to global integration potentiated by the world financial crisis. To be sure, there is clearly a relationship between the broader pattern mentioned first above and the second, more focused one. As I have indicated already, it would be odd if trends in the globalisation of public procurement were insulated from these larger movements affecting our world. Indeed, perhaps we should take a distinct, if arguably perverse, satisfaction in discovering that public procurement policy has achieved sufficient recognition in policy and political circles to be buffeted by these important developments in our social, political and economic universe.

[17] See eg SL Schooner 'Introduction: the Symposium "Drafting a Government Procurement Law: Lessons Learned from the United States"' (2002) 11 *Public Procurement Law Review* 99–151, including the papers that were presented at a visit by a Chinese delegation to the Government Procurement Law Program at the George Washington University in the spring of 2001. See specifically JI Schwartz, 'Learning from the United States' Procurement Experience: On "Law Transfer" and its Limitations' (2002) 11 *Public Procurement Law Review* 115–25; see also JI Schwartz, 'On Globalization and Government Procurement' in S Arrowsmith and M Trybus (eds) *Public Procurement: The Continuing Revolution* (The Hague, Kluwer Law International, 2003) 23–45.

[18] It seems apt to refer to this new more sceptical, less optimistic perspective as 'post-modern' because it parallels the development of the schools and perspectives in the arts that reacted against modernism, and often returned to historical modes of expression. The hope for a harmonised global system of procurement is here associated with modernism, which tended to obliterate distinctive national and historical styles. So too, the reaction against it can fairly be called 'post-modern', particularly as national characteristics and nationalist sentiment, including protectionism, are recognised as a more serious obstacle to harmonisation than was appreciated by the moderns. And to the extent that some have questioned the normative wisdom of a strong harmonisation regime, as is described in section V of this chapter, the label 'post-modern' seems even more appropriate.

Let me try to sketch here the basis for these claims, acknowledging that, at first blush, the pessimism expressed here about the prospects for convergence over the near to medium term appears unwarranted. Before doing so it seems useful to try to define our terms with somewhat more precision.

II. Convergence and Harmonisation, Defined and Distinguished

In this paper I endeavour to use the term 'convergence' to denote the phenomenon, descriptively and predictively, in which systems of procurement in modern or modernising economies will tend increasingly over time to resemble each other in their desiderata, requirements and procedures. In other fields of comparative legal studies, for instance, the study of the law governing corporations and other business entities, this is known as 'the Convergence Hypothesis'.[19] In comparative procurement studies, as in corporate law, related, but distinct, and more heroic claims are made that this phenomenon of convergence is inevitable, inexorable and normatively desirable. We should try to distinguish as carefully as possible between the more modest descriptive and predictive facets of this convergence claim and the stronger normative version of this claim. At the same time, because of temptation to believe with Voltaire's Dr Pangloss that this is, indeed, the best of all possible worlds, we should be alert to blurring the line between the two faces of convergence theory.

Two more introductory points about the term 'convergence' should be noted:

- First, we need to be aware that the convergence hypothesis in fields such as corporate law is scarcely settled doctrine.[20]
- Second, the convergence theory is sometimes seen as a normative dogma that is part of the triumphalist 'Washington Consensus' supporting liberal democracy, property rights and relatively unregulated capitalism that prevailed at the start of the of the twenty-first century, and was the target of attack by the anti-globalisation movement of the time around 11 September 2001.[21]

[19] See eg H Hansmann and R Kraakman, 'The End of History for Corporate Law' (2000–01) 89 *Georgetown Law Journal* 439, 439: 'The basic law of corporate governance – indeed most of corporate law – has achieved a high degree of uniformity across developed market jurisdictions, and continued *convergence* toward a single, standard model is likely' (emphasis added). See also S Berger, 'Introduction' in S Berger and R Dore (eds), *National Diversity and Global Capitalism* (Ithaca, Cornell University Press, 1996) 1; Schwartz, 'On Globalization and Government Procurement' (n 17) 23–45, especially 39–43.

[20] A particular challenge to the convergence hypothesis in corporate law is the operation of corporate law and culture in Japan. A recent issue of *The Economist* reports a new revision of Japan's corporate governance code aimed, *inter alia*, at getting Japanese firms to behave more like Western ones in a variety of respects. But the newspaper also notes a record of earlier similar – but unsuccessful – reform efforts tracing back a generation, concluding that '[g]rounds for scepticism are plentiful', as to whether this reform programme will be any more successful; 'Winds of Change' *The Economist*, 4 June 2015, 53–56, available at www.economist.com/business/2015/06/04/winds-of-change.

[21] See Schwartz, 'On Globalization and Government Procurement' (n 17) 29–43.

A bit of jurisprudential background is useful here: prominently in the pre-industrial period followers of natural law philosophies tended to the view that a divine providence had created a world in which there

By contrast, I use the term harmonisation in this paper to refer to deliberate policy efforts to establish interoperability and compatibility of desiderata, requirements and procedures for public procurement among nations. One might further distinguish between strong harmonisation, which presses for maximum uniformity and interoperability among national systems, and more modest versions of harmonisation. The latter seek to impose a framework or common core of requirements that establish a moderate degree of compatibility, while preserving some room for expression of national differences. For instance, Professor Sue Arrowsmith has approvingly referred to the desire to preserve 'national regulatory space for commercial and horizontal procurement policies'.[22] As Arrowsmith's work indicates, much of the debate over the recent past and the future direction of the EU Procurement Directives can be viewed in terms of the policy choice between strong harmonisation and more tempered versions of the harmonisation within the EU.[23]

was one right way to operate the institutions of government and the national and international economy. This was conceptualised much as the natural law philosophers concluded that there was one right understanding of the natural (physical, chemical, and biological) functioning of the world. This was the view that even in the sphere of social, economic and political law, man's God-given intelligence would, at least eventually, enable him to discern that correct regime. Moreover, these correct truths were universal – being divinely ordained – though left for man to discover, and unvarying over time and across societies. Thus, the content of economic, political and social governance was not a matter of national will, nor a matter of policy choice, but a matter of correctly understanding, using mankind's divinely granted faculties of reason and moral reason, what the correct regime is, which is inherent in the design of God's universe. Interestingly, in the realm of the early international law, reflected in the work of scholars such as Hugo Grotius and Samuel Pufendorf, this conception of the sources and nature of law was thought to be a resource that could enable nations to coexist in harmony, observing common universal rules; H Grotius, *De Jure Belli et Pacis* (1625); S Pufendorf, *De Jure Naturae et Gentium* (1672).

A curious echo of this kind of reasoning is found in the approach to law-making we call *common law formalism* in the common law tradition received as national law by the nascent United States. This view valorised the role of common law judges in devising, over time, a legal regime that approached perfect efficiency. Conversely, the contributions of legislators and regulators to the legal regime were viewed as imperfect and inefficient and to be reducing the efficiency of the common law legal regime. See W Blackstone, *Commentaries on the Laws of England* (1765) 63–92; W Eskridge and P Frickey, Historical and Critical Introduction to H Hart, Jr and A Sacks, *The Legal Process: Basic Problems in the Making and Application of Law* (St Paul, Minnesota 1995). In the modern era, beginning in the later 18th century, the common law formalist idea came under attack from the legal realists, most famously in Oliver Wendell Holmes, Jr's phrase 'the law is not a brooding omnipresence in the sky' – *Southern Pacific Co v Jensen*, 244 U.S. 205, 222 [1917]. In other words, law is made, not discovered, and entails policy choice, unlike the principles of the hard sciences, believed to be genuinely universal and immutable.

More recently still, a curious swing back towards the natural law view has emerged in some quarters of the law and economics movement. The proponents of this point of view argue not for universality and immutability because their guiding principles reflect God's will discerned, but because they embody uniquely efficient solutions to widely shared and persistent issues.

Readers should be aware that the convergence hypothesis has an association with the natural law view and the law and economic view of the nature and evolution of law.

[22] S Arrowsmith, 'The Purpose of the EU Procurement Directives: Ends, Means and the Implications for National Regulatory Space for Commercial and Horizontal Procurement Policies' (2012) 14 *Cambridge Yearbook of European Legal Studies* 1–47.

[23] As Caroline Nicholas explains in her paper for this conference, the UNCITRAL definition of harmonisation emphasises securing the interoperability of discrete systems of national law, whereas 'unification' denotes a more absolute convergence: 'the adoption by States of a common legal standard' – C Nicholas, 'UNCITRAL in practice: lessons for the west from other regions? Moving towards greater use of the UNCITRAL Model in member Countries' (Public Procurement Global Revolution VII Conference, 15–16 June 2015) 2.

III. Convergence Triumphant?

From the perspective of students of public procurement law and policy these are indeed productive and fascinating times. Indeed, it might seem, at first, that [2015] remains halcyon days for descriptive and predictive convergence theory, and advocates for strong harmonisation policies.[24] Consider, first, the profusion of important, even transformative, developments portending further global harmonisation of procurement regimes that the last six years – from 2009 to 2015 – have brought us:

- In 2009, the European Union adopted the Defence Directive, which was designed to significantly expand the scope of procurement by EU nations that is covered by the rules of the European single market, filling a gap previously created by the exclusions for defence and security-related procurement from the procurement regimes theretofore established by the EU.[25]
- In 2011, a major revision of the UNCITRAL Model Procurement Law was finalised and adopted. It promised to promote global harmonisation of procurement regimes, particularly in developing and transitional economies, and was intended, among other things, to make the UNCITRAL Model Law compliant with the World Trade Organization's Government Procurement Agreement (GPA), and to address modern electronic procurement techniques.[26]

[24] The reader should note with care the question mark appended to the title for this section of the current paper. Too often readers have overlooked the question mark appended to Francis Fukuyama's original version of his seminal essay, 'The End of History?' *The National Interest* (summer 1989). And Daniel Bell's earlier seminal 1960 collection of essays, *The End of Ideology* (n 6), which argued in effect that we all are, or all should become, technocrats now rather than ideologues, made claims that appear, with hindsight, premature. If Bell in fact believed that fundamental ideological or political arguments were obsolete (in the entire world – a reading that is at least contestable) the ensuing 58 years do not make his insight look prescient. Alternatively, the era about which he wrote, the 1950s, now appears to many to have been a temporary interlude (or 'era of good feeling') experienced at most in parts of the West rather than marking a permanent shift, worldwide. The anti-colonial movements of the 1960s and the wars of national liberation of the 1960s and beyond are only a part of what I have in mind here.

[25] Directive 2009/81/EC of the European Parliament and of the Council of 13 July 2009 on the coordination of procedures for the award of certain works contracts, supply contracts and service contracts by contracting authorities or entities in the fields of defence and security and amending Directives 2004/17/EC and 2004/18/EC [2009] OJ L216/76. As will be described in further detail below, the Defence Directive works to minimise the applicability of, and recourse by member nations to, the exemptions *allowed by* the EU Treaty (art 346 TFEU; formerly art 296 TEC) that permit them to exempt sensitive military equipment from the single market procurement where its inclusion would, in their judgement, threaten their essential security interests. In part the new mechanism works by emphasising and extending the heavy burden placed upon them (by European Court precedent) to justify invocation of this essential security interests exemption. In effect the 2009 Defence Directive operates by institutionalising the assumption that recourse to the art 346 exemption should be extraordinary so that a genuinely unified European defence market is established (Brussels, December 2010).

[26] UNCITRAL Model Law on Public Procurement, adopted 1 July 2011, available at www.uncitral.org/pdf/english/texts/procurem/ml-procurement-2011/2011-Model-Law-on-Public-Procurement-e.pdf. UN General Assembly Resolution 66/95 of 9 December 2011 recognising the revision of the UNCITRAL Model Procurement law includes the following statement of what was expected from the promulgation of the Revised Model Procurement Law:

> *Noting also* that the revised Model Law is expected to contribute significantly to the establishment of a harmonized and modern legal framework for public procurement that promotes economy, efficiency and competition in procurement and, at the same time, fosters integrity, confidence, fairness and transparency in the procurement process,

- Also in 2011, the GPA nations finalised agreement on a major revision of the Government Procurement Agreement,[27] which was formally adopted in 2012, and which came into force upon reaching the prescribed threshold for ratifications on 6 April 2014.[28]
- The long process of revision of the EU Public Sector Procurement Directive reached its culmination on 26 February 2014, with the adoption by the European Parliament of Directive 2014/24/EU.[29]
- Meanwhile efforts to bring China under the umbrella of the Government Procurement Agreement continued to grind forward, albeit with no clear end in sight.

In addition, a continuing series of events has drawn attention to on-going efforts to harmonise particular aspects of public procurement systems globally: suspension and debarment systems and procedures, as well as a range of anti-corruption procedures and sanctions.[30] A thread of particular note in these developments is the decision to make corruption sanctions in one nation a ground for automatic debarment in other nations.[31] As we shall see in section VI a heightened perception of pervasive corruption is a major

> *Convinced* that the revised Model Law will significantly assist all States, in particular developing countries and countries with economies in transition, in enhancing their existing procurement laws and formulating procurement laws where none presently exist, and will lead to the development of harmonious international economic relations and increased economic development,

(ibid 2). Caroline Nicholas' paper in this Conference takes off from the adoption of the Revised Model Procurement Law and explores the prospects for progress in harmonisation in light of the successes and the disappointments in the implementation of this Model Law; Nicholas, 'UNCITRAL in practice' (n 23).

[27] www.wto.org/english/docs_e/legal_e/rev-gpr-94_01_e.pdf. See S Arrowsmith and RD Anderson, *The WTO Regime on Government Procurement: Challenge and Reform* (Cambridge, Cambridge University Press, 2011), throughout, especially, RD Anderson and S Arrowsmith, 'The WTO regime on government procurement: past, present and future' in this collection at 3–58; JI Schwartz, 'International Protection of Foreign Bidders under GATT/WTO Law: Plurilateral Liberalization of Trade in the Public Procurement Sector and Global Propagation of Best Procurement Practices' in M Audit and S Schill (eds), *The Transnational Law of Public Contracts* (Brussels, Bruylant Publishers, 2016) 79–106.

[28] WTO: 2014 news items, 'Revised WTO Agreement on Government Procurement to come into force on 6 April 2014', available at www.wto.org/english/news_e/news14_e/gpro_11mar14_e.htm.

[29] Directive 2014/24/2014 of the European Parliament and of the Council of 26 February 2014 on public procurement and repealing Directive 2004/18/EC [2014] OJ L94/65. See S Arrowsmith, *The Law of Public and Utilities Procurement: Regulation in the EU and UK – Volume I*, 3rd edn (London, Sweet & Maxwell, 2014); also Arrowsmith, 'The Purpose of the EU Procurement Directives' (n 22).

[30] Recent conferences and presentations, just in the last year or so, and just in Washington, DC, include: The World Bank Global Forum on Law, Justice and Development, and The George Washington University Law School, et al, 'Suspension and Debarment Colloquium' (15 May 2014, at the World Bank); Transparency International USA, 'Corporate Compliance and Global Corruption: TI-USA's Report on Verification of Corporate Anti-Corruption Programs' (24 July 2014); OECD, The World Bank Group, et al, 'Launch of the OECD Foreign Bribery Report' (10 December 2014, at the World Bank); The World Bank Group et al, 'Exclusion and Debarment in the EU: The new regulatory regime under the revised EU Procurement Directives and the Current Member State Practice' (18 February 2015, at the World Bank); The George Washington University Law School, et al, 'Drivers of Corruption and Institutional Responses: Are Current Anti-Corruption Instruments Effective?' (25 March 2015); The World Bank Group, et al, 'Public Wrongs, Private Actions: Civil Lawsuits to Combat Corruption' (20 April 2015, at the World Bank); Transparency International UK, 'Suspension & Debarment: Strengthening Integrity in International Defence Contracting' (7 May 2015, at Covington & Burling).

[31] eg under amendments to Canada's Integrity Framework, effective 1 March 2014, '[s]uppliers who have received foreign convictions similar to the Canadian convictions listed in the Integrity Framework will be ineligible to obtain' contracts from or to engage in real property transactions with Public Works and

recruiting tool for absolutist and anti-democratic movements, including terrorism, which concentrate attention on anti-corruption efforts, resulting in extra emphasis paid to this facet of the larger project of harmonisation in public procurement.[32]

At first blush this impressive series of developments would certainly seem to portend a continuing march towards the goal of strong global harmonisation of significant public procurement regimes. Moreover, there was no shortage of optimistic commentary about the prospects for continuing progress on this front, particularly associated with the adoption of the new GPA.[33] However, as explained in the next section of this paper, another contrasting story could be told about the trend line of world developments bearing on convergence and harmonisation efforts affecting public procurement, and on the global project of economic integration more generally.

IV. Elements of the Counter-Narrative

Over the course of the last eight or so years there has been a series of events that might make one question whether the progress towards convergence and the prospects for harmonisation efforts were really leading to the harmonious future that had been envisioned by many in 2007. Addressed first are developments more narrowly tied to the field of public procurement. Thereafter we note developments that reflect political obstacles and resistance to convergence and harmonisation efforts affecting the whole range of global political and economic systems more generally. I note here only a few of the particulars that you are all familiar with.

A. Reverses and Obstacles to Harmonisation

First, as the other papers in this session will document with much more particularity, the project of harmonisation has met with some difficulties that exceed the optimistic assumptions of various harmonisation instruments. For instance, Caroline Nicholas, in her paper for this session relates that in drafting the revised UNCITRAL Model Law on Public Procurement

> it was agreed that countries at all levels of development should be able to use the best practice that the more developed countries contributed to the process, even if that best practice might assume levels of capacity, experience and governance that were not yet in place in all countries.[34]

Government Services Canada; www.tpsgc-pwgsc.gc.ca/ci-if/synopsis-backgrounder-eng.html. See generally on the pros and cons of automatic cross-debarment, CR Yukins, 'Cross-Debarment: A Stakeholder Analysis' (2013) 45 *George Washington International Law Review* 219.

[32] Particularly influential, at least in diverse intellectual circles in the United States, is S Chayes, *Thieves of State: Why Corruption Threatens Global Security* (New York, W.W. Norton & Company, 2015). Her work has garnered the attention of development professionals, national security and foreign relations experts, and military analysts, as well as procurement scholars.

[33] See generally many, but not all, of the contributions collected by S Arrowsmith and RD Anderson in their 2011 collection timed to reflect the new GPA, *The WTO Regime on Government Procurement: Challenge and Reform* (n 27).

[34] Nicholas (n 23) 2–3.

Yet she reports, certainly more in sorrow than in anger or triumph, that 'experience in using the Model Law has highlighted some areas in which more significant adaptation than was envisaged when the Model Law was drafted appears to be needed' and usefully identifies three major areas in which challenges have characteristically or recurrently arisen.[35] She concludes that even the tempered 2007 prediction of my colleagues, Steve Schooner and Chris Yukins, that strong harmonisation may be at least a generation away, is, based on recent 'experience in the UNCITRAL context' too optimistic as to 'both the scope and time frame of this convergence' and that 'in the meantime, additional policy guidance and dialogue will be necessary'.[36]

Second, responses to the world financial crisis and ensuing 'Great Recession' have reflected a temptation to give in to protectionism in the field of public procurement. As John Linarelli and I have each written elsewhere, the stimulus legislation enacted to address the immediate impact of the financial crisis in the United States was enacted with significant 'Buy American' restrictions on the expenditure of some of the funds made available.[37] Although proponents of free trade in public procurement managed to temper the original proposals of the protectionists, specifying that the 'Buy American' requirement should yield to the treaty commitments of the United States (which include both the GPA and various bilateral trade agreements that cover some part of public procurement), as Linarelli and I agree, the resurgence of the protectionist impulse in times of economic adversity was unmistakable. The only question is whether this episode shows, on balance, that the harmonisation project and the liberalisation of trade in the public procurement sector, is a glass that is alarmingly half-empty or encouragingly half-full. At least in the public procurement sector, the relatively negative assessment of those who have studied the vitality and limitations of the lessons world policy-makers deployed starting in 2008 that they had learned – or thought they had learned – from the Great Depression of the 1930s, has, ironically, proved to be, perhaps, still too positive.[38]

In 2009, Pascal Lamy, the Director-General of the World Trade Organization, called attention to the risks of protectionism in stimulus and public infrastructure investment

[35] ibid 4.

[36] ibid 22.

[37] J Linarelli, 'Global Procurement in Times of Crisis: new Buy American Policies and Options in the WTO Legal System' in Arrowsmith and Anderson (n 27) 773; JI Schwartz, 'Procurement in Times of Crisis: Lessons from US Government Procurement in Three Episodes of "Crisis" in the Twenty-first Century' in Arrowsmith and Anderson (n 27) 803, 825–29.

[38] See B Eichengreen, *Hall of Mirrors: The Great Depression, the Great Recession, and the Uses – and Misuses – of History* (Oxford, Oxford University Press, 2015). As the title may already suggest, Eichengreen's basic thesis is that the economic policy-makers in the United States and Europe learned some important lessons from the mistakes that were made in addressing the earlier crisis of the 1930s, but also drew some mistaken lessons, and had some critical blind spots in making policy to ameliorate the most recent financial crisis and recession in a manner ostensibly informed by the lessons of the earlier one. Nonetheless, in the procurement field, his assessment, focused on a broader canvas, to be sure, looks rather rosier than can be justified.

Specifically, he asserts what whereas '[g]overnments in the 1930s succumbed to the protectionist temptation', as a 'result of the lessons policy makers drew' from the lessons of the Great Depression, in addressing the world financial crisis starting in 2008 'they prevented the worst. After the failure of Lehman Brothers pushed the global financial system to the brink … [t]hey resisted the beggar-thy-neighbor [sic] tariffs and controls that caused the collapse of international transactions in the 1930s' (ibid 1–2). Moreover, he asserts that '[a]lthough there is no evidence that the [Smoot-Hawley] tariff had a significant negative impact on the American economy [in the 1930s], its ritual invocation helped policy makers resist the protectionist temptation in 2009' (ibid). As we can see, this was not entirely true with regard to the procurement sector.

programmes adopted in response to the world economic crisis.[39] He, too, has sought comfort in the notion that the GPA has stood as a safeguard against 'a rush to wholesale adoption of such measures'.[40]

Third, although more than 13 years have passed since China promised to move towards entry in the GPA when it was seeking admission to the World Trade Organization, China's accession to the GPA remains very much a work in progress.[41]

Fourth, although there were in 2015 significant multilateral negotiations in progress with respect to trade liberalisation that would include the public procurement sector, both across the Atlantic and the Pacific, the political prospects for enactment of 'fast-track' trade promotion authority legislation in the United States are cloudy at best, and have become embroiled in the larger partisan dysfunctionality of United States politics. Absent fact-track authority trade agreements are unlikely to pass the United States Congress. Specifically, such 'trade promotion authority' would be necessary as a practical matter for the United States to adhere to either of the major trade agreements presently being negotiated – the proposed Transatlantic Trade and Investment Partnership ('T-TIP') between the United States and the European Union and the proposed Trans-Pacific Partnership ('TPP') between the United States and major Pacific Basin nations.[42] But Democrats in the United States Congress have become extremely reluctant to support such trade liberalisation agreements, despite the support of a Democratic President, believing that they result in loss of domestic employment, while Republicans in Congress mostly support such trade liberalisation in principle but are reluctant to hand President Obama a victory on *anything* he seeks from Congress. There is a grave risk that the 'centre cannot hold'.[43] Indeed at latest writing, the Congress has proven unwilling to provide that authority that might enable successful negotiations on the Trans-Pacific Partnership.[44] And certainly this does not bode at all well for progress

[39] WTO, 'Overview of Developments in the International Trading Environment: Annual Report by the Director-General' (WT/TPR/OV/12 of 18 November 2009) para 140.

[40] P Lamy, 'Foreword', in Arrowsmith and Anderson (n 27) xxv–xxvii.

[41] See P Wang, 'Accession to the Agreement on Government Procurement: The Case of China' in Arrowsmith and Anderson (n 27) 92-116; Office of the United States Trade Representative, 'United States Welcomes Opportunities for US Suppliers Under Newly Revised WTO Government Procurement Agreement' (Press Release, December 2011) available at https://ustr.gov/about-us/policy-offices/press-office/press-releases/2011/december/united-states-welcomes-opportunities-us-suppliers.

[42] J Weisman, 'Obama's Trade Deal Faces Bipartisan Peril in the House' *The New York Times*, 31 May 2015, available at www.nytimes.com/2015/06/01/business/obamas-push-for-trade-deal-faces-bipartisan-peril-in-house.html?ref=politics.

[43] WB Yeats, 'The Second Coming' (see www.potw.org/archive/potw351.html). The grim overtones of the phase from the celebrated Yeats poem connotes a world spinning out of control and is used here, advisedly, to connote the fragility of the present situation. More particularly, it is also often used at least in domestic US political commentary to describe events like this where the left and right together can kill a proposal favoured by the centre. Scholar/politician, United States Senator, and Harvard professor, Daniel Patrick Moynihan famously employed it in his account of the failure in the 1960s of President Richard Nixon's proposed 'Family Assistance Plan'. Although he used the Yeats quote in the lectures that he delivered on the subject at Harvard, as the author vividly recalls, Moynihan's book recounting the same uses only an alternate phrase: 'The center … was overcome'; DP Moynihan, *The Politics of a Guaranteed Income: the Nixon Administration and the Family Assistance Plan* (New York, Vintage Books, 1973) 541.

[44] J Weisman, 'House Rejects Trade Measure, Rebuffing Obama's Dramatic Appeal' *The New York Times*, 12 June 2015, available at www.nytimes.com/2015/06/13/us/politics/obamas-trade-bills-face-tough-battle-against-house-democrats.html?hp&action=click&pgtype=Homepage&module=first-column-region&region=top-news&WT.nav=top-news.

between the United States and Europe on the T-TIP, particularly because the EU position in T-TIP negotiations has pressed the United States strongly for inclusion of much more sub-central government procurement, making progress on harmonisation and liberalisation of public procurement through that path both contentious, and particularly unlikely to bear fruit in the near term.[45]

B. Setbacks and Obstacles to Harmonisation in World Politics and Economics

One only has to read the newspaper to appreciate the drumbeat of events that suggest that the smooth march towards a harmonious world that would naturally tend to promote liberalisation of trade in the public procurement sector has encountered strong headwinds. The forces of division, divergence and dissonance appear stronger perhaps than at any time since the end of the Cold War. While these are largely outside the author's academic expertise, those attending this Conference are likely to be all too familiar with elements of this litany. While there is room to quarrel about the causation and the consequences of any particular item on the list below, it is likely that most of the readers of this paper could easily supplement it. Some of the developments of the years 2010-15 that reflect a trend towards divergence and disaggregation in the international theatre are:

- A distinct revival of Cold War tensions between Russia and the US and EU, including territorial conflicts affecting Georgia and Ukraine. Proposals aimed at closer integration of Ukraine with the EU appear to have been a trigger for the separatist conflict in Ukraine. We are back to jostling over duelling hegemonies and spheres of influence.
- The European project is threatened from many directions, which include:
  - The growing electoral strength of Eurosceptic and strong nationalist parties on both the right and left of political spectres in nations as diverse as Greece, Spain, France and the UK.
  - In the UK, the unexpected recent electoral triumph of the Conservative party with its promise to roll back EU treaties and hold a referendum on continued membership for the UK.
  - Again, in the UK, the strength of Scottish nationalism with the threat both to the unity of the UK itself and to majority support for EU membership for the UK.
  - The continuing crisis over Greek debt with the possibility of an exit from the Eurozone and the EU.
  - Going further back in time, the defeat over the course of the previous decade of the long effort to establish a European constitution that would have advanced the cause of further EU integration.

[45] See CR Yukins and JS Schnitzer, 'GPA Accession: Lessons Learned on the Strengths and Weaknesses of the WTO Government Procurement Agreement' (2015) 7 *Trade, Law and Development* 89, 118.

- The rise of competition between the United States and China for leadership in the sphere of regional development banks and other mechanisms for economic harmonisation in the Pacific Basin.
- Overarching all of these trends, of course, is a general resurgence of nationalism and national identity politics.

C. Divergence Within Harmonisation Frameworks

Yet another facet of the case for this less optimistic assessment of the prospects for strong harmonisation and strong convergence emerges from taking a closer look at some of the very items listed in section III of this paper which, at first blush, suggested that rapid progress in harmonisation between 2009 and 2014. Specifically, much of this apparent and real momentum may have been the residual inertia force and bureaucratic momentum of elite movements that had lost much of their democratic legitimacy in the wake of the shock of the Great Recession. Like a super-tanker or aircraft carrier changing course, it takes a distance and time for the changing course or flagging momentum of such international developments to be fully apparent.[46]

Moreover, some of the milestone achievements listed in section III, were, on closer analysis, actually meant to accommodate the centrifugal forces that were pushing national procurement regimes apart. Some instances are discussed below.

The package that led to the adoption of the new GPA had a strong emphasis on flexibility and on transitional regimes. These include the 'SDT', or 'Special and Differential Treatment' provisions intended to accommodate the 'development, financial, and trade needs and circumstances of developing countries and least developed countries'.[47] It is not meant as a criticism of these provisions to observe that to an extent they simply legitimate and possibly even perpetuate divergence, in the interest of reducing the degree to which the Government Procurement Agreement could be viewed as a 'rich nations' club'. Of course, by enabling developing nations to ramp up into gradual adherence to the full terms of the GPA, the SDT may indeed facilitate the enlargement of membership and assist in the gradual transition to fuller harmonisation. Certainly there is practical wisdom in offering developing nations an alternative to being forced to vault up a cliff face. But it remains to be seen both whether the availability of these SDT provisions is a successful inducement to wider GPA participation, and whether those so induced actually transition, albeit gradually, to full participation and thus harmonisation at the moderate level contemplated by the GPA.

Somewhat similar caveats could be voiced about the 'Future Work Programmes' that were also adopted along with the 2011 version of the GPA. These reflect growing international agreement that some consensus should be found about both (i) facilitating and encouraging the fuller participation of small and medium-sized enterprises in

[46] It is instructive that it took the better part of a decade for the leadership of the European Union to recognise that in the painstakingly negotiated efforts to further integrate under a European constitution they had outstripped popular and national support for the further political integration of Europe.

[47] Revised Agreement on Government Procurement (2011) art V.1.

government procurement, and (ii) assuring environmentally sustainable government procurement practices. At the same time, a critic could discern a moderate dose of either 'an agreement to disagree' or, more generously, an agreement to agree in the future. What is fair to say is that these Future Work Programmes enabled the new GPA to move forward – a genuine reflection of progress in moderate harmonisation efforts – while deferring the difficult task of finding meaningful common ground on these sensitive issues on which so much national disagreement has been possible. Convergence has not yet been achieved by any stretch of the imagination on these points. Progress has been made, globally, in securing consensus that the GPA should not rule out protection of environmental values. If the glass of harmonisation is filling slowly, the evidence of the new GPA together with its associated elements, is that it still is gradually filling, unevenly and in fits and starts.

Something similar could be said about the new market access commitments made by entities such as the United States. Other GPA nations that include sub-central procurement are invariably frustrated and puzzled by the limited degree to which the United States can offer liberalised access to the half of public procurement in the United States that is carried out at the level of state or local government. The strong constitutional commitment of the United States to its regime of federalism, in which the United States national government generally lacks authority to compel a state or a city to open its public procurement, is hard for our global partners to understand and credit. This point has also become a major stumbling block in the T-TIP negotiations, according to usually informed sources. And the same political environment that has placed congressional approval for trade promotion authority tantalisingly out of reach makes it unlikely that meaningful change will occur on this front at any near date.[48]

Even the new EU Directives, which Professor Sue Arrowsmith has argued go too far in the direction of forcing a common code of procurement on the EU nations, as is explained below, have certain elements of deregulation. For instance, by extending permission for member nations to engage in a form of what we Americans call competitive negotiation, the EU has continued to move in that direction, transcending the quite grudging step in this direction that took the form of the competitive dialogue under the previous iteration of the Directives. This particular development reflects, simultaneously aspects of convergence and undertones of divergence. It assuredly reflects a growing convergence between the United States and the EU, but when the Directives are implemented in national law a broader range of practices among EU member nations may result.

Finally, in recognising the complexity and dual-edged nature of some of the convergence developments noted at the outset, I would observe that the specialised focus on achieving harmonisation and/or convergence in the anti-corruption area and with

[48] My colleague, Professor Yukins, has suggested that a possible middle ground in the T-TIP negotiations (assuming that these can now go forward at all given expressed congressional hostility) would be for the United States to negotiate about an access commitment covering that share of state and local government procurement that is funded by federal government grant money. And this is worth exploring. But mandating state and local adherence to liberalised public procurement even by the grant condition mechanism would be both legally and politically controversial. See JI Schwartz, 'Etats-Unis/United States of America' in R Noguellou and U Stelkens (eds), *Droit Compare Des Contrats Publics/Comparative Law on Public Contracts* (Brussels, Bruylant, 2010) 613, 615–17 & fns 4–5.

regard to suspension and debarment practices has also produced its own counter-movement even before it has advanced very far. Specifically, in surveying anti-corruption developments around the world, *The Economist* claims that 'the cost and complexity of [anti-corruption] investigations are spiralling beyond what is reasonable'.[49] And a point of emerging global convergence – prioritising self-cleaning approaches that are meant to be less heavy-handed than governmental regulation or draconian sanctions – is tarred as 'a ravenous "compliance industry" of lawyers and forensic accountants who have never seen a local bribery issue that did not call for an exhaustive global review'.[50] Yet, ironically, the very same leader asserts that 'governments should lower costs by harmonizing anti-bribery laws and improving co-ordination between national probes'.[51] In the same vein the leader claims that

> anti-bribery laws should be amended to offer companies a 'compliance defence.' Specifically, if firms can show that they had sound anti-bribery policies, that they were making reasonable efforts to uphold them, that the wrongdoing did not involve senior managers and that they came forward to the authorities promptly, the penalties should be greatly reduced.[52]

D. Collateral Effects of the World Financial Crisis

A resurgence of protectionism in the context of national stimulus programmes and other responses to the financial crisis, as was noted above, was not the only impact of the financial crisis on harmonisation efforts. The economic downturn had a variety of salient secondary effects on procurement policies and efforts at their harmonisation. Heightened scepticism about the virtues and value of globalisation and of opening markets, and heighted political support for national preferences and exclusion of foreign offerors from competition for public procurement funds were accompanied by:

- A renewed attention to the need for public procurement reform, harmonisation and liberalisation of trade in public procurement to deliver, and be seen to deliver, improved value for money to governments and to the taxpayers that fund them. Of course, as noted below, it is in part this effort to align public procurement reform, politically, with the pursuit of good value, which had produced a sceptical reaction from Professor Sue Arrowsmith, in the context of her broader argument against strong harmonisation.[53]
- Increased concern about the cost of procedures that might be fastened upon governmental entities in the name of public procurement liberalisation and harmonisation.

[49] 'Daft on Graft' *The Economist*, 9 May 2015, 14.

[50] ibid.

[51] ibid.

[52] ibid. It certainly strikes the reader that much of what the editors of *The Economist* advocate is actually consistent with the thrust of the harmonisation and convergence movement in the anti-corruption sphere. But whether or not that is so, the fact of the reaction against what may at times be over-zealous or counterproductive anti-corruption efforts, does suggest that progress in this sector, like that affecting harmonisation in public procurement more broadly, will be episodic, iterative and inconsistent.

[53] See below, text accompanying nn 54–61.

This has produced the kind of attention to flexibility and allowance of scope for transitional regimes that is featured in the provisions accompanying the new GPA.[54]

- Increased attention to the accessibility of public procurement markets in nations and internationally, to small and medium-sized enterprises.[55]

V. A Nuanced Spectrum of Perspectives

I do not mean to suggest here that knowledgeable commentators have heretofore been uniformly or unrealistically optimistic about prospects for convergence. Indeed, there has been quite a range of opinions about the likelihood and time horizon for achieving convergence, as well as the desirability of strong harmonisation efforts. This literature reflects a divergence of views both on the predictive side and on the normative side: as to whether convergence was achievable and as to whether strong harmonisation efforts are desirable. At times this spectrum of views may have been clouded by the somewhat guarded terms in which different points of view have been expressed, but taking a close look, retrospectively, the disparity of viewpoints is clearly evident. What follows is a selective representation of some salient divergent points of view. At the same time it is not fair to say, in a revisionist mode, that no one ever held the viewpoint that now appears to have been unrealistically optimistic about the degree of harmonisation and convergence that might be achieved or the timetable on which it might be done.

It seems fair in particular to note that Professor Sue Arrowsmith has long been a sceptic about aggressive harmonisation particularly within the EU, as well as globally. At least as early as 2002, Arrowsmith had questioned whether 'a single body of procurement rules can ever be suitable for all [EU] Member States'.[56] By 2006 she argued that the costs and difficulties of attempting to embrace a true common code for procurement had been magnified by the enlargement of the membership of the EU.[57] Yet she perceived that she was fighting an uphill battle against an

> EC procurement regime [that] appears to be in a process of transition from one in which Member States have the main responsibility for procurement procedures subject to a broad EC framework, to one in which procedures are laid down by the EC with a limited area of discretion for Member States.[58]

Specifically she claimed that 'the costs of the' emerging EC 'regime are arguably disproportionate to the benefits' and that there are 'alternative means of pursuing Community objectives that could be equally, or only marginally less, effective, and that would not

[54] See above text accompanying n 47 ff (regarding Special and Differential Treatment provisions).

[55] See above text accompanying n 47 ff (regarding Future Work Programmes).

[56] S Arrowsmith, 'The EC Procurement Directives, National Procurement Policies and Better Governance: The Case for a New Approach' (2002) 27 *European Law Review* 3. If memory serves, Professor Arrowsmith made the argument reflected in the 2002 article in a talk coincident with the start of the 2001 Global Revolution II Conference.

[57] S Arrowsmith, 'The Past and Future Evolution of EC Procurement Law: From Framework to Common Code' (2006) 35 *Public Contract Law Journal* 337.

[58] ibid 384.

have such an adverse impact on national sovereignty in the area of procurement'.[59] Specifically, she decried the activism of the European Court of Justice (ECJ) in extending the reach of EU procurement law and tightening its grasp on national sovereignty. This approach both created undesirable 'uncertainty over the content of legal obligations' and raised concern that the trade liberalisation focus of the non-specialist judges of the ECJ will take insufficient 'account of the "practicalities of procurement"'.[60] She attributed to the Court a 'bias toward market integration above other policies'.[61] Even apart from the liabilities associated distinctively with this trend towards judicial elaboration of the EU law, she questioned 'the desirability of the current trend toward common rules'.[62]

A decade later, as that trend continued to be in evidence, Professor Arrowsmith continues to approach this matter from a similar perspective. To be more precise, two facets to her approach emerged: to continue to argue against unduly broad interpretations of the ambit of the EU procurement law where possible, and to criticise the path of the evolution of that law where the first branch was unsuccessful. As for the former, in her 2012 piece for the *Cambridge Yearbook of European Legal Studies*, Professor Arrowsmith argued for a narrowed understanding of the objectives and means of the European Procurement Directives.[63] Specifically, she argues against the view that the Directives are designed to standardise procurement procedures, to promote competition that replicates that of the private marketplace, or to promote securing best value for taxpayer money expended by governments. By contrast, she argues that the Directives seek to promote the internal EU market 'solely by three means prohibiting discrimination, implementing transparency, and removing barriers to access'.[64]

Most recently, perhaps recognising that her advocacy for a narrower approach to the remit of EU procurement law was falling on deaf ears in that her arguments had not been accepted in the adoption of the 2014 EU Procurement Directives, Professor Arrowsmith seems again to be arguing for an alternative to the current EU policy. In the 2014 edition of her treatise on procurement law in the EU and the UK, she identifies salient problems with the EU regime such as: undue inhibition of legitimate objectives of national policy, the complexity of the regime, and [undue] legal uncertainty, appealing for reconsideration of the current approach to EU procurement regulation.[65]

By contrast with Professor Arrowsmith, my colleague and Co-Director, Professor Christopher Yukins appears to be a strong advocate of the convergence hypothesis. He has argued that 'procurement systems, to a remarkable extent, seem to evolve in parallel' and that 'procurement rules – on either side of the Atlantic, and around the world – are increasingly, and extraordinarily, similar'.[66] Indeed, he claims that this has occurred

[59] ibid.

[60] ibid

[61] ibid 383.

[62] ibid.

[63] Arrowsmith (n 22).

[64] ibid 1.

[65] Arrowsmith, *The Law of Public and Utilities Procurement: Regulation in the EU and UK – Volume I* (n 29) 225. She devotes section 3-70 of this treatise to a 'Critique of EU Policy: The Case for a More Flexible Approach'; ibid 225–35.

[66] CR Yukins, 'Convergent Evolution: U. S. Government Contracting in the Context of Global Public Procurement', draft paper for presentation at the 'Global Governance Program: The Internationalization of Government Procurement Regulation' (Robert Shuman Centre for Advanced Studies, European University Institute Florence, Italy, December 2014) 2 (Manuscript on file with present author).

despite strong resistance by the United States to any overt openness to harmonisation on the part of the United States.[67] Calling the remaining differences between the US and EU procurement regimes 'minor, almost vestigial', he suggests that ideally they should as soon as possible be 'smoothed away, as unnecessary impediments to competition and trade'.[68]

If this enthusiastic embrace of strong harmonisation as the appropriate goal seems too ambitious, I would note that more nuanced approaches have been offered both before and after the onset of the world financial crisis, including by Professor Yukins. Ironically, an assessment that now appears both balanced and prescient was offered right on the eve of the financial crisis, jointly by my George Washington University colleagues, Professors Steve Schooner and Christopher Yukins.[69] At the time, Schooner and Yukins seemed to see convergence as the long-term goal, but they saw the path to getting there as a long one:

> [T]he most significant development in public procurement today may be the incremental opening of an increasing number of public procurement markets across the globe. Although this nascent trend will span decades, and no doubt will proceed in fits and start, we are heartened by what we see as increasing momentum.[70]

Their approach did not rely on an inevitable or inexorable automatic convergence; rather it attributes key roles to deliberate harmonisation policies. And it recognises multiple tools for harmonisation ranging from model procurement codes, through the procurement guidelines imposed by financial institutions such as the international development banks, to binding international agreements.[71] These authors map four developmental steps or stages that outline a gradual pathway towards eventual strong harmonisation or unification, a result which they concluded was then 'at least a generation away'.[72]

Recently, indeed at the previous iteration of this Conference, my George Washington University colleague Daniel Gordon articulated an approach which in some respects resembles Sue Arrowsmith's, favouring moderate or weak harmonisation instead of the strong version, and seeing little likelihood or need for full convergence. But the distinctive feature of Gordon's approach, elaborated in a presentation at the last iteration of this conference, is that although a framework of 'agreed minimum standards' is generally sufficient, he argues that different degrees of harmonisation are appropriate for different aspects of public procurement law, acknowledging that there are

[67] ibid 20-21.

[68] ibid 3.

[69] CR Yukins and SL Schooner, 'Incrementalism: Eroding the Impediments to a Global Procurement Market' (2007) 38 *Georgetown Journal of International Law* 529.

[70] ibid 532.

[71] ibid 556–64.

[72] ibid 558. The steps are: (i) political commitment to non-discrimination; (ii) (a moderate degree of) harmonisation through instruments such as the minimum standards of the GPA; (iii) rationalisation to ensure that national procurement systems employ best practices and in fact lead to good value; and (iv) institutionalisation: the integration of these harmonised, rationalised practices into the fabric of national law and implementation through building of the requisite institutional capacities; ibid 564–76. To the present reader it is not clear just how far along the spectrum of harmonisation – weak to strong, and convergence – this roadmap ultimately points. But what is clear is that Yukins and Schooner envision a process that is both gradual and iterative.

discrete areas in which 'shared practices are … definitely beneficial'.[73] Recognising that there are increasing similarities in public procurement systems, he cautions that '[t]hese similarities do not mean that we are moving toward a uniform public procurement system across the world'.[74] In particular he identifies the WTO's Government Procurement Agreement as a framework that establishes 'minimum standards for transparency, competition and accountability' while allowing for significant national differences. And he assigns an affirmative virtue to '[v]ariation among procurement systems' both because it permits states to use features adapted to their unique environment and because it encourages experimentation and innovation, which may ultimately lead to new international norms.[75] This idea of the dynamic creativity allowed by bounded diversity within an overarching framework, which is often associated with the virtues of a system of constitutional federalism in United States law, suggests that it is not just the values of national autonomy which argue for a limit on convergence and strong harmonisation.[76] Moreover, in Daniel Gordon's articulation, it suggests a rather complicated relationship between harmonisation, convergence and the improvement of global practice in procurement. Straight-jacketing national procurement systems by insisting on thoroughgoing harmonisation may actually retard the recognition of evolving best practices. Gordon also makes a strong practical contribution by identifying specific procurement policy areas in which seeking international uniformity is either unwise or unrealistic, and in any event is, in his judgement *not necessary* to move forward the state of procurement internationally.[77] Conversely, Gordon identified areas not requiring full convergence regarding the rules for procurement that nonetheless *would* benefit from more attention in harmonisation efforts. In particular, he calls for redoubled attention to (i) training of a professionalised acquisition corps of procurement personnel; (ii) increased focus on challenge/bid protest systems that can identify actual failures in practice to abide with the written rules adopted for procurement; and

[73] DI Gordon, 'Appreciating the Progress Made and Reflecting on the Challenges Ahead', presentation at the 'Global Revolution VI' Conference (Nottingham, UK, June 2013) (manuscript on file with present author).

[74] ibid 2; see also DI Gordon, 'Anti-Corruption Internationally: Challenges in Procurement Market Abroad – Part II: The Path Forward for Using Procurement Law to Help with Development and the Fight Against Corruption' (2013) *West Government Contracts Year in Review Conference Covering 2012 Conference Briefs* 4 (Thomson Reuters, 2013).

[75] Gordon, 'Appreciating the Progress' (n 73) 2.

[76] In his celebrated dissent in *New State Ice Company v Liebmann* 285 US 262, 311 (1932), US Supreme Court Justice Louis Brandeis wrote: 'It is one of the happy incidents of the federal system that a single courageous State may, if its citizens choose, serve as a laboratory; and try novel social and economic experiments without risk to the rest of the country'. Although written in dissent in 1932, this view – often denoted the 'laboratories of federalism' or 'laboratories of democracy' argument – has long since ascended into the firmament of accepted constitutional wisdom in the United States.

[77] These include, in his assessment:

- the timing of determination of offerors' qualification (before or after the determination of the merits of the offer);
- whether relative quality of past performance can be used as an award criterion;
- the permissibility of small business set asides;
- the need for a standstill procedure to allow filing of challenges after identification of the contract winner and before the formal award of the contract; and
- the nature and location of the forum authorised to hear challenges to procurement known as bid protest in the United States.

Gordon (n 73) 3–5.

(iii) professionalisation of contract management.[78] Finally, there is only one area that he identified, in which further harmonisation of applicable rules is a reasonably strong priority: development of an 'international norm calling for a fairly formal competition among holders of framework [agreements]' before actual orders are placed, comprehending a requirement for issuance of a written solicitation, 'identified and weighted evaluation criteria and a right to challenge the selection by disappointed bidders'.[79]

VI. What Should be Done; What Lies Ahead?

The nuanced, selective, patient and iterative approach to harmonisation advocated by Schooner and Yukins in 2007 and by Dan Gordon in 2013 appears to me to mark the way forward. The presentations and papers at this Conference from this session on implementation of the UNCITRAL Model Law, demonstrate that the hard work of harmonisation cannot be completed in an artificially short time period. At the same time, however, they reflect and potentiate the gradual accretion of practical wisdom as to how to effectively go forward with the work of procurement reform in a world of diverse nations with diverse national economies and political systems. I would argue that harmonisation of a different kind – let's call it 'common law harmonisation' – is actually occurring as serious professionals committed to the long-range goal of advancing open, competitive procurement, procurement that fosters both honest government and the attainment of good value exchange hard-won insights as to what does work, what can work, and what cannot work in a world of such diverse nations. I call this 'common law harmonisation'. The label was chosen because it has the quality, familiar to those whose legal tradition descends from the English common law, of iterative development in usually small steps that nonetheless yields reasonable determinate guidance over time. So what guidance can we take away?

First, accumulating experience teaches us that radical harmonisation is unlikely to succeed in the near to medium term; the diversity of nations with different institutional competences, histories and economic systems precludes that. Rather, a balance must be struck between accommodating national and developmental diversity and assuring reasonable openness to cross-border suppliers and reasonable assurance of fair treatment for all would-be suppliers. To use the terms that Sue Arrowsmith has employed in the EU context, *at least outside the EU*, a framework, rather than a common code, is what is wanted at this stage of globalisation of procurement.[80] It may well be that a higher degree of harmonisation can be achieved in the shorter term in regional procurement pacts that may be part of regional trade liberalisation among groups of nations that share sufficient commonality of legal traditions and institutional development.

[78] ibid 5-7.

[79] ibid 5.

[80] I deliberately leave to one side the question, addressed by Professor Sue Arrowsmith, whether the EU has struck correctly the balance for that group of 28 Member States. As noted earlier, her view is that even for the EU, the present Directives go too far in the direction of imposing a common code. Thus, I take her view to be that simplification of the overall EU regime would be possible, reducing materially the cost of procurement procedure and the associated litigation.

Second, the excessive cost associated both with high complexity in a procurement regime and with frequent revision of any national procurement regime, is a common insight that emerges from the experience of developed and developing nations and transitional economies alike. My own work has tried to demonstrate how excess complexity can arise in a sophisticated procurement regime. Ironically, we have seen in the United States how easily this can be an unintended consequence of efforts to offer simpler and quicker procurement vehicles, such as frameworks. Too often, in practice, these alternative vehicles are added to a long and growing list of available procurement procedures with the result that the procurement regime becomes unmanageably complex, or prone to bad practice. This is particularly so when the procurement regime must be implemented by an under-resourced, under-trained cadre of procurement professionals.[81]

A related insight that emerges from the experience of procurement reform in developing and transitional economies appears to be that the complexity of the most sophisticated Western procurement regimes may be simply too much for nations first undertaking to implement modern competitive public procurement procedures. It is striking that the full range of options offered by 2011 UNCITRAL Model Law on Public Procurement can appear overwhelming to many such nations, and the aggregate complexity of a procurement system would be increased if any nation attempted to implement the full range of options that the UNCITRAL law allows. Interestingly, again, this insight does not appear to me to be applicable only to developing and transitional economies. As I have written since the time that Hurricane Katrina demonstrated critical weaknesses in the US procurement regime a decade ago, even efforts to make available simpler, quicker procurement procedures can add to the aggregate complexity of the procurement system, making the task of competently using those tools very difficult. Similarly, the need for increased emphasis on, and resources for, procurement workforce training suggested both by Daniel Gordon and by Steve Schooner seems applicable to nations at all levels of development.

Moreover, our shared experience teaches that both in highly developed procurement regimes, as well as in developing and transitional economies the trade-off must be made between the benefits and costs of enhanced discretion, with the common observation that a procurement regime can become too complex and afford procurement officials too many choices of procurement procedure. So, for instance, we learn from Caroline Nicholas, that no nation should actually implement the 13 choices of procurement procedure afforded by the updated UNCITRAL Model Law. Even within a procurement regime that is well-established, as we have seen in the United States, procurement officials may well flee from the discretion offered by the procurement regime. As my colleague Daniel Gordon has shown, for instance, procurement officials in the United States are likely too prone, under the umbrella of our competitive negotiation procedure,

[81] J Schwartz, 'Perspectives on Public Procurement Reform in the United States' in G Marcou, L Folliot-Lalliot, D Gordon, S Schooner, J Schwartz and C Yukins (eds), *Le Controle des Marches Publics* (Paris, Bibliotheque de L'Institut de Recherche Juridique de la Sorbonne, 2009) 99; Schwartz, 'Regulation and Deregulation' (n 15); J Schwartz, 'Katrina's Lessons for Ongoing US Procurement Reform Efforts' (2006) 15 *Public Procurement Law Review* 363; Acquisition Advisory Panel, 'The Federal Acquisition Workforce', ch 5 in Acquisition Advisory Panel, 'Report of the Acquisition Advisory Panel to the Office of Federal Procurement Policy and the United States Congress' (January 2007) 325, available at www.acquisition.gov/sites/default/files/page_file_uploads/ACQUISITION-ADVISORY-PANEL-2007-Report_final.pdf.

to eschew discretionary trade-offs between price and quality that are permitted by the procedure. Instead they are likely to use a variation of competitive negotiation we call 'LPTA' – 'lowest price, technically acceptable' – which fails to take advantage of the ability fully to pursue best value, and instead seeks a result that minimises the likelihood of a successful challenge procedure brought by a disappointed would-be supplier.[82]

Another, related, unifying insight is the need for stability in the legal framework of a procurement regime, and the counterproductive effects of frequent changes in that regime. At all levels of development, the challenges to the procurement workforce and training of that workforce are dramatically magnified by frequent changes. Evgeny Smirnov of the European Bank for Reconstruction and Development made this point in the Global Revolution 7 panel on implementation of the 2011 UNCITRAL Model Law on Public Procurement; it is equally true in advanced procurement systems. This was a major theme that emerged from the work of the United States' Acquisition Advisory panel on which I served from 2005-07.[83]

There are other emerging developments that bear on the overall prospects for harmonisation, going forward. Certainly we have seen in the last year or so a renewed attention to the severe costs of corruption in nations both developed and developing. A new degree of urgency has attached to anti-corruption efforts with the argument made most prominently by Sarah Chayes that corruption threatens global security because it is a major driver of anti-democratic movements.[84] Of course anti-corruption is but one facet of public procurement reform and it has been argued at this Conference that a one-dimensional emphasis on the anti-corruption axis can undermine the pursuit of other values of procurement reform, including the pursuit of best value. Thus a tentative consensus insight that may form part of the emerging common law harmonisation might be that a one-sided emphasis on criminal prosecution as a solution for corruption is not sustainable. Rather it must be married to the long, hard work of building trustworthy institutions and training and retaining an experienced procurement workforce in order to achieve either both value for money spent and the maximum possible inhibition of corruption.

In the end, it appears that the work of harmonisation does move forward. It may often proceed in a 'two steps forward, one step back' mode. The hopes that some cherished a decade ago for early radical convergence do appear to have been unrealistic. But a more measured, selective, iterative and incrementalist pathway towards harmonisation remains viable. So, we have work to do. Let us continue.

[82] DI Gordon, 'Bid Protests: The Costs Are Real, but the Benefits Outweigh Them' (2013) 42 *Public Contract Law Journal* 489, 506.

[83] Acquisition Advisory Panel, 'Report of the Acquisition Advisory Panel to the Office of Federal Procurement Policy and the United States Congress' (n 81).

[84] See Chayes, *Thieves of State* (n 32).

5

The Harmonisation Process in Developing Countries

LAURENCE FOLLIOT-LALLIOT

I. Introduction

In the world of development, harmonisation used to be presented one or two decades ago as a goal that should be achieved in order to overcome the obstacles encountered by Development Aid.[1] The issue of harmonisation has been a recurrent question of the reform agenda discussed in international arenas when questioning how to improve procurement systems in developing countries. Despite efforts to harmonise the rules of the development partners with the Sustainable Development Goal (SDG)[2] number 17 on strengthening the means of implementation and revitalising the Global Partnership for Sustainable Development, and despite increasing convergence of international norms,[3] discussions continue about whether harmonisation is a goal or just an indirect consequence, good or bad, of the process of making aid effective for developing countries. Thus a constructive approach should look at several dimensions of the paradigm. Firstly, it should address its ultimate objectives: Why look for harmonisation in public procurement? Who will benefit from it? Secondly, it should analyse its coverage and boundaries: How far should harmonisation go? What should actually be harmonised? Is it about principles and foundations, or about rules (laws and regulations), or about practices? Are international institutions pursuing harmonisation for

[1] 'In 2016, total receipts by developing countries from donor countries of the Development Assistance Committee of the Organization for Economic Cooperation and Development (OECD), multilateral agencies and other key providers were $315 billion, of which $158 billion were ODA [official development assistance]'. Source: United Nations Economic and Social Council (UNECOSOC), 'Progress towards the Sustainable Development Goals – Report of the Secretary General' (UNECOSOC, E/2018/64, 10 May 2018) para 94, available at undocs.org/E/2018/64.

[2] The 2030 Agenda for Sustainable Development was adopted by all UN Member States in 2015 with 17 Sustainable Development Goals (SDGs) aiming at ending poverty and other deprivations through strategies that improve health and education, reduce inequality and spur economic growth – all while tackling climate change. Available at www.un.org/sustainabledevelopment/sustainable-development-goals/.

[3] Such as the EU Public Contracts Directives, the UNCITRAL Model law on Public Procurement, and the WTO's Government Procurement Agreement, for example.

the sake of development and/or competition? Today, controversies about harmonisation arise especially in light of recent efforts to ensure that a country's context is taken into account during national procurement reforms and the implication that there is no 'one-size-fits-all' solution to improving procurement outcomes at the country level.[4]

Despite years of debate about the merits of harmonisation in public procurement, diversity and fragmentation of models remain. Beyond the discussion between diversity versus harmonisation, there is a need to differentiate harmonisation from an international standpoint and harmonisation from the domestic perspective. This chapter will discuss the phenomena of public procurement harmonisation at the country level, specifically in the context of developing countries. It will explore the issue of harmonisation to try to understand (i) how harmonisation has been promoted from an international top-down perspective[5] but has become an unreachable goal in the field of public procurement; (ii) why it has not been a driver for reform in developing countries; and (iii) why now we may consider that it has been replaced by multipolar convergences.

II. The Unreachable Grail of Harmonisation in Public Procurement?

To be operative and effective, vertical harmonisation requires a pre-determined model accepted by all parties: a common set of requirements and milestones towards which all stakeholders can converge. Currently available sets of international standards belong to: (i) regional systems such as the EU Procurement Directives[6] and others (eg WAEMU,[7] COMESA[8] directives); (ii) Free Trade Agreements and the GPA;[9] (iii) the

[4] See ch 12 in this collection by C Yukins and S Williams-Elegbe.

[5] This chapter focuses on public procurement. Thus it will not address the theoretical issue of defining harmonisation against analogous notions such as standardisation. On this question, see J-F Gaudreault-Desbiens, E Mackaay, B Moore and S Rousseau, *Convergence, concurrence et harmonisation des systèmes juridiques* (Montréal, Éditions Thémis, 2009) 300.

[6] Directive 2014/24/EU of the European Parliament and of the Council of 26 February 2014 on public procurement and repealing Directive 2004/18/ECOJ L 94, 28.3.2014, p 65–242; Directive 2014/25/EU of the European Parliament and of the Council of 26 February 2014 on procurement by entities operating in the water, energy, transport and postal services sectors and repealing Directive 2004/17/ECOJ L 94, 28.3.2014, p 243–374; Directive 2014/23/EU of the European Parliament and of the Council of 26 February 2014 on the award of concession contracts Text with EEA relevance, OJ L 94, 28.3.2014, p 1–64.

[7] West African Economic and Monetary Union, UEMOA in French, regroups eight countries in West Africa, which have adopted three Procurement Directives (in French) harmonising the procurement rules above thresholds.

[8] The Common Market for Eastern and Southern African Countries has enacted a Procurement Directive in 2009 for its 22 member states. Available at fr.scribd.com/document/97282899/Comesa-Rules-and-Regulations.

[9] The Agreement on Government Procurement (GPA) consists of 19 parties covering 47 WTO members (counting the EU and its 28 Member States, all of which are covered by the Agreement, as one party). Another 32 WTO members/observers and four international organisations participate in the GPA Committee as observers. Ten of these members with observer status are in the process of acceding to the Agreement; www.wto.org/english/tratop_e/gproc_e/memobs_e.htm.

UNCITRAL Model Law on Public Procurement and its Guide to Enactment[10] whose stated purpose is to 'support the harmonization of procurement regulation internationally, and so to promote international trade'; (iv) the OECD Recommendation on Public Procurement;[11] (v) soft-law procurement regulations issued by multilateral development banks (MBDs), such as the World Bank's former guidelines and now regulations;[12] (vi) and other so called 'Principles' or 'Codes of conduct' customised to fit particularities of the private sector or of the public sector.

Although references to 'good' or 'best' practices adorn international declarations,[13] there is, in fact, no clear agreement on which of the international procurement standards[14] the harmonisation effort, if desirable, should be based, and what hierarchy among these standards should be established. However, 'standards or best practices'[15] tend to be presented in the public procurement field as interchangeable concepts reflecting the implicit mix between the legal and practical dimensions of these references.[16] How to establish the balance between efficiency and sustainability? The concept of transparency itself could be questioned: is it a principle or just a means to foster governance? All these still pending questions were not sufficiently researched in the fora of international organisations (IOs) while they were busy designing procurement models for developing countries with mixed results.[17] In the realm of the 2005 Paris Declaration, the first Methodology for Assessing Procurement Systems (MAPS)[18] tool was presented as a way to assess the existing elements of a procurement system against a defined set of standards, or baseline indicators, that are derived from an implicit model system. Despite such affirmation, the vacuum in the identification of these international standards, or even more, of this 'model system', created uncertainty and room for loose interpretation. At this point, we argue that the fragmentation of procurement standards is inherent in the lack of consensus at the international level; indeed, it resonates with the divergence among the 'goals' of harmonisation.

[10] The UNCITRAL Model Law on Procurement of Goods, Construction and Services (1994) and the UNCITRAL Model Law on Public Procurement (2011) with its Guide to Enactment, available at www.uncitral.org/uncitral/en/uncitral_texts/procurement_infrastructure/2011Model.html.

[11] Published in 2015, available at www.oecd.org/gov/public-procurement/recommendation/.

[12] World Bank, The Procurement Framework – Policy, Regulations, Guidance, 2016, available at www.worldbank.org/en/projects-operations/products-and-services/brief/procurement-new-framework.

[13] Such as the 2005 Paris Declaration on Aid Effectiveness (para 3.vi.): 'Defining measures and standards of performance and accountability of partner country systems in public financial management, procurement, fiduciary safeguards and environmental assessments, in line with broadly accepted good practices and their quick and widespread application'. Source: OECD, 'The Paris Declaration on Aid Effectiveness and the Accra Agenda for Action' (OECD, 2005/2008) 11, available at www.oecd.org/dac/effectiveness/34428351.pdf.

[14] S Arrowsmith, 'Public Procurement: An Appraisal of the UNCITRAL Model Law as a Global Standard' (2004) 53 *International & Comparative Law Quarterly* 17.

[15] Not to be confused with technical standards for which the question of standardisation is also a controversial issue. See H Schepel, 'The New Approach to the New Approach: The Juridification of Harmonized Standards in EU Law' (2013) 20 *Maastricht Journal of European and Comparative Law* 521.

[16] See SL Schooner and CR Yukins, 'Incrementalism: Eroding the Impediments to a Global Procurement Market' (2007) 38 *Georgetown Journal of International Law* 529.

[17] As denounced by S Evenett and BM Hoekman, 'International Cooperation and the Reform of Public Procurement Policies', World Bank Policy Research Working Paper 3720 (September 2005) 19, available at documents.worldbank.org/curated/en/324441468135312471/pdf/wps3720.pdf.

[18] OECD, 'Methodology For Assessing Procurement Systems (MAPS)' (OECD, February 2010) available at www.oecd.org/governance/ethics/Methodology-assessing-procurement-MAPS-Report-February-2010.pdf.

A. Divergence among the Goals of Harmonisation

Looking at the recent instruments and sets of rules produced at international level in the field of public procurement, two major trends have converged, or at least moved, to enhance the harmonisation process: the globalisation of trade which has stimulated the negotiations of trade treaties establishing common competition rules, and the role of IOs and the donor community in the management of development aid. Parallel but distinct, their scope of operation differs with the first trend mainly focused on developed countries, and the second trend specifically addressing issues encountered by developing countries.

i. Harmonisation as a Trade Goal

As a common feature, many of the international procurement instruments listed at the beginning of section II target the harmonisation or, at least, compatibility of domestic procurement rules with the international rules in order to promote competition and better access to governments' markets for foreign companies.[19] The harmonisation of procurement systems is perceived as a means to facilitate trade, by offering similar rules and conditions.[20] Although harmonisation may not be proclaimed upfront,[21] more often than not it is an implicit goal that can be discovered through an analysis of the provisions. Indeed, for Sue Arrowsmith 'It is clear … that UNCITRAL's mandate for adopting the Model Law is based on the potential for harmonized laws on public procurement to further the development of international trade'.[22] Furthermore, she insisted on the harmonisation purpose as being the generalisation of identical rules fostering trade: 'from the trade perspective, the Model's Law's potential as a harmonization instrument can be fully realized only if it is used by all types of states'.[23]

However, these different sets of standards differ in their motivation, scope and also legal impact. In terms of their legal force, some instruments are mandatory for their country members as soon as they are formally implemented into their national law (GPA, trade agreements, EU Procurement Directives, WAEMU Directives), whilst some are just solemn declarations of intention without any binding effect

[19] Previous work of the current author explored the impact of internationalisation and globalisation on domestic procurement rules: L Folliot-Lalliot, 'From the Internationalization of Rules to the Internationalization of Public Contracts: How International Instruments Are Reshaping Domestic Procurement Systems', ch 2 in M Audit and SW Schill (eds), *Transnational Law of Public Contracts*, 1st edn (Brussels, Bruylant, 2016) 23.

[20] RD Anderson and WE Kovacic, 'Competition Policy and International Trade Liberalisation: Essential Complements to Ensure Good Performance in Public Procurement Markets' (2009) 18(2) *Public Procurement Law Review*67.

[21] The implementation of this objective matured in initiatives such as the Integrated Framework involved in the ITC, IMF, UNCTAD, UNDP, World Bank, WTO and OECD. On the promotion of this idea, see WA Wittig, 'Public procurement and the Development Agenda' (WTO, 2002) available at www.wto.org/english/tratop_e/gproc_e/wkshop_tanz_jan03/itcdemo1_e.pdf.

[22] S Arrowsmith and C Nicholas, 'The UNCITRAL Model Law: Past, Present, and Future' ch 1 in S Arrowsmith (ed), *Reform of the UNCITRAL Model Law on Procurement: Procurement Regulation for the 21st Century* (West, 2009) 9.

[23] ibid 22.

(eg OECD Principles for Integrity in Public Procurement or Other OECD Guiding Principles on Public Procurement – Principles and codes of conduct[24]). These re-join the 'soft-law' category together with the UNCITRAL Model Law on Public Procurement and the UNCITRAL Legislative Guide on Privately Financed Infrastructure Projects,[25] whilst MDBs' procurement guidelines and regulations constitute an intermediary legal category, only gaining true legal force when they are incorporated into a binding loan agreement signed between the financial institutions and their client countries.

Considering the modus operandi of these standards, divergence is *de facto* the consistent common denominator. The GPA and other trade agreements are trade-only instruments, focusing on the opening of borders for trade and the stimulation of competition by a selective elimination of protectionism. If these instruments are trade models, and are used ultimately to foster harmonisation, their starting point is actually based on the principle of reciprocity: benefiting from the opening of borders is a privilege limited to the members of the treaty in question. In fact, it is the ability to circumvent existing barriers that defines the attractiveness of these trade agreements, where the main incentive for candidate countries is the enjoyment of preferential access. Soft-law instruments such as recommendations, principles and model laws, could be better vectors of harmonisation since they promote models and optimal norms that should be applied by all countries across their procurement system. However, most of the time, they miss the point as they try to promote an idealistic situation that barely reflects the current possibilities and capacities of the countries that are contemplating them. When it comes to the motivations engrained in these different international sets of standards, they fail to achieve the goal of harmonisation: trade instruments, either bilateral or plurilateral, despite a few adjustments for the least developed economies, are too often a way for the more active and exporting economies to gain access to markets, along with a surgical eradication of domestic preferences. In addition, they may sometimes operate with a multiplier effect, amplifying the existing strengths and weaknesses of both partners. Based on the principle of reciprocity, they refer to a limited or circumscribed harmonisation, reserved for the signatory parties.

ii. Harmonisation as a Goal for Donors in Development Aid

The harmonisation process launched by the IOs started from a very different standpoint. For many years, the World Bank and its followers[26] (regional MDBs, such as African Development Bank, Asian Development Bank, or Inter-American Development Bank, for example) had promoted their procurement guidelines as mandatory rules for borrowing countries. However the impact of these guidelines was limited

[24] eg CIPS Code of Conduct, available at www.cips.org/en/who-we-are/governance/cips-code-of-conduct/.

[25] Adopted in 2000 with legal recommendations added in 2003 www.uncitral.org/uncitral/en/uncitral_texts/procurement_infrastructure/2001Guide_PFIP.html.

[26] R Sanches and D Engel, 'The Role of Regional Multilateral Development Banks in the Internationalization of Public Contracts', ch 25 in Audit and Schill (eds), *Transnational Law of Public Contracts* (n 19) 661.

to specific projects,[27] although the 'National Competitive Bidding' (NCB) procedure imposed on countries presenting a 'risk' in International Competitive Bidding terms created a 'quasi-domestic public procurement framework for Open Competition'.[28] Reinforcing its advisory services, at the end of the 1990s, with 'Development Policy Lending' (DPL) replacing 'Programmatic lending', the World Bank deployed a new tool fostering recommendations for reform of domestic procurement rules and practices, after a thorough evaluation of the situation through the CPAR (Country Procurement Assessment Report) modality. As described by Bentchikou,

> gradually and oftentimes as a result of exposures to and transposition of certain broadly recognized open competitive bidding best practices, requirements formulated by the World Bank became incorporated into domestic regulatory frameworks, through procurement reforms assisted by institutional development projects.[29]

However, it is interesting to look at the history of this process, understanding how harmonisation of public procurement standards was presented as a solution to remedy some development issues. Within the ambit of the Millennium Development Goals (MDGs),[30] a Development Assistance Committee (DAC) Task Force on Donor Practices[31] was established in partnership with other development organisations in December 2000 for a two-year period. Several outputs of DAC's work demonstrated that fragmentation of rules and systems was at the core of many issues faced by developing countries.[32] Procurement was not the only public activity analysed. Public financial management, financial reporting and auditing were also concerned by this diagnostic exercise.[33] Dis-harmonisation or fragmentation was indeed an enshrined characteristic of development aid not only because of recurrent internal disorganisation of beneficiary countries, but also because of the lack of coherence among the donors' solutions, specifically in the area of their public procurement requirements.[34] Actually these

[27] F Bentchikou, 'World Bank Procurement: Contributions to the Harmonization of Public Contracts', ch 23 in Audit and Schill (n 19) 615.

[28] ibid 623.

[29] ibid 624.

[30] The Millennium Development Goals (MDGs) were the eight international development goals for the year 2015 that had been established following the UN Millennium Summit in 2000.

[31] Other than the World Bank, Heads of Procurement of MDBs and the WTO, members of DAC were only developed countries: Australia, Austria, Belgium, Canada, Denmark, Finland, France, Germany, Greece, Ireland, Italy, Japan, Luxembourg, the Netherlands, New Zealand, Norway, Portugal, Spain, Sweden, Switzerland, the United Kingdom, the United States, and the Commission of the European Communities, but 16 developing countries were also invited to participate in the discussions.

[32] OECD, *Harmonising Donor Practices for Effective Aid Delivery: Good Practice Papers – A DAC Reference Document*, DAC Guidelines and Reference Series (Paris, OECD Publications, 2003) available at www.oecd.org/development/effectiveness/20896122.pdf.

[33] These sectors are covered by several reports in the *Harmonising Donor Practices for Effective Aid Delivery* collection ((n 32). Around the same period, the adoption of the 'Equator Principles' illustrated the concern of the international community, including private actors such as banks, for reducing the cost of divergence in the financing of infrastructure projects. See A Meyerstein, 'Global Private Regulation in Development Finance: The Equator Principles and the Transnationalization of Public Contracting' in Audit and Schill (n 19) 799.

[34] OECD Harmonizing Donors Practices for Effective Aid Delivery – vol 3: Strengthening Procurement Practices in Developing Countries, p 11: 'Developing countries and donors will monitor and evaluate progress in implementing the Round Table guidance, in achieving the desired results and in promoting donor

procurement requirements increased transaction costs for developing countries since they were forced to manage several different sets of donors' rules when implementing internationally subsidised projects.

After the Monterrey Consensus,[35] in February 2003, the Rome Declaration on Harmonisation[36] set in motion 'an important international effort to harmonise the operational policies, procedures, and practices of the [donors'] institutions with those of partner country systems to improve the effectiveness of development assistance', and thereby contribute to meeting the Millennium Development Goals (MDGs). After that, and as further discussed in chapter 3 of this collection, the 2005 'Paris Declaration on Aid Effectiveness: Ownership, Harmonisation, Alignment, Results and Mutual Accountability' was clearly an attempt to streamline donors' public procurement rules, based on the DAC Reference Document 'Harmonising Donor Practices for Effective Aid Delivery'.[37] Thus, the Paris Declaration promoted[38] harmonisation and coordination on the donors' side, using work by the Heads of Procurement of the MDBs to harmonise their respective procurement guidelines and standardise procurement documents. They have adopted common standard bidding documents,[39] and, among at least few MDBs, they have organised cross-debarment of corrupt and fraudulent companies.[40]

In this context, it is interesting to note that harmonisation in public procurement was not initially imposed on developing countries. From a substantive point of view, harmonisation among donors' rules was understood as a means of achieving simplification and thus accelerating project implementation: 'Harmonisation leads to simplification, which in turn frees up resources that can be used to develop better local capacity that will allay donor fiduciary concerns'.[41] Simplification around donors' rules was presented as a desirable goal from both sides, namely donors and developing countries. Moreover, this simplification exercise was instrumental in the design of an idealistic

harmonisation and alignment around strengthened partner country procurement systems'; see also the Paris Declaration on Aid effectiveness (2005), point 3 on harmonisation: 'Donor countries and organisations co-ordinate their actions, simplify procedures and share information to avoid duplication', available at www.oecd.org/dac/effectiveness/45827300.pdf.

[35] UN, *Report of the International Conference on Financing for Development – Monterrey, Mexico, 18–22 March 2002,* A/CONF.198/11 (UN, 2003) available at archive.ipu.org/splz-e/ffd08/monterrey.pdf.

[36] This Declaration was endorsed by Ministers, Heads of Aid Agencies and other Senior Officials representing 28 aid recipient countries and more than 40 multilateral and bilateral development institutions. It can be found at https://europa.eu/capacity4dev/help/file/10146/download?token=-eDdSh5h.

[37] OECD and World Bank, *Harmonising Donor Practices for Effective Aid Delivery – Volume 3: Strengthening Procurement Capacities in Developing Countries,* DAC Guidelines and Reference Series (Paris, OECD Publishing, 2005) available at www.oecd.org/gov/ethics/34336126.pdf.

[38] Para 3: 'We reaffirm the commitments made at Rome to harmonise and align aid delivery'.

[39] Master Procurement Documents: Master Document for Procurement of Plant Design, Supply and Installation (February 2007) available at http://siteresources.worldbank.org/INTPROCUREMENT/Resources/MBD-PLANT-rev-JUN06-final-rev02-05-07.pdf.

[40] The Agreement for Mutual Enforcement of Debarment Decisions was signed between the African Development Bank, the Asian Development Bank, the European Bank for Reconstruction and Development, The Inter-American Development Bank and the World Bank, 2010, available at www.adb.org/documents/agreement-mutual-enforcement-debarment-decisions.

[41] OECD and World Bank, *Harmonising Donor Practices for Effective Aid Delivery – Volume 3: Strengthening Procurement Capacities in Developing Countries* (n 37) 25.

procurement system while, at the same time, the World Bank's Doing Business Report of 2004 was calling for a 'One-Size-Can-Fit-All' approach.[42] Indeed, the 2005 DAC Report on Strengthening Procurement Capacities in Developing Countries proclaimed: 'The third lesson is the need for agreement among developing countries and among donors over what constitutes a "good" procurement system and how this should be measured'.[43] Other parts of the Report refer to a 'model system',[44] a 'well-designed system'[45] reflecting the attempt to promote a unique procurement system which all countries should reach.

B. Towards the Alignment of Domestic Procurement Rules on MDB Models

Implicit harmonisation imposed on recipient countries, at least non-EU related developing countries,[46] was progressively introduced. The analysis of the narrative of the 2005 DAC Report on Strengthening Procurement Capacities in Developing Countries demonstrates that its original aim gradually moved from targeting harmonisation of donors' rules to the harmonisation of domestic procurement systems. This was in line with the Rome Declaration which had proclaimed that recipient countries, for their part, would undertake necessary reforms to enable progressive reliance by donors on their systems as they adopted international principles or standards and applied good practices.[47] Reform and upgrading of the domestic systems were presented as necessary drivers for change. In 2005, the DAC Report on Strengthening Procurement Capacities in Developing Countries illustrated this top-down approach:[48]

> Because few procurement systems are mainstreamed today in the sense recommended by the Round Table, the Strategic Framework also provides background and advice on the many new tools and techniques … This should be of use to governments when they design programmes involving mainstreaming elements and to help them overcome resistance to change.

In this context, the elaboration of the first MAPS tool a year later would also serve this objective of the harmonisation of domestic procurement legal systems. Presented as a tool,[49] it was affirmed that the assessment of developing countries' practices against a

[42] C McLiesh and S Djankov, *Doing Business in 2004: Understanding Regulation* (Washington DC, World Bank, the International Financial Corporation and Oxford University Press, 2004) XVI, available at documents.worldbank.org/curated/en/724511468762587518/Doing-business-in-2004-understanding-regulation.

[43] OECD and World Bank (n 37) 9.

[44] ibid 56.

[45] ibid 57.

[46] Elizabetta Morlino has demonstrated that Non-EU States in the area of influence of the EU, such as countries of the African, Caribbean and Pacific Group of States (ACP), have been subject to the 'europeanisation' of their procurement rules – E Morlino, 'Development Aid and the Europeanization of Public Procurement in Non-EU States', ch 26 in Audit and Schill (n 19) 689.

[47] See n 36.

[48] OECD and World Bank (n 37) 9.

[49] OECD, Methodology For Assessment Of National Procurement Systems, Version 4 (OECD, July 2006) 2, available at http://www.oecd.org/gov/ethics/37390076.pdf.

baseline qualified as 'a desirable "good practice standard"' would serve this purpose. In the aftermath of the Paris Declaration, using MAPS for its assessments, the World Bank launched the Pilot titled 'Use of Country Systems' (UCS) in 2008 with the aim of relying on the domestic procurement rules of selected countries for project operations. Welcomed by developing countries, this exercise which was initially designed to evaluate domestic rules against 'international standards'[50] turned out to be a comparison between the domestic rules and the World Bank standards, verifying whether local rules were 'consistent with the Procurement Guidelines and acceptable to the Bank'.[51] Alignment to the World Bank standards was implicitly required, and the whole programme finally failed to achieve its objectives.[52]

Under the auspices of the development community, these technical cooperation activities gave and still give to the MDBs some legitimacy in preparing prescriptive requirements in domestic public procurement procedures.[53] In this connection, Dr Loukas A Mistelis noted:[54]

> [S]everal other international organizations, such as the World Bank, the European Bank for Reconstruction and Development (EBRD), and the International Monetary Fund (IMF), demonstrated in a number of endeavors their interest in being involved in the lawmaking process or at least in the standard-setting. In principle, neither the World Bank nor the EBRD nor the IMF has any power to legislate and, hence, standard-setting is the appropriate form of involvement.

The abandonment of the UCS project in 2011[55] revealed the resistance of developing countries to the alignment effort. Ultimately, procurement tools of MDBs, although presented as bearers of international standards, cannot achieve harmonisation. Too rigid, the provisions contained in their procurement regulations, and former guidelines, were tailored first and foremost to fit the MDBs' own agendas and fiduciary obligations, ensuring fiduciary relevance and compliance of the financed projects. For many years, this idiosyncratic orientation led the MDBs to neglect some crucial (legal) issues

[50] World Bank, *Piloting Program in the Use of Country Procurement Systems: Second Progress Report* (Washington DC, The World Bank, 2010) 1, available at siteresources.worldbank.org/INTPROCUREMENT/Resources/278019-1311363656902/UCS_Second_Progress_Report_(Final_version)_(22_Dec_2010).pdf.

[51] Bentchikou, 'World Bank Procurement' (n 27) 624.

[52] World Bank, 'Strengthening Country Procurement Systems: Results and Opportunities – Report for the 4th High-Level Forum on Aid Effectiveness' (Washington DC, World Bank, 2011) 121, available at siteresources.worldbank.org/INTALBANIA/Resources/Strengthening_Procurement_Systems.pdf.

[53] On the pressure on developing countries, see C McCrudden and S Gross, 'WTO Government Procurement Rules and Local Dynamics of Procurement Policies: A Malaysian Case Study' (2006) 17 *European Journal of International Law* 151.

[54] LA Mistelis, 'Regulatory Aspects: Globalization, Harmonization' (Global Policy Forum, Fall 2000, v34(3) 1055–69) available at www.globalpolicy.org/component/content/article/163/28139.html.

[55] 'In the end, even the four countries (id: Brazil, Senegal, Mauritius, Rwanda) conditionally cleared to move to the project phase did not do so. Brazil was expected to move forward at the time of the final progress report but shifted course after deciding that the conditions imposed as a requirement for the use of country systems, which effectively created a hybrid, modified national procurement system, were too onerous'. See World Bank, *The World Bank and Public Procurement – An Independent Evaluation. Volume II: Achieving Development Effectiveness through Procurement in Bank Financial Assistance* (Washington DC, Independent Evaluation Group, World Bank, IFC and MIGA, 2014) 19, available at documents.worldbank.org/curated/en/971621468165867766/pdf/832100PUB0v20R00Box382076B00PUBLIC0.pdf.

pending for their client countries, whilst at the same time procurement guidelines were presented as standards to be implemented. However, it is not because a mechanism is robust in one environment that its transplantation will be proven effective in another. As an example, several client countries have, with the support of MDBs, transplanted the Bank's 'no-objection' system for the prior review of contracts,[56] duplicating red tape and pointless layers of bureaucratic oversight in a completely different legal and institutional environment, sometimes adding inappropriate layers in decentralised countries. By contrast, a vacuum in the MDBs legal framework could also negatively impact the success of copy-pasted procurement reform in the recipient countries. Thus, for many years, the procurement guidelines of MBDs have lacked effective rules for the establishment of a sophisticated complaint mechanism. The explanation can be found in the MDBs' own status: enjoying sovereign immunities[57] protecting them from any challenge to their decisions, even the challenge of the award of their own contracts, MDBs were not likely to design such process. Not surprisingly, their procurement guidelines lacked detailed provisions on challenge mechanisms. As a matter of fact, the new procurement framework of the World Bank,[58] launched in 2016,[59] expressly excludes setting mandatory requirements in countries' public procurement. This approach will prevent any reputational risk for the Bank: 'No mandatory specifications will be set, but rather the focus will be on producing targeted procurement guidance that better supports Borrowers and the private sector'.[60]

Finally and reflecting the multidimensional aspects of (international) public procurement, there is a lack of harmonisation because there are too many harmonisation tools and models conflicting among each other. Public administration and financial reforms attract many actors: international, local, public and private, such as consulting and other legal firms attracted by this expanding business. Assessment tools have flourished in all sectors, looking for similar signs of improvement. In 2016, 81 developing countries had undertaken national exercises to monitor development effectiveness.[61] In the field of public procurement[62] and Public-Private Partnerships (PPPs),[63]

[56] The 'no-objection' process requires the Bank's prior approval for main procurement steps and decisions in projects financed by the World Bank in client countries. See World Bank Guidelines Procurement under IBRD Loans and IDA Credits (May 2004 revised 2006 & 2010) art 2.18.

[57] HG Schermers and NM Blokker, *International Institutional Law: Unity within Diversity*, 5th rev edn (Leiden, Martinus Nijhoff Publishers, 2011) 599.

[58] New Procurement Framework and Regulations for Projects After July 1, 2016, available at www.worldbank.org/en/projects-operations/products-and-services/brief/procurement-new-framework.

[59] By contrast, the new procurement policy of the World Bank places emphasis on this issue: 'The Bank will significantly enhance its approach to procurement-related complaints'. See World Bank, 'Procurement in World Bank Investment Project Financing – Phase II: The New Procurement Framework' (World Bank, 11 June 2015) 5, available at wbnpf.procurementinet.org/sites/default/files/Board-Paper-phase-ii-the-new-procurement-framework.pdf.

[60] World Bank Board Paper, 'Phase II: the New procurement Framework' (11 June 2015).

[61] NECOSOC, 'Progress towards the Sustainable Development Goals' (n 1) para 144.

[62] World Bank Group, 'Benchmarking Public Procurement 2017: Assessing Public Procurement Regulatory Systems in 180 Economies' (Washington DC, World Bank Publications, 2016) available at pubdocs.worldbank.org/en/121001523554026106/BPP17-e-version-Final-compressed-v2.pdf.

[63] World Bank's Infrastructure, PPPs and Guarantees (IPG) Group and the Global Indicators Group, 'Procuring Infrastructure Public-Private Partnerships 2018' (Washington DC, World Bank, 2018), available at pppknowledgelab.org/documents/5453.

benchmarking tools[64] have been more recently prepared, all with an underlying standardisation effect, albeit the second MAPS tool tries better to take into consideration the country context. Despite repetitive references, including in the 2017 MAPS,[65] it is almost impossible to define what is meant by 'international standards' in public procurement.

III. Harmonisation and the Main Drivers for Reform at the Country Level

Before meeting the requirements of a potential agenda of harmonisation proposed either by the donor community or by the trade negotiators, developing countries need to succeed in their own reform process. However, slow results or real failures have illustrated that the attempts to reform domestic procurement systems have been less successful than expected (section III.A). We argue that whilst achievement of the harmonisation process was, and still is, not a goal of developing countries, seeking harmonisation could explain some of the failures or maladjustments of the domestic reforms (section III.B).

A. Lessons Learned from Procurement Reform Failures

Many reports are periodically produced to monitor the functioning of the procurement systems all over the world. We will not enumerate all of their findings. However, we will emphasise some of the pitfalls that could be related to the design of the procurement reforms. Quite often, designers of reforms tend to promote easy targets, introducing standard provisions, tools and techniques, while avoiding major issues because these may seem to be too difficult to grasp. However, 'like the elephant in the room', the definition of public procurement contracts is not even covered in several systems, or it is barely mentioned in laws and regulations, or it is just defined as a tautology: a public procurement contract is a contract signed by public bodies according to public procurement rules.[66] As exemplified by Switzerland, which has recently implemented a major reform for trade purposes mandated by its accession to the GPA,[67]

[64] P Triantafillou, 'Benchmarking in the Public Sector: a Critical Conceptual Framework' (2007) 85 *Public Administration* 829; J Raymond, 'Benchmarking in Public Procurement' (2008) 15 *Benchmarking: An International Journal* 782.

[65] 'The 2017 MAPS embodies high aspirational standards and serves as a guide toward reform, rather than setting out minimum standards that countries are universally required to attain'. See MAPS, 'Section I – User's Guide' (OECD, 2017) 5, available at www.mapsinitiative.org/methodology/MAPS-user-guide.pdf.

[66] This used to be the definition stated by the French Procurement Code until 2001: 'Les marchés publics sont des contrats passés, dans les conditions prévues au présent code, par les collectivités publiques en vue de la réalisation de travaux, fournitures et services' – (' Procurement contracts are contracts awarded, under the conditions provided for in this code, by public authorities by public authorities to carry out works, supplies and services'), Code des marchés publics, art 1, Décret 64-729 1964-07-17, JORF du 21 juillet 1964 p 6438.

[67] E Poltier, 'La commande publique portant sur des objets complexes: les solutions du droit actuel et du P-LMP, ainsi qu'un regard sur le droit de l'Union européenne', in *Verwaltungsorganisationsrecht – Staatshaftungsrecht – öffentliches Dienstrecht – Droit public de l'organisation – responsabilité des collectivités publiques – fonction publique, Annuaire 2016–2017*, 41 (e-book, Bern, 2017).

ignoring this essential step of the definition of procurement in its coverage has created room for uncertainty, inducing further issues.

Competition among legal systems is also at stake in the area of public procurement. For developed countries, which have elaborated their own legal environment, the legal global competition is also a factor to be considered. Although proclaiming the difference between common law and civil law systems is now part of any introduction to public procurement legal frameworks, its consequences are barely taken into consideration. Not only does it affect the hierarchy of norms in place in a country, as explained by the new MAPS, but it also impacts on the organisational structures, institutions and legal rules applied to the formation and execution of procurement contracts. This element could also explain why some countries turn to arbitration as a way to resolve contractual disputes while others are more reluctant to adopt this model, proactively promoted by 'international standards'.

In parallel with the debate between the common law versus civil law contexts, the task of harmonising public procurement systems might be harder now that domestic contract rules are more and more impacted by the revolution of international trade law. This revolution is affecting the scope of international commercial law, its sources and some substantive rules that may conflict with public procurement rules. Common issues, and grey zones, may call for different approaches from both sides, thus creating potential conflicts between public commercial trade and private commercial trade laws. On scope, one topical example can be found in the work conducted by the International Institute for the Unification of Private Law (UNIDROIT). The 2016 UNIDROIT Principles[68] now cover the performance of long-term contracts, addressing few issues encountered in public contracting, including by PPPs. Moreover, the stronger influence of private actors is illustrated by the promotion of commercial rules and concepts such as arbitration in the realm of public contracting. However, the harmonisation of private commercial law is still itself underway as the result of several initiatives but with no binding results so far.[69] A comparison with the pace of reform of harmonisation in the case of PPPs illustrates the issues encountered: whilst there is a real need for common rules and practices for the security of these long-term projects with frequent transnational dimensions, there remains strong resistance to harmonisation. Freedom of contract is regularly proclaimed as the main legal principle that should guide work in the field of PPPs, whilst real aims are more about maintaining discretion, free negotiation and private resolution of conflicts through arbitration. For the moment, the tenants of the status quo have successfully blocked the harmonisation process in the PPP area, as demonstrated by the UNCITRAL 2012 decision[70] not to launch the preparation of

[68] UNIDROIT – International Institute for the Unification of Public Law, *UNIDROIT Principles of International Commercial Contracts 2016* (Rome, UNDROIT, 2016) available at www.unidroit.org/instruments/commercial-contracts/unidroit-principles-2016. The 2016 edition of the UNIDROIT Principles covers virtually all most important topics of general contract law.

[69] JAE Faria, 'Future Directions of Legal Harmonisation and Law Reform: Stormy Seas or Prosperous Voyage?' (2009) 14 *Uniform Law Review* 5.

[70] Official Records of the General Assembly, Sixty-seventh Session, Supplement No 17 (A/67/17), para 120, and Sixty-eighth Session, Supplement No 17 (A/68/17), paras 327–31. See UNCITRAL – United Nations Commission on International Trade Law, *Yearbook – Volume XLIII:* 2012 (New York, UN, 2015) pt 1, and

a Model Law on PPPs but update as necessary all or part of the existing Legislative Guide,[71] by involving experts in the process.[72] Interestingly, if harmonisation of the PPP legal framework is still in its infancy, standardisation of PPP model contracts is flourishing. In the end, the normative space of public procurement law is subject to opposing forces with legal harmonisation driven by public (international and domestic) actors on the one side, and private actors promoting the expansion of international (private) commercial law on the other side.[73]

The identity of the promoters of the harmonisation effort merits attention. Interesting parallels could be established between public procurement and related public sector fields that have been well exposed to major reforms and a process of harmonisation. Auditing, with the instrumental role of the International Organization of Supreme Audit Institutions (INTOSAI) in promoting the International Public Sector Accounting Standards (IPSAS), is a good example of a successful on-going harmonisation process, even though implementing issues and diversity persist.[74] IPSAS have been adopted for years by several IOs, including the UN and its agencies, the OECD, the EU Commission, NATO and others. This uniformity among IOs is likely to influence developing countries when they contemplate promoting reforms of their accounting mechanisms. As observed by the academic approach of Global Administrative Law (GAL),[75] sectors such as auditing, sports, banking or the internet are other legal/economic areas affected by globalisation. Focusing on the regulation process and the formulation of rules, GAL[76] pinpoints the public or private origin of norms combined with their international or national origin. Whilst in some areas, 100 per cent of regulation emerges from private bodies (example: internet) or a mix of public and private bodies (examples: banking, or sports), public procurement could appear to be the result of a monopoly over public regulations enjoyed by public legislators. On the contrary, harmonisation

UNCITRAL – United Nations Commission on International Trade Law, *Yearbook – Volume XLIV*: 2013 (New York, UN, 2016) pt 1, available at www.uncitral.org/pdf/english/yearbooks/yb-2013-e/Yearbook_2013_e.pdf.

[71] UNCITRAL Legislative Guide on Privately Financed Infrastructure Projects (2000) (including Legislative Recommendations), and the UNCITRAL Model Legislative Provisions on Privately Financed Infrastructure Projects (2003) (n 25).

[72] Decision has been taken in July 2018 during UNCITRAL's Fifty-first Session in New York to conduct the update of the Legislative Guide. A new version should be presented to the 2019 session in New York.

[73] A Riles, 'The Anti-Network: Private Global Governance, Legal Knowledge, and the Legitimacy of the State' (Cornell Law Faculty Publications, Paper 36, 2008) available at scholarship.law.cornell.edu/facpub/36. About transnational contracts, Gilles Lhuilier observes that 'the private actors now "localise" themselves on singular "normative spaces"' in 'The Concept of "Normative Space"' in Les Cahiers d'Ebisu, Occasional Papers, 'Rethinking the Globalization of Law' n°3 (2013) 67, available at www.mfj.gr.jp/publications/_data/e-CahiersEbisu3_pp41-79_GlobalizationLaw_screen.pdf. This idea is also developed in his book: G Lhuilier, *Le droit transnational* (Paris, Dalloz, 2016).

[74] T Budding, G Grossi and T Tagesson, *Public Sector Accounting*, 1st edn (Abingdon, Routledge, 2015).

[75] S Cassesse (ed), *Research Handbook on Global Administrative Law* (Cheltenham, Edward Elgar Publishing, 2016).

[76] 'Global administrative law can be understood as comprising the legal rules, principles, and institutional norms applicable to processes of "administration" undertaken in ways that implicate more than purely intra-State structures of legal and political authority' – B Kingsbury and M Donaldson, 'Global Administrative Law' in *Max Planck Encyclopedia of Public International Law* (Oxford Public International Law, 2012), abstract accessible at www.iilj.org/publications/global-administrative-law/.

of public auditing standards has been prepared, since 2001, by a collaborative effort between the International Auditing and Assurance Standards Board (IAASB), a group of public and private sectors representatives under the auspices of the International Federation of Accountants,[77] and INTOSAI targeting the way public auditors should perform their controls over public financial processes.[78] IPSAS have been designed and applied since 2011 to the public sector by INTOSAI with a clear commitment towards harmonisation.

However, public procurement law cannot just borrow tools and models from the private sector and customise them for its purposes. Due to social policy considerations, to the necessary interactions with the private sector in the formation and performance phases of contracts, and ultimately because of its beneficiaries who are the users/citizens, public procurement finds itself exposed to multiple tensions, including the clash between public and private interests.

This conflict of sources is even more apparent on substantive issues, to the extent that there is a huge contrast between the over-regulated area of procurement rules, subject to the influences of different standards, and the lack of models regarding the execution of these contracts. Whilst the formation of public contracts and methods of procurement are heavily regulated by international public norms and rules, the performance of these contracts is still understood as an area where freedom of contract prevails. Here, it is no longer the word 'public' that is determinant, but the word 'contract', as if the design of these contracts were still entirely in the hands of the two parties, without any limitation or constraint. Many would like to portray the signature of the contract as an *instrumentum* defining the border between public law and private law, or what could be considered 'ruled and locked in' versus what is left to the parties' own decisions, which is at the core of the notion of privity of contract. This approach is illustrated by countries which apply ordinary/commercial law as governing law of procurement contracts, and considering that only the formation phase is mainly an administrative process. In fact, behind the preservation of the contractual freedom principle, there may reside one of the forces most resistant to harmonisation in public procurement law: the area of contract performance. However, one can ask if this still reflects the reality of contracts now subject to mandatory standard clauses, model clauses and other specific requirements or protections when they are entered into by public entities. Interestingly, general clauses of contract have proliferated, from public initiatives, IOs (World Bank and other MDBs' standard bidding documents contain such sets of mandatory clauses) and private initiatives (for example, FIDIC[79] templates). This harmonisation movement, apparently only technical, contrasts drastically with the ring-fencing of the content and performance of contracts through the recent revision of some international instruments, such as the UNCITRAL Model Law on Public Procurement in 2011

[77] IAASB Terms of References, available at www.iaasb.org/about-iaasb/terms-reference.

[78] However, the two legal traditions and conceptions of government, ie those of Anglo-Saxon countries and those of EU continental countries are still influential, with a principles-based approach for the first category and a rules-based approach for the second one. See E Caperchione, J Christiaens and I Lapsley, 'The Forward – The Primacy of, and Complexity of, Accounting for Government' (2013) 29 *Financial Accountability & Management* 349.

[79] Fédération Internationale des Ingénieurs Conseils (International Federation of Construction Engineers).

and the GPA in 2012. These international law products do not cover the administration and performance of the contracts, topics considered to be countries' monopoly in order to preserve their sovereignty. This choice illustrates how trade harmonisation in public procurement is State driven. For many years, the EU's procurement framework was based on the same idea that such areas were irrelevant for Directives targeting competition issues, and limited to the formation phase. The new 2014 EU public procurement 'package', which contains extensive provisions on modification and termination of contracts,[80] reveals *a contrario* that the harmonisation effort can no longer ignore both the content and the performance of procurement contracts. Missing this point does not preserve the independence of the countries' legal systems, but, in the meanwhile, the proliferation of private norms, arbitral solutions and investment law precepts are opportunely filling the gaps. Ignoring harmonisation of rules concerning the performance of public contracts could even be a dangerous choice from a public interest perspective.

Facing the disappointing results of procurement reforms, observers are critical about the effectiveness of the new norms and rules. The main issues are actually not found at the design level, but more at the level of implementation. Even if the new rule is consistent with international 'best standards' (see section II), its implementation may remain discretionary. Many denounce the perpetuation of inadequate practices ignoring the new regulations. Harmonisation of the rules will not suffice if there is no harmonisation of the practices. This finding can be relevant in the EU public procurement area where diverging interpretations (and application) of the procurement rules can still be noticed, despite the harmonisation effort of the EU Court of Justice.[81]

At the implementation level, too often the lack of commitment from developing countries endangers procurement reforms. Governments may endorse a reform promoted by an international organisation only because it is tied to financing they need. Domestic procurement regulatory agencies have been created, mostly along the pattern promoted by IOs, domestic rules have been enacted, civil servants have been trained, at least some of them, but practices lag behind expectations.

Too often as well, the human factor[82] remains neglected in the process of procurement reforms.[83] Whereas the topic of public procurement is rather technical, persons in charge of conducting the procurement reform are usually bureaucrats, who lack the power and legitimacy to make policy choices. Rational choice theory may also be

[80] Arts 72 and 73 of EU Procurement Directive 2014/23 (n 6).

[81] For an example of divergences in the implementation of the Remedies Directive in the EU, see S Torricelli, 'Uniformité et particularisme dans les transpositions nationales du droit européen des procédures de recours' in L Folliot Lalliot and S Torricelli (eds), *Contrôles et contentieux des contrats publics, Oversight and Challenges of Public Contracts* (Brussels, Bruylant, 2018) 481, 473–93.

[82] KS Doty, 'Economic Legal Reforms as a Necessary Means for Eastern European Transition into the Twenty-First Century' (1999) 33 *International Lawyer* 189, 196–97.

[83] C Léon de Mariz, C Ménard and B Abeillé, *Public Procurement Reforms in Africa, Challenges in Institutions and Governance* (Oxford, Oxford Scholarship Online, 2014) 176. Through their examination of 28 procurement reforms conducted in African countries, the authors concluded that 'the flaws and drawbacks in the reform of procurement generally resulted from the overly zealous focus on changing formal rules while neglecting informal and enforcement mechanisms'.

confronted by resistance to change within the procurement community. Even though the goals of the reform might call for a total revamp of the system, economic rents for individuals and institutions create oppositions and explain why reforms get stuck or miss their aim.[84] 'Capture' of the reform can also occur from a sociological point of view. This is actually a recurrent issue with the (sometimes) not so competent existing service in charge of writing the procurement regulation, which may be reluctant to acknowledge its deficiencies and oppose any transfer of its prerogatives to a new body. Quite often, individuals in key senior positions try to maintain their situation or even use the reform channel for expanding their personal status, rendering the reform counterproductive.[85] Adding civil society and private sector representatives to the body in charge of designing the reform might be a good solution, which is suggested from an international perspective. But it may only be a cosmetic move dissimulating the pivotal role of senior officials, without allowing nascent ideas to flourish.[86]

This leads to the general issue of the capacity-building effort[87] which must accompany any procurement reform. Not that capacity-building is usually ignored as a logical continuum after the legal and regulatory reform,[88] but there is too often a lack of comprehensive strategy. Such a comprehensive approach has only quite recently begun to be addressed by the OECD.[89] Long-term reform can only succeed with a sustainable capacity-building effort, which means training of young professionals and even students. However, these promising targets are frequently kept out of the scope of the procurement reform, because of a lack of funding and time constraints imposed by political agendas. Thus, ad hoc short-term training programmes are usually put in place for (few) randomly selected procurement specialists[90] who, sometimes, later on use the vacuum in the civil service law to boost their careers by moving to work for the private sector (or even for the MDBs) where their updated skills can be better rewarded. In many cases, developing countries do not have provisions against 'revolving doors' and mandatory years of work in the civil service; therefore, with low-paid jobs in government services, there is no effective solution against such permeability.

[84] ibid 117.

[85] The author refers here to personal experiences as advisor of MDBs concerning procurement reforms in several countries.

[86] On the power of former bureaucrats in blocking water reform, see MM Shirley and C Ménard, *Cities Awash: A Synthesis of the Country Cases: Thirsting for Efficiency, The Economics and Politics of Urban Water System Reform* (Amsterdam/New York, Pergamon, 2002) 15.

[87] 'Total ODA for capacity-building and national planning amounted to $20.4 billion in 2016 and represented 18 per cent of total aid allocable by sector, a proportion that has been stable since 2010. Of the total, Latin America and the Caribbean received $5.1 billion, sub-Saharan Africa received $4.6 billion and Southern Asia received $3.8 billion. The three main sectors assisted were public administration, environment and energy, which received a total of $10.2 billion'. Source UNECOSOC, 'Progress towards the Sustainable Development Goals' (n 1) para 140.

[88] This was already stated in 2005 in the DAC Report on Strengthening Procurement Capacities in Developing Countries: 'many previous programmes to develop procurement capacity have been low-level, too short term and donor driven and have mostly failed to address fundamental barriers to change, or make sustainable improvements. Theoretical work on capacity development that is being undertaken tells us that a more strategic, holistic approach is needed' – OECD and World Bank (n 37) 9.

[89] OECD, 'Developing Public Procurement Capacity in Europe' (2017) available at www.oecd.org/gov/public-procurement/publications/public-procurement-capacity-europe.pdf.

[90] Even worse: they can be the same procurement staff always beneficiating from the training offer, driven by the pecuniary benefits attached to the attendance of such events: I Sawadogo, 'La Fraude dans les marchés publics au Burkina Faso', GOMAP (ILO) 2018 (Masters degree thesis, not published).

B. Diversity of the Main Drivers for Reforms at Country Level

We argue that whilst the achievement of the harmonisation process was, and still is, not a goal for developing countries, trying to achieve it could explain some of the failures or maladjustments encountered in domestic procurement reforms. One of the several factors explaining the disappointing results in the attempt to reform/harmonise public procurement in developing countries is that too many objectives are at stake even from the international perspective.[91] Whilst the international community wants to promote the harmonisation of public procurement rules for the sake of global competition and/or local development, the emergence of procurement as a dedicated and cross-cutting function, the fight against corruption and for accountability, and the debate on trade, social and environmental considerations through sustainability and human rights protection are reasons that progressively contribute to enhancing the centrality of procurement. Public procurement is now recognised as improving public sector and governance at large, and it is now regarded not merely as a financial management activity incidental to the chain of governmental spending. A 'silo' approach of harmonisation is not possible anymore. As stated by Professor Christian von Bar about private law – but his words can be easily adapted to the procurement law area – 'a segmental approach to harmonization … disturbs the coherence of the interlocking concepts and principles in the national jurisdictions'.[92] As a consequence, developing countries may experience divergent pressures from conflicting harmonisation processes related to different sectoral policies designed at the international level (example: the safeguard policy[93]).

Rapid changes and evolutions also characterise the activities of the public sector, emerging both from new techniques available such as e-procurement and further developments of artificial intelligence, and from new legal solutions (framework agreements, competitive negotiations, or the Amazon web service for government initiative) may render the so called 'international standards' rapidly obsolete. Countries can now benefit from 'regulatory shopping', picking procurement rules according to their needs. This offer plays against the historical actors on the market of global regulations, forcing them to re-think their policies and practices. Standardisation, as it was articulated by the World Bank in its former procurement guidelines,[94] is not perceived today as an advantage but rather as an impediment. A similar movement can be noticed in the trade area with the latest revision of the GPA and of the UN soft-law products.

[91] For a stimulating presentation of these drivers at the domestic level, see SL Schooner, 'Desiderata: Objectives for a System of Government Contract Law' (2002) 11 *Public Procurement Law Review* 103.

[92] Professor Christian von Bar, Chairman of the Study Group on a European Civil Code, 'The Contribution of the Study Group on a European Civil Code to the European Convention' (2004) available at fr.scribd.com/document/286796508/about-the-study-group-pdf.

[93] Indeed, in aid development, financing for gender equality and environmental action is increasing – OECD, *Development Co-operation Report 2018: Joining Forces to Leave No One Behind* (Paris, OECD Publishing, 2018) 33, available at www.oecd-ilibrary.org/development/development-co-operation-report_20747721.

[94] Accessible at http://www.worldbank.org/en/projects-operations/products-and-services/brief/procurement-policies-and-guidance.

Furthermore, the political and economic dimensions of public procurement might have superseded its financial, legal and technical dimensions. Therefore, it may be useful to understand each domestic trade-off between procurement basic principles and system resilience that could block the reform's effectiveness. Integrity and anti-corruption policy provide a good example of this dissonance. For more than ten years, eradication of corruption has been a top priority on all MDBs' and donors' agenda with a worldwide effort engaging dozens of projects for millions of dollars.[95] It is actually one public policy area where there is convergence on the diagnostics and sharing of many solutions. However, the results are yet to appear since the methods used are still based on a 'silo' approach: pouring funds into legal reforms to enact anti-corruption laws, creating anti-corruption bodies and addressing the stakeholders' weaknesses while spreading capacity-building training. Everything seems to be in the right place and yet the mechanics do not work to match expectations of the international community. There is a need to look for explanations from a different perspective, with a holistic or systemic approach. Thus, the US has the most sophisticated and effective network of laws, regulations and institutions to prevent and sanction corruption and non-ethical behaviours attached to procurement procedures. However, this is the result of 150 years of history, a social aversion to mistrust and fraud, and even religious foundations.[96] Moreover, the anti-corruption procurement legal framework is supported by a strong back-up of criminal laws with dissuasive penal sanctions and civil remedies, notably by the False Claims Act, and administrative actions.[97] Before being presented as a safety net, this policy required layers of statutes and regulations, having been elaborated along the years, which shows that time is essential for successful reforms, even though this may be unwelcome to political and development agendas looking for quick wins.

Furthermore, it illustrates that efficient systems are based on checks and balances, not easily detectable. In the US, efficient bidding practices such as discretion and negotiations could not have been introduced without an administrative framing of the waivers policy, and a proficient back-up network of criminal laws and penalties. The margins of flexibility of the procurement system rely on this support network: effective institutions, and rules that are in place to detect misbehaviours and to punish behaviours when discretion is abused.

At the global level, the harmonisation attempt has to face increasing disparities between countries. Penetration by new actors in trade exchanges and protectionist positions maintained by ancient actors are new parameters that contribute to the changing environment of public procurement at global level, calling for constant adaptations and re-positioning at country level, in particular in the area of direct and indirect measures organising access of foreign companies to local procurement markets.[98]

[95] S Rose-Ackerman, 'Introduction: The Role of International Actors in Fighting Corruption' in S Rose-Ackerman and PD Carrington (eds), *Anti-corruption Policy: Can International Actors Play a Constructive Role?* (Durham – North Carolina, Carolina Academic Press, 2013) 3.

[96] S Rose-Ackerman, *Corruption and Government: Causes, Consequences, and Reform* (Cambridge, Cambridge University Press, 1999).

[97] US General Services Administration, Office of Inspector General, Office of Audits, 'Procurement Fraud Handbook' (December 2012) available at www.gsaig.gov/sites/default/files/misc-reports/ProcurementFraud-Handbook_0.pdf.

[98] J Gourdon, V Bastien and L Folliot-Lalliot, 'OECD taxonomy of measures affecting trade in government procurement processes', OECD Trade Policy Papers No 198 (Paris, OECD Publishing, 2017).

It is indeed interesting to look at the drivers for procurement reforms that are pursued by countries. Harmonisation of procurement rules and institutions is barely a goal by itself, except for countries engaged in regional integration. When it is contemplated, procurement reform is just perceived as a means to achieving better public policies such as productivity gains and budgetary savings (value for money), transparency and good governance, integrity and anti-corruption, and/or compliance with international instruments. These are effective triggers of reforms and drivers for change. They are more concrete goals than procurement harmonisation per se, and easier concepts to be explained to government officials in charge of public policy.

Furthermore, a country's territorial structure (centralisation versus deconcentration or decentralisation) is one important factor to be taken into consideration. Federalism can block the harmonisation process within the country itself as the US illustrates: even though the federal government contracts legal framework is one of the most sophisticated in the world, many of the States within the US are still lagging behind international standards, with heterogeneous rules, and a lack of coordination.[99] Intra-harmonisation may be the first step needed to be achieved before international harmonisation, whenever the institutional constraints created by the country's constitutional organisation limit the effectiveness of any comprehensive public policy.[100] In public spending, where local governments are overly keen to preserve their margins of autonomy, a trade-off will be needed among powers at regional, national and supranational levels. A long tradition of decentralisation will demand strong local procuring entities and adapted oversight bodies, even though economists would recommend centralisation and group purchasing. Indeed, the centrifugal forces at stake may play at the level of public entities, with ministries or semi-public entities such as state-owned enterprises sheltering specific procurement rules.

Identifying the actual procurement goal(s) of a country may be a promising avenue of analysis. For some countries, opening trade opportunities explains the twist of their procurement reform: some would like to join the GPA in order to attract more investors and escape geographical and political isolation. As a good example, Jordan's decision to be the first Arab country to join the GPA has been an effective engine for promoting public procurement reform during the last years. However, local resistance within the institutional framework against the required reforms remains despite several attempts to strengthen the domestic procurement framework.[101] At the world level, large public procurement markets around the world are still sheltered from becoming part of future liberalisation rounds, whilst other countries are bound by regional or bilateral trade agreements covering government procurement, such as the Sub-Saharan

[99] For regulations at State level in the US, see MJ Copeland (ed), *Guide to State Procurement: A 50-State Primer on Purchasing Laws, Processes, and Procedures*, 2nd edn (American Bar Association, 2016).

[100] J Broschek, 'Reforming Federal Systems: Insights from Australia, Canada, Germany and Switzerland' (Cahiers du CÉRIUM, Working Paper No 3, Centre d'études et de recherches internationales, Université de Montréal, 2014) available at https://cerium.umontreal.ca/fileadmin/Documents/FAS/CERIUM/Documents_PDF/2-Recherche/6-Cahiers/Cahier03.pdf.

[101] Audit Bureau of Jordan, Mazahreh, Jad Raji, 'Jordan – Public Procurement Reform Support Project: audited financial statement – January 1, 2015 – January 20, 2016' (Arabic, English) (2016) available at http://documents.worldbank.org/curated/en/115381481122798309/Jordan-Public-Procurement-Reform-Support-Project-audited-financial-statement-January-1-2015-January-20-2016.

African countries. Their procurement reforms were regionally market driven, mainly as suggested by MDBs[102] promoting an aggressive regional integration agenda as the best way to achieve development. Under the auspices of the WAEMU procurement directives, the eight West African countries needed to rewrite their domestic legislation and to reorganise their institutional layers by creating national regulatory bodies in charge of preparing procurement regulations and of reviewing complaints. In this connection, Stephen R Karangizi noted:

> This combined need to establish such national legal frameworks and to decentralise the procurement function to entities with a central authority providing policy direction were in fact two of the key challenges identified for public procurement reform in Africa at an international conference on public procurement reform in Africa held in Abidjan, Cote d'Ivoire in 1998[103] by the African Development Bank, the World Bank, UNDP and the International Trade Centre (ITC).[104]

So far these reforms have been deployed in the domestic legislation, but results are yet to come.

In the Middle East and North Africa Region (MENA), even though results are also expected through the economic turmoil, the governance trigger has been an evident accelerator of procurement reforms engaged after the 2011 uprisings in the region.[105] Many of the MENA countries have recently adopted, or are on the verge of adopting, procurement reforms as instruments for improving transparency and integrity. The movement could even be accelerated by the recently enacted Constitutions of Morocco, Egypt and Tunisia. Public policy reforms which were rather lagging behind in this region, compared to other regions, are now contemplated or reactivated by all MENA countries, but only when they enjoy a relatively stable political situation. Unfortunately, the instability and/or war situation has compromised the reforms already engaged. This specific finding illustrates the maladjustment of any procurement reform agenda in the context of fragile States. Not only is the unstable situation non-conducive to the success of any administrative reform under such terrible circumstances, but also, to be well implemented, a procurement reform needs to cover most of public purchasing, which is obviously not the case when the armed conflict requires

[102] W Odhiambo and P Kamau, 'Public Procurement: Lessons from Kenya, Tanzania and Uganda', OECD Working Paper No 208 (OECD, Dev/Doc[2003]06, March 2003) available at www.oecd.org/countries/uganda/2503452.pdf.

[103] Report of the Proceedings of the Conference on Public Procurement Reform in Africa – 30 November to 4 December 1998, Abidjan, Cote d'Ivoire-International Trade Centre UNCTAD/WTO, 9.

[104] SR Karangizi, 'Framework Arrangements in Public Procurement: a Perspective from Africa', ch 6 in Arrowsmith (ed), *Reform of the UNCITRAL Model Law on Procurement: Procurement Regulation for the 21st Century* (n 22) 243, 244.

[105] A 2015 World Bank report examines whether inequality or other factors contributed to the Arab Spring uprisings and economic stagnation, as well as to the ensuing conflicts. It concludes that expenditure inequality, relatively low and declining, could not have been a major factor, but wealth disparities (typically higher) could have. Instead, ordinary people, especially the middle class, were frustrated by the decline in living standards, related to the shortage of formal-sector jobs, the poor quality of public services and *lack of government accountability*. World Bank Middle East and North Africa Region – MENA Economic Monitor, *Inequality, Uprisings, and Conflict in the Arab World* (Washington DC, World Bank Group, 2015) available at documents.worldbank.org/curated/en/303441467992017147/pdf/99989-REVISED-Box393220B-OUO-9-MEM-Fall-2015-FINAL-Oct-13-2015.pdf.

exceptional acquisition procedures. This factor, which accentuated in recent years,[106] can also be retained as a partial explanation of harmonisation's failure, in addition to the economic situation affecting other countries, pushing them to hide behind a protectionist facade. In the end, a cost analysis of the pros and cons of harmonisation in public procurement is also considered by countries contemplating potential reforms.

IV. Conclusion: Harmonisation versus Multipolar Convergences

Searching for the best customised solutions for countries,[107] the procurement reforms could eventually, but not systematically, converge with solutions retained by other countries, achieving congruence versus harmonisation.[108] Understanding the historical, political, economic and social goals of any country would be a prerequisite to addressing the legal dimension of convergence. Linked to an increased circulation of ideas and concepts, an interdisciplinary exchange of techniques and practices, harmonisation could proceed 'from interaction that spontaneously occurs between different legal systems', as described by Louis Del Duca as '"osmotic" harmonization'.[109] And for analysing the legal dimension of harmonisation, as recommended by the Vice President of the Conseil d'Etat, the French Supreme Administrative Court, only the methodological posture of comparative law will allow a dynamic legal analysis of a specific practice or institution in place in one country, since such practices or institutions need to be contextualised and situated in their legal environment. Related to this Jean-Marc Sauvé noticed:

> In any field, the globalization cannot transforms itself in a successful harmonization process without this comparative lecture of the norms in the background of a technical rule. Comparative law is a lever serving harmonization because it helps to identify commonalities, consensus, and discrepancies among different legal systems.[110]

[106] According to the OECD, in 2016, more countries experienced some form of violent conflict than at any time in the last 30 years – OECD, *States of Fragility 2018* (Paris, OECD Publishing, 2018) available at www.oecd.org/dac/states-of-fragility-2018-9789264302075-en.htm. Underscoring the multidimensional factors of fragility, this OECD report calls for coordination of different financial flows in fragile context.

[107] The World Bank has switched towards this goal with its new Procurement Framework launched in 2016, putting an emphasis on more tailored, and context-specific approaches for fragile and conflict-affected states. 'This standardized approach is no longer considered the best fit for purpose and needs to be better tailored to different operating environments and project needs' – World Bank, 'Procurement in World Bank Investment Project Financing – Phase II: The New Procurement Framework' (n 58) 11. And also: www.worldbank.org/en/projects-operations/products-and-services/procurement-projects-programs.

[108] The term 'congruence' was used by Professor Joshua Schwartz in the context of US federal procurement contracts: JI Schwartz, 'Liability for Sovereign Acts: Congruence and Exceptionalism in Government Contracts Law' (1996) 64 *George Washington Law Review* 633.

[109] LF Del Duca, 'Developing Global Transnational Harmonization Procedures for the Twenty-First Century: The Accelerating Pace of Common and Civil Law Convergence' (2007) 42 *Texas International Law Journal* 625, 626.

[110] JM Sauvé, 'Comprendre et réguler le droit globalisé ou comment dompter la Chimère?' – Opening of the Conference 'Droit comparé et territorialité du droit' (Comparative Law and territoriality of the Law) (Paris, Conseil d'Etat, 20 May 2015), available in French at www.conseil-etat.fr/content/download/42968/372460/version/1/file/2015-05-17-Droit-compare-et-territorialite-du-droit.pdf.

Considering that harmonisation based on a single model is neither an achievable nor a suitable target, and indeed harmonisation cannot be unification,[111] one needs to consider the growing impact of multipolar subdivisions. Room for local adjustment and customised solutions has been acknowledged by the new procurement framework of the World Bank which entered into force in July 2016.[112] After having cancelled the first UCS programme in 2011, the Bank is drawn to reintroduce a lighter program: 'The Bank will streamline its requirements for the use of a country's own national procurement system' – but only for 'procurements of lower to moderate value/risk'.[113]

On the world scale, regional and sub-regional groups of countries are emerging, something Jürgen Basedow has named 'the dawn of inter-regionalism',[114] with countries working on convergent rules fostering trade or other common priorities. Indeed if governance is a top priority for several developing countries,[115] it is not considered as being a goal for developed countries, since it is already an existing component of their regimes.[116] The harmonisation process might be definitely compromised in developing countries. The new international development agenda should turn to achieving a balance between harmonisation and diversity in public procurement. Different aims, different paths, different pace should be the 'motto' in setting procurement reforms, even though there is consensus on basic procurement principles, transparency, equal access, equal treatment, efficiency, sustainability and integrity. This holistic approach will inevitably conflict with the harmonisation movement.

[111] 'More than ever before, it becomes evident that harmonisation is by no means synonymous with unification; harmonisation is a process which may result in unification of law subject to a number of (often utopian) conditions being fulfilled, such as, for example, wide or universal geographical acceptance of harmonising instruments, and with wide scope of harmonising instruments which effectively substitute all pre-existing law. To the extent that harmonisation of law is sporadic and incomplete, in practice, most harmonising laws are designed to work within and with existing laws'. L Mistelis, 'Is Harmonisation a Necessary Evil? The Future of Harmonisation and New Sources of International Trade Law', extract from I Fletcher, L Mistelis and M Cremona (eds), *Foundations and Perspectives of International Trade Law* (London, Sweet & Maxwell, 2001) 3–27, para 1-003, available at www.cisg.law.pace.edu/cisg/biblio/mistelis2.html.

[112] 'The Framework has been designed from the outset to be fit for purpose and to meet the diverse needs of Bank clients'. – World Bank, 'Procurement in World Bank Investment Project Financing – Phase II' (n 58) 3.

[113] ibid.

[114] J Basedow, 'Worldwide Harmonization of Private Law and Regional Economic Integration – General Report' (2003) 8 *Uniform Law Review* 31, 35.

[115] As it was presented for the first time by the World Bank, *Sub-Saharan Africa: From Crisis to Sustainable Growth. A Long-Term Perspective Study* (Washington DC, World Bank, 1989).

[116] 'Many of the elements which have been identified as being included in good governance are already part of Western legal systems, and therefore it has little to add to Western law. However, it does play an important part in jurisdictions elsewhere' – T Zwart, 'Good governance as a legal concept with a bite' (13 March 2009) (Contribution to conference) available at dspace.library.uu.nl/bitstream/handle/1874/308433/concept.pdf?sequence=1&isAllowed=y.

PART III

Meeting the Challenges on the Way: Untying Aid, Fighting Corruption and a New Entry: Sustainability

6

The Echternach Procession of Untying Aid

ANNAMARIA LA CHIMIA*

I. Introduction

This chapter deals with donors' practice of tying aid, that is aid granted on condition that goods and services for the aid-financed project will be purchased from companies based in the donor country only (when aid is fully tied), or in a small group of countries, usually including the donor and all (or some) recipient countries (aid is partially tied). Recipient countries, if they want the aid to be granted, have no other choice but to fulfil the tied condition even if it would be more convenient to acquire the goods or the services elsewhere. Given the importance of aid for development and, in some circumstances, for the day-to-day functioning of recipients' governments, very few countries are in a position to refuse aid, even if tied.[1]

Aid is *untied* when it is not subject to any geographical limitations on procurement.[2] Yet, even when aid is formally untied, participation in the aid tender is often *de facto* limited to suppliers, goods and services from the donor country only.[3] In this latter case, the aid is said to be *informally tied*. Informal tied aid is probably the most damaging form of aid tying since its impact cannot be monitored and safeguard mechanisms cannot be implemented to reduce the excessive costs of tying. The reasons for informal tying are manifold and they are related to the strong influence that the donor country can exercise when it disburses aid funds;[4] and to many of the problems linked to

* This chapter draws on the author's previous published work on tied aid and provides important updates in light of topical developments that have occurred in the aid context in recent years such as the work of the new Global Partnership for Effective Development Cooperation (GPEDC), the privatisation of aid, the rise of new donors and the recent turn to use aid to promote trade. For an extensive analysis of this topic, see A La Chimia, *Tied Aid and Development Aid Procurement within the Framework of EU and WTO Law: the Imperative for Change* (Oxford, Hart, 2013).

[1] Only a handful of recipients have objected to tied and refused aid offers. A Huliaras, 'The Tied Aid Paradox'. The author reports the cases of India and Eritrea; article cited in A La Chimia, *Tied Aid and Development Aid Procurement within the Framework of EU and WTO Law: the Imperative for Change* (Oxford, Hart, 2013).

[2] DAC, *Glossary* available at https://stats.oecd.org/glossary/detail.asp?ID=3089.

[3] Studies show that a great portion of aid is still informally tied. E Clay, M Geddes and L Natali, *Untying Aid: Is it Working? An Evaluation of the Implementation of the Paris Declaration and of the 2001 DAC Recommendation of Untying ODA to the LDCs* (Copenhagen, Danish Institute for International Studies, 2009) available at www.odi.org/sites/odi.org.uk/files/odi-assets/publications-opinion-files/6865.pdf.

[4] eg donors can ensure that aid is linked to domestic exports by providing detailed project design advice that influences the bidding process, for example by requiring very detailed specifications which might refer to a specific brand of product rather than to its general functions.

development procurement that have already been highlighted in chapter 3, such as donors' complex aid systems, the high number of donors present in one country and the multiplicity of rules applied. These factors can make it arduous for suppliers to find out, in due time, the basic facts of the aid projects (ie what aid projects are funded and where) and of the procurement process (ie what rules are applied, where tenders are advertised etc). Further, informal tying can be facilitated by poor procurement practices combined with – when not caused by – the systemic lack of competition that characterises aid procurement more generally.[5] Indeed, informal tying usually takes place at the procurement stage[6] and is facilitated by corruption, inexperience, lack of transparency and lack of instruments aimed at ensuring open competition in the procurement process. All these elements can lead to *de facto* discrimination in favour of donors' suppliers, even if this is not a formal policy, and can have repercussions in terms of the level of aid which is tied and the number of tenders effectively open to competition. Not surprisingly, it is often said that granting aid as budget support and using country systems could help eradicate informal tied aid, as can also the process of harmonising donors and recipients' rules.[7]

Concerns over the costs and over other negative consequences of tying aid – especially in terms of loss of recipients' ownership of the aid donated and of distortion of the nature of the aid (see section II) – have made of tied aid a central issue in the aid effectiveness debate and one of the most controversial aspects of aid granting.

After a first section dedicated to explaining what are the costs and effects of aid tying and why donors tie aid, this chapter will focus on the international initiatives to untie aid, highlighting the strengths and weaknesses of such initiatives. It will be argued that, despite some initial positive steps to untie aid undertaken during the first wave of the aid effectiveness initiatives, little has been done since. In fact the lack of strong and specific commitments to untie aid and the absence of a legally binding framework to liberalise aid procurement are leading to a return of tied aid masked under the guise of new forms of aid financing and donors' more recent ambiguity over the use of aid funding caused by recent 'uncertain political times'.

II. Tied Aid: Costs, Rationale and Data

A. Costs and Rationales

By restricting the number of companies that can participate in aid tenders and reducing the level of competition to a handful of suppliers, tying aid leads to an increase of the

[5] See s IV and ch 3 more generally; see also La Chimia, *Tied Aid within the Framework of EU and WTO Law* (n 1).

[6] As Tajoli argues 'This kind of informal tying is almost totally ruled out within competitive binding under multilateral aid procurement due to the surveillance of the World Bank and other international bodies'. L Tajoli, 'The Impact of Tied Aid on Trade Flows Between Donor and Recipient Countries' (1999) 8(4) *Journal of International Trade and Economic Development* 373–88, 374.

[7] See La Chimia (n 1) and ch10 in this collection. The use of countries' systems would solve the problems of the multiplicity of donors' rules and would give a much-needed advantage to local suppliers, more familiar with their own countries' rules than with donors' rules.

price of goods and services purchased, affecting value for money and undermining the overall efficiency of the aid donated (ie less is bought with the aid money). The OECD has estimated that tying aid increases the prices of the goods and services purchased of between 15 to 30 per cent.[8] In the case of food aid, the costs of tying aid can reach price surges of up to 50 per cent compared to local or triangular purchases.[9] Eurodad estimates that in 2016 the 'immediate costs of tying (*omissis*) was between $1.95 billion and $ 5.43 billion'.[10]

An increase in transportation costs can also be associated with the imposition of tied aid conditions: while the transportation costs can be low if the goods are purchased locally or regionally, they increase considerably when the goods have to come from the donor country. This is problematic when one considers that the transportation costs are borne, almost always, by the recipient country (this is often the case for food, where the food aid itself is provided as aid and is financed totally or partially by the donor – this depending on whether the aid is donated as a grant or as a soft loan – but the transportation costs are borne by the recipient).[11] Furthermore, the donor sometimes also restricts competition for the transportation of the aid goods. This is the case, for example, of food aid donated by the US, where legislation (PL 480) requires that '75% of USAID and 50% of USDA managed food aid be transported in "flag-carrying" vessels registered in the US'. It is evident therefore that the costs of tying go beyond the increase of the price of the goods purchased, significantly reducing the value of the aid.

Tying aid also has negative implications in terms of timeliness of delivery of the aid goods. Such delays can reach more than 60 per cent loss in timeliness compared to situations where the goods were procured locally.[12] This is problematic when the aid goods are perishable, as can be the case for food aid,[13] and when prompt delivery of aid goods is needed to respond to a famine and save the lives of thousands of people. For example, in 2011 during the Horn of Africa food crisis that affected Somalia, Ethiopia and Kenya, between 50,000 and 100,000 people, more than half of them children under five, died because of delays in the delivery of food aid.[14]

Yet, the costs of tying aid go beyond the increase in price and the delays in the delivery of the goods/services purchased. Negative effects of tied aid are associated with

[8] OECD, *Policy Brief: Untying Aid to the Least Developed Countries* (Paris, 2001). The increase often depends on the type of goods purchased.

[9] Triangular purchases are carried out in the same region or in a neighbouring country of the recipient of the aid – ie where the aid will be delivered.

[10] P Meeks/Eurodad: 'Development, Untied: Unleashing the Catalytic Power of ODA through Renewed Action on Untying' (Eurodad Publications, July 2018). These costs are said to be conservative estimates.

[11] See A La Chimia, 'Food Security and the Right to Food: Finding Balance in the 2012 Food Assistance Convention' (2006) 65(1) *International and Comparative Law Quarterly* 99–137.

[12] E Lentz, S Passarelli and C Barrett, *The Timeliness and Cost-Effectiveness of the Local and Regional Procurement of Food Aid* (Ithaca, Cornell University, 2012), who report that 'procuring food locally or distributing cash or vouchers results in a time savings of nearly fourteen weeks, a 62 percent gain in timeliness'.

[13] US Government Accountability Office, GAO-07-560, 'Foreign Assistance: Various Challenges Impede the Efficiency and Effectiveness of U.S. Food Aid' (2007), where it is reported that in some instances US food aid has arrived rotten.

[14] Unfortunately, there are many examples of delays in responding to warning signs of food crises causing deaths of thousands of people; see S Tisdall, 'East Africa's Drought: the Avoidable Disaster' *The Guardian*, 18 January 2012, available at www.guardian.co.uk/world/2012/jan/18/east-africa-drought-disaster-report.

the distortion of the nature of the aid donated and with misallocation of resources. When aid is tied it risks being unsuitable, from both a cultural and technical perspective, to meet the needs of the recipient country. This is because donors tend to fund goods and services that their suppliers are able to offer rather than goods and services needed by recipients of the aid. Tying aid therefore affects recipients' ownership of the aid and, as pointed out by Meeks, it could also fossilise situations of inequality, marginalisation and deprivation where local groups are not involved in the decision-making process for the spending and delivery of aid goods.[15]

Economists have also shown that tying aid induces fragmentation and poor coordination in donors' development policies.[16] Aid granted from different donors to the same sector often results in incompatible equipment, which require complex spare parts and training arrangements.[17] Further, tying aid can deprive local and regional companies of precious trade opportunities.[18] Aid is indeed a key driver for local and regional production and for job creation within the recipient countries.[19] By tying aid, recipient countries lose the opportunity to generate 'trade for aid'[20] in that tying frustrates the potential of aid to foster trade between developing countries – in many of these countries public bodies and, in particular, aid-financed projects, are major potential outlets for trade between neighbouring States.

Given the high costs of tying aid, why then do donors tie aid?

Both economic and political explanations have been offered to justify the tying of aid. From an economic perspective donors maintain that tying aid could advantage their economy by helping donors' exporters. However, economists have proven that the short-terms gains are far outweighed by the long-term costs.[21] Indeed, domestic industries might become dependent on the subsidy which tied aid represents and might become vulnerable if the aid were to be withdrawn in the future.[22] Moreover, the increase in exports does not automatically mean an increase in the overall welfare of the donor's nation. As Jepma argued, it is only the value added of the selective group of

[15] See also Meeks/Eurodad, 'Development, Untied' (n 10).

[16] O Morrissey and H White, 'How Concessional is Tied Aid?', CREDIT Research Paper No 93/13, 4.

[17] eg a survey in Kenya found more than 16 different kinds of water pump in use, each funded by a different donor country; Huliaras, 'The Tied Aid Paradox' (n 1) 13.

[18] J Clapp, *Hunger in the Balance: The New Politics of International Food Aid* (Ithaca, Cornell University Press, 2012) 7, 78–79. The author reports that in 2003 the USAID director, Natsios, tried to undertake local and regional purchase in Afghanistan because the country experienced surpluses as a result of US-funded agricultural assistance. He was unsuccessful, however, and 300,000 tonnes of US wheat were shipped to the country, causing the collapse of local wheat prices and forcing, the following year, local farmers to cultivate poppies for heroin production.

[19] See eg the case of Afghanistan where the untying of aid has been said to have boosted local production and generated new jobs. See S Gilmore, 'Afghanistan: Proof that Untied Aid really Works' *The Guardian*, 24 October 2011, available at www.theguardian.com/global-development/poverty-matters/2011/oct/24/afghanistan-untied-aid-creates-jobs.

[20] See La Chimia (n 1). The expression 'trade for aid' was there coined to expressly recall the WTO initiative to encourage members to donate 'aid for trade', ie to fund technical assistance programmes for developing countries, yet as I argue extensively in the book, the WTO neglects the positive effects that aid could have for trade in terms of stimulating and supporting local and regional production.

[21] See Tajoli, 'The Impact of Tied Aid on Trade Flows Between Donor and Recipient Countries' (n 6); O Morrissey and H White, 'How Concessional Is Tied Aid' (1993) CREDIT Research Paper No 93/13, University of Nottingham.

[22] CJ Jepma, *Inter-nation Policy Co-ordination and Untying of Aid* (Avebury, Brookfield USA, 1994) 16.

exporters that is increased and not the net effect on national welfare, which instead is negative.[23]

Donors also often argue that tying aid can have positive effects on their balance of payments and on the level of employment. Aid represents an outflow on the current account so by tying aid and increasing exports they hope to create inflows through stepping up the trade flow with the beneficiary country.[24] these assumptions have been disproven by economists who have shown that 'tying does not automatically increase trade flows'[25] and that 'it is very unlikely that aid tying produces significant macroeconomic benefits for domestic employment or balance of payment aggregates in the donor country'.[26]

From a political point of view, donors maintain that they would receive more support for their aid policies if the aid entailed an economic return for their country. By tying aid and showing that for every dollar spent on aid there is a return for the nation (as USAID used to advertise on its website) donors hope to obtain support at home for their aid policies. However, studies have shown that if people knew the real damaging consequences of tying aid and the negative consequences it has on the effectiveness of the aid, they would not support tied aid policies.[27]

The small and uncertain economic gains that could be brought from tying aid make it evident that the case for tying is more political than economic. Tying practices seem to be determined more by the pressure of the lobbies that would gain from the aid rather than by strategic trade policies.

That the case for tying is more political than economic is also shown by the fact that tying aid is often related to defensive concerns. Donors do not want their industries to be disadvantaged in foreign markets for aid granted from other donors to their national firms' competitors. Donors also maintain that if they take the lead by unilaterally reducing the amount of tying, their domestic industries would suffer in two respects: first their protection would disappear and, second, foreign competitors would achieve a better relative position.

Donors are locked in to the so-called 'prisoner's dilemma', a dilemma that can be resolved only if all countries act together to untie aid. Hence, multilateral institutions such as the World Bank, the United Nations and the OECD have a fundamental role to play in coordinating international policies. The international steps taken thus far to untie aid will be discussed in the following pages.

B. Data

Despite the negative effects of tied aid and the many commitments made by donors to untie aid (see further below section III) a high percentage of aid continues to be tied.[28] It has been reported that, of a total of USD 55 billion of aid spent through

[23] ibid 35.

[24] OECD, *Policy Brief* (n 8).

[25] Tajoli (n 6).

[26] Jepma, *Inter-nation Policy Co-ordination and Untying of Aid* (n 22); Morrissey and White, 'How Concessional is Tied Aid?' (n 16); Tajoli (n 6); F Lammerssen, 'Development Choices' (2001) *The OECD Observer* No 228.

[27] La Chimia n 1.

[28] E Clay, M Geddes and L Natali, *Untying Aid* (n 3).; see also La Chimia (n 1).

procurement in 2016, 'some US$25 billion of ODA [Official Development Assistance] was reported as tied'[29] in the same year. These data are said to be conservative estimates because of the opacity and lack of clarity of donors' reporting systems for tied aid and because of the prevalence of informal tying. Furthermore, OECD data do not include food aid and aid donated by new donors, such as China, who do not report data on tied aid at all.[30]

Commentators have long been very critical of the OECD data on tied aid,[31] how they are collected and reported.[32] Most donors do not report data 'in sectors in which tying of project aid might be expected, (such as) infrastructure, transport, industry and energy'.[33] This criticism has been exacerbated recently as a result of the OECD/DAC's failed attempt to reform its aid reporting systems and to agree on a new definitions of aid.[34] This has been especially problematic in the context of 'blended finance', ie when aid is mixed with private financing, and could have serious repercussions on the level of aid which is tied given that, as further discussed below, this new trend on privatisation of aid financing is leading to a further increase in the level of aid which is tied.[35]

In light of the opacity and inaccuracy of the data on untying aid collected by the OECD, another indicator often used by NGOs as a proxy to identify how much aid is tied is to look at the volume (in number and value) of contracts awarded to donors' suppliers. A high percentage of contracts awarded to home suppliers is regarded as an indication of a poor level of *de facto* untying, ie aid being informally tied. Such an approach, first adopted in 2010 by the organisation Publish What You Fund,[36] continues to be an important Metrix used by NGOs and CSOs. For example, Eurodad also uses this indicator and reports that 'only 4% of the 15 billion dollars' worth of aid contract awards reported to the DAC in 2014 went to suppliers in the poorest countries'.[37] The high number of tenders awarded to donors' companies is certainly a

[29] Meeks/Eurodad (n 10). Such data only relate to formal tied aid and it does not consider any aid that is informally tied

[30] ibid; Clay et al (n 3); OECD, 2018 Report on the DAC Untying Recommendation (11 June 2018).

[31] OECD recently reported that, in 2016, over 80% of aid covered by the OECD Recommendation was untied; see OECD '2018 Report on the DAC Untying Recommendation' DCD/DAC(2018)12/REV2, available at www.oecd.org/dac/financing-sustainable-development/development-finance-standards/DCD-DAC(2018)12-REV2.en.pdf.

[32] Clay et al (n 3); see also La Chimia (n 1).

[33] Clay et al (n 3).

[34] For a long time the OECD has been trying to agree on a new definition of ODA and to improve the data reporting system, including on aid tying, yet disagreement between donors, and with civil society, has proved reaching an agreement on a new definition difficult. For the controversy surrounding the new definition of ODA, see JB Atwwo, R Manning and H Riegler, 'Don't undermine the basic architecture of OECD/DAC statistics: a letter of warning' (21 December 2018) available at www.brookings.edu/blog/future-development/2018/12/21/dont-undermine-the-basic-architecture-of-oecd-dac-statistics-a-letter-of-warning/.

[35] See 2016 GPED monitoring report for a definition of blended finance; see also J Pereira, 'Blended Finance: What it is, how it works and how it is used for', Research Report (Oxfam/Eurodad, February 2017), available at https://eurodad.org/files/pdf/58a1e294657ab.pdf.

[36] This was the position taken by some NGO participants at the meeting held by the NGO Publish What you Fund and the ODI, on 'Untying, is it Working?' held in London on 5 March 2010.

[37] OECD DCD/DAC Report on the DAC Untying Recommendation, Table 5 (contract awards within the scope of the recommendation), analysis by value. Reported in P Meeks, *Unravelling Tied Aid Why aid must never be tied to donor country companies at the expense of women and men living in poverty*, available at https://eurodad.org/files/pdf/1546810-unravelling-tied-aid-1516803666.pdf. Similar equivalences have been drawn in the past by the think tank Publish What You Fund, ibid.

problem (especially for local suppliers) and it might be an indication of, at the very least, lack of 'healthy' competition within the recipients' market. It is also an evident sign of problems linked with accessing donors' tenders, especially for local suppliers. *In loco* suppliers should be, at least in principle, better placed to offer the goods and services required.[38]

However *simply and simpliciter* equating the number of contracts won by suppliers based in the donor country with the level of aid which is tied is problematic, ie a 'presumption of tying' whenever a home supplier wins a tender, should be avoided because it could be misinterpreting the facts (and hence misleading), and because it could be counterproductive from a policy perspective. It can be misleading because contracts might have been won legitimately by donors' suppliers because they offered better goods/services following an open tender. From a policy perspective, a 'presumption of tying' could undermine the efforts made by those donors who have *de jure* and *de facto* untied, but yet award contracts to home suppliers because home suppliers tender the best offers, and could lead to a paradoxical situation where donors don't want to award tenders to the home suppliers because they don't want to be 'perceived' as informally tying aid.[39] Further, this proxy might lead donors to stop reporting the nationality of suppliers who win aid contracts (and to a growing aversion for aid untying). The problems with aid contracts being awarded to donors' suppliers are complex and are linked to structural problems connected to the system of aid procurement more generally and to donors' contradictory approaches to aid procurement that, by undermining the credibility of the aid system more generally, impinge on suppliers' willingness to rely on it.

This is, however, not to say that looking at the nationality of suppliers winning aid tenders is not important and that such data do not disguise formal and informal tied aid practices; on the contrary, such information should be collected regularly and made public, but this should be combined with thorough and accurate investigations of the number and nationality of suppliers who participated in the aid tenders, with an assessment of the specifications and other conditions for participation in the procurement process, with interviews with local suppliers to identify both whether aid was really tied (formally and informally) and where the real problems in the tender process lie. Only a thorough assessment of the aid tender and the aid market would provide an understanding of the real causes that lie behind the high number of contracts won by donors' suppliers. Such an assessment would also allow the identification of ways to remove barriers to competition in the aid market. This is important because the solutions that could be put in place to overcome genuine obstacles that local suppliers face are very different from what could be done if the aid was in fact tied. Yet despite the importance of identifying how to make the aid market more competitive, and of rebutting any quick presumption of tying, such comprehensive investigations of aid procurement and aid data have not yet been carried out. Donors who are serious about

[38] As mentioned above when talking about informal tying, such problems might be linked to the rules used, the language for the tender, the publications and other transparency requirements etc.

[39] Procurement officials interviewed by the author reported that they had experienced situations where donors refused to provide the committed funds because the aid tender had been awarded, after an open competition, to a home supplier.

improving competition in the aid market and promote aid untying should consider investing adequate resources to explore these key issues.

III. From Donors' Pledges to Untie Aid to New Forms of Aid Tying

In the late 1990s an increased awareness of the damaging effects of tied aid and of its negative consequences on aid effectiveness led a broad network of development actors – international organisations and bilateral donors but also NGOs and other development experts – to put in place a series of initiatives at the international and regional level to untie aid.

A pivotal role in pushing forward the untying cause was played by donor members of the OECD/DAC. In 1999, the OECD/DAC was vested with a mandate to explore ways to liberalise procurement regimes in the aid context and to work on a Recommendation to untie aid.[40] In 2001, the Recommendation on Untying Aid to Least Developed Countries (LDC) was adopted.[41] The Recommendation entered into effect on 1 January 2002. It covers only aid to LDC and, from 2008, aid to Highly Indebted Poor Countries (HIPC).[42] The Recommendation excludes food aid from its coverage and does not apply to non-OECD/DAC donors, such as China, who are believed to grant a conspicuous amount of tied aid. Because of these exemptions from its coverage, the Recommendation[43] only covers 12 per cent of the total of aid that was donated; in monetary terms this implies that in 2016 'more than $20 billion out of the total $25 billion in tied ODA fell outside the scope of the DAC's Recommendations'.[44] Finally, the Recommendation is not legally binding. Its implementation relies on the goodwill of States, the effectiveness of peer pressure and the OECD/DAC monitoring role.

These limitations notwithstanding, the Recommendation is regarded as a milestone in the fight against aid tying as it is the first official recognition of the benefits and importance of untying aid. The Recommendation has had a deep resonance within the international community and its adoption sets in motion a series of events geared towards reaching a consensus to further untying aid. The Recommendation is expressly

[40] Attempts were made in the 1970s and 1980s to reach an agreement to untie aid but they proved unsuccessful. Even the OECD agreement on export credits and tied aid, agreed under the leadership of the US concerned over the excessive use of export credits and loans and soft loans to stimulate trade, did not actually cover aid. For an extensive account, see H Fuhrer, *The Story of Official Development Assistance* (OECD, Paris, 1996) 22 and F Lammersen, 'The Helsinki Arrangement: its Impact on the Provision of Tied Aid' (2001) 6 *International Journal of Finance and Economics* 69. See further La Chimia (n 1) ch 2; OECD, *Policy Brief* (n 8) 4. See also OECD, *The DAC Journal of Development Co-operation 2001 Report*, (Paris, 2002) 42.

[41] Some donors have gone a step further. eg the UK in 2002 unilaterally untied all its aid funds. In 2006, the EC adopted Regulation 1906/2006 which ensures that EU aid is untied on a regional level towards developing countries and on reciprocal conditions towards other donors (ie the EU will untie its aid only on condition that other donors equally untie).

[42] The inclusion of HIPC added further five countries to the original list of beneficiaries countries, which now reaches 57 countries.

[43] For an analysis of the OECD Recommendation, see A La Chimia, 'International Steps to Untie Aid: the OECD/DAC Recommendation' (2004) 13 *Public Procurement Law Review* 1.

[44] Meeks/Eurodad (n 10).

recalled in the UN Programme of Actions for the Least Developed Countries and in the Brussels Declaration, both unanimously adopted by the UN Assembly.[45]

As mentioned above, the OECD/DAC was not the only actor to play a part in the campaign to untie aid. Worthy of note are the initiatives undertaken by ActionAid, a UK-based NGO. ActionAid published a series of studies highlighting the costs of tying aid and lobbied the EU Commission to lodge a case in front of the Court of Justice of the European Union against those EU Member States that tied their aid. ActionAid argued that by tying aid EU Member States were breaching EC (now EU) law as they were restricting competition within the aid market and were indirectly subsiding their national companies via tied aid.[46] As a result of the ActionAid campaign, the Commission sent letters of notice to Italy and Denmark, the two Member States that were making regular use of aid tying. However when these States endorsed the OECD Recommendation, the Commission dropped the case, even though it never ascertained whether those States were actually implementing the Recommendation.[47] Despite the Commission's (DG Internal Market Directorate) reluctance to initiate legal action against its Member States, it remained very vocal in supporting and pushing forward the untying cause at the international level (thanks to the leadership of its DG Development Directorate).[48] In 2002, the Commission sponsored a new study on aid untying which demonstrated the benefits of aid untying and after a few months the Commission declared that 'untying aid must go further'[49] (ie beyond the Recommendation). On December 2005, the Council adopted a Regulation[50] based on a Commission proposal[51] on the access to Community External Assistance, providing for the further untying of Community external aid.

Other donors, such as the UK, were also very supportive of untying aid. For example, in 2001 the UK, recognising the benefits of untying aid and following the leadership of Michelle Clark, the development secretary at the time and a fervent promoter of untying aid, committed to unilaterally untie all its aid programmes and enacted legislation to ensure that aid could only be donated for poverty eradication purposes.[52]

[45] UN Assembly at Third United Nations Conference on the Least Developed Countries UN A/56/297 Brussels, May 2001.

[46] The campaign was led by Belen Vasquez and this author had the privilege to work alongside Mrs Vazquez at ActionAid when the campaign was launched.

[47] As the author has argued elsewhere, it took a very long time for all Member States to implement the Recommendation effectively and, to some extent, some Member States are still disregarding the Recommendation principles.

[48] As argued before by the author, the contradiction in the Commission's behaviour towards untying aid reflects the fact that the two directorates responsible for Internal Market and Development Cooperation had opposite views in relation to the need to push untying aid further.

[49] Writing Document of the Commission Service, 'Response to the challenges of Globalisation. A study on the International Monetary and Financial System and on Financing for Development' SEC (2002) 185 final, p 70.

[50] Regulation of the European Parliament and of the Council on *Access to Community External Assistance* PE-CONS 3642/1/ 5 published on 14 December 2005, OJ L344/1. In 2006, the 2005 Regulation was repealed and modified by Regulation 1905/2006.

[51] EC Commission Proposal for a Regulation of the European Parliament and of the Council *on the Access to Community External Assistance* COM(2004) 313 final.

[52] La Chimia (n 1).

At the broader international level (ie beyond the OECD and the DAC donors) untying has been linked to the achievement of the Millennium Development Goals (MDG) – specifically, the proportion of official development assistance that is untied is one of the indicators for monitoring progress towards the achievement of MDG 8 'Develop a global partnership for development'[53] (indicator 8.3 for goal N 8.)

The pro-untying momentum continued throughout the first wave of the 'aid effectiveness agenda'. As already pointed out in chapter 3, untying aid became a cardinal commitment within that agenda. In 2002, in Monterrey donors openly committed to 'further' untying aid (ie beyond the OECD Recommendation). At the time the days of aid tying seemed nearly over, donors could no longer continue 'business as usual'.

Untying aid also figured in the Paris Declaration on Aid Effectiveness[54] and the Accra Agenda of Action (AAA) agreed in Ghana in December 2008.[55] Both the Paris Declaration and the AAA recognised that untying aid increases aid effectiveness and exhorted donors to continue to make progress on untying aid (paragraph 31 of PD and paragraph 18 of the AAA). A specific indicator (indicator 8) was dedicated to untying aid. However, the commitment in Paris is one of progressive realisation and no other specific target is set. While in Accra donors seemed to be more specific than in Paris because they agreed to broaden the coverage of the Recommendation to HIPC (a commitment soon fulfilled by OECD/DAC donors) this effectively resulted only in eight countries being added to the list of countries covered by the Recommendation.

The AAA also called on donors to 'elaborate individual plans to untie their aid to the maximum extent' (paragraph 18 of AAA) and to increase local and triangular purchases, especially in the field of food aid. This move towards individual rather than collective efforts certainly signalled some disagreements among the participants to the Accra Forum over the extent to which aid can be untied and effectively marked the beginning of the end of the former momentum to untie aid.

Soon after Accra, two reports commissioned by the OECD, namely the report on the implementation of the Paris Declaration and the report on the status of untying aid, showed that donors were not fulfilling their commitments on untying aid and that an 'overwhelming proportion of aid continued to be tied'[56]

Donors' individual efforts also proved unsuccessful. For instance the EU decision to further untie aid subject to reciprocal agreements signed with donor countries effectively resulted in only one agreement being reached with Australia in over ten years since the adoption of the EU 2005 Regulation.[57]

After Accra, the 2011 Busan Partnership agreement stressed again the importance of untying aid, recognising that 'in addition to increasing value for money, untying can

[53] See UN official MDG site at www.un.org/millennium/declaration/ares552e.htm. See also the 2005 World Summit (Resolution adopted by the General Assembly A/RES/60/1, www.un.org/Docs/journal/asp/ws.asp?m=A/RES/60/1. See also http://siteresources.worldbank.org/DATASTATISTICS/Resources/MDGsOfficialList2008.pdf.

[54] The level of aid untied is one of the indicators for measuring aid effectiveness used by the Paris Declaration. Available at www.oecd.org/document/18/0,3343,en_2649_3236398_35401554_1_1_1_1,00.html.

[55] Untying is one of the four issues considered by donors in Accra (the other three are predictability, country systems and conditionality).

[56] Clay et al (n 3).

[57] See La Chimia (n 1) ch 6.

present opportunities for local procurement, business development, employment and income generation in developing countries'. The partnership urged development partners to 'accelerate efforts to untie aid' and to review 'plans to achieve this'. Importantly, the Partnership also called on donors to 'improve the quality, consistency and transparency of reporting on the tying status of aid'. In Busan, donors returned to expressing a preference for multilateral endeavour, although no specific targets or specific timelines were set. To date, these commitments remain unfulfilled.

After Busan the work on the aid effectiveness agenda now continues under the auspices of the Global Partnership for Effective Development Cooperation. The level of aid which is untied remains one of the indicators used to monitor the implementation of donors' commitments towards more effective development. The specific commitment on untying aid is framed in terms of progressive realisation and of goodwill endeavours; specifically, donors commit to continue 'progress over time'.[58] Again, there is no specific target and no timeline, undermining the strength and credibility of such a commitment. As explained above in section II, reporting on the level of aid which is untied remains optional and no clear definition and parameters have been agreed on how aid untying should be measured and reported.

Worryingly, the 2016 GPEDC report on the implementation of the Busan principles points to a potential increase in the level of aid which is tied driven by new forms of aid granting.[59] Specifically, the report states that '... other considerations, such as the increasing role of donor-country private sector firms in the delivery of development co-operation' seem to lie behind donors' reasons for not untying aid'. This is problematic considering that the trend to blend aid with private financing and to increase Public-Private Partnership (PPP) collaboration is growing in the development sector (especially since the explicit endorsement of this form of development cooperation by the SDGs (goal 17)). Studies show that the use of this type of financing is growing exponentially. For example, Ghossein et al show that China resorts extensively to Public Private Partnerships within the Road and Belt initiative.[60] Critics have warned against an increase of aid associated with private financing especially in light of the little scrutiny so far undertaken over the risks and consequence of this mode of financing for development.[61] Little is also known about procurement linked to the PPP contracts financed by China and other donors, the only certainty being that most contracts tend to be won by Chinese companies (it is unclear whether competition for such contracts is open to foreign suppliers or whether instead the procurement is tied – either formally or informally – to Chinese goods and services.[62]

Other political events also pose a challenge for aid donation and risk leading to a return of tied aid. Surprisingly, even donors historically in favour of untying aid seem

[58] OECD/UNDP, 2016 progress report on Global Partnership on Effective Development Cooperation, available at www.undp.org/content/dam/undp/library/development-impact/--2016%20progress%20report--Full=v6bis%20(e-book)%20FINAL.pdf.

[59] Meeks/Eurodad (n 10).

[60] T Ghossein, B Hoekman and A Shingal, 'Public Procurement in the Belt and Road Initiative', Working Paper, World Bank Publications, available at http://documents.worldbank.org/curated/en/143241544213097139/Public-Procurement-in-the-Belt-and-Road-Initiative.

[61] C Tan and L Cotula, Regulating Development Partnerships: PPPs, Blended Finance and Responsible Investment Provisions', available at https://investmentpolicyhub.unctad.org/Blog/Index/63.

[62] T Ghossein et al, above n 62.

now to be advocating a greater use of aid to promote trade. For example, soon after the decision of the UK to exit the European Union (a process known as 'Brexit') the then UK secretary for development cooperation, Priti Patel, unapologetically stated that UK aid should be used to foster trade with recipient countries and secure new trade deals and new trading partners post Brexit.[63] This intention has been repeated by other politicians in the post-Brexit era and has been exacerbated during the months of the increasing likelihood of a possible no-deal Brexit.[64] Such a U-turn from a country like the UK that has made of 'using aid for poverty eradication only' a flagship commitment for its aid agency (and who has entrenched such commitment in legislation) could have damaging repercussions on the whole development community. NGOs and other development experts have been quick to point out the damaging consequences of such an approach and have warned that such use of aid resources could contravene UK law. Yet, if the post-Brexit environment (provided Brexit goes ahead) continues to be hostile, the prospect of a return to a mercantilist past where aid is used for the exclusive interests of donors' only, seem real and this could have serious damaging consequences for effective aid delivery.

On the other side of the Atlantic, the situation is no more reassuring. President Trump's nationalist approach to international trade and foreign policy and its implication for public procurement in general have been extensively discussed in chapter 4. The effects of Trump's (short-sighted) foreign policy vision have not taken long to be felt in the development aid sector. Soon after Trump came to office, the US administration announced that it would withdraw support (and aid) from countries that do not 'share American values' and 'do not support American foreign policies'.[65] The negative consequences and the negative impact of such policies on many development projects (especially in the health and agricultural sectors) have been amply documented.[66] NGOs and other development actors are not receiving vital funding and thousands of people are not receiving support. Such an approach is clearly aimed at coercing recipients of US aid money to act to please the US, flying in the face of the objectives of ownership and alignment (described in chapter 3). Will this have an effect on tied aid? While it might be argued that Trump has not called for the implementation of 'buy American' policies in the aid sector as loudly as he has done in other procurement fields

[63] R Merrick, 'Foreign aid to be spent on helping to secure post-Brexit trade deals, Priti Patel says' The Independent, 24 October 2017, available at www.independent.co.uk/news/uk/politics/brexit-latest-foreign-aid-spent-trade-deals-priti-patel-international-development-secretary-a8017796.html.

[64] On 11 January 2019, the MP Boris Johnson called for the UK Department for International Development to be closed so that aid can be managed by the Foreign Ministry and be better aligned to UK trade interests. See www.ft.com/content/03bb726a-157d-11e9-a581-4ff78404524e.

[65] J Gerber, 'Trump wants to cut foreign aid to countries not voting with US at UN, including South Africa' *News24*, 30 April 2018, www.news24.com/SouthAfrica/News/trump-wants-to-cut-foreign-aid-to-countries-not-voting-with-us-at-un-including-south-africa-20180430.

[66] A Saldinger, 'How Trump's first year impacted developing countries' (21 December 2017) available at www.devex.com/news/how-trump-s-first-year-impacted-developing-countries-91775. eg the author reports that 'the most immediate impacts of Trump administration policy are being felt as the result of the expanded "global gag rule," or Mexico City Policy, which prohibits foreign NGOs that receive U.S. aid for global health programming to providing any abortion-related services, including referrals or counselling'. This has had as a consequence that organisations providing reproductive healthcare and other services have had their US funding cut, or they have been forced to turn down US funding to continue educating women about all of their options.

(see chapter 4), this is probably because he does not need to do so as US aid is mostly tied anyway and the commitments so far endorsed to untie aid are mainly soft-low commitments (indeed there is no legally binding commitment to prevent any donor from tying aid). As it will be argued in the next section, the lack of legally binding obligations to untie aid is one of the greatest weakness of all the international initiatives to untie aid undertaken thus far and the return to a new era of protectionism in the aid sector exposes the weakness of a system so far based on soft-law commitments and goodwill endeavours only.

IV. The International Legal Framework Applicable to Tied Aid

As Jepma has argued, tied aid contradicts the anti-statist development strategies that donor governments attempt to promote worldwide.[67] 'Donor policies seem to reflect a strange asymmetrical liberalism … (*omissis*) going against the very free-market principles that most donors are trying to encourage in developing countries'.[68] This contradiction is evident when one looks at the international legal framework for the liberalisation of international trade and the efforts that Western countries (ie donors) have gone through to promote trade liberalisation, to abolish subsidies and protectionism, even within the field of public procurement. An extensive analysis conducted by the author elsewhere has revealed that tied aid and development procurement in general are left out from international legal framework applicable to public procurement in general.[69] As argued before, the WTO legal system does not cover tied aid in any meaningful and substantial way. Indeed, nor do the GATT,[70] the major WTO agreement in trade in goods, or the GATS, the WTO agreements on trade in services, apply to tied aid. This is

> because of the exemption provided for government procurement by Article III.8 of GATT from the National Treatment and the Most Favoured Nation obligations (contained in Articles III and I of GATT). Since tied aid is implemented by government bodies and relates to government procurement GATT rules are not applicable to tied aid. A similar reasoning is applicable to the interpretation of GATS.[71]

However, the author has argued that there is a possibility that tied aid could be covered by the WTO disciplines on subsidies, regulated within the WTO framework, by the Agreement on Subsidies and Countervailing Measures (SCM Agreement) and by Article XVI of GATT. It was suggested that 'a plausible argument could be made that tied aid is covered by the SCM Agreement as a prohibited subsidy'. However, it would be very difficult in practice to apply the SCM agreement to tied aid given the difficulty of ascertaining whether a benefit has been granted when tied aid is implemented and in ascertaining whether a 'benefit exists' within the terms of that agreement.

[67] Jepma (n 22).

[68] Statement of the President Of the World Bank's, cited in Huliaras (n 1) 3.

[69] A La Chimia, 'Cui Bono? Scope, Rationales and Consequences of the Exemption for Development Procurement in the Revised Text of the GPA' (2016) 7(1) *Trade, Law and Development* 156–84.

[70] The reader is referred to the author's past work for a detailed account of those findings; see La Chimia (n 1).

[71] ibid.

The author has also investigated whether tied aid is compatible with the rules of the WTO Government Procurement Agreement (GPA). Unfortunately, however, the GPA does not apply to tied aid either, because of an explicit exception within the GPA coverage excluding tied aid from the range of the agreement (art II(3)(e)(i) and (iii)).

> The 2012 revised GPA contains a total exclusion for development aid and international assistance from the scope of its coverage. This is regrettable given that the enhanced transparency provisions and the stronger review mechanisms provided for in the new text of the GPA could have provided an opportunity to make development aid procurement more effective, transparent, and in line with modern procurement practices.[72]

In conclusion, the international legal framework applicable to procurement in general does not apply to the aid sector and cannot be used to refrain donors from tying aid.

The practice of aid tying offers one of the most contradictory pictures of the international community: on the one hand, Western countries who are also donors of aid are the most vocal members within the WTO in favour of trade liberalisation, yet these same countries, when acting as donors, condone, justify and practise protectionism within the aid sector via tied aid conditions. This is a contradiction that undermines the credibility of the international community and the reputation of donors. Arguably the process for purchasing goods and services funded by international assistance grants and loans should benefit from the same competitive and transparent rules which apply to public procurement in general. This could be done using the existing legislative framework which has been used to foster free trade and competition in other sectors of the economy and in public procurement in general. Development procurement should no longer be left out of regional and international agreements regulating public procurement.[73] If this was the case donors would not be able to retract easily from their commitment – or at least they would not be able to do so without it being noticed amidst the silence of the vast procurement community.

V. Conclusions

In the early 2000s, the untying of aid debate had gained momentum. The network of actors who played a role in the journey towards untying aid was broad and involved international institutions, NGOs and individual donors also. The end of tied aid seemed nearer than ever. The damage of aid tying had been officially recognised with the

[72] ibid. As argued elsewhere by the author, apart from the problems in terms of protectionism, and lack of coherence with the principles of free trade and market liberalisation the fact that the GPA does not cover tied aid causes many other problems in terms of the suitability of this agreement for developing countries. eg because aid is not covered by the GPA donors might be less keen to grant aid as budget support to those developing countries who become members of the GPA (because aid as budget support cannot be distinguished from other entries in the budget it would have to be covered by the GPA, therefore donors keen to tie aid might prefer to continue to manage aid themselves so to be able to apply the aid exception) – hence the exception becomes a deterrent to implement aid in an effective way. Further the exception of aid from the coverage of the agreement might undermine the negotiating position of developing countries willing to become members of the GPA given that most of their procurement is financed by aid and therefore they would have less to offer to other parties. See further La Chimia, 'Cui Bono' (n 69).

[73] La Chimia (n 69) 156–84.

adoption of the OECD Recommendation. Donors had now to justify *why* they were not untying aid. Few were the sectors where donors were not prepared to untie aid – this was mainly in the agricultural sector where the influence of the potent agricultural lobbies was clear. Only new donors, such as China, were not engaging in the untying debate. The positive momentum however did not last long. Paradoxically, Paris marked the decline of the 'untying aid momentum'. While the benefits of untying aid had been recognised at the international level and donors had acknowledged that they needed to untie aid, pressure was no longer exercised on donors to push untying aid within the development agenda. While untying aid remained on the list of commitments to make aid more effective, untying beyond the commitments made within the Recommendation was seen just a 'goodwill endeavour', drafted in terms of progressive realisation. Furthermore, little was done in terms of monitoring whether the commitments made were actually fulfilled.

From Paris to Busan no significant new commitments have been made to untie. It is disappointing, to say the least, that despite the many recognitions of the negative effects of tied aid, very little has changed in over 15 years since the adoption of the Recommendation and no further official commitment on untying has been made at the international level.

Recent studies reveal that aid continues to be substantially tied and that donors continue to make extensive use of informal tied aid. Further, a new surge of tied aid risks being caused by new forms of development cooperation and the absence of any monitoring mechanism and any definition to draw the boundaries of this new form of aid granting. At the international level, both the new wave of protectionism which characterises the policies of the Trump administration and the problems created by Brexit are taking a toll on aid policies – with aid often being seen ever more as an instrument to promote donors' foreign policy and economic interests rather than as an instrument to eradicate poverty. In this gloomy scenario and without any legislative – legally binding commitment – to untie aid the future of aid untying is more uncertain than ever. The only certainty which remains is that tied aid is one of the worst example of donors' aid practices and an aberrant contradiction with modern procurement practices and with the aid effectiveness principles. Now more than ever collaboration between donors is needed and, even though unlikely, donors should be called to fulfil their commitments and to reopen the dialogue to further untying aid.

Post scriptum: on 31 January 2019, as this chapter went to the publisher, the USA President Trump issued *Executive Order on Strengthening Buy-American Preferences for Infrastructure Projects*, which encouraged federal grantees to 'Buy American' when purchasing iron, aluminum, steel and certain manufactured products for infrastructure projects funded by federal grants. Tied aid is back, now more than ever.

7

Corruption and Procurement: Recalibrating the Sights

PETER TREPTE

I. Introduction

There is little doubt that corruption can and does flourish in the context of public procurement but, as we have argued previously,[1] there is nothing inexorable about the phenomenon and it is important not to treat as an inevitable consequence of the procurement function what is essentially an avoidable by-product of such activity. It was argued that the procurement function is not the cause of corruption but merely provides an opportunity for corruption. The causes of corruption lie elsewhere and may be conditioned by any number of factors such as low pay, commercial usage, culture, state of market development, political rent-seeking and so forth. These various factors provide an explanation for what causes (motivates) corruption in all sectors of society and, in the context of public procurement, will also disclose the propensity of the potentially corrupt to seize the opportunities for corruption offered by the procurement function. Corruption in the context of public procurement is more likely to be a reflection of corruption within a given society more generally.

It is also clear that public procurement regulation is used extensively to address corrupt activities in public procurement although it is doubtful that it is, as Dekel suggests, the primary objective[2] which trumps the other objectives mentioned (economic efficiency and equal opportunity). The objectives sought to be achieved by any system of public procurement regulation will very much depend on the context and this is particularly true of the developing world, the subject of development aid, where the strategic choices made are critical to the success of any procurement reforms undertaken. Despite the emphasis the multilateral development banks (MDBs) have put on the

[1] P Trepte, 'Transparency and Accountability as Tools for Promoting Integrity and Preventing Corruption in Procurement: Possibilities and Limitations' (OECD, GOV/PGC/ETH[2005]1) available at www.oecd.org/officialdocuments/publicdisplaydocumentpdf/?cote=GOV/PGC/ETH(2005)1&docLanguage=En.

[2] O Dekel, 'The Legal Theory of Competitive Bidding for Government Contracts' (2008) 37 *Public Contract Law Journal* 237, 258.

objective of anti-corruption in the last 20 years or so (discussed below), their main objective, as stated in their respective Articles of Agreement, is a fiduciary one to 'ensure that the proceeds of any loan are used only for the purposes for which the loan was granted, with due attention to considerations of economy and efficiency and without regard to political or other non-economic influences or considerations'.[3] The current focus of some of the MDBs is on value for money and fitness for purpose[4] and, while anti-corruption continues to figure, this is done so either as part of the drive towards value for money or pursued as an inevitable but auxiliary action. In the United States, Schooner has identified nine goals of public procurement regulation one of which (among the three 'overarching principles') is integrity.[5] By contrast, the Procurement Directives of the European Union do not mention integrity as an objective, seeking rather, as the context would dictate, the promotion of the internal market through prohibiting discrimination, implementing transparency and removing barriers to access.[6] Similarly, the fundamental aim of the World Trade Organization's Government Procurement Agreement (GPA) 'is to mutually open government procurement markets among its parties'.[7] The first Recital of the revised GPA (2012) recognises 'the need for an effective multilateral framework for government procurement, with a view to achieving greater liberalization and expansion of, and improving the framework for, the conduct of international trade', although the sixth Recital also recognises the importance of transparent measures for avoiding corrupt practices.[8]

This is not to say that integrity and the fight against corruption does not have a critical role to play in public procurement regulation; on the contrary, it is a very effective tool, in so far as it goes,[9] and the statement above that the cause of corruption lies largely outside the procurement function serves to demonstrate the limitation of public procurement regulation in combating corruption. It can close off opportunities for corrupt behaviour but cannot address motivations outside that function. Crucially, the war on corruption as played out through public procurement regulation should not overshadow or indeed diminish the attainment of other goals sought in any given context. In all of the sources cited above, the various objectives of public procurement regulation are presented as potentially complementary or contradictory[10]

[3] Art III, s 5(b) of the Articles of Agreement of the International Bank for Reconstruction and Development (the World Bank) and largely replicated in the comparable documents of the regional development banks such as the African Development Bank, the Asian Development Bank and the Inter-American Development Bank. See also ch 12 of this volume (by Yukins and Williams-Elegbe); and P Trepte, 'All Change at the World Bank: The New Procurement Framework' (2016) 25 *Public Procurement Law Review* 121, 122.

[4] See ch 12; Trepte, 'All Change at the World Bank' (n 3); and V Sharma, 'An Update on Procurement Reforms at the African Development Bank' (2016) 25 *Public Procurement Law Review* 151.

[5] S Schooner, 'Desiderata: Objectives for a System of Government Contract Law' (2002) 11 *Public Procurement Law Review* 103.

[6] S Arrowsmith, 'The Purpose of the EU Procurement Directives: Ends, Means and the Implications for National Regulatory Space for Commercial and Horizontal Procurement Policies' (2012) 14 *Cambridge Yearbook of European Legal Studies* 1.

[7] GPA website: www.wto.org/english/tratop_e/gproc_e/gp_gpa_e.htm.

[8] Text of the revised GPA available at: www.wto.org/english/docs_e/legal_e/rev-gpr-94_01_e.htm.

[9] Trepte, 'Transparency and Accountability' (n 1).

[10] See also P Trepte, *Regulating Procurement: Understanding the Ends and Means of Public Procurement Regulation* (Oxford, Oxford University Press, 2004).

and the effects of favouring one over the others need to be taken into account when developing any strategy for procurement reform. The danger of over-emphasising corruption over economic efficiency or value for money has been highlighted previously[11] and this chapter relies on the same premise. The implications for aid effectiveness flow from the same concerns.

The purpose of this chapter is to critically assess the measures commonly taken to address corruption both through public procurement regulation *stricto sensu*, ie through the rules regulating the procurement function of procurement officers, as well as through broader mechanisms which may also apply in the procurement context such as debarment mechanisms, capacity-building initiatives and the development of codes of conduct. The aim is to demonstrate that the traditional approaches are limited or partially misconceived and that it is time to revisit the mechanisms adopted with a view to developing a more sophisticated approach. However heretical this may seem given the interests vested in the promotion of anti-corruption through public procurement regulation, there seems little merit in perpetuating a system which has demonstrably failed to deliver results or whose results are defined not by effectiveness but by heads counted. This is not an exercise in dismissing the objective of fighting corruption but in seeking ways of improving the chances of success.

II. Corruption as a Principal/Agent Problem

The public procurement function has frequently been seen as creating a principal/agent problem.[12] Under this analysis, governments consist, broadly speaking, of politically elected and non-elected members. The non-elected members make up the bureaucracy or apparatus of government and it is they who are, in most cases, responsible for the efficient functioning of government. Whilst the elected members make the policy decisions of government, it is the bureaucracy which carries out those policies in concrete form and ensures that the whole apparatus is in a position to fulfil the routine and policy tasks assigned to it. These two actors, the government (represented by the politicians) and the bureaucracy (represented by the government's procuring agencies), stand in an agency relationship: the government as principal, the bureaucrat as agent. Procurement decisions are, absent any political interference, largely made and carried out by the bureaucracy, specifically by procurement officers (agents) within the bureaucratic hierarchy.

[11] Trepte (n 1).

[12] G Becker and G Stigler, 'Law Enforcement, Malfeasance, and the Compensation of Enforcers' (1974) 3 *Journal of Legal Studies* 1; E Banfield, 'Corruption as a Feature of Government Organization' (1975) 18 *Journal of Law and Economics* 587; S Rose-Ackerman, 'The Economics of Corruption' (1975) 4 *Journal of Public Economics* 187; R Klitgaard, *Controlling Corruption* (Berkeley, CA, University of California Press, 1988); Trepte, *Regulating Procurement* (n 10) ch 2 (63–122); O Soudry, 'A Principal-Agent Analysis of Accountability in Public Procurement', ch 19 in KV Thai and G Piga (eds), *Advancing Public Procurement: Experiences, Innovation and Knowledge Sharing* (PrAcademics Press, Boca Raton, 2006) 432; Dekel, 'The Legal Theory of Competitive Bidding' (n 2); C Yukins 'A Versatile Prism: Assessing Procurement Law Through the Principal-Agent Model' (2010) 40 *Public Contract Law Journal* 63; and G Racca and C Yukins, 'Introduction. Steps for Integrity in Public Contracts' in G Racca and C Yukins (eds), *Integrity and Efficiency in Sustainable Public Contracts* (Brussels, Bruylant, 2014) 1.

The importance of this from the perspective of public procurement is that it reveals that the interests of principal and agent may not be identical and are likely, over time, to diverge, ie even if the presumed interest of the principal is to pursue the interests of the electorate/taxpayers, the agent may have his or her own interest. In terms of procurement, the agent is closer to the procurement process and will consequently hold more information with regard to the market and the suppliers than the principal. It is the procurement officer (agent) who holds all the relevant information concerning the transaction and the ability of the agent to act in his or her own interest is based on the fact that he or she holds information which is not available to the principal. There is, in economic terms, an 'informational asymmetry'. The agent holds information related to the process, the bidders and the products. He or she is, therefore, at an informational advantage vis-à-vis the principal and will be able to use this advantage for, *inter alia*, personal gain. In Klitgaard's terms,[13] the agent has a monopoly over the information and alone makes the procurement decision. It is the exploitation of this position which would enable him or her to enrich himself or herself at the expense of the government and, therefore, society.

From this perspective, it is clear that public procurement regulation can be used to curb corruption in procurement and the mechanism is also fairly obvious: reducing the informational asymmetries as a means of simultaneously reducing the opportunities for corruption, generally by imposing transparency and accountability requirements. This is done by focusing rules on those areas where the agent has most discretion (and most information) notably in specifying requirements, in selecting the procurement method or procedure to be used, in inviting and receiving tenders, in evaluating those tenders and in making the decision to award the contract. Additional tools used to guarantee accountability in procurement are the provisions relating to recording and reporting which will support supervision. Even where complaints are not made, the verifiability of transparent processes will serve to reduce the opportunity for corruption and enhance accountability.[14]

The advantage of agency theory is that it identifies the mechanism which allows procurement officers to engage in corrupt activities. It does not explain the causes of corruption any more than does the more procurement specific literature but it does show how the opportunities for corruption arise. Indeed, it may be that the principal/agency theory only explains one of the avenues through which opportunistic corruption may take place, ie where an agent may grasp the opportunity to exploit the informational asymmetry he or she possesses. Borrowing from transaction cost economics, Williamson[15] described opportunism as 'self-interest seeking with guile' so that, given the opportunity, [economic] agents may serve their own interests rather than those of the other party [to the contract]. The same could be said of the self-interest of the agent over the interests of the principal. Williamson later elaborated the concept of opportunism in terms of 'the incomplete or distorted disclosure of information, especially

[13] R Klitgaard, 'International Cooperation against Corruption' (1998) 35 *Finance & Development* 3.
[14] For a detailed discussion, see Trepte (n 1).
[15] OE Williamson, *Markets* and *Hierarchies: Analysis and Anti-trust Implications: A Study in the Economics of Internal Organization* (New York, The Free Press, 1975) 28.

to calculated efforts to mislead, distort, disguise, obfuscate, or otherwise confuse'[16] which offers a temptingly wicked description of the actions of corrupt procurement officers.

If, as suggested here, agency theory only explains how *opportunistic* corruption may take place, that begs the questions of, first, how to explain other instances of corrupt behaviour in the procurement context and, second, whether the approaches taken to combating opportunistic corruption are also sufficient effectively to address other forms of corruption that may arise in public procurement.

III. Identifying the Target

The comfort provided by agency theory in identifying both the mechanism giving rise to opportunistic corruption as well the mechanisms that may be used to minimise or prevent that opportunism is based, however, on a narrow view of corrupt activities and conceals the difficulties inherent in isolating and addressing its myriad manifestations. It assumes that corruption is easily identifiable and immutable whereas this is very far from being the case. 'Corruption' is something of a moving target, hard to define and even harder to measure. Ignoring those difficulties does not make the problem disappear and applying the same but ever stronger remedies to recognised symptoms does not cure the malady or 'cancer' to use the epithet chosen by a former World Bank president.[17] Indeed, failing to recognise the problems of definition and measurement, it is argued, exacerbates those problems and leads to the ineffectiveness of the cure.

Notwithstanding its ancient pedigree,[18] corruption has eluded a single neat (and accurate) definition and this remains true despite the relatively recent frenzied interest in the phenomenon in the context of public procurement. Its persistence over time also suggests that what we now see as a higher incidence of corruption is less a question of degree than one of visibility. It has probably always been there, maybe in the same degree, but it is our interest in it, the greater transparency of procedures and our obsession with measuring it that gives the impression that corruption is a bigger problem than it was (or is). But identifying what we mean by corruption is key if we mean to fight it.

Anechiarico and Jacobs[19] point out that the concept of corruption has expanded greatly over the twentieth century to embrace more types of corruption both as a result

[16] O Williamson, *The Economic Institutions of Capitalism: Firms, Markets, Relational Contracting* (London, Macmillan, 1985) 47.

[17] James D Wolfensohn, speaking at the 1996 World Bank Group (WBG) Annual Meetings: 'Annual Meetings Address by James D. Wolfensohn, President, The World Bank, October 1st 1996' (available at http://documents.worldbank.org/curated/en/135801467993234363/pdf/99712-WP-Box393210B-PUBLIC-1996-10-01-People-and-Development.pdf) and articulated in World Bank, 'Helping Countries Combat Corruption: The Role of the World Bank' (Washington DC, World Bank, 1997) available at www1.worldbank.org/publicsector/anticorrupt/corruptn/corrptn.pdf.

[18] Bardhan traces literature on the subject back to fourth century BC India: P Bardhan, 'Corruption and Development: A Review of Issues' (1997) 35 *Journal of Economic Literature* 1320.

[19] F Anechiarico and J Jacobs, *The Pursuit of Absolute Integrity: How Corruption Control Makes Government Ineffective* (Chicago, University of Chicago Press, 1996).

of perception and as the result of legislation.[20] They state that '[m]uch conduct that was legal a generation ago is now corrupt; yesterday's "honest graft" is today's illegal "conflict of interest"'.[21] They cite an official of the New York City Department of Investigation who explained that the Department's definition of corruption since the 1970s has included the 'subversion of fairness, of distributive and common justice, and of equal opportunity' and opine that, 'under this definition, even acknowledged error leading to waste could be corrupt'. It is thus quite possible that corruption has not become a greater problem than it has always been (which our greater awareness of the problem would suggest); only that what we now see as 'corruption' (given the widening of the definition of the term) can be labelled as such and prosecuted. One of the constant challenges of any anti-corruption programme is the attitude of the public. Where members of the public have become tolerant of corruption or are resigned to its existence (eg in the case of facilitation payments which have become mere transaction costs), then it is likely that instances of such corruption will go unchallenged. When attitudes begin to change, so too does the willingness of the public to challenge instances of corruption, so that those practices that have always existed will suddenly become targets of challenge. Again, the targeted corrupt practices have not just emerged; they have only then emerged as legitimate targets of challenge.

This progression from what is seen by one generation as permissible to what is seen by another as corrupt also has broader implications for governance and public administration in general. Bardhan remarks[22] that

> [s]ometimes one invokes legality and almost interchangeably uses the word 'corrupt' and 'illicit' in describing a transaction. But just as clearly not all illegal transactions are corrupt, nor are all instances of corruption or bribery illegal (as when you tip the maitre d' to get a better table at a restaurant than other customers, or in the much more important cases of gift-giving by lobbyists to politicians, campaign contributions to Political Action Committees, or post-retirement jobs in private firms to bureaucrats of agencies meant to regulate them). Similarly, one should keep a distinction between 'immoral' and 'corrupt' transactions. When you pay a blackmailer, you may consider him immoral, but you are paying to stop him from revealing some information which may be unpleasant for you but which may be neither illegal nor corrupt. On the other hand, one can think of instances of corruption and bribery which some people may not regard as immoral (particularly those for whom end justifies means), as when you bribe a policeman not to torture a suspect.

Notwithstanding the importance of a clear definition for the purposes of enforcement, there are few legislative (criminal code) definitions of corruption. The same is largely true of the common law where 'corruption' as an offence in itself is barely recognised. The term 'corruption' is usually used more as shorthand to refer to a basket of other more precise offences rather than as a term of art in itself. Legal acts (laws, acts of parliament, anti-corruption legislation and criminal codes, etc) instead rely on a mix of specific offences and crimes that together are 'popularly' considered as corruption. These will

[20] Johnston also makes the point that our understanding of corruption has narrowed since classical times where it was more a question of the moral health of whole nations: M Johnston, 'The Search for Definitions: the Vitality of Politics and the Issue of Corruption' (1996) 48 *International Social Science Journal* 321.

[21] Anechiarico and Jacobs, *The Pursuit of Absolute Integrity* (n 19) 6.

[22] Bardhan, 'Corruption and Development' (n 18) 1321.

include such offences as those of embezzlement, theft, bribery, facilitation payments and various types of fraud or misrepresentation. Such precise definitions, however, often fail to capture the whole range of activities which would be considered corrupt. Nepotism, patronage and other forms of favouritism, for example, also undermine good administration or due process and, whilst such activities are considered corrupt, they may not feature as specific offences or crimes in what might be considered the anti-corruption legislation in force.

Bribes, of course, are seen as the pre-eminent form of corruption in the public sector. These are paid by people to public officials in an attempt to persuade them to exercise their authority in a way which favours them above others. These are often used to obtain certain rights, such as permits or licences, but will also be paid where the public officer has the power to provide the payer with access to certain economic activities they would not otherwise be able to pursue. Bribes are sometimes used to refer to payments of relatively large amounts given to senior officials (decision-makers) to obtain a favourable decision where no right or claim to such decision exists. They are often contrasted with 'facilitation payments' which is a term more often used to refer to relatively smaller amounts paid to lower level officials to accelerate or facilitate a decision to which the payer has a legal claim (eg customs clearance) but which may be unduly delayed or withheld pending some payment. In this context, a distinction is often made between 'grand' and 'petty' corruption, essentially referring to the scale and amount of the bribes at issue. Despite the apparent scale of reprehension, both of these would generally be considered forms of corruption and will constitute illegal behaviour in most countries which prohibit corruption.

There is a clear distinction, however, between these 'categories' of bribe. 'Facilitation payments' may be made to encourage public officers to carry out duties they are obliged to carry out in any event, ie it is not a question of encouraging them to do anything which would otherwise be unlawful, but merely to do their job. Such payments may be made to speed up the processing of documents, for example. Such payments should be contrasted with those made to induce public officers to do something which they are not otherwise required to do and which may be unlawful. This might include processing applications for benefits, for example, that the applicant is not entitled to receive. In procurement terms, examples might be a payment to ensure that tender documents are released on time and a payment to secure the early release of tender documents (eg before an advertisement has been placed).

Bribes may also be 'paid' in any number of ways. This could take the form of a money payment, entertainment or the promise of future employment for example.[23] Anechiarico and Jacobs[24] state that

> [m]oney, however, can be transferred to government officials as a gift, honorarium, or investment opportunity. Payoffs need not be pecuniary. They can involve sexual favors, campaign support, or promises of high-flying jobs or run-of-the-mill favors. The favor need not be bestowed on the official personally; it may even be given to a member of the official's family or to a friend or lover.

[23] Trepte (n 10) 71.
[24] Anechiarico and Jacobs (n 19) 4.

The breadth of possibilities are unbounded[25] which simply serves to make identifying a single corrupt act ever more difficult.

Bribery is far from the only form of corruption despite being its most obvious manifestation. Embezzlement is another word for theft but applies most often in the context of public officials who use their public positions to perpetrate their crimes. This may consist of simply siphoning off funds into personal accounts (no doubt well camouflaged) but can also be carried out in a procurement context where the funds are paid, for example, to complicit contractors where there is no bribe by the contractor to obtain the benefit of the contract, but the contract is awarded to the corrupt contractor (for an adequate direct payment, cut of the proceeds or for an elevated bid price) on the understanding that payments will be made to the official for contract variations (additional costs, for example) that he makes. Similarly, the embezzlement may take the form of fictitious contracts to 'dummy' or 'shell' companies owned (ultimately) by the official (the contract need not be fictitious – the official could simply ensure through abusing his position that 'his' company wins).[26] Theft can also take place on a smaller scale by public officers misusing and stealing office equipment and supplies. The scale does not make it any less theft even though a certain amount of such thievery is often tolerated. Public officials can also abuse their positions for personal gain in other corrupt ways. Insider dealing is a clear example of fraudulent (corrupt) behaviour which is often strictly sanctioned. Improper affiliations with private sector firms, such as contractors or advisors in the industry, also pose conflict of interest issues which can amount to corrupt practices, although these are often dealt with through codes of conduct or ethical rules.

With so many permutations, many have sought, particularly international regulators, to develop what may be called a working definition which covers the multitude of sins and which is intended to enable discussion to take place over the means to combat corruption. The common denominator that emerges from the literature is some variant of the 'abuse of public office for private gain.'[27] Despite what appears to be fairly universal consensus on this general definition, its usefulness may be questioned. It certainly demonstrates its inadequacy as a means of expressing collusion as an example of corruption as the MDBs would have us believe.[28] Collusion is a supply side agreement between

[25] For a comprehensive account of corruption in government, see S Rose-Ackerman, *Corruption and Government: Causes, Consequences and Reform* (Cambridge, Cambridge University Press, 1999).

[26] See J Campos and S Pradhan (eds), *The Many Faces of Corruption: Tracking Vulnerabilities at the Sector Level* (Washington DC, World Bank, 2007) which provides a comprehensive exploration of how to be corrupt.

[27] Bardhan (n 18) 1321; Anechiarico and Jacobs (n 19) 4; Rose-Ackerman, *Corruption and Government* (n 25) 91; Klitgaard, 'International Cooperation' (n 13) 4; A Schleifer and R Vishny, 'Corruption' (1993) 108 *Quarterly Journal of Economics* 599, 599; D Kaufmann, 'Corruption: the Facts' (1997) *Foreign Policy* 114, 114; Transparency International, 'The Anti-Corruption Plain Language Guide' (Berlin, Transparency International – the global coalition against corruption, July 2009) 14 available at www.transparency.org/whatwedo/publication/the_anti_corruption_plain_language_guide; World Bank, 'Helping Countries Combat Corruption' (n 17) 8.

[28] World Bank, 'Procurement Regulations for IPF Borrowers: Procurement in Investment Project Financing – Goods, Works, Non-Consulting and Consulting Services (Washington DC, World Bank, July 2016, revised November 2017 and August 2018) Annex IV, available at https://policies.worldbank.org/sites/ppf3/PPFDocuments/Forms/DispPage.aspx?docid=4005&ver=current; The European Bank for Reconstruction and Development, 'Procurement Policies and Rules – Procurement Policies and Rules for projects financed

providers and does not involve (other than where a public official is also involved) the abuse of public office for the private gain of the public office holder. They are different concepts and manifest themselves at different levels of the market. Collusion (bid-rigging) is also an issue in public procurement but conflating it with corruption and seeking to combat it in the same way is surely mistaken. But that is a different story.

In broader terms, this working definition can be no more than shorthand for the primary transaction which is targeted by anti-corruption measures in the case of 'official' corruption. When setting out those measures, regulatory provisions fall back on the more precise definitions of the individual offences which fall within this generic definition. In framing remedial actions and designing tools to address those offences, the working definition is an irrelevance. The danger is, that over-reliance on such convenient definitions will mask the nature of the target being pursued and undermine the effort to prevent it.

IV. Sizing Up the Target

Notwithstanding our inability to define the concept with sufficient precision, there has been a recent feverish predilection for seeking to measure it. The inherent irreconcilability of this approach appears to have gone largely unnoticed. But one has to ask how, if we do not know what we are measuring and thus cannot measure it accurately, can we hope to design appropriate tools to combat it. As Andersson and Heywood[29] put it,

> the definitions of corruption matter greatly, and for two main reasons: first, they determine what we are trying to capture when we measure corruption; second, they condition the manner in which we understand the nature of the problem and, as a result, how we develop strategies to combat corruption.

Information about the target of regulation is nonetheless crucial, and one of the problems in knowing the extent of corruption is the difficulty in being able to measure it. It may well be that one of the reasons that there is no consensus on the effects of corruption is precisely because there has historically been little information on the extent of corruption and, therefore, an inability of commentators to identify the precise effects. Indeed, the amount of time spent on searching for a definition is arguably disproportionate to the amount of empirical data available but, of course, the very lack of data could be the reason that so much time has been spent on theoretical debate without significant results on the ground. Similarly, the lack of data meant that it was difficult to address the best means and practical methods of tackling or combating corruption

by the European Bank for Reconstruction and Development' (London, European Bank for Reconstruction and Development, revised October 2014) para 2.9, available at www.ebrd.com/news/publications/policies/procurement-policies-and-rules.html; and almost identical definitions in the rules of the Asian Development Bank, The African Development Bank and the Inter-American Development Bank.

[29] S Andersson and PM Heywood, 'The Politics of Perception: Use and Abuse of Transparency International's Approach to Measuring Corruption"(2009) 57 *Political Studies* 746, 750.

even if corrupt activities could be properly identified. The changing face of corruption also makes it almost impossible to provide reliable and accurate data on the incidence of corruption.

A number of early studies attempted to base their findings on some empirical data.[30] This, however, appears to have been very much data collected ad hoc, ie specifically for the purposes of the study in question or, alternatively, conclusions drawn from a wider, more non-specific analysis. Hard data, which may be achieved through such things as forensic accounting techniques, may well be able to identify instances of corrupt practices and the mishandling of funds but the resulting data is necessarily entity specific and not general enough to provide an indication of the level of corruption in a sector or a country.

A more recent study by D'Souza and Kaufmann[31] relies on statistics collected specifically for the purpose of studying, from an econometric point of view, key factors related to the incidence and magnitude of public procurement bribery. They utilise survey data from over 11,000 firms operating in 125 countries provided by the World Economic Forum from their Executive Opinion Survey 2006. It is clear, however, that, though not isolated, this is not a common undertaking although the search for data is obviously growing. The authors cite a number of previous empirical studies based on one or a limited number of countries which examine general bribery or corruption rather than the specific determinants of bribery in procurement and it is not clear that there had been any previous studies analysing factors associated with such bribery based on a cross-country survey. As recently as 2014, Søreide admits that, despite an expansion in corruption literature 'few impact evaluations have provided results of general applicability. Even experts' knowledgeable of the most up-to-date research do not know how anti-corruption initiatives should optimally be designed'.[32]

Many forms of corruption measurement rely on data collected by business-related organisations. One of the more recent developments has been the emergence of investment climate surveys which consider a range of country variables that affect the desirability for firms of making investments in those countries.[33] One example of these is the Business Environment and Enterprise Performance Survey (BEEPS), which is a joint initiative of the European Bank for Reconstruction and Development and the World Bank. It operates specifically in Eastern and Central Europe (ECA) and its results are based, to date, on five rounds of surveys. It is used to collect firm-level data on a broad range of issues about the business environment and performance of firms,

[30] P Mauro, 'Corruption and Growth' (1995) 110 *Quarterly Journal of Economics* 681; A Lanyi, 'Measuring the Economic Impact of Corruption: A Survey' (Center For Institutional Reform And The Informal Sector [IRIS] at the University of Maryland, The IRIS Discussion Papers on Institutions & Development, Paper No 04/04, February 2004) available at http://unpan1.un.org/intradoc/groups/public/documents/apcity/unpan024055.pdf – Lanyi provides an extensive survey of the studies which have sought to measure corruption and the methods they have adopted.

[31] A D'Souza and D Kaufmann, 'Who Bribes in Public Contracting and Why: Worldwide Evidence from Firms' (2013) 14 *Economic of Governance* 333.

[32] T Søreide, *Drivers of Corruption: a Brief Review* (Washington DC, World Bank, 2014) 45, available at https://openknowledge.worldbank.org/handle/10986/20457.

[33] See Lanyi, 'Measuring the Economic Impact' (n 30) 6.

including business-government relations, firm financing, labour, infrastructure, informal payments and corruption, and other topics such as training and innovation. The fifth round of the BEEPS in 2012-16 covered 16,566 enterprises in 32 countries of Eastern Europe and Central Asia.[34]

An alternative to the data obtained from firm-level surveys consists of seeking to measure 'perception' at a broader level. This appears to be the preferred approach of the donor community but does not, by definition, make the data collected any more precise or relevant. With few exceptions, the empirical studies focus on broad issues of corruption outside the public procurement arena and it is not different with surveys of perceptions which gather and aggregate data from a wide range of interlocutors. One of the most well-known aggregate measures is the Corruption Perceptions Index (CPI), published each year by Transparency International (TI), an international NGO dedicated to the fight against corruption.[35]

The annual CPI first released in 1995, is the best known of TI's tools. It has been widely credited with putting TI and the issue of corruption on the international policy agenda. The CPI ranks more than 180 countries (in the 2017 CPI) in terms of perceived levels of corruption, as determined by expert assessments and opinion surveys. In recent years, TI has also developed other corruption measurement tools to complement the CPI. The Bribe Payers' Index (BPI) assesses the supply side of corruption and ranks corruption by source country and industry sector. The Global Corruption Barometer (GCB) is a public opinion survey that assesses the general public's perception and experience of corruption in more than 60 countries around the world.[36]

The CPI 2017 itself is an aggregate indicator that brings together data from various sources. Up to 2012, the CPI was based on perceptions of corruption in each country/territory, *relative* to the other countries scored and ranked on the index. The index captured the rank position of each country in each data source, so that country scores were highly dependent on the changes in scores of the countries around it in the index. From 2012, the *unaltered* scores from each of the data sources are used, providing greater transparency on how the CPI scores have been constructed and allowing the scores to capture changes over time. They are no longer relative but country specific. Unlike previous CPIs, the score is also now based *only* on data which falls within the previous year with no spill-over beyond that period. This also means that data from 2012 onwards will not be comparable to data collected in other years.

The CPI 2017 is calculated using 13 different data sources from 12 different institutions ('experts' and business executives) that capture perceptions of corruption within the past two years on a number of corrupt behaviours in the public sector, including bribery, diversion of public funds, use of public office for private gain, nepotism in the civil service and State capture. The methodology follows four basic steps: selection of source data, rescaling source data, calculating the average and then reporting a measure for uncertainty.

[34] Results of the fifth round (2012–16) are available at https://ebrd-beeps.com/data/2012-2016.

[35] The annual results may be found on the TI website: www.transparency.org.

[36] Further information on these tools and on the results of the annual surveys are available at www.transparency.org/research/bpi/overview.

The results of this process are presented by a score which is given to each country. The higher the score, the lower the level of the perception of corruption in the country; the lower the score, the higher is the level of perception. The results are presented in a league table form and have traditionally been seen as a comparative assessment.

The country's position in the league table has frequently been used both by donors and regulators to justify additional intervention, and by countries themselves, where possible, to demonstrate improvements. The annual revision of the rankings is quite often used in this way, although this may well change given the amendments to the methodology which, from 2012, no longer provides *relative* scores. As Galtung[37] states,

> [t]he CPI has been cited in thousands of newspaper articles. It is cited almost on a daily basis. In some contexts, as illustrated above, it can be credited with influencing a country's political trajectory. The CPI was a watershed in the mid-1990s. It contributed towards the formation of a global movement and widespread consensus against corruption. The CPI was a formidable instrument in raising awareness about the international scope and shared burden of corruption and driving corruption onto the front pages of newspapers throughout the developing world. The CPI levelled the playing field by comparing, for the first time, disparate and distinct countries on the same scale. The international shaming that ensued, encouraged a race to the top, i.e. to lower levels of corruption. The race was on the international stage for some … and for some selected countries at the bottom of the league table (eg Bangladesh, Nigeria and Paraguay) it has spurred a determination to shed the label of being 'one of the world's most corrupt countries'.

Despite the apparent success, the CPI has been heavily criticised. Galtung[38] addresses what he sees as seven major failings with the CPI process although, since that article was written in 2005, some of those failings will have been palliated by the greater number of countries now subject to CPI scrutiny (176 in 2012). Similarly, the change in methodology introduced in 2012 will also have the effect of minimising the comparative nature of the index. The failings he levels at the CPIs are that they: only punish the takers, not the givers or abetters; are based on irregular and uncontrolled country coverage; are biased samples: more than 90 per cent of the world is missing; are based on imprecise and sometimes ignorant sources; are far too narrow and based on an imprecise definition of corruption; do not measure trends and cannot reward genuine reformers; make countries guilty by association, notably through aid conditionality. Andersson and Heywood[39] also highlight the difficulties with the measurement methods used in the CPI. They refer, for example, to the fact that the CPI measures 'perceptions' rather than actual cases of corruption; to the lack of common understanding in comparing such perceptions; and to the false sense of accuracy conveyed by such precise results.

Of potentially greater concern, however, is the danger presented by over-reliance on the league table nature of the CPI results, notably by the donor community.

[37] F Galtung, 'Measuring the Immeasurable: Boundaries and Functions of (Macro) Corruption Indices' in C Sampford, A Shacklock, C Connors and F Galtung (eds), *Measuring Corruption* (London, Ashgate, 2006) 108.

[38] ibid 109.

[39] Andersson and Heywood, 'The Politics of Perception' (n 29) 752.

The importance and credence given to the CPI in the developing world has already been highlighted by Galtung.[40] Andersson and Heywood point out, further, the potential pitfalls of such reliance:

> One potential consequence of the prevailing orthodoxy on both measuring and fighting corruption is that those countries most affected may become caught in a vicious circle: as aid becomes increasingly conditional on the adoption of Western-defined measures to combat corruption, so those countries with the least resources to implement 'good governance' stand to suffer most from the withdrawal of precisely the support they need to stand any realistic chance of tackling corruption. Alongside a poverty trap, we may now be witnessing the emergence of a 'corruption trap' in which, once corruption becomes systemically embedded, it may be virtually impossible for countries to secure the kind of aid that could help them put in place policies to promote the very development that is supposed to provide the best protection against corruption.[41]

Kenny[42] provides a clear example of such a trap in practice. He explains that the US' Millennium Challenge Corporation (MCC) imposes a 'hard hurdle' on its activities by denying aid to countries that rank poorly on corruption perception indices, ie those that find themselves in the bottom half of their income group as regards the control of corruption. He considers the hurdle

> a weak incentive to reform because it is difficult to know what policy levers move the control of corruption needle, and it is a weak tool for aid effectiveness because a fuzzy corruption indicator is (unsurprisingly) weakly related to development outcomes.

Whether based on hard data of some sort or on perceptions, none of the results are without flaw.[43] In selecting interlocutors, it will be impossible to avoid bias since those taking part may be influenced by the very position that led to their selection (eg as a patient or a bidder). If, as bidders, they have been responsible for paying bribes, their honesty in responding to questions may not always be assumed. Bias may be a particular danger in the case of perception surveys where those taking part may be influenced by hearsay or by newspaper and other reports. Surveys are also rather sector specific and relate to particular areas of activity, eg the business sector in the case of the CPI,[44] with the results extrapolated more generally. Even in the case of hard data what is most often being measured is not the level of corruption defined as a single concept but a series of indices which serve as proxies for corruption. In the case of Mauro's study,[45] for example, it was an indicator defining, *inter alia*, the degree to which business transactions involve questionable payments.[46] In the final analysis, such reports will in some cases

[40] Galtung, 'Measuring the Immeasurable' (n 37).

[41] Andersson and Heywood (n 29) 760.

[42] C Kenny, *Results not Receipts: Counting the Right Things in Aid and Corruption* (Washington DC, Center for Global Development, 2017) 100. See also C Arndt and C Oman, *Uses and Abuses of Governance Indicators* (Paris, Development Centre of the OECD/OECD Publishing, Paris, 2006) available at www.oecd-ilibrary.org/development/uses-and-abuses-of-governance-indicators_9789264026865-en.

[43] Lanyi (n 30).

[44] Andersson and Heywood (n 29) 753.

[45] Mauro, 'Corruption' (n 30).

[46] See also M Mironov and E Zhuravskaya, 'Corruption in Procurement and the Political Cycle in Tunneling: Evidence from Financial Transactions Data' (2016) 8(2) *American Economic Journal: Economic Policy* 287,

be able to express the level of corruption generally but will be unable to distinguish between different types of corrupt behaviour.[47]

Even assuming that there were substantive merit in the perception results achieved from these perceptions-based indices, the reliability of such data is open to question both for the reasons explained above as well as because there is often a weak correlation between perception and reality.[48] Heywood and Rose[49] point to a series of Eurobarometer studies of the attitude of Europeans to corruption. The latest, conducted in September 2011, found that a strikingly high proportion of EU citizens (74 per cent, on average) saw corruption as a 'major problem' in their country, yet, personal experience of corruption remained strikingly low, with an overall average of just 8 per cent of respondents having been asked to pay any form of a bribe for access to services during the preceding 12 months.[50] Perceptions of corruption also appear to be influenced by the absolute level of corruption rather than the relative level[51] so that, even if the number of corruption incidents per person in the population is identical, a country with a larger population is more likely to have a worse perceived level of corruption. One wonders what happens to the perception of corruption in those countries where anti-corruption efforts are successful, leading to a higher number of prosecutions and greater visibility through reporting. The irony is that those countries seeking to address corruption may be perceived, as a result of the higher visibility of anti-corruption actions, as being more corrupt.

Given the emphasis placed on the annual results of the CPI and the importance given in practice to the evolving position of a country in the 'league table' which, as stated above, has frequently been used both by countries themselves to demonstrate improvements and by donors and regulators to justify additional intervention or even deny aid (*cf* MCC above), one would expect to see significant movement in the annual results which might reflect the anti-corruption efforts that have taken place. Heywood and Rose[52] conducted a regression analysis to test the assumption. The result of comparing the data from 2000 and 2011 demonstrated a remarkable consistency in the results during that period suggesting no substantive change over time. They conclude that 'there has been virtually no substantive change to two of the main perception-based measures of corruption over a period of more than a decade, a finding that seriously undermines their utility as analytic tools'.[53] It may thus come as no surprise that TI's

who measure the amount of cash tunnelled illegally out of firms around the time of regional elections and relate it to the probability that these firms obtain procurement contracts from the government.

[47] Andersson and Heywood (n 29) 751; D Donchev and G Ujhelyi, 'What Do Corruption Indices Measure?' (2014) 26 *Economics and Politics* 309, 320.

[48] D Treisman, 'What Have We Learned About the Causes of Corruption from Ten Years of Cross-National Empirical Research?' (2007) 10 *Annual Review of Political Science* 211; D Treisman, 'What Does Cross-National Empirical Research Reveal about the Causes of Corruption?', ch 7 in PM Heywood (ed), *Routledge Handbook of Political Corruption* (Abingdon, Routledge, 2015) 95.

[49] PM Heywood and J Rose, '"Close but no Cigar": the Measurement of Corruption' (2014) 34 *Journal of Public Policy* 507, 510.

[50] See also BA Olken, 'Corruption Perceptions vs. Corruption Reality' (2009) 93 *Journal of Public Economics* 950; R Rose and W Mishler 'Experience versus Perception of Corruption: Russia as a Test Case' (2010) 11 *Global Crime* 145.

[51] Donchev and Ujhelyi, 'What Do Corruption Indices Measure?' (n 47) 322.

[52] Heywood and Rose, '"Close but no Cigar": the Measurement of Corruption' (n 49) 513 ff.

[53] ibid 514.

website, in introducing the results of the 2017 survey, states that '[t]his year's Corruption Perceptions Index highlights that the majority of countries are making little or no progress in ending corruption … compared to recent years, this poor performance is nothing new'.[54] It appears that the anti-corruption efforts of the last 20 years have not achieved the intended result, at least not one that is measurable. Whilst there may be a number of reasons why this is so, basing decisions concerning aid allocation on perceptions indices – potentially creating the 'corruption trap' discussed above – is hardly a recipe for improving aid effectiveness.

V. A Proliferation of Targets

One of the disadvantages of examining corruption through the prism of agency theory is that it focuses attention on the agent, the procurement officer. Indeed, it is arguable that it is this very focus that has led to solutions based on improving governance and reinforcing institutions. If the problem lies with the agent, then the answer must be found (*sic*) in weak governance structures and this is surely what has led to the emphasis of strengthening (or introducing) a robust procurement legal and regulatory framework, the hallmark of donor-driven procurement reforms. The 'Washington Consensus',[55] which drove much of the procurement reforms from the 1980s onwards, was centred on improving governance, and corruption was seen as a clear example of poor governance which diminished aid effectiveness. As explained above, there is little or no evidence to show that imposing stronger procurement rules (better governance) has diminished the incidence of corruption or improved aid effectiveness, which puts the whole exercise into question. The issue may well be that it is not always the agent that is the problem and the Weberian[56] ideal of agents serving democratically elected principals is not always achieved.

Political corruption,[57] for example, is generally associated with the principals, either politicians or senior public officials, not agents.[58] It is often associated with the electoral cycle and relates primarily to election funding, or with the direct effort to buy a politician's vote or decision, either in a parliamentary vote or outside of it (such as in a parliamentary committee). Party political financing is a particular problem which manifests itself in most countries, both developed and developing.[59] Corruption in political finance takes many forms, ranging from vote buying and the use of illicit

[54] www.transparency.org/news/feature/corruption_perceptions_index_2017.

[55] See ch 3.

[56] M Weber, *Economy and Society* (New York, Bedminster Press Incorporated, 1968).

[57] Rose-Ackerman, 'The Economics of Corruption' (n 12); J Andvig and O Fjeldstad with I Amundsen, T Sissener and T Søreide, 'Corruption: A Review of Contemporary Research, Report R 2001/7 (Bergen, Chr. Michelsen Institute Development Studies and Human Rights, 2001)' available at www.cmi.no/publications/861-corruption-a-review-of-contemporary-research.

[58] The most dramatic recent example may be Brazil's Operation Car Wash ('*Lava Jato*'), which implicated a number of politicians and senior government officials: see https://en.wikipedia.org/wiki/Operation_Car_Wash.

[59] Rose-Ackerman (n 25) 132 ff.

funds to the sale of appointments and the abuse of state resources. Not all are illegal. Political corruption often also appears as lobbying or as extortion, but also through 'revolving door' moves of senior politicians directly into high business positions, often in companies whose activities were previously regulated or controlled by the same politician.[60]

One particularly pernicious form of political corruption is known as regulatory capture. As a body of politicians, the government, as principal, may well have priorities other than social welfare, not least of which will be the desire for re-election. This is a fundamental aspect of political corruption. As Buchanan[61] points out, these personal priorities may well affect the regulatory policies of the government they represent. The assumption that the government always acts in the public interest (or the interests of the electorate) has been cast into doubt by the emergence of a body of literature relating to the positive theory of regulation which emphasises the role of interest groups in the formation of public policy.[62]

According to Stigler,[63] regulation is not instituted in the public interest, ie for the protection and benefit of the public at large or some large or small subclass of the public, but is acquired for industry and designed and operated primarily for the latter's benefit. Members of an industry have more incentives than dispersed consumers to exercise political influence and have a higher per capita stake in the outcome of regulation. The smaller the group, the higher the per capita stake and the greater is the incentive to affect the regulatory outcomes.[64] This is not restricted to industry groups and may apply equally to other interest groups such as those promoting certain social goals or cleaner technologies. Capture represents the ability of industry to influence or shape the regulatory framework to its own advantage, ie its capacity to influence the very rules of the game through affecting the content of applicable laws, regulations and other measures.[65]

The procurement process can be distorted at a higher hierarchical level through the influence exerted by senior government officers and parliamentarians, not only for political but also personal gain. The absence of corruption depends, in some ways on the existence of a 'benevolent principal' or 'principled principal'.[66] Corruption exists, so the story goes, when a benevolent principal delegates decision-making power to a

[60] On patronage and political corruption, see P Blunt, M Turner and H Lindroth, 'Patronage's Progress in Post-Soharto Indonesia' (2012) 32 *Public Administration and Development* 64.

[61] JM Buchanan, 'Rent Seeking and Profit Seeking' in JM Buchanan, RD Tollison and G Tullock (eds), *Toward a Theory of the Rent-Seeking Society* (Texas A& M University Press, 1980) 3.

[62] Trepte (n 10) 82–83.

[63] GJ Stigler, 'The Theory of Economic Regulation' (1971) 2(1) *The Bell Journal of Economics and Management Science* 3.

[64] M Olson, *The Logic of Collective Action: Public Goods and the Theory of Groups* (Harvard University Press, 1965).

[65] See, for an empirical study on the real world effects of state capture, J Hellman, G Jones and D Kaufmann, 'Seize the State, Seize the Day: State Capture, Corruption, and Influence in Transition' (2003) 31 *Journal of Comparative Economics* 751.

[66] A Persson, B Rothstein and J Teorell, 'Why Anticorruption Reforms Fail – Systemic Corruption as a Collective Action Problem' (2013) 26 *Governance: An International Journal of Policy, Administration, and Institutions* 449.

non-benevolent agent.[67] But the principal need not be benevolent. He may also be corrupt. The involvement of politicians and senior officials in the procurement processes is generally referred to as political – as opposed to bureaucratic – corruption.[68] It may be that senior officials in the government and politicians are complicit in the activities of the corrupt agents. Rose-Ackerman[69] explains that this can operate in at least two ways: bottom-up or top-down. In the bottom-up version, low level or 'street level' officials collect the bribes and share them with their superiors. These may start as pay-offs to secure the silence of the superiors but may become institutionalised. In the top-down version, it is the corrupt superiors who buy the silence of their subordinates by sharing the spoils. But there need not be complicity. Bureaucrats may simply be at the mercy of the politicians or senior officials and forced to do their bidding without sharing in the spoils. These situations are likely to arise, for example, in those countries where corruption has become entrenched. Once corruption has taken root, it is difficult to eradicate. It is a vicious circle emphasising the fact that 'corruption is a contagious phenomenon'.[70] As an accepted way of doing business, it may become entrenched as a cultural necessity with the consequent desire of all participants to conform.[71] Once the incentive for small-time corruption at the level of agent has been created, it has a tendency to develop further up the hierarchy through 'self-interested complicity'[72] and for increasingly higher stakes. The higher the rank of the official involved, the higher the pay-off and the more interactive it becomes, the greater the risk that the practice of corruption becomes entrenched and systemic. The result is an environment in which corruption becomes accepted and regulated by a complex series of relationships of patronage and mutual dependency between suppliers, procurement agents and their superiors, and which is extremely difficult to unravel.[73] Corruption has become systemic.

From a regulatory perspective, agency theory, which suggests that greater regulatory controls be placed on the agents (by principled principals), becomes useless as an analytical tool since there will simply be no actors willing to monitor and punish corrupt behaviour.[74] Evidence suggests,[75] nonetheless, that agents (procurement officers), far from fearing the introduction and enforcement of robust procurement regulations, welcome them as a means of providing a shield against higher level civil servants or politicians seeking to influence procurement decisions, ie when faced with calls to award contracts to certain bidders, the agents are able to point to procurement rules which require them to follow and apply transparent procedures guaranteeing

[67] TS Aidt, 'Economic Analysis of Corruption: A Survey' (2003) 113:491 *The Economic Journal* F632, F635.

[68] See Rose-Ackerman (n 12); J Andvig and Fjeldstad et al, *Corruption: A Review* (n 57).

[69] S Rose-Ackerman (n 25) 82.

[70] O Cadot, 'Corruption as a Gamble' (1987) 33 *Journal of Public Economics* 223, 239.

[71] A Antoci and P Sacco, 'A Public Contracting Evolutionary Game with Corruption' (1995) 61 *Journal of Economics* 89.

[72] A phrase borrowed from Cadot 'Corruption' (n 70) 239.

[73] Trepte (n 1) 9.

[74] Persson, Rothstein and Teorell, 'Why Anticorruption Reforms Fail' (n 66) 452; Andvig and Fjelstad et al (n 57).

[75] From interviews conducted by the author for an Asian Development Bank project in 2011 (Impact Assessment of Procurement Reforms, TA-6317, unpublished).

objectivity and non-biased award decisions. There is thus likely to be a practical benefit in imposing procurement rules, even where the problem lies not with the agent but with the principal. On the other hand, the strength of that shield will clearly depend not only on the 'corruptness' of the superior (ie on how unprincipled the principal is) but also on the power of the superior and on the security of the agent's employment. Faced with a choice between making a poor procurement decision (to the benefit of a superior officer) and losing his job and means of supporting his family, the agent may well opt to comply with his instructions. Where there are penalties imposed on the agent for non-compliance with the procurement rules,[76] his decision may need to take account of the costs and benefits of paying the penalty (for non-compliance) and losing his job (for failing to follow his superior's instructions), although it may also be the case that the superior has means of protecting the agent in the event of detection. The superior escapes penalty in any event since, formally, he is probably not implicated in the formal decision-making process covered by the procurement rules. Increasing the penalties imposed on the agent for failing to comply with the procurement rules places the agent in an invidious position but does nothing to punish the superior whose only challenge remains finding the next scapegoat.

Recent research[77] suggests that the weakness of stronger regulation is reflected in reality. In an empirical study conducted in Hungary investigating corruption risk associated with the expenditure of EU funds, the authors found that even though public procurement using EU funds faces considerably more stringent regulation than domestic law, their use posed much greater corruption risks when compared with procurement using domestic funds. The large-scale institutionalised corruption that was identified in the study typically did not operate between lower level bureaucrats and private individuals but, rather, through contractual relationships which benefit the highest echelons of the political and business elite. Thus the higher officials (essentially the political principals) were able to evade the procurement regulations designed to constrain the corrupt activities of the agents. This provides a good example of how stringent procurement rules designed to curb the agent are redundant when faced with unprincipled principals.

'Corruption', in the broad sense, may arise between principal and agent even in the absence of any explicit lack of principle on the part of the principal. One of the benefits of relying on the shorthand definition of corruption ('abuse of public office for private gain') is that it allows us to look beyond bribery of the procurement officer as the defining characteristic of corruption. Whilst such bribery may represent the popularly held view of corruption in procurement, it is far from being its only manifestation. This issue goes far beyond the fine distinctions to be made between bribes and facilitation payments or bribes and gifts[78] and raises some fundamental questions on how corruption functions in the context of public procurement.

[76] These appear more and more frequently in the procurement laws of developing countries. The issue is considered further below.

[77] M Fazekas, L King and I Tóth, 'Hidden Depths. The Case of Hungary', ch 6 in A Mungiu-Pippidi and B Rothenstein (eds), *Controlling Corruption in Europe: The Anticorruption Report, Vol 1* (Opladen, Barbara Budrich Publishers, 2013) 74.

[78] On this, see Rose-Ackerman (n 25) ch 6.

The weakness of agency theory and concepts of political corruption are that they focus on the shortcomings of the State and on governance within the State and cannot successfully incorporate other causes of corruption which arise not from the machinery of State but from the country context: the dynamics of local culture, traditions and the political economy.

> Corruption is not simply about rent seeking and economic advantage … The issue needs, for example, to be placed within a wider politico-historical context which looks at the utility of corruption as a means of maintaining power structures and systems of political control in particular national contexts.[79]

Without investigating their historical roots, how are the existence and multiplicity 'of such diverse practices as *baksheesh* in Arab countries, *hongbao* in China, *matabiche* in Central Africa, la *propina* or la *mordida* in Latin America, *pots de vin* in France, and back-handers and graft in the rich Anglo-Saxon countries' to be explained?[80]

Nepotism and patronage are not easily categorised as consequences of the principal/agent paradigm and they are not either, at least not necessarily, a form of political corruption. They may well be, on the other hand, a cultural phenomenon, a tradition, arising out of the political economy of a particular country. In lesser populated economies, the near impossibility of avoiding family and neighbours in the State to business sector gives rise to what we might call favouritism arising from family or tribal ties based on a system of reciprocal obligation and trust, and underpinned by notions of duty, trust and reputation. Take, for example, the far from isolated '*wantok*' (a pidgin word derived from 'one talk', meaning those that speak the same language) system in Papua New Guinea where preferences of all sorts are provided to members of one's *wantok* neighbours. Such practices are common throughout the world and have a strong influence on how bureaucrats respond to their own kin.

That is not to say that corrupt activities are determined exclusively by culture, ie that corrupt activities are somehow considered to be legitimate. Rothstein,[81] citing others,[82] states that 'ordinary people in severely corrupt systems usually do not internalize corrupt practices as morally legitimate acts. Instead, they usually condemn corruption as morally wrong and put the blame on "the system" for forcing them to take part in corruption'. This is a defining characteristic of collective action.

Where corruption in a society is entrenched or has become systemic either because it is based on political corruption – where the problem arises from complicity between principals and agents or principals and their captors – or because it flows from complex personal, social or tribal relationships, the problem can no longer be characterised as

[79] E Brown and J Cloke, 'Neoliberal Reform, Governance and Corruption in the South: Assessing the International Anti-corruption Crusade' (2004) 36 *Antipode* 272, 290.

[80] E Brown and J Cloke, 'Neoliberal Reform, Governance and Corruption in Central America: Exploring the Nicaraguan Case' (2005) 24 *Political Geography* 601, 609, citing a December 2000 article by P Abramovici in the *Johannesburg Mail*.

[81] B Rothstein, 'Anti-Corruption: The Indirect "Big Bang" Approach' (2011) 18 *Review of International Political Economy* 228, 232.

[82] R Karklins, *The System Made Me Do It: Corruption in Post-Communist Societies* (Armonk, NY, M.E Sharpe, 2005); S Widmalm *Decentralisation, Corruption and Social Capital: from India to the West* (Thousand Oaks, SAGE Publications, 2008).

a principal/agent problem but as one deriving from collective action. Punishing the agent becomes ineffective, first, because it is not the agent that should be the target but, second, the (benevolent) principal who would be expected to control the agent is itself complicit or, indeed, the one and only perpetrator. The political elite often takes the lead in developing and maintaining the corrupt system[83] and such leadership will mostly implicate all of those who operate within the system. As collective action, corruption benefits all of those involved and none has interest in 'rocking the boat'. Even if all are aware of the costs of corruption and the benefits of removing it, the bonds may be too strong and the one that seeks to break out of the web may simply miss out on the spoils while achieving nothing in terms of changing the system. In Rothstein's words: 'who wants to be a sucker?'[84] Since corruption is seen as so widespread, being incorrupt often makes little sense.[85] Marquette likens this to what Bandura calls 'selective moral disengagement' through a 'diffusion of responsibility': 'Where everyone is responsible, no one really feels responsible. Collective action, which provides anonymity, is still another expedient for weakening moral control. Any harm done by a group can always be attributed largely to the behaviour of others'.[86]

VI. Caught (Trapped) in the Crosshairs

Notwithstanding the inability to identify or measure corruption properly or to identify the perpetrators hidden behind the procurement officer, modern procurement regulation continues to focus primarily on the agent and to seek ever stricter means of reducing his ability to benefit from the position which provides him the opportunity to be corrupt. Whilst agency theory may provide a means of understanding how opportunistic corruption might arise in this context (and provide some solutions), it does not provide a similar framework for understanding the workings of political corruption, capture or the consequences of collective action. This does not, however, appear to slow the march of the corruption crusade.

Agency theory does not throw up corruption as the only result of the agency relationship and informational asymmetries. The interests of principal and agent may diverge for other, no less damaging, reasons as well. Principals depend on agents to execute their tasks properly but elected officials do not always know who actually carries out such tasks. That is dependent on the civil service and the quality of the civil servants depends on their recruitment. Procurement rules can regulate the activity of the agents but it cannot regulate the quality of those carrying out the activity. One cannot regulate for competence. In some ways, procurement regulation overcomes part of this problem

[83] M Johnston, *Syndromes of Corruption: Wealth, Power and Democracy* (Cambridge, Cambridge University Press, 2005).

[84] B Rothstein, *Social Traps and the Problems of Trust* (Cambridge, Cambridge University Press, 2005) 4.

[85] H Marquette, '"Finding God" or "Moral Disengagement" in the Fight against Corruption in Developing Countries? Evidence from India and Nigeria' (2012) 32 *Public Administration and Development* 11.

[86] A Bandura, 'Selective Moral Disengagement in the Exercise of Moral Agency' (2002) 31 *Journal of Moral Education* 101, 107.

by setting out what must be done from a procedural point of view so as to minimise potential incompetence on the part of the agent. By controlling the process rather than by defining the outcome, the principals are able to assure compliance without specifying, or even necessarily knowing, what substantive outcome is most in their interest.[87] Poor results may continue but 'bad' procurement is not always the result of bad intentions: it could just be the result of incompetence. Procurement rules may be voluminous and complicated and, especially in developing countries, relatively new. The addition of new tools (electronic procurement) or new trends (social, environmentally friendly and sustainable procurement) make the task of understanding them no less easy. The proliferation of rules (of the donors and MDBs) in addition to national rules cause confusion and create tensions. This adds to a lack of knowledge and competence and is one of the key issues discussed in this book for rendering aid, notably in the context of procurement, less effective.

The government itself is not generally renowned for its efficiency and the absence of a profit motive deprives government of a reliable measure of efficiency.[88] Notwithstanding any lack of probity on his part, the agent may simply become careless for he has no incentive to do otherwise. Equally deleterious is the agent who, far from being careless, strives to meet the public interest. He or she sees it as his or her duty to get the best results; the problem is that the 'best' result in his mind is the best product, almost invariably the more expensive. This leads to 'gold-plating' where there is a danger that contract specifications are overstated and that the government obtains products which are far above what is needed, leading to greater costs. The lack of profit motive is reflected in the desire to provide the highest service regardless of the increased costs of doing so.

It should be added that the agent himself or herself is also at an informational disadvantage. Whilst he or she may have more information concerning the markets and the suppliers than his or her principal, suppliers will also have rather more information – about themselves, each other and the market – than the agent. This raises a further series of issues with which procurement regulation is also concerned[89] and it may be argued that the complementary role of procurement regulation is to assist the procurement agent in overcoming this informational disadvantage through facilitating his search for the information he or she needs (through imposing competition) and not only to prevent the misuse of that information.

It must be recognised that poor procurement is not always the result of a lack of integrity or of nefarious corrupt practices. It may be the result of ignorance, incompetence or government inefficiency, at the very least. Indeed, empirical research appears to support such a view. Bandiera et al[90] conducted an experiment in Italy, analysing purchases of standardised goods by Italian public bodies which could be purchased essentially through a framework agreement operated by a national procurement

[87] MD McCubbins, RG Noll and BR Weingast, 'Administrative Procedures as Instruments of Political Control' (1987) 3 *Journal of Law, Economics and Organization* 243, 244.
[88] Trepte (n 10) 77.
[89] ibid 85.
[90] O Bandiera, A Prat and T Valletti, 'Active and Passive Waste in Government Spending: Evidence from a Policy Experiment' (2009) 99 *American Economic Review* 1278.

agency or independently, where at given periods of time those products were not available on the framework due to the different start and end dates of agreements covering each of the products. The objective was to investigate whether differences in prices were the result of 'active waste' (defined as waste that entails direct or indirect benefit for the public decision-maker, eg through corruption, whereby the public official inflates the price paid for a certain good in exchange for a bribe) or 'passive waste' (defined as waste whose presence does not benefit the public decision-maker and deriving from a variety of sources, eg an absence of skills to minimise costs or a lack of incentive to minimise costs). They postulated that, on the basis that active waste was eliminated in the central framework agreement, any difference in the prices achieved when a central framework agreement was not operational would be a function of: (i) the propensity of the specific public body to engage in active waste, and (ii) the ability of the public body to avoid passive waste. When, on the other hand, a central framework agreement was operational, the probability that a public body buys from a central framework is a decreasing function of active waste, but an increasing function of passive waste. Following analysis of a dataset covering 21 generic goods purchased by 208 public bodies between 2000 and 2005, the authors found that their results

> were consistent with the hypothesis that, in aggregate, most waste in the procurement of generic goods by the Italian public sector is not due to corruption but to inefficiency. Our results do not in any way imply that corruption is not an important issue in public procurement in Italy. They just indicate that passive waste seems to have an even larger effect.[91]

Another possible cause of passive waste identified by Bandiera et al consists in the excessive regulatory burden that may make procurement cumbersome and increase the average price that the public body pays. Kelman's seminal work based on a study of government procurement of computer technology[92], clearly demonstrates the dangers of applying strict rules inappropriately: '[i]n an environment too complex to be reducible to simple rules or in one that changes more rapidly than the rules can be changed, a decision-making system that depends on rules invites disaster'. The risk of imposing 'regulatory handcuffs'[93] on procurement officers is that eager reformers run the risk of developing regulations which do not limit themselves to reducing the opportunities for corruption but go further by imposing regulations which eliminate any possibility for the procurement agent to exercise his or her discretion. Whilst the possession of discretion provides an opportunity for corruption, it is only the *abuse* of that discretion that may amount to corruption. The possession and proper use of discretion is the very function of the competent procurement officer. Anechiarico and Jacobs also maintain that it is possible for an overzealous anti-corruption campaign to have negative effects for public administration:

> the anti-corruption machinery has had profound, complicating, and often negative implications for the organization and operation of public administration. It constrains decision makers' discretion, shapes priorities, and causes delays that undermine efficiency. The irony

[91] ibid 1281.

[92] S Kelman, *Procurement and Public Management: the Fear of Discretion and the Quality of Government Performance* (Washington DC, AEI Press, 1990) 88.

[93] Trepte (n 10) 104.

> of corruption control is that the more anticorruption machinery we create, the more we create bureaucratic pathology and red tape. In essence, both corruption and corruption control contribute to the contemporary crisis in public administration.[94]

The effect of misguided regulation is everywhere to be seen: in the fear of procurement officers to take decisions without hierarchical approval; in the focus in processing expenditure rather than in exploring needs and defining outcomes; in the application of lowest cost awards as opposed to best value award; in fear of auditors who favour cost reduction at the expense of quality; in blind adherence to compliance rather than achieving competence. As Kenny remarked bluntly:

> If corruption is a cancer, the chemotherapy of ring fencing – special procurement rules and financial procedures with heavy donor oversight – may in some cases be worse than the disease. As important, there is limited evidence that it kills the cancer cells.[95]

Removing discretion, rather than curbing the abuse of that discretion, is tantamount to reducing procurement to a clerical function which is a notion that runs counter to all procurement reform initiatives aimed at making aid effective. Reformers in the developing world are seeking to emulate the procurement professions of (some of) the developed world by seeking to create a cadre of professional procurement officers with the skill, training and experience to conduct efficient and professional procurement. But reducing the procurement function to a mechanical application of rules negates such an attempt and often results in a complete lack of necessary discretion on the part of the agent. The result is likely to be a series of 'bad' procurement decisions devoid of any judgement or skill on the part of the officer and yet, this is exactly what is needed if procurement is to be become more effective.[96] Whilst it is important, especially where rules are new or amended, to provide training which focuses on compliance with regulatory rules, this focus often ignores issues related to the quality of procurement, which requires more than simply compliance. It also requires greater competence, in the sense that optimum results will be achieved by procurement officers with the requisite skills, knowledge and experience, as well as the ability to use the procurement tools made available by the applicable legal framework. Concentrating on competence training as a means of enhancing the capacity of procurement officers to carry out procurement efficiently and effectively will elevate procurement above the clerical function it is sometimes considered to be and emphasise the professionalism needed to achieve positive outcomes.[97]

One rather pernicious and unfortunate fallout of anti-corruption zealotry is the growing trend in developing countries to impose financial penalties (and incarceration) on procurement officers (but no other civil servants) for a failure to comply with procurement rules. To be clear, these are not penalties imposed for having carried out

[94] Anechiarico and Jacobs (n 19) xv.

[95] C Kenny, *Results not Receipts: Counting the Right Things in Aid and Corruption* (Washington DC, Center for Global Development, 2017) 88.

[96] See eg ch 15, where Gutman argues for greater technical expertise for higher quality outcomes and ch 11, where Meyer argues for improved professionalisation.

[97] P Trepte, 'Building Sustainable Capacity in Public Procurement', ch 12 in S Arrowsmith and R Anderson (eds), *The WTO Regime on Government Procurement* (Cambridge, Cambridge University Press, 2011) 377.

corrupt activities. Those criminal offences are usually dealt with explicitly and referred to the relevant authorities. They are not linked to the payment of compensation to tenderers. They are imposed directly on government entities or, more often than not, on individual procurement officers. Since those officers are also generally subject to the disciplinary rules applicable to civil servants, they would apply in addition. No, these are administrative penalties imposed for failing to follow the rules, for misunderstanding the novel procurement rules which are barely understood by those drafting them either and for which the procurement officer is poorly equipped in terms of training (especially given the problems caused by rotation in the civil services). They are effectively imposed for lack of competence. It is difficult to see any justification.

If a penalty is imposed on the procuring entity, for example, the fine itself is paid to another government entity (or government-funded entity such as a court). This may be an effective way of financing other government entities but it is merely a mechanism for moving money around the government. The result of such a fine on the procuring entity could, however, be disastrous. Given that procurement budgets are generally granted based on estimates which are then reduced by appropriations committees or parliament, it may be that after paying the fine there is no longer sufficient budget to proceed with the procurement as planned or at all. No doubt the procuring entity would wish to avoid this, if only to maintain its budget for the following year[98] but the only people who are really harmed by this are the public who may have been expecting, for example, the construction of a new hospital.

Where fines are imposed on the procurement officer then there may also be more generalised negative consequences. The possibility will certainly act as a disincentive to take on the position of procurement officer (especially where other civil servants are not subject to the same dangers), will certainly discourage any risk taking (in the form of exercising discretion), and could impede the creation of a professional procurement cadre: it is curious that, notably in reform countries, where new rules are introduced, where capacity is low, where training is generally insufficient, where precious little advice is given, where procurement officers are not offered increased salaries or conditions of employment, they should then be fined for making mistakes, fines which may often be greater than their monthly or even annual salaries.

Such penalties would not operate to prevent corruption since acts of corruption attract their own and different penalties and courses of action. They operate only to intimidate procurement officers and discourage recruitment and the development of competence in procurement.

Despite the obvious shortcomings of reliance on agency theory as the sole basis for procurement regulation designed primarily to combat corruption, there appears to be little change in the solutions proposed by members of the donor community and few indications that the approach is working.[99] They continue to rely on incremental

[98] Which, following the perverse logic of government financing, may now need to be increased.

[99] In a survey conducted among Norwegian business leaders with significant experience from international trade Søreide concluded that the impact of rules on the challenge of corruption has regularly been overestimated. 55% of the survey respondents did not think tender rules could prevent corruption and only 6% considered them an efficient obstacle to corruption: T Søreide, 'Grey Zones and Corruption in Public Procurement: Issues for Consideration', ch 6 in OECD, *Fighting Corruption and Promoting Integrity in*

institution-strengthening as a means of improving governance even though, as explained above, it is often the very people that are expected to guarantee institutional strength who are the main culprits. The principals may be in the best position to institute anti-corruption policies but they may also be the ones who stand most to gain from the corrupt system. As Johnston commented in 2005: 'Calls for "political will" in countries whose leaders rule with impunity look increasingly like a bad joke'.[100] Whilst donors, notably the MDBs (see chapters 12 and 13, are moving to a more flexible and contextualised approach striving for value for money, their recent change of heart is far removed from the big bang approach envisioned by Rothstein[101] as the solution to the problem of collective action. In the case of anti-corruption policy, the solutions continue to rely on incrementalism and the gradual improvement of the institutions.[102] The instruments of change are formalistic and technocratic.

VII. Targeting the Bribe Givers

The focus on corrupt actions, and notably on bribes as the foremost example of such actions, leads to other possibilities for challenge. A new'ish favourite[103] in the anti-corruption arsenal consists in targeting and punishing those who offer or pay bribes to government officials by way of a process of debarment, ie by barring bidders, usually temporarily, from participation in contract award procedures where they have been found guilty (or in some cases merely suspected)[104] of bribe giving (among other things[105]). There is no doubt that this brings a glow of satisfaction to those who catch out wayward bidders but the mechanism is not without its problems, even assuming that we are in the presence of principled principals unconcerned with protecting bribe takers.

The difficulty of defining corruption, explained above, applies equally to the individual crimes defined in legislation that make up the general concept of corruption. Notwithstanding the nature of bribes as extending beyond mere cash payments (making them hard to discover and prosecute), it is noteworthy that, in anti-corruption legislation, bribery is conceived primarily, but not exclusively by any means,[106] as a crime

Public Procurement (Paris, OECD Publishing, 2005) 51, 55, available at www.oecd-ilibrary.org/governance/fighting-corruption-and-promoting-integrity-in-public-procurement_9789264014008-en.

[100] Johnston, *Syndromes of Corruption* (n 83) 184.

[101] Rothstein, 'Anti-Corruption' (n 81).

[102] An approach recommended by Johnston (n 83).

[103] Debarment is not a new phenomenon but is one which appears to have been resurrected only recently: S Schooner, 'The Paper Tiger Stirs: Rethinking Suspension and Debarment' (2004) 13 *Public Procurement Law Review* 211.

[104] S White (ed), *Procurement and Organised Crime: an EU-wide Study* (London, IALS, 2000) 8, which indicates that, at least in some European countries, suspicion is (or was, at the time of writing) sufficient.

[105] See eg C Swan and B Manka, 'Risky Business: Does Debarring Poor Performers Mitigate Future Performance Risk?' Third International Conference on Public Procurement Law Africa, organised by the African Procurement Law Unit at Stellenbosch University (1–2 November 2018) available at http://ssrn.com/abstract=3287348.

[106] There are many, and an increasing number, of high-profile prosecutions of bribe takers also.

perpetrated by the bribe giver.[107] Not all legislative acts dealing with bribery cover bribe takers,[108] ie those receiving bribes, and even those that do,[109] generally describe it as *passive* as opposed to *active* bribery suggesting that, in some way, the action and thus the consequent crime flows in one direction only and that the bribe taker is in some way a (rather fortunate) bystander. The focus of debarment, of course, is necessarily only on the bribe giver and little attention is given to the bribe taker. In considering debarment mechanisms, we sometimes appear to be facing a victimless crime. Under the FCPA, for example, Tillipman points out that, since the crime consists in the active giving or offering of a bribe, 'FCPA liability may attach even if the corrupt act does not succeed in its purpose'.[110] This focus on only one side of the equation is evident in many jurisdictions, including in the efforts of the World Bank, one of the prime movers in the field of debarment in the world of development aid.

This may be illustrated by a relatively recent speech given by the then Vice President for Integrity at the World Bank, Leonard McCarthy.[111] In his speech, McCarthy explained that

> [a] few years ago we received an allegation from a losing bidder on a World Bank-financed project who complained that a government project official made a 'pay-to-play' demand[112] … It turns out the man who solicited the bribe had dealings with other companies who had paid him far more substantial amounts to win contracts. In the end, the World Bank debarred five suppliers from Europe and Africa for a combined total of more than 15 years. Two additional suppliers from Asia, one of whom was acting as an agent seeking 5% of the contract value, are also facing sanctions proceedings.

What is interesting from the perspective of this chapter is that the speech discussed action against seven bidders but made no further mention of the man who solicited the bribes – clearly the common denominator and, probably, initiator of all the bribes in question. This is not to suggest that no action was taken; only that it is not mentioned. But therein lies the problem. The main function of the Bank's Integrity Vice Presidency (INT) is to identify and prosecute bidders, ie the bribe givers, but not the bribe takers. Indeed, it has no jurisdiction to prosecute public officials in borrowing member countries, even were it to hold evidence of bribe taking on their part. Action against bribe

[107] It is perhaps curious that, in surveys of perception, the questions appear to be framed in terms of bribe takers rather than bribe givers, the implicit suggestion being that bribes are paid only when required, rather than that they may be used proactively as a means to secure contracts: Andersson and Heywood (n 29) 753.

[108] See eg OECD Convention on Combatting Bribery of Foreign Officials in International Business Transactions (1997), the US' Foreign Corrupt Practices Act 1977 (FCPA): 15 U.S.C. § 78dd-1 ff.

[109] See eg the UK's Bribery Act 2010 (s 2); the United Nations Convention against Corruption (UNCAC) in art 15(b). In the case of the UK's Bribery Act 2010, the Guidance issued in 2011 by the UK Ministry of Justice is largely silent on the issue of passive bribery although it is referred to in passing: www.justice.gov.uk/downloads/legislation/bribery-act-2010-guidance.pdf.

[110] J Tillipman, 'Foreign Corrupt Practices Act Fundamentals', *Briefing Papers*, No 08-10 (Thomson Reuters/West, September 2008) 5.

[111] Keynote Address by Leonard McCarthy: 'The Dawning of New Era in Anti-Corruption Enforcement' at the 2nd Annual Global Anti-Corruption & Compliance Summit, Amsterdam, Netherlands (6 April 2017) available at www.worldbank.org/en/news/speech/2017/04/06/keynote-address-by-leonard-mccarthy-the-dawning-of-a-new-era-in-anti-corruption-enforcement.print.

[112] The important point being made in the speech was that the bribe in question was very small but that by investigating this bribe, further and higher bribes were detected.

takers, if any, is taken elsewhere.[113] A search of INT's website[114] and of its Annual Reports[115] reveals little or no data on measures or actions taken by the World Bank or other institution (national or otherwise) against bribe takers.[116] The data available on these websites present only one side of the picture. The other half of the story is missing. At best, this is just a question of balance and could be remedied by better or more coordinated reporting of *all* the results of bribery cases, both for bribe givers and bribe takers.[117] At worst, it is evidence that some of the symptoms of bribery are being treated with gusto but that the root causes are being ignored. The shotgun of choice appears to be single barrelled. Maybe the self-styled corruption 'hunters' supported by the World Bank should consider the advice of Wikipedia, viz that 'Single-barrel shotguns have always been popular as an inexpensive alternative to double-barrelled shotguns ... [but] [t]hey are not widely used in shotgun sports, as most events require the ability to quickly fire two successive shots'.[118]

It would be unfair and inaccurate, however, to suggest that the World Bank and other donors are not concerned with bribe takers. In the same speech, McCarthy also stated that he

> would be remiss if [he] didn't point out that the private sector is just one part of the equation. Governments need to uphold the rule of law, ensure their institutions function properly and provide for the well-being of their citizens.[119]

This also illustrates the problem with tackling bribe takers. They are generally part of the government administration and responsibility for their actions rests with those governments, ie it becomes a problem for the governments that receive the funds. We have discussed above the likelihood (or not) of action by governments in situations of collective action where corruption has become entrenched. But from the Bank's point of view, it also means that, in some cases, the bribe takers may be senior members of the government and simultaneously the interlocutors of the donors. They are not only interlocutors, of course, but the 'owners' of the Bank and executive directors of the member countries sit on the board that approves the very loans that give rise to the opportunities for bribery. This then ostensibly makes tackling the issue a very political one. That is not to say that the Bank has not tried to tackle the issue.

Though making earlier appearances in Bank reports,[120] the fight against corruption became a particular focus of the Bank under the presidency of James Wolfensohn,

[113] And action is sometimes taken, often in a dramatic way: see the *Lava Jato* case referred to in n 58. The publicity surrounding the affair was intense and gives the impression that a large coordinated war is being waged against bribe takers. However, this is one of only a few examples that have entered the public consciousness and is conspicuous more by its novelty than by its frequency.

[114] www.worldbank.org/en/about/unit/integrity-vice-presidency.

[115] Available on the website.

[116] The same is true in the case of other MDBs which have similar mandates.

[117] Assuming that some action is actually taken against bribe takers.

[118] en.wikipedia.org/wiki/Single-shot.

[119] Above, n 111.

[120] R Agarwala, R Heaver, D Lallement, G Lamb, P Landell-Mills, S Ozgediz and M Shirley, *World Development Report 1983 – World Economic Recession and Prospects for Recovery; Management in Development; World Development Indicators* (Oxford, Oxford University Press – Published for The World Bank, 1983).

notably in his 'cancer of corruption' speech[121] and articulated in a 1997 policy document.[122] It took a mainly holistic approach seeking to strengthen governance and public sector management, to improve economic policies and legal/judicial systems, and to develop and implement specific anti-corruption measures. Crucially, it also suggested that it would 'take corruption into account more explicitly in its decisions on country operations'.[123] In 1997, Wolfensohn went so far as to say that 'If a government is unwilling to take action despite the fact that the country's development objectives are undermined by corruption, then the Bank Group *must* curtail its level of support to that country'.[124] Whilst this overall approach was criticised as leading to the fight against corruption being seen as an end unto itself, thus compromising the Bank's broader public sector reform agenda, it was the more crusading aspects of a subsequent President, Paul Wolfowitz, which attracted more ire, notably in respect of his tendency to withdraw or suspend loans to countries considered to be corrupt.[125] Apart from undermining the country's immediate ability to meet the challenges for which the loan was intended (eg health, poverty reduction, etc), this approach could also run the risk of 'labelling' countries as corrupt and thus undermining their attractiveness as recipients of aid. This recalls one of the problems identified with the use of Transparency International's CPI which may also lead to such labelling, causing what Andersson and Heywood have called the 'corruption trap'.[126]

In some ways, the World Bank's approach to fighting corruption may have become a victim of this history. The political dimension of fighting corruption when the subject of the actions taken is the country itself, ie where funds are withheld if the country in which the project is located is regarded as corrupt, means that those actions become too sensitive, if not impossible, to take. The Bank's Articles of Agreement[127] prevent overtly political actions, and challenging countries and their governments directly may be seen as overstepping the mark. As the 1997 policy document itself recognised,

> corruption can be addressed by Bank staff as an economic concern within the framework already approved by the Board for governance issues. This framework provides scope for the Bank to help countries by advising on economic policy reform and strengthening institutional capacity. However, the Bank's mandate does not extend to the political aspects of controlling corruption ... So while the Bank's mandate provides scope for the institution to help countries control corruption, it shapes the way in which the Bank may respond.[128]

Whether as a direct result of these events or not, the activities of the Bank have tended to concentrate on these governance and institutional issues. In the case of procurement,

[121] 'Annual Meetings Address by James D. Wolfensohn' (n 17).

[122] World Bank, 'Helping Countries Combat Corruption' (n 17).

[123] ibid 51.

[124] World Bank Group, Board of Governors, 1997 Annual Meetings, Hong Kong, China, 'Address by James D. Wolfensohn to the Board of Governors of the World Bank Group, at the Joint Annual Discussion' (Press Release No 4, 23–25 September 1997) 9. Full text available at www.imf.org/external/am/speeches/pdf/pr04e.pdf.

[125] H Marquette, 'The World Bank's Fight against Corruption' (2007) 13(2) *Brown Journal of World Affairs* 27, 31.

[126] Andersson and Heywood (n 29) 760.

[127] Art IV, s 10 of the IBRD Articles of Agreement.

[128] World Bank, 'Helping Countries Combat Corruption' (n 17) 25.

this led to the strengthening of the Procurement Guidelines,[129] the creation of INT and the enforcement of the Bank's integrity provisions, primarily in the context of debarment.[130] As we have seen, these actions address bribe givers, not bribe takers. It might even be considered naïve to believe that, as banks, the MDBs would be prepared to take action against their own customers (and owners), especially given the overwhelming need to ensure disbursement to achieve development goals.[131] When it comes to tackling bribe takers, the MDBs' (and donors') approach becomes decidedly more general and imprecise. One assumes that if bribery has been detected in a debarment case,[132] there must also be some evidence of who received the bribe.[133] As indicated above, however, no data is provided on the fate of the bribe taker in debarment cases. In respect of misprocurement cases,[134] the ultimate sanction available to the MDBs against borrowers where corruption has been discovered in their projects, the same is true; there is no or very little *publicly* available information on the level and incidence of misprocurement, although it has clearly been declared on occasion.

Rather, efforts are concentrated on improving more general measures such as financial disclosure, detecting illicit financial flows (IFF) and tax evasion. Whilst countries will receive financial support in implementing their own anti-corruption mechanisms, it is up to them to design and implement the measures taken and there are a number of international agreements and conventions which seek to provide models for the introduction and enforcement of anti-corruption tools.[135] Ultimately, the success of such measures will also depend on the willingness of countries to prosecute wrongdoers and the existence of principled principals. Despite some high-profile examples of success in prosecuting politicians and senior officials,[136] these appear to be the exception rather than the rule.

The positive effect of concentrating on bribe givers is clear for all to see and 'contractor-bashing' as a motivation for debarment is clearly gaining traction in some jurisdictions.[137] It is likely also to embarrass the countries in which bribery has

[129] Now 'Procurement Regulations' (2016, revised 2017 and 2018); see n 28.

[130] P Dubois, P Ezzeddin and CD Swan, 'Suspension and Debarment on the International Stage: Experiences in the World Bank's Sanctions System' (2016) 25 *Public Procurement Law Review* 61.

[131] Marquette, 'The World Bank's Fight against Corruption' (n 125) 33. See also CE Weaver, 'Reforming the World Bank: Promises and Pitfalls' (2007) 13(2) *Brown Journal of World Affairs* 55.

[132] Even if the burden of proof is reduced to a civil ('balance of probabilities') rather than criminal one ('beyond reasonable doubt') – World Bank, 'Procedure: Bank Procedure: Sanctions Proceedings and Settlements in Bank Financed Projects' (Catalogue No MDCAO6.03-PROC.106, issued 28 June 2016, effective 1 July 2016) s 8.02, available at http://siteresources.worldbank.org/EXTOFFEVASUS/Resources/3601045-1377105390925/Procedure_Bank_Procedure_Sanctions_Proceedings_and_Settlements_in_Bank_Financed_Projects(6.28.2016).pdf.

[133] This is clear from McCarthy (n 111). Of course, the person receiving the bribe in the first instance may not be the ultimate beneficiary but that is a further complication, not a reason to ignore the recipient.

[134] Which would be accompanied by loan cancellation, suspension or acceleration. For a description of the possibilities, see S Williams-Elegbe, *Public Procurement and Multilateral Development Banks: Law, Practice and Problems* (Oxford, Hart Publishing, 2017) 200.

[135] See eg S Williams and A Eyo, 'Fighting Corruption in Public Procurement through the OECD: a Review of Recent Initiatives' (2009) 3 *Public Procurement Law Review* NA103-113.

[136] *cf* the *Lava Jato* (n 58).

[137] J Tillipman, 'The Congressional War on Contractors' (2013) 45 *George Washington International Law Review* 235.

taken hold. As a deterrent or punishment,[138] counting scalps sends a clear message to potential perpetrators and signifies success, at least in terms of the number of prosecutions. Whether that success extends to reducing or eradicating corruption is less certain.

The approach seems to be to dry up the supply of bribes in the hope that the demand will disappear. In other sectors of the economy, a limited supply generally has the opposite effect, of increasing demand, and, therefore, prices, ie what people are willing to pay or, in other words, the desirability of the objective. If the same supply conditions prevail throughout a given market, it is arguable that there could be an effect on the demand side. However, where conditions are not the same (eg where different anti-bribery laws apply to bidders in different countries), the effect is likely to be to move supply to those countries where it can continue with less risk, on the premise that corruption is a game of risk which diminishes as the threat of detection or prosecution increases.[139]

There are some real concerns with the approach that focuses only on bribe givers. It assumes not only that the bribe taker is some sort of jejune recipient but that the bribe giver in some way needs to pay the bribe in order to win the contract. In other words that, without the bribe, he would lose the contract. Whilst that may be true in many cases, it is also untrue in many others. It is not only incompetent bidders who may be tempted to bribe.[140] Even where the bidder is certain of his ability to execute the contract on the best terms, he may be tempted to offer bribes in circumstances where it is known that the only means of obtaining any contract is by way of bribe. The bidder will be prepared to do whatever it takes to win the contract,[141] even if he would have won the contract absent the corruption. Indeed, he may be the best placed to win the contract since, arguably, the most efficient firm will win the bid because of its ability to manipulate its higher profit margin to offer the highest bribe.[142]

In other cases, the 'bribe' is little more than a transaction cost in the sense that payment is due to the purchaser by any successful bidder, ie payment is made by the successful bidder (sometimes after the event), *whether or not* it would have won the contract without the bribe. In Indonesia, this type of payment is so common that it has a name: *traktir* (literally, a 'treat').[143] It is a gift for having been given the contract and it is understood and accepted as such. It is not given by incompetent bidders who would otherwise lose the contract; it is paid by the best bidders who have successfully won the contract by means otherwise fair and square. As such, it is perfectly possible that, even where a bribe is paid, the 'best' bidder will still win the bid since whoever wins will be forced to pay the bribe. In situations such as these, catching and blacklisting individual

[138] A distinction that lies at the heart of defining the purpose of debarment.

[139] *cf* Cadot, 'Corruption as a Gamble' (n 70).

[140] Trepte (n 10) 74.

[141] PJ Beck and MW Maher, 'A Comparison of Bribery and Bidding in Thin Markets' (1986) 20 *Economics Letters* 1.

[142] ibid.

[143] Interestingly, such a payment also makes an appearance in the UK's Bribery Act 2010: where, in s 2(4) Case 5, 'R requests, agrees to receive or accepts a financial or other advantage *as a reward* for the improper performance (whether by R or another person) of a relevant function or activity' (emphasis added).

bidders (the most incompetent ones in concealing their activities) will merely remove one or more bidders from the equation and possibly deprive the purchaser of the most efficient or 'best' bidder. At the same time, it is unlikely that this would have any effect at all on the system which creates the incentive to bribe, viz the requirement that bribes will always be paid. In such a situation, the satisfaction of knowing that a payer of bribes has been caught out does nothing to eradicate the systemic corruption and may even divert attention from its continuing existence.

There are some additional consequences. In smaller developing economies or even in economies, developing or otherwise, which are hard to reach (geographically), removing just one or two bidders is likely to reduce the pool of bidders to the detriment of the government purchaser. Where the 'bribe' is real, in the sense that it was paid by an incompetent bidder in order to win a contract it would otherwise have lost, this may serve to protect the government. Where, however, the bribe is some form of transaction cost as described above, the effect is to reduce choice and competition and provides little benefit. Further, it is known that the effects of debarment can be serious for firms, especially smaller ones, and may lead to a significant loss of business if not bankruptcy,[144] an effect exponentially increased when the effects of the MDBs' cross-debarment (the practice of debarring bidders from project funded by all MDBs once they have been debarred by one of them[145]) are taken into account. Where debarment is the result of a transaction cost, the result of cross-debarment is devastating but the effect on aid effectiveness, whatever the result, is tangible.

The focus on debarment may thus be seen both as a diversion and a distraction. It is a diversion because the emphasis is on numbers caught with success inevitably being measured by how many are caught. It may give the impression that corruption is being reduced but the bribe takers remain. If bribes are a transaction cost, then plenty more will be paid by those not stupid enough to be caught. But if, because of the country context, there are not plenty more bidders to pay the bribe, the supply market will have been weakened. In some countries, that may be fatal.

It is a distraction because debarment and the debarment process upon which it relies becomes an end in itself. The machinery of debarment becomes an exercise in ensuring that, legally, the process is as efficient as possible, creating an industry around the idea of debarment which takes on a life if its own.[146] Perfecting the system obscures the purpose of avoiding corruption[147] and gives way to crusades which deflect attention from that goal.[148] This particular brand of *omphaloskepsis* consists in the over-indulgent contemplation of the procedural rules at the expense of the wider concern with eradicating corruption. Debarment, as with procurement regulation in general is not well served by a one-size-fits-all approach. It also calls for greater sophistication.

[144] See eg J Tillipman, *The Foreign Corrupt Practices Act & Government Contractors: Compliance Trends & Collateral Consequences*, Briefing Papers (Aug 2011) available at https://papers.ssrn.com/sol3/papers.cfm?abstract_id=1924333.

[145] Information on the MDBs' agreement on cross-debarment is available at http://lnadbg4.adb.org/oai001p.nsf/.

[146] The extent of this industry is illustrated by S Williams-Elegbe, *Fighting Corruption in Public Procurement: A Comparative Analysis of Disqualification or Debarment Measures* (Oxford, Hart Publishing, 2012), but this is also only a relatively small part of that industry which has proponents in most countries.

[147] There are other purposes, of course, such as punishing fraud, misrepresentation and poor contractor performance.

[148] Tillipman, 'The Congressional War on Contractors' (n 137).

VIII. Concluding Remarks

From an aid effectiveness perspective, the incorporation of anti-corruption measures into public procurement regulation has slotted very conveniently into the good governance agenda implying, as it does, stricter, more robust rules to control the actions of corrupt procurement officers. There is little doubt that this mechanism addresses opportunistic corruption by reducing the opportunities for corrupt practices and increasing the likelihood of detection but it is a very blunt instrument in the face of corrupt practices which are not directly affected by the procurement process itself, viz those that do not emerge from a direct misapplication of the rules, that are carried out independently of the procurement process or that are perpetrated by persons other than the procurement officer. The very difficulty in providing a compelling definition of corruption means that many forms of corruption are simply not addressed within this framework.

Despite continuing attempts to quantify the problem, there is little in the way of precise evidence in respect of corruption within the procurement context. There also appears to be an assumption that all poor procurement is the result of corruption, even where much of it can be more properly traced to incompetence or inefficiency. There may be specific studies which reveal corrupt practices in given situations but these tend to be very case specific and the results cannot be extrapolated further. There is much more in the way of perception measurement and analogy, so that, faced with the multiple forms of corruption, it is not at all clear what precisely is being measured. Similarly, there is little or no evidence that any of the measures adopted in the anti-corruption crusade have reduced corruption; indeed, it may be that there has been no change. That is not to say that corruption does not exist in the procurement context; such a conclusion would be highly unlikely. Nevertheless, we have to admit that we do not know what we are measuring and so cannot identify how much corruption there actually is, where it arises or how well it is being addressed through the approaches taken to date. Given this lack of solid foundation, those approaches should themselves be subject to serious scrutiny, for fear of making matters worse.

Perhaps the most glaring shortcoming of agency theory which underpins the good governance agenda in the case of procurement is its failure to reveal the true identity of the corrupt. It assumes that the perpetrator is the procurement officer, as agent, but by focusing on the procurement officer, sight is lost of other actors, notably the politicians and senior government officials who are either the 'victims' of State capture or the primary actors of corrupt practices. After all, it is rarely the procurement officer that has a Swiss bank account or villa in the south of France. Such luxuries are the spoils amassed by the kleptocrats at the very top of government. The theory also fails to recognise the complex relationships that generate systemic corruption based on collective action which deprives most of the tools employed to date of their anti-corruption effects. They are aimed at the wrong targets.

Notwithstanding the opacity of the targets, the traditional approach has been to apply more of the same, in the belief that there is a single solution to a single problem. The favoured mechanisms are increased and stricter forms of regulation which seek to control the corrupt actions of the procurement officer (often the wrong target) but which, at the same time, create regulatory handcuffs which deprive the agent of the ability to perform better, by minimising or removing discretion (rather than only controlling the abuse of that discretion) and reducing the procurement function to a clerical function requiring only compliance with a set of inadequate rules. The anti-corruption crusade, whilst demonstrating no reduction of corruption in procurement, has effectively banished initiatives based on competence, professionalism, performance and value for money. Whereas modern procurement systems seek to improve outcomes, these traditional approaches deprive procurement officers of the flexibility and discretion needed to achieve those outcomes. There is a need to re-think this approach.

The focus on bribes has similarly led to a one-size-fits all approach. The recent appetite for debarment as a means of curbing bribery focuses mainly on the bribe giver, for the most part ignoring the other participant in any bribery equation, the bribe taker. This is so, even where the bribe taker takes the initiative, a particular problem in the face of unprincipled principals, where bribes are not mechanisms to obtain contracts by poor performers, where they have become transaction costs paid by any successful bidder or where they are culturally expected. Whereas the scalp counting that ensues will gratify anti-corruption zealots, corruption will not always have been reduced but bidders and procurement markets, especially in lesser developed countries, may be badly affected to the detriment of the public purchaser.

Whilst this all suggests that we need to take a more intelligent approach to the means of addressing corruption in procurement, it is also clear that the knowledge and understanding we need to do so is lacking. In the absence of a solution based on Rothstein's 'big bang',[149] there is a pressing need to take more account of (country or sector) context and to identify the type of corruption at play. This applies not only to the form of corruption taking place (bribes, more complex forms of subversion, nepotism etc) but also to the identity of the corrupt (procurement agents, senior officials or politicians) and to the extent of corruption (opportunism, systemic etc). This requires data and a lot of it but, without the relevant information, applying the same arsenal is simply likely to miss the target and, at the same time, undermine better procurement. The irony is that a governance-based anti-corruption agenda appears, at least in the procurement context, to have made aid less effective to the extent that better (more efficient and effective) procurement (in terms of better outcomes or value for money) is a measure of that effectiveness.

MDB procurement reform is currently moving in the direction of a more outcomes-based approach[150], at least in the case of some of the MDBs, but the approach to anti-corruption measures in procurement has not changed in line with this new overall tack; the approach remains as it always has been. While the effects of such an approach are likely to be harmful to 'good' procurement even in a compliance-based environment, the effect of such an approach in a competence (or performance or outcomes) based approach is likely significantly to undermine the desired objectives. No matter that the procurement officer is now given the tools to conduct strategic procurement

[149] Rothstein (n 81).
[150] See ch 12 (Yukins and Williams-Elegbe) and ch 15 (Gutman).

effectively, unless he is afforded a real possibility to exercise that new-found flexibility (by his superiors, the politicians, State capturers, his family, his clan, the public etc), corrupt behaviour which is not addressed effectively by those same rules will still find a way of depriving the public purse of the value for money it desires.

To complement this more enlightened approach to procurement reform, there is an urgent need also to upgrade the approach to combating corruption through the procurement process. This needs to be an evidence-based approach and one which identifies the real incidences of corruption in a given context, either at country or sector level. Evidence-based approaches are clearly not unknown[151] but appear, in this context, to have been limited to the measurement of corruption (discussed above) rather than to an identification of the types of corruption being perpetrated. Without a proper diagnosis, the symptoms may well be misinterpreted and the cure all but useless. It will not be an easy task nor a cheap one but the current approach, applying the same remedy to all situations, is demonstrably not working. In each context, evidence needs to be collected and the types of corrupt practices mapped so as to provide a better understanding of where the problem lies and thus enable a set of remedies to be designed that can address those problems. Where corruption can be traced to procurement officers, the traditional approach might suffice; where it is traced to politicians and senior officials then action needs to be taken against those perpetrators outside the procurement regulation at least to the extent that such regulation applies only, as it does in most cases, to the civil servants directly implicated in the procurement process and not to the politically elected principals. Where MDBs are unable to do this, better support needs to be given to borrower countries to allow them to establish and implement appropriate actions provided, of course, that the problem does not lie at the highest level. In such cases, no amount of window dressing is likely to suffice. Despite, for example, the great hopes that many have had for the creation of Anti-Corruption Commissions, they have, with a few notable exceptions, been a disappointment both to the people of developing countries and to their development partners.[152] Where collective action has rendered corruption systemic, then maybe only a wholesale and dramatic change of the system will succeed in changing attitudes. In the case of debarment, where bribe givers are merely responding to the requirements of bribe takers, the latter also need to be brought to account so as not to skew the markets further.

There has never been an easy answer to combating corruption in public procurement and the task will become no easier. But seeking to address a problem which is not correctly identified and whose scope and effects have not been accurately measured

[151] For a recent call for such an approach, see OECD Strategic Approach to Combating Corruption and Promoting Integrity (Paris, 2018) 18, available at www.oecd.org/corruption/OECD-Strategic-Approach-Combating-Corruption-Promoting-Integrity.pdf.

[152] See eg J Heilbrunn, 'Anti-Corruption Commissions Panacea or Real Medicine to Fight Corruption?' (Washington DC, World Bank Institute, 2004); UNDP, 'Institutional Arrangements to Combat Corruption: A Comparative Study' (Thailand, UNDP, 2005) available at http://regionalcentrebangkok.undp.or.th/practices/governance/documents/Corruption_Comparative_Study-200512.pdf; EU Anti-Corruption Report COM(2014) 38 final (03.02.14) available at https://ec.europa.eu/home-affairs/sites/homeaffairs/files/e-library/documents/policies/organized-crime-and-human-trafficking/corruption/docs/acr_2014_en.pdf.

deprives those seeking to remedy the problem of any meaningful weapons with which to tackle the problem effectively. Worse, the pursuit of inappropriate remedies risks undermining the pursuit of better procurement, a goal which is becoming ever more demanding as the focus moves from compliance to improved outcomes. It is time for the anti-corruption agenda to move in line with the procurement agenda and borrow from the MDB reforms so that it too becomes more fit for purpose.

8

Sustainability and Public Procurement

ROBERTO CARANTA AND CAROL CRAVERO*

I. Introduction

It is widely acknowledged that public authorities must act in a transparent and corruption-free way and are accountable to the taxpayers and to society at large when handling public money. It is not just a 'question of matching supply and demand'[1] as it may be for a private procurement. In fact, unlike private sector procurement, 'public procurement is a business process within a political system with distinct consideration of integrity, accountability, national interest and effectiveness'.[2] As a consequence, public entities have to ensure cost-efficiency and best value for money in their purchasing activities. This is generally achieved through an adequate level of competition guaranteeing the respect of non-discrimination and equal treatment among bidders.

However, public procurement has long been a policy tool. For instance, '[u]ntil the recent attempts made through regional procurement agreements and the WTO Government Procurement Agreement (GPA) to restrict discriminatory purchasing, the use of procurement to promote national industrial objectives was an important feature of the procuring policies of most developed countries'.[3] The push to open national procurement market to foreign suppliers goes beyond the GPA and regional agreements or, more recently, bilateral free trade agreements (FTAs). International Competitive Bidding (ICB) has long been the preferred procurement method for multilateral

* Roberto wrote ss III.A, III.B, III.D, III.G and IV, and Carol wrote ss II, III, III.C, III.E and III.F. The Introduction and Conclusions have been written together.

[1] R Roos, *Sustainable Public Procurement. Mainstreaming sustainability criteria in public procurement in developing countries* (Lüneburg, Centre for Sustainability Management – Leuphana Universität Lüneburg, 2012) 1, available at www2.leuphana.de/umanagement/csm/content/nama/downloads/download_publikationen/Roos_Sustainable%20Public%20Procurement.pdf.

[2] WA Wittig, 'Building Value Through Public Procurement: A Focus on Africa' (Ninth International Anti-Corruption Conference, Durban, South Africa, 10–15 October 1999) 3, available at http://9iacc.org.s3-website.eu-central-1.amazonaws.com/papers/day2/ws2/dnld/d2ws2_wwittig.pdf.

[3] S Arrowsmith, J Linarelli and D Wallace Jr, *Regulating Public Procurement: National and International Perspectives* (The Hague, Kluwer Law International, 2000) 238.

development banks (MDBs).[4] In these contexts a preference for price – or for criteria that might easily be translated into price, such as post sale warranties or services – was seen as instrumental to avoid discrimination.

The focus on economic development again led to an economic efficiency rationale for procurement, focused essentially on price. Environmental concerns however soon started getting traction in policy agendas. Public procurement was seen as an important tool to try and address those concerns. More recently, the power of public procurement as a lever has been invoked and at times used to answer to wider sustainability goals.

This chapter considers the evolution, at the international level, of the focus of procurement from economic goals to broader social and environmental goals, taking into account the contribution made to this evolution by the UN's Millennium Development Goals (MDGs) and Sustainable Development Goals (SDGs). In particular the chapter shows how these goals are and can be employed in procurement through the application of environmental and social policies (development, labour, human rights, SMEs, etc).

The purpose of this chapter is to provide an understanding that buying practices are being developed beyond pure economic efficiency. Thus, the notion of sustainable public procurement will first be sketched, linking it to the MDGs and SDGs (section II). The important role played by a number of international organisations, including MDBs, in making public procurement (more) sustainable will then be analysed (in section III). Among the many and different issues that sustainable public procurement (SPP) raises, the question how its benefits, and consequently aid effectiveness, are to be measured, will be briefly addressed (in section IV). Short conclusions will close the chapter also providing a short account of the role SPP can play in a development context (section V).

II. Sustainable Public Procurement (SPP) and the UN Development Goals

Sustainable public procurement (SPP) means somewhat different things in different jurisdictions or institutional environments. The 2017 UNEP (which has recently changed its name to 'UN Environment') research titled *Global Review of Sustainable Public Procurement*[5] states that:

> SPP policies are still most commonly associated with environmental concerns, but a broader scope is progressively being adopted. Public and private procurers increasingly support the

[4] eg World Bank 'Guidelines – Procurement of Goods, Works, and Non-Consulting Services under IBRD Loans and IDA Credits & Grants by World Bank Borrowers' (January 2011, revised July 2014), which were applicable until 1 July 2016, available at http://pubdocs.worldbank.org/en/492221459454433323/Procurement-GuidelinesEnglishJuly12014.pdf.

[5] UN Environment, *Global Review of Sustainable Public Procurement 2017* (United Nations Environment Programme, 2017) IX, available at https://wedocs.unep.org/bitstream/handle/20.500.11822/20919/Global-Review_Sust_Procurement.pdf?sequence=1&isAllowed=y.

> idea that sustainable procurement is about more than just purchasing more environmentally friendly products. Most national governments that participated in this study have SPP commitments that cover both environmental and socio-economic issues. Some governments, particularly in Asia, focus exclusively on environmental issues, and are not yet considering the socio-economic dimension. However, others prioritise an impressive range of socio-economic and ethical issues in addition to focusing on the environment. As in 2013, energy conservation continues to be a top priority globally, along with resource efficiency and climate change mitigation. Among the main socio-economic issue areas, diversity and equality have grown in prominence compared to 2013. This suggests an evolution from a focus on the social issues most closely tied to economic performance, for example employment and business development, towards the inclusion of issues related to human wellbeing and social justice.

This broader definition of sustainable procurement follows to a significant extent the evolution of the concept of development, which over time has been understood and interpreted as encompassing notions that go beyond economic development.[6] It is outside the scope of this chapter to dwell on the concept of development and its evolution, but it suffices here to say that while the concept of development has originally been associated mainly with the *economic* development approach, this approach is no longer sufficient and adequate to encompass the multifaceted nature of development. The disruptive nature of economic development against ecological systems and social stability has highlighted the need to adopt a more holistic approach encompassing human development and environmental protection.[7] Whereas quality of life and subjective well-being are increasingly taken into account as crucial components of development, the concept of development itself has been reshaped towards paying greater attention to social and environmental dimensions. This has led to a new formulation of the concept in terms of sustainable development (SD).

According to the 1987 definition in 'Our Common Future', also known as the 'Brundtland Report', SD is the 'development that meets the needs of the present without

[6] The mainstream concept of measuring development by economic growth has been challenged by, *inter alia*, economist and philosopher Amartya Sen. Inspired by Adam Smith, Karl Marx and Aristotle, A Sen adopted the so-called 'capability approach' under which (i) human life is seen as a set of 'doings and beings' (called 'functionings'), and (ii) the evaluation of the quality of life is related to the assessment of the capability to function. This 'valuational exercise cannot be done by focusing simply on commodities or incomes that help those doings and beings, as in commodity-based accounting of the quality of life'. On the contrary, the focus is on human achievement and freedom, and on the need for reflective – rather than mechanical – evaluation. Accordingly, A Sen argued that human development is about the expansion of citizens' capabilities. See eg A Sen, *Development as Freedom* (Oxford, Oxford University Press, 1999). See also E Neumayer, 'Human Development and Sustainability' (United Nations Development Programme, Human Development Reports, Research Paper 2010/05, June 2010), available at http://hdr.undp.org/sites/default/files/hdrp_2010_05.pdf. Neumayer has analysed the linkages existing between the two broad concepts of human development and sustainability proposing a practical way in which the measurements of human development and sustainability can be linked with each other. His most important policy conclusion is 'that countries of high to very high human development face the double task of achieving strong sustainability by severing the link between high human development and strongly unsustainable carbon emissions and helping other countries, particularly those with low levels of human development, to achieve weak sustainability in the first place and strong sustainability eventually' (see also E Neumayer, *Human Development and Sustainability* (2010) 2, available at SSRN: https://ssrn.com/abstract=1711867).

[7] See, *inter alia*, Sen, *Development as Freedom* (n 6); Neumayer, 'Human Development and Sustainability' (n 6).

compromising the ability of future generations to meet their own needs',[8] which implies the consideration of social and environmental impacts of economic activities. This definition has marked the starting point of an awareness-raising process about the pressing problems linked to economic development and the consequent urgent need for global intervention. Accordingly, SD has first and foremost been dissociated from the concept of a mere economic growth disruptive to social and environmental dimensions. It has been designed as a structure balancing on three interdependent and mutually reinforcing pillars, which are economic development, social development and environmental protection.

The need to take into account all the social and environmental facets and impacts of development has also been reflected in the formulation of the 2000–15 UN's Millennium Development Goals (MDGs)[9] and the subsequent 2015–30 Sustainable Development Goals (SDGs).[10]

Far from being considered as mere economic goals, MDGs and SDGs encompass the environmental protection and social inclusion issues. However, significant differences between the two can be emphasised. Whereas the MDGs have set eight international development goals ranging 'from halving extreme poverty to halting the spread of HIV/AIDS and providing universal primary education, all by the target date of 2015',[11] the 17 SDGs go further by adopting a more holistic approach covering poverty reduction and inequality, sustainability and economic growth with job creation.[12]

In doing so, both MDGs and SDGs require 'combined efforts of all, governments, civil society organizations and the private sector, in the context of a stronger and more effective global partnership for development'.[13] Furthermore, one of the most significant

[8] The World Commission on Environment and Development, Report on 'Our Common Future', 41 available at www.un-documents.net/our-common-future.pdf.

[9] See www.un.org/millenniumgoals/. The MDGs were the international development goals for the year 2015 that had been established following the Millennium Summit of the United Nations in 2000, through the adoption of the United Nations Millennium Declaration. The MDGs were formulated as follows: (i) to eradicate extreme poverty and hunger; (ii) to achieve universal primary education; (iii) to promote gender equality and empower women; (iv) to reduce child mortality; (v) to improve maternal health; (vi) to combat HIV/AIDS, malaria and other diseases; (vii) to ensure environmental sustainability; and (viii) to develop a global partnership for development.

[10] See 'The Sustainable Development Agenda' at www.un.org/sustainabledevelopment/development-agenda; see also the 'United Nations Environment Programme and the 2030 Agenda: Global Action for People and the Planet', available at https://wedocs.unep.org/bitstream/handle/20.500.11822/9851/-The_United_Nations_Environment_Programme_and_the_2030_Agenda_Global_Action_for_People_and_the_Planet-2015EO_Brochure_WebV.pdf.pdf?sequence=3&isAllowed=y.

[11] www.un.org/millenniumgoals/bkgd.shtml.

[12] See 'The Sustainable Development Agenda' at www.un.org/sustainabledevelopment/development-agenda. SDGs are the following: (i) no poverty; (ii) zero hunger; (iii) good health and well-being for people; (iv) quality education; (v) gender equality; (vi) clean water and sanitation; (vii) affordable and clean energy; (viii) decent work and economic growth; (ix) industry, innovation and infrastructure; (x) reducing inequalities; (xi) sustainable cities and communities; (xii) responsible consumption and production; (xiii) climate action; (xiv) life below water; (xv) life on land; (xvi) peace, justice and strong institutions; and (xvii) partnerships for the goals.

[13] The words of the UN Secretary-General BAN Ki-moon, available at www.un.org/millenniumgoals/bkgd.shtml. He further states: 'The Millennium Development Goals set timebound targets, by which progress in reducing income poverty, hunger, disease, lack of adequate shelter and exclusion – while promoting gender equality, health, education and environmental sustainability – can be measured. They also embody basic

areas of progress made by the SDGs is the recognition of their universal nature meaning that they apply to all countries and actors, whereas the MDGs were intended for action in developing countries only.[14] This reflects the fact that MDGs were likely to be largely determined by countries of the Organisation for Economic Cooperation and Development (OECD) and international donor agencies, whereas the SDGs have been produced by detailed international negotiations that have involved middle-income and low-income countries as well.[15]

However, combining these three dimensions (ie economic, social and environmental) in a unique concept is not without risks. If the main challenge is about the scope of such a notion, the risk is to have (always) a prevailing dimension. Trying to find a balance between the three dimensions has been one of the core objectives of the call for a 'climate justice', which incorporates the well-known concept of 'social justice'[16] together with climate issues. This approach has the merit of clearly showing the linkages existing between social well-being and the environment. Nevertheless, it overlooks the fact that these two pillars are not the same, and, moreover, they are even quite different. If environmental protection refers to global concerns, social issues are usually linked to a specific local context. For instance, provisions on working conditions or vulnerable workers' inclusion usually have specific national boundaries.

In a remarkably parallel development, the evolution from economic to sustainable development has been mirrored in the integration of sustainability considerations in public procurement, thus giving rise to the SPP discourse.

Among the 17 SDGs, a direct reference to sustainable public procurement is made in SDG 12 on sustainable consumption and production (SCP)[17] and, more specifically, in its target 12.7, which emphasises the promotion of 'public procurement practices that are sustainable, in accordance with national policies and priorities'.[18] Under indicator 12.7.1, progress and compliance to this target are measured through assessing the number of countries implementing SPP policies and action plans.[19]

It is particularly significant that SPP has been placed under SDG 12, given that SCP 'is about promoting resource and energy efficiency, sustainable infrastructure, and providing access to basic services, green and decent jobs and a better quality of life

human rights – the rights of each person on the planet to health, education, shelter and security. The Goals are ambitious but feasible and, together with the comprehensive United Nations development agenda, set the course for the world's efforts to alleviate extreme poverty by 2015'.

[14] See 'The Sustainable Development Agenda' at www.un.org/sustainabledevelopment/development-agenda.

[15] J Sandler Clarke, '7 reasons the SDGs will be better than the MDGs', *The Guardian*, 26 September 2015, available at www.theguardian.com/global-development-professionals-network/2015/sep/26/7-reasons-sdgs-will-be-better-than-the-mdgs.

[16] C McCrudden, *Buying Social Justice: Equality, Government Procurement, & Legal Change* (New York, Oxford University Press, 2007) 13ff.

[17] According to the SDG 12: 'Sustainable consumption and production is about promoting resource and energy efficiency, sustainable infrastructure, and providing access to basic services, green and decent jobs and a better quality of life for all. Its implementation helps to achieve overall development plans, reduce future economic, environmental and social costs, strengthen economic competitiveness and reduce poverty' (www.un.org/sustainabledevelopment/sustainable-consumption-production).

[18] See https://sustainabledevelopment.un.org/sdg12.

[19] ibid.

for all'.[20] This calls for a shift towards economic practices that are more compatible with the environment and social aspects. In fact, as emphasised by Rita Schwarzelühr-Sutter, Parliamentary State Secretary in the Federal Ministry for the Environment, Nature Conservation and Nuclear Safety of Germany, implementation of SDG 12 'needs a structural shift', implying a change of the 'still widespread "business-as-usual" mode'.[21] Accordingly, public procurement may become a powerful instrument to implement sustainable consumption, since 'The public sector has the power to provide incentives for market players to focus more on sustainability and to support the market of green products'.[22]

The traditional competition-based framework poses a challenge for SPP. The reasons can be summarised in two main categories: on the one hand, the contradiction between fundamental principles (eg equal treatment) and horizontal or strategic objectives of public procurement (social and environmental concerns) and, on the other hand, the contradiction between the three SD pillars.

As to the latter, the coexistence in a unique concept – that of SD – of three heterogeneous components, namely the economic, social and environmental dimensions, has a significant impact when it comes to the integration of SD in public procurement. In fact, if it is true that SPP 'is where the concept of sustainable development and public procurement meet',[23] then the multidimensional nature of SD has to fit with the cross-sectional public procurement area.

Integrating SD into public procurement means that linkages with social and environmental objectives have to be considered by public entities. More specifically, when adopting a SPP-based approach, public entities have to look beyond the simple price/cost of the purchases and take into account different kinds of social and environmental considerations. Their purchasing decisions should be shaped (not necessarily at the same time) by at least four different goals, namely:

> i) to minimize any negative impacts of goods, works or services across their life cycle and through the supply chain for example, impacts on health and well-being, air quality, generation and disposal of hazardous material, ii) to minimize demand for resources for example, reducing purchases, using resource-efficient products such as energy-efficient appliances, fuel-efficient vehicles and products containing recycled content, iii) to ensure that fair contract prices and terms are applied and respected that meet minimum ethical, human rights and employment standards, and iv) to promote diversity and equality throughout the supply chain by for example, providing opportunities for small and medium sized enterprises (SMEs) or by supporting training and skill development.[24]

This list of goals shows that the framework in which public entities operate is quite complex. Complexity is due to, at least, three main issues. First, too many different and

[20] See again www.un.org/sustainabledevelopment/sustainable-consumption-production/.

[21] R Schwarzelühr-Sutter, 'Sustainable Strategic Procurement: Can the State Be a Role Model for Sustainable Consumption?' (25 July 2018) available at http://sdg.iisd.org/commentary/guest-articles/sustainable-strategic-public-procurement-can-the-state-be-a-role-model-for-sustainable-consumption.

[22] ibid.

[23] Roos, *Sustainable Public Procurement* (n 1) 2.

[24] Roos (n 1) 2, referring to C Berry, *The Sustainable Procurement Guide: Procuring Sustainably Using BS 8903* (London, British Standards Institute, 2011) 3–4.

(to some extent) conflicting objectives (mixing environmental and social concerns) are laid down with a certain degree of variation between national and international policy priorities;[25] secondly, there is a high number of policies, tools and legal instruments regulating SPP (one estimate lists 300 different tools);[26] thirdly, there is no common guiding framework enabling public entities to easily incorporate sustainability into their day-to-day procurement tasks. Finally, tools are of different nature and legal force, ranging from soft law to hard law, and come from different legal frameworks (national, regional and international).

This complexity and the existing interconnections between pillars makes it more and more difficult for different actors – such as policy-makers, decision-makers, public entities, private sector, researchers and civil society – to get an easy and clear picture of the state of play of SPP. This obviously affects the behaviour of the different actors involved in the public procurement process, for instance when defining priorities and needs, when choosing the applicable provision, when interpreting the norms, when including green and social criteria in the tender documents, when formulating a socially-responsible or green bid, when evaluating bids, or when participating in one or more stages of the whole process as stakeholders.

Treating SPP as (among others) an economically inefficient tool, or as a concept operating against full and open competition, or – on the contrary – as a 'strategic' objective of public procurement (as defined by the EU), clearly has an impact on the effectiveness of international policies promoting SD in and through public procurement. Indeed, including social and green considerations in public procurement 'involves not just changes in the legislation, it requires changes in procurement practices'.[27]

III. Making Public Procurement (More) Sustainable: The Role of the International Organisations

Several international organisations, including MDBs, have played and are playing a relevant and growing role in fostering SPP translating the MDGs, now SDGs, into action and actual practice. There is a growing awareness about the 'need to go beyond the lowest price and stop procuring products or services which are cheap only because the costs to the environment [and to the society] have been externalised'.[28] This awareness has been spread out by international organisations even if in different ways and with different focuses. If environmental concerns are becoming an integral part of almost every international policy, social issues still encompass claims that are too inhomogeneous to be kept together within one unique category. In other words, considering social aspects in public policies and especially in public procurement, would need both

[25] S Arrowsmith, 'Horizontal Policies in Public Procurement: a Taxonomy' (2010) 10 *Journal of Public Procurement* 149.

[26] Roos (n 1) 10.

[27] R Caranta, 'Helping Public Procurement Go Green: The Role of International Organisations' (2013) 8 *European Procurement & Public Private Partnership Law Review* 49.

[28] ibid 2–3.

specific measures and general prioritisation policy in order to meet all (but, obviously, not at the same time) social needs that are at stake (eg working conditions, vulnerable workers' inclusion, minority-owned business' promotion, etc).

Different international organisations have played and are playing a role in shaping green and/or social with procurement practices.[29] Their role 'does not necessarily involve here the drafting of international treaties or other hard law instruments',[30] since they usually use soft-law language, by developing recommendations, guidelines, best practices, as well as by providing technical assistance and training to procurement authorities.[31] All these are 'instances of soft legal integration which are presently quite at the core of the much more general development of a global administrative law'.[32] The activity of international organisations in this area is at times anticipated, and often supported by quasi- or non-governmental organisations.[33]

In the following subsections, a number of examples will be analysed, starting from the UN system, then the main tools on trade harmonisation specifically related to public procurement (WTO-GPA, UNCITRAL Model Law and OECD) at global level, and finally a very relevant instance of regional integration (the EU).

A. The UN System: From Words to Action

The role played by the UN in shifting the focus from economic to sustainable development has already been analysed in section II. In 2012, at the UN Conference on SD (Rio+20), the 10-Year Framework of Programmes on Sustainable Consumption and Production Patterns (10YFP) was adopted as a global framework for action to accelerate the shift towards SCP in both developed and developing countries.[34]

Moreover, the UN system is also a major buyer at global stage. Aggregated data for 2016 (the latest available) points to a total expenditure of almost USD 50 billion.[35] In 2011, four organisations in the UN system drafted a guide titled 'Buying for a Better World: A Guide for Sustainable Procurement for the UN System'. These international organisations are: (i) UN Environment, whose mission is to 'provide leadership and encourage partnership in caring for the environment by inspiring, informing, and enabling nations and peoples to improve their quality of life without compromising

[29] ibid.

[30] ibid.

[31] ibid. See also eg J Salzman, 'The Organization for Economic Cooperation and Development's Role in International Law' (2012) 43 *The George Washington International Law Review* 255, 276.

[32] ibid; see also A von Bogdandy, P Dann and M Goldmann, 'Developing the Publicness of Public International Law: Towards a Legal Framework for Global Governance Activities' (2008) 9 *German Law Journal* 1375, and more generally the contributions collected by A von Bogdandy et al (eds), *The Exercise of Public Authority by International Institutions: Advancing International Institutional Law* (Heidelberg, Springer, 2010).

[33] O Perera, N Chowdhury and A Goswami, 'State of Play in Sustainable Public Procurement' (Winnipeg, International Institute for Sustainable Development, November 2007) available at www.iisd.org/pdf/2007/state_procurement.pdf.

[34] The UN Conference on SD (Rio+20) took place in Rio de Janeiro, Brazil on 20–22 June 2012. See https://sustainabledevelopment.un.org/rio20.html. The earlier actions are analysed by G Clark, 'Evolution of the Global Sustainable Consumption and Production Policy and the United Nations Environment Programme's (UNEP) Supporting Activities' (2007) 15 *Journal of Cleaner Production* 492.

[35] www.unsystem.org/content/FS-F00-05.

that of future generations';[36] (ii) the UN Office for Project Services (UNOPS), which is the central resource for the UN system in procurement and contract management, including civil works and infrastructures;[37] (iii) the International Labour Organisation (ILO), which is 'responsible for drawing up and overseeing international labour standards';[38] and (iv) the ITC-ILO, which is the training centre for ILO with a large campus in Turin (Italy) and a unit devoted to sustainable development and governance focusing, among other aspects, on public procurement.[39]

According to the guide referred above, there are five main concepts towards sustainability, namely: (i) SD; (ii) climate change; (iii) resource efficiency and green economy; (iv) human rights; and (v) SPP. The latter considers the economic, social/labour and environmental consequences of public procurement in all its stages. Whereas the social and labour factors include 'recognizing equality and diversity, observing core labour standards, ensuring fair working conditions, increasing employment and skills, developing local communities and their physical infrastructure', the environmental factors include 'natural resource use and water scarcity, emissions to air, climate change and biodiversity over the whole product life cycle'.[40]

This implies a number of efforts in adapting national public procurement frameworks to the SD challenges since a standard SPP approach cannot be applied. Accordingly, SPP

> should be applied in phases adopting a step-by-step approach, through small incremental steps at a pace determined by the degree of maturity of the supply market, the development of a policy framework, staff training, and by the degree of readiness of the organization to achieve sustainability.[41]

The guide explains also how to apply sustainability principles at each stage of the procurement process, namely: procurement planning, requirement definition, sourcing, evaluation, and contract management. As a key point, it is stressed that, beyond good SPP policies, 'specific expert advice should be integrated into the procurement cycle, so as to improve delivery of the planned sustainable outcome'.[42]

B. UN Environment's Special Role

Besides working to recast its own consumption method following SPP principles, the UN is involved in encouraging and helping procuring entities to follow suit. The UN Environment Programme (UNEP), which has recently changed its name into 'UN Environment', is the leading UN organisation working on SPP and on sustainability issues

[36] www.unenvironment.org/about-un-environment.

[37] www.unops.org.

[38] www.ilo.org. ILO is the only 'tripartite' UN agency that brings together representatives of governments, employers and workers to jointly shape policies and programmes promoting decent work for all.

[39] www.itcilo.org. The ITC-ILO provides training and other services to develop human resources and institutional capabilities.

[40] UN Environment Programme (UNEP), United Nations Office for Project Services (UNOPS), International Labour Organisation (ILO) and the ILO's International Training Centre (ITC ILO), 'Buying for a Better World: A Guide for Sustainable Procurement for the UN System' (2011) 14, available at www.ungm.org/Areas/Public/Downloads/BFABW_Final_web.pdf.

[41] ibid 13.

[42] ibid 33.

more generally. A leading early initiative was made in the framework of the Marrakech Process, a global multi-stakeholder process to support the implementation of SCP. The Process responds to the call of the Johannesburg Plan of Implementation (World Summit on Sustainable Development, 2002) to support the regional and national initiatives to accelerate the shift towards SCP patterns. The first meeting took place in Marrakech, Morocco in June 2003, hence the name of the process.

In 2005 an international Task Force on SPP was launched at the initiative of the Swiss government within the framework of the Marrakech Process. It created an approach for implementing SPP in both developed and developing countries, known as the Marrakech Task Force (MTF) Approach to SPP.[43] In 2008, the Swiss government and UN Environment with the support of the EU Commission and other organisations designed a project to roll out this approach in up to 14 countries worldwide. Among the activities pilot countries were expected to undertake was the development of technical specifications and other contract conditions incorporating sustainable procurement considerations.[44]

The mandate of the MTF on SPP ended in 2011 and UN Environment is now the custodian of the MTF Approach to sustainable public procurement. Taking stock of that approach, in 2012 UN Environment published the 'Sustainable Public Procurement Implementation Guidelines' providing advice on steps to adopt SPP practices based on practical experience in applying the MTF on SPP approach in a number of countries.[45]

More recently, UN Environment has launched a specific SPP programme as part of the 10YFP initiative.[46] Among the different activities undertaken, the 2015 SPP principles deserve specific mention.[47] They have been developed to guide both law and policy-makers. Finally (so far) in 2017 UN Environment published its second 'Global Review of Sustainable Public Procurement' examining the state of SPP policies and practices undertaken by national governments worldwide in the previous five years, based on research conducted between 2015 and 2016, among 41 national governments and more than 200 SPP stakeholders.[48]

C. From SPP Reluctance to SPP Promotion: The Case of the UNCITRAL Model Law on Public Procurement

The United Nations Commission on International Trade Law (UNCITRAL) has adopted the 'Model Law on Public Procurement' (Model Law) in 1994, then revised in 2011 with

[43] https://esa.un.org/marrakechprocess/.

[44] eg 'Plan Nacional de Compras Públicas Sustentables (2012–2016)' of Uruguay: for information, see www.cncs.com.uy/compras-publicas-sustentables-en-uruguay/; see also Clark, 'Evolution of the Global Sustainable Consumption and Production Policy' (n 34) 495.

[45] Available at www.unenvironment.org/explore-topics/resource-efficiency/what-we-do/capacity-building-spp-developing-countries.

[46] www.unenvironment.org/explore-topics/resource-efficiency/what-we-do/one-planet-network.

[47] Global Action for Sustainable Consumption and Production – 10 YFP, 'The Sustainable Public Procurement Programme of the 10-Year Framework of Programmes (10YFP SPP Programme): Principles of Sustainable Public Procurement (March 2015) available at www.oneplanetnetwork.org/sites/default/files/10yfp-spp-principles.pdf.

[48] UN Environment, *Global Review of Sustainable Public Procurement 2017* (n 5).

the purpose of modernising and harmonising national public procurement laws and regulations.[49]

As to the SPP, under the so-called 'socio-economic policies', article 2(o) refers to 'environmental, social, economic and other policies … authorized or required by the procurement regulations or other provisions of law' of a certain State 'to be taken into account by the procuring entity in the procurement proceedings'. This definition is 'not intended to be open-ended' and has the purpose of ensuring that 'socio-economic policies *(a)* are not determined on an ad hoc basis by the procuring entity, and *(b)* are applied across all government purchasing, so that their costs and benefits can be seen'.[50]

Accordingly, article 9 of the Model Law allows procuring entities to impose environmental qualifications, and ethical and other standards that could include fair trade requirements in the qualification criteria. More specifically, as the procuring entity considers appropriate and relevant in the circumstances of the particular procurement, suppliers or contractors shall, *inter alia*:

> have the necessary professional, technical and environmental qualifications, professional and technical competence, financial resources, equipment and other physical facilities, managerial capability, reliability, experience and personnel to perform the procurement contract;
>
> [and] … meet ethical and other standards applicable in this State.

Despite this recognition, socio-economic policies seem to be still under suspicion. In fact, while opening up domestic public procurement to international competition is explicitly mentioned by the Model Law as a goal for public procurement systems, enhancing sustainability is not. In fact, as it is well known, 'The Model Law … contains procedures and principles aimed at achieving value for money and avoiding abuses in the procurement process. The text promotes objectivity, fairness, participation and competition and integrity towards these goals'.[51]

Moreover, many sections of the Guide to Enactment of the UNCITRAL Model Law on Public Procurement manifest some concern that SPP might hinder fair competition and international trade. More specifically, when dealing with socio-economic policies, the Guide to Enactment states that 'The pursuit and implementation of these policies may have an impact on the performance of the procurement system itself, as, in essence, they are implemented through restrictions on competition for a particular procurement', which 'can bring additional costs to procurement, as it may increase the ultimate price paid'.[52] Accordingly, as it involves exceptions to full and open competition, the promotion of socio-economic policies through procurement systems is 'therefore to be considered an exceptional measure' under the Model Law.[53]

[49] UNCITRAL, *Model Law on Public Procurement [2011]* (New York, UN, 2014) available at www.uncitral.org/pdf/english/texts/procurem/ml-procurement-2011/2011-Model-Law-on-Public-Procurement-e.pdf.

[50] UNCITRAL, *Guide to Enactment of the UNCITRAL Model Law on Public Procurement [2012]* (New York, United Nations, 2014) 59.

[51] www.uncitral.org/uncitral/en/uncitral_texts/procurement_infrastructure/2011Model.html.

[52] UNCITRAL, *Guide to Enactment [2012]* (n 50) 6 (point 14).

[53] ibid 6 (point 16).

D. WTO-GPA: Still in Denial?

According to the GPA's website, 'The GPA is a plurilateral agreement within the framework of the WTO, meaning that not all WTO members are parties to the Agreement. At present, the Agreement has 19 parties comprising 47 WTO members'[54] (the EU accounting for 28 members). Most of the members are developed countries.

The GPA, even in its 2012 revised text (that came into force in 2014),[55] is still a traditional trade liberalisation instrument. It does not address the issues facing sustainable procurement, and this is potentially hindering the development of this area of the law at national level.[56]

Negotiations to revise the GPA also resulted in the adoption of a package of work programmes intended to assist in improving the implementation and administration of the revised Agreement and in laying the ground for further reform. Among these work programmes, one is focusing on SPP. The 2012 decision initiating the SPP work programme still belies concerns that shifting the focus on sustainability will hinder the more traditional goals and instruments linked to market liberalisation.

The 2012 decision indeed recognises that several parties to the GPA 'have developed national and sub-national sustainable procurement policies'.[57] However, it reaffirms 'the importance of ensuring that all procurement is undertaken in accordance with the principles of non-discrimination and transparency as reflected in the Agreement'.[58] On this basis the work programme shall focus on:

> (a) the objectives of sustainable procurement; (b) the ways in which the concept of sustainable procurement is integrated into national and sub-national procurement policies; (c) the ways in which sustainable procurement can be practiced in a manner consistent with the principle of 'best value for money'; and (d) the ways in which sustainable procurement can be practiced in a manner consistent with Parties' international trade obligations.[59]

The mission of the SPP work programme initiated by the 2012 decision is to

> identify measures and policies that it considers to be sustainable procurement practiced in a manner consistent with the principle of best value for money and with Parties' international trade obligations and prepare a report that lists the best practices of the measures and policies.[60]

E. The OECD-MAPS and SPP

In 2017, the OECD Secretary-General, Angel Gurría, together with the EU Commissioner for Internal Market, Industry, Entrepreneurship and SMEs, Elżbieta Bieńkowska,

[54] www.wto.org/english/tratop_e/gproc_e/gp_gpa_e.htm, also providing additional information on GPA.

[55] The revised WTO-GPA is available at www.wto.org/english/docs_e/legal_e/rev-gpr-94_01_e.htm.

[56] See JJ Pernas-García, *Contratación pública verde* (Madrid, La Ley, 2011) 38 ff; S Arrowsmith, 'Application of the EC Treaty and Directives to Horizontal Policies: a Critical Review', ch 4 in S Arrowsmith and P Kunzlik (eds), *Social and Environmental Policies in EC Procurement Law: New Directives and New Directions* (Cambridge, Cambridge University Press, 2009) 147.

[57] The full text of the 2012 decision initiating the SPP work programme is available at www.wto.org/english/tratop_e/gproc_e/annexe_e.pdf.

[58] ibid.

[59] ibid.

[60] ibid.

affirmed that public procurement is 'not a back-office function anymore, but a crucial pillar for delivering government services, and a strategic one for tackling climate change'.[61] Similarly, the 2015 recommendation of the OECD Working Party on Leading Practitioners on Public Procurement (LPP) refers to public procurement as a tool to deliver what are (still often) called secondary policy objectives such as 'sustainable green growth, the development of small and medium-sized enterprises, innovation, standards for responsible business conduct or broader industrial policy objectives'.[62]

However, for a long time the OECD 'Methodology for Assessing Procurement Systems' (OECD-MAPS), which is the common benchmarking tool analysing strengths and weaknesses of national public procurement systems, has not addressed issues relevant for SPP. As a consequence, the concept of SPP has mainly been neglected. This has been true especially for public procurement reforms in developing countries.[63]

Initially developed in 2003–04, the OECD-MAPS has been revised between 2015 and 2018 in order to 'respond to current public procurement challenges, the evolution of international standards and country demands'[64] in line with the UN SDGs, and especially SDG 12 calling for the promotion of sustainable procurement practices. The new 2018 OECD-MAPS has been defined by the OECD itself as 'a universal tool to catalyse and accelerate the implementation of modern, efficient, sustainable and more inclusive public procurement systems in all countries'.[65] Consistent with this, value for money has been expressly linked to 'the basic goal' that every procurement system should achieve by 'providing the required goods, works, and services in an economic, efficient, effective and sustainable way'.[66]

A direct reference to SPP is made in the first pillar of the 2018 MAPS focusing on the national 'legal, regulatory, and policy framework', which analyses if and to what extent the legal framework reflects the country's secondary/horizontal policy objectives (eg SD) and international obligations. More specifically, the new sub-indicator 3(a) entitled 'Sustainable Public Procurement (SPP)' assesses whether:

a) the country has adopted a policy and an implementation plan to implement Sustainable Public Procurement (SPP) in support of national policy objectives,
b) the legal and regulatory framework includes provisions on the inclusion of sustainability criteria in public procurement; and
c) those provisions are balanced against primary objectives of public procurement and ensure value for money.[67]

[61] As quoted by L Casier, 'How to Implement Strategic, Smart, Sustainable Public Procurement' (29 June 2017) available at www.iisd.org/blog/how-implement-strategic-smart-sustainable-public-procurement.

[62] OECD, 'Recommendation of the Council on Public Procurement' (2015) available at www.oecd.org/gov/ethics/OECD-Recommendation-on-Public-Procurement.pdf. See also Casier, 'How to Implement Strategic, Smart, Sustainable Public Procurement' (n 61).

[63] Roos (n 1) LXXVI (Annexures).

[64] 'Public consultation on the revised Methodology for Assessing Procurement Systems (MAPS)' available at www.oecd.org/gov/ethics/public-consultation-methodology-assessing-procurement-systems.htm.

[65] See the 2018 MAPS at http://www.mapsinitiative.org/methodology/.

[66] OECD, 'Methodology for Assessing Procurement Systems (MAPS)' Version of 2018, available at http://www.mapsinitiative.org/methodology/. See also OECD, 'Methodology for Assessing Procurement Systems (MAPS)' Version of 2016 (Draft for Public Consultations, July 2016) 2, available at www.oecd.

[67] ibid 31.

In other words, 'SPP should be embedded in programs that are part of the country's sustainable development strategy' and the horizontal 'objectives should be consistent with primary objectives of public procurement such as economy, efficiency, and transparency'.[68] What is most interesting is that sub-indicator 3(a) explicitly requires, among others, that the national framework is based on a 'well-balanced application of sustainability criteria to ensure value for money'.[69] In this context, horizontal policies objectives are defined as being:

> [A]ny of a variety of objectives of an economic, environmental and social nature (such as sustainable green growth, the development of small and medium-sized enterprises, innovation, standards for responsible business conduct or broader industrial policy objectives), which governments increasingly pursue through use of procurement as a policy lever (sometimes referred to as 'secondary' policies, in contrast with the so-called 'primary' objectives of delivering goods and services in a timely, economical and efficient manner).[70]

Sub-indicator 3(a) also mentions some key factors that should be taken into account when focusing on SPP implementation, namely:

> [T]he capacity and training/development needs of the procurement workforce, the development and application of new tools and techniques, prioritisation of measures, impact assessment methodologies to measure the effectiveness of SPP, and the provision of guidance material. It is also necessary to decide which institution is best suited to manage and oversee the nationwide deployment of SPP and/or whether new institutions need to be established (e.g. certification institutions or product-testing facilities).[71]

Sub-indicator 3(a) finally refers to a specific SPP supplementary module (in addition to the OECD-MAPS),[72] showing that SPP is increasingly considered as a (more and more crucial) component of public procurement systems, even if it always has to be balanced with value for money and efficiency considerations.[73]

F. Multilateral Development Banks (MDBs): How Far Are They Going with SPP in Developing Countries?

As already mentioned, the SPP goal reflects the need to spread sustainable development considerations in all public policies (including public procurement) at all levels in order to make sustainable development a more effective tool. However, the SPP goal is still in potential conflict with other aims, such as ensuring competition, integrity and public savings as far as possible.[74] A sound public spending is usually the core

[68] ibid 31.
[69] OECD, 'Methodology for Assessing Procurement Systems (MAPS)', Version of 2018 (n 66) 33.
[70] ibid 77.
[71] ibid 33.
[72] ibid 33.
[73] ibid.
[74] R Caranta, 'Sustainable Procurement', ch 7 in M Trybus, R Caranta and G Edelstam (eds), *EU Public Contract Law. Public Procurement and Beyond* (Brussels, Bruylant, 2014) 165–90; A Sanchez-Graells, *Public Procurement and the EU Competition Rules* (Oxford, Hart Publishing, 2015); G Piga and T Tatrai, 'Supporting Social Considerations through Public Procurement: Economic Considerations' in G Piga and T Tatrai (eds),

objective of public procurement policies. This is true especially when it comes to MDBs. Considering that they basically provide funding to States which in turn enter into public procurement processes, MDBs have the strong interest to make sure that this money is properly and efficiently spent. As a consequence, sustainability dimensions have often been left out from their public procurement policies.

For instance, the World Bank (WB) has only recently developed a specific 'Procurement Guidance on Sustainable Procurement'.[75] Adopted at the end of 2016, the Guidance illustrates how sustainability priorities can be reflected at each stage of a public procurement process financed by the Bank itself through an Investment Project Financing (IPF), the purpose of which is to promote poverty reduction and SD.[76] In this framework, procurement is described as supporting 'borrowers to achieve value for money (VfM) with integrity in delivering sustainable development'.[77] Despite SD apparently being designed as being the final objective of an IPF, it is still not considered as a must-have component of a 'good' public procurement and neither as core procurement principle of the Bank (unlike value for money, economy, integrity, fit for purpose, efficiency, transparency and fairness).[78] Moreover, the integration of SD in public procurement is 'at the Borrower's discretion'[79] and must be 'agreed with the Bank' (point 5.12 of WB Procurement Regulation).[80] This approach may be explained by the difficulties that borrowers (generally, developing countries or upper middle-income economies) face in adopting SPP. Challenges may be linked to several different factors, such as – among others – the market (un)readiness and/or (un)responsiveness in relation to the sustainability needs in developing countries.

The 2016 WB Procurement Guidance on SPP is an example of the growing global attention to the 'three-dimensional thinking' in public procurement.[81] However, even if it explains how to include SPP considerations in different stages of the public procurement process, it remains reluctant as to making room for sustainability among key public procurement principles. Moreover, SD has been listed among the 'procurement arrangements that are inherently risky' (Section 3.1, Annex 2) and for which a prior

Public Procurement Policy (London, Routledge, 2016); M Trybus, 'Supporting Social Considerations through Public Procurement: a Legal Perspective' in G Piga and T Tatrai (eds), *Public Procurement Policy* (London, Routledge, 2016); C McCrudden, *Buying Social Justice* (n 16).

[75] World Bank, 'Procurement Guidance: Sustainable Procurement – An introduction for practitioners to sustainable procurement in World Bank IPF projects' (Washington, World Bank, November 2016), available at http://pubdocs.worldbank.org/en/788731479395390605/Sustainable-Procurement-Guidance-FINAL.pdf.

[76] ibid. Investment Project Financing (IPF) is defined as follows: 'the Bank's financing of investment projects that aims to promote poverty reduction and sustainable development. IPF supports projects with defined development objectives, activities, and results, and disburses the proceeds of Bank financing against specific eligible expenditures'.

[77] ibid 1. See also The World Bank, 'Procurement Guidance: Project Procurement Strategy for Development – Short Form Detailed Guide' (Washington DC, World Bank, July 2016), available at http://pubdocs.worldbank.org/en/633801467334323120/PPSD-Short-Form-July-26.pdf.

[78] ibid. This is set out in detail in s III.C of the 'Bank Policy: Procurement in IPF and Other Operational Procurement Matters' (Catalogue Number OPSVP5.05-POL.144, issued 7 November 2017, effective 1 July 2016, last revised 2 November 2017), available at https://policies.worldbank.org/sites/ppf3/PPFDocuments/a3656cb78847417b886f11fa0235216e.pdf.

[79] ibid 3.

[80] World Bank, 'Procurement Regulations for IPF Borrowers' (2018) 17.

[81] ibid.

review is required even for procurements below the applicable mandatory thresholds (this together with 'the use of negotiations in a competitive procurement process for goods, works and non-consulting services, BAFO, competitive dialogue, and the application of sustainable procurement').[82]

A similar approach is shared by the African Development Bank (AfDB). According to the 2015 AfDB 'Procurement Policy for Bank Group Funded Operations', good procurement can facilitate the realisation of 'socio-economic and environmental sustainability policy objectives' at the national level.[83] If this does not clearly take into account the possibility that good public procurement might be SPP, it is still the first step in recognising the SPP role in national public procurement. This is stated by paragraph 1.6.6 of the 2015 AfDB 'Methodology for Implementation of the Procurement Policy', which recognises that 'many of its Borrowers have developed policies to promote sustainability with a view to improve the lives and well-being of their citizens, or to protect the environment', through the use 'of environmental and socially responsible procurement (ESRP), preference margins, local content, set asides, offsets, provisions in labour laws to encourage fair-wages and gender sensitive policies'.[84]

Although the AfDB recognises the SPP benefits as 'not limited to the procurement entity or the end users' but going 'beyond to communities and the public at large', it maintains a suspicious-looking attitude vis-à-vis SPP. Indeed, the AfDB must ensure that borrowers' requests for inclusion of sustainability requirements meet two criteria, namely: (i) requests have to be 'consistent with its own policies; and (ii) they do not adversely impact the procurement principles' (paragraph 1.6.6 of the 2015 AfDB 'Methodology for Implementation of the Procurement Policy').

The WB's and the AfDB's examples show that SPP is turning into one of those procurement considerations that cannot be totally overlooked. This also applies to developing countries. However, in relation to developing countries, two main limits are evident: on the one hand, there are reality-based limits (eg the market unreadiness and/or unresponsiveness in relation to the sustainability needs) and, on the other hand, MDBs' reluctance-oriented limits. Since MDBs have the strong interest to make sure that their money is properly and efficiently spent, 'a right balance' is generally required 'between considerations of competition, fairness and transparency while ensuring that the other national objectives of sustainability and socioeconomic development are also taken into account'.[85] In other terms, the priority seems to be here the consideration of the transactional costs and efficiencies at every stage of the procurement in order to ensure decisions that optimise value for money.

[82] World Bank, 'Procurement Regulations for Borrowers Procurement in Investment Project Financing' (working draft), Section 3.1, Annex 2, available at https://consultations.worldbank.org/Data/hub/files/consultation-template/procurement-policy-review-consultationsopenconsultationtemplate/materials/annex_f_-_procurement_regulations_for_borrowers.pdf.

[83] AfDB 'Procurement Policy for Bank Group Funded Operations' (2015) 5, available at https://www.afdb.org/fileadmin/uploads/afdb/Documents/Policy-Documents/Procurement_policy_for_bank_group_funded_operations.pdf.

[84] AfDB 'Methodology for Implementation of the Procurement Policy' (2015) 10 available at https://www.afdb.org/fileadmin/uploads/afdb/Documents/Policy-Documents/Procurement_policy_for_bank_group_funded_operations.pdf.

[85] ibid para 3.1.2.

G. The EU: Sustainability Promoted to Strategic Goal of Public Procurement

EU institutions act as contracting authorities. However, the EU is much more relevant in that it lays the rules under which public procurement is managed in the Member States. In this subsection the latter and more impactful role will be examined first. The EU law applicable to EU institutions as contracting authorities will be analysed later in this subsection.

The different considerations relating to the environment, to social policy, and to SMEs – or at least the first two – have traditionally been labelled as secondary considerations in opposition to economic efficiency being the primary objective of public procurement legislation and policy. The chosen adjective implied passing a judgement on relevance and was challenged. The term 'horizontal policies' was the suggested alternative.[86] The 2011 European Commission 'Green Paper on the modernisation of EU public procurement policy: Towards a more efficient European Procurement Market' instead referred to 'complementary objectives', in a way putting sustainability on the same footing as other objectives, including economic efficiency.[87]

The Green Paper opens with a reference to the Europe 2020 strategy for smart, sustainable and inclusive growth.[88] Public procurement is said to play a key role in this by (i) improving framework conditions for business to innovate, making full use of demand side policy; (ii) supporting the shift towards a resource efficient and low-carbon economy, for instance 'by encouraging wider use of green public procurement'; and finally (iii) improving the business environment, especially for innovative SMEs.[89]

While the 2004 Public Procurement Directives[90] took stock from the early case law and allowed some scope for SPP,[91] the 2014 reform package,[92] again building on a most

[86] S Arrowsmith and P Kunzlik, 'Public Procurement and Horizontal Policies in EC Law: General Principles', ch 1 in Arrowsmith and Kunzlik (eds), *Social and Environmental Policies in EC Procurement Law: New Directives and New Directions* (n 56) 35 ff; see also, highlighting the difficulty in distinguishing between the two sets of considerations, ME Comba, 'Green and Social Considerations in Public Procurement Contracts: A Comparative Approach', ch XI in R Caranta and M Trybus (eds), *The Law of Green and Social Procurement in Europe* (Copenhagen, Djøf Publishing, 2010) 307 ff.

[87] European Commission, 'Green Paper on the modernisation of EU public procurement policy: Towards a more efficient European Procurement Market', Brussels, 27.1.2011, COM(2011) 15 final.

[88] European Commission, 'Communication from the Commission: EUROPE 2020 – A strategy for smart, sustainable and inclusive growth', Brussels, 3.3.2010, COM(2010) 2020 final.

[89] R Caranta, 'The Changes to the Public Contract Directives and the Story they Tell about how EU Law Works' (2015) 52 *Common Market Law Review* 391, 394.

[90] European Parliament and Council Directive 2014/24/EU of 26 February 2014 on public procurement (OJ L 94, 28.3.2014, 65–242) and repealing Directive 2004/18/EU (OJ L 134, 30.4.2004, 114–240).

[91] Pernas-García, *Contratación pública verde* (n 56); R Caranta, 'Sustainable Public Procurement in the EU' in Caranta and Trybus (eds), *The Law of Green and Social Procurement in Europe* (n 86) 15; Arrowsmith and Kunzlik, 'Public Procurement and Horizontal Policies in EC Law' (n 86) 30 ff McCrudden (n 16) 97 ff; J Arnould, 'Secondary Policies in Public Procurement: the Innovations of the New Directive' (2004) 4 *Public Procurement Law Review* 187–97.

[92] European Parliament and Council Directive 2014/24/EU of 26 February 2014 on public procurement (OJ L 94, 28.3.2014, p. 65–242) and repealing Directive 2004/18/EU (OJ L 134, 30.4.2004, p. 114–240), European Parliament and Council Directive 2014/23/EU on the award of concession contracts and European Parliament and Council Directive 2014/25/EU on procurement by entities operating in the water, energy, transport and postal services sectors and repealing Directive 2004/17/EU.

relevant judgment of the Court of Justice,[93] much strengthened the provisions on SPP, including adding brand new rules on life-cycle costing and making the use of ecolabels easier.[94]

In a limited number of cases the EU goes beyond enabling contracting authorities to buy sustainable goods and services and directs them to do so.[95] This is the case, for instance, with Regulation (EC) No 106/2008 (the so-called EU Energy Star Regulation),[96] which introduced obligations on contracting authorities to require in their public contracts a certain level of energy efficiency, and with Directive 2009/33/EC on the promotion of clean and energy-efficient vehicles, which introduced obligations on contracting authorities to take energy or other environmental impacts into account in their public procurement decisions.[97]

Other measures call on the public sector to play an exemplary role in the field of energy efficiency (Directive 2012/27/EU on energy efficiency) and by promoting resource-efficient public buildings for instance because of low or zero primary energy consumption (Directive 2009/28/EC on the promotion of the use of energy from renewable sources, and Directive 2010/31/EU on the energy performance of buildings).[98]

The SPP provisions in Directive 2014/24/EU, including those on labels and on life- cycle costing, have been mostly duplicated in the Financial Regulation applicable to the general budget of the Union and its rules of application last reformed in 2018.[99] Articles 160 and following of the Financial Regulation regulate contracts financed in

[93] Case C-368/10, *Commission v Netherlands (Max Havellar)* ECLI:EU:C:2012:284.

[94] See the works collected by B Sjåfjell and A Wiesbrock (eds), *Sustainable Public Procurement Under EU Law: New Perspectives on the State as Stakeholder* (Cambridge, Cambridge University Press, 2016); see also DC Dragos and B Neamtu, 'Sustainable Public Procurement in the EU: Experiences and Prospects' in F Lichère, R Caranta and S Treumer (eds), *Modernising Public Procurement: The New Directive* (Copenhagen, Djøf Publishing, 2014) 302 ff.

[95] See European Commission, 'Green Paper on the modernisation of EU public procurement policy' (n 87) 41 ff; see the discussion by P Trepte, 'The Contracting Authority as Purchaser and Regulator: Should the Procurement Rules Regulate what we Buy?' ch 3 in GS Ølykke, C Risvig-Hansen and CD Tvarnø (eds), *EU Public Procurement – Modernisation, Growth and Innovation: Discussions on the 2011 Proposals for Procurement Directives* (Copenhagen, Djøf Publishing, 2012) 85.

[96] European Parliament and Council Regulation (EC) 106/2008 of 15 January 2008 on a Community energy-efficiency labelling programme for office equipment (OJ L 39, 13.2.2008, 1–7).

[97] European Parliament and Council Directive 2009/33/EC of 23 April 2009 on the promotion of clean and energy-efficient road transport vehicles (OJ L 120, 15.5.2009, 5–12). See further European Parliamentary Research Service Blog, 'Review Of The Clean Vehicles Directive [EU Legislation in Progress] available at https://epthinktank.eu/2018/02/02/review-of-the-clean-vehicles-directive-eu-legislation-in-progress.

[98] European Parliament and Council Directive 2012/27/EU of 25 October 2012 on energy efficiency (OJ L 315, 14.11.2012, 1–56), amending Directives 2009/125/EC and 2010/30/EU and repealing Directives 2004/8/EC and 2006/32/EC Text with EEA relevance. European Parliament and Council Directive 2009/28/EC of 23 April 2009 on the promotion of the use of energy from renewable sources and amending and subsequently (OJ L 140, 5.6.2009, 16–62) repealing Directives 2001/77/EC and 2003/30/EC. European Parliament and Council Directive 2010/31/EU of 19 May 2010 on the energy performance of buildings (OJ L 153, 18.6.2010, 13–35). See also Recital 95 of European Parliament and Council Directive 2014/24/EU (OJ L 94, 28.3.2014, 65–242), see also Recital 100 of European Parliament and Council Directive 2014/25/EU (OJ L 94, 28.3.2014, 243–374); see also DC Dragos and B Neamtu, 'Sustainable Public Procurement in the EU' (n 94) 310 ff.

[99] Regulation (EU, Euratom) 2018/1046 of 18 July 2018 on the financial rules applicable to the general budget of the Union, amending Regulations (EU) No 1296/2013, (EU) No 1301/2013, (EU) No 1303/2013, (EU) No 1304/2013, (EU) No 1309/2013, (EU) No 1316/2013, (EU) No 223/2014, (EU) No 283/2014, and Decision No 541/2014/EU and repealing Regulation (EU, Euratom) No 966/2012 [2018] OJ L193/1.

whole or in part by the EU budget. These include external action contracts to which the Procedures and Practical Guide (PRAG) applies, namely to both procurement and grant award procedures applying to EU external actions financed from the general budget of the Union and the European Development Fund (the EDF).[100]

IV. Measuring Sustainability

There is much discussion as to efficiency – or even effectiveness – of multiple public procurement goals.[101] The debate has distinct political overtones and the limited data available, especially concerning social considerations, makes it difficult to validate conflicting claims.[102] This notwithstanding, the amount of data available is growing, especially concerning traditional sectors such as construction.[103] However, benefits of sustainable public procurement are said to include spill-over effects on general well-being and market readiness to supply, for instance, greener alternatives. These benefits are harder to quantify (but not impossible).[104]

Principle 6 of UN Environment's 2015 SPP principles (see above section I.A) builds on the other principles focusing on monitoring and measuring. It indicates:

> SPP monitors its outcomes and results.
>
> Continuous improvement is only possible if the outcomes delivered through SPP are known. Using monitoring and evaluation systems to measure outcomes is essential for tracking progress as well as identifying areas for improvement. Outcomes can include environmental performance such as reduced emissions, reduced material use and reduced waste generation; economic outcomes such as cost savings (including non-tangible benefits and costs), job creation, wealth creation, and transfer of skills/technology; and social outcomes such as minority empowerment, poverty reduction, and good governance.[105]

Also objectivity is an explicit requirement for addressing sustainability concerns in some regional frameworks for public procurement. This is certainly the case with the EU. For instance, article 68 of Directive 2014/24/EU on life-cycle costing (LCC) provides that the method used for the assessment of costs imputed to

[100] See art 1.1. of the European Commission, Procedures and practical guide PRAG (2018), available at https://ec.europa.eu/europeaid/work/procedures/index_en.htm_en.

[101] See eg the divergent appraisals in the contributions collected at the initiative of the Konkurrensverket/ Swedish Competition Authority in *The Cost of Different Goals of Public Procurement* (Västerås, Västra Aros, 2012).

[102] See however the recent work by A Aschieri, *Public-Private Partnerships and Sustainable Development in the European Union*: Another Reason to Foster the Promotion of PPPs as Viable Alternatives in the Delivery of Public Services and Infrastructure (Maastricht-Turin, Datawyse/Universitaire Pers Maastricht, 2017).

[103] eg AX Sanchez et al, 'Evaluation Framework for Green Procurement in Road Construction' (2014) 3(2) *Smart and Sustainable Built Environment* 153.

[104] eg T Simcoe and MW Toffel, 'Government Green Procurement Spillovers: Evidence from Municipal Building Policies in California' (2014) 68 *Journal of Environmental Economics and Management* 411.

[105] Global Action for Sustainable Consumption and Production – 10 YFP, 'The Sustainable Public Procurement Programme of the 10-Year Framework of Programmes (10YFP SPP Programme): Principles of Sustainable Public Procurement (March 2015) available at www.oneplanetnetwork.org/sites/default/ files/10yfp-spp-principles.pdf.

environmental externalities shall be based on objectively verifiable criteria.[106] Objectivity is however implicit in the general principles framing public procurement, such as non-discrimination, equal treatment, and transparency.[107]

Enhancing objectivity in assessing and measuring the benefits of SPP is probably needed to make SPP itself acceptable from an international trade law point of view.

Life-cycle assessment (LCA) and LCC represent important steps in making sustainable purchase objective and non-discriminatory. The development of the international standards for LCA (ISO 14040:1997, ISO 14041:1999, ISO 14042:2000, ISO 14043:2000) was an important step towards consolidating procedures and methods of LCA. Their contribution to the general acceptance of LCA by all stakeholders and by the international community was crucial. In 2006, new international standards of LCA, ie the new ISO 14040 and ISO 14044, were already introduced. LCC requires an additional step which is probably essential to meet objectivity obligations.

Since 2017 these specific documents have been supplemented by ISO 20400:2017. This provides guidance to organisations, independent of their activity or size, on integrating sustainability within procurement, as described in ISO 26000.

LCC-based labels, allowing easy assessment of the environmental or social quality of goods and services, are expected to go a long way towards making SPP attractive for procurement officials, including in developing countries where those officials might be not as professionalised as elsewhere.[108]

V. Conclusions: The Way Forward

SPP has made enormous progress during the past decade. Still lot needs to be done, both at policy level and through a workable SPP toolkit.

At the highest policy level, an effort of coordination between (so many) different approaches of (so many) organisations should be made in order to reduce the risk of weakening the effectiveness of actions fostering SD. Moreover, SDG 12 gives a special attention to green concerns even more so than to social issues. Reducing resource use, degradation and pollution is likely to be its core target. In fact, the promotion of human and labour rights along global supply chains is not explicitly taken into account in SDG12, while supply chains are mentioned to the limited extent that they should be considered in view of the prevention of food losses.

Therefore, when dealing with public procurement, a holistic approach should be used by going beyond the specific reference of SPP in SDG 12. The implementation of SPP seems to be strongly linked to other goals, such as SDG 8 on decent work and economic growth, SDG 9 on industry, innovation and infrastructure, and SDG 11 on

[106] See D Dragos and B Neamtu 'Sustainable Public Procurement: Life Cycle Costing (LCC) in the New EU Directive Proposal' (2013) 8 *European Procurement & Public Private Partnership Law Review* 19.

[107] CH Bovis, *EU Public Procurement Law* (Cheltenham, Edward Elgar Publishing, 2012) 48.

[108] Professionalisation has wide importance in developing countries (and beyond). See NP Mrope, 'The Effect of Professionalism on Performance of Procurement Function in the Public Sector: Experience from the Tanzanian Public Entities' (2017) 5(6) *International Journal of Business and Management Review* 48.

sustainable cities and communities. For instance, although no reference is made to SPP in SDG 8, SPP might play a pivotal role in requiring businesses to create the conditions that allow people to have quality jobs that stimulate the economy while not harming the environment.[109] The same is true for SDG 9, under which SPP could be crucial in relation to investments in infrastructure, transport, irrigation, energy and information and communication technology,[110] as well as for SDG 11 focusing on efficient urban planning and management practices in order to deal with the challenges brought by urbanisation.[111]

To translate policy into SPP practice it is necessary to go beyond guidance documents. Further developing LCA, LCC, and labels is seen as the most effective tool in leading to the uptake of SPP.

Concerning developing countries, fostering SPP means taking into account their special situation and needs. Today these countries still very much depend on Official Development Aid (ODA). This aid is still often *de facto* tied favouring firms from the donors' countries.[112] One possible way to foster SPP in developing countries while untying aid would be to promote short supply chains which reduce carbon footprint. ODA procurement may also be used to prod local companies in developing countries to comply with social standards concerning workers' rights. Besides helping sustainable development in the developing countries, this will contribute in preparing local companies to compete at global level without having recourse to social dumping. Requiring labels should instead phased in gently since it might favour companies from developed countries and local ones will need time to conform to Western standards. The above measures may contribute in making SPP solutions familiar to local procurement officials in developing countries while at the same time widening the production base for sustainability-oriented industry.

[109] www.un.org/sustainabledevelopment/economic-growth. SDG 8 provides that 'A continued lack of decent work opportunities, insufficient investments and under-consumption lead to an erosion of the basic social contract underlying democratic societies: that all must share in progress'.

[110] See UN SDG 9 at www.un.org/sustainabledevelopment/development-agenda.

[111] www.un.org/sustainabledevelopment/cities.

[112] See the discussion by A La Chimia, *Tied Aid and Development Aid Procurement in the Framework of EU and WTO Law. The Imperative for Change* (Oxford, Hart, 2014), and the OECD '2018 Report on the DAC Untying Recommendation' DCD/DAC(2018)12/REV2, available at www.oecd.org/dac/financing-sustainable-development/development-finance-standards/DCD-DAC(2018)12-REV2.en.pdf.

PART IV

Strengthening Developing Countries' Systems: Turning the Tide?

9

The Evolution of the Methodology for Assessing Procurement Systems (MAPS)

LENA DIESING AND PAULO MAGINA

I. Introduction

The Methodology for Assessing Procurement Systems (MAPS) is the most relevant tool to evaluate countries' public procurement systems to identify areas for improvement. MAPS as a policy tool offers an interesting case study of the genesis of a comprehensive and international policy tool, as well as its governance. Conceptualised in the development policy community more than a decade ago, the tool has recently been overhauled to re-emerge as a universal assessment for countries in all contexts.

Decisions to conduct a MAPS assessment have been sparked by reasons as different as fiduciary considerations in a development finance context on the one hand, and reform orientation on the other hand. Analysing the use and impact of MAPS as a policy tool can offer interesting insights for policy-makers, practitioners and scholars alike – both with regards to public procurement issues specifically, as well as policy-making in general. To what extent does the international policy environment influence an implementation-oriented tool? What impact can be expected from a tool targeting country systems? To what extent do the results from a tool like MAPS enable judgements about policy-making on an international level?

With occasion of the revision of MAPS completed in 2018, it is time to take stock of the tool's history: its evolution and past use. This chapter recapitulates on the origins of the tool, and how it was subsequently used. The overarching question explores the differences between the originally intended use, ascribed utilisation, and areas where MAPS was able to create the most relevant impact.

The main argument of this chapter is that there was a mismatch between the conceptualisation of MAPS as a diagnostic tool, and the role MAPS later had as an aggregate policy indicator for development progress. MAPS emerged out of the aid effectiveness agenda, in an effort to strengthen country systems and to increase the use of country systems (UCS). Monitoring of international commitments showed, however, that the UCS principle did not gather pace. MAPS was used frequently and probably improved country systems by informing reforms. However, there is no indication that the introduction and use of MAPS led to an increased use of country systems. MAPS has been renewed, with a focus on public procurement reform – in all countries, not just those who receive donor funding.

MAPS has not been the subject of ample research. Academic research mentions MAPS in the context of public procurement reform as well as in studies related to UCS. Some of these analyses come from academia with a link to the international development policy community.[1] Most studies emerged out of the policy context itself as background studies for international discussions and meetings on the subject.[2] In addition, many of the more than 100 MAPS assessments that have been conducted are not available publicly. Therefore, in tracing the history of MAPS, the authors relied on a review of policy documents from the context of MAPS' creation until today, interviews with participants that have been following the evolution of MAPS since the beginning, as well as speeches and discussions in a policy setting. All external observers spoke in an unofficial role and as public procurement experts, and not as representatives of institutions.

This chapter is structured in four sections (apart from the current introductory section): Origins; Uptake of the pre-2016 versions; Revision; Conclusion. In section II we will trace back the origins of MAPS in the development policy community in the early 2000s. Section III analyses how MAPS had been used until the recent revision process was started in 2015. Following this analysis, section IV details the goals of the revision process that has led to an updated MAPS, and the milestones towards this update. The concluding section outlines the lessons MAPS offers with regards to similar processes.

II. Origins

This section provides the background of the Methodology for Assessing Procurement Systems (MAPS), going back to its origins. The origins are intricately linked with the aid effectiveness agenda adopted by the donor community in the late 1990s and early 2000s. Initially developed in 2003–04, MAPS evolved in parallel to the international aid effectiveness agenda which is marked by a series of High-Level Fora and agreements on development assistance since the Paris Declaration in 2005.[3] Procurement has been indirectly a topic from the beginning, given that procurement is central to delivering development projects, and given that it is effective procurement where effective development assistance crystallises.

[1] See eg C Léon de Mariz, C Ménard and B Abeillé, *Public Procurement Reforms in Africa: Challenges in Institutions and Governance* (Oxford, Oxford University Press, 2014); CL Pallas, and J Wood, 'The World Bank's Use of Country Systems for Procurement: A Good Idea Gone Bad?' (2009) 27 *Development Policy Review* 215.

[2] See eg OECD, 'Compendium of Country Examples and Lessons Learned from Applying the Methodology for Assessment of National Procurement Systems: Sharing Experiences' (2008) 9(4) *OECD Journal on Development*, DOI: http://dx.doi.org/10.1787/journal_dev-v9-art2-en; OECD, *Aid Effectiveness 2011: Progress in Implementing the Paris Declaration*, Better Aid (Paris, OECD Publishing, 2012) available at DOI: http://dx.doi.org/10.1787/9789264125780-en; OECD/UNDP, *Making Development Co-operation More Effective: 2014 Progress Report* (Paris, OECD Publishing, 2014) available at http://dx.doi.org/10.1787/9789264209305-en.

[3] See the OECD website, 'The High Level Fora on Aid Effectiveness: A history', at www.oecd.org/dac/effectiveness/thehighlevelforaonaideffectivenessahistory.htm.

In fact, MAPS evolved to be considered one of the main, commonly accepted tools to assess public procurement systems. This development is linked to a general trend: developing countries were increasingly taking charge of their own development strategies. The result was an increased demand for using the countries' own systems to implement projects. This demand had to be balanced against donors' worries about safeguarding taxpayers' money. With regards to public procurement, MAPS was included into the efforts towards increased aid effectiveness as a tool for enhancing public procurement systems and for monitoring progress in doing so.[4]

The OECD Development Assistance Committee (DAC) recognised the need for a benchmarking tool for partner countries' procurement systems during the implementation of the 2001 DAC Recommendation on Untying Official Development Assistance to the Least Developed Countries.[5] In an effort to increase the effectiveness and efficiency of official development assistance (ODA), DAC members agreed to untie their development assistance. 'Untying aid' means that goods, services and works purchased with ODA should increasingly be open to international competition; fewer and fewer ODA-financed projects should be tied to a requirement to purchase in the donor country.[6] A DAC note on the implementation of the recommendation to untie ODA states that 'DAC members will work with partner countries to identify needs and to support efforts' to promote 'local and regional procurement in partner countries'.[7] In order to support the practical untying of aid, aside from the commitments on paper, countries saw the need to improve country procurement systems. A diagnostic tool was identified as potential assistance to doing so.

Two types of policy communities were involved in creating MAPS and later in shaping the uptake of MAPS, and, broadly, two streams of events were intertwined: a working group was founded that focused primarily on public procurement and the development of MAPS – the 'World Bank/OECD Development Assistance Committee (DAC) Procurement Roundtable' initiative.[8] In addition, a broader, more overarching community devised principles for development assistance in general, which culminated, for example, in the Paris principles for aid effectiveness and the related High Level Fora and Declarations (see further description in the following paragraphs.) While early discussions took place simultaneously, the evolution of MAPS as a procurement tool became increasingly part of the discussions around more general principles of

[4] 4th High-Level Forum on Aid Effectiveness (29 Nov–1 Dec 2011, Busan, Korea), 'Strengthening Country Procurement Systems: Results and Opportunities', available at http://siteresources.worldbank.org/INTALBANIA/Resources/Strengthening_Procurement_Systems.pdf; A Ayoung, N Bikondo and A Motamedi, 'Background Paper: Review of World Bank's Procurement Policies and Procedures. Use of Procurement Country Systems' (World Bank, February 2013) available at https://consultations.worldbank.org/Data/hub/files/meetings/Procurement_Policies/Background_Paper_on_Use_of_Country_Systems.pdf.

[5] OECD DAC Recommendation on Untying OECD Legal Instruments Official Development Assistance to the Least Developed Countries and Highly Indebted Poor Countries (2014) available at https://legalinstruments.oecd.org/public/doc/140/140.en.pdf.

[6] A La Chimia, *Tied Aid and Development Aid Procurement in the Framework of EU and WTO Law: The Imperative for Change* (Oxford, Hart Publishing, 2013).

[7] OECD/DAC, Working Party on Financial Aspects of Development Assistance, 'Implementing the DAC Recommendation on Untying Official Development Assistance to the Least Developed Countries', DCD/DAC/FA (2001) 3.

[8] OECD, MAPS Methodology for Assessing Procurement Systems, available at www.oecd.org/gov/public-procurement-methodology-assessing-procurement.htm.

Public Financial Management (PFM). As part of these discussions, MAPS became part of the more general principles set out in the Paris Declaration (2005).[9] The succession of these international high level fora on development relate to MAPS in three ways. First, the commitments coming out of these meetings sparked the development of the MAPS indicators/methodology. Second, MAPS – already in place – offered indicators to monitor the commitments. Third, broader goals of the development declarations, such as UCS, offered a justification for undertaking more MAPS assessments. These levers both influenced the use of MAPS and were influenced in turn by the outcome of the MAPS assessments. Table 1 summarises the main events that are described in more detail in the following paragraphs.

Table 1 Timeline: MAPS Development in the Context of the Aid Effectiveness Agenda

Date	Event	Policy Community
March 2002	Monterrey Financing for Development Conference and 'Monterrey Consensus'[10]	Aid Effectiveness
January 2003	Launch of the World Bank/OECD Development Assistance Committee (DAC) Procurement Roundtable	Public Procurement
February 2003	1st High-Level Forum on Aid Effectiveness, Rome, and 'Rome Declaration'[11]	Aid Effectiveness
December 2004	First publication of a public procurement benchmarking methodology (aka MAPS) as part of the Johannesburg Declaration, Conclusion of Roundtable	Public Procurement
March 2005	2nd High-Level Forum on Aid Effectiveness, Paris, and 'Paris Declaration'[12]	Aid Effectiveness
May 2008	Arusha Statement of the OECD DAC Joint Venture on Procurement	Public Procurement
September 2008	3rd High Level Forum on Aid Effectiveness, Accra, and 'Accra Agenda for Action' (AAA)[13]	Aid Effectiveness
November 2011	4th High-Level Forum on Aid Effectiveness, Busan, and the 'Global Partnership for Effective Development Cooperation' (GPEDC)[14]	Aid Effectiveness

(continued)

[9] OECD DAC Recommendation on Untying OECD Legal Instruments Official Development Assistance to the Least Developed Countries and Highly Indebted Poor Countries (n 5).

[10] UN, Monterrey Consensus on Financing for Development (2002) available at www.un.org/esa/ffd/wp-content/uploads/2014/09/MonterreyConsensus.pdf.

[11] OECD, Rome Declaration on Harmonisation, in: Harmonising Donor Practices for Effective Aid Delivery (2003) 10, available at www.oecd.org/dac/effectiveness/31451637.pdf.

[12] OECD, 'The Paris Declaration on Aid Effectiveness: Five Principles for Smart Aid' (undated) available at www.oecd.org/dac/effectiveness/45827300.pdf.

[13] OECD, 'Paris Declaration and Accra Agenda for Action', available at www.oecd.org/dac/effectiveness/parisdeclarationandaccraagendaforaction.htm.

[14] OECD, 'Fourth High Level Forum on Aid Effectiveness', available at www.oecd.org/dac/effectiveness/fourthhighlevelforumonaideffectiveness.htm. See also the website of the Global Partnership on Effective Development Cooperation at effectivecooperation.org.

Table 1. (*Continued*)

Date	Event	Policy Community
	Cusco Declaration of the OECD DAC Task Force on Procurement[15]	Public Procurement
October 2013	Meeting on the Task Force on Procurement, Rabat[16]	Public Procurement
April 2015	Global Public Procurement conference, Manila	Public Procurement
June 2015	First meeting of the Stakeholder Group on the Revision of MAPS	Public Procurement
July 2015	3rd International Conference on Financing for Development and the 'Addis Ababa Action Agenda' (AAAA)[17]	Aid Effectiveness
September 2015	Sustainable Development Goals (SDGs)[18]	General

Source: authors' compilation.

In parallel, the first stepping stones for the later aid effectiveness agenda were laid in 2002. The Monterrey Consensus of March 2002[19] mentioned the need to increase country ownership in technical assistance programmes, including through public procurement. The First High-Level Forum in Rome (February 2003)[20] outlined principles of aid effectiveness for the first time. An effort to use country systems in the implementation of development projects crystallised as part of this new focus. Procurement was only indirectly mentioned: e-procurement was considered as one of the key areas of technological progress that could boost aid effectiveness.[21]

As a consequence of what was previously explained, the Methodology for Assessing Procurement Systems was developed by the joint World Bank/ECD Development Assistance Committee (DAC) Procurement Roundtable initiative, which was a multi-stakeholder approach led jointly by the OECD and the World Bank that brought

[15] OECD/DAC Task Force on Procurement, The Cusco Declaration of the OECD/DAC Task Force on Procurement, 'Strong Procurement Systems for Effective States' (undated) www.oecd.org/dac/effectiveness/48425963.pdf.

[16] See the OECD calendar of events at www.oecd.org/fr/sites/mena/gouvernance/calendarofevents.htm; Royaume du Maroc, Trésorerie Générale du Royaume, Allocution d'ouverture de Monsieur Noureddine Bensouda, Trésorier Général du Royaume, Réunion du groupe de travail de l'OCDE sur les marchés publics, Rabat, 7 and 8 October 2013, 'Task Force on Procurement Meeting' at www.tgr.gov.ma/wps/wcm/connect/f0310c67-ce8c-46ef-b351-e1d4859e1a62/Task+Force+on+procurement+meeting+.pdf?MOD=AJPERES&CACHEID=f0310c67-ce8c-46ef-b351-e1d4859e1a62.

[17] UN, 'Addis Ababa Action Agenda of the Third International Conference on Financing for Development (Addis Ababa Action Agenda)' (New York, UN, 2015) available at www.un.org/esa/ffd/wp-content/uploads/2015/08/AAAA_Outcome.pdf.

[18] See https://sustainabledevelopment.un.org/.

[19] UN, Monterrey Consensus on Financing for Development (n 10).

[20] OECD, Rome Declaration on Harmonisation (n 11).

[21] See the OECD website, 'The High Level Fora on Aid Effectiveness: A history' (n 3); OECD, Rome Declaration on Harmonisation (n 11).

together developing countries, as well as bilateral and multilateral donors from 2003–04. Their aim was to develop a set of tools and standards to guide improvements of procurement systems, and to monitor progress on related commitments. The roundtable launched its work in a January 2003 meeting in Paris. Initially, the roundtable focused on four areas:

1. develop research about the benefits of good public procurement practices (establishing the rationale for focusing on public procurement reform);
2. agree on standards to benchmark progress of public procurement reform (set targets for countries' reforms and follow up achievements);
3. build capacity in public procurement systems (develop a strategy for capacity-building, based on the World Bank's Country Procurement Assessment Reviews, CPAR); and
4. develop monitoring and evaluation mechanisms for reform progress (closely related to no 1, as evaluation and monitoring results can support research and provide arguments to focus on reform).

According to the protocol,[22] the discussions focused closely on practical aspects of public procurement reform. Benchmarks as possible tools were discussed to make progress more concrete for each individual country. No high-level aggregates were discussed. The goal for donors to rely on countries' system is mentioned only marginally.[23]

The negotiations of the DAC Procurement Roundtable were concluded with the 'Johannesburg Declaration'. It is one of the main outcomes of the roundtable. The Declaration was issued in December 2004 by the countries and organisations that were part of the roundtable process.[24] The parties committed to three goals: (i) to improve procurement capacity; (ii) to base this capacity-building on diagnostics, prioritising and monitoring; and (iii) to focus on measurable performance and impact. The aspect of country ownership and UCS played a role in the commitments. However, this aspect was only one of three considerations informing the commitments, aside from prioritising public procurement reform and increasing effectiveness of the ways in which procurement systems are developed. To do so, countries committed to improving measurement and diagnostics.

The diagnostic framework mentioned as the second goal of the Johannesburg Declaration essentially corresponds to the indicator framework that became the MAPS. The first version is featured as a chapter in a 2005 OECD DAC report titled: 'Harmonising Donor Practices for Effective Aid Delivery – Volume 3: Strengthening

[22] OECD, 'Strengthening Procurement Capacities in Developing Countries: Summary Report of the OECD/DAC – World Bank Round Table, Paris, 22–23 January 2003' (2003) 4(2) OECD Journal on Development, available at www.oecd.org/dac/effectiveness/2500769.pdf.

[23] On this point, see ibid nr 22, 10.

[24] Australia, Austria, Belgium, Canada, Denmark, Dominican Republic, Ethiopia, European Commission, France, Germany, Ghana, Iceland, Indonesia, Ireland, Italy, Japan, Madagascar, Morocco, Mozambique, Nicaragua, Netherlands, Norway, Philippines, Portugal, Senegal, South Africa, Spain, Sri Lanka, Sweden, Switzerland, Tanzania, Uganda, Vietnam, United Kingdom, United States, African Development Bank (AfDB), Crown Agents for Overseas Governments and Administrations, Ltd., The Global Fund, Ideas Centre, International Development Law Institute, International Monetary Fund, International Trade Centre, Nordic Development Fund, Sahel Club of West Africa, UN, United Nations Conference on Trade and Development (UNCTAD), United Nations Development Programme (UNDP), United Nations World Food Programme, West African Economic and Monetary Union (UEMOA), World Bank, World Trade Organization.

Procurement Capacities in Developing Countries'.[25] Prior to its standalone publication as Methodology for Assessing National Procurement Systems in 2006, MAPS was referred to under different titles, such as 'OECD DAC benchmarking tool'.[26] (Fourth High-Level Forum on Aid Effectiveness, 2011)

Meanwhile, public procurement received expressed attention in the following High-Level Forum and the resulting declaration: the Second High-Level Forum took place in 2005 in Paris, under the title 'Joint Progress towards Enhanced Aid Effectiveness'.[27] In addition to deepening previous commitments related to harmonisation, the 2005 Paris Declaration[28] includes demands related to country ownership, alignment, managing for results and mutual accountability. Strengthening national procurement systems was prioritised and included as a common goal of donors and partner countries.

In detail, the commitment included goals to:

1. assess systems based on mutual standards, design reforms accordingly, and monitor progress made based on the reform strategy and assessment;
2. provide sufficient means to implement reforms; and
3. share lessons learned on reform efforts.

The first goal (assessing systems and creating standards) constitutes the basis for MAPS. The methodology describes what it means to assess national procurement systems against a commonly agreed standard, and provides indications for what it means to improve them. The goal also links MAPS to UCS policy, even though the initial constituting documents do not necessarily place this at the centre of MAPS. The burden of the commitment was on the donors, who agreed to use countries' procurement systems if they met commonly agreed standards, and to coordinate and harmonise their efforts among themselves. Countries were expected to take charge of the procurement reforms.

The Paris Declaration included indicators that made it possible to monitor the commitments. MAPS became a central element. On procurement, there were two indicators:

1. Reliable procurement systems (Indicator 2b in the Paris Declaration monitoring framework): by 2010, one-third of partner countries should have moved up at least one measure in the MAPS scale (at the time a four-point scale A to D).[29]
2. Using country procurement systems (Indicator 5b in the Paris Declaration monitoring framework): 80 per cent of donors should have used a country's procurement system by 2010, and there should have been an increase in the percentage of aid using country systems, depending on the MAPS score received by the country.[30]

[25] OECD, 'Harmonising Donor Practices for Effective Aid Delivery – Volume 3: Strengthening Procurement Capacities in Developing Countries' (OECD, DAC Guidance and Reference Series, 2005) available at www.oecd.org/gov/ethics/34336126.pdf. See also, 4th High-Level Forum on Aid Effectiveness, 'Strengthening Country Procurement Systems: Results and Opportunities' (n 4) 105.

[26] Pallas and Wood, 'The World Bank's Use of Country Systems for Procurement' (n 1) 218.

[27] See also the OECD website, 'The High Level Fora on Aid Effectiveness: A history' (n 3).

[28] OECD, 'The Paris Declaration on Aid Effectiveness and the Accra Agenda for Action' (undated), available at www.oecd.org/dac/effectiveness/34428351.pdf.

[29] OECD, *Aid Effectiveness 2011: Progress in Implementing the Paris Declaration* (n 2) 47.

[30] OECD, 'The Paris Declaration on Aid Effectiveness: Five Principles for Smart Aid' (n 12) 2. Also OECD, *Aid Effectiveness 2011: Progress in Implementing the Paris Declaration* (n 2).

As detailed in the next section, there was limited progress on use of country systems, according to these indicators. In addition, it has to be noted that when the indicators were developed, MAPS was a mere two years old. That means MAPS in its application and its indicator framework had not been thoroughly vetted, tested or consolidated. Instead, it has to be considered a first attempt at creating a tool to assess procurement systems. The close proximity between the first conceptualisation and the introduction as (aggregate) indicator to monitor the implementation of commitments concerning use of country systems makes it difficult to determine the true initial character and purpose of MAPS. Was MAPS developed to promote use of country systems? Or was MAPS developed to build public procurement systems? Considering the 'founding documents' referenced above, it appears that MAPS was more committed to reforms and improvements of systems. The documents do not state a commitment to UCS policy for which a tracking mechanism needed to be found.

Following the Paris Declaration, the Accra Agenda for Action (AAA), issued at the Third High-Level Forum on Aid Effectiveness in 2008,[31] aimed at deepening previous commitments. In doing so, the AAA focuses efforts on four main areas: (i) ownership, (ii) inclusive partnerships, (iii) delivering (measurable) results and (iv) capacity development. With regards to procurement, the AAA committed donors to use countries' systems more frequently, and to achieve higher transparency and value for money.[32] In the follow-up to the AAA, the political dimensions of use of country systems were increasingly appreciated. As a consequence, beyond supporting the technical decision-making around the question whether to use country systems or not, stakeholders raised awareness of the importance of public procurement with the political leadership in the run-up to the next High-Level Forum.

The grouping that had been known as the Procurement Roundtable had originally concluded its work in 2004 with the Johannesburg Declaration (see above). Given the international interest in aid effectiveness and the role of public procurement therein, the grouping continued its work, but in changing set-ups that built on linkages between public procurement and public financial management. First, the OECD DAC Joint Venture on Procurement focused on the further development of the MAPS. In the margins of the 2008 AAA, the Joint Venture issued the 'Arusha Statement'. This statement reiterated the importance of public procurement for the implementation of the goals of the 2005 Paris Declaration as a whole, and specifically emphasised the role of MAPS to do so. Use of country systems was one of seven focus points identified in the implementation of the Paris Declaration – separate from the two focus points relating to the use of MAPS.[33]

Second, the OECD DAC Task Force on Procurement continued the procurement-related work around aid effectiveness in the run-up to the next High-Level

[31] UN, 'Addis Ababa Action Agenda of the Third International Conference on Financing for Development (Addis Ababa Action Agenda)' (n 17).

[32] OECD, 'The Paris Declaration on Aid Effectiveness and the Accra Agenda for Action' (n 28).

[33] OECD/DAC Working Party on Aid Effectiveness, Joint Venture on Procurement, 'The Arusha Statement of the OECD/DAC Joint Venture on Procurement, Arusha, The United Republic of Tanzania, May 5–7, 2008, "To Support the Implementation of the Paris Declaration Principles by Building Reliable Public Procurement Systems"' (2008) available at www.oecd.org/dac/effectiveness/final%20Arusha%20Statement%20May%2026,%202008%20ENGLISH.pdf.

Development Meeting. The Fourth High-Level forum on Aid Effectiveness in Busan (2011) resulted in the Global Partnership for Effective Development Cooperation (also referred to as Busan Partnership for Effective Development Cooperation).[34] Public procurement was less centrally featured; focus was on increasing partnership and cooperation between developing countries and development assistance providers of all types, beyond the DAC donors that had been traditionally at the heart of the High-Level Fora. The Global Partnership for Effective Development Cooperation (GPEDC) is being monitored on a regular basis, including against indicators about use of country systems. The indicator for use of country systems builds on the previous indicator, but combining the previously separate indicators for PFM and public procurement. Reference to improved procurement systems and MAPS specifically was dropped. Instead, the World Bank's Country Policy and Institutional Assessment (CPIA) serves as the data source. Baseline target was 49 per cent of aid channelled through country systems.[35]

In the context of the Busan High Level Meeting, the Cusco Declaration of the Task Force on Procurement commented on priorities in strengthening public procurement systems, but almost left out the emphasis on use of country systems. The last point in the declaration called for a 'pragmatic approach in [the] progressive use of country systems'.[36] The Task Force on Procurement met again in October 2013, in Rabat, Morocco, following requests from multiple parties to continue the global dialogue on public procurement. The goal of the meeting was to determine concrete steps to ensure a continuation. The group agreed to begin the revision of MAPS, and set out first ideas on the direction that this update should take. In addition, the meeting focused on strengthening peer learning between countries, including by the commitment to establish an informal Global Public Procurement network.[37]

Renewed commitments to strengthening public procurement systems were made in the global development-related agreements of 2015, notably the Sustainable Development Goals (SDGs) and, leading up to the SDGs, the Addis Ababa Action Agenda (AAAA).[38] While these international agreements stand in the tradition of the efforts of improving how development assistance is delivered, and the UCS principle remained as an ideal way of implementing development projects, there was less emphasis on this topic. Instead, procurement is increasingly perceived as a lever to achieve sustainability. The complexity of decision-making in the context of development policy was appreciated.

The AAAA was issued at the Third International Conference on Financing for Development in July 2015; and the SDGs were issued in September that year. The AAAA commits signatories to strive for transparent public procurement systems that

[34] See OECD website at www.oecd.org/development/effectiveness/busanpartnership.htm.

[35] Global Partnership for Effective Development Co-operation, 'Monitoring Guide 2015–2016: Monitoring the effective development co-operation commitments' (October 2015) available at http://effectivecooperation.org/wp-content/uploads/2015/10/2015-Monitoring-Guide_-final1.pdf.

[36] OECD/DAC Task Force on Procurement, The Cusco Declaration of the OECD/DAC Task Force on Procurement, 'Strong Procurement Systems for Effective States' (n 15).

[37] OECD, 'The Paris Declaration on Aid Effectiveness and the Accra Agenda for Action' (n 28).

[38] UN, 'Addis Ababa Action Agenda of the Third International Conference on Financing for Development (Addis Ababa Action Agenda)' (n 17).

'reinforce sustainable development' as a strategic tool.[39] The SDGs emphasise the role of public procurement in achieving sustainable development outcomes even more: Goal 12, which looks at sustainable consumption, features a specific target (12.7) on sustainable procurement: 'Promote public procurement practices that are sustainable, in accordance with national policies and priorities'.[40] In addition, target 16.6 called for the development of 'effective, accountable and transparent institutions', which includes public procurement systems.[41] MAPS re-gained importance in parallel. As described in section III of this chapter (on the revision of MAPS), the process to revise the tool and adapt it to today's challenges gained momentum around the same time.

III. Uptake of the Pre-2016 Versions

This section follows the uptake of MAPS until the revision. This view is necessary to understand why a revision of MAPS was later undertaken, what objectives this review pursued, and *why* these objectives were chosen in the way they were chosen. This section follows the use of the pre-2016 versions of MAPS. First, it analyses the intentions behind launching MAPS assessments. A second step mirrors these intentions with the actual outcomes of MAPS assessments. Finally, it looks at the criticisms of MAPS; criticisms that on the one hand emerged out of this realistic look at the purpose of MAPS and that on the other hand led to the revision of MAPS.

A. Why MAPS was Initially Developed

MAPS was used for different purposes, with some goals receiving more attention than others. While some of the goals were achieved, others were not – and often not those that where most frequently quoted as the reasons behind MAPS.

Concretely, the following were the goals behind the development and application of MAPS:

1. start and follow reform processes;
2. provide a benchmark in support of use of country systems; and
3. harmonisation and mutual accountability.

i. First Goal: Start and Follow Reform Processes

Regardless of the commitment to increased use of country systems, countries have always strived to improve their systems due to the immediate benefits that reforms

[39] ibid.

[40] See the website of the United Nations Sustainable Development Knowledge Platform, Sustainable Development Goal 12, 'Ensure sustainable consumption and production patterns', at https://sustainabledevelopment.un.org/sdg12.

[41] See the website of the United Nations Sustainable Development Knowledge Platform, Sustainable Development Goal 16, 'Promote peaceful and inclusive societies for sustainable development, provide access to justice for all and build effective, accountable and inclusive institutions at all levels', at https://sustainabledevelopment.un.org/sdg16.

have. For example, countries hoped to make their public procurement processes more efficient and capitalise on the very tangible monetary savings associated with that. Through self-assessments MAPS offered a way to support reforms in three aspects: first, an assessment using MAPS highlights where new reforms could be targeted; second, it helps to justify difficult changes to a sceptical public or political leadership; and third, repeated assessments could offer a way to monitor progress.

ii. Second Goal: Provide a Benchmark in Support of UCS

While the concept of UCS is closely related to improved country procurement systems, it became a goal in itself – a 'badge of honour' in development finance – and an incentive to develop public procurement systems in itself. As stated in the first version of MAPS, as well as the Johannesburg Declaration, one purpose of MAPS was to support greater use of country systems. The UCS concept is based on the idea that any public system works like a muscle: the more it is used, the stronger it gets. As a consequence, providers of development cooperation should use a country's own system to implement their projects, which makes the projects also more sustainable, rather than using donor-owned structures. Use of country systems usually comprises three areas: beyond the national procurement systems, use of country systems also looks at the national budget execution procedures, as well as and the national auditing procedures.[42]

Donors may strive to transfer more money directly to countries, but – due to pressures to account for their spending vis-à-vis taxpayers – only with assurance that a country's system is indeed up to the task and will not recklessly squander the money. MAPS is a tool to address exactly this issue: it assesses a system against agreed standards, and provides a way to communicate the results of this analysis easily. More importantly, it signals the status in a manner that can easily be communicated. That means that the fiduciary aspect of assessing procurement systems has a very high significance for donors. Donors thus have an incentive to pay for MAPS assessments, to be repeated rather more often than not, to be able to produce an up-to-date assessment. A partner country can have an interest in the increased independence that the UCS principle offers, ie receiving the 'approval stamp' for being able to undertake procurement independently.

iii. Third Goal: Harmonisation and Mutual Accountability

A third motive emerged on a procedural level: while all parties acknowledged the need for assessments, be it for fiduciary reasons or to kick-start reforms, as a self-assessment or with external support, different stakeholders preferred different approaches to doing an assessment. This put a burden on all parties. Assessments had to be repeated because individual assessments were not comparable and usually satisfied only the needs of the donor who launched the assessment. Consequently, countries had to repeatedly conduct similar assessments; donors repeatedly paid for them. The need for a common approach became apparent. This includes not only harmonisation of the assessments,

[42] OECD/UNDP, *Making Development Co-operation More Effective: 2014 Progress Report* (n 2) 47.

but also trying to create a vehicle to establish mutual accountability. The harmonised approach to assessments would render repeated assessments futile. In addition, harmonisation would provide an agreed standard towards which reform should work. Finally, harmonisation promised a way to compare approaches to the UCS policy, to which the donors had committed. This created a way to monitor success with regards to use of country systems.

B. The Outcomes of MAPS Assessments

i. What Remained of these Intentions?

These different goals illustrate different drivers behind the MAPS, and also how different these drivers are. In fact, put figuratively, the different motivations pull into different directions. The development impact is one driver; measurement for the sake of measurement is another. The international commitments ask for improvements in certain indicators, but it has not been proven that these indicators accurately represent the actual improvement in the systems.

Nevertheless, MAPS was in demand, as evidenced by the quantity of assessments: since its creation in 2004–05, observers estimate that at least several dozen but likely over 90 countries were assessed using the MAPS. Most of the countries were assessed more than once: either because donors repeated the assessment, or because several donors each conducted at least one MAPS-based assessment for their specific purposes in the same country. In addition, assessments were launched to support the monitoring efforts of the Paris Declaration (notably indicator 2b) and, in this context, to show progress over time.

However, compared with the goals of the assessment as stated above, MAPS was only partially successful, despite the broad application. On the one hand, countries were indeed able to progress with their procurement reform agendas. On the other hand, the availability of a benchmark to prepare use of country systems did not actually translate into more use of country systems. In the meantime, while MAPS was increasingly accepted as the standard for assessing procurement systems, assessments did not provide a sufficient basis to monitor overall progress, nor did they foster mutual accountability or reliability.

In essence, the use of MAPS in the decade following its launch in 2005 until the revision can be associated with two antagonistic observations:

1. use of country systems did not substantially increase; and
2. several countries reformed their systems.

a. Progress on Use of Country Systems Remained behind Targets

MAPS, as an indicator, is related to use of country systems in two ways: one, the multilateral development banks (MDBs) decided to grant use of country systems status based on a country's MAPS score. Two, as mentioned above, aggregated MAPS scores were used as an indicator for the commitments in the high-level development declarations. The expected result would be that donors use country systems over time because they now have a tool – MAPS – that would make it safe for them to do so. MAPS would enable donors in two parallel ways: one, to help make an informed decision to use the assessed procurement systems, and two, to be able to combine efforts and co-fund reform programmes on the basis of commonly shared assessments. In addition, the quality of public procurement systems would be expected to increase, given that a tool – MAPS – would now highlight promising areas for reform and therefore make reforms more efficient. Neither expectation was confirmed.

The initial target related to use of country systems specified in 2005 in the Paris Declaration envisioned that 80 per cent of official development assistance would be channelled through partner country's own systems.[43] In addition, the aggregated scores of the MAPS assessments should increase one measure on the four-point scale for one-third of the partner countries.[44] However, repeated monitoring of the commitments in the Paris Declaration in 2008 and 2011 showed that countries hardly progressed.[45] The baseline (2005) had been 40 per cent; by 2007, only 43 per cent of aid was channelled fully through country procurement systems, and by 2011 only 45 per cent. The 2011 monitoring report on the Paris Declaration cites credibility, efficiency and effectiveness as the reasons for which donors require using their own procurement rules.[46] Aside of the percentage of aid, a survey among donors found that in 2011, 60 per cent of the donors responding to the survey were not using country systems despite the international commitment six years earlier.[47] In addition, the 2011 monitoring report on the Paris Declaration found that not enough MAPS assessments were available to reach a substantive conclusion, so the target had to be dismissed:

> No targets are presented for indicators 2b (reliable procurement systems) and 5b (use of country procurement systems) as the sample of countries for whom [*sic*] data on the quality of systems are available is too small to allow for meaningful analysis.[48]

Overall, as observers note, even under ideal circumstances, these results are testimony to the fact that the indicators and associated goals were too ambitious. Timelines for reforms were too short to achieve meaningful progress in the countries given the time that was necessary to plan, fund and implement projects before impact could materialise. Expectations were equally unrealistic with regards to the number of MAPS assessments that would be available over a given timeframe, taking into account that the quite complex MAPS assessments took considerable time and resources to manage. In addition, repercussions of the global financial crisis starting in 2008 contributed to the already negative direction at a critical juncture and likely contributed to the loss of momentum as priorities shifted.

The 2011 monitoring report on the Paris Declaration noted that MAPS assessments were often of a 'one-off nature', which would not lend itself to discover trends. In fact,

[43] OECD, 'The Paris Declaration on Aid Effectiveness: Five Principles for Smart Aid' (n 12).
[44] OECD, *Aid Effectiveness 2011: Progress in Implementing the Paris Declaration* (n 2) 47.
[45] ibid 47.
[46] ibid 47.
[47] 4th High-Level Forum on Aid Effectiveness, 'Strengthening Country Procurement Systems: Results and Opportunities' (n 4) 16.
[48] OECD, *Aid Effectiveness 2011: Progress in Implementing the Paris Declaration* (n 2) 19.

Table 2 highlights the small sample size of MAPS assessments included in the survey that was conducted as a basis for monitoring the Paris commitments.

Table 2 Quality of Country Procurement Systems. Indicator 2b (2007–10)

Score	2007 No. of countries	2010 No. of countries
Very strong – A	–	–
B	7	1
C	9	4
Weak – D	1	–
Number of countries scored	17	5

Source: OECD, *Aid Effectiveness 2011: Progress in Implementing the Paris Declaration* (2012) (n 2) 47.

Half a decade later, the picture was equally bleak, as evidenced by the 2016 Monitoring Report related to the commitments as part of the Global Partnership for Effective Development Cooperation (GPEDC). The commitments monitored in this report were issued in the Busan High-Level Meeting in 2011.[49] Indicator 9 in the monitoring framework for the GPEDC contained the commitments for public procurement as related to use of country systems, which was to increase use of country systems in those countries with a certain score in the MAPS-related CPIA, without stating a more concrete goal.[50] The 2016 Monitoring Report found that 50 per cent of aid was channelled through country systems. This report groups together the use of country systems related to budget execution, financial reporting, auditing and procurement. However, when considering procurement systems only (ie dismissing systems for budget execution, financial reporting and auditing unlike other indicators), the use of countries' own procurement systems decreased: use of procurement systems to channel aid fell from 39 per cent in 2010 to 37 per cent in 2015. The targets to increase use of country systems were set as a proportion of the aid not yet channelled through country systems, with a larger proportion to be attained for better developed systems (those with a higher CPIA score.) Donor countries had committed to using country systems for as much as 83 per cent of aid.[51]

Similar conclusions were reached by the World Bank in an evaluation report in February 2013 related to its UCS policy.[52] After three years of implementation, the evaluation report found that only a limited number of countries achieved a limited clearance for use of country systems. The report attributes the outcome to 'un-reconciled views on the program's objectives' and a lack of incentives for all parties

[49] OECD/UNDP, *Making Development Co-operation More Effective: 2016 Progress Report* (Paris, OECD Publishing, 2016), available at http://dx.doi.org/10.1787/9789264266261-en.

[50] Global Partnership for Effective Development Co-operation, 'The Monitoring Framework of the Global Partnership for Effective Development Co-operation: Indicators and Targets' (undated) available at http://effectivecooperation.org/wp-content/uploads/2015/05/GPEDC-Monitoring-Framework-10-Indicators.pdf.

[51] OECD/UNDP, *Making Development Co-operation More Effective: 2016 Progress Report* (n 49).

[52] Ayoung, Bikondo and Motamedi, 'Use of Procurement Country Systems' (n 4).

to work towards use of country systems.[53] Similar assessments of earlier projects came to the same conclusion.[54]

As noted by observers, an additional aspect to be considered in this context is that there seemed to be different ideas of what exactly means 'using country systems'. The UCS principle was interpreted along a continuum of effort: does 'using country systems' mean to hand over the management of a process to the partner country's authorities fully or just transferring limited elements?

These results highlight a paradox: even though donors now had the MAPS as a tool at hand there was limited improvement. One conclusion from this is that MAPS had little effect on the UCS policies.

b. Several Countries have Successfully Used a MAPS Assessment to Foster Public Procurement Reforms

Many countries began a longer-term reform process, often spanning more than a decade, by undertaking a MAPS assessment. MAPS mostly served as a stocktake to determine strengths and weaknesses of the public procurement system in the respective country. Based on that, priorities of the public procurement reforms were determined – such as whether the legal framework needed to be strengthened or whether the tasks of the public procurement body should be reviewed. In Senegal, the results of a MAPS assessment served to appease critics who claimed any elaborate public procurement regulatory system would slow down procurement processes more than it would help to render the procurement cycle more efficient. In Zambia, the Zambian Public Procurement Authority (ZPPA) was able to argue for the need of reforms in the public procurement system, because MAPS summarised the shortcomings into an easily comprehensible assessment result. Other examples include Rwanda, which conducted a self-assessment using MAPS, and the Philippines, where MAPS was transformed into a monitoring tool to evaluate progress against the public procurement reform strategy. In the West African Economic and Monetary Union (WAEMU) member states, MAPS assessments were used to highlight disparities among the countries' procurement systems. This enabled the countries to harmonise their systems through reforms.[55]

ii. The Problem of Good Data as the Basis for Monitoring Remained

As mentioned above, the monitoring report for the Paris Declaration[56] dismissed the use of country systems target due to a lack of assessments that could be drawn upon for analysis. In fact, only the piloting assessments of the MAPS, conducted in the mid-2000s, were gathered in a publicly available space. However, a study on use of country systems prepared for the 2011 Busan High-Level Forum assesses that the use

[53] ibid 16.

[54] Léon de Mariz, Ménard and Abeillé, *Public Procurement Reforms in Africa* (n 1) 92–102, 119–21.

[55] 4th High-Level Forum on Aid Effectiveness, 'Strengthening Country Procurement Systems: Results and Opportunities' (n 4). In addition, these experiences were expressed in the High Level Meeting on the Revision of the MAPS: From Consultation to Implementation (Dakar, Senegal, 8–9 November 2016.

[56] OECD, *Aid Effectiveness 2011: Progress in Implementing the Paris Declaration* (n 2) 47.

of MAPS had 'become widespread',[57] that repeated assessments had been undertaken and allowed to monitor progress on public procurement reforms. The common practice has been that each donor conducts their own country assessments as they saw fit to plan their projects, changing the methodology as needed and without publishing them beyond the parties involved in the concrete planning for projects and financing. This individualised application of MAPS also prevented a true harmonisation of assessments, and their exchange. Often, countries were assessed repeatedly by different donors – using similar, yet not identical, assessment methodologies based on MAPS.[58]

Indeed, a report tabled at the Busan High-Level Forum highlighted 'issues of concern with regards to donor behaviour',[59] including donor coordination and the degree of use of country systems. This suggests that repeated assessments of the same country were conducted and country systems were used infrequently.

C. Shortcomings and Criticisms

The application of MAPS revealed several shortcomings of the methodology, and criticism ensued.

Some were related to the practical implementation, others had their origin in the conceptualisation. Three aspects were named by countries that were assessed with the MAPS, by the sponsors of the assessments (ie, the development banks), as well as by independent experts who observed the application and drew their conclusions. Criticisms were gathered in the stakeholder group on the revision of MAPS as a starting point to improvements. These aspects are discussed below.

i. MAPS Remained Donor-driven

The overwhelming majority of assessments seems to have been conducted by the MDBs, as noted in interviews with stakeholders and as suggested by a compendium of country cases.[60] In addition, only few countries that would be assessed with MAPS had been involved the creation of MAPS. Some institutions incorporated MAPS into their approval processes for UCS mechanisms, but observers noted that the consultation process around this was structured to make feedback and involvement difficult.[61] The approach in which MAPS assessments were conducted usually followed a similar pattern: the need for an assessment would depend on the provision of financing – and not necessarily be related to the country's needs to use an assessment to pursue reforms. In addition, donors often demanded slightly changed versions of MAPS to

[57] 4th High-Level Forum on Aid Effectiveness, 'Strengthening Country Procurement Systems: Results and Opportunities' (n 4) 17.

[58] Discussions in the MAPS stakeholder group on the revision of the MAPS to prepare the revised MAPS version.

[59] 4th High-Level Forum on Aid Effectiveness, 'Strengthening Country Procurement Systems: Results and Opportunities' (n 4) 17.

[60] OECD, 'Compendium of Country Examples and Lessons Learned from Applying the Methodology for Assessment of National Procurement Systems: Sharing Experiences' (n 2).

[61] Pallas and Wood (n 1).

match with internal guidelines, resulting in several similar, yet not identical assessments of the same country. That said, the donor's incentive and ownership remained larger than the country's, which was potentially mostly motivated by not losing development finance by foregoing a MAPS assessment. Once launched, a public procurement expert, hired as a consultant, would prepare the assessment remotely and then spend a maximum of a month in the target country to gather information and do the MAPS analysis. The conclusions of the assessment were equally conducted remotely. As a consequence, country ownership remained low, as well as an acceptance of the results of the MAPS assessments. In turn, the recommendations of the MAPS assessment would not be used to conduct reforms.

ii. Mandatory Scoring Proved Counterproductive

Many country representatives reported that their 'MAPS Score' had been the result of lengthy negotiations. Supposedly neutral experts were the ones undertaking the actual assessment indicator by indicator. However, country representatives, representatives of development banks and the experts argued about the decimal points of the final MAPS score. The reason why these minor differences in the MAPS score caused such heated discussion hinges on the weight these scores have in determining the approval for use of country systems. A minor difference in the MAPS score would determine whether the country was able to receive funds under a more liberal UCS policy or not. However, the MAPS indicator and scoring system did not actually match the granularity of the banks' decision-making structure with regards to use of country systems approval.

In this respect, MAPS became a source of conflict about a result that had little effect on a country's long-term improvements. MAPS reduced the progress of a public procurement system to a score, and this score determined the availability of funds. High stakes were matched with a relatively vague assessment concept. In fact, the ability to achieve reforms did not matter as long as the score improved. In addition, the score inherently benchmarked countries. Even if a country undertook reforms that were impressive for their context, they could still have a bad score or only minor improvements in terms of the MAPS scale. That means that countries have an incentive to favour changes that would reflect easily in big improvements on the MAPS scale (typically legal reforms), but no incentive to undertake those reforms that would result in definitely important changes in other terms (such as capacity, strategic policy objectives, savings, less corruption, etc).

iii. MAPS Measured Compliance rather than Performance

The MAPS indicator framework was structured in a way that favoured an analysis of whether a country met a certain qualitative standard. This was a static 'yes/no' analysis of the characteristics of a country's public procurement system. The central question, therefore, became: 'Does the country have a certain law, institution or process in place?', and not how well these features worked in practice.

For several years from 2006 to 2010, MAPS included optional 'Compliance and Performance Indicators' (CPIs), to be distinguished from the mandatory 'Baseline Indicators' (BLIs). The BLIs were mandatory and focused on formal compliance of the system, whereas the CPIs focused on performance, and were introduced to mitigate the fact that performance was largely unaccounted for. The names do not reflect the fact that the CPIs were largely quantitative indicators, whereas the BLIs were often qualitative. Given the optional nature, as well as challenges to retrieve quantitative evidence, few MAPS assessments applied the CPIs and this aspect remained neglected. The mere existence of laws hardly paints a picture of the way in which a public procurement system fulfils its original purpose. Decisions – be it about use of country systems or reform strategies – on the basis of compliance will always be less relevant than decisions based on performance monitoring and evidence-based policy-making.

iv. Conclusions on the Success and Failure of MAPS

In conclusion, it appears that both the success and failure of MAPS hinged on its unforeseen use as an indicator.

Considering early documents around MAPS, producing an indicator and tracking UCS policy does not appear to be at the heart of the existence of MAPS. Instead, MAPS was drawn on when the need to track this policy in the wake of international commitments became desirable. The original focus – kick-starting reforms – slipped out of sight. With the Sustainable Development Goals and the Addis Ababa Action Agenda, use of country systems in its previous design became less prominent, and equally the use of MAPS to track it.

IV. Revision

As discussed in the previous section, MAPS was most successful where it was used in the context of public procurement reforms. Despite repeated assessments and progress on the MAPS-scale, the amount of ODA channelled through country systems remained behind targets. In addition, the application of MAPS repeatedly presented the same challenges, regardless of context. Different stakeholders called on a revision of MAPS. The most recent revision confirms the shift towards reform, emphasising the universality of the concept underlying MAPS.

The revision of MAPS was largely driven by an informal stakeholder group. This stakeholder group builds on a history of similar groupings that had been formed and abandoned in parallel with the high-level development fora of the 2000s, as mentioned above. The MAPS revision process was structured as an informal exchange, driven by stakeholders who have used or will use MAPS in the future. The Stakeholder Group on the Revision of MAPS guided the revision process. First discussions about a MAPS revision took place in 2013, emerging out of the World Bank and the OECD. First stocktakes of how MAPS had been used were conducted; options for revising MAPS were explored in several meetings, for example in Rabat in 2013. During this meeting, stakeholders referred back to the unfinished aspects of the Task Force on Procurement from 2011. The MAPS revision started concretely in the spring of 2015, at a global public procurement conference in Manila, Philippines (20–21 April 2015). Subsequently, interested stakeholders met periodically to discuss the process of the MAPS revision and first drafts of the updated tool. Meetings were coordinated by the OECD, acting as an informal MAPS Secretariat, and supported in different ways by the members of the stakeholder group. The stakeholder group came to include representatives from countries, bilateral and multilateral development assistance providers, international organisations, and other interested experts and parties, proving to be a unique gathering of international and regional players to develop a common good, under the same understanding.[62]

The stakeholder group shared the objectives of the MAPS revision. To summarise, the reasons for the revision were the following:

1. evolution of public procurement within public policy and development policy;
2. increasing importance of performance over compliance;
3. improving coordination; and
4. emphasising the universality of the MAPS approach.

A. Evolution of Public Procurement within Public Policy and Development Policy

Public procurement as a policy and research area has progressed substantially in recent years. The most immediate reason why a revision of MAPS was called lies in this progress. It goes beyond the scope of this chapter to describe this development in detail; to simplify heavily, public procurement as a government function developed from an administrative function to a strategic function. In the past, public procurement was considered as the simple purchasing of goods, services and works for the government. Now, in the majority of the cases, the strategic aspects of this activity are being highly appreciated and accounted for when developing public procurement systems. Countries actively use the governmental purchasing power in a more general understanding, pursuing strategic goals beyond the narrow ones of the past. This, however, has made the public procurement function much more complex than before, requiring more sophisticated legal and institutional frameworks and, in turn, requiring an assessment of the quality of the public procurement system that takes account of that.

International frameworks have been reflecting this shift: most notably, in 2015, the OECD developed a new standard for public procurement systems. This standard was adopted by the OECD member countries through the OECD Recommendation of the

[62] Representatives from the following countries and organisations participated in the exchanges of the stakeholder group: Afghanistan, African Development Bank (AfDB), Agency for Public Management and eGovernment (Difi) in Norway, Asian Development Bank (ADB), Australia's Department of Foreign Affairs and Trade, Global Affairs Canada, Caribbean Development Bank (CDB), Chile, Council of Europe Development Bank (CEB), Colombia, European Bank for Reconstruction and Development (EBRD), European Investment Bank (EIB), European Commission, Expertise France, Georgia, GIZ – commissioned by the German Federal Ministry for Economic Cooperation and Development, Inter-American Development Bank (IADB), Islamic Development Bank (IsDB), Organisation for Economic Cooperation and Development (OECD), Philippines, Senegal, SIGMA (Support for Improvement in Governance and Management), United States Agency for International Development (USAID), World Bank, Zambia, as well as independent public procurement consultants.

Council on Public Procurement.[63] This recommendation is based on 12 principles, without prioritising any principle:

- access;
- accountability;
- balance;
- capacity;
- efficiency;
- e-procurement;
- evaluation;
- integration;
- integrity;
- participation;
- risk management; and
- transparency.

These principles describe in an aspirational way how a state-of-the art public procurement system should look. They cover the entirety of the procurement system and the entirety of the public procurement cycle. Together with many other international standards (EU Public Procurement Directives, 2014; UNCITRAL Model Law, 2011; WTO/GPA, 2014)[64] and the procurement frameworks of the MDBs, MAPS is inspired by this approach, as it moved away from the benchmark model (defining minimum requirements) towards a principles-based approach.

B. Increasing Importance of Performance over Compliance

A second development is related to this evolution in approaches to public procurement. Generally, the quality of a system was increasingly based on performance considerations which cannot be assessed by applying a 'checkbox-style' assessment. Instead of assessing mere *de jure* compliance, assessors and policy-makers are increasingly interested in qualitative evaluations, taking into account *de facto* performance. In turn, because of this greater interest, more data has been gathered. This facilitates performance-based

[63] See www.oecd.org/gov/public-procurement/recommendation.

[64] Directive 2014/23/EU of the European Parliament and of the Council of 26 February 2014 on the award of concession contracts [2014] OJ L94/1; Directive 2014/24/2014 of the European Parliament and of the Council of 26 February 2014 on public procurement and repealing Directive 2004/18/EC [2014] OJ L94/65; Directive 2014/25/EU of the European Parliament and of the Council of 26 February 2014 on procurement by entities operating in the water, energy, transport and postal services sectors and repealing Directive 2004/17/EC [2014] OJ L94/243; UNCITRAL Model Law on Public Procurement (UN doc A/66/17 Annex I) (As adopted by the United Nations Commission on International Trade Law on 1 July 2011) available at www.uncitral.org/uncitral/en/uncitral_texts/procurement_infrastructure/2011Model.html; World Trade Organization, Revised Agreement on Government Procurement [2014] available at www.wto.org/english/docs_e/legal_e/rev-gpr-94_01_e.htm.

assessments in a way that was not possible before. The revised MAPS now includes indicators that support this aim, while the previous version of MAPS was not designed to conduct this type of assessment.

C. Improving Coordination

A third development that sparked the revision of MAPS was the insight that coordination around assessments and reform was necessary. As detailed in the previous sections, countries were faced with an increasing burden to undergo repeated, cumbersome assessments. A revision of the MAPS should introduce changes that facilitated self-assessments, and reduce the burden of repeated assessments. Stakeholders to the MAPS revision have hoped to improve coordination around MAPS assessments to exploit synergies, thereby reducing individual costs for assessments and alleviating assessment fatigue on the part of the countries. One ambition has been to revise MAPS in order to create a stronger basis for mutual recognition of assessments, by making the assessments more comparable and possibly by creating an independent party that would supervise the assessment processes. Previously, two assessors might not arrive at the same conclusions in the same country. This concept of 'mutual reliance' was a strong component of the discussions and a large motivation to devote resources to the revision.

D. Universality of the MAPS Approach

The fourth reason for revising MAPS was to stress the universality of the underlying aim of MAPS: to assist and support countries in improving their public procurement systems. Giving priority to this universal goal also contributed to ensuring the relevance of MAPS in the future when countries evolve. Many countries that benefited from previous MAPS assessments indeed graduated from their status as developing country into mid-income range (such as Chile or Colombia). Constantly striving to improve their public procurement systems, their systems outgrew the previous MAPS. At the same time, the MAPS indicator framework, targeting the entire procurement system, harbours great potential for more advanced reform. This aspect is framed by the launch of the Sustainable Development Goals (SDGs) in September 2015, defining a universal set of aims, valid for all countries. The revised MAPS is aligned with this standard: instead of providing a low common denominator or benchmark, the revised MAPS provides aspirational goals that constitute a good public procurement system, applicable to all countries irrespective of development level or economic strength.

One tangible way to allow for this universal applicability in any given country context was realised by introducing optional modules in addition to a 'core' MAPS tool that focus on assessing the main (common and basic) features of a procurement system. In fact, MAPS was expanded to a 'suite' model, with indicator frameworks for specific and particular topics of a public procurement system that can be added to the assessment as needed, therefore providing a more comprehensive vision of the system.

At the time of writing, six optional modules were being developed, on the following topics:

- agency-level assessments;
- e-procurement;
- professionalisation;
- public-private partnerships and concessions;
- sector market analysis; and
- sustainability.

This list is not self-limitative. These topics were developed taking into consideration the priorities and current trends in the implementation of optimal procurement systems. Additional optional modules may be added in the future, as per proven demand from countries or institutions.

The revised 'core' MAPS tool consists of several elements, at the heart of which is the revised indicator framework. The MAPS has 14 indicators with 55 sub-indicators. The 14 indicators are allocated to four areas, or 'pillars' (see Figure 1):

1. the legal, regulatory and policy framework;
2. institutional framework and management capacity;
3. procurement operations and market practices; and
4. accountability, integrity and transparency.

Figure 1 Elements of the Methodology for Assessing Procurement Systems (MAPS)

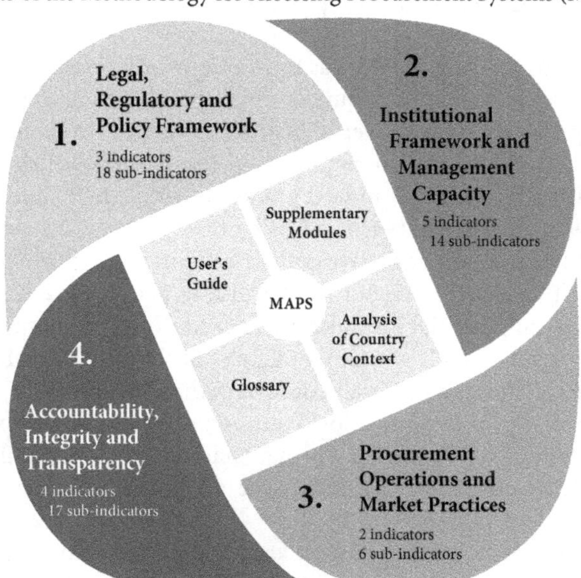

Source: www.mapsinitiative.org.

In line with the overarching principles stated above, the indicators and sub-indicators provide assessment criteria (ie, a description of an aspirational, ideal setting) according to which the assessors appraise the procurement system in all its aspects. There are qualitative and quantitative assessment criteria. A central element of the assessment is the identification of gaps, and among them the gaps that represent a critical problem ('red flags').

Following the substantive review of the MAPS indicator system, the first draft of the revised MAPS was vetted. In the summer of 2016 (from August to October), the draft was publicly available for comment on an OECD website;[65] the draft was also widely circulated in the public procurement and policy communities. Overall, 25 comments were received from 35 countries, agencies, civil society organisations, and procurement experts from five continents. Some contributions were submitted jointly. In addition to the solicitation of comments remotely, the MAPS draft was first presented and discussed with a larger audience in a November 2016 meeting in Dakar, Senegal, co-organised by the Senegalese public procurement authority 'Authorité de Régulation des Marchés Publics' (ARMP) and the OECD.[66] The intention has been to create an inclusive revision process, as evidenced by this broad public consultation in addition to the already very representative stakeholder group on the revision of the MAPS. The feedback has been overall positive. In general, comments acknowledge positively some innovations in MAPS which responded to the criticisms and goals described earlier (such as the removal of scoring, the development of supplementary modules rendering MAPS flexible, quantitative indicators, and most notably including an analysis of the country context to frame the assessment), finally turning it into a truly universal tool to be applied in all countries. Further improvements were called for with respect to addressing some questions of policy-making, as well as technical aspects related to the concrete formulation of indicators. A summary of the feedback can be accessed at the consultation website.[67]

In the first half of 2017, MAPS was tested in a limited number of countries, both developed and developing (Norway, Chile and Senegal). These assessments were not mainly intended to just evaluate a country's public procurement system, but rather followed the goal of testing whether the revised MAPS methodology worked in practice and in what areas it had to be improved. The lessons learned from these testing exercises were taken up together with the feedback of the public consultation in a final version of the revised MAPS, which was provided in late 2017.

V. Conclusion

The original goal of the MAPS, to assist countries in reforming their public procurement systems through diagnostics, re-emerges in the current revision process. This chapter has argued that MAPS was never conceptualised as a fiduciary tool or a compliance tool to facilitate UCS policy. Instead, the main driver behind the creation

[65] See the OECD website on the consultation on the revised Methodology for Assessing Procurement Systems (MAPS), www.oecd.org/governance/ethics/public-consultation-methodology-assessing-procurement-systems.htm.

[66] See brochure for the event at www.oecd.org/corruption/ethics/Revision-of-the-MAPS-meeting.pdf.

[67] ibid.

of MAPS has been to develop a diagnostic tool to support country reforms. However, MAPS was developed in a time and in a context that favoured use of country systems, and MAPS appeared as a good means to implement it and evaluate progress. A tool to assess fitness for use of country systems would have needed to be developed specifically for this purpose and differently from MAPS. In fact, because MAPS as such was not fit for the purpose, the MDBs developed their own tools that they felt were more adequate in assessing a country's fitness for use of country systems. In doing so, however, they missed incorporating their clients' and their specific goals in the tool. This, in turn, was to render the tool inaccurate and the goal of UCS policy unattainable.

Valuable insights emerge from analysing the history of MAPS, the way MAPS was used, and how the application evolved. These insights are particularly relevant for the creation of future policy tools, assessment methodologies or impact evaluations on an aggregate level. However, studying the evolution of MAPS also points to governance and policy coordination challenges in an international context in general. Lessons can be broadly grouped into two areas:

1. lessons related to the specific agenda of MAPS as a tool; and
2. lessons related to the process within which MAPS was created and embedded.

A. Lessons Related to the Specific Agenda of MAPS as a Tool

Lessons related to the specific agenda of MAPS as a tool also relate to the structure and the content of the MAPS methodology and indicator framework. As the argumentation in this chapter emphasises, there was a mismatch between the purpose assigned to MAPS and its capabilities as defined by the design of the indicator framework. The purpose of MAPS – and in particular the limits of it – did not seem to be clearly defined and communicated when the methodology as such was consolidated during the practical application. In the following years of implementation, the purpose of MAPS was stretched to become an aggregate indicator for commitments that were not related to the initial purpose of the tool to provide country-level diagnostics. As a consequence, the specific design of MAPS indicators were adequate for the purpose of system diagnosis, but not fit for the superimposed purpose of aggregate indicator. In short, MAPS indicator design – with an emphasis on the level of granularity – did not match the intended purpose.

For the creation of new policy tools, this means that the clear definition and communication of the purpose and capabilities of such tools is crucial. Following the definition of a purpose, the methodology should be designed in a way to honour this purpose. The purpose should not be stretched after the creation of the tool without adapting the methodology.

B. Lessons Related to the Process within Which MAPS was Created and Embedded

Lessons related to the process within which MAPS was created and embedded hinge on management challenges. MAPS has been a commendable example of collective action: organisations responded proactively to a need, creating a new tool. However, the structures that drove the creation of MAPS remained relatively informal, without sustainable institutionalised support that would take charge of steering matters related to the implementation and management of MAPS as a tool, its purpose and wide application (as mentioned above). In addition, the negotiations to develop MAPS, clarify areas of ambiguity, and set the objectives remained largely associated with this initial group of stakeholders. In fact, during the practical application of the previous MAPS, ie in the phase where MAPS was consolidated with regards to its purpose, there was no institution that could have facilitated an inclusive discussion about any changes to the original approach of MAPS, or defended the original agreements, and that is a lesson to take forward.

In the creation of new policy tools, stakeholders should focus on three things. First, stakeholders should create a sustainable support structure that can maintain the guardianship for the tool and any related agreements beyond the initial phase of creation. Second, no matter how this support structure is designed, it should have a clear and realistic mandate to follow up on the initial development phase, and be resourced accordingly, allowing also for close monitoring of its impact. Third, any considerations around the creation of the tool and its future should be structured in an inclusive manner, involving those stakeholders that are concerned by the tool.

Taking these lessons as a starting point, there are many open questions and ample room for further research. A systematic analysis of the use of MAPS by development banks could shed light on the impact of MAPS. Which countries were assessed, for what purpose, and with what kind of results? Also, the availability of MAPS assessments will be decisive to improve their acceptance, dissemination and recognition. In addition, the uptake of the new and revised MAPS will be an interesting case study in itself.

10

The Use of Country Systems

ANNAMARIA LA CHIMIA AND SOPE WILLIAMS-ELEGBE

I. Introduction

The reliance on country systems in the procurement process for funded contracts is a crucial part of the aid effectiveness agenda. The reliance on borrower procurement systems in donor-financed contracts is expected to help align aid projects with national priorities; increase developing countries' ownership of the aid; assist aid recipient countries to develop their procurement and public financial management systems; improve domestic procurement capacity; and thus improve aid delivery outcomes. The commitment to use country systems was described as having the potential to be one of the 'most significant policy changes' for multilateral development banks (MDBs)[1] and, one can argue, also for all donors and for development procurement in general.

Country systems may be described as national arrangements and procedures for public financial management, procurement, audit, monitoring and evaluation, and social and environmental procedures.[2] Central to the use of a country system commitment that stems out of the aid effectiveness agenda is the requirement that countries own a set of procurement rules and procedures that meet 'mutually agreed standards' that 'satisfy all donors'.[3] An adequate procurement system often involves a transparent, competitive, efficient and non-corrupt procurement system.

When recipient countries' systems do not meet the 'mutually agreed' quality standards (and, one could argue, do not satisfy donors' expectations) they are encouraged to implement procurement reforms. In many developing countries, implementing procurement reforms to fulfil this criterion will require significant efforts. Efforts which are 'rewarded' not only by the many advantages for the country linked to an efficient

[1] CL Pallas and J Wood, 'The World Bank's Use of Country Systems for Procurement: A Good Idea Gone Bad' (2009) 27(2) *Development Policy Review* 215, 218. These authors argue that the driver for the use of country systems is not limited to the aid effectiveness agenda, but is also in response 'to pressure from certain borrowers and to maintain market share in the face of competition from other lenders'.

[2] OECD, 'Country Systems, and Why We Need to Use Them' in E Deutscher (ed), *Development Co-operation Report 2010* (Paris, OECD Publishing, 2010) 45.

[3] The Second Meeting of the OECD DAC Task Force on Procurement, 4–6 May 2011, Cusco, Peru, available at www.unpcdc.org/media/218131/pcdc_notes_-_2nd_meeting_oecd-dac_task_force_on_procurement_in_cusco_may-2011.pdf.

procurement system, but also by the possibility to then use those systems 'to administer donor-financed procurement'.[4] Hence the possibility to use country systems when purchasing aid goods and services offers an incentive to recipient countries to reform their procurement system.[5] When one considers that in some countries over 50 per cent of national expenditures are financed by donors one can appreciate how substantial this 'indirect' incentive is.[6]

As anticipated in chapter 3, encouraging developing countries to implement institutional reforms aimed at improving governance – in this case by promoting the use of country systems and subordinating such use to those systems being compliant with 'mutually agreed standards'[7] – donors not only tried to address the more immediate problems associated with aid ineffectiveness, such as aid not being aligned to national priorities and the increased administrative burdens for developing countries, but they also tried to address the root causes of aid ineffectiveness, ie those linked to weak institutions and poor governance. They did so by encouraging developing countries to put in place procurement reforms.[8] Moreover, the benefits of improving country systems would be felt beyond aid procurement by 'improving all government expenditures not just those funded by donors';[9] ensuring recipients make better use of their own resources and ultimately eliminating the need for aid itself. Hence, the commitment to use country systems probably reflects, better than any other commitment within the aid effectiveness agenda, donors' intention to address the institutional and structural problems linked to aid ineffectiveness (see further chapter 3). The use of country systems is, arguably, the most evident manifestation of donors using procurement to address the micro and macro problems linked to aid donations.

It must be stated that in the provision of aid, donors will often use some aspects of a country's systems but not all, and the domestic aspects relied upon by donors depend on the type and modality of aid being granted. When aid is granted as programme, project or emergency aid, the process for purchasing the goods, services and works (ie development aid procurement) differs between donors. Some donors tend to impose their own procurement rules on recipient countries (as is the case with MDB-financed

[4] ibid.

[5] The use of country systems is by no means the only reasons why developing countries would or should reform their systems but it is certainly an incentive for them to do so. eg the survey conducted for the Task Force on Procurement by Pamela Bigart, Kirsten Ejlskov-Jensen, and Rita Roos reveals that interviewed countries had indicated as one of the most common factors to kick-start procurement reforms 'donor pressure, or donor assessments that reveal weaknesses in the system'. The survey also makes known that amongst the incentives to initiate procurement reforms, the developing countries interviewed listed 'to satisfy the demands of donors' and 56% of them said 'their reforms had been prioritised jointly with donors'. See P Bigart, K Ejlskov-Jensen and R Roos, 'Strengthening Country Procurement Systems: Results and Opportunities, A report for the OECD/DAC Task Force on Procurement', 8 (file with the author).

[6] For an extensive analysis of direct and indirect incentives to implement procurement reforms in developing countries, see A La Chimia, 'Donors' Influence on Developing Countries' Procurement Systems, Rules and Markets: a Critical Analysis' in S Arrowsmith and G Quinot (eds), *Public Procurement Regulation in Africa* (Cambridge, Cambridge University Press, 2013).

[7] See OECD, 'The Paris Declaration on Aid Effectiveness and the Accra Agenda for Action' (OECD, 2005/2008) available at www.oecd.org/development/effectiveness/34428351.pdf.

[8] See La Chimia, 'Donor's Influence on Developing Countries' Procurement Systems, Rules and Markets' (n 6).

[9] ibid.

projects), whilst others ask recipients to use a procurement agency based in the donor country (this is the option chosen by some bilateral donors, including Italy for example). On other occasions, donors prefer to conduct the procurement process themselves (for example, the UK) while delegating other aspects of the procurement cycle, such as project management and monitoring, to the recipient. Moreover, the same donor might follow different approaches depending on the recipient it is dealing with. It also needs to be noted that where donors fail to coordinate, different (and multiple) procurement arrangements and rules might apply in the same recipient country at the same time; one for each donor would not be unusual. When one considers the number of donors operating at one given time in each recipient country, one can easily understand the problems created for the recipient. For example, it has been reported that in 2002 there were 25 bilateral and 19 multilateral donors and about 350 NGOs operating in Vietnam, for over 8000 projects.[10] Although the donors' and the recipient government's procurement procedures often have common objectives and principles, the donors' procurement procedures are very different from those of the recipient's in terms of the devolution of decision-making power to local agencies, procurement thresholds and specific awards and payments methods.[11]

The situation is however different when aid is provided through budget support, where there is little choice but for the donor to rely on the country's systems in the management and disbursement of these funds,[12] since the aid donated by the donor cannot be distinguished from the recipient's budget. For this reason, one of the indicators that can be used to assess whether donors are using – or increasing their reliance on – country systems, is to monitor the level of aid donated as budget support.[13] Donors' commitment to donate aid as budget support is an indication of donors' trust in a recipient's financial management system. For example, in 2016, donors committed to grant 50 per cent of aid to Afghanistan as budget support.

As discussed in chapter 3,[14] one of the reasons why donors believe it appropriate to impose their procurement rules or alternative procurement arrangements on recipients is because they consider recipients' procurement institutions and public management systems to be weak and prone to corruption.[15] However, the 'parallel' procurement systems used by donors create duplication, increase transaction costs, hamper alignment with country priorities and ownership, and constrain efforts to strengthen national capacity.[16] Furthermore, duplications of donors' rules and of procurement arrangements create problems for suppliers based in recipient countries as well. Indeed suppliers' capacity to participate towards aid procurement opportunities will be significantly undermined by the multiplicity of aid agencies operating in their country. Local suppliers will struggle to familiarise themselves with the different agencies and rules

[10] La Chimia (n 6).

[11] ibid.

[12] OECD, 'Country Systems, and Why We Need to Use Them' (n 2) 46.

[13] La Chimia (n 6).

[14] See also extensively S Williams-Elegbe, *Public Procurement and Multilateral Development Banks: Law, Practice and Problems* (Oxford, Hart Publishing, 2017) ch 2.

[15] D Dollar and L Pritchett, *Assessing Aid – What works, What doesn't and Why* (New York NY, Oxford University Press, 1998).

[16] ibid.

and will be at a disadvantage compared to suppliers based in donor countries. As it has been argued elsewhere 'donors' complex development cooperation systems hamper the possibility of establishing a sound procurement environment where international, regional and local competition can take place'.[17] It is not surprising therefore that the competition level in aid contracts is often poor with the market being dominated by a handful of foreign suppliers.[18]

The use of multiple donor systems and practices places a resource and capacity burden on aid recipients and borrowers. It is in light of these concerns that the development community began to pursue an agenda to rely more on recipient systems for funded procurements.[19] As further explained in section II, the use of country systems agenda has had a checkered history, and there is evidence that in the 1980s, the World Bank first attempted a slight, if informal move towards the use of country procurement systems where appropriate for Bank-financed contracts.[20] However, the actual reliance on country systems in Bank-funded contracts was few and far between during this decade, but this set the stage for the introduction of the Country Procurement Assessment Reports (CPARS) as well as the formal acknowledgement of the necessity to rely on country systems where appropriate. Twenty years later, the Monterrey Consensus and subsequent development fora galvanised donors led by the World Bank and other MDBs to pursue the agenda that had been unsuccessful in earlier decades. As will be discussed further below, the desire to rely on national procurement systems led the World Bank to conduct an extensive piloting programme to examine the modalities for the use of domestic country systems in Bank-funded contracts, and to determine the level of robustness that could suffice for the Bank to allow reliance on a domestic procurement system in Bank-funded procurements.[21]

It must be noted that despite the emphasis placed on the use of recipients' country systems by the Paris Declaration and the Accra Agenda of Action (AAA), and the recognition that 'bypassing country systems reduces the sustainability of development programs and undermines a partner countries capacity to manage its own development agenda',[22] the use of country systems has not increased by any significant extent in recent years and of all the components of the aid effectiveness agenda, the use of country systems has probably been the least successful initiative, to the extent that the lack of reliance on recipients' systems is often the most significant parameter used to proclaim the end of the aid effectiveness crusade.

For example, although use of country systems was included as a clause in the 2011 World Bank's procurement guidelines, there are very few cases in which a borrower's

[17] La Chimia (n 6).

[18] See ICAI report Achieving value for money through procurement Part 1: DFID's approach to its supplier market A performance review November 2017, available at icai.independent.gov.uk/wp-content/uploads/ICAI-Procurement-review-DFID%E2%80%99s-approach-to-its-supplier-market.pdf; see also in this collection La Chimia, tied aid, ch 6.

[19] Williams-Elegbe, *Public Procurement and Multilateral Development Banks* (n 14) ch 9.

[20] Operations Policy and Country Services, *The World Bank's Procurement Policies and Procedures: Initiating Discussion Paper* (Washington DC, The World Bank, 29 March 2012) 3; Pallas and Wood, 'The World Bank's Use of Country Systems for Procurement' (n 1) 216–19.

[21] S Williams-Elegbe, 'The Evolution of the World Bank's Procurement Policy: Reform and Coherence for the 21st Century' (2016) 16(1) *Journal of Public Procurement* 23. See also Pallas and Wood (n 1) 221–22.

[22] N Coulson, 'Using Country Systems – Is It All or Nothing?' (1 April 2011) quoted in La Chimia (n 6) 237.

procurement system was deemed appropriate for use in *international* bidding in an MDB-funded project. This chapter examines the importance of the use of country systems, using the World Bank as a case study. The chapter will explain why country systems are good for development (section II) and the history of the commitment to use country systems within the aid agenda (section III), providing an updated account of the use of country systems thus far. The final sections in the chapter will examine the World Bank's approach to the use of country systems, and the reasons for the limited success of its earlier approaches as well as the Bank's new approach to relying on country systems under its 2016 procurement regulations.

II. The Importance of a Reliance on Country Systems

The importance of country systems to international development was detailed in an OECD report, which states:

> It is certainly true that the way in which aid has been delivered in the past – for example, when donors create their own mechanisms for implementing development rather than using partner countries' systems – has risked undermining the sustainability of development efforts. By bypassing the government's existing systems, these parallel systems can contribute to the country's continued dependency on donors. Bypassing a country's decision-making bodies can undermine these institutions and hence the accountability of the government towards its own citizens. These risks need to be considered alongside donors' own concerns as they make efforts to increase their use of country systems in the delivery of aid.[23]

The use of country systems has been proven to build sustainable capacity for a country to develop, implement and account for its policies to its citizens and parliament.[24] Using country systems especially in public procurement is important beyond the delivery of aid as procurement expenditures account for a significant proportion of government spending, and can be up to 70 per cent of GDP in developing countries.[25] Thus, an efficient and effective procurement system will increase the likelihood of a country meeting domestic developmental aspirations and goals and will improve social and economic outcomes. As was stated by the World Bank, 'strengthening country procurement systems is core to improving the development effectiveness of public expenditure, whether it be financed with taxes, with World Bank funds, or with resources from other partners'.[26]

Relying on country systems also helps avoid duplications in procurement purchases, especially if the use of country systems is associated with aid being granted as budget

[23] OECD, 'Country Systems, and Why We Need to Use Them' (n 2) 44.

[24] UNDP, 'Moving towards the use of country systems for procurement in Bangladesh: A case study' (2009) available at unpcdc.org/media/22472/moving%20towards%20use%20of%20country%20systems%20for%20procurement%20in%20bangladesh.pdf.

[25] UNDP, *Public Procurement Capacity Development Guide* (Procurement Capacity Development Centre, Capacity Development Group, and Bureau for Development Policy, 2010) available at www.undp.org/content/dam/aplaws/publication/en/publications/capacity-development/undp-procurement-capacity-assessment-users-guide/Procurement%20Capacity%20Assessment%20Guide.pdf.

[26] World Bank, *Use of Country Systems in Bank-Supported Operations: Proposed Piloting Program* (Washington DC, World Bank, 2008) available at siteresources.worldbank.org/INTPROCUREMENT/Resources/UseOfCountrySystemsFinalApprovedVersionForDisclosure-June20-2008.pdf.

support rather than as individual project or programme aid. When donors fail to coordinate they might end up funding similar (or the same) project and purchase the same goods/services, making some of the purchases redundant and unnecessary. As a result, tenders are often cancelled at the last minute, wasting what are already limited capacities.[27] Lack of coordination and duplication of procedures between donors mean that sometimes aid money is not spent at all and the donor simply withdraws the funding. The use of country systems – and the granting of aid as budget support to which the use of country systems is often associated – avoids such duplications and waste of resources.

The benefits of a reliance on national procurement systems were summarised by Ayoung as follows:

> The use of national systems promises to alleviate the load on recipient countries of having to deal with multiple policies, in particular procurement rules; make it easier for donors to co-finance operations; and in the long run reduce the transaction costs for the countries. Most importantly, it also provides a strong incentive for countries to bring their systems to an acceptable standard and thus scale up development by improving the return on all government expenditures not just those funded by donors.[28]

It may be noted that a reliance on country systems is not an easy exercise and despite its proven long-term benefits, there are several risks presented by this idea, which are often in opposition to donors' own internal policies and politics. These are detailed by the OECD to include the risks of loss of funds to fraud or corruption (the fiduciary risk); the risk that the funds will not be used for the stated developmental project (the development risk); the risk to the donors' reputation if their efforts are not recognised or the blame they may face where something goes wrong (the reputational risk); and the delays that the use of country systems may occasion to the deployment of funds (the delay risk).[29] These risks raise several concerns for donors, and an aversion to these risks may be partly responsible for the slow pace of progress in relation to the use of the country systems agenda. In many cases, the responsibility of bilateral donors to their governments and domestic taxpayers means that such donors must ensure that the development financing they provide is not exposed to an unacceptable level of risk.[30]

In deciding to transition to the use of country systems, there are several issues that are required to be addressed by both donors and borrowers. In the first place, the donor must understand properly the nature of the country system,[31] to understand whether the system is sufficiently robust and is properly aligned with international practices,

[27] eg this has been recognised recently, in Afghanistan's development strategy. See Islamic Republic of Afghanistan, 'Afghanistan National Peace and Development Framework (ANPDF) 2017–2021', available at extwprlegs1.fao.org/docs/pdf/afg148215.pdf.

[28] A Ayoung, 'Background Paper Review of the World Bank's Procurement Policies and Procedures: Use of Procurement Country Systems' (Washington DC, The World Bank, 2013) 3, available at consultations.worldbank.org/Data/hub/files/meetings/Procurement_Policies/Background_Paper_on_Use_of_Country_Systems.pdf.

[29] OECD (n 2) 48.

[30] UNDP, 'Moving towards the use of country systems for procurement in Bangladesh' (n 24).

[31] Note that there is debate as to what constitutes the element of a procurement system. Should it be limited to rules, regulations and the institutional framework, or should it take into account the broader environment that impacts the functioning of the procurement system? See Ayoung, 'Background Paper Review' (n 28) 6–7.

or at least, the practices the donor is accustomed to.[32] The system here refers to institutional arrangements for the procurement function, leadership and accountability structures and the legislative, policy and operational frameworks. The existing gaps in the system must also be mapped.

Secondly, the donor must understand the existing capacities within the system for managing or deploying funds and undertaking the required functions and tasks. In other words, whether the existing manpower in the country (or more precisely, in the particular agency), can cope with implementing the required functions to a standard acceptable to the donor? This is particularly important, where the function is of a specialist or technical nature, such as procurement in the construction, IT, energy, healthcare or water/sanitation sectors.

Thirdly, once both the system and the capacities have been mapped, the donor needs to assess the level of risk presented by the system and existing capacities, determine if the risk level is acceptable; and further develop risk mitigation strategies, where required. In cases where an intolerable level of risk is presented, the donor may of course decide not to use the country system, until there is an improvement in the system. For this reason the promise of donors' use recipients' system is often used to allure recipient countries to improve and reform their procurement systems.

Fourthly, the donor must also review its own capacity to manage the nature of the interaction that will be had with borrowers, where country systems are being utilised. The differences in the nature and the level of interaction often require a novel approach that may be difficult to implement, without organisational, institutional, operational and structural variations in the donors.

It is for this reason that, as further explained in the next section, the use of country systems has been subordinated to recipients being able to ensure that the aid will be spent for the 'agreed purposes' and to the systems conforming to 'mutually agreed' standards and processes.[33] Only when these two conditions are met will recipient countries will be able to lead the aid procurement process.

Donors have often relied on the same tools[34] to assess a country system, understand the level of compliance within the system, assess the level of risk, and also determine appropriate risk mitigation strategies. As will be discussed chapter 9, in 2016, both the OECD and the World Bank revised the existing assessment tools.[35]

III. The Use of Country Systems in the Aid Effectiveness Agenda

As mentioned earlier, the first attempt at promoting the use of country systems was made by the World Bank in the 1980s.[36] However, this initiative had little success and

[32] Note that in some cases, the scope of an assessment is limited to an agency, sector or region.

[33] Paris Declaration (PD) (n 7) paras 17, 18, 19 and 28.

[34] These tools are the Methodology for Assessing Procurement Systems (MAPS) and the Country Procurement Assessments (CPAR).

[35] This tool is referred to as the Methodology for Assessing Alternative Procurement Arrangements (MAAPA).

[36] Williams-Elegbe (n 14) 241.

it was only with the launch of the aid effectiveness agenda in Monterrey in 2002 that donors' pledge to use country systems became a key part of the aid effectiveness initiative. Although the first commitments made in Monterrey were general and focused more on enhancing recipients' ownership of the aid process and increasing recipients' capacities for leading the process, Monterrey is nonetheless important as it laid the foundation for a process that reached maturity in Paris with the endorsement of the Paris Declaration on Aid Effectiveness. Starting with the Monterrey Consensus, the international development community stated that:

> 43. Recipient and donor countries, as well as international institutions, should strive to make ODA more effective. In particular, there is a need for the multilateral and bilateral financial and development institutions to intensify efforts to:
>
> - …
> - **Enhance the absorptive capacity and financial management of the recipient countries to utilize aid** in order to promote the use of the most suitable aid delivery instruments that are responsive to the needs of developing countries and to the need for resource predictability, including budget support mechanisms, where appropriate, and in a fully consultative manner;
> - Use **development frameworks that are owned and driven by developing countries** and that embody poverty reduction strategies, including poverty reduction strategy papers, as vehicles for aid delivery, upon request;
> - **Enhance recipient countries' input into and ownership of the design, including procurement**, of technical assistance programmes; and increase the effective use of local technical assistance resources;

The Rome Declaration on Harmonisation lent further credence to procurement reform, capacity-building and the use of country systems initiatives and stated that:

> We in the donor community have been concerned with the growing evidence that, over time, the totality and wide variety of donor requirements and processes for preparing, delivering, and monitoring development assistance are generating unproductive transaction costs for, and drawing down the limited capacity of, partner countries. We are also aware of partner country concerns that donors' practices do not always fit well with national development priorities and systems, including their budget, programme, and project planning cycles and public expenditure and financial management systems. We recognise that these issues require urgent, coordinated, and sustained action to improve our effectiveness on the ground.
>
> We attach high importance to partner countries' assuming a stronger leadership role in the coordination of development assistance, and to assisting in building their capacity to do so. Partner countries on their part will undertake necessary reforms to enable progressive reliance by donors on their systems as they adopt international principles or standards and apply good practices. The key element that will guide this work is a country-based approach that emphasizes country ownership and government leadership, includes capacity building, recognises diverse aid modalities (projects, sector approaches, and budget or balance of payments support), and engages civil society including the private sector.

As discussed in chapter 3, a series of parallel initiatives specifically targeted at procurement were being undertaken by the same actors involved in the High-Level Fora. These initiatives, first organised by the Procurement Roundtable and then by the Joint Venture on Procurement and the Joint Procurement Task Force, were held between development partners, including the MDBs.[37] One such initiative culminated in the adoption of the 2004 Johannesburg Declaration.[38] The Johannesburg Declaration, in recognising the fact that improvements in country procurement systems would '(i) produce enormous benefits towards efficient use of public resources … and (ii) facilitate harmonization and aid effectiveness by enabling greater reliance on well performing country systems for delivery of development assistance', considered that urgent action was needed in the following areas:

- Accord public procurement reform a higher strategic priority.
- Improve the effectiveness of the approaches and techniques used to develop procurement system capacity.
- For aid funded procurement, move towards greater reliance on national systems that conform to internationally recognized standards, or are moving successfully in that direction.

In addition, under the Johannesburg Declaration, the partners committed to:

- Work to strengthen country procurement system capacity at the institutional, organizational and professional levels using new approaches and techniques, which strongly emphasize country ownership.
- Do this by carrying out careful systems-wide diagnostics at the country level, identifying priority areas of weakness, and designing realistic reform programmes based on the results that are closely and flexibly monitored during implementation.
- Focus on measurable improvements in the performance and impact of procurement systems.

From the above, it can be seen that the Johannesburg Declaration included a commitment to the adoption of a diagnostic tool as the agreed international standard for assessment of national procurement systems. Following the conclusion of the Roundtable initiative, the Joint Venture for Procurement was established under the coordination of the OECD/DAC Working Party on Aid Effectiveness. The Joint Venture subsequently developed a methodology for the application of baseline and compliance and performance indicators to be used in the assessment of domestic procurement systems. This tool, discussed in detail in chapter 9, is referred to as the Methodology for Assessing Procurement Systems (MAPS), which was utilised in the assessment of procurement systems that were candidates for reform.[39] The commitments within the Johannesburg Declaration were consolidated by the Paris Declaration on Aid Effectiveness, endorsed in Paris at the Second High-Level Forum on aid effectiveness in 2005 and by the AAA agreed in Accra in 2008. Indeed, both the Paris Declaration and the AAA placed special emphasis on encouraging donors to let recipient countries use their country systems when implementing aid projects. However, the possibility

[37] OECD/DAC, 'Strengthening Procurement Capacities in Developing Countries: Summary Report of the OECD/DAC – World Bank Round Table, Paris, 22–23 January 2003' (Washington DC, World Bank, 2003) available at www.oecd-ilibrary.org/development/strengthening-procurement-capacities-in-developing-countries_journal_dev-v4-art16-en.

[38] OECD, 'A Framework for Developing Effective Procurement Systems in Developing Countries: The Johannesburg Declaration' (Paris, OECD, 2004) available at www.oecd.org/gov/ethics/34269704.pdf.

[39] OECD, *Methodology for Assessing Procurement Systems* (Paris, OECD, 2018) available at www.mapsinitiative.org/methodology/MAPS-methodology-for-assessing-procurement-systems.pdf.

of using country systems, as a means to enhance aid effectiveness, is conditional on recipients' procurement systems being able to ensure that the aid will be spent for the 'agreed purposes' (paragraph 17 of the Paris Declaration) and to the systems conforming to 'mutually agreed'[40] [between donor and recipient] standards and processes (paragraphs 28 and also 18 and 19). Only when these two conditions are met will recipient countries be able to use their systems and lead the aid procurement process. Furthermore, both the Paris Declaration and the AAA refer to the need to develop diagnostic tools to ascertain the suitability of those systems to lead on procurement. In particular, the AAA further establishes that 'Developing countries and donors will jointly assess the quality of country systems in a country-led process using mutually agreed diagnostic tools'.[41] As further analysed in chapter 9, a detailed methodology for assessing the suitability of recipients' procurement system has been developed by the OECD (ie MAPS) the latest version of which was released in 2018.[42]

The text of the Paris Declaration expanded and clarified the obligations of donors and recipients in relation to the use of country systems and the following paragraphs are particularly pertinent:

> 20. Partner countries commit to:
>
> - **Carry out diagnostic reviews that provide reliable assessments of country systems and procedures.**
> - On the basis of such diagnostic reviews, **undertake reforms** that may be necessary to ensure that national systems, institutions and procedures for managing aid and other development resources are effective, accountable and transparent.
> - Undertake reforms, such as public management reform that may be necessary to launch and fuel sustainable capacity development processes.
>
> 23. Partner countries commit to:
>
> - Integrate specific capacity strengthening objectives in national development strategies and pursue their implementation through country-led capacity development strategies where needed.
>
> 28. Partner countries and donors jointly commit to:
>
> - Use **mutually agreed standards and processes to carry out diagnostics, develop sustainable reforms and monitor implementation.**
> - Commit sufficient resources to support and sustain medium and long-term procurement reforms and capacity development.
> - Share feedback at the country level on recommended approaches so they can be improved over time.
>
> 29. Partner countries commit to take leadership and implement the procurement reform process.

[40] For criticism of these 'mutually agreed standards', see A La Chimia, *From Monterrey to Bussan, via Paris and Rome* (forthcoming).
[41] Accra Agenda of Action (AAA) (n 7) para 15.
[42] OECD, MAPS (2018) (n 39).

30. Donors commit to:

- **Progressively rely on partner country systems for procurement when the country has implemented mutually agreed standards and processes** (Indicator 5).
- Adopt harmonised approaches when national systems do not meet mutually agreed levels of performance or donors do not use them.

The use of country systems reveals, more than any other commitment within the aid effectiveness agenda, the importance of the procurement-specific initiatives developed in parallel with the High-Level Fora. As it can be seen above the Paris Declaration incorporates in the aid agenda many of the procurement-specific commitments endorsed by the Johannesburg Declaration. This trend and parallelism continues with other procurement-specific initiatives. After the Paris Declaration but just prior to the AAA, the May 2008 meeting of the Joint Venture on Procurement issued the Arusha Statement, which reiterated donor commitments made at Paris to provide 'sufficient resources to support and sustain medium and long term procurement reforms and capacity development'.[43]

After Arusha, in September 2008 the AAA confirmed the commitments made under the Paris Declaration and further highlighted the areas where more was required to be done by both donors and recipients. The AAA placed a 'special emphasis on encouraging donors to let recipient countries use their procurement systems when implementing aid projects',[44] and remains till date the most comprehensive statement by the development community on this issue. In particular, in order to strengthen and increase the use of country systems, donors agreed 'to use country systems as the first option for aid programmes' (AAA paragraph 15, point a) and should donors choose to use another option and 'rely on aid delivery mechanisms outside country systems (including parallel project implementation units), they will transparently state the rationale for this and will review their positions at regular intervals' (AAA paragraph 15, point b).

The Agenda also confirmed the need to assess country systems and develop diagnostic tools to assess those systems.

With these multilateral commitments to rely on country systems,[45] the MDBs made another attempt to implement this agenda through a pilot project conducted by the

[43] Arusha Statement of the OECD/DAC Joint Venture on Procurement, 'To Support the Implementation of the Paris Declaration Principles by Building Reliable Public Procurement Systems' (2008) para 3, available at www.unpcdc.org/media/4140/global%20jv%20on%20procurement.pdf.

[44] La Chimia (n 6) 252.

[45] Further commitments have been made since Busan; eg in the Communique of the First High Level Meeting of the Global Partnership for Effective Development Cooperation, Mexico 15–16 April 2014, it was stated that 'Looking ahead, we encourage recipient countries to continue promoting domestic reform and development agendas that contribute to the social and economic wellbeing of citizens and encourage donors to fully support these efforts. In this context, we agree to strengthen our actions to continue enhancing country ownership and leadership by aligning and tailoring aid to the national development agenda and context. In particular, we agree to invigorate efforts to strengthen and use country systems as the default approach and promote assessment and dialogue on the extent to which their use is appropriate, consider budget support in the appropriate mixture of delivery instruments, continue untying aid, enhance the localization of development cooperation, including by promoting local procurement, and support partner countries' ambitions to better coordinate, assess and manage the plurality of aid'. See 'The First High

World Bank between 2008 and 2011. However, the pilot was not very successful in determining a way forward for the use of country systems agenda.[46]

The initial objective of the pilot was to propose a methodology by which 'national procurement systems would be relied upon for ICB contracts in countries that have achieved procurement standards equivalent to those embodied in the Bank's Procurement Guidelines and have demonstrated capacity to carry out such procurement'.[47] The methodology was to be used to identify a group of countries, in which national procurement systems were of sufficient quality and capacity to achieve generally the same results in terms of economy and efficiency as could be achieved through the application of the World Bank's procedures.[48]

The components of the methodology used in selecting countries and projects were detailed as follows:

- (i) An assessment of the quality of country procurement systems, using the knowledge the Bank has gained through public finance management assessments, Country Procurement Assessment Reviews, procurement reform programs, and the application of the OECD/DAC Procurement Benchmarking Tool;
- (ii) A detailed examination of the extent to which the country's procurement policies are equivalent to and consistent with the principles of the Bank's procurement policies as set out in its Procurement Guidelines;
- (iii) A review of compliance with the country's policies and procedures, and the past performance and overall capacity of the government agencies designated to be responsible for the proposed projects to be covered by country pilots;
- (iv) An assessment of the fiduciary risks of pilot projects;
- (v) Launching of a process of limited national competitive bidding for the selection of consultants in the pilot countries;
- (vi) Incorporating a strong program of gap-filling analysis and capacity building in procurement; and
- (vii) Maintenance of a regular reporting framework, an international advisory panel, and a transparent mechanism for the continued participation of stakeholders during the pilot program.[49]

By the conclusion of the pilot in 2011, none of the countries in the pilot were unconditionally cleared to be eligible for the Bank to rely on their systems for Bank-funded procurements.[50] The second progress report in December 2010 stated that the

Level Meeting of the Global Partnership for Effective Development Cooperation, Mexico 15–16 April, 2014', available at effectivecooperation.org/wp-content/uploads/2015/01/MEMORIA-FINAL.pdf.

[46] See World Bank, *Use of Country Procurement Systems in Bank-supported Operations: Proposed Piloting Program I* (R008-36/3) (Washington DC, World Bank, 2008); World Bank, *Piloting Program in Use of Country Systems: First Progress Report* (SecM2009-513) (Washington DC, World Bank, 2009); World Bank, *Use of Country Procurement Systems in Bank-Supported Operations: First Progress Report on the Piloting Program* (R2009-0314 and IDA/R2009-0317) (Washington DC, World Bank, 2009) and World Bank, *Piloting Program in the Use of Country Procurement Systems: Second Progress Report* (Washington DC, World Bank, 2010), available at siteresources.worldbank.org/INTPROCUREMENT/Resources/278019-1311363656902/UCS_Second_Progress_Report_(Final_version)_(22_Dec_2010).pdf.

[47] World Bank, *Use of Country Systems in Bank-Supported Operations: Proposed Piloting Program* (n 26).

[48] ibid.

[49] ibid.

[50] World Bank, *The World Bank and Public Procurement: An Independent Evaluation Vol II Achieving Development Effectiveness through Procurement in Bank Financial Assistance* (Washington DC, IEG/World Bank, 2014) 10–12, available at ieg.worldbank.org/Data/reports/Procurement_Vol_II_02_04_2014.pdf.

piloting programme had proved challenging and had 'not been a success' from the perspective of its original objective, which was to use country procurement systems in individual projects.[51] It was evident that no project using country procurement systems would be approved before the scheduled end of the programme on 30 June 2011, and the Bank decided that the programme would not be extended beyond that date.[52] One effect of the pilot however, was that a paragraph was included in the 2011 procurement guidelines, which provides for the use of country systems in circumstances related to the pilot.[53]

In concomitance with the World Bank pilot, the second report on the implementation of the Paris Declaration Paris Declaration, was issued by the OECD.[54] The report strikes another blow to the future prospects of using country systems and future hopes of seeing this commitment being developed further. Indeed the report proved that no progress was being made on the use of country systems, and the data showed that donors were not increasing the use of country systems at the pace that was originally hoped for. The report illustrated that progress towards the use of country systems was very slow and 'even when there are good-quality country systems, donors often do not use them, despite the recognition that using country systems promotes their development'. It also reported

> a moderate increase in the use of partner country's procurement systems by donors over time. For the 32 countries participating in both the 2006 and 2011 Surveys, use of country procurement systems increased from 40% of aid for the government sector in 2005, to 43% in 2007 and 44% in 2010.[55]

Other studies also denounce the fact that donors are not fulfilling their promises of using country systems, despite the fact that many of the countries studied had implemented the required procurement reforms.[56]

While the use of the country systems commitment was initially conceived as a means to implement the ownership principle and to overcome fragmentation and lack of coordination of donors' practices, the subordination of the use of country systems to those systems reaching 'mutually agreed standards' and the identification of those standards, with donors' procurement, with donors' standards, with donors' regulation, effectively ended up resembling (voluntarily or involuntarily) just another legislative imperialist project (one of the many pursued by the MDBs in the past). As anticipated in chapter 3, alignment and harmonisation had been reduced to transporting donors'

[51] World Bank, *Piloting Program in the Use of Country Procurement Systems: Second Progress Report* (n 46).

[52] World Bank, *The World Bank and Public Procurement: An Independent Evaluation Vol II* (n 50) 10–12.

[53] See World Bank, Guidelines: Procurement of Goods, Works, and Non-Consulting Services under IBRD Loans and IDA Credits & Grants by World Bank Borrowers (World Bank January 2011) para 3.20 at go.worldBank.org/1KKD1KNT40, which state that 'The Use of Country Systems (UCS) refers to the use of the procurement procedures and methods contemplated in the public procurement system in place in the country of the Borrower that have been determined to be consistent with these Guidelines and acceptable to the Bank under the Bank's Use of Country Systems Piloting Program. They may be used by Borrowers in pilot projects that have been approved by the Bank under such Piloting Program'.

[54] OECD/DAC, *Aid Effectiveness 2005–10: Progress in implementing the Paris Declaration* (OECD, 2011) available at effectivecooperation.org/wp-content/uploads/2016/03/2011%20Report%20on%20Monitoring%20the%20Paris%20Declaration%20ENGLISH.pdf.

[55] ibid.

[56] See eg B Ellmers, *Tapping the Potential? Procurement, Tied Aid and the Use of Country Systems in Uganda* (EURODAD, 2010).

regulatory framework into developing countries' system. Therefore, it is no surprise that the World Bank pilot on the use of country systems failed. No country could meet the high standards set in the pilot.

It was with the negative findings of the second OECD survey that donors and recipients approached the fourth and final HLF held in Busan in 2011. In Busan, the commitment to use country systems was reiterated. Specifically point 19 of the Busan Partnership for development states:

> 19. The use and strengthening of developing countries' systems remains central to our efforts to build effective institutions. We will build on our respective commitments set out in the Paris Declaration and Accra Agenda for Action to:
>
> a) Use country systems as the default approach for development co-operation in support of activities managed by the public sector, working with and respecting the governance structures of both the provider of development co-operation and the developing country.
>
> b) Assess jointly country systems using mutually agreed diagnostic tools. Based on the results of these assessments, providers of development co-operation will decide on the extent to which they can use country systems. Where the full use of country systems is not possible, the provider of development co-operation will state the reasons for non-use, and will discuss with government what would be required to move towards full use, including any necessary assistance or changes for the strengthening of systems. The use and strengthening of country systems should be placed within the overall context of national capacity development for sustainable outcomes.

As explained in detail in chapter 3, the Busan Forum was followed by the Global Partnership for Effective Development Cooperation (GPEDC). Again the commitment to use country systems remained high on the agenda of the Global Partnership. As further explained in chapter 3, one of the objectives of the GPEDC is to monitor the implementation of the Partnership commitments and to share best practices. To this end a very useful dashboard was developed where the country-by-country findings of the monitoring reports on the implementation of the Partnership commitments are presented and made publicly available.[57] Importantly, one of the indicators for monitoring progress on the implementation of the Partnership programme is the level of aid which is administered using country systems (namely indicator 9b). Since results for the reports conducted in previous years are also available, one can easily compare the data and see whether the level of the indicator (in our case, use of country systems) has increased or decreased over the years.

It needs to be noted that data is only available for a selected number of countries and often not all data is available for all reporting years. These limitations notwithstanding, the dashboard remains a valuable instrument that provides credible information on the aid agenda and, in this case, the use of country systems commitment.

Whilst it is outside the scope of this chapter to present the findings of the report on the use of country systems for each country, however some examples might be useful. For example Senegal registered a level of 31.2 per cent of use of country systems in 2010; this went down to 22 per cent in 2014 and then increased again to 31.8 per cent which is slightly above the level registered in 2010. This data show that donors are not

[57] See dashboard.effectivecooperation.org/viewer.

consistent in using country systems and progress is only marginal. Egypt was over 50 per cent in 2010 and declined to just above 27 per cent in 2016. There are also positive results, so for instance, Colombia registered a very low level of use of country systems in 2010, just above 6 per cent, but recorded a level of 34.3 per cent in 2016.

Interestingly the dashboard also presents data on donors, showing whether and to what extent donors are fulfilling their commitments. Again two limitations need to be noted from the outset: first, the number of donors for whom data is available is limited (for example the MDBs are not represented at all); and second, not all indicators are available for all donors (by way of example, no data on indicator 10 linked to tied aid is available for China). Again, the (available) data shows that as far as the use of country systems is concerned, the level remains low (the US for example reaches only 21 per cent in 2016), and generally does not change significantly over the three years surveyed (2010, 2014, 2016). The level of the use of country systems sometimes slightly decreases (Italy for example registers levels above 56 per cent in 2014 and decreases to 51 per cent in 2016), and only in exceptional cases registers a substantial increase (the level of the use of country systems registered for Sweden for example goes from 49 per cent in 2014 to 63 per cent in 2016).

The positive examples notwithstanding the use of country systems remains limited and is far from being used as the 'default option' to purchase aid-funded goods and services as agreed in Accra and Busan by donors.

IV. The Use of Country Systems under the World Bank 2016 Procurement Regulations – Alternative Procurement Arrangements

Although the World Bank pilot did not prove to be the success originally hoped for it provided a lot of lessons, which were taken into account in the World Bank's revision of its approach to use of country systems in 2016. As was detailed by Ayoung:

> First, the Piloting Program's 'all-or-nothing' approach – that is, the country's system in toto was considered to have passed or failed the benchmark – limited the number of countries that could participate in the piloting program: only four countries, out of the starting twenty, were conditionally approved at the end of Stage II, subject to a set of corrective actions to be approved and adopted by the borrower. Second, a sequenced and measured approach to the use of country systems would be a more likely successful approach. Such an approach would be to use those well-performing segments of the borrower's procurement system while continuing to focus efforts on improving the rest of the system and those related areas such as public administration, budgeting and financial management, as needed. Third, there would always be inconsistencies when comparing national regulations with international institutions' procurement policies, as their respective objectives are typically trying to achieve different results. Such lessons were used to shape future initiatives on new ways to increase the Bank's use of country systems such as the recently approved PforR lending instrument and the Bank's ongoing review of its procurement policy.[58]

[58] Ayoung (n 28) 16.

One lesson that has been adopted by the World Bank in the 2016 review of its procurement framework is an approach to assessing borrower capacity that focuses on the capacity of individual borrower agencies and not on the capacity of the country as a whole.

In 2016, the World Bank introduced some changes to the manner in which it may rely on other procurement systems in a Bank-funded procurement. The 2016 regulations introduced the prospect for the Bank to rely not only on domestic procurement systems, but to also rely on the procurement rules and procedures of another multilateral or bilateral organisation.[59] These arrangements are now referred to by the Bank as 'alternative procurement arrangements'. In addition, the Bank created a detailed methodology to assess the use of alternative procurement arrangements.[60]

The World Bank's 2016 procurement regulations provide as follows:

> At the Borrower's request, the Bank may (subject to its policies and rules, and applicable fiduciary and operational requirements), agree to:
>
> a. …
> b. may rely on and apply the procurement rules and procedures of an agency or entity of the Borrower.[61]

Where a borrower wishes to rely on its domestic procurement rules and procedures in a Bank-funded procurement, it will be required to include a proposal to that effect in a document referred to as the Project Procurement Strategy for Development (PPSD). This document is defined as a 'a project-level strategy document, prepared by the Borrower, that describes how procurement in IPF operations support the development objectives of the project and deliver VfM'.[62] It is required to be prepared by the borrower as part of the project preparation process, to be reviewed and agreed upon by the borrower and the Bank.[63]

In relation to the proposal to rely on the domestic system for a funded procurement, the borrower is required to provide via the PPSD, a 'justification of the proposed procurement arrangements based on market analysis, risk and operating context and the project's particular circumstances'[64] and shall consider the following factors in assessing its ability to implement the procurement:

> a. procurement capacity to carry out the procurement process from planning to contract management;

[59] World Bank, Bank Policy: Procurement in IPF and Other Operational Procurement Matters (Washington DC, World Bank, 2017), s IIIF, available at policies.worldbank.org/sites/ppf3/PPFDocuments/a3656cb78847417b886f11fa0235216e.pdf; World Bank, Procurement Regulations for IPF Borrowers (Washington DC, World Bank 2016) para 2.4, available at pubdocs.worldbank.org/en/178331533065871195/Procurement-Regulations.pdf.

[60] World Bank, Draft Guide to the APA Assessment: Methodology to assess Alternative Procurement Arrangements in Borrower Implementing Agencies for Procurements Financed under IPF (Washington DC, World Bank, 2016) available at pubdocs.worldbank.org/en/634391468437110489/Alternative-Procurement-Arrangements-Guide-to-the-Assessor.pdf.

[61] World Bank, Procurement Regulations for IPF Borrowers, para 2.4.

[62] ibid Common Abbreviations and Defined terms.

[63] ibid Annex V, s 2.1.

[64] ibid Annex V, s 2.3.

b. experience in implementing similar projects, track record level of success and lessons learned;
c. contract management capacity; and
d. complaints management systems.[65]

There are three hurdles a borrower may face in proposing to the Bank that it be permitted to use its domestic procurement framework in a funded contract. The first is that the borrower's procurement framework may not be inconsistent with the Banks 'policies, rules, and applicable fiduciary and operational requirements'. The second is that the borrower must be able to justify its desire to use its domestic procurement framework 'based on market analysis, risk and operating context and the project's particular circumstances',[66] and the third is that it must have the necessary capacity, experience and an acceptable remedial system.

It may be the case that the first and the third hurdles will be the most difficult for a borrower to overcome. The first may be a matter of the borrower's PFM system and perhaps ideological compatibility between the Bank's approach and the borrower's approach to procurement,[67] whilst the second will necessitate the existence of a domestic procurement framework that is acceptable to the Bank. This will depend on an assessment of the borrower's procurement framework and its existing procurement capacity, and examining the risks presented by both. As was discussed above, there are several risks that are presented by a commitment to rely on the borrower's procurement systems – the fiduciary risks, development risk, reputational risks and delay risks,[68] and before the Bank or any donor will agree to the use of a domestic system, it will want to provide risk mitigation strategies to ensure that the development financing provided is not exposed to an unacceptable level of risk.[69] In cases where an intolerable level of risk is presented, the donor may of course decide not to use the country system, until there is an improvement in the system.

An important aspect of the third hurdle, which may prove problematic in some developing countries is the existence of an 'acceptable remedial system'. In 2016, the Bank significantly modified its approach to the remedies that are available to participants in a funded procurement;[70] and this new approach requires borrowers to do significantly more in providing remedies under funded procurements than they hitherto had to.

The efficacy of the procurement remedial system in a number of African countries had earlier been questioned, especially in relation to the limited nature of remedies available where a breach of the procurement rules is substantiated;[71] but there is evidence to suggest that these systems are improving both in terms of access and the

[65] ibid Annex V, s 3.4.
[66] ibid Annex V, s 2.3.
[67] eg will a system that is designed to pursue social objectives (and is thus discriminatory) like the South African system be thought of as being compatible with the Bank's requirements?
[68] OECD (n 2) 48.
[69] UNDP (n 24).
[70] Williams-Elegbe (n 14) ch 11.
[71] G Quinot, 'A Comparative Perspective on Supplier Remedies in African Public Procurement Systems' in Quinot and Arrowsmith (eds), *Public Procurement Regulation in Africa* (n 6).

nature of remedies provided.[72] The upshot is that borrowers will be required under the new Bank regulations to provide a forum for complaints by participants in a funded contract, respond to those complaints timeously and provide adequate remedies, including amending procurement decisions, where complaints are substantiated.[73]

Once the borrower can overcome these hurdles in its PPSD, the document is submitted to the Bank, and reviewed and approved by the Bank if it is acceptable to the Bank.

V. Methodologies for Assessing Procurement Systems by the World Bank: The MAAPA

As seen from the above, a borrower seeking to rely on its domestic system will have to have the necessary capacity and experience to do so. The Bank will thus conduct an assessment of the borrower's procurement system and capacities. The assessment of a procurement system relies on several diagnostic tools. The World Bank has recently developed a new Methodology for Assessing Alternative Procurement Systems (MAAPA).

The MAAPA was developed under the Bank's new procurement framework to assist the Bank with 'identifying, assessing and agreeing acceptable alternative procurement arrangements (APAs) in Borrower implementing agencies'.[74] It is important to note that the MAAPA is designed to assess the borrower's agencies, and whilst it considers the national procurement system, the MAAPA assessment is not intended to approve countries' procurement arrangements.[75] It thus has a different thrust and a narrower scope from the OECD MAPS.

The findings of a MAAPA will be used to justify Bank decisions in relation to the use of country systems – referred to as alternative procurement arrangements (APA).[76] It must be noted that a successful MAAPA assessment is a crucial element of the justification for seeking to rely on the domestic procurement system as may be proposed in the PPSD document discussed above. Thus, the MAAPA assessment must necessarily have been conducted prior to the development of the PPSD document.

The MAAPA is intended to assess the legal and regulatory framework as well as the capacity and the capability of a borrower-implementing agency.[77] The MAAPA is based on the MAPS, with the inclusion of another pillar, which relates to procurement operations and the use of minimum standards.[78] Considering the narrower focus of this methodology the addition of an extra pillar seems surprising, to say the least. The MAAPA is comprised of five pillars, each one covering several dimensions or facets of a procurement system. The pillars and dimensions are reproduced in Table 1.

[72] A Engelbert, M Kaltenborn and N Reit-Born, *Effective Corruption Control: Supplier Remedies in Public Procurement in Kenya, Uganda and Tanzania – a Comparative Analysis of Mechanisms and their implementation*, Ua Ruhr Studies on Development and Global Governance 68 (Berlin, Logos Verlag, 2016).

[73] Williams-Elegbe (n 14) ch 11.

[74] World Bank, Draft Guide to the APA Assessment (n 60) s I.

[75] ibid s I.

[76] ibid s III.

[77] ibid s I.

[78] ibid s I.

Table 1 MAAPA Pillars and Dimensions

PILLAR	DIMENSIONS
Legal, regulatory and policy framework	Public procurement legislation, policy, regulations, general conditions of contract, sustainability.
Institutional framework and management capacity	Procurement planning, payments, functional normative/regulatory body, institutional development capacity, conflict of interests, national procurement statistics, staff performance, training.
Procurement administration and market practices	Procurement competence, safekeeping of records, procurement review and controls, partnerships.
Integrity and transparency of the public procurement system	Internal and external controls, audit, complaints mechanism, access to information, fraud and corruption, record keeping.
Procurement operations	Procurement methods, advertising, tender documentation and technical specifications, bidding process, model tender documents, pre-qualification, evaluation and award criteria, procurement performance, dispute resolution, risk management.

Prior to the conduct of an assessment, the Bank conducts an initial feasibility study to review the national environment, publicly available information, any complaints received by the Bank and any prior fraud and corruption allegations. This review, once completed, determines whether the Bank will proceed to a full MAAPA assessment.[79]

The feasibility study is a high level review of the national environment in which the agency operates; information available online; any complaints received by the Bank; and fraud and corruption allegations against the borrower agency.[80] The feasibility study determines if the agency has the potential capacity and capability to lead on procurement activities using its own procurement arrangements in a manner that is acceptable to the Bank.[81] It is essentially a desk-based analysis that consists of a review of the national environment and the agency's past performance.[82]

Once the feasibility study is completed, a recommendation is issued to determine whether to undertake a full assessment, and if not, why this is the case.[83] Where it is recommended that a full MAAPA assessment is undertaken, this assessment determines whether the borrower agency can use its own arrangements for procurements financed by the Bank.[84] The assessment considers whether the borrower agency's procurement arrangements, including procurement performance and governance, 'provide reasonable assurance that the Bank's financing will be used for the intended purpose(s), and in accordance with the Bank's Core Procurement Principles'.[85]

[79] ibid s IV.
[80] ibid s IV.
[81] ibid s IV.
[82] ibid s IV.
[83] ibid s IV.
[84] ibid s II.
[85] ibid s II.

The crux of a MAAPA assessment is whether the assessed system meets minimum standards in relation to its procurement. An agency needs to meet all the minimum standards for it to be approved for APA. The agency has to meet the minimum standards for each requirement under each indicator.[86] The results of the assessment will be used to inform a decision on the effectiveness of procurement arrangements at the agency level.[87]

The assessment itself is conducted in three stages: step A assesses the regulatory framework at national and agency level; step B assesses quantitative evidence; and step C assesses qualitative perceptions of the system.[88] Thus, the results obtained from the step A assessment are then assessed in steps B and C. Each of the five pillars is evaluated using the three-part assessment methodology.[89]

The outcome of the MAAPA is crucial to the use of country systems as it determines whether the Bank will permit that agency at the project level to

> rely on the procurement rules and procedures of the implementing agency for the specific project. Individual procurements will be subject to post review carried out by the Supreme Audit Institution within the country or an independent audit by a leading audit institution to determine performance and the future ongoing use of the agency's APA.[90]

The MAAPA thus determines if the entire procurement process as well as the procurement review will be subject to national rules and institutions. It is in essence a wholesale devolution of the entire procurement process to the borrower's system.

Where it is recommended that an agency's procurement arrangements are suitable for APA, the agency will be approved for future use for Bank-financed projects, and the agency's procurement arrangements will then be considered for future Bank-financed projects, if it is the most appropriate approach as subsequently incorporated in the PPSD.[91] The use of the agency's procurement arrangements could be for all the procurements under a project or just for certain elements of the project.[92] Once it is approved, the borrower agency will be able to utilise its domestic procurement framework for funded contracts for a two- to three-year period.

It may be noted that where an agency undergoes a full assessment and does not meet the minimum standards, an action plan is required to be produced which 'highlights the areas of the assessment that the agency didn't meet and therefore, would need to address before these elements can be re-assessed and the agency potentially being conditionally approved'.[93]

It may be stated here that it is not likely that many agencies will fail an assessment as the criteria for selecting agencies to be assessed requires that selected agencies are 'high performing, has good process and procedures, and a good track record of delivering Bank financed projects'.[94] It is also stated that it is 'very important to select high

[86] ibid s III.
[87] ibid s III.
[88] ibid s IV.
[89] ibid s IV.
[90] ibid s II.
[91] ibid s IV.
[92] ibid s IV.
[93] ibid s II.
[94] ibid s IV.

performing agencies for which the assessment's results are likely to be positive'.[95] It is thus the case that the selection process and the initial feasibility study will weed out any agencies that are unlikely to meet the minimum requirements and any assessments will lead to an agency's qualification for APA.

What the new MAAPA seems to have done is to build in its own success factors. Unlike the use of country systems pilot which was not able to clear any countries after assessment, as detailed above, the MAAPA approach ensures that there will be a very high, if not absolute success rate for agencies that undergo the assessment. This has both practical and psychological implications. The practical implication is that there will finally be a full reliance on domestic systems for contracts subject to international bidding – the holy grail of Bank procurement methods. The psychological implication is that the development community will now record successes in the area of the aid harmonisation agenda that has so far eluded substantial gains.

VI. Conclusion

The chapter has shown that although the use of county systems is one of the most significant commitments made by donors under the aid effectiveness agenda, practice still lags behind and donors make little use of country systems to purchase aid-funded goods and services.

This chapter has attempted to offer an updated account of donors' international commitments on the use of country systems; examine the World Bank's approach to the use of country systems as well as examine the new methodologies for assessing procurement systems developed by the World Bank. It was shown that the methodology developed by the World Bank has a narrower focus as it assesses borrower agencies and not a country system, unlike the OECD MAPS. The implications of the Bank's approach, is that more agencies that are identified as 'high performing' will be cleared for the use of country systems, but it also represents a move away from a holistic approach that looks at systems and not just agencies, and may not do much for the wholesale reform of borrower procurement systems.

[95] ibid s IV.

11

Maturity Model for Institutional Development of Procurement Units in Indonesia*

JEANMARIE MEYER†

'I was taught that the way of progress was neither swift nor easy.'

Marie Curie

I. Introduction

A. The Compact

In November 2011, the United States of America, through the Millennium Challenge Corporation (MCC)[1] signed a compact with the Government of the Republic of Indonesia (GoI) granting USD 600 million to fund three projects: (i) the Green Prosperity Project;[2] (ii) the Community-Based Health and Nutrition Project;[3] and (iii) the Procurement Modernisation Project – with a particularly ambitious objective

* Any opinions or arguments expressed within this chapter are solely those of the author. None of the information contained within this chapter should be construed as either an expressed or implied endorsement by the Millennium Challenge Corporation or the US government.

† The author wishes to acknowledge the contribution of Jamie Meacham for his research and input into the sections on the Background on Maturity Modelling and Structure of Maturity Models.

[1] The Millennium Challenge Corporation (MCC) is an independent US foreign aid agency that is helping lead the fight against global poverty. Created by the US Congress in January 2004, MCC provides time-limited grants to eligible partner countries to promote economic growth, reduce poverty and strengthen institutions. For further information about MCC and the MCC Compact with the Government of Indonesia, see www.mcc.gov.

[2] The Green Prosperity Project supported activities in renewable energy and natural resource management intended to reduce reliance on fossil fuels, improve land management practices, protect natural capital and complement efforts to reduce emissions from deforestation and environmental degradation.

[3] The Community-Based Health and Nutrition Project supported activities to reduce stunting and low birth weight and improve sanitation in communities.

of improving the effectiveness and efficiency of the Indonesian public procurement system by supporting the institutional development of procurement units staffed with well-trained procurement professionals equipped with modern technical and procedural procurement tools. Project implementation began in April 2013 and ended in April 2018.[4] This chapter tells the story of how what became known as the maturity model for institutional strengthening of procurement units became the focal point of the Procurement Modernisation Project. It describes how the maturity model was created and guided the strategy and approach to procurement modernisation in Indonesia.

B. The Indonesian Public Procurement System

While the Indonesian public procurement system is operationally decentralised, it is uniform legally with all public procurement, including national and subnational procurement, regulated by Presidential Decree. In 2016, Indonesia expended about USD 42billion through public procurement.[5] With an estimated population of 261 million, this huge system operates in vastly different circumstances as Indonesia is the world's largest island nation with more than 13,000 islands spread over two continents.

In 2007, Presidential Decree PerPres 106[6] established the National Office of Public Procurement (LKPP[7]) to set procurement policy and monitor implementation of procurement regulation across the country. The President signed PerPres 54[8] in 2010 followed by PerPres 70[9] in 2012. Together these decrees mandate significant public procurement reforms throughout Indonesia. The Procurement Modernisation Project was designed to support implementation of the legal and institutional reforms set out in these Presidential Decrees.

II. Background

A. The Procurement Modernisation Project

Mirroring the large footprint of public procurement, the Procurement Modernisation Project (PM Project) was broad and complex. Built on the fundamental premise that

[4] After a compact is signed there is a period of time for the partner country to satisfy certain conditions to enactment before implementation begins. This period varies among compacts but often takes 12 months or more. Once a compact comes into force, the funds are available for implementation. By US law, the implementation period of an MCC compact is strictly limited to five years with no exceptions.

[5] See the website of the Indonesian National Office of Public Procurement at http://monev.lkpp.go.id/.

[6] Regulation of the President of the Republic of Indonesia Number 106 of 2007 on the National Public Procurement Agency at JDIH Lembaga Kebijakan Pengadaan Barnag/Jasa Permerintah, available at jdih.lkpp.go.id.

[7] Acronym for its title in Bahasa Indonesian: Lembaga Kebijakan Pengadaan Barang/Jasa Pemerintah.

[8] Regulation of the President of the Republic of Indonesia Number 54 of 2010 on the Procurement of Public Goods and Services at JDIH Lembaga Kebijakan Pengadaan Barnag/Jasa Permerintah, available at jdih.lkpp.go.id.

[9] Regulation of the President of the Republic of Indonesia Number 70 of 2012 on Second Amendment to the Regulation of the President Number 54 of 2010 on Procurement of Public Goods and Services at JDIH Lembaga Kebijakan Pengadaan Barnag/Jasa Permerintah, available at jdih.lkpp.go.id.

procurement is a strategic function of government, all of the several activities under the project and outlined briefly here led to that objective. The compact granted a total USD 75 million to fund PM Project activities.[10] These funds were applied to establish dedicated procurement units in government entities throughout Indonesia and to provide extensive support to nurture their organisational growth. The project defined procurement as a profession, identified 77 competency standards of the procurement professional and developed and delivered 43 procurement and organisational skills training modules mapped to these professional competencies. Over 1000 persons participated in the training programme that also established local training institutions and developed local trainers. Along with establishing proactive procurement institutions and a skilled procurement workforce, the project modernised the procedural and technical tools of procurement. A Procurement Information Management System modernised data collection and business intelligence collecting procurement data from across the country through a secure i-cloud system and delivering reports directly into the office of the President of Indonesia. The system has built-in fraud filters that can block transactions or send red flag alerts when problems are detected. It also includes an e-catalogue system populated with goods and services procured through modern framework contracting policies and procedures that the project helped develop and pilot. Additionally, the project funds were applied to help develop and pilot new procurement policies, procedures and model bidding documents for procuring Public-Private Partnerships. The PM Project also conducted extensive research to provide a foundation for the GoI to adopt practices promoting environmentally and socially sustainable public procurement in Indonesia. A brief discussion of these various activities of the PM Project follows and then this chapter will focus on the development of the maturity model which proved to be an important tool in implementing the PM Project.

i. Institutional Strengthening

The PM Project fostered the professionalisation of procurement institutions by supporting the establishment of efficient and effective procurement services units (PSUs) dedicated to the procurement function within national and local spending units of government. Forty-four PSUs representing all levels and forms of government and geographically spread over the length and breadth of the country participated in the programme (Pilot PSUs). Designing and implementing this assistance proved particularly challenging in both scale and substance. The strategy and approach for institutional development of the PSUs in the PM Project is the primary focus of this chapter.

ii. Professional Workforce Development

Additionally, for PSUs to serve a strategic function, the procurement workforce needed to be trained to a professional level of knowledge and skills. Building a substantial cohort of procurement professionals in Indonesia was a core component of the project.

[10] Originally budgeted at USD 50 million, another USD 25 million of the compact funds were subsequently reallocated to the project.

The professional development programme delivered formal training and mentoring in both organisational and procurement skills.

The procurement skills training programme adopted a competency-based training approach focused on building the skills and knowledge necessary to perform the duties of a procurement professional. The training programme is mapped to a sophisticated schema of 77 competencies that the project team identified from a study of several procurement systems.[11] Each competency is identified as either a core competency or elective, and categorised at basic, intermediate or advanced level of professional skill. The training programme consists of six modules each for basic,[12] intermediate[13] and advanced[14] levels, plus nine speciality courses[15] that build specialised skills at the advanced level. The competency mapping is very complex as a single module will build skills in multiple competencies and, conversely, skills in a single competency item will be developed over several modules. The basic level programme aims to develop understanding of the procurement process and build skills in basic procurement planning, risk identification and operational procurement. The intermediate level programme builds on the foundation learned during the basic training but from a more analytical

[11] The word 'profession' means different things to different people and this is especially true in the context of procurement. The PM Project adopted an approach consistent with the definition stated by Professions Australia – Australian Council of Professions, an association of professional organisations in Australia: 'A profession is a disciplined group of individuals who adhere to ethical standards and who hold themselves out as, and are accepted by the public as possessing special knowledge and skills in a widely recognised body of learning derived from research, education and training at a high level, and who are prepared to apply this knowledge and exercise these skills in the interest of others' (www.professions.com.au/about-us/what-is-a-professional). This definition led to the more challenging question: what special knowledge and skills would be suitable for the development of the procurement profession in Indonesia? To answer this question, the project conducted a detailed review of established and recognised standard procurement and purchasing programmes from the private as well as the public sectors, and then focused analysis on three programmes: (i) Chartered Institute of Purchasing and Supply (CIPS at www.cips.org/en); (ii) Association for Contract and Commercial Management (IACCM at www.iaccm.com); and (iii) Australian Government Public Sector Procurement Training Package (AusGov Procurement]) as well as the Australian Nationally Recognised Training in Purchasing (AusGov Purchasing]). The competency framework of each of these programmes was broken down into three levels: competency fields, competency subfields and competency items. These were then compared across size, fields, subfields, skills and levels. Based upon the findings in this study, the project identified 77 competency items.

[12] The six modules are titled: Applying Basic Procurement Principles; Planning Simple Procurement; Developing Solicitation Documentation; Receiving and Evaluating Bids; Managing Procurement Documentation, Records and Contract Files; Procurement Management Information Systems (PMIS) and Framework Agreements.

[13] The six modules are titled: Planning & Developing Complex Procurement; How to Develop Cost Estimates and Why; How to Calculate Total Cost of Ownership (TCO) and Why; How to Develop & Interpret Specification; How to Select Appropriate Contracting Models; How to Implement & Manage Contracts.

[14] The six modules are titled: Planning & Implementing Strategic Procurement; Undertaking Framework Contracting; Identifying & Managing Risk in Complex Procurement; Managing Strategic & Complex Contracts; Developing & Conducting Bid Evaluations for Large/Complex Procurement; Fraud Schemes & Indicators.

[15] The nine modules are titled: Conducting International Procurement; Procurement of Professional Services & Appropriate Selection Procedures; Procurement of Works & Appropriate Selection Procedures; Contract Administration (Works Contracts); Procurement of Pharmaceuticals & Appropriate Selection Procedures; Procurement of Medical Equipment & Appropriate Selection Procedures; Supply Chain Management; Procurement of IT & Appropriate Selection Procedures; Procurement as a Strategic Government Function for Senior Managers.

approach and introduces more complex procurement processes. A participant achieves the status of procurement professional only after successful completion of all modules at the basic and intermediate level. Then, at the advanced level the participants develop more strategic skills and competence in managing high-value and complex procurements.

To complement the formal training programme, the project also supported a mentoring programme. During monthly visits to the Pilot PSUs, the mentors assisted the PSU staff to apply the newly acquired skills and knowledge in their work activity and assessed whether the participants demonstrated competency in the target skills and knowledge defined in the competency framework. The mentors also used these visits to test the effectiveness of the training programme and develop ideas for improving the materials.

In addition to the procurement skill training, the PSU staff gained organisational skills through training and mentoring programmes. This 12-module programme facilitated the organisational transition to the new procurement institutional model developing skills in change management, performance planning and management, customer relations and stakeholder management, knowledge management, leadership in procurement management, and organisational risk management.

During the five-year life of the project, over 500 persons attained procurement professional status each receiving over 700 hours of procurement and organisational skills training and mentoring, and over 300 of these persons received additional advanced training in highly specialised procurement skills. In addition, nearly 450 persons with roles in the procurement cycle outside of the PSUs received training appropriate to their function in procurement with particular emphasis on training budget officers in procurement planning and training sector experts in contract management. The project also developed and delivered a programme of three courses for auditors[16] and special training programmes for developing and operating procurement training centres and for developing and administering a virtual network for procurement professionals.

iii. Procurement Management Information System

To serve a strategic function, procurement professionals require modern technical and procedural tools to deliver effective procurement outcomes efficiently. The PM Project delivered a modern state of the art Procurement Management Information System (PMIS) capable of pulling together procurement information from every spending unit in the country into a data warehouse programmed to analyse and correlate data into useful information about the operation of this system from planning to contract management. The PMIS includes functions for planning, tendering and contract management, plus an e-catalogue component.[17] The PMIS also incorporates an elaborate scheme of

[16] The three modules are titled: How to Audit Strategic Procurement (Red Flags of Procurement Fraud Schemes); How to Conduct Probity Audits; How to Conduct Effective Audits of Procurement and What are the Soft Skills Required.

[17] See the Indonesian national public procurement agency website at www.lkpp.go.id/v3/en for more information about the PMIS.

filters developed in the context of the PM Project to detect fraud schemes. Capable of blocking certain transactions and sending red flags alerts that there may be a problem with the bidding or payment activity, this leading-edge component is understood to be the most elaborate system of fraud filters of any country procurement system.

iv. Framework Contracting

An important component of PMIS is the e-catalogue system. To populate the catalogue, the PM Project helped LKPP develop procedures for framework contracting and piloted these in several PSUs around the country. The pilot programme provided intense training and mentoring in procurement planning and developing bidding documents for framework agreements.

v. Public-Private Partnerships

The PM Project also supported the development of procurement procedures and standard bidding documents to support the government's Public-Private Partnerships (PPP) initiative. To advance capacity in the application of these new PPP procedures and tools, the project delivered an intense formal training and mentoring programme along with providing technical support for several pilot PPP projects. Although LKPP had been granted authority to develop competitive bidding procedures for PPPs, the general responsibility for PPPs rested elsewhere in government. Before the PM Project began, the importance of procurement procedures and the procurement professional in PPPs was not well understood or appreciated. This mind-set changed substantially as the PM Project activity was implemented and LKPP became a leading partner in the PPP initiative.

vi. Sustainable Procurement

Finally, the PM Project supported a broad study of sustainable public procurement (SPP) issues in Indonesia and socialised the findings to lay the foundation for further development and implementation of environmentally and socially sustainable procurement policies and procedures. The study found that the state of SPP in Indonesia was very elementary. There was no overarching strategy, policies, regulations, guidelines or tools. There was a board lack of familiarity with SPP concepts and very limited number of suppliers providing SPP products and services. Given the current state of SPP, the study recommended that the government develop a National SPP Action Plan to be implemented over five years. It also provided a detailed framework for development of the plan to include strategies: (i) for market engagement; (ii) to increase awareness; (iii) for capacity development; (iv) to improve regulations especially in context of product standards and labelling; and (v) for development of SPP public procurement tools including SPP tender procedures and bidding documents, a 'green' e-catalogue, supplier data base and adoption of life-cycle analysis and costing.

B. Institutional Strengthening of Procurement Service Units

The PM Project was designed to support the implementation of the legal and institutional reforms of newly enacted Presidential Decrees on Public Procurement in Indonesia. These regulations included a mandate that permanent and independent PSUs be established throughout the government, at national and subnational levels. Translated into reality, this meant that over 600 PSUs would need to be established in central ministries, regional offices, provinces, districts, cities and public institutions across Indonesia. Aside from the requirement that the units be permanent and independent, the regulations left a blank slate. There was no mention of organisational standards, expected roles and responsibilities of the PSUs, nor a requirement that the PSU staff be permanent and dedicated to the procurement function. Moreover, even the requirement for 'permanent and independent' was a vague notion that was complicated to define and implement. The PSUs needed roots in the organisation that were not easily dissolved by political whim and it needed to have reporting lines that went directly to the highest officials in the spending unit, independent from the control of and domination by the user groups yet there was no precise vision or strategy for how this could be achieved within the various types and levels of public entities.

Aside from the magnitude of the task of establishing PSUs, fundamental challenges to implement this mandate existed. First, it was clear that the regulatory gaps were not intended simply to provide flexibility but rather reflected a lack of consensus among policy-makers on basic fundamental questions as to what a PSU should be and should do. Second, when the regulations were issued, procurement was not even designated a functional position within the civil service. It was merely an ad hoc function assigned arbitrarily as needed. Given these handicaps out of the starting gate, the task of PM Project assistance was basic: to provide assistance in defining the path to establishing professional PSUs at national and subnational levels. Sequentially, the core objectives and implementation strategy for PSU institutional strengthening were simple to identify although not easily implemented or achieved:

- Establish procurement as a functional position in civil service.[18]
- Select and engage a cohort of Pilot PSUs that reflect the geographic diversity and institutional circumstance such that the programme could be replicated throughout Indonesia.
- Establish permanent PSUs with full-time workforces in the newly engaged Pilot PSUs.

[18] As a condition of the compact, the GoI agreed to establish procurement as a functional position in the civil service. Although this condition was fulfilled in 2012, the position was established at low grades with associated low compensation levels reflecting the low regard at that time of procurement as simply an administrative function. This complicated project implementation making it more difficult to attract talented personnel to staff the PSUs. However by the end of the PM Project there was a growing recognition that procurement was a strategic government function and the Ministry of State Apparatus and Bureaucratic Reform agreed to raise the grades and compensation for procurement positions in 2018.

- Develop and implement a mentoring programme to develop the newly established PSUs into effective procurement organisations and establish a new PSU model that could be replicated throughout Indonesia.[19]
- Develop and deliver a comprehensive organisational training programme to build leadership and organisational skills of at least 500 PSU staff in the Pilot PSUs to create a core group of procurement professionals that could implement and replicate the new PSU organisational model.
- Design, develop and deliver all aspects of the PSU institutional strengthening programme in close coordination with LKPP and Pilot PSUs to ensure sustainability after the compact period.

III. Maturity Modelling

Following a rigorous process for selecting the first group of Pilot PSUs,[20] 29 spending units each signed a Memorandum of Understanding to participate in the institutional strengthening activity of the PM Project. The spending units were at various stages of establishing a PSU because, when the compact began serious implementation in late 2013, many of the spending units were already attempting to comply with the mandate to organise a PSU. As might be expected, the Pilot PSUs, in their attempts to set up PSUs, exemplified a sundry range of approaches to establishing a PSU. During the selection process, it became clear that a sophisticated tool was needed, one capable of providing not only baseline assessment data but also a bespoke roadmap for the institutional strengthening of each particular PSU. Following a study of various procurement assessment tools available in 2013,[21] the project team did not find a useful tool to generate the

[19] The PM Project included a comprehensive programme for on-site mentoring in both organisational and procurement skills. This coaching was a follow-up to the formal training programme, eg once the PSU's staff completed the classroom training for developing and tracking performance indicators, a mentor travelled to the PSU site and helped the PSU set up and implement its performance tracking system. Similarly the procurement skills mentors provided on-the-job coaching to the PSU in applying new skills learned in the classroom to his or her procurement tasks.

[20] An additional 15 Pilot PSUs came into the PM Project in 2016.

[21] The following models, representing a range of authors from academic to private and public sectors, were reviewed: United Nations Development Program Capacity Assessment Framework authored by the United Nations Development Program; MSU+ authored by Michigan State University and NEVI, Netherlands Association of Purchasing Management; SKI Model authored by National Procurement Ltd – Denmark; Procurement Maturity Model authored by National Rural Electric Cooperative Association – USA; Procurement Maturity Assessment authored by Southern Universities Purchasing Consortium (SUPC); Procurement Enabler Diagnostic authored by Bain & Company; Methodology for Assessing Procurement Systems (MAPS) authored under Organisation for Economic Co-operation and Development with support of international development banks and bilateral donors; Capability Maturity Model Integration authored by Carnegie Melon University; Global Fund Procurement & Supply Management Assessment Tool authored by Global Fund; The OGC Procurement Capability Framework authored by the Office of Government Commerce, the precursor of the United Kingdom Crown Commercial Service. (All files cited are with the author.) In general the public sector and donor models focused more on the country-wide overall system, which was too high a level for the purposes of the PM Project. Moreover many of the factors in these models are within the control of central policy, regulatory or legislative bodies and not the spending units or the procuring services units. While the private sector models generally focused at a lower level and on the operational process, they did not provide the level of granularity needed for newly developing entities.

desired information. Most public sector tools provided a top-down approach, focused on the legal and policy structure of a country's procurement system but not on an institutional, operational, bottom-up assessment to define and build institutional capacity. After determining the need to create a new assessment tool, the project team decided to build upon the well-developed discipline of maturity modelling. As maturity models are designed to focus assessment at the organisational level, looking at people, processes and operating structures, this provided a foundation that could be used to produce not only an assessment of each individual PSU but also a bespoke roadmap for institutional development.

A. Background on Maturity Modelling

Maturity modelling has been applied extensively to measure a myriad of functions, organisations, technical capabilities and people. Typically the process of maturity modelling is used to assess objectively the maturity of a given process, function or organisation against descriptions of increasing levels of maturity. The first recognised maturity model is the Capability Maturity Model (CMM),[22] created by Carnegie Mellon University in collaboration with US Department of Defense. Its initial objective was to standardise functions by comparing similar organisations against a consistent framework. CMM applies a five-level structure with increasing levels indicating an increasing level of maturity. The CMM levels are labelled: (i) Initial, (ii) Repeatable, (iii) Defined, (iv) Managed and (v) Optimising. Many next generation maturity models drew inspiration from the structure of CMM.

While maturity modelling has spread across numerous disciplines and organisational types, even in the context of purchasing, maturity modelling as applied to public procurement is not well developed. Despite extensive research, the project team found no replicable model that could be refined to meet the needs and goals of the PM Project. Thus the project team concluded that the maturity model for PSU development needed to be an original piece of custom-built work and that pre-existing models would provide only ideas for structure and inspiration for typical areas of organisational development.

B. Structure of Maturity Models

At the most basic level, a maturity model requires both a focus area (what is being measured) and a maturity scale (the progressive standard of measurement). Typically a model will have four or five levels of maturity development and a description of what the focus area looks like at each level. During assessment, the organisation will be reviewed for each focus area and assigned a level of maturity that most closely matches its current state of organisational development.

Table 1 illustrates a maturity model structure for spend analysis.

[22] CMM is a registered trademark of Carnegie Mellon University.

Table 1 Maturity Model Structure for Spend Analysis

Area of focus	Maturity Level				
	Basic	Improving	Established	Advanced	Leading Practice
Spend Analysis[23]	Spend Analysis is not undertaken in a systematic manner.	Spend Analysis is conducted to prepare for a tender.	Spend Analysis is conducted continuously throughout the year.	Spend Analysis is embedded in the process of category planning and developing procurement strategy.	Spend Analysis is automated and available to procurement team in real-time through a procurement dashboard.

This example shows how a maturity model is constructed at the measurement level. Complexity is added to models by increasing the range or depth of the focus areas and also by layering focus areas into larger sub-groups. This enables very precise measurement in each focus area while also providing a more holistic view of the organisation's development. While the project team discovered that there is no uniformity in maturity models, it identified five key structural elements from various models as building blocks for shaping the maturity model for PSU development (Table 2).

Table 2 Building Blocks for Shaping the Maturity Model for PSU Development

Structural Element	Description
Domains	A domain is the highest level focus area of a maturity model and describes the commonality between the lower level areas being measured within that domain.
Indicators/Sub-Indicator	These are the lower levels within the models and go down to the next level of granularity after domains. The number of levels (Indicators/sub-indicators/sub-sub-indicators) depends on the structure and complexity of the model.
Assessment Level	Most models have 4–5 assessment levels or maturity levels, typically 1 being the lowest and 4–5 being the highest. There is no consistent nomenclature for maturity levels.
Scoring System	The scoring system refers to how results of the measurement are translated into output maturities for the high levels of the model. Typically models follow either an average scoring mechanism, a strict-step scoring mechanism, or there is no defined scoring system.
Support tool	Typically models will come with some tools to support assessment. These are typically user guides and spreadsheets or online tools to facilitate assessment.

[23] Spend Analysis is the process of collecting, categorising and evaluating expenditure data.

IV. Development of Maturity Model for Procurement Service Unit Strengthening

The story of the development of the Maturity Model for PSU strengthening (PSU Maturity Model) might be its most unique feature. The model was not developed by academics or policy-makers sitting in an office, meeting room, or library and then pushed out for reality on the ground to mould itself to the model. No, the PSU Maturity Model has a far more distinctive birth, being the creative product of watershed work over five years by hundreds of people representing several countries and multiple disciplines, with diverse skills, experience, perspectives and interests.

The PSU Maturity Model had a humble beginning at a workshop in 2013, on the island of Lombok, across the bay from Bali, Indonesia. This first workshop for representatives of the 29 newly selected Pilot PSUs marked the beginning of implementation of the PM Project. The model introduced at the workshop had just two key areas labelled 'Human Resource Capacity Development' and 'Organisational Maturity Development'. The former was layered with three indicators and the latter with six but there were five levels of maturity defined for each. The entire model fit on a dozen power point slides.

The participants enthusiastically embraced the tool, filling the room with charts and post-it notes, as each assessed their own PSU's level of maturity and developed their own roadmap to success. Although the initial self-assessments were highly inflated, it was clear to the project team that a valuable tool to drive the project forward had been conceived. As institutional strengthening mentors began their visits to help each PSU construct a more realistic assessment, the initial assessments were revised, most down to level one, with a clear roadmap to improve maturity. More importantly, most of the participating PSUs began the practice that continues today of posting progress in their offices and celebrating with pride and satisfaction every time a post-it note moves to the next level of maturity.

The next major milestone in development of the PSU Maturity Model came from a workshop in Bali in 2015. After the formal workshop ended, members of the project team, including international and national experts, met informally for a few intense days of brainstorming. Based upon what had been learned in the context of all the PM Project activities to that time, and especially in organisational training and mentoring, the project team settled upon the basic framework for the PSU Maturity Model that has endured.

The revised PSU Maturity Model is built on three layers: Domains, Indicators and Sub-indicators. There are four Domains: Institutional, Management, Operational and Personnel. Although the definitions have been modified slightly to reflect development of the model, these Domain labels remained unchanged. At the next level there are 11 Indicators. Similarly, there has been no change in the labels of these Indicators but the definitions have been changed slightly from the 2015 version to the final version issued March 2018. Table 3 lists the Domains and Indicators of the revised PSU Maturity Model.

Table 3 Domains and Indicators

Domains	Indicators
Institutional	Organisational, Ethical Culture, Stakeholders
Management	Leadership and Culture, Performance
Operational	Information Systems, Risk, Process
Personal	Competency, Staffing, Career

The third layer, the Sub-indicators, has experienced more change. The 'Bali' version had over 60 Sub-indicators, then at one point their number increased to over 70 Sub-indicators and the final version posts 53 Sub-indicators. Additionally, the 'Bali' version retained the five levels of maturity but gave the levels new titles to reflect better the evolving concepts of development: *Reactive*, *Compliant*, *Proactive*, *Strategic* and *Innovative*. This progression sends an important message that merely conducting procurements in strict compliance with regulations is not sufficient. Compliant is only the second level of institutional maturity. Although the 'Bali' version represented a quantum leap in developing the PSU Maturity Model, it was just the prelude to the next step in development of the model. The hardest part was ahead.

The next stage of development of the PSU Maturity Model faced several major challenges. First, it was not easy to develop meaningful definitions for each of the Domains, Indicators, and especially, the Sub-indicators. Second, and more challenging, how should the levels be defined for each Sub-indicator? Experience in applying the earlier version of the model made clear that vague, subjective qualitative descriptions led to confusion, debate and overstating maturity while yielding less useful roadmaps for the PSUs. Third, once the levels were well defined, what was the source of evidence to support that the level was achieved? For some Sub-indicators the evidence would be obvious, but for many Sub-indicators, especially at higher levels of maturity, it was more difficult to settle upon a reliable source of proof. Finally, how would the project team socialise the new 'Bali' version of the PSU Maturity Model which made far-reaching changes to the version that the PSUs had embraced and nearly worshipped as their little post-it notes travelled along the path to maturity? It would take nearly another three years of experimenting, discussing, re-thinking, redoing, evaluating, re-evaluating, cajoling and persuading combined with plain hard work before the PSU Maturity Model was deemed final and ready to be converted into an online tool to foster the institutional development of PSUs across all of Indonesia. Progress in procurement is neither swift nor easy.

V. The 2018 Maturity Model for Procurement Service Unit Strengthening

How can procurement move from the forgotten, neglected, under-valued, under-resourced, low status function to a strategic function of government? The journey is long and steep. If governments acknowledge that public procurement is a broad and complex function but vital to the operation of government and the delivery of public services, then the function must reside in strong, well-resourced organisational structures and be managed by thoroughly trained procurement professionals. Just as the function is complex, so too is the road to institutional maturity. A single snapshot of the focus areas of the PSU Maturity Model makes no pretence that the road is easily traversed. Consider too that each of the focus areas is fully defined with 53 Sub-indicators precisely described to five levels of maturity coupled with an explanation of how the level is achieved and proven. No, the PSU Maturity Model is not a simple tool, but to suggest that less is required would be compromising or, worse, truly forsaking the objective.

A. Structure of PSU Maturity Model

It is worth noting that this 'snapshot' of the scope of the PSU Maturity Model is also a visualisation of most activities of the PM Project.[24] The project supported the development of nearly all of the Sub-indicators set out in the model. Table 4 shows the four Domains layered with 11 Indicators and 53 Sub-indicators, and Table 5 provides descriptions for Indicators.

Table 4 The Four Domains layered with Eleven Indicators and Fifty-three Sub-indicators.

Domain	**1. Institutional**				
Indicator	**1. 1. Organisational**				
Sub-indicators	*1.1.1.* Legal Status	*1.1.2.* Leadership Authority	*1.1.3.* Tasks and Roles of PSU	*1.1.4.* PSU Organisational Structure	*1.1.5.* Standard Operating Procedures
	1.1.6. Staffing Adequacy	*1.1.7.* Funding Adequacy	*1.1.8.* Material Resources		
Indicator	**1.2. Ethical Culture**				
Sub-indicators	*1.2.1.* Code of Conduct for Procurement	*1.2.2.* Legal Protection	*1.2.3.* Personnel Sanctions	*1.2.4.* Transparency	
Indicator	**1.3. Stakeholders**				
	1.3.1. Internal Customer Management	*1.3.2.* Vendor Management	*1.3.3.* Public Relations Management		

(continued)

[24] PM Project also supported development of Public-Private Partnerships and Sustainable Procurement which are not captured in the model.

Table 4 ***(Continued)***

Domain	**2. Management**				
Indicator	**2.1. Performance**				
Sub-indicators	*2.1.1.* Performance Indicators	*2.1.2.* Procurement Performance Planning and Target Setting	*2.1.3.* Performance Management	*2.1.4.* Document Management	
Indicator	**2.2. Leadership and Culture**				
Sub-indicators	*2.2.1.* Leader Stakeholder Outreach	*2.2.2.* PSU Internal Collaboration	*2.2.3.* Strategic Vision		
Domain	**3. Operational**				
Indicator	**3.1. Process**				
Sub-indicators	*3.1.1.* Planning	*3.1.2.* Vendor Qualification	*3.1.3.* Evaluation Criteria	*3.1.4.* Tender Review	*3.1.5.* Contract Standardisation
	3.1.6. Consultation Mechanism	*3.1.7.* Contract Administration	*3.1.8.* Contract Management	*3.1.9.* Monitoring and Evaluation	*3.1.10.* Debriefing
Indicator	**3.2 Risk**				
Sub-indicators	*3.2.1.* Conflict of Interest Framework	*3.2.2.* Fraud Framework	*3.2.3.* Whistle-blower System	*3.2.4.* Managing Exclusive Relationships	*3.2.5.* Non-Performance
	3.2.6. Financial Due Diligence	*3.2.7.* Blacklisted Suppliers	*3.2.8.* Environmental Risks	*3.2.9.* Complaint System	
Indicator	**3.3. Information Systems**				
Sub-indicators	*3.3.1.* Systems Implementation	*3.3.2.* Data Processing and Data Analysis	*3.3.3.* Information Communication Technology Infrastructure	*3.3.4.* Information Communication Technology Risk Management	
Domain	**4. Personnel**				
Indicator	**4.1. Competency**				
Sub-indicators	*4.1.1.* Human Resource Capacity Assessment	*4.1.2.* Human Resource Training	*4.1.3.* Technical Advisory and Knowledge Transfer		
Indicator	**4.2. Career**				
Sub-indicators	*4.2.1.* Reward and Incentive	*4.2.2.* Career Planning	*4.2.3.* Compensation		
Indicator	**4.3. Staffing**				
Sub-indicators	*4.3.1.* Staff Planning	*4.3.2.* Staff Recruitment			

Table 5 Indicators Defined

Domains	Indicators	Description
Institutional	1.1 Organisational	Assesses the organisational maturity by reviewing the legal structure, funding, presence of material resource and ability to influence the spending unit effectively.
	1.2 Ethical Culture	Assesses the independence of the PSU, the provision to both protect and sanction individuals, and the broader ethical culture of the unit.
	1.3 Stakeholders	Assesses the approach to critical relationships: internal customers, vendors, governance bodies and the public.
Management	2.1 Performance	Assesses the monitoring process, the management of records, and how performance is managed through key indicators and budgetary responsibility.
	2.2 Leadership and Culture	Assesses the leadership of the unit and the extent to which it delivers a strong strategy and a culture of trust and responsibility.
Operational	3.1 Process	Assesses the operational procurement process through the entire procurement from planning to contract closure and the extent to which the PSU is committed to ensuring that the execution of each process is to a high-level standard.
	3.2 Risk	Assesses the approach to identifying, classifying, mitigating and safeguarding against a range of different risks, both internal and external.
	3.3 Information Systems	Assesses the development of information systems strategies, the adoption of eProcurement techniques, and the availability of the infrastructure requirements to enable process execution efficiencies and excellence.
Personnel	4.1 Competency	Assesses the efforts taken to assess the competencies within the unit, planning for competency development, and the focus on skills developments.
	4.2 Career	Assesses how well the career path through the unit is defined and how compensation, rewards and incentives are used to motivate staff to progress through the defined path.
	4.3 Staffing	Assesses the staff planning and selection processes in place to build effective procurement capabilities.

The model divides each of these eleven Indicators into Sub-indicators. There are a total of 53 Sub-indicators and each of these is then defined at five levels of maturity. Table 6 shows the descriptions of maturity levels.

Table 6 Level Descriptions

Levels	**Overall Description**
Level 1 - Reactive	PSU is not fully established and is in the process of developing its structure, people and processes to be compliant with the relevant regulations and requirements.
Level 2 - Compliant	PSU is compliant to PSU regulation and the current regulations in place for public sector procurement.
Level 3 - Proactive	PSU has started to develop and enhance its procurement process over and above the legislative requirements.
Level 4 - Strategic	PSU has developed a strategic approach to procurement, is acting as a partner to spending units and drives strong external collaboration with external stakeholders.
Level 5 - Innovative	PSU brings an innovative approach to procurement, is a champion of best practice for procurement in the Indonesian government and consistently drives self-improvement and innovation throughout all of its activities.

The assessment of each PSU is conducted at the Sub-indicator level yielding a very precise assessment of the overall strengths and weaknesses of the PSU. The following examples selected from each of the 11 Indicators illustrate how Sub-indicators are defined at each level of maturity (Tables 7–18).

Table 7 Example of Sub-indicator Defined at Five Maturity Levels from Domain 1, Indicator 1.1

Domain 1: Institutional

Indicator 1.1: Organisational

1.1.3 **Task and Role of PSU**	This Sub-indicator assesses the list of tasks and roles that are assigned to the PSU. Key question: What is the scope of the task and role of the PSU?
Level 1	No well-defined tasks and roles for the PSU.
Level 2	PSU's tasks and roles are limited to the selection process.
Level 3	PSU's tasks and roles are expanded to coordinate with the entities who are responsible for procurement planning.
Level 4	PSU's tasks and roles are expanded to coordinate with all entities that are involved in procurement to cover the integrated procurement process chain in its entirety (including budgeting, procurement planning, and contract management). The PSU also has the role of protecting its staff from legal risk.
Level 5	PSU's tasks and roles not only cover the integrated procurement process management but also include an additional value-creating role that might include building and developing the capabilities of other PSUs, providing full legal protection to the PSU's staff through a dedicated and comprehensive legal function embedded within the PSU, and managing an IT system that enables innovative improvement of the procurement system.

Table 8 Example of Sub-indicator Defined at Five Maturity Levels from Domain 1, Indicator 1.2

Domain 1: Institutional

Indicator 1.2: Ethical Culture

1.2.1 Procurement Code of Conduct	This Sub-indicator assesses how the PSU develops and implements a code of conduct. Key question: How is the procurement code of conduct established and to what extent is it implemented?
Level 1	PSU has little awareness of the importance of a code of conduct for procurement. No structured approach to implement a code of conduct.
Level 2	PSU is aware of the importance of a code of conduct for procurement but the PSU adheres only to any generic policies of conduct in force within the spending unit.
Level 3	PSU has developed a specific procurement code of conduct that provides the best fit to their operative conditions and procurement context.
Level 4	PSU has developed a specific procurement code of conduct that provides the best fit with their operative conditions and procurement context. The code of conduct is formalised within the entire spending unit and is binding on personnel that are involved in the procurement process beyond the PSU, and aspires to set standards of behaviour and build a culture of procurement integrity throughout the entire spending entity.
Level 5	PSU has developed a specific procurement code of conduct that provides the best fit with their operative conditions and procurement context. The code of conduct is formalised within the entire spending unit and binding on personnel that are involved in the procurement process beyond the PSU, and aspires to set standards of behaviour and build a culture of procurement integrity throughout the entire spending entity. PSU adopts innovative approaches to enforce compliance with the code of conduct, such as establishing an ethical committee to supervise and administer compliance with the code of conduct, and it has a procedure for reporting violations of the code of conduct. The code of conduct is reviewed and updated periodically.

Table 9 Example of Sub-indicator Defined at Five Maturity Levels from Domain 1, Indicator 1.3

Domain 1: Institutional

Indicator 1.3: Stakeholders

1.3.1 Internal Customer Management	This Sub-indicator assesses the PSU's initiatives to manage their internal customer relationship. Key question: What are the initiatives taken by the PSU to manage their internal customers?
Level 1	PSU does not recognise the importance of establishing relationships with internal customers.
Level 2	PSU builds relationships with internal customers through a formal correspondence mechanism.
Level 3	PSU conducts stakeholder analysis as a basis for PSU staff to establish relationships with internal customers.
Level 4	PSU has implemented a cycle of internal customer satisfaction surveys that includes deploying the surveys and using the feedback to improve satisfaction and the quality of relationships with internal customers.
Level 5	Collaboration between the PSU and internal customers is well-established and reflected through the development of effective and strategic procurement plans.

Table 10 Example of Sub-indicator Defined at Five Maturity Levels from Domain 2, Indicator 2.1

Domain 2: Management

Indicator 2.1: Performance

2.1.1 Performance Indicators	This Sub-indicator assesses the PSU's approach in determining procurement performance indicators to be managed. Key question: What indicators are used to assess procurement performance?
Level 1	PSU has limited awareness of the importance of procurement performance indicators as an essential part of performance management and procurement management in general. Hence no full application of any performance indicator.
Level 2	PSU has a strict adherence to national policy on procurement performance management indicators. Hence, they use only performance indicators that are suggested by national policy: efficiency (gap between owner estimated value and contract value) and budget absorption.

(continued)

Table 10 ***(Continued)***

Level 3	PSU has full understanding of procurement performance management essentials and uses performance indicators that cover four procurement outcome areas: timeliness, cost-effectiveness, quality and service level.
Level 4	PSU has fully utilised multiple procurement performance indicators that cover four procurement outcome areas (timeliness, cost-effectiveness, quality and service level) and has linked these to organisational performance indicators.
Level 5	PSU has utilised multiple performance indicators that cover four procurement outcome areas (timeliness, cost-effectiveness, quality and service level) and these are aligned with organisational objectives. PSU is also able to formulate additional performance indicators to promote value creation and continuous improvement.

Table 11 Example of Sub-indicator Defined at Five Maturity Levels from Domain 2, Indicator 2.2

Domain 2: Management

Indicator 2.2: Leadership and Culture

2.2.3 **Strategic Vision**	This Sub-indicator assesses the mechanism and scope of strategic planning by the PSU. Key question: How does the PSU establish a strategic plan and what is covered in its strategic plan?
Level 1	PSU has no annual programme plan.
Level 2	PSU participates in the annual programme plan for the spending unit but there is no particular section that covers planning for procurement operations.
Level 3	PSU participates in the annual programme plan for the spending unit and there is a particular section that covers planning for procurement operations.
Level 4	PSU has an annual programme plan that has become a strategic long-term plan (five-year plan) covering not only a vision for procurement operations but also a plan to improve and strengthen the PSU.
Level 5	PSU has a strategic plan that puts the development of the PSU as one of the priority areas of the spending unit strategy. The strategic plan also has been well-established and acknowledged, and it incorporates others in the spending unit who have roles in the procurement function.

Table 12 Example of Sub-indicator Defined at Five Maturity Levels from Domain 3, Indicator 3.1

Domain 3: Operational

Indicator 3.1: Process

3.1.7 Contract Administration	This Sub-indicator assesses the role of the PSU in contract administration. Key question: To what extent is the PSU involved in contract administration actions?
Level 1	PSU has no contract register or Standard Operating Procedures (SOP) for contract administration.
Level 2	PSU maintains a contract register and has SOP on contract administration (including contract amendment, contract termination, settlement of contractual disputes, and administration of warranties).
Level 3	PSU maintains a contract register and has SOP on contract administration (including contract amendment, contract termination, settlement of contractual disputes, and administration of warranties) and has consistently applied the SOP as well as periodically performing internal reporting and monitoring. The SOP also includes more detailed procedures for administering the dispute process, managing critical contract issues, and actions for damages.
Level 4	PSU maintains a contract register and has SOP on contract administration (including contract amendment, contract termination, settlement of contractual disputes, and administration of warranties) and has consistently applied the SOP as well as periodically performing internal reporting and monitoring that cover wider procurement stakeholders. These procedures include controls and provide for continuous analysis of the contract provisions so that the procurement function runs more strategically.
Level 5	PSU maintains a contract register and has SOP on contract administration (including contract amendment, contract termination, settlement of contractual disputes, and administration of warranties) and has consistently applied the SOP as well as periodically performing internal reporting and monitoring that cover wider procurement stakeholders. These procedures include controls and provide for continuous analysis of the contract provisions. PSU consistently documents issues and major problems in contract administration in order to mitigate risk of contract issues. The SOP also requires monitoring of contract performance and performance management processes.

Table 13 Example of Sub-indicator Defined at Five Maturity Levels Domain 3, Indicator 3.1

Domain 3: Operational

Indicator 3.1: Process

3.1.8 Contract Management	This Sub-indicator assesses the implementation of a contract management function. Key question: To what extent is a contract management function being implemented?
Level 1	PSU does not perform any contract management functions.
Level 2	PSU performs a contract management function but this is limited to monitoring of contract implementation.
Level 3	PSU monitors and evaluates the management of contracts.
Level 4	PSU performs a strategic contract management function which includes identification of contract priorities, accountability of contract management and identification of target benefits on each contract.
Level 5	PSU performs a strategic contract management function that is enhanced with a feedback mechanism from procurement stakeholders including vendors in order to make further improvement in contract management.

Table 14 Example of Sub-indicator Defined at Five Maturity Levels from Domain 3, Indicator 3.2

Domain 3: Operational

Indicator 3.2: Risk

3.2.1 Conflict of Interests Framework	This Sub-indicator assesses the policy being applied to manage conflict of interest within the procurement process. Key question: How is conflict of interest being managed within the procurement process?
Level 1	PSU and the spending unit have no formal policy to manage conflicts of interests.
Level 2	PSU and spending unit have a basic policy to identify and avoid conflicts of interests in the procurement process.
Level 3	PSU and spending unit have comprehensive policies to identify and avoid conflicts of interests, especially in the bid evaluation process, and have sanctions for violations of policies.
Level 4	PSU and spending unit have comprehensive policies to identify and avoid conflicts of interests, especially in the bid evaluation process, and there are sanctions for violations of policies. The policies on conflicts of interests are incorporated in standard training programmes so that the policies are well understood.
Level 5	PSU and spending unit have comprehensive policies to identify and avoid conflicts of interests, especially in the bid evaluation process, and there are sanctions for violations of policies. The policies on conflict of interests are incorporated in standard training programmes so that the policies are well understood and there is a process for continuous improvement and innovation in identifying and preventing or mitigating conflicts of interests.

Table 15 Example of Sub-indicator Defined at Five Maturity Levels from Domain 3, Indicator 3.3

Domain 3: Operational

Indicator 3.3: Information Systems

3.3.2 **Data Processing and Data Analysis of Information System**	This Sub-indicator assesses the coverage of procurement data processing and data analysis process performed by the PSU. Key question: To what extent does the PSU conduct procurement data processing and data analysis?
Level 1	PSU does not conduct consistent procurement data processing and analytics.
Level 2	PSU conducts basic procurement data processing and analytics but this activity is limited to collecting, compiling and reporting procurement process data.
Level 3	PSU conducts enhanced procurement data processing and analytics that includes collecting, compiling and analysing the data to be utilised as an information feed for performance management.
Level 4	PSU conducts advanced procurement data processing and analytics that includes collecting, compiling and analysing the data to be utilised as an information feed for performance management as well as a reference point for strategic decision-making.
Level 5	PSU conducts advanced procurement data processing and analytics that includes collecting, compiling, and analysing the data to be utilised as an information feed for performance management as well as a reference point for strategic decision-making. PSU also participates in the PSU network where the PSUs collaborate to improve data processing and analysis continuously.

Table 16 Example of Sub-indicator Defined at Five Maturity Levels from Domain 4, Indicator 4.1

Domain 4: Personnel

Indicator 4.1: Competency

4.1.1 **Human Resource (HR) Capability Assessment**	This Sub-indicator assesses the mechanism of the PSU in performing HR Capability Assessment Key question: How does the PSU perform its HR Capability Assessment?
Level 1	PSU does not apply a particular standard to assess staff capability consistently.
Level 2	PSU applies consistent procedures to assess HR capability based on basic procurement technical skill/competency requirements.
Level 3	PSU applies consistent procedures to assess HR capability based on national procurement specialist technical skill/competency requirements.

Table 16 ***(Continued)***

Level 4	PSU applies consistent procedures to assess HR capability based on national procurement specialist technical skill/competency requirements and additional organisational and managerial skills.
Level 5	PSU applies consistent procedures to assess HR capability based on international or global procurement standards in technical and managerial skill/competency requirements.

Table 17 Example of Sub-indicator Defined at Five Maturity Levels for Domain 4, Indicator 4.2

Domain 4: Personnel

Indicator 4.2: Career

4.2.2 **Career Planning**	This Sub-indicator assesses the mechanism of developing career plans for the PSU staff. Key question: How does the PSU develop career plans for their staff?
Level 1	PSU does not develop career development plans.
Level 2	PSU develops basic career development plans that track career progression based on regulation criteria with emphasis on tenure.
Level 3	PSU develops procurement specialist career development plans that involve the HR function to enable multi-factor career progression that includes performance factors as well as tenure.
Level 4	PSU develops procurement specialist career development plans that involve the HR function to enable multi-factor career progression that includes performance factors as well as tenure. PSU also develops advance career planning that includes succession planning and integration with training programmes.
Level 5	PSU develops procurement specialist career development plans that involve the HR function to enable multi-factor career progression that includes performance factors as well as tenure. PSU also develops advance career planning that includes succession planning and integration with training programmes. The career development plan reflects the leader's vision and strategy for the future development of the PSU.

Table 18 Example of Sub-indicator Defined at Five Maturity Levels for Domain 4, Indicator 4.3

Domain 4: Personnel

Indicator 4.3: Staffing

4.3.1 **Staffing Plan**	This Sub-indicator assesses the mechanism of developing a staffing plan for the PSU. Key question: How does the PSU develop a staffing plan for its organisation?
Level 1	PSU does not establish an adequate staffing plan.

(continued)

Table 18 ***(Continued)***

Level 2	PSU establishes an adequate staffing plan that focuses on the necessary quantity of procurement staff according to workload analysis.
Level 3	PSU establishes an enhanced staffing plan that focuses on the requirements of both quantity and quality (individual capability) of procurement staff according to workload analysis.
Level 4	PSU establishes an advanced staffing plan that focuses on the requirements of both quantity and quality (individual capability) of procurement staff according to workload analysis, as well as career progression plan and succession plan.
Level 5	PSU establishes an advanced staffing plan that is not only based on historical data but also uses a forecast process to ensure adequate staffing for future needs.

The assessment of maturity requires that findings are rooted in facts and based upon hard evidence. The definition of maturity levels for each Sub-indicator identifies concrete stepping stones to maturity. The next piece of the maturity model puzzle is the description of the evidence and where to find it. This information is based upon the experience gained conducting the assessments of the Pilot PSUs. Table 19 presents an example of a Sub-indicator defined at five maturity levels with the suggested source of information to support the assessment finding.

Table 19 Example of Sub-indicator Defined at Five Maturity Levels with Source Documents for Assessment

Domain 3: Operational

Indicator 3.2: Risk

3.2.2 Anti-Fraud Framework[25]	This Sub-indicator assesses the PSU's risk culture as shown by the anti-fraud framework coverage implemented within their system. Key question: To what extent does the PSU develop and implement an anti-fraud framework as the manifestation of the organisation's risk culture?	
		Source Documents
Level 1	PSU has no formal anti-fraud risk management framework and has only an ad hoc approach to anti-fraud initiatives.	N/A

(continued)

[25] The PM Project organisational and procurement skills training programme included multiple courses that supported the PSUs competency in risk management and procurement fraud issues: Basic Risk Management, Identifying & Managing Risk in Complex Procurement; Fraud Schemes & Indicators. The PM Project also included a special three-course programme for auditors that included: How to Audit Strategic Procurement (Red Flags of Procurement Fraud Schemes).

Table 19 ***(Continued)***

Level 2	PSU has developed anti-fraud risk management tools including policies and process for reporting fraud. The organisation in general has limited awareness of anti-fraud risk management objectives.	Regulation/Policy on anti-fraud risk management
Level 3	PSU has fully implemented a functional anti-fraud risk management framework. The PSU has already embedded risk awareness, key risk behaviours, and general awareness on risk and outcomes within its organisation, and risk management is viewed positively.	1. Regulation/Policy on anti-fraud risk management 2. Guidance on anti-fraud risk management culture
Level 4	PSU has already implemented a fully integrated anti-fraud risk management framework that has been aligned directly with the goals of the spending unit. The whole spending unit is driven by risk and outcomes to guide all their activities as they understand risk tolerance and treatment.	1. Regulation/Policy on anti-fraud risk management 2. Guidance on anti-fraud risk management culture
Level 5	PSU has already fully implemented an enhanced anti-fraud framework that includes a framework for control with automation[26] on potential fraud alert systems and tools, hence enabling a proactive approach in deterring fraud and identifying fraudulent activities in a timely manner.	1. Regulation/Policy on anti-fraud risk management 2. Guidance on risk culture 3. Risk management report 4. Anti-fraud risk early warning system

[26] The PMIS system funded by the PM Project incorporates a state of the art fraud filter system that can block certain transactions and send alerts when red flags are identified.

B. The PSU Maturity Model in Action

The PSU Maturity Model began as a tool to help the project team get their heads around the task of establishing a PSU. At the onset of the project, many in Indonesia and outside observers believed that the mandate to establish a unit dedicated to the procurement function would not be taken seriously and would be nothing more than a new label for doing business as usual. One truth was clear to everyone: to break the status quo, mind-sets must change at many levels within the spending unit. How was the PM Project going to light the fire and build enthusiasm? That foundation was essential. While the PSU Maturity Model was introduced as a *tool to organise assistance* in establishing PSUs and as a *tool to assess* where and how to start, it also became the *aspirational tool* that ignited the fire and guided the way to change and then, surprisingly, it became a *tool of persuasion*, igniting political will to put money and resources into strengthening PSUs.

Hope and progress began with simple post-it notes of many colours. These were introduced at the first workshop in 2013 and continue to endure for years as important locally owned flags of progress. Moving from the early simple PSU Maturity Model to the sophisticated and complex tool that evolved was not an easy transition, especially at first, but soon the revised tool was embraced and its advantages appreciated. The more precise tool yielded reliable and specific information making it difficult for Indonesian officials to ignore the reality of the neglected state of the procurement function. Moreover, the precision of the tool targeted deficiencies and made clear exactly what needed to be done to advance the symbols of progress, namely the post-it notes moving from level to level along the road to maturity for each Sub-indicator, Indicator and Domain. This precision was both effective and efficient. The PM Project targeted assistance specifically to the needs of each PSU, and each PSU knew how and where to focus its efforts to strengthen the organisation's structure and operations. Each PSU could also use its detailed roadmap to construct specific, justified and persuasive requests from political leaders for the resources it needed.

But then, something unplanned and unexpected happened. The mayor of a major Indonesian city with a PSU participating in the project attended a conference as part of the PM Project programme. When he asked why he was not speaking at the conference while other mayors were touting their stories about the developing PSU in their own organisation, he was informed of the results of the PSU Maturity Model assessment and about the slow progress being made by his city's PSU. Because the results produced by the PSU Maturity Model assessment were precise, clear and irrefutable, he did not question but responded that we would be speaking at the next conference. His prediction became reality. Using the roadmap generated by the PSU Maturity Model tool, his staff were able to define clearly the support needed from him and over the next six months the post-it notes flew, charting much accelerated progress. The competition was on as more and more heads of spending units recognised the political benefit to their image and agenda of supporting procurement modernisation which translated into higher scores on the PSU Maturity Model assessment. Local buy-in, local assessment, local ownership and local pride in progress fuelled by healthy competition are all hallmarks of the Indonesian PSU Maturity Model in action.

The PSU Maturity Model also became an important tool to spread the reforms that the PM Project infused into the Indonesian procurement system. A critical condition of MCC's investment is the partner country's commitment to sustain the outcomes of a project. The sustainability plan begins even before the compact is signed, but comes into clearer focus in the final years and months of the compact. As the success of the PSU strengthening activity became increasingly apparent, the MCC agreed to invest additional funds to increase the probability of the reforms to spread beyond the Pilot PSUs. The PSU Maturity Model was converted to an online version making the tool more accessible to all PSUs across the country. To facilitate progress to maturity, the online tool includes lessons learned and case studies that describe how Pilot PSUs overcame particularly difficult obstacles in their path to institutional maturity. This online tool also enables LKPP to track the developmental progress of the more than 600 PSUs across the country and identify where progress is lacking or stalled.

MCC also provided financial support to establish an institutional strengthening programme of 'peer to peer' mentoring to continue after the PM project ended. The demand was there as non-pilot PSUs were already seeking support from LKPP and the Pilot PSUs. However with nearly 600 non-pilot PSUs needing assistance, the programme of support needed to be more formalised. If a Pilot PSU was awarded a 'Center of Excellence' (COE) status[27] in PSU development based upon attaining an advanced level of maturity in several key indicators, that PSU became eligible to be trained as a Champion PSU to mentor other PSUs along the path to maturity. In 2017, LKPP held four regional workshops inviting non-pilot PSUs along with the Champion PSUs from the region. Using the PSU Maturity Model tool, the mentors from the Champion PSUs began to help the non-pilots assess their PSUs and develop roadmaps for development.

Another milestone occurred in February 2018, when the mayor of the city of Jayapura invited heads of all of the spending units and PSUs throughout Papua and West Papua, Indonesia, 44 in total, to convene in Jayapura and begin the journey to strengthen their PSUs and become a COE in PSU development under the guidance of the city of Jayapura PSU. Jayapura attained COE status faster than any of the other Pilot PSUs and also completed the mentor training programme to become a Champion COE for PSU development. This event in Jayapura marked the first time that one of the Pilot PSUs organised and hosted a major programme itself, and set out a formal process of mentoring other PSUs along the journey to become a COE. The journey to COE is difficult as it requires the PSU to attain substantial institutional maturity in 22 of the 53 Sub-indicators spread across all four Domains: Organisational, Management, Personnel and Process development. Mentoring a PSU through the process is a heavy lift. The key tool, now proven, is the PSU Maturity Model.

VI. Conclusion

To improve the efficiency and effectiveness of public procurement, what is more important, training the people or strengthening the institution? Is 'both' the correct

[27] 30 of the 44 Pilot PSUs attained Center of Excellence Status by March 2018.

answer? The PSU Maturity Model illuminates that procurement is a function of many facets. Perhaps there is no factual, irrefutable evidence that strengthening procurement institutions will lead to savings and better quality in procurement outcomes, but those involved in the PM Project would argue: institutional strengthening is the foundation for efficiency and effectiveness of public procurement, not less important than programmes aimed exclusively at training. From a long-term sustainable development perspective, building strong institutional homes with prestigious status for procurement is arguably more critical. Even when a participant had learned a new skill in the classroom, he or she hesitated to apply the skill unless the institutional environment was supportive. This consistent restraint suggests that the success of aid effectiveness in the context of procurement reform and modernisation is at risk if institutional strengthening is ignored or does not receive the elevated priority it merits.

Can change happen in the classroom? The PM Project participants that completed the entire procurement and organisational skills training programme received 30 modules of formal training. Each module was two or three full days of classroom work. This was a serious formal training programme. Yet, even though the training programme was designed to develop skills through exercises and case studies, the mentoring programmes in institutional strengthening and in procurement skills pushed the 'needle' of change. This was particularly true in changing the organisational culture and mind-set within the spending unit and the PSU. The PSU strengthening mentors were experts in facilitating change management; they were not procurement experts. With every site visit these mentors held the PSUs accountable for progress on the journey to institutional maturity. Equally important, the mentors learned about barriers to progress. Many of the problems that surfaced proved to be serious barriers 'strangling' PSU development. Finding solutions was critical to project success. Resolving one highly serious and unexpected legal barrier took years, substantial additional resources, and the involvement of the highest officials in government. This experience offers convincing evidence that an investment in institutional mentoring along with organisational development training is nearly essential to reform the operation of a procurement system.

The PSU Maturity Model was designed and developed in Indonesia and for Indonesia with dedicated, enthusiastic Indonesians owning the PSU Maturity Model. The trainers in the classroom and the institutional strengthening mentors were critical 'components' of the development process. They continually monitored how well the PSU Maturity Model tool was working. Constantly learning from this feedback, the project team, including trainers and mentors, filled out the details and made adjustments to the PSU Maturity Model tool.

The PSU Maturity Model belongs to the procurement system of Indonesia. Indonesians own it, not in terms of copyright, but more importantly in terms of content and culture. Notwithstanding this fact, much of the model can be embraced by systems outside Indonesia. To make the model generic and readily adaptable requires only a modest level of effort. It is the cultural nuances, however, that make the PSU Maturity Model work, so replicating the success of Indonesia may not come easily. The PSU Maturity Model was not perceived by the Indonesians as a script written by some 'authorities' in far-off places. Rather, it was built with their enthusiastic cooperation and informed input based upon their own experiences and knowledge of local conditions. This suggests that to impose a model suppressing local ownership will not lead to equally successful results as those experienced in Indonesia. While reinventing the entire maturity model structure may not be necessary, the Indonesian experience powerfully indicates that a successful maturity model tool must be adapted, developed and refined with full participation and support of the users along the neither swift nor easy journey to progress.

PART V

The Path of Donors' Reforms

12

The World Bank's Procurement Framework: An Assessment of Aid Effectiveness

CHRISTOPHER R YUKINS AND SOPE WILLIAMS-ELEGBE

I. Introduction

In 2016, the World Bank formally implemented a massive reform[1] of the guidance it applies to procurements conducted under World Bank-financed projects.[2] Other multilateral development banks have followed the World Bank's example in harmonising their procurement rules to those of the World Bank in the past,[3] and so the Bank's new Procurement Framework is likely to shape the procurement policies of the other multilateral development banks,[4] as well as other international institutions. Moreover, because of the prominent role that the World Bank plays in shaping procurement policy, the Bank's reforms have had a profound impact on procurement in many countries around the world.[5]

The Bank's reforms involved a 'once-in-a-generation systematic reform and culture change', with a new emphasis on capacity-building in borrower nations and 'hands-on' implementation support from the Bank, as well as oversight through Bank guidance

[1] See eg C Swan and S Harutyunyan, 'Multilateral Development Banks in an Era of Procurement Reform: How Larger Development Goals Are Shaping Revamped Approaches to Procurement' (2016) 58(14) *The Government Contractor* 111.

[2] For an overview of how the World Bank manages its financed projects through the project cycle and the procurement process, see S Williams-Elegbe, *Public Procurement and Multilateral Development Banks – Law, Practice and Problems* (Oxford, Hart Publishing, 2017) ch 5, 77–103.

[3] ibid 59 (discussing harmonising efforts of other multilateral development banks to follow World Bank's earlier procurement guidelines).

[4] In 2015, as the World Bank's reforms were unfolding, the African Development Bank announced approval of its own new procurement framework, which is built on many of the same policies that undergird the World Bank's Procurement Framework. See eg African Development Bank, 'AfDB Approves the New Bank Group Procurement Framework' (Press Release, 14 October 2015) (Board of Directors of the African Development Bank Group approved the Bank's new procurement framework) available at www.afdb.org/en/news-and-events/afdb-approves-the-new-bank-group-procurement-framework-14817.

[5] See eg S Williams-Elegbe, 'The World Bank's Influence on Procurement Reform in Africa' (2013) 21(1) *African Journal of International and Comparative Law* 95.

and regulations.[6] The reforms were built on strikingly novel statements of policy, and included new procurement regulations to implement the many reforms, from enhanced complaints procedures to improved competitive procedures.

II. Measures of Aid Effectiveness

The Bank's reforms were done against a backdrop of strong demands from across the world to improve the 'effectiveness' of development aid.[7] Those concerns were synthesised in two landmark documents, the Paris Declaration on Aid Effectiveness (2005) and the Accra Agenda for Action (2008).[8] With regard to capacity in procurement for development,[9] the Paris Declaration called for:

- strengthening partner (ie recipient) nations' operational frameworks and capacities in their own country systems (including their procurement systems);
- respecting and bolstering partner nations' leadership in their development;
- reducing duplication and redundancies due to special demands from donors; instead, donors committed to use 'country systems and procedures to the maximum extent possible';
- fighting corruption and a lack of transparency, which erode public support, slow mobilisation and divert vital resources;
- setting mutually agreed frameworks to allow reliable assessments of country systems; and
- specifically with regard to procurement, donors and partner nations pledged to strengthen national procurement systems and support reforms, and to use mutually agreed standards and processes for assessment; donors committed to '[p]rogressively rely on partner country systems for procurement when the country has implemented mutually agreed standards and processes'.

The Accra Agenda for Action followed on the Paris Declaration. The Accra Agenda confirmed that donors would 'strengthen and use developing country systems to the maximum extent possible', and would work to ensure 'that their procurement procedures are transparent and allow local and regional firms to compete'.[10] Donors and

[6] World Bank, 'Procurement in World Bank Investment Project Financing – Phase II: The New Procurement Framework' (11 June 2015) 1–4, available at https://wbnpf.procurementinet.org/sites/default/files/Board-Paper-phase-ii-the-new-procurement-framework.pdf.

[7] For a broader discussion of the aid effectiveness agenda and its effect on the multilateral development banks' policies, see Williams-Elegbe, *Public Procurement and Multilateral Development Banks* (n 2) ch 9, 'The Aid Effectiveness Agenda: Harmonisation, Tied Aid and Use of Country Systems' 217–42.

[8] Available at www.oecd.org/dac/effectiveness/parisdeclarationandaccraagendaforaction.htm.

[9] See eg B Ellmers, European Network on Debt and Development (Eurodad), 'How To Spend It: Smart Procurement for More Effective Aid' (Brussels, Eurodad, September 2011) (report based on six country case studies on procurement, aid untying and using country systems) available at http://eurodad.org/files/pdf/4639-how-to-spend-it-smart-procurement-for-more-effective-aid-.pdf.

[10] See eg African Development Fund, 'Implementing the Paris Declaration Commitments and Building on the Accra Agenda for Action: Background Paper' (ADF-11 Mid-Term Review, October 2009,

developing countries were to respect agreed anti-corruption principles, including those under the UN Convention Against Corruption. Developing nations also were to fight corruption by 'improving systems of investigation, legal redress, accountability and transparency in the use of public funds'.

Using the Paris Declaration and the Accra Agenda for Action as background to assess the World Bank's recent procurement reforms as a matter of 'aid effectiveness', this chapter focuses on key aspects of the reforms. The chapter proceeds in seven sections. In section III, the chapter provides a short history of the 2016 reforms. In section IV, the chapter reviews the key principles that frame the reforms. In section V, the chapter reviews the implementing guidance and regulations. Section VI reviews new challenges which may emerge, given the trajectory of the Bank's reforms. Summing up the Bank's new measures, section VII concludes by assessing how these procurement reforms may, on balance, affect aid effectiveness in the Bank's projects in the coming years.

III. History of the Reforms

The World Bank was established by the Bretton Woods Agreement, to provide reconstruction aid in the wake of the destruction of World War II.[11] The World Bank includes 189 member countries, represented by the Board of Governors, who are generally the finance ministers for member nations and who meet once a year. The Board of Governors delegates specific duties to 25 executive directors, who work on-site at the Bank. The nations that are the largest shareholders in the Bank each appoint their own executive directors, while the other member countries are represented by elected executive directors. The executive directors make up the Board of Directors of the World Bank, and they oversee high-level policy-making at the Bank – including policies regarding procurement.[12]

The World Bank Group is made up of five institutions, two of which are the focus of the procurement policies reviewed in this chapter: the International Bank for Reconstruction and Development (IBRD), which typically lends to middle-income countries, and the International Development Agency (IDA), which provides grants and interest-free loans to the poorest countries. When the World Bank provides support for projects through these institutions, it requires that the resulting procurements be conducted under certain policies and procedures mandated by the Bank.[13]

The World Bank launched the use of International Competitive Bidding (ICB) in 1951, and then promulgated procurement guidelines for use on its funded projects, founded on the Bank's fiduciary obligations[14] to ensure sound management of its funds

Helsinki, Finland) available at www.afdb.org/fileadmin/uploads/afdb/Documents/Generic-Documents/BP%20Implementing%20Paris%20Accra.FINAL.EN.pdf.

[11] World Bank, 'History', available at www.worldbank.org/en/about/archives/history.

[12] See generally World Bank, 'Organization', available at www.worldbank.org/en/about/leadership.

[13] See S Williams-Elegbe, 'The Changes to the World Bank's Procurement Policy and the Implications for African Borrowers' (2014) 1 *African Public Procurement Law Journal* 22.

[14] As the World Bank's new 'Procurement Regulations' note, the 'Bank is required by its Articles of Agreement to "make arrangements to ensure that the proceeds of any loan are used only for the purposes for which the loan was granted, with due attention to considerations of economy and efficiency and without regard to

pursuant to its Articles of Agreement.[15] The Bank issued its first written procurement rules to provide guidance for staff in 1961, and in 1964 the first formal instructions on their use were approved by the Bank's Board of Executive Directors. The first formal instructions on selecting consultants, used primarily for large engineering projects, were issued in 1966,[16] and the Bank began requiring the use of standard bidding documents in 1993.[17]

As these processes evolved over the decades, the Bank began to employ a 'no-objection' device for approving procurement methods and outcomes.[18] Because the Bank is not a party to the procurement contract – it is only a bank, or financier – the Bank formally does not 'approve' a procurement approach, but does not object: the Bank provides a formal notice of 'no objection' at critical junctures in the acquisition process.[19]

By 2012, when the latest reforms launched, the World Bank had developed two sets of guidelines[20] for borrowers to follow when conducting procurement in Bank-financed projects: the 'Procurement Guidelines' (known colloquially as the 'red book', because of the colour of the booklet's cover), which governed the procurement of goods, works, and non-consulting services,[21] and the 'Consultant Selection Guidelines' (the 'green book'), which were to be used when consulting services were procured.[22] Over many decades, the world procurement community relied on these guidelines extensively, both for use in World Bank projects[23] and as templates for broader procurement reform. At the same time, though, the guidelines were often criticised[24] – especially the 'red book', for too narrowly emphasising competitions based on low-price, not best value – and in 2011, when the guidelines were updated, the World Bank decided to launch a review of its procurement policies.[25] As the Bank put it, although for 'over 50 years the

political or other non-economic influences or considerations'" – World Bank, 'Procurement Regulations for IPF Borrowers' (Washington DC, World Bank, July 2016, revised November 2017, and August 2018) para 1.2, available at http://pubdocs.worldbank.org/en/659511533066042959/Procurement-Regulations-2017.pdf.

[15] See eg P Trepte, 'All Change at the World Bank? The New Procurement Framework' (2016) 25 *Public Procurement Law Review* 121, 122 (discussing history and Articles of Agreement).

[16] World Bank, Operations Policy and Country Services, 'The World Bank's Procurement Policies and Procedures: Policy Review – Initiating Discussion Paper' (29 March 2012) [hereinafter 'Initiating Discussion Paper'] 2, available at http://siteresources.worldbank.org/INTECA/Resources/257896-1335553632562/Initiating-Discussion-Paper-Eng.pdf.

[17] ibid 3.

[18] ibid 2, fn 4.

[19] For an example of how the 'no-objection' process worked in World Bank financed procurements before the reforms implemented in 2016, see eg World Bank, 'The World Bank Operations Manual: Bank Procedures – Procurement, BP 11.11' (January 2011, revised April 2013).

[20] See eg Williams-Elegbe (n 2) 58–64.

[21] See eg World Bank, 'Guidelines: Procurement of Goods, Works, and Non-Consulting Services under IBRD Loans and IDA Credits by World Bank Borrowers' (January 2011, revised July 2014) available at http://pubdocs.worldbank.org/en/492221459454433323/Procurement-GuidelinesEnglishJuly12014.pdf.

[22] See eg World Bank, 'Guidelines: Selection and Employment of Consultants under IBRD Loans and IDA Credits by World Bank Borrowers' (January 2011, revised July 2014) available at http://siteresources.worldbank.org/INTPROCUREMENT/Resources/Consultant_GLs_English_Final_Jan2011_Revised_July1_2014.pdf.

[23] See eg A Green, *International Government Contract Law* (Eagan MN, West, 2017) § 5:5 (available on Westlaw).

[24] See eg EW Debevoise and CR Yukins, 'Assessing the World Bank's Proposed Revision of Its Procurement Guidelines' (2010) 52(21) *The Government Contractor* 180.

[25] See 'Initiating Discussion Paper' (n 16) viii.

Bank's procurement approach ha[d] been a model of good international practice', as 'procurement has matured as a profession in an environment of globalization and rapid information exchange, the Bank's global procurement leadership ha[d] fallen behind good international practice and need[ed] to be modernized'.[26]

After several years of preparations[27] and meetings with thousands of shareholders,[28] including governments, representatives of the private sector, trade bodies, civil society organisations (CSOs) and non-governmental organisations (NGOs),[29] the World Bank's Board of Executive Directors approved the new Procurement Framework,[30] which became effective in July 2016.

IV. Central Principles of the New Procurement Framework

The reforms launched in 2011 ultimately went far beyond merely revising the World Bank's Procurement Guidelines. Framed as a new 'procurement framework' which took effect in July 2016,[31] the reforms marked, in many ways, entirely new approaches for the World Bank, and for the broader development community. While the World Bank's new procurement framework is implemented through a complex suite of documents available on the World Bank website, the key principles that underpin the new framework are set forth in a master policy statement titled 'Bank Policy: Procurement in IPF (Investment Project Financing) and Other Operational Procurement Matters'.[32]

The Bank's policy document explains the core principles and goals of the new procurement framework, and outlines some of the means used. The policy states:

> Procurement in IPF operations supports Borrowers to achieve value for money with integrity in delivering sustainable development. To achieve this vision, the Bank seeks assurance from Borrowers that acceptable procurement arrangements are applied to the financial resources it provides to Borrowers, and supports Borrower countries in enhancing and implementing sound procurement systems and institutions. The Bank may support country capacity building at the level of the project or as part of the country dialogue, using a range of measures – funding, technical support, and hands-on expanded implementation support (in selected cases) – depending on the specific context of the country, sector, agency, or project.[33]

[26] World Bank, 'Procurement in World Bank Investment Project Financing – Phase II: The New Procurement Framework' (n 6) 11.

[27] ibid 12 (describing preparatory steps over three-year process).

[28] See eg, Trepte 'All Change at the World Bank?' (n 15) 121.

[29] See World Bank, 'Procurement in World Bank Investment Project Financing – Phase II: The New Procurement Framework' (n 6) 1–2.

[30] World Bank, 'New World Bank Procurement Framework Approved' (Press Release, 21 July 2015) available at www.worldbank.org/en/news/press-release/2015/07/21/world-bank-procurement-framework.

[31] See eg Williams-Elegbe (n 2) 64–76; Swan and Harutyunyan, 'Multilateral Development Banks in an Era of Procurement Reform' (n 1).

[32] World Bank, 'Bank Policy: Procurement in IPF and Other Operational Procurement Matters' (Catalogue Number OPSVP5.05-POL.144, issued 7 November 2017) available at https://policies.worldbank.org/sites/ppf3/PPFDocuments/a3656cb78847417b886f11fa0235216e.pdf.

[33] ibid 2.

As this overview reflects, the core purpose of the procurement guidance – oversight through management requirements, to ensure the Bank's funds are well spent – remains unchanged from the earlier era of the Bank's 'red' and 'green' procurement guidelines. This core goal stems from the Bank's fiduciary obligation to its contributing shareholders, to safeguard the funds entrusted to the Bank for development. Beyond that core goal, however, this new framework looks to new tools, especially capacity-building, to bolster the Bank's oversight, direction and support for procurement in borrower nations.

To frame this new approach, the policy document sets forth key principles used in the Bank's procurement framework. Some of these are considered in the following paragraphs.

Although it is tucked away in the Bank's array of guiding principles, '*fit for purpose*' was arguably the most important guiding principle for Bank officials in reshaping the Bank's oversight of procurement. The Bank's policy document explains that 'fit for purpose' applies to both 'intended outcomes and … procurement arrangements', and it means 'determining the most appropriate approach to meet the project development objectives and outcomes, taking into account the context and the risk, value, and complexity of the procurement'. By refocusing oversight on the projects and problems that pose the greatest risk,[34] and by allowing borrowers to use a broader array of procurement tools to accomplish purchasing goals, the principle of 'fit for purpose' has played a powerful role in the Bank's new procurement framework.

The Bank's policy emphasises '*value for money*' – the principle that demands the 'effective, efficient, and economic use of resources', with an 'evaluation of relevant costs and benefits, along with an assessment of risks', and 'non-price attributes and/or life cycle costs'. In a procurement framework that stresses value for money, the policy notes that '[p]rice alone may not necessarily represent value for money'.[35]

The policy introduces the principle of '*economy*', a term which might normally be associated with efficiency or even parsimony, but which the Bank's policy applies to a much more diverse array of concepts, such as sustainability, quality and non-price attributes and/or life-cycle costs. To make sense of this principle, perhaps it is better to see it as a euphemism for change – as a signal that the Bank is willing to embrace a range of ideas that were irreconcilable, traditionally, with rigid competitions based on lowest price alone. This new principle of 'economy', it should be stressed, goes beyond mere flexibility in procurement method – it specifically allows borrowers to integrate 'sustainability criteria' (which, depending on the national context, could span from 'green' procurement to local economic development goals) in 'support of the Borrower's own sustainable procurement policy', a new approach that could, in effect, allow borrowers to close off competition from abroad, and use purchasing to advance social and political goals closer to home.

The policy's approach to '*integrity*' reflects both the promise and the limitations of the Bank's role, and also builds on the Bank's increasing concerns about corruption.[36]

[34] See eg World Bank, 'Procurement in World Bank Investment Project Financing – Phase II: The New Procurement Framework' (n 6) 7 (focus on high-risk projects).

[35] ibid 3.

[36] See Williams-Elegbe, 'The Changes to the World Bank's Procurement Policy' (n 13) 25–26.

Probably inevitably given the diversity of its stakeholder community, the Bank's approach is more instrumental than normative: its policy does not approach integrity as an end in itself, but rather as a means to ensure the 'use of funds, resources, assets, and authority according to the intended purposes and in a manner that is well informed, aligned with the public interest, and aligned with broader principles of good governance'. The Bank's approach thus deals with corruption more as an agency problem[37] – a problem of diverting public resources for personal ends – than as a symptom of social collapse. As a practical matter, this leaves the Bank standing somewhat apart from the social and political forces gathering against corruption around the world. At the same time, though, this approach allows the Bank to focus on improving the effectiveness of the procurement functions the Bank is nurturing in the developing world, by treating 'integrity' more clinically as a means of reducing performance risk and reputational risk in procurement, and as a means of reducing fiduciary risk in development.

The Bank's approach to '*transparency*' in its policy document reflects the Bank's sometimes awkward role as a multilateral development institution caught between politics and practical necessity. Outside the Bank, the 'open government' movement treats transparency as an absolute, on the assumption that unflinching openness will transform governance to make it much more responsive to citizens' needs and views.[38] While the Bank voices support for open government,[39] its policy treats transparency in a more traditional, instrumental way, as a means of ensuring open communications among an existing network of contractors, officials and stakeholders. The policy calls for transparency to allow an 'appropriate review of … procurement activities, supported by appropriate documentation and disclosure'. Transparency, the Bank's policy says, requires that 'relevant procurement information be made publicly available to all interested parties, consistently and in a timely manner, through readily accessible and widely available sources at reasonable or no cost' (ie, online), that there be 'appropriate reporting of procurement activities' (to ensure accountability and effective oversight), and that confidentiality provisions in contracts be used only where justified (to ensure that private imperatives do not overwhelm public goals of transparency). The Bank's policy thus reflects the traditional push-and-tug over transparency between established stakeholders in the procurement community, and leaves for another day the emerging question of whether all public functions, including procurement, should be fully transparent.

The Bank's policy's approach to '*fairness*' is perhaps the most telling. For the Bank, 'fairness' is not an agonised normative matter; it is, instead, a rolling effort to manage competing demands among the Bank's many stakeholders. To reconcile those demanding voices, the Bank stresses the need for open competitive procurement – the traditional answer for 'fair' procurement – and defines fairness largely in terms of

[37] See eg CR Yukins, 'A Versatile Prism: Assessing Procurement Law Through the Principal-Agent Model' (2010) 40 *Public Contract Law Journal* 63 (applying agency theory to procurement).

[38] See eg Open Government Partnership, 'Open Government Declaration' (September 2011) (discussing principles of open government) available at www.opengovpartnership.org/open-government-declaration.

[39] World Bank, 'Open Government' (Brief, 18 June 2015) (Bank's adherence to principles of open government) available at www.worldbank.org/en/topic/governance/brief/open-government-global-solutions-group.

process, not norms. 'Fairness', for the Bank, refers to affording bidders equal opportunity and treatment, and distributing rights and obligations fairly between borrowers and suppliers, bidders, consultants and contractors. Finally, fairness means 'credible mechanisms for addressing procurement-related complaints and providing recourse' (a topic we will return to below, in our discussion of the Bank's procurement complaints mechanism).

The Bank's policy document also touches on more practical concerns in implementing the new procurement framework. The policy discusses '*Alternative Procurement Arrangements*', under which the Bank may agree to rely upon the procurement rules of another multilateral agency or organisation, may agree to allow that other organisation to take the lead in implementing and monitoring a project's procurement, or may even rely directly on the procurement rules of a borrower nation's responsible agency. These 'Alternative Procurement Arrangements' are discussed further below, in section V.

Finally, and importantly, the policy confronts *conflicts of interest* – which were, ironically, the concerns which launched some of the Bank's earliest procurement reforms in the decades after World War II.[40] The Bank's policy extends explicitly now to both personal conflicts of interest and what are commonly known as 'organisational' conflicts of interest (a conflict of interest a firm may have, for example, in drafting specifications against which that same firm may later bid).[41] Importantly, the Bank's policy says that 'all parties involved in the Procurement Process [shall] not have a conflict of interest, *unless such a conflict has been resolved in a manner acceptable to the Bank*' (emphasis added).[42] This last point is important, because it makes the Bank the ultimate arbiter on issues of conflicts of interest – a sound approach if the goal is to contain reputational and operational risk from conflicts of interest, but with serious potential issues, practically and structurally. Read strictly, this policy means that any issue of conflict of interest would need to be vetted by the Bank, which is a practical impossibility given the vast reach (and overwhelming complexity) of the Bank's work. From a policy perspective, this policy (again, if read strictly) would place the Bank in the role of what is known as a 'third-party' monitor – a trusted observer that oversees a threatening situation which may yield conflicts of interest and deviant behaviour.[43] When a third-party monitor fails, that failure can be catastrophic precisely because of others' reliance; making a commitment to review all conflicts of interest thus may be too taxing for the Bank, and may in practice leave its stakeholders with a false sense of security and oversight. We will return to this topic again below, in section V.

[40] See 'Initiating Discussions Paper' (n 16) 2.

[41] See eg United Nations Commission on International Trade Law, 'UNCITRAL Model Law on Public Procurement' (2011) art 21, available at www.uncitral.org/pdf/english/texts/procurem/ml-procurement-2011/2011-Model-Law-on-Public-Procurement-e.pdf; US Federal Acquisition Regulation, Subpart 9.5, 48 Code of Federal Regulations Subpart 9.5; Debevoise and Yukins, 'Assessing the World Bank's Proposed Revision of Its Procurement Guidelines' (n 24) citing DI Gordon, 'Organizational Conflicts of Interest: A Growing Integrity Challenge' (2005) 35 *Public Contract Law Journal* 25); P Braun and C Birespek, 'Conflicts of Interest in Public Award Procedures: Deloitte Business Advisory NV v. Commission of the European Communities' (2008) *Public Procurement Law Review* NA53 (European case law and rules regarding firms' conflicts of interest).

[42] World Bank, 'Bank Policy: Procurement in IPF and Other Operational Procurement Matters' (n 32) 4.

[43] See Yukins, 'A Versatile Prism' (n 37) 65 and fn 34.

V. Key Elements of the World Bank's Procurement Framework

As noted, although touted as an attempt to simplify procurement oversight at the World Bank, the Procurement Framework was in fact presented as a highly complex suite of inter-related policies and requirements. Key policies were reviewed above; here, we will address important regulations and guidance in the Procurement Framework, focusing on those – specifically, the new 'Procurement Regulations' – that appear to relate most directly to aid effectiveness goals per the Paris Declaration and the Accra Agenda for Action.

The document at the heart of the new Procurement Framework is the 'Procurement Regulations', which set basic requirements for procurement done by borrowers. As before, the new 'Procurement Regulations' keep the Bank at arm's length from the borrower's procurement contract itself: they explain that the Legal Agreement which frames the borrower's obligation to the Bank stands apart – as the Bank stands apart – from the borrower's procurement contract with a vendor.[44] At the same time, the 'Procurement Regulations' make clear the Bank's unshakeable oversight over the borrower's contracting: the 'Regulations' closely guide the borrower's procurement when the borrower uses Bank financing, and the 'Regulations' explicitly state that even if a borrower's contractor with a vendor is *not* financed by the Bank but is part of a Bank-financed project, the borrower may adopt other procurement rules and procedures *only* if 'if the Bank is satisfied that … the rules and procedures will fulfill the Borrower's obligations to carry out the project diligently and efficiently'.[45]

The 'Procurement Regulations' provide crucial guidance on a number of initiatives which relate directly to aid effectiveness, including Alternative Procurement Arrangements (which would, in principle, allow borrowers to use their own procurement rules), complaints (the Bank's form of bid challenges, and an opportunity for the Bank to exercise oversight over troubled procurements), anti-corruption measures and procurement methods.

A. Alternative Procurement Arrangements (APAs)

One of the most conspicuous reforms in the new Procurement Framework was the Bank's endorsement of Alternative Procurement Arrangements (APAs), by which the Bank will allow borrowers to use their own procurement rules if they meet certain criteria. The Bank's embrace of APAs follows an extended period of trial and failure, during which the Bank launched a pilot programme to assess borrowers' use of their own national procurement systems for major Bank-financed projects. (Smaller procurements can be done using National Competitive Bidding [NCB], under the borrower's

[44] World Bank, 'Procurement Regulations for IPF Borrowers' (2016, revised 2017 and 2018) (n 14). Also referred to as 'Regulations'.

[45] ibid para 2.3.

existing rules.) The 'Use of Country Systems' (UCS) initiative largely failed,[46] probably in part because the Bank expected borrowers, in order to be eligible, to use procurement systems that mirrored the Bank's own procurement guidelines.[47]

The apparent failure of the 'Use of Country Systems' initiative did not, however, end the concept, because allowing borrowers to use their own systems was a core element of internationally recognised aid effectiveness goals (discussed in section II, above). The Bank's Procurement Framework called for the use of APAs to allow borrowers (or their agencies) to use APAs, subject though to strict assessment requirements. Specifically, the Bank's 'Procurement Regulations' provide that the Bank may allow borrowers to use their own procurement rules for specific agencies or procuring entities, subject to the Bank's requirements.[48]

The Bank has developed draft assessment standards, based upon the Organisation for Economic Co-operation and Development (OECD) Methodology for Assessment Procurement Systems (MAPS), adjusted to include an additional element which assesses procurement operations. The proposed approach also would use data from past procurements, and input from the private sector and CSOs, to assess whether the nominee agency (or country) is an appropriate candidate for an APA.[49] More on the assessment methodology is presented in chapters 9 and 10 of this book.

B. Anti-Corruption Measures

The 'Procurement Regulations' under the Bank's new framework reflect a mix of old and new anti-corruption strategies. The Bank's anti-corruption measures have, over time, gathered strength as the Bank has come to see corruption as a major obstacle to development.[50] And as the Bank allows its borrowers to use more sophisticated and riskier methods of procurement, such as competitive dialogue (discussed below), the anti-corruption systems deployed by the Bank's borrowers will become more important.

The Bank's 'Procurement Regulations' embrace an emerging strategy to check corruption: monitoring by independent third parties. Under the new 'Regulations', when procurement strategies (such as competitive dialogues) present additional risk,[51]

[46] See eg CL Pallas and J Wood, 'The World Bank's Use of Country Systems for Procurement: A Good Idea Gone Bad?' (2009) 27 *Development Policy Review* 215 (discussing the Bank's earlier efforts to allow borrowers to use their country systems for procurement, as part of broader initiatives to improve aid effectiveness).

[47] See Trepte (n 15) 128–31 (discussing the history of the World Bank's 'Use of Country Systems' initiative in detail); Williams-Elegbe (n 2) 251–56 ('Use of Country Systems' initiative).

[48] 'Procurement Regulations' (n 14) para 2.4 ('At the Borrower's request, the Bank (subject to its policies and rules, and applicable fiduciary and operational requirements), may agree to … rely on and apply the procurement rules and procedures of an agency or entity of the Borrower').

[49] See World Bank, 'Draft Guide to the APA Assessment: Methodology to assess Alternative Procurement Arrangements in Borrower Implementing Agencies for Procurements financed under IPF' (World Bank, July 2016) available at http://pubdocs.worldbank.org/en/634391468437110489/Alternative-Procurement-Arrangements-Guide-to-the-Assessor.pdf.

[50] See Williams-Elegbe (n 2) 178–87 (history of World Bank's efforts against corruption in procurement).

[51] When preparing a Project Procurement Strategy for Development (PPSD) (the precursor to a formal procurement plan), available at http://pubdocs.worldbank.org/en/847531467334322069/PPSD-Long-Form.pdf, borrowers are expected to assess whether 'any proposed additional oversight (e.g. probity assurance)' is

borrowers may retain a 'Probity Assurance Provider', an 'independent third party that provides specialist probity services for concurrent monitoring of the Procurement Process'.[52] These monitors may be private firms or may come from CSOs.[53]

The Probity Assurance Providers may work closely with Bank staff who provide 'Hands-On Expanded Implementation Support' (HEIS) when borrowers have urgent capacity constraints.[54] The HEIS assistance is itself arguably an anti-corruption device, for it allows Bank officials to be involved directly in drafting procurement documents, assessing proposals, observing dialogues and negotiations, and drafting evaluations and award documentation – thus providing both capacity support and monitoring with experienced Bank staff. Although Bank officials providing HEIS assistance are not to usurp the key decision-making to be done by borrowers, such as the procurement award decision, the HEIS assistance can assist borrowers 'to deliver effective procurement processes beyond the normal implementation support' the Bank would provide.[55]

Otherwise, the Bank's anti-corruption measures were generally strengthened but not radically changed by the 2016 reforms.[56] Fraud and corruption concerns were given special prominence in the new complaints procedures (see below), so that those will gain special attention from the Bank and the borrower as they arise.[57] The conflict of interest provisions in the new 'Procurement Regulations',[58] for example, generally track those of the prior 'Procurement Guidelines'.[59] As it was noted above in the discussion of the Bank's guiding principles, the Bank's approach to integrity remains instrumental, still largely removed from more normative questions such as public censure.[60] Furthermore, the anti-corruption sanctions that the Bank undertakes are focused on specific (and past) acts of contractor misconduct,[61] and not more broadly on ensuring that performance and reputational risks are reduced in Bank projects on an on-going basis.[62]

required, eg 'due to risk in the proposed procurement arrangements (such as use of negotiations, competitive dialogue)' – World Bank, 'Project Procurement Strategy for Development: Short Form Detailed Guide' (World Bank, July 2016) 43, available at https://wbnpf.procurementinet.org/sites/all/themes/npf/misc/documents/PPSD-Short-Form-Final-June-30.pdf; see also Williams-Elegbe (n 2) 83–84 (describing PPSD).

[52] See 'Procurement Regulations', Common abbreviations and defined terms (n 14).

[53] For an interview describing CSOs' efforts to monitor procurement in various projects around the world, see 'Interview with Christopher Yukins and Donal O'Leary, Sabine Engelhard and Lars Jeurling of the Partnership for Transparency Fund (PTF)' (2018), available at www.youtube.com/watch?v=-lNnM-AH67s.

[54] World Bank, 'Bank Guidance: Procurement Hands-on Expanded Implementation Support' (Catalogue Number OPS5.05-GUID.167, issued 3 August 2016) para III.A.7, available at https://policies.worldbank.org/sites/ppf3/PPFDocuments/3c801309d23748bd932e756bf58468ac.pdf.

[55] ibid s III.A.

[56] See Williams-Elegbe (n 2) 187–215 (detailed review of anti-corruption measures in Bank-financed procurement).

[57] See 'Procurement Regulations' (n 14) para 3.31.

[58] See ibid para 3.14.

[59] See World Bank, 'Guidelines: Procurement of Goods, Works, and Non-Consulting Services' (2011, revised 2014) (n 21) para 1.6 ff.

[60] See Williams-Elegbe (n 2) 215–16.

[61] See eg 'Procurement Regulations' (n 14) Annex IV para 2.2.

[62] See eg CR Yukins, 'Rethinking the World Bank's Sanctions System' (2013) 55(42) *The Government Contractor* 355; P Dubois, P Ezzeddin and C Swan, 'Suspension and Debarment on the International Stage: Experiences in the World Bank's Sanctions System' (2016) 25 *Public Procurement Law Review* 61; JS Schnitzer and CR Yukins, 'Combating Corruption in Procurement – Debarment Present and Future' in UNOPS, 'Future Proofing Procurement' (2016) 26 (discussing how different anti-corruption strategies address different classes

C. Focusing Oversight on Procurement Risk

A cornerstone to the Bank's new Procurement Framework – the logical extension of the 'fit for purpose' principle discussed above – is to focus the Bank's oversight and reviews[63] on high-risk and/or high-value procurements.[64] The process for triggering a review is complex:

> Procurement risk is assessed independently, based on factors such as perceived capacity in the borrower agency, market conditions and the procurement approach to be used.[65]

That perceived risk ('low' to 'high') is then assessed against a sliding dollar scale; high-risk projects, for example, will trigger a review at lower dollar value.[66]

Thus, the procurement risk is very much assessed *from the Bank's perspective* – the reviews focus on addressing the Bank's fiduciary obligations and the need to mitigate risk in the procurement itself, not on the performance risks that the project (or its beneficiaries) may face.

The Bank's 'Procurement Procedure' appears to confirm that focus, because it *mandates* reviews when certain procedures which the Bank considers inherently risky (such as competitive dialogue)[67] are used.[68] These risks are not necessarily linked to the borrower's performance risk; instead, these are risks tied to a potential failure of the *procurement itself*, ie a failure to purchase best value.

D. Procurement-Related Complaints

The Bank's new Procurement Framework included important reforms to the Bank's procedures for handling procurement-related complaints.[69] Under the reformed process, procurement-related complaints are to be submitted to the borrower in

of risk, reputational versus performance) available at www.bhrinlaw.org/documents/2015-asr-supplement.pdf. For a broader discussion of debarment systems used around the globe, see S Williams-Elegbe, *Fighting Corruption in Public Procurement: A Comparative Analysis of Disqualification or Debarment Measures* (Oxford, Hart Publishing, 2012).

[63] See eg Williams-Elegbe (n 2) 190–92.

[64] See eg 'Procurement Regulations' (n 14) para 3.5.

[65] World Bank, 'Project Procurement Strategy for Development – Long Form Detailed Guidance' (Washington DC, World Bank, July 2016) ss IV–V, available at http://pubdocs.worldbank.org/en/847531467334322069/PPSD-Long-Form.pdf.

[66] See eg World Bank, 'Bank Procedure: Procurement in IPF and Other Operational Procurement Matters' (Catalogue Number OPS5.05-PROC.138, issued 21 July 2018, effective 1 August 2018), Annex I, available at https://policies.worldbank.org/sites/ppf3/PPFDocuments/Forms/DispPage.aspx?docid=4004&ver=current; Williams-Elegbe (n 2) 191.

[67] World Bank, 'Project Procurement Strategy for Development – Long Form Detailed Guidance' (n 65) 17.

[68] World Bank, 'Bank Procedure: Procurement in IPF and Other Operational Procurement Matters' (n 66) 25–26; 'Procurement Regulations' (n 14) Annex II.3.

[69] See 'Procurement Regulations' (n 14), paras 3.26 to 3.31 and Annex III; World Bank, 'Procurement-related Complaints: How to complain', 2nd edn (Washington DC, World Bank, January 2017) available at http://pubdocs.worldbank.org/en/975671478891365829/Complaints-Guidance-FINAL-Revised.pdf (discussing complaints arising in connection with contracts where the Bank's Standard Procurement Documents [SPDs] apply); Williams-Elegbe (n 2) 284–91 (noting improvements from 2011 Procurement Guidelines to the complaints process under the 2016 Procurement Framework).

a timely manner, and the borrower is to track and address those complaints. The borrower is to resolve the complaints under the procedures set forth in Annex III to the 'Procurement Regulations' (for procurements covered by the Bank's Standard Procurement Documents), under national complaints procedures agreed upon by the Bank (for national competitive bidding [NCB]), or, for Alternative Procurement Arrangements (discussed above), under complaints procedures agreed upon by the Bank.[70] Where the procurement is subject to prior review, the Bank is required to examine the remedial action proposed by the borrower in a timely fashion.[71]

The World Bank's complaints procedure operates, in a very loose sense, like 'bid protest' or 'remedies' procedures in national systems: the complaints procedure allows bidders to complain to the government running the procurement of failures in contract formation, and (in some cases) the Bank will play a monitoring role. Complaints (bid challenges) are sometimes viewed as anti-corruption devices, but given the institutional constraints on any complaints body – they typically lack investigative authority or police powers, and have a specialised focus on procurement – these reviewing bodies are probably better viewed as guardians of the procurement process. Many nations now have bid challenge systems in place to supervise their own procurement systems,[72] and the Bank's complaints procedure builds on those institutions while providing, to a limited extent, another layer of review at the Bank.

In framing reforms to the complaints procedure, the Bank noted that many in the private sector had requested much stronger Bank involvement when complaints arose regarding Bank-financed procurements; the private sector argued that a more robust complaints process would build private confidence in Bank-financed procurement, which in turn would encourage stronger competition.[73] To address these concerns, the Bank agreed to dedicate senior staff to advise on and expedite procurement-related complaints.[74] Under the new Procurement Regulations, all complaints regarding an International Project Finance (IPF) operation must be reported to the Bank (including for national procurements and procurements done using 'Alternative Procurement Arrangements'). Debriefings to bidders regarding the bases for award are required, and standstill periods (to allow for a debriefing and, if necessary, a complaint) are now required under the Bank's standard selection documents. Complaints regarding contract awards are monitored by the Bank, and, for post-award disputes regarding contract performance, the Bank will facilitate dispute resolution.

The new complaints process still appears to be a work in progress, and the normal remedies afforded by a bid challenge system generally are not available in the

[70] 'Procurement Regulations' (n 14), paras 3.26 to 3.30; World Bank, 'New Procurement Framework: Procurement-related Complaints' (Private Sector Webinar) Slide 12, available at http://pubdocs.worldbank.org/en/690521503326539557/Webinar-Handling-Procurement-Related-Complaints.pdf.

[71] 'Procurement Regulations' (n 14) Annex III, para 3.9.

[72] Complaints systems are required, eg, by art 9 of the United Nations Convention against Corruption, available at www.unodc.org/documents/treaties/UNCAC/Publications/Convention/08-50026_E.pdf, and by art XVIII of the WTO's revised Government Procurement Agreement, available at www.wto.org/english/docs_e/legal_e/rev-gpr-94_01_e.htm. See generally DI Gordon, 'Constructing a Bid Protest Process: Choices Every Procurement Challenge System Must Make' (2006) 35 *Public Contract Law Journal* 427.

[73] See World Bank, 'Procurement in World Bank Investment Project Financing – Phase II: The New Procurement Framework' (n 6) 5–6.

[74] ibid 6.

Bank's own process.[75] While the Procurement Framework puts the basic elements of a bid challenge system in place (eg borrowers' debriefings are called for, interested parties are clearly defined, a standstill period is required, 'business standard' deadlines are set, and there is an established process), the new framework, out of the Bank's normal institutional deference, will leave the review largely to the borrower nation.[76] There is no regular or transparent means of tracking complaints brought to the Bank, and there are no published decisions from the Bank to shed light on how the law is developing, or how recurring issues will be addressed. To the extent the complaints process remains immature and incomplete, sophisticated bidders frustrated with a Bank procurement may turn first to the traditional alternative – private requests for intercession by the Bank.

The gaps in the Bank's complaints process may be felt most keenly on those projects that now will fall outside the Bank's close review, as the Bank focuses its oversight and resources on its highest-risk, highest-value projects (see above). The projects newly pushed to the periphery probably will still be just as important to the agencies involved, and just as strategically vital to the vendors competing for that work; the agencies and vendors, however, will no longer have the same benefit of Bank oversight. This makes it more likely that there will be a sort of centrifugal movement, away from the Bank's central control, as vendors and other stakeholders seek out solutions for the problems that inevitably emerge.

One obvious place to go will be the bid challenge forums in the borrowing nations. The Bank's Procurement Framework almost predicts that – it leaves the complaints process in the hands of the borrower nations. But the Bank's Procurement Framework has no special place for building capacity in the bid challenge institutions emerging around the world, and the Bank's own still incomplete complaints procedures say much about the Bank's own apparent ambivalence about bid challenges.

If vendors confronting corruption on Bank-financed projects cannot resolve problems in the bid remedies systems of the borrowing nations, they may seek help from the rapidly growing network of anti-corruption agencies called for by various international anti-corruption instruments,[77] and bolstered by new anti-corruption laws, such as those in the United Kingdom[78] and France.[79]

If vendors encounter more prosaic problems – if they face not corruption, but simple bureaucratic collapse – and they cannot rely on bid remedies systems of borrower nations, vendors may possibly turn to relief under bilateral investment treaties. Under certain circumstances, those treaties allow for investor-state disputes (which may be administered, ironically, through one of the World Bank's own institutions,

[75] See eg Williams-Elegbe (n 2) 291 ('it is a misnomer to talk of remedies in the traditional sense in the context of bidders on a Bank-funded procurement').

[76] See eg Trepte (n 15) 149.

[77] See generally S Wickberg, Transparency International, 'Best Practices for Anti-Corruption Commissions' (Transparency International, 2013) available at www.transparency.org/files/content/corruptionqas/Best_practices_for_anti-corruption_commissions_2.pdf.

[78] UK Bribery Act 2010, available at www.legislation.gov.uk/ukpga/2010/23/contents.

[79] Loi No 2016-1691 du 9 décembre 2016 relative à la transparence, à la lutte contre la corruption et à la modernisation de la vie économique (commonly known as the 'Sapin II' law) available at www.legifrance.gouv.fr/eli/loi/2016/12/9/2016-1691/jo/texte.

the International Centre for the Settlement of Investment Disputes [ICSID]), and those types of disputes may emerge as an alternative remedy for investors frustrated with World Bank-financed procurements that now fall outside the narrowed band of review by the Bank.[80]

While it is difficult to predict what pathway frustrated vendors may take, what is clear is that the Bank's narrowed oversight, including its highly deferential complaints process, may have collateral effects which cannot be resolved simply by building capacity in borrower nations. Problems emerge in even more mature procurement systems (there are thousands of bid challenges brought in North America and Europe every year, for example), and the Bank's new, narrower approach to oversight is likely to have spillover effects as contracting problems go unresolved in the normal course. The Bank's more focused approach to oversight allows the Bank to focus resources on its points of highest risk, and in effect leaves more authority to borrower nations to police other projects – an outcome that *seems* consonant with the Paris Declaration and the Accra Agenda for Action, but which in practice could have a negative impact on Bank-funded projects.

E. Sustainable Procurement

The Bank's Procurement Framework includes new provisions allowing for sustainable procurement strategies,[81] such as the special procedures outlined in Annex VII to the 'Procurement Regulations'. Sustainability, in the Bank's view, extends to economic, environmental and social factors, and the Bank 'encourages Borrowers to actively consider and apply sustainable procurement, where appropriate'.[82] Although the Bank's new framework allows borrowers to incorporate sustainability goals in procurement in an approach reminiscent of the European Union's,[83] the Bank still considers sustainability a procurement risk which will trigger a prior review.[84]

The Bank's cautious approach to sustainability reflects a narrow path the Bank must tread. There is broad support internationally for many of the goals of sustainability, such as addressing climate change and improving socio-economic conditions. At the same time, however, 'sustainability' remains only loosely defined,[85] and

[80] See eg Y Kryvoi, 'Bribery, Corruption, and Fraud in Investor-State Disputes: How Should Tribunals Approach Economic Crimes?' (Posting on Kluwer Arbitration Blog, 10 August 2018) available at http://arbitrationblog.kluwerarbitration.com/2018/08/10/bribery-investor-state.

[81] See eg World Bank, 'Sustainable Procurement: An introduction for practitioners to sustainable procurement in World Bank IPF Projects' (Washington DC, World Bank, November 2016) available at http://pubdocs.worldbank.org/en/788731479395390605/Sustainable-Procurement-Guidance-FINAL.pdf; Williams-Elegbe (n 2) 155–57; Trepte (n 15) 133–34.

[82] 'Procurement Regulations' (n 14), para 5.12 and Annex VII para 2.3.

[83] See Trepte (n 15) 133–34.

[84] See eg World Bank, 'Bank Procedure: Procurement in IPF and Other Operational Procurement Matters' ((n 66) 21 (World Bank Team Leader is to prepare 'a memorandum … seeking … approval to include Borrower's sustainability requirements (i.e., the application of social and economic criteria) in World Bank-financed procurement'); ibid Annex I para 2.2 ('irrespective of the contract value, the following procurement activities are subject to the Bank's procurement prior review … (c) sustainable procurement').

[85] See eg J Gutman, 'Publication Review – Public Procurement and Multilateral Development Banks: Law, Practice and Problems' (2018) 27 *Public Procurement Law Review* 96, 99.

sustainability goals can be used by procuring agencies for less lofty purposes, such as favouring advanced firms uniquely able to meet emerging sustainability goals.[86] The Bank's ambivalence is reflected in Annex VII to the Bank's 'Procurement Regulations', which allow sustainability goals but stress that 'sustainable procurement requirements should be based on evidence (i.e., with supporting data), and on existing social-label criteria, eco-label criteria, or information collected from stakeholders in industry, civil society, and international development agencies'.[87] By demanding a documented, rational basis for sustainability goals, one informed by best practices and standards, the Bank apparently hopes to limit the risks of discrimination and corruption that sustainability might otherwise present.

F. New Procurement Methods – Including Competitive Dialogue

While the Bank's Procurement Framework has endorsed a number of innovations in procurement methods, from a technical standpoint perhaps the most important is the Bank's embrace of competitive dialogue. Other methods were already gaining traction – framework agreements were allowed under the prior 'Procurement Guidelines' and electronic reverse auctions were already being addressed in practice by the Bank[88] – but the World Bank's decision to accept competitive dialogue as a procurement method was a marked change, as many Bank officials had long been quite hostile to competitive dialogue and the corruption risks it brings. Although the new 'Procurement Regulations' allow other new procurement methods as well,[89] our focus here is on competitive dialogue both because it sheds light on what shaped the World Bank's new Procurement Framework, and it helps predict the role the Bank's new framework will play in international development in the coming years.

The Bank's acceptance of competitive dialogue followed parallel developments around the world, such as the European Union's embrace of competitive dialogue (and competitive procedure with negotiation, its close cousin) in the European Procurement Directives,[90] the inclusion of a form of competitive dialogue in the 2011 rewrite

[86] See eg R Roos, Deutsche Gesellschaft für Internationale Zusammenarbeit (GIZ), 'Sustainable Public Procurement in LICs [Low-Income Countries] – Implications for Ongoing World Bank Procurement Review' (Bonn, Deutsche Gesellschaft für Internationale Zusammenarbeit (GIZ) GmbH, 2013) vii ('There is also the perceived risk of SPP [Sustainable Public Procurement] creating unfair competitive advantage for few (often large, international) firms able to comply with SPP standards') available at https://consultations.worldbank.org/Data/hub/files/meetings/Procurement_Policies/SPP_in_LICs.pdf.

[87] 'Procurement Regulations' (n 14), Annex VII para 2.4.

[88] See eg World Bank, 'e-Reverse Auction Guidelines for MDB Financed Procurement' (December 2005) available at https://openknowledge.worldbank.org/bitstream/handle/10986/19058/883170WP0eReve00Box385191B00PUBLIC0.pdf?sequence=1&isAllowed=y.

[89] See eg Trepte (n 15) 134–38; Williams-Elegbe (n 2) 131–42.

[90] EU Procurement Directive: Directive 2014/24/2014 of the European Parliament and of the Council of 26 February 2014 on public procurement and repealing Directive 2004/18/EC [2014] OJ L94/65, arts 29–30; see also Crown Commercial Service (CCS), 'The Public Contracts Regulations 2015 & The Utilities Contracts Regulations 2016, Guidance on changes to procedures (Competitive procedure with negotiation, competitive dialogue & innovation partnerships)' (October 2016) available at https://assets.publishing.service.gov.uk/government/uploads/system/uploads/attachment_data/file/560264/Guidance_on_Changes_to_Procedures_-_Oct_16.pdf; Office of Government Commerce (OGC), UK Government, 'Competitive

of the UN Commission on International Trade Law (UNCITRAL) model procurement law,[91] and the shift of much of US federal contracting to a more liberal form of competitive dialogue, called 'competitive negotiations', under the Federal Acquisition Regulation.[92]

All these methods call for competitive multilateral negotiations, in which the purchasing agency enters into a 'dialogue' with each offeror, either in writing or orally, through which each offeror can present a unique solution to the purchasing agency's stated requirements. This is a dramatic change from classic open tendering (called 'sealed bidding' in the United States federal system),[93] which proceeds from the assumption that the government customer can define its needs with precision and then award (generally speaking) based on low price.

The shift internationally from open tendering (traditionally, the default method) to competitive dialogue reflects, in many ways, passage over a technological divide. In a more primitive age, it made sense for a government to specify a uniform solution for its requirements, and then to award a contract for that uniform solution to the lowest bidder. Rapidly advancing technology has changed that calculation, however, and competitive dialogue allows procuring agencies to choose among technologically advanced solutions – solutions which may be idiosyncratic precisely because they are technologically advanced, and so do not lend themselves to low-price bidding against a defined set of requirements. Competitive dialogue also gives government customers a 'window' into emerging technologies, because vendors engaged in a competitive dialogue with a government customer will be more willing to disclose their advanced solutions in a closed environment of private exchanges. Finally, because competitive dialogue (unlike traditional tendering) allows the government to choose among a more diverse array of potential solutions, it is more likely that the chosen solution – the awardee – will better 'fit' the government's actual requirements.

In economic terms, competitive dialogue thus helps mitigate the principal-agent issues (discussed above) that normally burden public procurement. By allowing the public buyer to engage directly with many diverse solutions in the marketplace through multilateral negotiations, competitive dialogue can mute the distorting self-interest of the intermediary, the contracting official, who traditionally might default to a uniform, inflexible solution to allow an award to a low bidder. Competitive dialogue allows for a more nuanced balancing of price and quality, and allows buyers to access diverse emerging technologies, and thus may reduce performance risk for the buyer. (Conversely, the traditional strong preference for open tendering could retard development, by forcing public buyers back onto simpler, uniform solutions.)

Dialogue in 2008 – OGC/HMC joint guidance on using the procedure' (HM Treasury and OGC, 2008) available at http://webarchive.nationalarchives.gov.uk/20130102211752/http://www.hm-treasury.gov.uk/d/competitive_dialogue_procedure.pdf.

[91] UNCITRAL Model Law on Public Procurement (n 41) art 49 (request for proposals with dialogue).

[92] See FAR pt 15, 48 Code of Federal Regulations pt 15; CR Yukins, 'The U.S. Federal Procurement System: An Introduction' (2017) *Upphandlingsrättslig Tidskript* 69, 81–84, available at www.urt.cc/?q=node/187.

[93] See FAR pt 14, 48 Code of Federal Regulations pt 14. See generally J Cibinic Jr, RC Nash Jr and CR Yukins, *Formation of Government Contracts*, 4th edn (Riverwoods, IL, Wolters Kluwer Legal, 2011) ch 4.

At the same time, however, competitive dialogue almost certainly increases *reputational* risk, for both the buyer and the financier (here the World Bank), precisely because it *is* a dialogue. The exchanges between offerors and the government customer typically take place privately, and open an array of opportunities for corruption. World Bank policy-makers know that, and though many officials argued that they opposed competitive dialogue because it is too complex for young procurement systems, in fact that reputational risk may have been a major reason for the Bank's longstanding opposition to competitive dialogue.

The Bank's embrace of competitive dialogue thus tells us much. The fact that the Bank resisted competitive dialogue for so long gives us some insight into the Bank's keen sensitivity to reputational risk; that is natural, given the Bank's exposure to criticism (often from those hostile to its philanthropic mission) and the deeply corrosive effect that corruption (a risk with any competitive dialogue) can have on the Bank. At the same time, the fact that the Bank *did* eventually embrace competitive dialogue because the Bank realised it was falling out of step with emerging best practices, and the fact that the Bank's change of heart has helped persuade others to embrace competitive dialogue as well, confirmed the important role the Bank plays in defining and modelling best practices in procurement.

G. Capacity Development

The Bank's roles in defining best practices and driving reform in procurement go hand-in-hand with the Bank's commitment to building capacity. In procurement, building capacity means helping governments and societies do procurement better, to ensure that those governments can buy the best possible goods and services for the people they serve.[94] Capacity-building can mean training and counselling government personnel, and it can mean building understanding in the private sector as well, among contractors and their personnel, and in the institutions and professions that support the procurement system. Recognising all these aspects, the World Bank and other multilateral development institutions have long supported capacity-building efforts in the developing world, and strengthening capacity is a building block to effective aid.

In a series of declarations and commitments,[95] the international development community has recognised the importance of capacity-building to successful

[94] See eg United Nations Development Programme (UNDP), 'Public Procurement Capacity Development Guide' (New York, United Nations Development Programme, October 2010) available at www.undp.org/content/dam/aplaws/publication/en/publications/capacity-development/undp-procurement-capacity-assessment-users-guide/Procurement%20Capacity%20Assessment%20Guide.pdf; S Williams-Elegbe, 'Beyond UNCITRAL: The Challenges of Procurement Reform Implementation in Africa' (2014) 25 *Stellenbosch Law Review* 209, 210–15; Williams-Elegbe (n 2) 249–50; CR Yukins and R Macdonald, 'Capacity Building in Public Procurement: Burma/Myanmar – A Case Study' (2015) 44 *Public Contract Law Journal* 749.

[95] See eg OECD, 'Recommendation of the Council on Public Procurement' (2015) art IX, available at www.oecd.org/gov/public-procurement/recommendation/OECD-Recommendation-on-Public-Procurement.pdf.

procurement policy. One of the most comprehensive plans for building capacity was published by the OECD in 2015, in a model built around a 'steering committee' of stakeholders brought together to build capacity in procurement:

1. *Provide leadership: Creating the steering committee*

The first step is to create the steering committee, to include all relevant stakeholders to co-ordinate all activities as well as the strategy.

2. *Identify the issues: Assessing the public procurement workforce*

This diagnostic step is necessary to assess the current needs in terms of institution capacity, staff competency and the education system.

3. *Establish perspective: Identifying the goals*

The steering committee should identify and prioritise the goals in terms of people and institutions, professionalising the procurement function and jobs.

4. *Seek solutions: Finding the appropriate training solutions*

The strategy recommends different types of training in terms of duration, institutions and format, depending on the needs.

5. *Design the programme: Drafting the strategic action plan*

The strategic action plan should include scheduled objectives, actions, and timeframe, while identifying the beneficiaries of the actions.

6. *Include training: Drafting the training action plan*

The training action plan will depend on the needs, and should focus on training solutions for designated individuals and institutions.

7. *Remember resources: Financing the strategy*

The financing is a key step for the success of the implementation of the strategy. The steering committee should consider different options and models from internal and external donors.

8. *Monitor the results: Learning and adapting*

The last step is important to identify best practices or unsuccessful solutions with constant adaptation of the trainings.[96]

The OECD 'Roadmap' explained how building capacity would reinforce each key pillar in a sound public procurement system, including (i) simple and clear rules that ensure access to procurement opportunities; (ii) effective institutions to plan and manage public contracts; (iii) appropriate tools for electronic procurement; (iv) suitable, skilled human resources – procurement officials, in other words; and (v) competent contract management.[97] The 'Roadmap' reflects the 'top-down' approach

[96] OECD, 'Roadmap: How To Elaborate a Procurement Capacity Strategy' (OECD, 2016) 6, available at www.oecd.org/governance/ethics/Roadmap-Procurement-Capacity-Strategy.pdf. Janos Bertok, Head of the Public Sector Integrity Division, and Paulo Magina, Head of the Public Procurement Unit at the OECD, played important roles in preparing the OECD 'Roadmap', with Kenza Khachani, an OECD policy analyst.

[97] ibid 5.

to capacity-building generally favoured by large institutions engaged in procurement: a government-focused, centralised effort to identify and instil key training goals in procurement, typically built around an established system of rules.[98]

At least in principle this traditional approach to capacity-building in procurement, which works best from an established base of rules, put the World Bank in a quandary: having endorsed a broadening use of borrower nations' procurement systems, and having recognised the need to support capacity-building under the new procurement framework,[99] which set of rules would form the foundation of the Bank's capacity-building – the Bank's new procurement regulations or the borrower nations' own rules? The answer appears to be a 'fit for purpose' approach, which focuses first on a borrower nation's own capacity needs and not on training in the World Bank's procurement regime. The World Bank's 'Bank Directive – Procurement in IPF and Other Operational Procurement Matters' describes how support to borrowers for their procurement capacity-building will be structured, through direct support at the project level or as part of a country-wide initiative.[100] With regard to its own procurement framework, the World Bank has posted various learning resources on its website,[101] though not as part of a fixed curriculum, and the Bank has co-sponsored a 'MOOC' (a 'massive open online class') to provide low- or no-cost online training in the Bank's new procurement framework.[102]

What the Bank's new initiatives did not address, however, is probably the next historical phase in capacity-building, as the educational institutions in borrower nations mature and can provide procurement training in a private marketplace. In that 'bottom-up' environment, individuals make career decisions to advance in procurement, whether (for example) as contracting officials, vendor employees, investigators, lawyers, auditors or accountants. To advance their careers, those individuals will seek

[98] See eg UNDP, 'Public Procurement Capacity Development Guide' (n 94). The OECD 'Roadmap' notably cited the US Defense Acquisition University (DAU), probably one of the world's largest institutions dedicated to procurement training (n 96) 96. In federal fiscal year 2017, eg, DAU received approximately USD $138.3 million in funding to train the defence acquisition workforce – US Office of the Undersecretary of Defense (Comptroller), Chief Financial Officer, 'Operation and Maintenance Overview Fiscal Year 2019 Budget Estimates' (March 2018) 147, available at https://comptroller.defense.gov/Portals/45/Documents/defbudget/fy2019/fy2019_OM_Overview.pdf. The training at DAU is focused on ensuring that the thousands of members of the Defense Department's acquisition workforce are trained in the US government's complex web of policies, rules and procedures for acquisition – see eg DAU, '2016–2019 Strategic Plan – FY 16 Organizational Plan: Shaping the Future' (2016) available at www.dau.mil/about/PublishingImages/Special%20Interest%20Areas/StrategicPlan.pdf.

[99] See eg World Bank, 'Procurement In World Bank Investment Project Finance Phase I: A Proposed New Framework' (revised 18 October 2013) 25 ('strengthening client institutional capability is a central theme of the proposed new framework and capacity building efforts and procurement reforms would form part of the Bank's larger country engagement, the resources for which would be part of the country dialogue and priorities') available at http://siteresources.worldbank.org/PROCUREMENT/Resources/ProcurementProposedNewFrameworkOctober2013Final.pdf.

[100] World Bank, 'Bank Directive – Procurement in IPF and Other Operational Procurement Matters' (Catalogue Number OPS5.05-DIR.145, issued 9 November 2017) 6, available at https://policies.worldbank.org/sites/ppf3/PPFDocuments/95d59b3ec7a84a8782207aa0609dea0d.pdf.

[101] eg World Bank, 'e-Learning Platforms', available at https://wbnpf.procurementinet.org/e-learning-programs.

[102] World Bank et al, 'Certificate Program in Public Procurement (MOOC)' available at www.procurementlearning.org/certificate-program-public-procurement-cppp.

out education in a private educational marketplace (which may still include public institutions, such as universities) that responds to that demand. The private marketplace for capacity-building imposes far higher transaction costs (individuals must seek out, assess and purchase the training, and those offering training must market and sell continuously, in a rapidly evolving environment with generally loosely defined standards). But those offering training in that 'bottom-up' private marketplace can adapt much more readily to change, and the professionals who emerge from that 'bottom-up' capacity-building system are deeply invested in their training and committed to the procurement field – and that, in turn, may mean that those individuals are more likely to resist corruption and embrace reform.

VI. Possible Responses to the Bank's Shifting Role as a Monitor

By focusing the Bank's oversight on the points of greatest risk in the Bank's loan portfolio, the World Bank's procurement reforms are logical and efficient but open new areas of potential conflict.

The chief risk involves the Bank's oversight itself. By design, the Bank has positioned itself as a third-party monitor in its projects around the world; by approving important milestones in those projects through the 'no-objection' process, it serves as a monitor for its many stakeholders, including both its shareholders and its borrowers. The economic literature teaches us that a third-party monitor is uniquely trusted and other parties may rely too heavily, if anything, on the impartial monitor – a situation which can be highly disruptive if the third-party monitor fails in its role.[103] To avoid this type of chaotic collapse, it will be important for the Bank to be transparent, and to explain clearly the new boundaries of its monitoring role.

A good example of this problem is the Bank's new complaints process, for monitoring bid challenges in borrower countries. As the discussion above reflects, the Bank's involvement remains very much that of a third-party monitor, and unlike corruption (which may elicit a debarment from the Bank directly through the sanctions system), a failure of procurement process will be monitored, but not necessarily remedied, through the expanded complaints process at the Bank. This uncertainty regarding the Bank's oversight may engender friction with both vendors and borrowers, as each set of stakeholders jockeys for the Bank's intercession or acquiescence. While that dynamic may bolster Bank officials' tactical leverage in any given procurement, the uncertainty of the new structure also may, over the long term, erode the Bank's perceived authority as a monitor.

[103] Yukins (n 37) 70–71. For other perspectives on agency theory in public procurement, see A Chrisidu-Budnikagnieszka and J Przedańskajustyna, 'The Agency Theory Approach to the Public Procurement System' (2018) 7(1) *Wroclaw Review of Law, Administration & Economics* 154, available at https://doi.org/10.1515/wrlae-2015-0059; O Azfar, 'Disrupting Corruption', ch 8 in A Shah (ed), *Performance Accountability and Combating Corruption*, Public Sector and Accountability Series (Washington DC, The International Bank for Reconstruction and Development/The World Bank, 2007) 255, available at http://siteresources.worldbank.org/PSGLP/Resources/PerformanceAccountabilityandCombatingCorruption.pdf.

Resolving this problem – making clear the boundaries of the Bank's oversight – will be made more complicated by the Bank's likely shift over the coming decades to relying more heavily on borrower country procurement systems. The Bank's new framework, as noted, will take a highly variable approach to that shift to country systems, and it is likely that some borrowers' robust procurement systems will be approved long before others', and the approved systems will garner less oversight from the Bank. In practice, this may mean that the Bank's direct oversight will grow more uneven over the coming years, potentially varying from country to country or even from agency to agency within the same country. To ease this problem, it will be important for the Bank to be highly transparent regarding the scope, and practical reach, of its oversight of any given project.

VII. Conclusion: The World Bank's Procurement Framework and Aid Effectiveness

As the discussion above reflects, the World Bank's new Procurement Framework was, in the words of one highly respected expert, more 'evolutionary' than 'revolutionary'.[104] Reform had been a near-constant in World Bank procurement over many decades, and as one former World Bank procurement official noted, the Bank, 'to address its client countries concerns and to improve the overall effectiveness of its actions', had long 'attempted to develop a procurement policy beyond its narrow fiduciary responsibility'.[105] The question, then, is how the latest iteration of reform, the Bank's Procurement Framework, measures against international goals for aid effectiveness.

Even before the Paris Declaration and the Accra Agenda for Action, the Bank's procurement policies sought to 'establish modern and simplified procurement rules, to harmonise public procurement rules among donors and to build procurement capacity in Bank's client countries'.[106] Drawn against that history of reform, the Paris Declaration and the Accra Agenda for Action marked important inflection points in development policy internationally,[107] and they provide useful benchmarks to assess the Bank's most recent procurement reforms, in terms of aid effectiveness.

In keeping with the Paris Declaration and the Accra Agenda for Action, the World Bank's recent procurement reforms clearly set out to strengthen borrower nations' operational capacity in procurement. The Bank's capacity-building efforts, as noted, focus first on building capacity under borrowers' own systems, and not merely in the Bank's procurement regime. The Bank's reforms also respect borrowers' leadership in their own

[104] Trepte (n 15) 121.

[105] J-J Verdeaux, 'The World Bank and Public Procurement: Improving Aid Effectiveness and Addressing Corruption' (2006) 15 *Public Procurement Law Review* NA179.

[106] ibid.

[107] See eg L Chandy, 'It's Complicated: The Challenge of Implementing the Paris Declaration on Aid Effectiveness' (Brookings, 22 September 2011) available at www.brookings.edu/opinions/its-complicated-the-challenge-of-implementing-the-paris-declaration-on-aid-effectiveness.

development. Borrowers assess the risks inherent in their own projects, and even when Bank personnel are called in to provide direct support, that assistance will be structured to preserve borrowers' decisional autonomy. When problems arise in contract formation, the Bank generally will defer to the borrower nations' own complaints system.

That said, the Bank's procurement regime remains highly prescriptive. The Bank's oversight turns largely on the Bank's perceived risk – not necessarily on the project risks for the borrower or the affected citizens. The Bank has retained its right to prior review where borrowers use what the Bank views as inherently risky methods or criteria, such as competitive dialogue or sustainability, and those risks are clearly viewed from the Bank's perspective as a fiduciary for its shareholders.

With regard to the use of country systems – a key pillar of the aid effectiveness agenda – the Bank's Procurement Framework remains a promise unfulfilled. 'Alternative Procurement Arrangements', the current name for the use of country systems, have still not been formalised. Jeff Gutman, a senior fellow at the Brookings Institution and former official at the Bank, remains pessimistic about the initiative's prospects:

> From the first High Level Forum on Aid Effectiveness and the Rome Declaration (2003), to the Paris Declaration of the second Forum (2005), then the Accra Agenda for Action (2008) and the Busan Accord (2011), generally the OECD donors and the MDBs committed to a range of principles and initiatives. While the intensely negotiated communiques did have a significant impact on the harmonisation of policies and procedures, including for procurement, the parallel focus on the use of country systems was vague, more of a politically correct right-minded statement. As a participant in the Accra negotiations, it was clear to the current reviewer that the high-level donor officials did not have any specific target or understanding about what country systems implied whether for public financial management, environmental and social safeguards or procurement. This became evident during the various attempts at the World Bank to pursue country systems for procurement.[108]

What *seems* to be slowing Alternative Procurement Arrangements is a lingering concern with corruption. Where corruption exists, the Paris Declaration noted, 'it inhibits donors from relying on partner country systems'.[109]

There may, though, be a deeper problem – an uneasy sense that allowing borrowers to use their own country systems may have a centrifugal, diffusing effect on a vigorously centralised World Bank procurement system. The same strong concerns arose in the US procurement system when the Federal Aviation Administration was allowed to write its own regulations to supersede the Federal Acquisition Regulation (FAR),[110] which had been unified since 1984, and more recently as 'Other Transaction Authority' (a sort of blanket waiver from the FAR) gained broader acceptance among federal agencies.[111]

[108] See Gutman, 'Publication Review – Public Procurement and Multilateral Development Banks: Law, Practice and Problems' (n 85) 97.

[109] The Paris Declaration on Aid Effectiveness and the Accra Agenda for Action (2005 and 2008), para I (4v), available at https://www.oecd.org/dac/effectiveness/34428351.pdf.

[110] See eg R Allen and CR Yukins, 'Bid Protests and Contract Disputes Under the FAA's New Procurement System' (1997) 26 *Public Contract Law Journal* 135.

[111] See eg S Maucione, 'OTA Contracts Are the New Cool Thing in DoD Acquisition' (Federal News Radio, 19 October 2017, available at https://federalnewsradio.com/acquisition/2017/10/ota-contracts-are-the-new-cool-thing-in-dod-acquisition.

In the US system, as in the Bank, there is an abiding concern that fracturing a uniform regulatory regime will weaken the overall system.

The World Bank's new Procurement Framework is, in sum, a step on the road to reform, and not an end point. The Framework earns mixed grades when assessed against the traditional measures of aid effectiveness, but it does reflect important reforms in how the Bank oversees and directs procurement in Bank-financed projects, and in how the Bank accommodates and nurtures procurement systems in the developing world.

13

Harmonisation and Reforms at Other Multilateral Development Banks

PETER TREPTE

I. Introduction

The harmonisation of the procurement rules of the multilateral development banks (MDBs) has been mentioned in several chapters of this book, notably chapters 3, 4, 5 and 12, and is, of course, one of the key principles of the Paris Declaration discussed in chapter 3; a holy grail as Folliot-Lalliot puts it.[1] This chapter is provided more in the way of a supplemental note on the MDB harmonisation process and on its effects on the procurement reforms taken by a number (but not all) of the other MDBs subsequent to the reforms undertaken by the World Bank[2] and discussed in the previous chapter 12.

'Where the World Bank leads, the other MDBs will follow' has been something of (a rather unfair) refrain for some time,[3] although it may have some truth in the sense that, as a matter of practice, the resources of the World Bank ensured that it was in a better position to carry out more policy research and garner more manpower thus providing the groundwork that could be shared by all. Certainly, there is a little to be gained from 'reinventing the wheel' so that, given their later births,[4] the original Procurement Guidelines of the regional MDBs were largely taken from those of the existing World Bank. The process continues and even the rather new Asian Infrastructure and Investment Bank (AIIB), based in China, also appears to have, in large part, followed the lead of the World Bank (in this case of its new procurement framework whose creation coincided with the establishment of the AIIB), although this may also be due to its intention/need to enter into co-financing operations with other MDBs[5] which would make application of the same or similar procurement rules much

[1] Ch 3, s II.

[2] Formally, the International Bank for Reconstruction and Development (IBRD) and its satellites, such as the International Development Association (IDA).

[3] Ch 12, s I.

[4] eg IBRD (1945), IADB (1959), AfDB (1964), ADB (1966), EBRD (1991), AIIB (2016).

[5] J Górski, 'Regulation of Government Procurement by the AIIB: Convergence with other Multilateral Development Banks and The Impact on the Liberalization of Procurement Markets and Sustainability of Government Contracts' (2017) 44 *Syracuse Journal of International Law and Commerce* 251–328, 269.

more sensible. Over the years and based on their own experiences in their different regions and, in the case of the European Bank for Reconstruction and Development (EBRD), of providing both Sovereign and non-Sovereign loans, those procurement rules began to take on their own characteristics and were thus not identical. Nevertheless and independently of the harmonisation imperatives of the aid effectiveness agenda discussed in chapter 3, the MDBs had begun working on (re-) harmonising their rules and documents. Whilst this process may have been overtaken by events (notably by the Paris Declaration and its subsequent iterations), it was a process that was already well underway.

II. The MDB Harmonisation Process

In terms of the harmonisation of MDB procurement policies and procedures, efforts have been on-going since at least 1998–99 through a forum for procurement harmonisation established at the level of the Heads of Procurement (HOPs) of the MDBs,[6] aiming to provide a coherent mechanism for procurement cooperation between MDBs, international financial institutions and key development partners. The key actors in this process have been the Asian Development Bank (ADB), African Development Bank (AfDB), Black Sea Trade and Development Bank (BSTDB), Caribbean Development Bank (CDB), Council of Europe Development Bank (CEB), European Bank for Reconstruction and Development (EBRD), European Investment Bank (EIB), Inter-American Development Bank (IADB), International Bank for Reconstruction and Development (IBRD) and the Islamic Development Bank (IsDB).

Meetings of the HOP forum have taken place every six to nine months since its establishment and, acting through various working groups designated to work on different topics (eg procurement guidelines and standard bidding documents), took some significant steps towards harmonisation, in particular achieving substantial harmonisation of the MDBs' procurement guidelines, in principle at least, and the standardisation of bidding documents for the procurement of goods, works, small works, plant design supply and installation, and consultant's request for proposals. These meetings also provided an opportunity for dialogue and cooperation on a wide range of other issues relating to the application of good procurement procedures and practice and led to common positions on a number of matters including electronic government procurement (eGP),[7] fraud and corruption,[8] debarment and, in particular cross-debarment,[9]

[6] See Comprehensive Review of the AFDB's Procurement Policies and Procedures: Summary of Literature on Harmonization in Public Procurement (AFDB 2014), 2, available at www.afdb.org/fileadmin/uploads/afdb/Documents/Procurement/Project-related-Procurement/Summary_of_Literature_on_Harmonization_in_Public_Procurement.pdf; S Williams-Elegbe, *Public Procurement and Multilateral Development Banks: Law, Practice and Problems* (Oxford, Hart Publishing, 2017) 227.

[7] E-Tendering Requirements for MDB Financed Procurement: http://siteresources.worldbank.org/INTPROCUREMENT/Resources/E-Tendering_Requirements_for_MDB_Loans-Grants_and_Credits_November_2009.pdf.

[8] International Financial Institutions Anti-Corruption Task Force: https://www.afdb.org/fileadmin/uploads/afdb/Documents/Generic-Documents/Uniform_Framework_for_Combatting_Fraud_and_Corruption.pdf.

[9] Agreement for Mutual Enforcement of Debarment Decisions: http://lnadbg4.adb.org/oai001p.nsf/0/F77A326B818A19C548257853000C2B10/$FILE/cross-debarment-agreement.pdf.

Public-Private Partnerships (PPPs),[10] local procurement[11] and private sector transactions[12] and allowed for exploration of approaches to such things as the position of countries in fragile and conflict situations and on procurement reform in member countries where the MDBs would often carry out joint diagnostic assessments especially in the case of jointly financed projects.

In the case of the procurement rules of the MDBs, the HOP process of harmonisation of policy guidelines led to a gradual alignment and convergence between the policies, with the World Bank versions serving as the standard[13] although, to be fair, it has to be said that the working group process entailed considerable debate over the concerns raised by the participants. Where agreement could not be reached on specific issues or clauses, each of the MDBs would take their own approach. This often happened in the case of provisions such as the use of language and currencies. One notable example in terms of procurement methods was the use of two envelope single stage procedures which were permitted by, for example, the ADB but not, at the time, by the World Bank (although that has now changed in the World Bank's new framework). In this way, the pre-2016 Procurement Guidelines[14] of, at least the World Bank,[15] ADB,[16] AFDB[17] and IADB[18] were almost identical, subject to some minor inconsistencies on specific issues of concern in the different regions. Even the rules of the EBRD,[19] despite the slightly different operational context which includes loans to the non-Sovereign sector, were very similar in content.

Much harmonisation work was also carried out on the standard bidding documents which accompanied the procedures and policies of the various MDBs. This resulted in a set of 'Harmonised Master Procurement Documents' to reflect what were considered 'best practices' and intended to be used as a basis by the MDBs for issuing a standard procurement document for each individual institution.[20] Based on an initial

[10] Procurement Guidance for MDB Public Sector PPP engagements: http://siteresources.worldbank.org/INTPROCUREMENT/Resources/MDB_ProcurementPrinciplesApplicableToPublicSectorTransactions.pdf.

[11] Requirements for Local Procurement in Borrowing Countries (August 2003): http://siteresources.worldbank.org/PROCUREMENT/Resources/localproc.pdf.

[12] MDB Procurement Principles applicable to Private Sector Transactions (October 2012): www.bstdb.org/MDB_ProcurementPrinciplesApplicableToPrivateSectorTransactions.pdf.

[13] AFDB, 'Comprehensive Review' (n 4) 5.

[14] The Guidelines references relate to goods, works and non-consulting services. A similar process was undertaken in the case of consulting services, notably the bidding documents, but these Guidelines, in any event, demonstrate a much higher level of congruity.

[15] Guidelines for the Procurement of Goods, Works, and Non-Consulting Services (January 2011, revised July 2014): http://pubdocs.worldbank.org/en/492221459454433323/Procurement-Guidelines EnglishJuly12014.pdf.

[16] Rules and Procedures for Procurement of Goods and Works (2008, revised July 2012): www.afdb.org/fileadmin/uploads/afdb/Documents/Procurement/Project-related-Procurement/Rules%20and%20Procedures%20for%20Procurement%20of%20Goods%20and%20Works%20%28May%202008%20Edition%20Revised%20July%202012%29.pdf.

[17] Procurement Guidelines (April 2015): www.adb.org/sites/default/files/procurement-guidelines-april-2015.pdf.

[18] Policies for the Procurement of Goods and Works financed by the Inter-American Development Bank (March 2011): http://idbdocs.iadb.org/wsdocs/getdocument.aspx?docnum=774392.

[19] Procurement Policies and Rules (PP&R) (2014): www.ebrd.com/news/publications/policies/procurement-policies-and-rules.html.

[20] AFDB, 'Comprehensive Review' (n 4) 5.

selection of baseline documents (for goods, small and large works and plant), taken from different MDBs, the working groups discussed the documents in detail and opted for the formulation that was most representative in terms of best practices, and which the participating institutions would use collectively. Each document was presented to the HOPs for approval, following which the HOPs designated the new document as the Harmonised MPD. Four Harmonised MPDs were created through this process: for Goods; Small Works; Works; and Plant Design, Supply and Installation. Following this phase, the task became one of ensuring consistency and alignment between the four MPDs so that they would share a common structure and appearance. This was largely achieved save for the general conditions of contract which were too different in the case of each MPD. A generic master document was prepared to guide further harmonisation efforts and two further MPDs followed, on the procurement of non-consultancy services and a standard form of Requests for Proposals (RFP) for consultancy services, respectively. The existing pre-qualification guidance was not amended. The documents that were harmonised through this process were:

- Master Standard Request for Proposals (October 2011);
- Generic Master Procurement Document (July 2008);
- Master Document for Procurement of Small Works (July 2008);
- Master Procurement Documents – Prequalification Documents for Procurement of Works and User's Guide (May 2003);
- Master Document for Procurement of Works (July 2008);
- Master Document for Procurement of Goods (July 2008); and
- Master Document for Procurement of Plant Design, Supply, and Installation (February 2007).

Thus, by about 2014, it could be said that the procurement rules of the IBRD and the regional MDBs,[21] together with their key standard bidding documents, were largely harmonised in terms of content and, in most cases, structure. Only the PP&R of the EBRD had a different feel but, even then, the content was very similar. It seemed that one of the critical commitments of the Paris Declaration, namely harmonisation of donor rules, had been achieved, at least at a technical level.

As explained above, the harmonisation work was carried out in a meticulous fashion and, in the case of the standard bidding documents (SBDs), in particular, discussing 'in detail and extensively, section by section, clause by clause, the formulation that was most representative in terms of best practices'.[22] The result, of course, was a series of carefully wrought texts that were acceptable to all and which did not tolerate deviation. Given the very small differences between the texts ultimately adopted

[21] The rules of the regional banks not referred to explicitly above were rather more diverse. The CDB's Guidelines for Procurement (2006) (www.caribank.org/work-with-us/procurement/resources) are also almost identical to the unrevised guidelines of the IBRD and the IBRD rules are reflected quite closely in the IsDB's Guidelines for Procurement of Goods and Works under Islamic Development Bank Financing (May 2009, amended February 2012) available at www.ipkb.gov.tr/assets/data/files/kilavuzlar/islam-kalkinma-bankasi-finansman-mal-alim-ve-insaat-isleri-satin-alma-kilavuzu.pdf and the BSTDB's Procurement Principles and Rules, available at www.bstdb.org/project-procurement.

[22] AFDB, 'Comprehensive Review' (n 4) 6.

by the different MDBs, those differences became very important, however minor in reality, in distinguishing between the MDBs and their approaches so that the application of their respective procurement rules became very prescriptive. Strict compliance with those different MDB documents became even more important because of those small differences.

The MDBs ensured compliance with their own rules through a series of *ex ante* and *ex post* reviews, depending essentially on the value and complexity of the contracts, as well as on the extent to which reliance had been placed on national procurement systems under national competitive bidding (NCB) procedures. NCB was applied to lower value contracts when the MDB considered that the borrower's procurement system was acceptable and the threshold for NCB usage was set at various levels (by each MDB and in relation to each country and sometimes sector) depending on, *inter alia*, country capacity and the degree of acceptability of its systems as measured by an MDB assessment, more frequently now based on a MAPS assessment. The NCB threshold established, therefore, the point at which an MDB decided that it could rely on national systems rather than apply the full force of its own Procurement Guidelines and standard bidding documents using International Competitive Bidding (ICB) procedures. Use of NCB was also a mechanism for the MDBs to impose conditionalities on borrowers to ensure that their practices and institutions conformed to the MDBs' notions of good governance.[23]

As explained by Trepte,[24] in the case of the World Bank (but the same is true of other MDBs as well), the increased use of NCB procedures was accompanied by increased supervision by way of random *ex post* reviews by the Bank of smaller, less complex contracts to verify that they had been let according to the Bank's Guidelines, instead of *ex ante* (prior) review of all contracts through the bidding process by the Bank and its no objection prior to award and signature. The rules became more restrictive and procedural to provide for the various possibilities permitted at national level by reference to pre-defined limits according to the country, contract size and procurement method. Procurement became more standardised and this was reflected in the project documentation with the MDBs mostly requiring the use of SBDs for ICB,[25] based on the harmonised documents described above.

The result of such a relatively long evolution in the design and harmonisation of the procurement rules, fuelled by project-specific concerns, supervision, standardisation and, latterly, a concern with integrity,[26] has led to a set of relatively complex and prescriptive rules applying to Bank-funded procurement. They are concerned primarily with ensuring compliance and leave little room for more strategic procurement based on outputs and performance. As admitted in the World Bank's Initiating Discussion Paper (which set the scene for the review of its procurement framework):

> their complexity and prescriptiveness [of the Procurement Guidelines], while reflecting the complex nature of procurement, limits their positive impact, particularly in borrowing

[23] See further ch 3.

[24] P Trepte, 'All Change at the World Bank? The New Procurement Framework' (2016) 25 *Public Procurement Law Review* 121, 123.

[25] A range of SBDs was provided on the Bank's website (http://web.worldbank.org/WBSITE/EXTERNAL/PROJECTS/PROCUREMENT/0,,contentMDK:20062006~menuPK:84284~pagePK:84269~piPK:60001558~theSitePK:84266,00.html) and on the websites of the other MDBs.

[26] See ch 7.

> countries that lack capacity. The Guidelines remain largely rules-based and driven by compliance with specific procedures.[27]

The harmonisation process has indeed resulted in MDB rules which appear very similar, if not identical, but this has led to a high level of standardisation and prescription which is exacerbated by an environment of compliance which effectively dismisses the use of any country system which does not also conform to the negotiated standard. It is perhaps little wonder that the Paris Declaration commitment to use country systems has failed so dismally.[28]

III. Post-2016 MDB Reforms

The year 2016 has been chosen as a watershed year because this is when the World Bank's major reform of its own procurement framework became operational. This is discussed extensively in chapter 12. The World Bank itself described it as 'a once-in-a-generation systematic reform and culture change',[29] presaging a significant shift from its pre-2016 harmonised position. The question for current purposes is whether the other MDBs are following suit in order to remain harmonised or whether the road that led to harmonisation of MDB rules is at an end.

It would be too ambitious to try to carry out a comprehensive comparison of the position of each of the MDBs against the reforms carried out by the World Bank but even that statement implies that there is much to compare. Rather, we will consider a few selected issues which might be said to be key characteristics of the changes brought about. Even before that, however, we can point out that two of the major MDBs involved in the previous harmonisation process have not entered into any reforms subsequent to the World Bank reforms in order to bring them into line and appear to have no intention of doing so. The EBRD's Director of Procurement,[30] for example, believes that its PP&R has served it well and that there is no need to change them in response to the World Bank's revised framework, although that is not to say the policy does not need to change to remain up-to-date and introduce similar levels of flexibility. IADB also does not appear to be envisaging any changes to its procurement rules at this stage and intends to maintain and strengthen its focus on the use of country systems in its region[31] (which also consists in applying NCB at given thresholds). A search of the websites

[27] The World Bank's *Procurement Policies and Procedures: Policy Review Initiating Discussion Paper* (29 March 2012) 9, available at http://siteresources.worldbank.org/INTECA/Resources/257896-1335553632562/Initiating-Discussion-Paper-Eng.pdf.

[28] Trepte, 'All Change at the World Bank?' (n 24) 129; ch 10.

[29] Procurement in World Bank Investment Project Financing, Phase II: The New Procurement Framework (11 June 2015), ('The Board Paper'), para 1, available at: http://consultations.worldbank.org/Data/hub/files/consultation-template/procurement-policy-review-consultationsopenconsultationtemplate/phases/phase_ii_the_new_procurement_framework_-_board_paper.pdf.

[30] J Jackholt, 'The Procurement Policies and Rules and the Procurement Activities of the European Bank for Reconstruction and Development' (2016) 25 *Public Procurement Law Review* 172–78, 174.

[31] A Salazar and M López, 'The Inter-American Development Bank: Reform to Build Up and Increase the Use of National Procurement Systems in Latin America and the Caribbean' (2016) 25 *Public Procurement Law Review* 164–71.

of the BSTDB,[32] CDB[33] and the IsDB[34] reveals no intention to revise their current procurement rules. Any change by the World Bank away from the harmonised position of its pre-2016 procurement framework is thus already a move away from the harmonisation so far achieved and in a direction that several MDBs have decided not to follow, at least, not yet.

Two of the regional banks, namely the ADB and the AfDB, have carried out reforms after 2016, and the AIIB, which was established just around about 2016, appears to have been inspired, in drafting its own procurement rules, by the World Bank's new procurement framework. Does this mean, therefore, that in respect of these three MDBs at least, harmonisation has been maintained? It seems not.

In terms of structure, much has changed. Previously, all the MDBs operated on the basis of an almost identical set of procurement guidelines. The wave of reforms has changed that. The World Bank, the ADB and the AIIB now operate on the basis of a policy document which is relatively brief, accompanied by a set of rules applicable to borrowers (called Regulations in the case of the World Bank[35] and the ADB[36] and an Interim Operational Directive in the case of the AIIB[37]). In the case of the AfDB,[38] there is also a policy document, although this is a much longer document and contains much of what is relegated to the Regulations at the World Bank and ADB and the Directive in the case of the AIIB. This policy document of the AfDB is accompanied by a Methodology for Implementation, Operations Procurement Manual and a Toolkit. In the case of the ADB, a significant structural change includes the amalgamation of the rules on goods, works and non-consulting services and the rules on consulting services into one single document. There is much to commend this approach since most of the provisions in both sectors were and are very similar, with major differences only appearing in the evaluation methods, though maintaining some of the old terminology may well cause confusion and somewhat undermines the significance of the change. Whilst it may be said that structure is of minor importance if the content is the same, it must also be remembered that the point of harmonisation in this context, as explained in chapter 3, is to counter the fragmentation of the application of multiple procurement rules and thus reduce the capacity erosion caused to procurement officers in those countries. The new legal frameworks of these MDBs look quite different from one another and from the previous documents still maintained by the other MDBs, so that it is clear that procurement officers in the borrowing countries will need to familiarise themselves with several new procurement frameworks. This is a retrograde step in terms of the de-fragmentation achieved before 2016.

All of these four new procurement frameworks take a principles-based approach, seeking to overturn the prescriptive compliance-based approach of the previous Procurement Guidelines, and the ADB, AfDB and the AIIB have all adopted the two new principles explicitly introduced by the World Bank, namely 'value for money'

[32] www.bstdb.org/about-us/how-we-operate/procurement.
[33] www.caribank.org/work-with-us/procurement/resources.
[34] www.isdb.org.
[35] www.worldbank.org/en/projects-operations/products-and-services/brief/procurement-new-framework.
[36] www.adb.org/documents/procurement-guidelines.
[37] www.aiib.org/en/policies-strategies/.
[38] www.afdb.org/en/projects-and-operations/procurement/new-procurement-policy/.

and 'fitness for purpose', although it may be argued that there is nothing new in the concept of value for money. There is, however, something new in the way that each of the MDBs has defined these principles. While keeping more or less to the same script, there are slight but significant differences in the definitions which may well provide plenty of material for legal dissent. See, for example, the alternative definitions of value for money:

> *Section III.C.1 of the World Bank Policy*: The principle of value for money means the effective, efficient, and economic use of resources, which requires an evaluation of relevant costs and benefits, along with an assessment of risks, and non-price attributes and/or life cycle costs, as appropriate. Price alone may not necessarily represent value for money.
>
> *Section 3.1.5 of the AIIB Directive*: The procurement process enables the Recipient to obtain optimal benefits with the resources utilized. This may include not only the initial costs, but also costs over the economic life of the procured item, the quality of the output, fitness-for-purpose (see paragraph 3.1.6 below), timeliness, and the achievement of other socio-economic and environmental development objectives of the Recipient.
>
> *Section III.5(vi) of the ADB Regulations*: This principle enables the borrower to obtain optimal benefits through effective, efficient, and economic use of resources by applying, as appropriate, the Core Procurement Principles and related considerations, which may include life-cycle costs and socioeconomic and environmental development objectives of the borrower. Price alone may not sufficiently represent value for money.
>
> *Section 2.3 of the AfDB Policy*: The procurement process should ensure that the Borrower obtains optimal benefits with the resources utilized. This may include not only the initial costs but also those over the economic life of the procured item, the quality of the output, fitness for purpose, timeliness, and the achievement of other development objectives of the Borrower. Value for Money (VfM) is driven by the four broad principles of economy, efficiency, effectiveness, and equity. In supporting VfM, the Bank discharges its broader mandate of maximizing development effectiveness while minimizing exposure to fiduciary risk through enabling its Borrowers to undertake cost-effective and efficient procurement.

These definitions have many similarities and may or may not be interpreted identically in practice but, since the same pattern is evident in almost all of the definitions, it means that users of the rules will need to be able to distinguish and differentiate between them to the extent that they need to satisfy the relevant MDBs of their compliance with the applicable framework. Again, procurement officers will not be able to rely on their knowledge of just one of these systems; they will need to be familiar with whichever is being applied.

One of the novelties of the World Bank reforms is the greater emphasis placed on the planning phase in order to ensure better outcomes and these planning requirements go some way to revealing the primary objectives of the reforms of each of the MDBs since they disclose the intended purpose of the procurement. Each of the MDBs that have amended their rules after 2016 have also placed an increased emphasis on planning, though perhaps not quite to the same extent as the World Bank. However, the reasons for improved planning do not appear to be identical and reflect rather the different concerns of the various MDBs.

For the World Bank, the planning phase of procurement is a fundamental part of its effort to modernise its procurement approach to accommodate and better support the use of various modern procurement methods in support of development outcomes.[39] The key to this approach lies in the Project Procurement Strategy for Development (PPSD) which must be created for each project. The optimum procurement approach for each operation will be based on the findings from an analysis of the project needs, market, risks and other influencing factors identified through a PPSD and the new procurement framework will support the delivery of better procurement outcomes by expanding the number of approaches and methods that can be used, reflecting modern international good practice. It thus plays a key role in ensuring value for money and fitness for purpose but is also very much focused on the selection of the most appropriate procurement methods which, as we shall see below, have been expanded.

In the case of the ADB, the new strategic approach was less about applying more flexible methods to achieve better outputs than about reducing overall procurement time and improving quality and delivery systems.[40] ADB had already initiated, in 2014, a Midterm Review (MTR) action plan to improve ADB operational efficiency and effectiveness.[41] Implementation of these actions was encouraging and these latest amendments were designed to build upon these successes. Thus, 'the framework, grounded in achieving optimal value for money (VfM) for DMCs, will enable ADB and its DMCs to increase development effectiveness by reducing overall procurement time and improving the quality of procurement outcomes in ADB-financed projects'.[42] The weak delivery system was identified as the main culprit for long procurement decision-making and delays in contract implementation and it was the need to improve that delivery system that led to the overall approach requiring 'greater emphasis on procurement planning during the project design stage, with increased depth of focus on market and country circumstances and capacity constraints, risk based transaction due diligence during bidding and a more engaged contract administration and management process'.[43] Whilst, therefore, the ADB reforms are also based on better planning and preparation, the aims are rather different so that the issues taken into account and the consequential actions are likely to differ from those that would emerge from a similar planning process under, say, the World Bank's PPSD.

Despite referring to similar concerns to the World Bank in terms of improving the outcomes of procurement, the AfDB deals much less in detail with the issue of procurement planning.[44] The provisions are much the same as they were in its previous Procurement Guidelines. In its initiating Board Memorandum,[45] the AfDB framework, more than the others, emphasises two things in particular: greater use of

[39] World Bank Board Paper (n 29) 1.

[40] ADB Policy Paper: Improving Procurement Performance in ADB Projects through Second Generation Procurement Reforms (March 2017) 5, available at www.adb.org/sites/default/files/institutional-document/295616/policy-paper-procurement-framework.pdf.

[41] See www.adb.org/sites/default/files/institutional-document/176137/s2020-mtr-reforms-ea.pdf.

[42] ADB Policy Paper (n 40) 2.

[43] ibid 3.

[44] AfDB Policy Document (n 38) 25.

[45] Board Memorandum: Comprehensive Revision of the ADB's Procurement Policy Procedures and Processes (October 2015): hwww.afdb.org/fileadmin/uploads/afdb/Documents/Policy-Documents/Comprehensive_revision_of_the_ADB's_procurement_policy_procedures_and_processes.pdf.

country systems and the maintenance of fiduciary compliance. The headline objective is to 'support development effectiveness within an acceptable fiduciary compliance framework'.[46] The procurement framework is designed to enhance country systems 'in order for them to obtain optimal value for money based on mutually supporting and reinforcing principles of economy, efficiency, effectiveness and equity. This is achieved using processes and procedures that are competitive, fair and transparent;.[47] So, there is a very clear emphasis on the four key principles[48] as well as a clear awareness of risk management. These are also features common to the other MDB reforms but to a lesser degree.

The AIIB is perhaps the closest to the World Bank in its use of careful planning, although the project delivery strategy (PDS) of the AIIB Directive is 'a simplified equivalent' of World Bank's PPSD[49] requiring prior market research to develop an understanding of the relevant sectors and potential tenderers, how the market works and how this may impact the approach to the market and methods used to procure and assess issues that affect the risks and VfM of the project.

It is to be noted that the World Bank's emphasis on the PPSD for the selection of the appropriate procurement method is also a reflection of the broader choice now given to borrowers. This is perhaps one of the most noticeable and visible changes brought about by the framework both in terms of terminology and substance. A distinction is now drawn between the approved selection methods to be used and the way in which the market is approached. As a result, the method now known as Requests for Bids may be conducted using open or limited competition. When conducted by way of open competition, Requests for Bids could be carried out either by way of international competition (effectively, the old ICB) or national competition (effectively, the old NCB) and in single or multiple stages.

The Regulations identify four main approved selection methods: Request for Proposals (RFP); Requests for Bids (RFB); Requests for Quotations (RFQ);[50] and Direct Selection. The pre-qualification and post-qualification provisions are also maintained. The former two-stage procedure has been removed but seemingly replaced by two new methods, the new Requests for Proposals and Competitive Dialogue, which appear to address similar concerns depending on the degree of complexity. The other two novelties introduced in the context of competitive bidding procedures are (i) the use of best and final offers (BAFOs) and (ii) the now permitted use of negotiations, which is limited to international competitive procurement subject to prior review and held in the presence of an independent third party.

The remaining MDBs have not amended their procurement methods in the same way, although there have been changes. In the case of the AfDB, Open Competitive Bidding (OCB) is now a generic term which encompasses International Competitive Bidding (ICB) and National Competitive Bidding (NCB). The framework also foresees Limited Competitive Bidding (LCB), Direct Procurement (DP) and Force Account

[46] ibid 3.

[47] ibid 8.

[48] V Sharma, 'An Update on Procurement Reforms at the African Development Bank' (2016) 25 *Public Procurement Law Review* 151–63, 155.

[49] Górski, 'Regulation of Government Procurement by the AIIB' (n 5) 300.

[50] Formerly called 'shopping'.

(construction). LCB methods cover Limited International Bidding (LIB) and Shopping or Request for Quotations (RFQ). Apart from some minor changes in nomenclature, these are the same as the previous methods.

ADB has gone a little further with changes in terminology. It has also opted for Open Competitive Bidding (OCB) but, unlike the AfDB, no longer distinguishes between ICB and NCB although OCB may be advertised at both national and international levels. ADB also provides for LCB, Direct Contract, RFQ and Force Account. In addition it provides for framework contracts and electronic reverse auction. These latter two are also permitted by the other MDBs.

The AIIB has also remained rather conservative in the options it provides and has remained faithful to the pre-2016 suite of methods. The principal procurement methods include international open competitive tender (IOCT) (also renamed), National Competitive Tendering (NCT), selective tendering, direct contracting, Request for Quotations (RFQ) as well as e-procurement and procedures for the award of PPPs and concessions.

It is quite clear, therefore, that procurement officers will now need to make themselves familiar with an array of different methods[51] even if, in reality, they are not so very different in substance. From the harmonisation perspective this again leads to fragmentation and tends to unravel the pre-2016 efforts at alignment. That is not to say that some of the changes are not highly beneficial; only that they may have negative effects for aid effectiveness where the renewed multiplicity of procurement methods increases the learning curve for procurement officers who need to be aware of the procurement rules of all MDBs that operate in their country.

We could investigate many of the other changes brought about by the World Bank reforms and compare them to changes made to the procurement frameworks of other MDBs but the result is likely to be the same. The amendments are not identical and, in some cases, are very different. The rules are now significantly less harmonised than they were before 2016.

IV. The End of Convergence?

There is no doubt that the pre-2016 versions of the MDB procurement rules were relatively harmonised, thanks in large part to the HOP harmonisation process which preceded the Paris Declaration. It is also true, however, that harmonisation came at a cost. The standardisation that resulted from the harmonisation process led to a rather prescriptive set of rules which, combined with the high degree of supervision by the MDBs and their concern with the application of their own rules or a country system which reflected their own rules led to a highly rigid, compliance-based system. There was little flexibility and little room to allow country context to be taken into account into the design and implementation of funded procurement activities.

[51] The matrices (for goods, works, non-consulting services and consulting services) of methods provided in the Bank's Regulations, available at http://pubdocs.worldbank.org/en/178331533065871195/Procurement-Regulations.pdf, 34 and 47, appear to indicate that there are well over 150 permutations of methods and approaches to market, significantly more than the number of previous methods permitted.

It may be that the harmonisation eased the burden of procurement officers in the way intended by the aid effectiveness agenda but it also replaced it with a very standardised and prescriptive system of procurement. It is questionable whether that consequence also improves aid effectiveness. The World Bank and the other reforming MDBs obviously think not. Their reforms, though not identical, all move in the direction of flexibility and customisation (for different reasons) suggesting that the one-size-fits-all result of harmonisation is not the way forward. Despite reiterating their commitment to harmonisation, their actions show that the MDBs are currently heading in quite another direction.

Convergence is not the hallmark of the post-2016 reforms even if there remains a commonality in the principles applied. Maybe, over time, the other MDBs will rally around the World Bank but, at present, the road to harmonisation is bifurcating in numerous directions at several points along the way.

Addendum

Since drafting this chapter, the Inter-American Development Bank has also initiated a public consultation to expand its current procurement policies picking up, in part, some of the reforms introduced by the World Bank: see https://www.iadb.org/en/procurement/idb-procurement-policies-expansion.

14

Aid Effectiveness and Public Procurement – The USAID Experience

JUN JIN AND RONALD WIETECHA*

As discussed in the first three chapters, public procurement is an important tool in promoting and advancing development objectives such as those described in the various multilateral aid effectiveness agreements.[1] This chapter looks at one bilateral development partner's organisational and practical experiences in attempting to modify its procurement processes and policies to better align with the aid effectiveness goals of increased local engagement, greater use of partner country systems, and greater focus on sustainability and country ownership.

I. Brief Introduction to USAID

Established in 1961 under the Administration of President John F Kennedy, the United States Agency for International Development (USAID) is the lead foreign assistance arm of the US government (USG). USAID has a semi-autonomous relationship with the US Department of State and advances the development prong of the USG's three-pillar 'Diplomacy-Development-Defense' National Security Strategy. Although the USG implements a fragmented approach to development with more than 20 different agencies and departments implementing some form of foreign assistance,[2] USAID represents more than one-half of the USG's overall official development assistance as measured by the Organisation for Economic Cooperation and Development's Development Assistance Committee (OECD/DAC).[3]

* Any views expressed in this chapter are solely those of the authors in their private capacity and are not intended to represent the views of the US government.

[1] See eg the Paris Declaration on Aid Effectiveness (2005) and the Accra Agenda for Action (2008) available at www.oecd.org/dac/effectiveness/34428351.pdf as well as the Busan Partnership for Effective Development Cooperation (2012) available at www.oecd.org/dac/effectiveness/Busan%20partnership.pdf.

[2] See OECD, 'OECD Development Assistance Peer Reviews: United States 2011' (Paris, OECD Publishing, 2013) 43, available at www.oecd.org/dac/peer-reviews/48434536.pdf.

[3] See C Tarnoff and ML Lawson, 'Foreign Aid: An Introduction to U.S. Programs and Policy' (Congressional Research Service, 2018) available at www.fas.org/sgp/crs/row/R40213.pdf.

One can think of procurement as it relates to USAID in at least four different ways: (i) as a modality using a partner government's public procurement systems to implement programmes – entrusting USAID funds to partner governments who channel such funds through their own procurement systems, applying their own laws, regulations, policies and practices to perform specific activities as set forth in direct government financing agreements between USAID and a partner country; (ii) as an implementation modality through programming parallel to a partner government's own activities – USAID uses direct procurements as a primary means of implementing USAID's programmes via entering into direct contracts (and grants) with implementers (typically, for-profit and non-profit organisations) who receive USAID funding to perform activities to advance development objectives in any given country or sector; (iii) as a vehicle to promote and support local actors – entering into direct funding relationships with local contractors and non-profit entities to bolster local economic growth, increase local non-governmental technical, financial and administrative capacity of organisations who, along with their governments, are the heart of sustainability as the local actors who will 'own' the country's future development path; and (iv) as a set of capacity-development activities to support developing countries in strengthening their own public procurement systems – providing assistance (technical, logistical, etc) to partner country governments and non-governmental organisations (NGOs) to improve the legal, regulatory, policy, administrative, enforcement, compliance and performance aspects of their procurement systems within a broader framework of public financial management, public administration and governance and economic reform strategies.

This chapter covers these four different aspects of procurement from USAID's perspective and, in particular, how at least the last two aspects contribute to efforts to improve both the delivery of US foreign assistance and to help countries establish functional and effective procurement systems to effect good governance, eliminate extreme poverty and promote economic growth.

II. Evolution of Promoting Local Ownership and Procurement Systems

Using partner government procurement systems as an aid modality to implement development activities was a major feature of one of USAID's recent and comprehensive reform efforts called USAID Forward.

A. USAID Forward

In 2010, USAID initiated an ambitious reform agenda called USAID Forward.[4] USAID Forward was a conscious attempt by the Agency to better align with international

[4] See USAID, 'USAID Policy Framework, 2011–2015' (Washington DC, USAID) 32, available at www.usaid.gov/sites/default/files/documents/1870/USAID%20Policy%20Framework%202011-2015.PDF.

initiatives addressing aid effectiveness.[5] USAID Forward recognised that the Agency's practice of financing a small group of primarily US contractors and NGOs to implement its development activities did not adequately align with the country-led and -owned goals of the Paris Declaration on Aid Effectiveness (Paris Declaration) and the Accra Agenda for Action (AAA).[6] USAID Forward was also borne out of a sense that USAID's modalities and past practices were not always optimally tailored to contribute to attainment of the Millennium Development Goals (MDGs) via a locally-owned model based upon general precepts of sustainable development.[7]

The technical elements of USAID Forward were developed by a blended group of career Agency personnel and recently appointed political leadership that naturally led to the United States' positions and views expressed in its participation in the Busan Partnership Agreement for Effective Development Cooperation in 2011 (Busan Partnership).[8] Other driving factors that further facilitated strong support within the USG for USAID Forward were the Presidential Policy Directive (PPD)[9] on Global Development and the then-recently initiated Quadrennial Diplomacy and Development Reviews (QDDR).[10] Both the PPD and QDDR gave USAID the mandate to undertake comprehensive and fairly radical structural and operational changes in order to make its assistance more effective, efficient, sustainable and in better alignment with the aforementioned international efforts on aid effectiveness.[11]

The primary and most widely publicised component of USAID Forward was the technical-level initiative called Implementation and Procurement Reform (IPR).[12] IPR used a rationalised approach to organisational change that recognised how USAID operated in 2010 while at the same time articulating a vision for what USAID intended to achieve by 2015. To make US foreign assistance more cost-effective and ultimately sustainable, IPR articulated six objectives for building more local capacity at both the governmental level and within civil society, as well as by simplifying and streamlining policies and procedures to work with a broader range of development partners. These six objectives recognised the realities of USAID's legal and other operational limitations[13] while mandating that the Agency operate as closely in alignment

[5] See eg S Reichle, 'USAID Reforms Aim to Strengthen Local Institutions and Systems' (2012) available at https://blog.usaid.gov/2012/12/usaid-reforms-aim-to-strengthen-local-institutions-and-systems.

[6] See n 1.

[7] See eg D Eckerson, 'How a New USAID Was Born' (2013) available at https://blog.usaid.gov/2013/03/how-a-new-usaid-was-born.

[8] See n 1.

[9] Presidential Policy Directive on Global Development, available at https://obamawhitehouse.archives.gov/the-press-office/2010/09/22/fact-sheet-us-global-development-policy.

[10] www.state.gov/s/dmr/qddr.

[11] USAID recognises that the Paris Declaration and AAA articulated the central insight 'that external aid investments are more likely to catalyze sustained development processes when they reinforce a country's internally determined development priorities (country ownership) and arrangements (country systems)' – USAID, 'Local Systems: A Framework for Supporting Sustained Development' (Washington DC, USAID, 2014) 3, available at www.usaid.gov/sites/default/files/documents/1870/LocalSystemsFramework.pdf.

[12] See eg 'USAID Policy Framework, 2011–2015' (n 4) 35, '*Building* Local Capacity'.

[13] The PPD formally recognised that United States 'cannot do all things, do them well, and do them everywhere'. See The White House, Office of the Press Secretary, 'Fact Sheet: U.S. Global Development Policy' (22 September 2010) available at https://obamawhitehouse.archives.gov/the-press-office/2010/09/22/fact-sheet-us-global-development-policy.

with the Paris Declaration, AAA and Busan Partnership to achieve the MDGs as those limitations permit. In doing so, USAID's approach was somewhat unique and noteworthy in that USAID defined 'local entity' for purposes of localising its aid more broadly than just public sector financial and procurement systems.[14] At the same time, USAID defined very broadly the types of entities with which it would be attempting to build both financial and collaborative partnerships: local and international, private and public, national and international.

These definitional and operational parameters resulted in six somewhat compartmentalised objectives for IPR:

1. strengthen partner country capacity to improve aid effectiveness and sustainability;
2. strengthen local civil society and private sector capacity to improve aid effectiveness and sustainability;
3. increase competition and broaden USAID's partner base;
4. use USG resources more efficiently and effectively;
5. strengthen collaboration and partnership with bilateral donors, multilateral and international organisations to increase synergies and avoid duplication; and
6. rebuild USAID's internal technical capacity and rebalance the workforce.

As a management tool, USAID's leadership instituted Agency-wide targets to measure USAID's progress against these objectives by 2015. Based on a detailed analysis in 2010 of obligations over the prior three fiscal years in order to determine baseline figures, the targets, implementation plan and timelines were determined based on best estimates of the time it would take to modify legislation, regulations and policies and train staff.[15] Emphasising that the targets were applicable to the entire Agency and not necessarily applicable to each individual bilateral programme or each Mission, the Agency indicated the targets were intended to be realistic.[16] Those targets were as follows:

1. increase programme fund obligations from less than 10 per cent to 20 per cent through partner country systems in at least 25 countries;
2. increase the amount of direct grants to local non-profit organisations from 2.46 per cent to 6 per cent of its programme funds; increase the number of local non-profit partners from 424 to 1000; increase the amount of programme-funded direct contracts to local private businesses from 0.83 per cent to 4 per cent; and increase the number of partners from 322 to 600;

[14] Local Systems Framework (n 11) 3.

[15] USAID, Building Local Development Leadership: USAID's Operational and Procurement Plan, 2011 [no longer publicly available Agency working document contemporaneously referenced extensively by USAID and various commenters]. See eg USAID, USAID Forward Achievements, 5 May 2011, available at pdf.usaid.gov/pdf_docs/PDACS876.pdf; InterAction, 'More Effective Capacity Building Within USAID Forward', (2012) 4, available at www.interaction.org/sites/default/files/InterAction%20-%20%20Effective%20Capacity%20Building%20in%20USAID%20Forward%20-%20Oct%202012.pdf; C Dunning, 'Is Local Spending Better? The Controversy over USAID Procurement Reform' (Center for American Progress, November 2013) available at www.americanprogress.org/wp-content/uploads/2013/11/ProcurementReform.pdf; and R Blue, 'Evaluation of the Implementation of the Paris Declaration: United States Government Synthesis Report' (Virginia, Social Impact, Inc., 2011) 27–29, available at pd-website.inforce.dk/content/pdf-countryreports/usa1.pdf.

[16] ibid.

3. obligate 5 per cent of its programme funds through contracts with US small and/or disadvantaged businesses and increase the number of partners to 300;
4. increase the percentage of fixed-price contracts for commodities and equipment to 75 per cent and for other types of contracts to 20 per cent;
5. revise Agency policies and guidelines to facilitate working with bilateral and multilateral donors in co-funding of projects and contributions to multi-donor trust funds; and
6. rebuild its internal technical capacity and strengthen its acquisition and assistance workforce by requesting legislative authority to establish a working capital fund (WCF) that charges 1 per cent of all Agency obligations to cover the entire costs of the Agency's Acquisition and Assistance staff and fund the administrative changes needed to achieve the procurement reform.

Most noteworthy from a procurement and aid effectiveness perspective is that the IPR targets for Objectives 1 and 2 were combined to form a 'top-line indicator' (TLI) to measure the Agency's progress towards its reform goals. The TLI called for an increase to 20 per cent use of partner government systems and an increase to 10 per cent financing of local for-profit and non-profit organisations. Progress towards the combined '30% by 2015' TLI has been tracked annually.[17]

Several aspects of the 30 per cent TLI target raised some concerns, both internal and external to USAID.[18] One concern stemmed from how the TLI was announced and socialised.[19] For example, a clear message that did not emerge until 2012 was whether the target was a hard target or purely 'aspirational'. While the message that the target was Agency-wide had accompanied the announcement of the targets, it remained unclear to Agency personnel whether individual Mission Directors would nonetheless be held accountable, for example in their annual performance evaluations, for progress towards meeting the 30 per cent target. Because a more direct and unequivocal message about the IPR target being 'aspirational' was not announced in formal Agency communications at its inception, scepticism, confusion and concern lingered for some time thereafter both inside and outside the Agency.[20]

The other primary concern expressed about the establishment of a TLI was whether it distorted USAID's decision-making on a granular development level, leading to inadvisable risk-taking or, worse, counterproductive results.[21] Even though another component of USAID Forward included a complete overhaul of USAID's programme cycle and project design processes, the 30 per cent IPR target was accused of leading USAID to retrofit activity and project designs into less-than-ideal instruments with

[17] As of 13 October 2016, USAID reported obligating 27% of its funding to local entities in 2015; USAID, 'Shared Progress, Shared Future: Agency Financial Report – Fiscal Year 2016' (Washington DC, USAID) 7, available at www.usaid.gov/sites/default/files/documents/1868/USAIDFY2016_AFR_508.pdf.

[18] See eg R Rosenkranz, 'Common ground on local procurement' (Devex, 26 July 2012) available at www.devex.com/news/common-ground-on-local-procurement-78769?utm_source=website&utm_medium=text&utm_campaign=linking_strategy.

[19] See eg Dunning, 'Is Local Spending Better?' (n 15).

[20] See eg P Troilo, 'In Washington, questions linger over risks and rewards of new aid model' (Devex, 21 May 2012) available at www.devex.com/news/in-washington-questions-linger-over-risks-and-rewards-of-new-aid-model-78262.

[21] See eg Dunning (n 15).

'local entities' that may or may not have a level of accountability for the activities to be implemented.[22]

Despite being largely unfounded,[23] these criticisms and concerns over the 30 per cent target led to increasing scrutiny of USAID Forward and IPR specifically from a variety of stakeholders, including the US Congress, the Government Accountability Office,[24] USAID's Inspector General[25] and a number of stakeholders from the contractor and NGO community.[26] Some have even posited that the IPR target controversy was merely an inevitable result of USAID's shift from being an operational agency to a contracting firm in the late 1990s.[27]

B. IPR to Local Solutions

Based in part on the recognition that IPR contained too narrow a focus on the means for implementing localised development rather than the rationale and purpose for localised, more effective aid, the Agency evolved IPR into a re-branded, re-focused initiative called Local Solutions (LS) in 2013.[28] LS was a conscious attempt to harmonise the various efforts under USAID Forward into a cohesive, systems-focused reform effort re-dedicated to the principle of sustainability and eventually eliminating the further need for US foreign assistance. LS intended to combine experience with revised project design, the mechanisms developed for direct financing with local implementers, the enhanced collaboration with other development actors and institutions, and the streamlined, more efficient tools to build USAID's internal capacity to address development challenges within systems rather than just organisations. As such,

[22] ibid 7.

[23] See eg United States Government Accountability Office (GAO), 'Foreign Aid: USAID Has Taken Steps to Safeguard Government-to-Government Funding but Could Further Strengthen Accountability', Report to Congressional Requesters, GAO-15-377 (Washington DC, June 2015) available at www.gao.gov/assets/680/670659.pdf. See also Dunning (n 15) 2 (lack of legal recourse against local entities has been mitigated by USAID's effective due diligence).

[24] GAO, United States Government Accountability Office, 'Foreign Aid: USAID Has Increased Funding to Partner Country Organizations but Could Better Track Progress', Report to the Committee on Foreign Relations, US Senate, GAO-14-355 (Washington DC, April 2014) available at www.gao.gov/assets/670/662596.pdf; and GAO, 'Foreign AID: USAID Has Taken Steps', GAO-15-377 (n 23).

[25] USAID, Office of Inspector General (OIG), 'Review of USAID's Partner-Country and Local Organization Assessments Under Implementation and Procurement Reform', Report No 9-000-13-003-S (Washington DC, 7 June 2013) available at https://oig.usaid.gov/sites/default/files/2018-06/9-000-13-003-s_0.pdf; and USAID OIG, 'Review of Stage 2 Risk Assessments for the Latin America and Caribbean Region Under Local Solutions', Report No 1-598-14-001-S (RIG/San Salvador, 30 September 2014) available at https://oig.usaid.gov/sites/default/files/2018-06/1-598-14-001-s.pdf.

[26] See eg Dunning (n 15) 6; and L Piccio, 'Behind on 30 percent local spending target, USAID eyes "100 percent sustainability"' (Devex, 22 June 2015) available at www.devex.com/news/behind-on-30-percent-local-spending-target-usaid-eyes-100-percent-sustainability-86389.

[27] See eg RESULTS Educational Fund, Discussion Paper 3 of 3: USAID Forward. Towards Collaborative Support to Global Education: A Review of the U.S. Pledge to the Global Partnership for Education (Washington, DC, 2013) 8, available at www.results.org/uploads/files/Towards_Collaborative_Support_to_Global_Education_-_Discussion_Paper_3_of_3_-_USAID_Forward.pdf.

[28] See eg L Piccio, 'Elizabeth Warfield's Vision for USAID Local Solutions' (Devex, 22 June 2015) available at www.devex.com/news/elizabeth-warfield-s-vision-for-usaid-local-solutions-86392?utm_source=website&utm_medium=box&utm_campaign=linking_strategy.

through LS, USAID intended to deliver sustainable development outcomes through better programme design and implementation to strengthen the actors within systems and those systems themselves.[29]

i. Local Systems Framework

The central policy statement of LS was a document titled 'Local Systems: a Framework for Supporting Sustained Development' (Local Systems Framework).[30] The Local Systems Framework sets forth 'a vision and a framework for advancing sustainable development that relies on thinking and working more systemically' to focus 'more on how we use 100 percent of our resources to strengthen and sustain local systems rather than just the share that goes directly to local partners'.[31] The Local Systems Framework also called for the development of system development best practices, rationalising the Agency's risk management practices and developing tools to measure and evaluate its system-focused efforts.[32] Rather than focusing solely on fiduciary risk and accountability for funds expended through local entities, the Local Systems Framework calls for examining various risks involved in particular local system interventions in an even-handed way to ensure USAID's 'potential investments are assessed in the same way for the results they will generate, the risks they face, and the rewards they offer'.[33]

ii. An Emerging Approach to Supporting Country Systems

The Local Systems Framework summarises the Agency's approach to development of and through systems.[34] The Local Systems Framework defines 'local system' as '[e]ach set of interconnected actors whose collective actions produce a particular development outcome'.[35] Notably, the Local Systems Framework recognised that developing local systems includes the participation and ownership of local entities but does not preclude the involvement or participation of external actors.[36] Further, the Local

[29] Local Systems Framework, above n 12 ('sustaining development outcomes depends on the sustainability of the local system, its built-in durability and a level of adaptability that allows actors and their interrelationships to accommodate shocks and respond to changing circumstances').

[30] Local Systems Framework (n 11).

[31] ibid fn 10.

[32] 'These steps include: (1) adhering to good practice in engaging local systems […]; (2) modifying the Agency's risk assessment process to take better account of rewards as well as risks and to ensure that we are able to direct our resources where they are most likely to catalyse sustained development; and (3) broadening our results architecture to track our contributions to the strength and sustainability of local systems'. ibid I.

[33] ibid 14.

[34] 'The focus on local systems is rooted in the reality that achieving and sustaining any development outcome depends on the contributions of multiple and interconnected actors. Building the capacity of a single actor or strengthening a single relationship is insufficient. Rather, the focus needs to be on the system as a whole: the actors, their interrelationships, and the incentives that guide them. Realizing improvements in development outcomes emanates from increasing the performance of multiple individual actors and the effectiveness of their interactions. And sustaining development outcomes depends on the sustainability of the local system; specifically, its built-in durability and adaptability that allows actors and their interrelationships to accommodate shocks and respond to changing circumstances'. ibid Executive Summary, I.

[35] ibid 3.

[36] The Local Systems Framework notes that 'local system' means 'those interconnected sets of actors that jointly produce a particular development outcome'. The 'local' in a local system 'refers to actors in a partner

Systems Framework also defines sustainability in terms of systems, rather than entities, recognising sustainability requires both (i) increased performance of individual actors and the effectiveness of their interactions as well as (ii) durability and adaptability of the actors and the system.[37]

Consequently, USAID's perspectives on and approaches to the sustainability and effectiveness goals of locally-owned and -led development embodied in the Paris Declaration, AAA and Busan Partnership have evolved, adapted and deepened over the past seven years.[38] While still a work in progress, the Agency's current policy represents a rational, measured attempt to end the need for development assistance through a localised, inclusive intervention model.[39] Under the current Administrator, USAID has renewed its commitment to increase local engagement and prioritise sustainability,[40] although, the Agency determined in October 2017 that the USAID Forward agenda had been sufficiently institutionalised to be termed 'legacy'.[41]

III. USAID's Use of Country Systems

A. History and Evolution

USAID's direct engagement with partner country systems, including those involving procurement, have changed and evolved along with the Agency's understanding, experience and policy framework about aid effectiveness and best practices. Most notably, USAID has struggled with the degree to which the use of country systems to implement development activities may or may not strengthen those systems, the fourth form of procurement described in the introduction.

At the beginning of the fourth quarter of the twentieth century, USAID engaged partner country systems primarily through the use of two mechanisms. In what USAID

country' who are 'local' to the outcomes they jointly produce. The Local Systems Framework also notes that, 'As development outcomes may occur at many levels, local systems can be national, provincial, or community-wide in scope'. ibid 3.

[37] Sustainability is 'the ability of a local system to produce desired outcomes over time. Discrete projects contribute to sustainability when they strengthen the systems' ability to produce valued results and its ability to be both resilient and adaptive in the face of changing circumstance'. ibid 4.

[38] The Busan Partnership 'added an important nuance: Effective and inclusive country ownership means that development priorities are established in ways that are broadly responsive to citizen needs and aspirations. Inclusive country systems also recognize that all parts of society – certainly governments, but also civil society, the private sector, universities and individual citizens – have important resources, ideas and energy that are essential to sustaining development'. ibid 2–3 (recognising a movement in the discourse from a focus on government systems towards a model that recognises sustainable development as a product of contributions from all parts of society).

[39] 'As designed, these policies permit USAID to work toward its goals of strengthening local system capacity, country ownership, and sustainability while providing reasonable assurance that U.S. resources are being used as intended'. GAO, 'Foreign Aid: USAID Has Taken Steps', GAO-15-377 (n 23) 27.

[40] See eg M Igoe, 'Exclusive interview: Mark Green says "America will continue to play its role in the world"' (Devex, 26 September 2017) available at www.devex.com/news/exclusive-interview-mark-green-says-america-will-continue-to-play-its-role-in-the-world-91021.

[41] See eg www.usaid.gov/usaidforward: 'As of October 2017, we are no longer updating information, including collecting indicators, on this legacy effort'.

termed 'non-project' assistance (NPA), USAID financed partner governments' budgets either in non-specific budgetary assistance called 'cash transfers' or through sector-specific arrangements collectively known as Sector Program Assistance (SPA).[42] Both of these non-project financing mechanisms relied on a distinction from the general accounting principles used by the US Federal Government in which expenditures and costs are attributed to particular activity or project purposes. To wit, the NPA name originated based upon the recognition that USAID's disbursements under these types of mechanisms were legally unrelated to or untraceable to particular costs or expenditures of a development activity, objective or purpose. While cash transfers were typically used primarily in exigent economic circumstances to address some unforeseen or out-measured budgetary situation,[43] SPA arrangements were used in the 1980s and 1990s to remove sector-level development barriers and incentivise sector-wide development outcomes using a combination of macroeconomic analysis and targeted benchmark monitoring.[44] USAID generally relied upon the partner country's systems under SPA arrangements, subject only to a few externally imposed requirements necessary to verify USAID's disbursement had reached its intended destination.[45] Although the Agency's use of SPAs declined dramatically after the 1990s, the authority for NPA, including SPA arrangements or other mechanisms, has become of greater interest to USAID and its stakeholders in light of the recent resurgence of performance-based and results-based financing and the degree to which such mechanisms use country systems.[46]

The other primary mechanism by which USAID engaged with partner country systems prior to the twenty-first century was through a procurement-focused mechanism titled Host Country Contracting (HCC).[47] HCC is generally a project-level mechanism by which USAID reimburses costs associated with individual contracts awarded by the partner country government. While generally speaking, USAID 'uses' partner country systems through the partner government's procurement actions under HCC, the rules USAID imposes in HCC financing are largely the same procedures and standards as USAID uses itself under the US Federal Acquisition Regulation.

[42] See USAID's 'Program Assistance' policy paper (Washington DC, USAID, 1996) available at www.usaid.gov/sites/default/files/documents/1870/prog_asst.pdf.

[43] See eg 22 USC § 2346.

[44] USAID's 'Program Assistance' paper (n 42) s 1.1.

[45] Legally, the funds are no longer USG funds once applied to the general SPA purpose for which they were disbursed, so the development-focused activities those funds enabled are no longer subject to the procurement and other legislative restrictions imposed on US-appropriated funds. See eg Automated Directives System (ADS) – 'ADS Chapter 624 Host Country-Owned Foreign Currency' (USAID, partial revision, 21 December 2011) available at www.usaid.gov/sites/default/files/documents/1868/624.pdf.

[46] See eg s 7026 of Public Law No 114-113 (Fiscal Year 2016 Appropriation Act). See also R Perakis and W Savedoff, 'Does Results-Based Aid Change Anything?' (Center for Global Development, 18 February 2015) available at www.cgdev.org/blog/does-results-based-aid-change-anything; World Bank, 'Results-Based Financing (RBF) and Results in Education for All Children (REACH)' available at www.worldbank.org/en/programs/reach; AM Grittner, 'Results-based financing Evidence from performance-based financing in the health sector' (Bonn, Deutsches Institut für Entwicklungspolitik, 2013) available at www.oecd.org/dac/peer-reviews/Results-based-financing.pdf; Instiglio, 'What is Results-Based Financing?' available at www.instiglio.org/en/results-based-financing.

[47] See eg 'ADS Chapter 305 Host Country Contracts' (USAID, partial revision, 23 December 2011) available at www.usaid.gov/sites/default/files/documents/1868/305_0.pdf.

Consequently, HCC can roughly be characterised as an externally-imposed system operated by a partner government, or, in many cases, a project-dedicated implementation unit thereof. Additionally, USAID retains very close oversight and approval requirements under HCC such that the procurement process is not truly owned or managed by the partner government. While there have been a few, isolated examples of partner governments adopting USAID's HCC system for all of their procurements, HCC arguably does not truly rely upon or use partner country systems. Consequently, it is a fair conclusion that HCC is generally not the 'first option' for implementing development activities described by the Paris Declaration, AAA and Busan Partnership.

B. Automated Directives System Chapter 220

As outlined in IPR Objective 1, USAID intended to align with the US and international aid effectiveness goals by increasing its use of reliable partner country systems.[48] The key word in this statement is the word 'reliable'. To satisfy critics and address stakeholder concerns about accountability and integrity, USAID clearly understood it would need a sufficient level of due diligence to be able to assert that it was only financing institutions that meet certain minimum standards and that such financing enhanced, rather than undermined, USAID governance programmes. Consequently, USAID developed the first iteration of its Public Financial Management Risk Assessment Framework (PFMRAF) in 2011 to enable a new modality for financing development project activities directly through partner government procurement and implementation systems. While it is arguable whether the statements at the time equating the *use* of partner country systems for implementing development interventions with *strengthening* partner country systems were true, the development of a pre-financing assessment like the PFMRAF was clearly a necessary component of USAID's commitment to directly finance partner country systems in an accountable manner.[49] The PFMRAF and all other policies and procedures pertaining to direct government-to-government (G2G) financing are found in USAID's Automated Directives System (ADS) Chapter 220.[50]

i. USAID's PFMRAF

USAID's pre-financing assessment tool, the PFMRAF, began as an attempt by the USAID Chief Financial Officer to manage fiduciary risk inherent in directly financing development activities implemented by assistance recipient governments. It was

[48] Automated Directives System (ADS) ch 220, containing the policy directives and required procedures for determining the suitability of using partner country systems for implementation of USAID-funded assistance, was initially titled 'Use of Reliable Partner Country Systems for Direct Management and Implementation of Assistance', https://pdf.usaid.gov/pdf_docs/PDACS875.pdf. See also J Glennie, 'Localising aid: can using local actors strengthen them?' (England, Overseas Development Institute, 2012) 35, available at www.odi.org/sites/odi.org.uk/files/odi-assets/publications-opinion-files/7789.pdf.

[49] The first two versions of ADS ch 220 were titled 'Use of Reliable Partner Country Systems for Direct Management and Implementation of Assistance'. The third version of ADS ch 220 changed the title in 2014 to 'Use and Strengthening of Reliable Partner Government Systems for Implementation of Direct Assistance'.

[50] Located at www.usaid.gov/sites/default/files/documents/1868/220.pdf.

developed in late 2010 and early 2011 as a two-stage inquiry to facilitate accountability and due diligence for USAID Missions prior to disbursing funds to partner governments that could allow USAID to track its funding to actual costs incurred by the implementing government entity or ministry.[51]

a. PFMRAF Process

The PFMRAF consists of two stages: the Stage 1 Rapid Appraisal yields a country-level, relatively quick and arguably general portrait of the partner government's Public Financial Management (PFM) environment while the Stage 2 Risk Assessment is an institutional-level examination using transaction sampling and other in-depth analyses of the particular funding flow involved in a prospective USAID-financed G2G development activity. The processes and tools used in the PFMRAF are contained in the PFMRAF Manual[52] and are intended to manage USAID and the partner government's resources, expectations and relationships through an initial, high-level screening prior to a more in-depth transaction-level assessment.

The Stage 1 Rapid Appraisal, as its name suggests, is intended to allow a USAID Mission to make a determination after a few weeks' worth of dedicated effort by an internal, interdisciplinary team about whether to engage in further deliberations with the partner government about G2G financing.[53] The Stage 1 Rapid Appraisal relies in part on existing reports such as those produced through the Public Expenditure and Financial Accountability (PEFA) assessment and the Methodology for Assessing Procurement Systems (MAPS). The findings and conclusions from these reports are then corroborated by first-hand interviews with a variety of stakeholders both within and external to the partner government. Stage 1 of the PFMRAF results in a report primarily consisting of answers to a 40-question checklist and a recommendation either to proceed or not to proceed to the Stage 2 Risk Assessment for particular activities being designed. If proceeding to Stage 2 is recommended, the Rapid Appraisal report will also identify areas of the partner government's PFM system involved in potential USAID-financed activities that warrant further examination because of particular risk concerns identified in the Stage 1 inquiry.

At the heart of the PFMRAF is the Stage 2 Risk Assessment Questionnaire, which is a 9-section, 86-question a la carte menu of PFM areas from which individual activity designers are to develop customised survey tools based on which questions are relevant and material to the particular activities, entities and funding flows involved in the development project's design. From the answers to the customised questionnaire,

[51] See USAID, 'USAID FORWARD Implementation & Procurement Reform Achievements' (5 May 2011) available at pdf.usaid.gov/pdf_docs/PDACS876.pdf.

[52] USAID, 'Public Financial Management Risk Assessment Framework (PFMRAF) Manual – A Mandatory Reference for ADS Chapter 220' (USAID, 2014) available at www.usaid.gov/sites/default/files/documents/1868/220mae.pdf.

[53] According to the PFMRAF Manual, the Stage 1 Rapid Appraisal is 'designed to answer key fundamental questions: • What is the overall PFM operating environment in the partner country? • Are public accountability institutions and related support mechanisms sufficiently viable to support G2G? • Is the level of fiduciary risk manageable enough to justify a more in-depth Stage 2 Risk Assessment(s)?' (ibid 8).

the Stage 2 report will include a risk mitigation plan by which the risks identified by the Risk Assessment questionnaire are to be treated in the G2G activity, if approved.[54] Depending on the status of the overall project in which the G2G activities are being designed, either the G2G activity, including the risk mitigation plan, is approved as part of the project appraisal process or the project appraisal document is amended to include the Authorization for the Use of Partner Government Systems (AUPGS) if the non-G2G activities are designed and approved before the G2G activities are fully designed.

While not technically independent of the project appraisal document, the AUPGS identifies the formal risk mitigation requirements that are either incorporated into the activity design or made part of the financing agreement.[55] While the AUPGS and its risk mitigation plan can identify PFM capacity-development and strengthening needs, the dedicated purpose and primary function of the Stage 2 assessment and report, as well as the AUPGS and risk mitigation plan, are to document USAID's due diligence and determine what treatment(s) will be used to mitigate the identified risks and weaknesses sufficiently to adequately account for the partner government's expenditures of USAID funding. Because such treatment is inherently a component of both the project design and the resulting financing agreement, USAID's policies and procedures for G2G financing were updated in July 2014 to more closely align the PFMRAF with USAID's project design guidance.[56]

Because of political concerns that USAID's IPR and LS intentions to increase the amount of financing directly to partner governments for development activities could result in unwanted degradation of democracy, human rights and governance (DRG) trends in recipient countries, the PFMRAF includes elements in both Stages 1 and 2 designed to specifically examine what effect, if any, the proposed G2G financing may have on the DRG conditions in the recipient country.[57] This 'democracy credit check' evolved from a go/no-go determination to a parallel 'DRG Review' process grafted onto the PFMRAF processes whereby Missions examine what mitigation measures, if any, USAID may employ to keep its financing from bolstering the anti-democratic, authoritarian and repressive actions of certain entities in certain regimes. As with the

[54] On p 16, the PFMRAF Manual notes: 'As a U.S. Government agency, USAID's risk appetite is necessarily conservative. That stance has implications on USAID's risk appetite, measurement and treatment. A deeply conservative stance removes the possibility of "toleration" of a risk. Instead, all risks are "treated" even if the treatment is non-intrusive and not staff intensive. The best example of non-intrusive and non-staff intensive risk treatment is an ex post audit with follow up to recover unallowable costs. The audit can be contracted out, even to a partner government agency if the risk assessment says that agency is competent and independent. Accordingly, USAID's conservative posture will drive the range of treatment, ranging from risk monitoring, to transfer, to termination. It will not include "toleration" or "acceptance." This contrasts with other organizations whose minimum risk posture may be acceptance or toleration of low impact, low probability risk events'. ibid 16.

[55] ADS 220.3.4.1 instructs that, 'The AUPGS is an addendum to the PAD ["Project Appraisal Document"] which documents the due diligence requirements and associated fiduciary risk mitigation plan for using PGS ["Partner Government Systems"]. The AUPGS establishes USAID's and the partner government's fiduciary risk management strategy and guidelines for the life of the respective project'. See n 50.

[56] See eg Recommendation 1 of GAO-15-377 (n 23).

[57] The procedures developed for the PFMRAF DRG review are intended to prevent USAID financing directly to governments from enabling those governments to erode democracy, human rights and governing accountability at the expense of their people.

PFMRAF itself, which also contains questions concerning public accountability and governance, the DRG Review process is intended to lead to a graduated approach whereby additional levels of granularity are examined as projects become more detailed in their design.[58]

Shortly after the creation of the PFMRAF by USAID, the US Congress included a new provision in its fiscal year (FY) 2012 annual appropriations law to require an assessment of partner government systems for direct G2G financing.[59] The law has since been expanded to include additional pre-financing requirements that must be met by a partner government before USAID may disburse funds under G2G arrangements.[60] The original statutory requirements applicable to FY 2012 and FY 2013 appropriations[61] to be used for G2G financing were relatively straightforward: an assessment must be performed to determine that the implementing agency or ministry receiving assistance has the systems required to manage such assistance and any identified vulnerabilities or weaknesses of such agency or ministry have been addressed.[62] Of particular note was the statute's statement that 'no level of acceptable fraud is assumed'.[63] Whether or not this phrasing actually means such, many within USAID understood the Section 7031 statutory language to be ratification by Congress of the PFMRAF Manual statements that USAID's risk appetite was conservative to the point of obviating fiduciary risk tolerance or acceptance.[64]

Since FY 2014, Section 7031 has retained all of the requirements from the 2012 and 2013 appropriation acts but also acquired three additional pre-financing requirements.[65] One new requirement was that 'the government of the recipient country is taking steps to publicly disclose on an annual basis its national budget, to include income and expenditures'.[66] Also added was a requirement that the recipient government is in compliance with the principles elsewhere in the Act that penalise recipient governments which do not exempt US foreign assistance from recipient government taxation.[67] Finally, the requirements from FY 2014 to the present have included a determination that 'the recipient government is taking steps to protect the rights of civil society, including freedom of association and assembly'.[68] As preconditions to any G2G financing by

[58] See ADS 220.3.2 (n 50).

[59] See s 7031 of Public Law No 112-74 (FY12).

[60] See eg s 7031 of Public Law No 113-76 (FY14), Public Law No 113-235 (FY15) and Public Law No 114-113 (FY16).

[61] The FY 2013 Appropriations Act carried over the FY 2012 Appropriations Act requirements via a continuing resolution in lieu of an Appropriation Act.

[62] Other requirements in FY 2012 s 7031 included that the recipient agency or ministry employs and utilises staff with the necessary technical, financial and management capabilities and has adopted competitive procurement policies and systems; and that there are effective monitoring and evaluation systems in place to ensure that such assistance is used for its intended purposes. The statute also expressed a preference for cost-based assistance and required special notification to Congress of any cost-based G2G assistance over USD 10 million.

[63] s 7031 of Public Law No 112-74 (FY12) (a)(1)(A)(iv).

[64] PFMRAF Manual (n 52) 16.

[65] By its own terms, s 7031 in each Appropriation Act applies only to the fiscal-year specific funds appropriated by that Act.

[66] (a)(1)(A)(v) in FY14 & 15, (a)(1)(A)(vi) in FY16.

[67] (a)(1)(B) in FY14-16.

[68] (a)(1)(E) in FY14-16.

the USG, these new requirements have been fulfilled by an interagency determination process led by the US Department of State. This is largely due to the USG-wide aspect of the determinations required about the recipient government, and in part due to the fact that other USG agencies such as the Centers for Disease Control (under the Department of Health and Human Services) have also engaged in direct financing of partner governments. Consequently, consistency and efficiency have consolidated some of the US government's G2G assessment requirements while the more technical, implementing entity or ministry-specific assessments of capacity remain under the control and responsibility of individual US government agencies.[69]

The end result of the statutory developments from 2012 regarding G2G assistance is that the number of countries in which USAID engages in G2G financing has plateaued and, within those countries, the number of government partner entities does not appear to have greatly expanded or is likely to do so in the near future.[70]

b. Roles and Responsibilities of Key USAID Actors

The renaissance of direct government financing by USAID was led by the Chief Financial Officer within USAID's Management Bureau. Partly because the IPR initiative had been originally placed by Administrator Rajiv Shah under the leadership of the USAID General Counsel and partly because the new form of engagement with partner governments was strewn with the legal and accountability pitfalls noted above, the initial generation and use of the PFMRAF, ADS 220 and G2G activities were primarily performed by field-based lawyers and accountants.[71]

In 2014, USAID revised ADS 220 to clarify the roles of other Mission personnel in G2G assistance, including programme officers, contracting officers and technical officers. While ADS 220 had previously noted the conduct of the PFMRAF processes involved a 'whole of Mission' approach and exhorted Missions to form interdisciplinary teams for the endeavour, the reality was that the necessary level of risk comfort,

[69] One of the interesting differences between the PFMRAF and s 7031 assessment requirements is that the PFMRAF places greater emphasis on fiduciary risks while s 7031 appears to require assessment of the implementing entity's level of technical capacity and suitability for purposes that the PFMRAF is not designed to measure directly.

[70] In the State Department's 5 October 2016 determination, 42 countries met the three FY14-16 eligibility prongs of s 7031, which has been actually reduced to 38 countries eligible for new G2G financing after 12 October 2017. See eg USAID, 'FY 2018 Statutory Checklists' (2018) 11, available at www.usaid.gov/sites/default/files/documents/1876/200sbs.pdf (referencing an interagency assessment process). According to the Congressional Research Service, 35 USAID Missions had completed a Stage 1 Rapid Appraisal by 2015, of which 27 had continued to Stage 2 assessments. Congressional Research Service, 'U.S. Agency for International Development (USAID): Background, Operations, and Issues' (2015) 46, available at https://www.everycrsreport.com/files/20150721_R44117_69c9e1bd162abe4a9a6fd338ee3730f009436c6d.pdf. Of those countries in which Stage 2 assessments were being performed, there were 147 Stage 2 assessments done as of 2015. ibid. This was well short of the number of countries in which USAID intended to focus its USAID Forward efforts in 2013, which were 79 (www.usaid.gov/usaidforward/usaid-forward-draft/frequently-asked-questions). USAID works in well over 100 countries worldwide (www.usaid.gov/who-we-are).

[71] See eg USAID OIG, Report No 9-000-13-003-S (n 25) 5-6 (finding of lack of sufficient oversight by the Office of the Chief Financial Officer Risk Management Team over Stage 2 Assessments).

knowledge and confidence were most often found among the financial and legal personnel.[72] It was only after a policy emphasis change and Mission experience in developing adequately-defined agreements and activity designs that the technical and programmatic expertise was recognised as a necessary feature of the G2G form of engagement.[73]

Ironically, the expansion of these G2G teams and the corresponding support of policy guidance led to a recurring complaint and criticism that G2G assistance is highly labour intensive and creates management burdens for Missions above what they experience when using contractors or grantees to implement development activities.[74]

c. Types of G2G Assistance and Funding/Implementing

As noted above, USAID has essentially two forms of G2G financing mechanisms at its disposal: project assistance and non-project assistance. Non-project assistance involves the disbursement from the USG for a partner government's benefit without regard to tracking or attribution to particular costs or expenditures. On the other hand, project assistance is generally the method of reimbursing partner governments for actual or estimated costs.[75] As a general matter, both programme assistance and G2G project assistance envisioned by ADS 220 arguably involve the use of partner country systems. These two types of disbursement to a partner government directly from USAID can also be distinguished from USAID's old, disfavoured form of project assistance involving partner governments described above, Host Country Contracting, in which a partner government is required to follow USAID's own procurement and other procedural rules and USAID typically pays the partner government's contractor without any disbursement to the partner government.

In passing Section 7031, Congress sought to more closely regulate USAID's direct disbursement of funds to partner governments, affecting both non-project assistance (budget and sector support) as well as the new project form of G2G assistance for which the PFMRAF had been developed.[76] Because the statute applies only to 'direct government-to-government assistance', HCC project assistance, which USAID's aid effectiveness aspirations had no interest in reviving, was left unaffected by Section 7031.[77] In passing Section 7031, Congress also expressed a clear

[72] See eg USAID, 'The Capable Partners Learning Agenda on Local Organization Capacity Development' (Learning Agenda)13 (describing the gap between 'program culture' and 'compliance culture' in USAID) available at https://usaidlearninglab.org/sites/default/files/resource/files/Executive%20Summary_Learning%20Agenda.pdf.

[73] *cf* Recommendation 5 of OIG Report No 9-000-13-S (n 25) 3, with FN 14 of GAO-15-377 (n 23).

[74] See s 2.23 of 'Program Assistance' policy paper (n 42), noting G2G is management intensive due to the very wide-ranging activities USAID management is required to perform – from policy dialogue, to general programming of financial resources, to monitoring. See also Learning Agenda (n 72) 13, describing IPR/LS as labour-intensive.

[75] See eg 'Program Assistance' policy paper (n 42).

[76] See eg FY12 Appropriations Act, s 7031 (a)(2), which notes that Congress considers G2G assistance to include both the project form and non-project form, the latter of which was already for decades subject to its own statutory requirements such as those found in FY12 Appropriations Act, s 7026, titled 'Separate Accounts'.

[77] FY12 Appropriations Act, s 7031 (a)(1).

policy preference for the project form of G2G assistance.[78] Moreover, the fiscal year 2014 and subsequent versions of Section 7031 have included a prohibition on using US disbursements to pay for international financial institution debt, one of the most frequent components of programme assistance.[79] While none of the above restrictions are themselves fatal to non-project assistance, USAID's use of any form of non-project assistance, in the form of programme assistance, budget support or cash transfers, has not substantially increased as a result of its USAID Forward efforts to increase direct financing of partner governments.[80]

Instead of increasing budget support or sector-specific programmes financed on other than a cost basis, USAID has devoted most of its G2G efforts since the inception of USAID Forward to project assistance financing mechanisms. The two primary modalities of G2G project assistance are cost reimbursement agreements and fixed amount reimbursement agreements (FARAs).[81] The primary distinction between the two modalities is that cost reimbursement involves USAID paying actual costs incurred by the partner government implementing entity and payments based on estimated costs that do not change based on the actual costs for producing outputs or their associated milestones. While not completely analogous to different contract types, the fixed amount reimbursement mechanism is conceptually based on the idea of a fixed-price contract whereby payment is expressly made for a completed development output rather than the component inputs to the development output.

While the FARA mechanism had been around for decades, it had been limited to tangible, easily identifiable and verifiable types of outputs such as small-scale construction (schools) or textbooks prior to IPR, the PFMRAF, and its incorporation into ADS 220.[82] When IPR placed a 30 per cent funding target on G2G (and local NGO) financing, the use of FARAs expanded to include outcomes and milestones rather than just the traditional outputs. This was partly due to a perception that, like a fixed-price contract, FARA financing shifts enough of the fiduciary risk to the partner government, and that rigorous, comprehensive and potentially expensive mitigation of accounting and other procedural risks identified in the PFMRAF assessments was largely unnecessary. This interpretation was further bolstered by the ADS 220 policy exempting

[78] See eg FY12 Appropriations Act, s 7031 (a)(1)(B)(ii), which states 'such assistance should be made on a cost-reimbursable basis'. See also FY12 Appropriations Act, s 7031 (a)(2), which exempts project G2G assistance up to USD 10,000,000 from further specific consultation and notification requirements. The effect of this is that Congress clearly indicated it wants to review and be involved in all forms of non-project G2G assistance while it abstains from the same level of scrutiny of project G2G assistance under the USD 10,000,000 threshold.

[79] See eg FY14 Appropriations Act, S7031 (a)(6) ('None of the funds made available by this Act may be used for any foreign country for debt service payments owed by any country to any international financial institution').

[80] See eg GAO-15-377 (n 23) Table 2 at 19 (NPA agreements were less than 3% of G2G agreements randomly reviewed by GAO).

[81] ibid.

[82] The FARA mechanism was treated relatively succinctly in an attachment to USAID, 'ADS Chapter 317 Procurement under Fixed Amount Reimbursement Activities' (USAID, partial revision 6 October 2011) available at www.usaid.gov/sites/default/files/documents/1868/317.pdf, with the guidance unchanged since before 2000 (www.usaid.gov/sites/default/files/documents/1868/3176s.pdf).

FARA mechanisms under USD 10 million from the PFMRAF Stage 2 assessment.[83] However, official Agency thinking on the subject has subsequently recognised that shifting fiduciary risk may have inverse effects on programmatic risk.[84] As a result, the official guidance on the use of the FARA mechanism, as updated in 2014 to align the mechanism with the PFMRAF, provides what greater flexibility the Agency's overall accountability footprint allows, and captures best practices learned from recent Agency experience by placing the guidance in ADS 220.[85]

The other project assistance G2G financing mechanism, cost reimbursement, in which USAID reimburses the partner government for its actual implementation costs, was new in the sense that USAID lacked any detailed policy guidance for it when IPR began.[86] Arguably, the PFMRAF had been designed primarily for the cost reimbursement financing mechanism in that the PFMRAF assesses the ability of another government's financial management system to track and account for costs in accordance with USAID funding rules as expressed in the financing agreement. Additionally, the cost reimbursement financing mechanism is how USAID primarily finances all of its other implementing partners under contracts and grants with the private sector, multilateral public international organisations and other sovereign, bilateral donors. Moreover, cost reimbursement G2G could be argued to be better suited to the relative financial positions of a G2G development assistance context: payment based on costs generally results in the financing party, in this case, USAID, absorbing more of the performance risk than its generally less solvent development assistance recipient government partners. Finally, accounting for actual costs and expenditures is how the US and other governments generally track their finances, so cost reimbursement G2G financing would arguably be the most collaborative and tightest form of public sector development implementation. However, despite the familiarity and these advantages, the mechanism remains less commonly used by USAID than the FARA financing mechanism in USAID's G2G financing.[87]

ii. GAO and Inspector General Reports on G2G and PFMRAF

USAID's aid effectiveness efforts in public financial management and public procurement under IPR and LS have been reviewed twice by the US Government Accountability

[83] The exception for a FARA from the PFMRAF Stage 2 does not obviate the need for an assessment that complies with the applicable Appropriation Act's s 7031(a) assessment. Additionally, the current version of ADS ch 220 states that the FARA exception to Stage 2 expired beginning in FY18. See ADS 220.3.3.1 b.(2) (n 50).

[84] See eg Local Systems Framework (n 11) 13 (recognising that decision-making based on risk assessment requires a comparative risk analysis among different types of risk).

[85] See USAID, 'Government to Government Implementing and Funding Mechanisms Fixed Amount Reimbursement – A Mandatory Reference for ADS Chapter 220' (USAID, new edn, 28 July 2014) available at www.usaid.gov/sites/default/files/documents/1868/220mah.pdf.

[86] The first two versions of ADS ch 220 mentioned the existence of the cost reimbursement mechanism but provided no detailed explanation or guidance on how it was to be used. The third version of ADS ch 220 added a mandatory reference on its use. See USAID, 'Government to Government (G2G) Implementing and Funding Mechanisms Cost Reimbursement Projects – A Mandatory Reference for ADS Chapter 220 (USAID, new edn, 28 July 2014) available at www.usaid.gov/sites/default/files/documents/1868/220mag.pdf.

[87] See GAO-15-377 (n 23) fn 28 (FARA more commonly used than cost reimbursement).

Office (GAO)[88] (the USG's external auditor) and twice by the USAID Office of Inspector General (OIG)[89] with a third review by the OIG in 2016 for which a report has not yet been issued. These reviews have generally found USAID's policies either adequate or having been sufficiently improved since inception, but have also consistently noted flaws in implementation and/or oversight.

According to the GAO, 'USAID's policies guiding the processes that missions follow to plan, implement, and monitor and evaluate G2G assistance generally reflect an international consensus on how best to achieve development outcomes as well as accepted accountability standards'.[90] However, the GAO noted that implementation of those policies was lacking and recommended the following actions:

1. develop an action plan to improve the timeliness of risk assessments so that these assessments can better inform project planning;
2. develop an action plan to ensure that monitoring and evaluation (M&E) plans for G2G assistance activities incorporate risk mitigation measures;
3. disseminate information to missions regarding best practices for coordinating risk assessments with other donors;
4. identify the factors contributing to late submission of required audits and develop a strategy to improve on-time audit submission and follow-up; and
5. develop and disseminate guidance on assessing the effects of G2G assistance on partner-country capacity, ownership and sustainability, including through the identification of indicators and evaluation approaches.[91]

Similarly, the USAID OIG noted initial weaknesses in USAID's policy implementation without faulting the overall conceptual framework of the PFMRAF. Generally, both USAID's OIG and the GAO have noted weaknesses in implementing G2G guidance, though, not expressly, any inherent weaknesses in the G2G modality itself.[92]

While USAID has expressed an interest in pursuing a strategy that both uses and strengthens partner government procurement systems, the degree to which the Agency will be able to distinguish between the two in practice remains unclear.[93] What remains to be seen is whether USAID's approach to the aid effectiveness principle of using partner government systems to implement development activities actually leads to increased capacity or system strengthening and, if so, whether the approach is worth pursuing further or expanding.[94]

[88] GAO reports (n 24 and n 25).

[89] USAID OIG reports (n 25).

[90] GAO-15-377 (n 23) 27.

[91] ibid 28. At the time of publication, Recommendations 1 and 3 have been closed through subsequent Agency action.

[92] See eg Congressional Research Service (n 70) 46.

[93] See Local Systems Framework (n 11) 5:'USAID is committed to employing all of our development resources to strengthen and use local systems'.

[94] See eg Recommendation 5 of GAO-15-377 (n 23): 'develop and disseminate guidance on assessing the effects of G2G assistance on partner-country capacity, ownership, and sustainability, including through the identification of indicators and evaluation approaches'.

IV. Domestic Preferencing Requirements, Aid Untying and Source and Nationality Reforms

With respect to the second and third forms of procurement noted in the introduction, USAID's own procurement and the promotion of local sources within it have undergone significant changes in recent times.[95]

A. Domestic Preferencing Requirements

The evolution of domestic preferencing requirements applicable to US foreign assistance is not linear or easy to track. Prior to 1961, US government-financed foreign aid procurements were untied. However, from the time of the authorisation of the Foreign Assistance Act of 1961 (hereinafter sometimes referred to as 'the Act')[96] to the present day, tied aid policies applicable to US foreign assistance provide a clear indication of some of the competing and some would say 'dissonant'[97] objectives of foreign aid.[98]

The Act states as a principal objective of US foreign policy 'the encouragement and sustained support of the people of developing countries … and to build the economic, political, and social institutions which will improve the quality of their lives'.[99] Although not stated prominently in the Act, certain administrative provisions evidence political support for providing economic opportunities, including subsidies, to US domestic organisations to provide goods and services financed by the foreign aid budget. Because of a balance of payments crisis in the late 1950s and early 1960s, the US Congress included in its passage of the Act a strong preference for procurement from the US unless the President determined that the benefits of less costly procurement from outside of

[95] President Donald Trump has expressed his intention to change USG policy on domestic preferencing via his issuance of the Buy American/Hire American Executive Order on 27 April 2017. See www.whitehouse.gov/the-press-office/2017/04/18/presidential-executive-order-buy-american-and-hire-american. The impact of such Order on domestic preferencing as it relates to foreign aid is yet to be determined.

[96] 22 U.S.C. § 2151 ff (Public Law 87-195 as amended) (the 'Act').

[97] The following Congressional testimony by Former USAID Administrator James Atwood in 1996 demonstrates the significance of domestic preferencing to explain how US foreign assistance benefits the US economy:

> USAID has particular importance in expanding new markets for the U.S. economy.… Most of the growth in U.S. exports continues to come from countries in the developing world and countries in transition from state-dominated economies to free market economies.… This growth supported roughly 1.9 million jobs in the United States. That translates into over 4 million jobs for Americans. Developing countries are particularly good customers for our high-value exports.…

(Cited in HV Milner and DH Tingley, 'The Political Economy of U.S. Foreign Aid: American Legislators and the Domestic Politics of Aid' (2010) 22 *Economics & Politics* 200, 204.

[98] This chapter attempts to discuss the general rule regarding preferences in US foreign assistance and does not address in detail certain specific types of tied aid provisions enshrined in law, such as manufactured vehicles, pharmaceuticals, food aid, engineering and construction services and agricultural commodities, each of which possesses special preferencing rules.

[99] s 101 of the Foreign Assistance Act, 22 U.S.C. § 2354 ff.

the US outweighed the economic harm of untying. Specifically, Section 604(a) at the time read as follows:

> Funds made available under this Act may be used for *procurement outside the United States only if* the President determines that *such procurement will not result in adverse effects upon the economy of the United States* or the industrial mobilization base, with special reference to any areas of labor surplus or to the net position of the United States in its balance of payments with the rest of the world, which outweigh the economic or other advantages to the United States of less costly procurement outside the United States, *and only if the price of any commodity procured in bulk is lower than the market price prevailing in the United States at the time of procurement*, adjusted for differences in the cost of transportation to destination, quality, and terms of payment. [emphasis added].

From 1961 until 1990, USAID operated under a default US-only system of procurement preferences with certain ad hoc flexibilities to purchase from non-US providers as deemed necessary in accordance with the parameters of Section 604(a).

In 1990, in another wave of domestic preferencing, the US State Department issued a cable known as the Buy American Policy of 1990 to further tie procurements to the US only, categorically excepting the recipient country from eligibility, except for small-scale procurements too small to attract the interest of US contractors.

Despite the general trend towards the tying of US foreign aid during this early period, Congress did provide some flexibility to executive agencies regarding domestic preferencing to carry out foreign aid programmes. In 1991, Congress added Section 496 (Development Fund for Africa) to the Act,[100] rendering Section 604(a) of the Act inapplicable to procurements funded out of the Development Assistance and Global Health accounts for activities targeted to Sub-Saharan Africa.[101] Specifically, Section 496 provided as follows:

> (n)(4) PROCUREMENT OF GOODS AND SERVICES. – In order to allow the assistance authorized by this section to be furnished as effectively and expeditiously as possible, section 604(a) of this Act, and similar provisions relating to the procurement of goods and services, shall not apply with respect to goods and services procured for use in carrying out this section ….

In essence, Section 496 provided USAID the ability to expand eligibility[102] for Development Assistance and Global Health account-funded procurements in Sub-Saharan Africa to all non-foreign policy-restricted countries, a substantial step in the way of untying US foreign assistance towards the subcontinent.

Shortly after the passage of Section 496, in 1992, Congress again sought to tighten Section 604(a) of the Act to further restrict non-US procurements beyond the original 1961 version. This effort resulted from concerns expressed about using US foreign aid

[100] 22 U.S.C. § 2293.

[101] The US budget includes a number of distinct foreign aid accounts, including those titled 'Development Assistance', 'Global Health', 'International Disaster Assistance' and the 'Economic Support Fund', to name a few.

[102] Other foreign and disaster assistance legal authorities provide additional and parallel flexibility regarding procurement and other requirements and restrictions. eg s 104(c)(4) of the Act provides the legal authority for the President (delegated to the USAID Administrator) to notwithstand any other provision of law that restricts assistance to foreign countries for certain types of health programming.

to subsidise German and Japanese vehicle manufacturers.[103] Early drafts bills conceived by the Senate Appropriations Committee attempted to create a rigid scheme that would have tied foreign aid procurements almost exclusively to US providers. But after both the House of Representatives Appropriations Committee and the Senate Appropriations Committee convened in 'Conference',[104] the proposed new Section 604(a) legislation (see immediately below) that eventually resulted was similar language to that found in Public Law 102–511 (also passed in 1992) relating to Support for the Economic and Democratic Development of the Independent States of the Former Soviet Union, which became codified as Foreign Assistance Act Section 498B(h).[105]

The final 1992 (and current) version of Section 604 as signed into law reads as follows:

> (a)(1) LIMITATIONS ON PROCUREMENT OUTSIDE THE UNITED STATES. - Funds made available for assistance under this Act may be used by the President for procurement—
>
> (A) *only in the United States, the recipient country, or developing countries; or*
> (B) *in any other country but only if—*
>
> (i) *the provision of such assistance requires commodities or services of a type that are not produced in and available for purchase in any country specified in subparagraph (A); or*
> (ii) the President determines, on a case-by-case basis, *that procurement in such other country is necessary—*
>
> (I) *to meet unforeseen circumstances*, such as emergency situations, where it is important to permit procurement in a country not specified in subparagraph (A); or
> (II) *to promote efficiency in the use of United States foreign assistance resources, including to avoid impairment of foreign assistance objectives.*

[103] See Floor Debate relating to discussion of Senate Amendment No 2712 (to strengthen 'Buy American' provisions of Foreign Assistance Act) to House Resolution 5368 (1993 Foreign Operations Appropriations Bill). In addition to ss 604(a), 496, and 498B(h) of the Act, the Congress passed other domestic preferencing requirements covering specific types of procurements, including the infrastructure services (s 604[g] of the Act), agricultural commodities (s 604(e) of the Act), pharmaceuticals (FAA s 604[X]) and motor vehicles (s 636[i] of the Act), to name a few. Known by USAID as 'restricted commodities', these procurements follow special rules that can be waived under certain conditions.

[104] 'Conferencing' as known in the US Congress is a procedural step whereby the respective committees of the lower house (the House of Representatives) and the upper house (the Senate) meet to reconcile competing legislative proposals and then take back to their respective chambers to approve before sending to the President one 'Conferenced' bill for signature into law.

[105] s 498B(h) of the Act reads as follows:

> PROCUREMENT RESTRICTIONS. - Funds made available for assistance under this chapter may be used for procurement—
>
> (1) in the United States, the independent states of the former Soviet Union, or a developing country; or
> (2) in any other country but only if—
>
> (A) the provision of such assistance requires commodities or services of a type that are not produced in and available for purchase in any country specified in paragraph (1); or
> (B) the President determines, on a case-by-case basis, that procurement in such other country is necessary—
>
> (i) to meet unforeseen circumstances, such as emergency situations, where it is important to permit procurement in a country not specified in paragraph (1), or
> (ii) to promote efficiency in the use of United States foreign assistance resources, including to avoid impairment of foreign assistance objectives.

(2) For purposes of this subsection, the term 'developing countries' shall not include advanced developing countries. (emphasis added)

Despite the intentions of the Senate Appropriations Committee in 1992, the eventual language of the Act resulted in providing USAID with certain additional flexibilities not included in the original 1961 version. Thus, although the Senate Appropriations Committee originally intended to create a default fully tied aid scheme, the final outcome is one that expresses certain preferences not so dissimilar from the policy followed by USAID from 1961 to the early 1990s while providing additional flexibility (eg procuring from worldwide sources to 'avoid impairment of foreign assistance objectives') that did not exist in statute up until this point.

Based upon the new Section 604(a), in 1996, USAID promulgated an external regulation at 22 C.F.R. Part 228 (titled 'Rules on Source, Origin and Nationality for Commodities and Services Financed by USAID', hereinafter sometimes referred to as 'Regulation 28').[106] This new regulation set forth detailed policies, rules and procedures to operationalise Section 604(a) and other domestic preferencing requirements applicable to USAID. Regulation 28 also included reference to a USAID Geographic Code Book to establish groups of countries deemed eligible to compete for specific USAID procurements. Every USAID activity financing discrete procurements would thereafter include an 'Authorized Geographic Code' to indicate eligibility to provide goods and services under the activity. The primary Authorized Geographic Codes at that time were as follows: (1) the US (Authorized Geographic Code '000'); (2) non-advanced developing countries excluding the partner country (Authorized Geographic Code '941'); and (3) any country excluding foreign policy restricted countries (Authorized Geographic Code '935').

Although USAID now possessed clear statutory authority under Section 604(a) of the Act to expand the universe of eligible countries for procurement to include the US, the partner country, and non-advanced developing countries, due to political sensitivities in the early 1990s and a continuing unfavourable balance of payments status, the Agency retained its Buy America Policy of 1990 via its internal policy and regulations so that the default Authorized Geographic Code up until 2011 was 000 (US only), even to the exclusion of local sources within the partner country, except for small-scale procurements.

B. USAID Forward and the Localisation of Aid

In the early years of President Barack Obama's Administration starting in 2010, the Agency began to take significant and specific steps to walk the walk on its previous commitments under the Paris Declaration on Aid Effectiveness and its progeny. Such steps included providing support to local actors (partner country governments, the private sector and non-governmental and civil society organisations) via establishing direct financing relationships and providing support to strengthen such local organisations as going concerns.

[106] See www.gpo.gov/fdsys/pkg/CFR-1997-title22-vol1/pdf/CFR-1997-title22-vol1-part228.pdf.

One concrete step to further its commitments under USAID Forward was to evolve its policy on tied aid. In 2010, USAID issued a substantially revised external regulation operationalising these requirements and corresponding internal regulations to create a default regime that served to 'untie' procurements of goods and services.

The Agency pursued a revision to its former 'Source, Origin and Nationality' rule at 22 C.F.R. Part 228 to encourage greater local participation in the implementation of development activities financed by USAID procurements. This revision aligned its rule with the statutory authority in Section 604(a) of the Act to create a default pool of eligible countries for procurement to include the US, the partner country, and any non-advanced developing country (referred to in USAID-speak as Authorized Geographic Code 937) as measured based upon the World Bank's per capita income statistics. Therefore, since 2011, all USAID requests for proposals posted on the USG's portal for procurement opportunities (www.fbo.gov) at the very least should include a reference to Code 937. In certain instances, the Agency may expand the list of eligible countries to Code 935 (worldwide).

The practical impact of expanding procurement opportunities is that local and regional companies may submit bids and win contracts, delivering best value in the following ways: (1) generating revenue to support local economies and promote economic growth in the countries where USAID operates; (2) tapping into the expertise of entities that possess a greater understanding of local context that may give them comparative advantage versus international firms in implementing USAID programmes; (3) giving local actors the opportunity to build upon or develop technical, financial and other expertise as an organisation to meet development challenges so as to position some entities to conduct such work in the future, whether externally funded from donors or via internal governmental or private sector-funded resources; and (4) delivering goods and services at lower costs compared with international firms due to the ease of mobilisation, reduction in international recruitment and reduced travel costs.

In its 2011 Peer Review of the United States, the Development Assistance Committee of the Organisation for Economic Cooperation and Development (OECD/DAC) acknowledged USAID's significant reforms to untie aid, noting a decrease in tied aid from 68 per cent in 2005 to 32 per cent in 2009.[107] The OECD/DAC Peer Review also recommended:

> To get the best value for money, and strengthen the capacity of local partners, the U.S. should further ensure that its bidding processes are open to non-US companies (in particular in Least Developed Countries and Highly Indebted Poor Countries) so that local companies truly benefit from the USAID procurement reform.

At the same time that USAID revised its external and internal regulations and policy regarding local and regional untying, USAID also revised significantly the existing policies and procedures to facilitate more direct funding relationships (typically via grants versus contracts) between USAID and local NGOs. The theory in a nutshell behind this

[107] OECD, 'OECD Development Assistance Peer Reviews: United States 2011' (Paris, OECD Publishing, 2013) 69, available at www.oecd.org/dac/peer-reviews/48434536.pdf.

approach to sustainable development is that by engaging more directly with local NGOs and supporting their organisational capacity to manage their affairs (financial, administrative and technical), such NGOs will represent the long-term presence in-country and will serve increasingly important roles within society long after USAID withdraws from the country.[108] Congress provided USAID with statutory authority to limit certain grant opportunities to local NGOs.[109] USAID engaged in a streamlining exercise to simplify the requirements imposed upon recipients of USAID grants (eg not requiring an Ethiopian NGO to comply with certain US requirements only applicable in a domestic US context, such as the Fair Labor Standards Act[110] which sets a mandatory minimum wage, overtime pay, recordkeeping and child labour standards).

C. Untying Recommendation and ADS Chapter 221

With the establishment of the 2001 Untying Recommendation, the OECD/DAC member countries agreed to the establishment of a WTO GPA-like non-discrimination provision whereby the DAC development partners would open up most of their Official Development Assistance (ODA)-funded procurement opportunities to contractors from other DAC countries on a *de jure* basis. Although the Recommendation is a non-binding, non-treaty 'gentleman's agreement', the USG (primarily through USAID as the lead USG agency that provides the lion's share of the USG ODA allocation) signed up to the 2001 Recommendation and issued internal Agency rules in its Automated Directives System (ADS) to operationalise the commitments made by the USG in signing up to the Recommendation.

ADS Chapter 221 requires the Agency to 'untie' (meaning open up procurement opportunities to virtually all countries) for certain covered contracts valued greater than 700,000 in Special Drawing Rights (SDRs)[111] executed in the Least Developed Countries (LDCs) or non-LDC Heavily Indebted Poor Countries (HIPCs). Covered categories for purposes of USAID compliance with the Untying Recommendation include the following:

- Capital projects (eg, transport, power, water).
- Capital equipment.
- Capital-related supplies and services.
- Discrete physical commodities.

Although this policy requires USAID to untie large capital assistance in LDCs and non-LDC HIPCs, ADS 221 is somewhat narrow in its application and does not apply to a significant portion of USAID funding. USAID may open up opportunities for other

[108] See USAID Local Systems Framework at www.usaid.gov/sites/default/files/documents/1870/LocalSystemsFramework.pdf for more information.

[109] See s 7077 of the 2012 Foreign Operations Appropriations Act, Public Law No 112-74.

[110] See 29 U.S.C. § 201, *et seq.*

[111] See www.imf.org/external/np/exr/facts/sdr.HTM for more information about SDRs. As of the time of writing, 1 SDR = USD 1.41 or EUR 1.24.

activities not covered under the Untying Recommendation on a programmatic, country, or case-by-case basis in accordance with its underlying legal and regulatory authorities. Some examples where USAID established worldwide eligibility to bid on and perform contracts include country reconstruction programmes in Iraq and Afghanistan as well as the Southeast Asian Tsunami reconstruction effort. However, despite opening up USAID procurement opportunities worldwide in those instances, the 2011 OECD/DAC Peer Review notes that US firms won 89 per cent of USAID untied contracts as required under ADS 221. This statistic provides support to those critical of untying efforts on the basis that *de jure* untying is not sufficient on its own as it does not in actuality lead to *de facto* untying and produce the attendant benefits of untying (greater efficiencies, cost savings etc).

V. USAID Efforts to Support Countries in Procurement Reform

Regarding the fourth form of procurement described in the introduction, USAID has made targeted, modest efforts to support countries in reforming their own procurement systems. The Foreign Assistance Act[112] and related legislation provide the general statutory authority for USAID to provide support to countries in strengthening public financial management (including public procurement).[113] For instance, Section 133 – Programs to Encourage Good Governance – notes that such activities shall include, to the extent appropriate, projects and activities that 'support the establishment of audit offices, inspectors general offices, third party monitoring of government procurement processes, and anti-corruption agencies'.[114]

Over the years, USAID has supported public procurement reform efforts, both through establishing 'global public goods' and by working at country level to provide technical assistance on a range of areas, from establishing organic procurement legislation to institutional capacity-development to supporting Public-Private partnership legal frameworks.[115] A few examples of such support efforts are described immediately below.

[112] 22 U.S.C. § 2151 ff.

[113] See eg s 102 of the Act (22 U.S.C. § 2151-1).

[114] A number of other references in the Act mention supporting public procurement in the developing world, including the following:

- s 104A(d)(1)(K)(viii) Assistance to Combat HIV/AIDS – 'assistance to facilitate widespread access to microbicides for HIV prevention, if safe and effective products become available, including financial and technical support for culturally appropriate introductory programs, procurement, distribution, logistics management, program delivery, acceptability studies, provider training, demand generation, and post-introduction monitoring'.
- s 104A(d)(6)(G)(iii) – 'encourage fair and transparent procurement practices among partner countries'.

[115] It warrants brief mention here that USAID support to developing countries to strengthen their own procurement systems is not necessarily motivated by the possibility that future USAID assistance can or will take the shape as direct G2G assistance, as discussed earlier in this chapter under the rubric of aid effectiveness. Rather, the main motivations for providing support to countries on procurement in any given instance are to strengthen governance, accountability and economic growth.

On global public goods, as extensively explained in chapter 9 in this collection, USAID has actively promoted and supported the work of the Methodology for the Assessment of Procurement Systems Working Group since 2004. USAID has also provided financial and technical support to the World Bank's Global Indicators Group to the implement the Benchmarking Public Procurement (BPP)[116] and Procuring Infrastructure Public-Private Partnerships[117] initiatives. Aligned with the World Bank's annual flagship Doing Business[118] report, the purpose of the BPP assessment is to capture the perspective of the private sector, civil society, academia etc over various aspects of a country's public procurement system, including the timeliness of procurement processes and the effectiveness of the complaint mechanism to challenge contract award decisions or other pre-award aspects of decisions made by procuring entities. The World Bank initially piloted the BPP assessment across 10 countries in 2015, expanded the survey to 77 countries in 2016, and 180 countries in 2017. The 2017 Doing Business report included an annex on public procurement and one possible significant result of the BPP initiative is the incorporation of public procurement as a permanent indicator to the overall Doing Business survey. The Procuring Infrastructure PPP report assesses country regulatory frameworks for procuring PPPs and identifies areas for potential reform 'to achieve more transparent, competitive, and efficient PPP procurement systems and where appropriate, increase private sector participation in infrastructure and service delivery'.[119]

At country level, USAID has assisted countries to implement new procurement laws and strengthen procurement regulatory bodies to fulfill their mandates. In Nigeria, since the early 2000s, USAID provided support to the Government of the Federal Republic of Nigeria to adopt its first Public Procurement Act. Signed into law by President Olusegun Obasanjo in 2007, the new procurement legislation replaced a motley collection of Treasury circulars and other guidance that provided immense opportunity for inconsistency, graft and inefficiency. As a federal republic with 36 sovereign States and a Federal Capital Territory with their own constitutionally-provided powers, Nigeria also sought to modernise its procurement legislation at the State level due to the decentralised form of government and the fact that much of the budget allocations and authority fell to the States. Under the Economic Governance Reform Project, USAID, along with the World Bank, the United Kingdom's Department for International Development, and the United Nations Development Programme supported the Federal Government in socialising States with a Model Procurement Code in hopes of eventual adoption. USAID supported nationwide workshops, training States on the principles of public procurement regulation and advising a select number of States, including Bauchi, on specific aspects of the draft legislation. Since that time, most of the 36 States have adopted their own procurement codes and have begun to develop institutional arrangements to handle the large procurement budgets under their authority.

[116] See https://bpp.worldbank.org/en/BPP-data.

[117] See https://bpp.worldbank.org.

[118] Launched in 2002, the World Bank Group's Doing Business project provides an objective measure of regulations applicable to SMEs across 190 economies. See www.doingbusiness.org for more information.

[119] See https://bpp.worldbank.org.

In Liberia, through its Governance and Economic Management Support Project, USAID provided years of support to the Government of Liberia, including the Public Procurement Concession Commission (PPCC) and a number of ministries, departments and agencies (MDAs) to comply with and implement the Public Procurement and Concessions Act of 2005 (revised in 2010). USAID/Liberia worked with MDAs to develop procurement plans (many for the first time), holding procurement clinics with both procurement officers and MDA senior officials to establish procurement plans jointly. USAID/Liberia provided tools to assist PPCC in monitoring implementing agencies' compliance with the law. USAID/Liberia also supported the development of a Handbook for Practitioners (Works, Consulting Services, Non-Consulting Services, Education, Health, ICT, Framework Contracting). The Handbook provides useful information for the benefit of procurement staff in carrying out their functions in accordance with the Public Procurement and Concessions Act and accompanying regulations. USAID/Liberia supported 14 MDAs in improving the quality of procurement documentation to create an audit trail. Such steps have helped to establish a culture of transparency and accountability in procurement.

In Pakistan, the Government of Pakistan (GOP) enacted a new law and regulatory body via the Public Procurement Regulatory Authority Ordinance in 2002. Shortly thereafter, the GOP issued procurement rules for all procuring entities at the national level, established an internet portal to house procurement notices and procurement plans, and established a National Institute of Procurement to train GOP procurement officials. In 2013, under its Assessment and Strengthening Program, USAID/Pakistan facilitated the formation of an Advisory Group on Public Procurement to provide a forum for all GOP procuring entities to share experiences and harmonise procurement practices. USAID/Pakistan also supported the following: (i) development of a National Procurement Strategy to establish a public procurement reform roadmap; (ii) a Learning Management System to offer cost-effective online training on a variety of procurement topics; (iii) updated rules and standard bidding documents; and (iv) e-procurement initiatives to increase the functionality of the Public Procurement Regulatory Authority website. The Mission chose to support a few specific subnational government entities, including supporting the Baluchistan Provincial Government in strengthening its newly formed Public Procurement Regulatory Authority and the Government of Sindh to implement its ambitious Capacity Building Plan as a leader in procurement reform in Pakistan.

USAID has also placed an emphasis on greater accountability and transparency in procurement through various 'democracy and governance' sector projects. For example, soon after the Government of the Philippines enacted its Government Procurement Reform Act in 2002, USAID worked with Procurement Watch, an NGO, and the government's Procurement Policy Board to formulate rules and regulations to implement the new procurement law. The new rules and regulations established a legal basis to tackle corruption, introduce efficiencies and limit unwarranted discretion in the procurement process. USAID supported consultative workshops with a wide array of stakeholders, trainings on the proper interpretation and implementation of the law for bids and award committee members and observers, and launching an electronic reporting system. USAID's support led directly to the issuance of the Operational Guidelines on Handling

Feedback and Complaints Submitted by Bids and Awards Committee Observers[120] and a primer which outlined the key procedures and steps in filing feedback and complaints resulting from public bidding activities.

USAID also supported the civil society organisations focused on tackling corruption in the public sector, some of whom became members of the Transparency Board, a Government of the Philippines-led entity that reviews certain government procurements. USAID worked with the Government of the Philippines' Ministry of Education to facilitate the involvement of civil society organisations to monitor the procurement and dissemination of textbooks to elementary schools throughout the country.

In Kenya, USAID supported the Government of Kenya's (GOK) public financial management reform programme from 2005, focusing on increasing transparency and accountability in public procurement. USAID advised the Kenyan Public Procurement Oversight Authority (PPOA) during its incipient stages to establish an organisational and management framework. USAID also provided support to the GOK to initiate e-procurement procedures. USAID co-financed the development of a Citizen's Guide to Public Procurement to educate citizens on the laws, rules and procedures governing procurement, particularly as they relate to the use of proceeds from the Constituencies Development Fund,[121] an allocation from the National Government to finance a range of projects identified by local communities across primarily the education, health, water and security sectors.

In Tanzania, USAID implemented a governance project to improve the effectiveness of the Government of Tanzania's (GOT) Public Procurement Regulatory Authority (PPRA). The overall project objectives included strengthening civil society's capacity to understand the procurement process and play a watchdog role and hold the GOT to account for the proper use of public resources, to deepen citizenry appreciation of the value for money in public procurement, and to expand PPRA's operational and outreach capacity. Instead of directly procuring the services of a technical assistance provider, USAID utilised a direct partner government financing (use of country systems) modality via a cost reimbursement agreement with PPRA. Although not necessarily intentional, this project merged the two objectives of supporting capacity-development of the PPRA while at the same time using the GOT's own procurement rules and institutions to both manage and oversee USAID's contribution and procure goods and services to implement the project. Under the project, USAID provided financial support to PPRA and wraparound technical assistance to support the implementation of PPRA's medium-term strategic plan. USAID aligned the project around the GOT's goals by addressing both the 'supply' and 'demand' side of public procurement. On the supply side, the project supported the GOT (including at the regional level) in increasing its capacity to implement the law and conduct efficient and effective procurement. On the demand side, the project encouraged PPRA to work with civil society organisations, including media, to improve citizen understanding of public procurement and provide a channel to report irregularities.

[120] A revised version of the Operational Guidelines can be found at http://pubdocs.worldbank.org/en/488821434986536867/Philippines-GPRA-Procurement-Observers-Guide-2014.pdf.

[121] As of 2015, the Constituencies Development Fund modified its name to the National Government Constituencies Development Fund (NG-CDF) to specify its focus on National Government functions.

USAID has also assisted countries to improve capacity in procuring infrastructure through Public-Private Partnerships (PPP). One example is under the Vietnam Competitiveness Initiative under which USAID supported the Government of Vietnam's Ministry of Planning and Investment (MPI) in its early stages to develop a government-wide PPP programme to build capacity at all government levels to promote private sector investment and technical capacity in infrastructure development in a more transparent, market-based and efficient manner. Along with the Asian Development Bank, the World Bank and other donors, USAID provided technical expertise with lessons learned from other countries to establish a stable legal framework, a fair and transparent procurement process, and internal capacity-development to manage a complex undertaking.

In 2010, the Prime Minister issued Decision 71 to promulgate the Regulation for Pilot PPP Infrastructure Investment Projects.[122] Due to the lack of accompanying guidance to implementing agencies to identify and assess potential projects in a fair and methodical manner, USAID supported country-wide stakeholder consultations, assisted in the development of technical operation guidelines, conducted preliminary assessments of several potential PPP projects, and helped establish funding vehicles to facilitate the preparation of projects by implementing agencies in Vietnam.

VI. Challenges and Opportunities to USAID Going Forward

A. New Skillset for Foreign Service Personnel to Provide Capacity Support

Increased visibility and interest by a broad array of stakeholders from partner countries to development partners to civil society organisations to academia to the private sector to improve public procurement creates significant opportunities to support sustainable development. USAID's renewed focus under USAID Forward's Local Solutions initiative promises to attract greater resources to local actors and their role in establishing and maintaining functional systems, including procurement.

USAID would do well to establish new employment categories for procurement professionals and employ local nationals who would possess a long-term, continuous view on procurement reform in-country. These professionals could work across sectors, assessing country public financial management (including procurement) systems to inform USAID country teams about opportunities to support country procurement systems, while also carrying out sector-specific objectives. Such individuals would also assume the day-to-day responsibility of collaborating with a wide range of country stakeholders to support procurement reform.

Creating a new cadre of in-house, local national procurement experts would enable USAID to 'walk the walk' in support of country procurement systems. Such a pivot may

[122] See http://vietnamlawmagazine.vn/decision-no-71-2010-qd-ttg-public-private-partnership-investment-gets-go-ahead-in-key-sectors-2853.html.

engender resistance due to the longstanding modus operandi of using direct contract and grant mechanisms to for-profit and non-profit organisations to implement development activities without genuine alignment around a country-led and country-owned strategy. Relying upon local experts who are well-versed in local systems, challenges and opportunities would facilitate and encourage greater USAID engagement with partner country governments and other actors interested in supporting procurement reform.

B. Procurement within the Broader Governance Landscape

Within the US and in other 'developed' countries, many foreign aid officials view procurement as an administrative and technocratic function often to be scapegoated when things go wrong and a 'necessary evil'. Many public financial management practitioners consider procurement as a stand-alone set of mechanical and bureaucratic rules and procedures and do not think of procurement as an integral part of a country's public financial management system. Procurement champions face an uphill battle in persuading decision-makers to devote precious foreign aid resources to support procurement reform.

In line with its Local Solutions initiative, USAID would do well to continue its pivot towards assessing partner country procurement systems with an eye to supporting capacity-development efforts as well as possibly using such systems to implement its aid programmes in the not-so-distant future.[123] Since 2010, USAID's Center of Excellence on Democracy, Rights and Governance has actively promoted the concept of cross-cutting programming, making the case that any activity, from treating HIV-positive patients in Haiti to providing textbooks to primary school children in Cambodia to building rural feeder roads in Rwanda, needs to take into account the importance of improving governance as a part of service delivery for USAID's assistance to have a sustainable impact upon the partner country in the future. And for the examples above, one can easily grasp the critical role that procurement (purchasing and delivering pharmaceuticals, textbooks and construction services) plays in ensuring that governments fulfil one of their main functions, namely the provision of basic goods and services.

In any country, USAID faces a choice: it could design an activity and award a contract to a private sector entity (US or non-US) to build a gravity sewer system in parallel with a partner government's own programme; *or* it could work with the partner government with an eye in the near or medium term to provide financial and technical support to the partner government to be able to receive USAID and other donor funding one day to procure the needed goods and services, monitor and supervise the contract, ensure quality and best value, and benefit from the fruits of good procurement and good governance. Even in instances where a partner government's procurement and financial management systems lack capacity and credibility and do not provide sufficient confidence to donors (and often partner country governments themselves), USAID and the partner country would benefit from a project that acknowledges the

[123] See Glennie, 'Localising aid' (n 48) for a thoughtful discussion of strengthening systems and sustainability through the transfer of funding to local as opposed to international actors.

importance for the responsible line ministries or other procuring entities to improve their capabilities to use government resources to carry out their mandates.

A good example of a well-considered cross-cutting programming is the USAID/ Tanzania Public Sector System Strengthening (PS3) Project. The PS3 Project combines aspects from four different sectors (health, education, agriculture and governance) into one project focused on improving public sector service delivery. Through the project, USAID acknowledged its important role in supporting the Government of Tanzania to strengthen governance at both national and local government area (LGA) levels to use resources transparently, enabling citizen engagement in planning and monitoring, resulting in improved outcomes across all sectors. One aspect of the project focuses on strengthening LGA-level procurement systems to increase efficiency and transparency and facilitating LGA-civil society mechanisms to establish social accountability monitoring across all sectors, including monitoring significant LGA procurements.

VII. Conclusion

USAID's experience in increasing aid effectiveness via public procurement tools is mixed. On the one hand, USAID's pivot over the past ten years to reduce domestic preferencing requirements, from supporting the Untying Recommendation to revising its source and nationality rule, has arguably led to increased efficiencies and best value in regards to USAID direct-financed procurements of goods and services to achieve developmental outcomes. Additionally, its modest increase in the use of country procurement and other public financial management systems as an aid modality empowers partner countries to use external revenues in close alignment with their own rules and priorities. However, USAID faces challenges in supporting capacity-development in public procurement reform due to funding allocations focused more on health, education, peace and security, and environmental sectors and less on democratic and economic governance, thus squeezing out opportunities for USAID to invest greater resources to support partner countries desiring donor support to improve their public procurement systems. USAID would do well to design projects in a cross-sectoral manner that incorporates aspects of improving country procurement systems, rather than engaging in helicopter-style assistance via its own contractors that provides immediate outputs (eg increased number of children vaccinated) while leaving the country with no better capacity to raise revenue, budget for, procure and deliver such vaccines.

Finally, USAID is subject to extensive regulation and scrutiny that places a premium on accountability and measurable results that take precedence over multilateral aid effectiveness objectives. Consequently, the flexibility and adaptability needed to completely harmonise USAID's procurement processes with broader aid effectiveness goals will require on-going exploration within the context of USAID's political, operational and practical constraints.

PART VI

The Road Ahead

15

Development Outcomes and Procurement Reform

JEFFREY GUTMAN

I. Introduction

Ask stakeholders what should be the main objective of procurement reform being pursued by the donor community and especially the multilateral development banks (MDBs) and you are certain to hear a wide range of responses. Some may refer to the need for greater efficiency and speed in the process and others may refer to reducing corruption and increasing transparency. Some may speak about promoting local small and medium-sized enterprises (SMEs) while others speak of environmental sustainability. And some may talk of greater innovation while others talk of greater use of local procurement systems. These perspectives can all be subsumed under the term 'aid effectiveness' but they miss the ultimate objective of ensuring the quality of investment outcomes – an approach to procurement that leads to the best possible development outcome. A development outcomes approach to procurement offers a 'holistic' perspective to the whole procurement cycle from upstream design and specifications through bid and award to contract management and implementation. This chapter defines what is meant by focusing on outcomes and, most importantly, its implications for the measurement of the impact and the evaluation of the success or failure of the reforms.

One of the major changes in development aid over the last ten years has been to enhance the focus on outcomes of aid. Whereas traditional approaches to measuring success tended to emphasise the efficiency of mobilising inputs, such as the mobilisation of contractors, and outputs, the final accounting of the physical outputs, such as kilometres of road built, the emphasis is now on defining the actual outcomes or impacts achieved through those investments, such as improved access to employment, commerce and education opportunities. Projects now provide results frameworks and matrices to be monitored during implementation. Procurement, however, has often been seen as an administrative or technical input rather than a strategic instrument for achieving outcomes. Focus has been heavily directed at the bid and award process, its transparency, level of competition and time required for processing. But it is clear that even a very efficient and transparent bid and award process does not necessarily translate into a successful investment outcome. Promoting local small and medium-size contractors will not necessarily translate into quality outcomes. These are important and valid elements and secondary objectives but they do not reflect the primary investment objective.

While recent reforms approved at the World Bank[1] and at the African Development Bank (AfDB)[2] have begun the change towards an outcome perspective, the challenge going forward will be to embed this through the implementation of the reforms, the focus of capacity-building efforts and the measurement of success. Worldwide attention to achieving 'value for money' (VfM) and the focus on a more diversified menu of procurement approaches that are 'fit for purpose' are clearly directed at the quality of outcomes. This represents a substantial change for the procurement community and the development community more broadly including governments, donors and civil society.

II. Defining Reform Objectives

A. Evaluating Past Policy

The basis for any major reforms to the provision of aid and related financing begins with an evaluation of the existing situation. In the case of procurement reform, the World Bank followed an extensive process of review and consultation. The number of background papers and breadth of consultations complemented by one of the most ambitious evaluations executed by the Bank's Independent Evaluation Group[3] offer an unprecedented volume of materials on the issue of public procurement and aid. A parallel though more limited review and evaluation was undertaken by the African Development Bank.[4] The results reflect the complex nature of the issues surrounding public procurement and the perspectives of different stakeholders. What seems to be missing, however, is an assessment of whether procurement is sufficiently contributing to development outcomes.

There is no argument that MDB procurement policy has contributed substantially to aid effectiveness. The application of International Competitive Bidding (ICB), first introduced in the 1950s, in which sources from around the world compete to provide works, goods and services at the evaluated least cost, has withstood the test of

[1] World Bank, *Procurement in World Bank Investment Project Financing, phase II: The New Procurement Framework* (Washington DC, The World Bank Group, 2015).

[2] African Development Bank, *Board Memorandum, Comprehensive Revision of the ADB's Procurement Policy, Procedures and Processes* (The African Development Bank, 2015).

[3] These include the World Bank procurement policy consultations and the World Bank Independent Evaluation Group review, which can be found via the respective sites: http://consultations.worldbank.org/consultation/procurement-policy-review-consultations; https://ieg.worldbankgroup.org/evaluations/world-bank-group-and-public-procurement.

[4] Independent Development Evaluation (IDEV), African Development Bank, *Operational Procurement Policies and Practices of the African Development Bank: An Independent Evaluation* (Abidjan, African Development Bank, 2014).

time. Client country surveys have recognised the value of MDB procurement policy by government officials, civil society and the private sector.[5] It has brought clarity to the rules applied, transparency to the process and consistency across a wide range of country contexts. It has led to worldwide competition and to the development of local industries in developing countries. In Financial Year (FY) 2013, the World Bank data for civil works contracts awarded through ICB (see Figure 1) indicated that over 80 per cent were awarded to local or regional contractors from developing countries in every region except Africa.[6] What is noteworthy is the singular focus on the process of bid and award with an assumption if that is handled well, development outcomes will be successful.

Figure 1 Percentage of Internationally Bid World Bank Civil Works Contracts Won by Local and Regional firms, FY 2013[7]

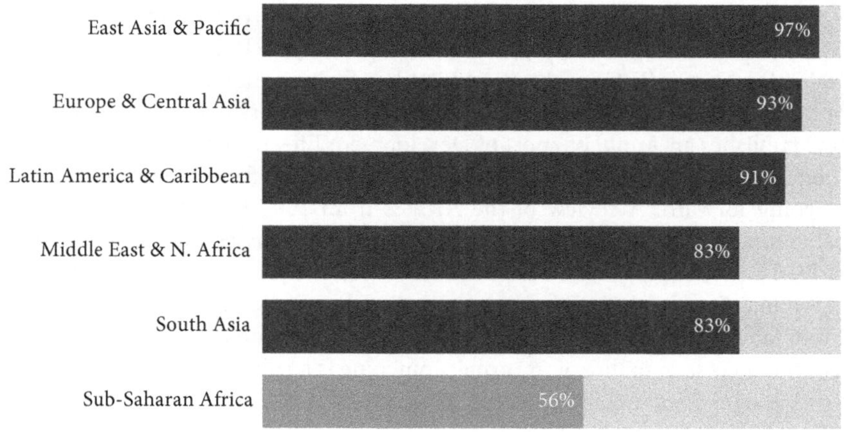

This perspective is reinforced by the four principles that underpin the previous procurement policies of the World Bank and their equivalent at the other MDBs:

1. the need for economy and efficiency in the implementation of the project, including the procurement of the goods and works involved;
2. the Bank's interest in giving all eligible bidders from developed and developing countries the same information and equal opportunity to compete in providing goods and works financed by the Bank;
3. the Bank's interest in encouraging the development of domestic contracting and manufacturing industries in the borrowing country; and
4. the importance of transparency in the procurement process.[8]

[5] Independent Evaluation Group World Bank, *The World Bank and Public Procurement: An Independent Evaluation* (Washington DC, The World Bank Group, Washington, 2014).

[6] C Zhang and J Gutman, 'Aid Procurement and the Development of Local Industry: A question for Africa' (Brookings Global Economy & Development Working Paper 88) (Washington DC, June 2015) available at www.brookings.edu/research/aid-procurement-and-the-development-of-local-industry-a-question-for-africa.

[7] ibid.

[8] World Bank, 'Guidelines: Procurement of Goods, Works, and Non-Consulting Services under IBRD Loans and IDA Credits & Grants by World Bank Borrowers' (Washington DC, The World Bank Group, 2011) 2 (fn omitted).

Evaluating procurement against these four principles ignores the overall contribution to ensuring the realisation of project outcomes. These principles are directed at how the procurement is carried out in terms of bid and award.

A review of annual procurement reports from the World Bank illustrates this issue. Looking at the reports from 2006 to 2011, there is arguably no substantive reference to project outcomes.[9] Instead, the discussion is mainly process-driven; in particular, there is an emphasis on the level of complaints and number of misprocurement cases. Similarly, in the 2011 report by the African Development Bank, the focus is on the process rather than the outcomes. For example, the principle of economy and efficiency is measured by the cost and time required to conduct the bid and award. The principles of equal opportunity and transparency are measured in terms of publication, competitive procedures and bidder participation as well as complaint handling. There is no mention of ultimate results.

While such a limited focus might be expected of the procurement community, one would expect a broader emphasis on development effectiveness by the Independent Evaluation Group (IEG) of the World Bank, a freestanding unit that reports to the Bank's Board and is tasked with providing an objective assessment of the Bank's work. The IEG publishes an Annual Report of Development Effectiveness (ARDE) that evaluates the outcomes of completed projects and draws lessons for achieving development results going forward. A review of the ARDEs from 1997 to 2009, however, reveals (at best) sporadic mention of the issue of procurement in assessing project outcomes. Similarly, the first (2011)[10] and second (2013)[11] editions of the African Development Bank's Annual Development Effectiveness Review have failed to address procurement in an outcomes-based framework. Nobody seems to ask the obvious question: 'How much of the success or failure of the project outcome is attributable to how the procurement was designed and executed?'

B. Setting the Basis for Reform

Even more disconcerting is the response of stakeholders during World Bank worldwide reform consultations. As illustrated in Figure 2, of the 25 procurement topics raised, the highest number of responses were directed at 'delays and responsiveness' of procurement policies and procedures while 'development effectiveness and impact' received the least responses. It is doubtful that this means that stakeholders are satisfied with the development impact of present policies but the lack of such discussion of the linkages represents an important missing piece in evaluating procurement.

[9] Available at https://ieg.worldbankgroup.org/ieg-search?keys=ARDE.

[10] Available at https://www.afdb.org/fileadmin/uploads/afdb/Documents/Project-and-Operations/ADER%20%28En%29%20-%20Websafe.pdf.

[11] Available at https://www.afdb.org/fileadmin/uploads/afdb/Documents/Project-and-Operations/ADER-%20Annual%20Development%20Effectiveness%20Review%202013.pdf.

Figure 2 Frequency of Procurement Topics Raised During Consultations[12]

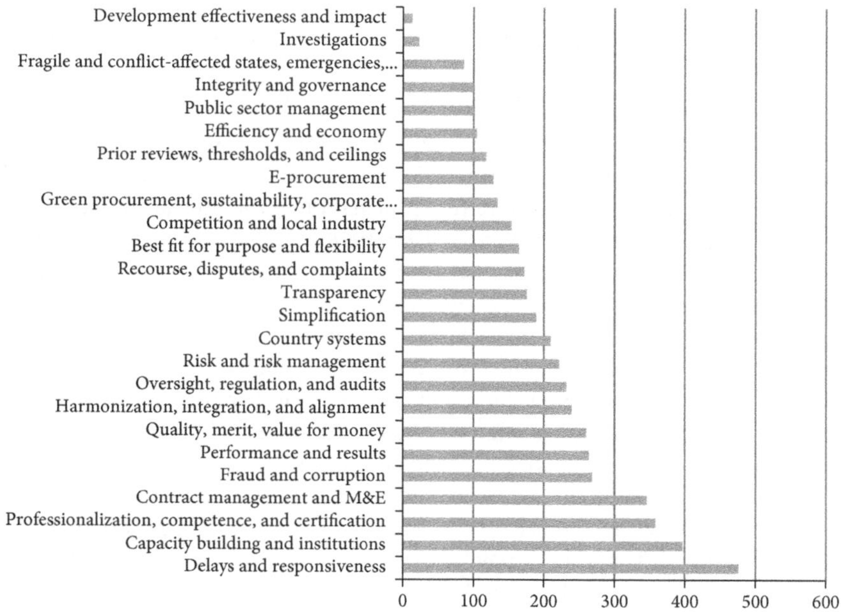

More significantly, the World Bank IEG conducted a comprehensive review of procurement policy and practices in 2014.[13] Yet, despite a volume purportedly devoted to 'Achieving Development Effectiveness through Bank Procurement', there is no assessment of the actual impact on project outcomes. Instead, the IEG concentrates on the economy and efficiency of the bid and award process. There are glimpses of examples that come close to illustrating how rigid application of its policies has negatively affected the final project outcome, including a failed loan for the supply of vaccines during an influenza epidemic in Mexico.[14] But these examples are few and anecdotal. They are not discussed in the context of developing a framework for analysing the impact on development effectiveness. In short, there is no consideration of how changes would affect outcomes.

Instead, the IEG drops the proverbial 'ball' and declares:

> Regarding development impact and the Bank's own lending, IEG finds that present Bank guidelines are broadly adequate instruments for Bank lending, including new areas of lending. IEG finds that there is need for review of select provisions, for example on consultant

[12] World Bank, 'Procurement Policy Review: Feedback from Consultations with External Stakeholders – Summary of Comments Submitted Online' (Washington DC, The World Bank Group, 2013) available at https://consultations.worldbank.org/Data/hub/files/consultation-template/procurement-policy-review-consultationsopenconsultationtemplate/materials/procurementpolicyreviewexternalstakeholders feedbackexecutivesummary_1.pdf.

[13] Independent Evaluation Group World Bank, *The World Bank and Public Procurement: An Independent Evaluation, Appendixes to Volume II: Achieving Development Effectiveness through Procurement* (Washington DC, The World Bank Group, 2014).

[14] ibid.

> selection or new and complex forms of procurement such as information and technology projects or public private partnerships (PPPs). Bank procurement processes, in contrast, are time consuming and have posed difficulties because of inflexibilities in interpretation. Process change requires better monitoring, clear standards, and changes in incentives that would lead to the exercise of reasonable judgment and less risk aversion.[15]

Within this statement are clues to more fundamental weaknesses in procurement that are not mentioned – weaknesses with serious implications for outcomes. The IEG evaluation does look at certain sectors (eg information and communications technology, or ICT, and Community Driven Development, or CDD) and assesses whether past procurement in these areas has led to poor or limited outcomes. ICT procurement has been a continuing challenge worldwide as the procurement profession has had to contend with the fast-moving changes in the sector. In 2006, the World Bank reviewed 23 projects financed by the Bank that included substantial ICT components. It found serious weaknesses in procurement planning, contributing to the finding that 77 per cent of these projects were rated less than satisfactory.[16] The IEG's evaluation in 2011 echoed the same findings that 'procurement is a major constraint to implementing ICT projects'.[17] It pointed to the inadequacy of applying Bank procurement policies, designed for infrastructure, to ICT procurement and the lack of appropriate technical expertise in the Bank. While ICT may be the most dramatic example of procurement failure due to inadequate policies and technical capacity, the question arises as to whether procurement approaches have also led to suboptimal results and possibly failures in other sectors.

The 2014 evaluation by the Independent Development Evaluation (IDEV) group of the African Development Bank offered a similar finding on their procurement policy. IDEV rated the policy as 'satisfactory':[18]

> Policy was perceived most favourably, an outcome that may surprise some. The various sources of evidence indicate that the Bank's rules and procedures provide a sound framework for fair and relatively corruption-free competition for contracts. Government procurement entities and private industry, however, find them complicated. Policies do not reflect the latest evolution related to value for money, green procurement and gender either. The overall rating for policy is satisfactory, but this is tempered in practice by the finding that the application of these policies does not reach the same standard as the policy framework.

While the AFDB IDEV overall finding is similar to that of the World Bank's IEG, the tone represents a distinct difference. The Evaluation states, 'The fact remains, however, that although most aspects of procurement performance were found to be at least moderately satisfactory, the overall results are well below the standards the Bank should

[15] Independent Evaluation Group World Bank, *The World Bank and Public Procurement: An Independent Evaluation* (Washington DC, The World Bank Group, 2014) 1.

[16] Quality Assurance Group, 'Quality of Information and Communication Technology (ICT): Components in Bank Projects' (Washington DC, The World Bank Group, 2006).

[17] Independent Evaluation Group World Bank, *The World Bank and Public Procurement: An Independent Evaluation, Appendixes to Volume II: Achieving Development Effectiveness through Procurement* (Washington DC, The World Bank Group, 2014).

[18] Independent Development Evaluation (IDEV), *Operational Procurement Policies and Practices of the African Development Bank: An Independent Evaluation* (Abidjan, African Development Bank, 2014).

set and meet as Africa's premier development institution'.[19] The recommendations emphasise the importance of focusing on other stages of the procurement cycle, both upstream in terms of design, and downstream, in terms of contract management, beyond a singular focus on bid and award. Lastly, IDEV raises a basic question that could lead one to a focus on development outcomes: 'The importance of Value for Money merits one inescapable conclusion: the Bank and its members and stakeholders urgently need to agree on what indicators are needed and work together to establish and maintain reliable databases for measuring results'.[20] Unfortunately, the question is left vague.

What is needed is a change in the nature of the conversation on development aid procurement with a focus on the actual outcome of the investment and the role that procurement plays in that outcome. Such a focus would provide a basis for assessing the varying perspectives and concerns of stakeholders. It facilitates a discussion of the relative trade-offs between secondary objectives and the comparison of the related costs and benefits, risks and rewards, of alternative approaches. The next section looks at the important change in the language of the policies under the reforms.

III. Will the Reforms Address Outcomes?

Despite the lack of attention to investment outcomes by the MDBs' independent evaluation departments and during the consultations, the good news is that the language used in the revised policies and related documents reflects the broader impact objective. The question remains as to whether the reforms will be implemented accordingly and evaluated on an outcome basis. The discussion below looks at the change in vision and principles while the subsequent three sections set forth their implications for an outcome-based approach to procurement.

It begins with the 'vision'. 'Procurement in IPF [Investment Project Financing] operations supports Borrowers to achieve value for money with integrity in delivering sustainable development'. This is the stated vision in the World Bank policy.[21] The policy then moves from the traditional process-oriented principles of economy/efficiency, effectiveness, domestic industry development, equal opportunity and transparency to a more comprehensive set (Table 1).

Table 1 World Bank's Core Procurement Principles[22]

1. Value for money	The principle of value for money means the effective, efficient, and economic use of resources, which requires an evaluation of relevant costs and benefits, along with an assessment of risks, and non-price attributes and/or life cycle costs, as appropriate. Price alone may not necessarily represent value for money.

(continued)

[19] ibid.

[20] ibid.

[21] World Bank, 'Bank Policy: Procurement in IPF and Other Operational Procurement Matters', revised 2 November 2017 (Catalogue Number OPSVP5.05-POL.144) (Washington DC, The World Bank Group, 2017) 2, available at https://policies.worldbank.org/sites/ppf3/PPFDocuments/a3656cb78847417b886f11fa0235216e.pdf.

[22] ibid 3–4.

Table 1 ***(Continued)***

2. Economy	This principle of economy takes into consideration factors such as sustainability, quality, and non-price attributes and/or life cycle cost as appropriate, that support value for money. It permits integrating into the Procurement Process economic, environmental, and social considerations that the Bank has agreed with the Borrower. It also permits augmenting identified sustainability criteria with specific criteria in support of the Borrower's own sustainable procurement policy.
3. Integrity	The principle of integrity refers to the use of funds, resources, assets and authority, according to the intended purposes and in a manner that is well informed, aligned with the public interest, and aligned with broader principles of good governance. The Bank requires that all parties involved in the Procurement Process, including without limitation, Borrowers and sub-Borrowers (and other beneficiaries of Bank Financing); bidders, consultants, contractors and suppliers; any sub-contractors, sub-consultants, service providers or suppliers; any agents (whether declared or not); and any of their personnel, observe the highest standard of ethics during the Procurement Process of Bank-financed contracts, and refrain from fraud and corruption, as that term is defined in the Anti-Corruption Guidelines.
4. Fit for Purpose	The principle of fit for purpose applies both to the intended outcomes and the procurement arrangements in determining the most appropriate approach to meet the development objectives and project outcomes, taking into account the context and the risk, value, and complexity of procurement.
5. Efficiency	The principle of efficiency requires that Procurement Processes are proportional to the value and risks of the underlying project activities. Procurement arrangements are generally time-sensitive and strive to avoid delays.
6. Transparency	The principle of transparency requires that the Borrower and the Bank enable appropriate review of the procurement activities, supported by appropriate documentation and disclosure. Transparency requires: (i) that relevant procurement information be made publicly available to all interested parties, consistently and in a timely manner, through readily accessible and widely available sources at reasonable or no cost; (ii) appropriate reporting of procurement activity; and (iii) the use of confidentiality provisions in contracts only where justified.
7. Fairness	The principle of fairness refers to: (i) equal opportunity and treatment for bidders and consultants; (ii) equitable distribution of rights and obligations between Borrowers and suppliers, bidders, consultants and contractors; and (iii) credible mechanisms for addressing procurement related complaints and providing recourse. Open competitive procurement is the Bank's preferred procurement approach, whenever possible to maximize fairness of opportunity to bid. Whenever is possible, the Bank requires that eligible individuals and firms be given the same opportunities to compete for Bank-financed activities.

Most importantly is the placement of 'value for money' as the first principle. Though expressed differently, the AfDB's emphasis in its Vision and Principles[23] is consistent. Vinay Sharma, former Director for Procurement at the AfDB:

> VfM takes into account not only the initial and/or life cycle costs and quality, but also factors such as risk, proportionality, predictability, sustainability, flexibility, innovation, timeliness and targeted outcome of procurement during the entire procurement cycle. The VfM approach is not intended to monetize benefits and cost for each factor but should assess whether the relevant procurement meets what has been characterized in the literature as the 'five rights' (i.e. right price, right quality, right quantity, right timing and right source) and whether the entire exercise ultimately delivers desired outcomes in a cost effective manner.[24]

While the vision and principles recognise the importance of focusing on the quality of investment results, there are three key areas that need to be addressed to realise such a vision in practice. These areas are discussed in the following sections.

IV. Implications of an Outcomes-Based Approach: Looking beyond Bid and Award

The most significant implication of applying an outcomes-based approach to procurement policy is that it is immediately apparent that a singular focus on the bidding and award stage of the cycle, as embedded in traditional MDB policies, is seriously inadequate. Applying an outcomes-based approach to evaluating the development effectiveness of procurement requires a 'holistic' assessment, looking at the whole procurement cycle, from design and planning to bid and award, to contract management and implementation. Evaluating the strengths and weaknesses of the procurement process necessitates careful consideration of each stage in the cycle (Figure 3).

Figure 3 Main Phases of the Procurement Cycle[25]

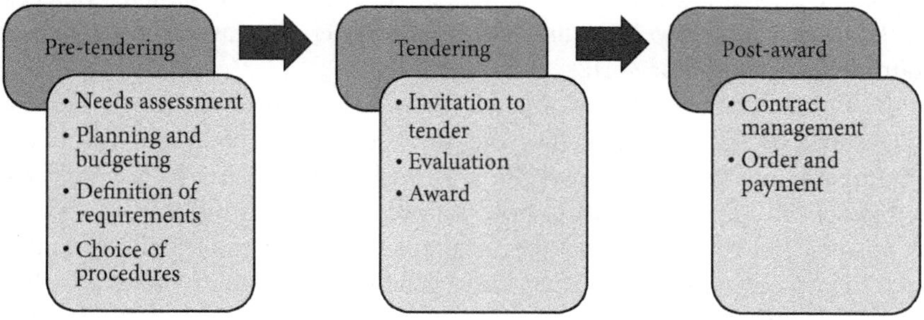

[23] Available at www.afdb.org/en/projects-and-operations/procurement/new-procurement-policy/.

[24] V Sharma 'An update on procurement reforms at the African Development Bank', paper presented at *Public Procurement: Global Revolution VII* at University of Nottingham, UK, June 2015.

[25] OECD, 'Principles for Integrity in Public Procurement' (2009).

First, design of the process and the crafting of specifications, or 'pre-tendering', represent the translation of the project concept into practical actions. Then the bid and award, or 'tendering', process ensures the participation of qualified suppliers at a competitive price. Finally, the contract management and implementation, or 'post-award' stage, ensures that what was planned is what is ultimately provided, with appropriate adaptations to circumstances. Moreover, success and compliance at one stage are necessary but not sufficient to ensure a good outcome. As stated in the World Bank's 2012 updated governance strategy:

> Traditional approaches have been based on the notion of best practice procedures. Such approaches overwhelmingly focus on regulations covering selection and evaluation procedures of suppliers, contractors, and service providers. Evidence shows that such a focus on procedures in the absence of a clear definition of procurement performance objectives can lead to reduced accountability and possibly poor results.[26]

While IEG and IDEV do raise the concern about the relative imbalance toward bid and award, their recommendations fall short of redressing this bias. There could be two main reasons for this imbalanced perspective and reluctance to incorporate, especially the contract management stage, into the policies. The first reason is that the bid/award process is clearly considered to be within the professional responsibility of the procurement expert, whereas the design and execution stages represent a grey area in which the technical expert has greater involvement. In the European Union (EU) Procurement Directives, United Nations Commission on International Trade Law (UNCITRAL) Model Law on Public Procurement and World Trade Organization (WTO) Global Procurement Agreement, the role of the procurement expert ends with the award.

A second reason is that the interests of private sector firms are mainly directed at the bid and award stage of the process. Such firms represent the core constituency that monitors and reacts to changes in MDB policy and practice. Understandably, they want to ensure that they have the opportunity to compete and that the process is fair and transparent. Donor countries' representatives on the MDB boards similarly reflect such interests as market access to MDB financing is often referred to as a crucial justification for countries' support to the MDBs.

From a broader development practice perspective, however, one is faced with such questions as the following: how did the bed nets get delivered without anti-malarial treatment; why did the website crash; what contributed to the early failure of the road? Each question points to potential weaknesses beyond the bid and award, either upstream in the design and specifications or downstream in the execution or delivery. In fact, the bid and award may have been fully compliant in these cases, but the project still ultimately failed. The operation was a success, but the patient unfortunately died. It is the whole chain that must be considered to ensure the right outcomes and to assess when outcomes fall short of expectations.

[26] World Bank, 'Strengthening Governance: Tackling Corruption – The World Bank Group's Updated Strategy and Implementation Plan' (Washington DC, The World Bank Group, 2012).

A. Design Stage

Upstream in the procurement cycle, the design stage is when the specifications are established and the type of bidding process is determined. A good knowledge of the supplier market for goods, works and services is essential. Also, the project team for the client country and the MDB must make judgements about whether the acquisition is relatively straightforward or whether other considerations – such as life-cycle costing, maintenance concerns or spare parts – should be taken into account. The team must also decide whether other objectives should be considered, such as environmental factors or the preferential treatment of certain subsets of the population, and, if so, how to quantify or monetise such factors.

A key consideration is whether the investment involves a complex or rapidly changing sector for which one wants to consider alternative solutions and for which the client agency may not have sufficient expertise. This determination could require interaction with the industry of suppliers ensuring timely adaptation of new technology or promoting and inviting innovation in proposals.

It is seldom, if at all, that post-project reviews actually look back at this stage to determine if a better result could have been achieved. What is apparent is that the project team at this stage should encompass more than just the procurement professional; rather, the technical expert(s) must also have a significant role. Yet, this critical stage remains a grey area in terms of responsibility, guidance, expertise and hence, accountability.

B. Contract Execution Stage

The most serious blind spot of past MDB policy is the lack of attention to what happens after the contract is awarded. Downstream in the procurement cycle, contract management and execution is recognised by all as crucial; yet, despite the 'bureaucratic hype' on delivery, this essential stage is usually ignored as an element of procurement. The technical experts assume that the procurement staff is still monitoring while the procurement staff believes their responsibility ended with the award.

While the MDBs emphasise the importance of integrity during bid and award, there is clear evidence that contract execution represents an equal if not greater threat to governance with serious consequences for outcomes and integrity. In 1991, Klitgaard offered a stylised model for representing corruption via the following formula:[27]

Corruption = **M**onopoly + **D**iscretion – **A**ccountability

When there is a lack of competition and a high amount of discretion in the decision-making process, combined with a low degree of accountability (and/or transparency), the risk of corruption is high. It is clear that this formula has influenced the rules governing the bid and award stage, which encourage competition, limit discretion and foster a high degree of transparency to enhance accountability. In terms of the downstream

[27] R Klitgaard, 'International Cooperation Against Corruption' (1998) 35(1) *Finance and Development* 3.

dynamics, however, the tables are turned. During contract execution, the selected supplier has a virtual monopoly and there is greater discretion on the part of the responsible parties, often leading to a lack of credible oversight of materials or cost overruns. Furthermore, unless the deficiencies during contract execution are immediately visible, the results of a given project will not be clear until years afterwards, limiting any accountability of the participating parties.

A further sign of inadequate attention given to contract execution is the lack of transparency by the MDBs. During the efforts to reform disclosure policy at the World Bank in 2010[28] (and subsequently in the other MDBs), a key controversial target was the disclosure of the Bank's supervision report regarding the status of project implementation. Despite all the transparency of the preparation and bidding documents and processes for a given project, the supervision report (now referred to at the World Bank as the Implementation Status and Results Report or ISR), generally issued twice a year per project, was not disclosed. The concern of staff was that such disclosure would jeopardise the candour in reporting if it were to be made public. Potentially serious but unconfirmed concerns about fraud and corruption or other potential risks might be withheld. In the end, most of the MDBs have agreed to disclose supervision reports while highly sensitive internal 'deliberative' issues are recorded but not made public. Despite the information now being disclosed, however, the format of the reporting is quite inaccessible to all but the most knowledgeable of practitioners and there is a concern that the 'deliberative' net is being cast well beyond the original spirit of the reforms.

Charles Kenny's research over the past decade has revealed what is at stake when the oversight of contract execution is ignored. In his 2006 paper, he argues that 'it's [*sic*] not how much you divert, but how you divert it that matters'. He stresses the importance of not confusing the financial and economic costs of bribe payments: 'The major damage done by corruption is probably not the narrow financial loss of bribe payments but the economic cost in terms of skewed spending priorities, along with substandard construction and operation'.[29] The use of substandard materials shortening the useful life of a road can seriously impact the economic benefits more substantially than the financial value of the bribe to a supervisory official. Estimating the costs and benefits of various approaches to fighting corruption should determine where to direct anti-corruption resources. In this case, it would appear that there would be greater returns through more attention being paid to contract implementation.

The failure to address contract management is increasingly being recognised in developed and developing countries. In 2013, the OECD Public Governance Review on integrity in public procurement found: 'Despite the risks involved in the contract management phase, few countries have taken active steps to supervise contractors' performance and integrity'.[30] The EU Anti-Corruption Report of the European

[28] World Bank, 'Bank Policy: Access to Information' (Washington DC, The World Bank Group, 2015) available at http://pubdocs.worldbank.org/en/393051435850102801/World-Bank-Policy-on-Access-to-Information-V2.pdf.

[29] C Kenny, 'Measuring and Reducing the Impact of Corruption in Infrastructure', Policy Research Working Paper 4099 (Washington DC, The World Bank Group, 2006) 16.

[30] OECD Public Governance Reviews, *Implementing the OECD Principles for Integrity in Public Procurement: Progress Since 2008*, OECD Public Governance Reviews (Paris, OECD Publishing, 2013) 83.

Commission found that 'while the efficiency of control mechanisms concerning pre-bidding, bidding and award phases has improved in Member States, the implementation (post award) phase is less closely monitored'.[31] The EU report finds that 'construction, energy, transport, defence [*sic*] and healthcare sectors appear to be most vulnerable to corruption in public procurement'.[32]

The World Bank's own experience confirms the risks of not sufficiently monitoring contract execution. Ben Olken has done serious work in estimating the level of corruption in rural roads construction under World Bank-financed village development projects in Indonesia. By conducting an engineering post-review of a number of roads and comparing the results to what was actually charged, he estimated a loss of 24 per cent of the expenditures.[33] Similarly, the Bank's Integrity Department's (INT) Detailed Implementation Review (DIR) for the Indian Health Sector 2006–07[34] documented the lack of focus on the deliverables and its results. Yet, despite this recognition of the vulnerability during contract execution, INT's caseload remains concentrated on fraud and corruption in bid and award. Only 20 per cent of its Final Investigation Reports (FIRs) related to issues arising during contract execution.[35]

C. New Initiatives

Recognition of this imbalance has led to a series of initiatives in recent years. One is the Construction Industry Transparency Initiative (CoST).[36] CoST is a country-focused effort to increase transparency in the delivery of construction projects. Through a partnership between the country (combination of government, private sector and civil society stakeholders) and international organisations, the initiative focuses on raising transparency throughout the project cycle from preparation, through bid/award and during contract implementation. It attempts to identify key information to be shared and how to make that information accessible and understandable to stakeholders. The implications for the improved governance and accountability have been tested through a three-year pilot in eight countries and launched more broadly in 2012.

A related initiative to enhance transparency is the Open Contracting Partnership (OCP).[37] This is an NGO that advocates policies for greater disclosure and related monitoring of public contracts – including those for the procurement of goods, works and services – at all stages of the contracting cycle. Its efforts include increasing public

[31] European Commission, *Report from the Commission to the Council and the European Parliament: EU Anti-Corruption Report* (Brussels 3.2.2014 COM [2014] 38 final) 33.

[32] ibid 27.

[33] BA Olken, 'Monitoring Corruption: Evidence from a Field Experiment in Indonesia', National Bureau of Economic Research Working Paper Series, Working Paper 11753 (2005) available at www.nber.org/papers/w11753. Published under the same title: (2007) 115 *Journal of Political Economy* 200.

[34] Department of Institutional Integrity (INT), World Bank, 'Detailed Implementation Review: India Health Sector 2006–2007' (Washington DC, The World Bank Group, 2007).

[35] Personal communication with World Bank Integrity Unity (April 2014).

[36] www.constructiontransparency.org.

[37] www.open-contracting.org.

disclosure of and accessibility to contract data, enhancing the quality of information on contracting, and promoting public participation in and monitoring of the contracting process. In January 2014, the OCP announced the development of the Open Contracting Data Standard, a common standard for publishing contract-level data,[38] with a view towards eventually complementing the International Aid Transparency Initiative (IATI) data standard for project-level aid spending data.[39]

What these efforts illustrate is the importance of a 'holistic' approach to the procurement cycle if one is to ensure the quality of outcomes. The MDBs' reforms must address all stages of the cycle if the procurement process is to remain an effective instrument in the toolkit for good governance. Such an approach should guide the relative level of resources assigned to each stage and the appropriate level of compliance versus discretion as discussed in the next section.

D. Reform Response

Although the policy and background documents recognise the issue of contract management and implementation and the lack of oversight, there is little effort to address it. There are several elements of the World Bank reforms that offer an opportunity to address the downstream stage. The policy is guided by a risk-based approach to deciding where and when the Bank should expend greater direct resources and review as opposed to the traditional more mechanical determination based on the value of the tender/contract. One could expect that the estimate of risk during contract implementation would be useful based on an assessment of clarity and capability for project monitoring. But this is not mentioned.

At the heart of this gap is an uncertainty between the role of the Bank and the role of the client country/executing agency and the role of the procurement expert versus other technical experts for contract management. The World Bank policy is targeted at Bank responsibility and the role of procurement staff. A more comprehensive presentation of the relative roles of stakeholders, beyond what is already incorporated, is needed to understand the relative responsibilities of the various parties and staff (country and donor institution) at each stage.

V. Implications of an Outcomes-Based Approach: Balancing Discretion versus Compliance

A. Conflicting Messages

The most difficult and contentious debate in public procurement is the tension between those who favour tighter compliance versus those who argue for greater discretion.

[38] L Marchessault, 'Open Contracting Data and International Aid Transparency: the Potential for Complementarity', Open Contracting Blog, 18 March 2014, available at www.open-contracting.org/2014/03/18/open_contracting_data_and_international_aid_transparency.

[39] Available at https://iatistandard.org/en/guidance/preparing-data/.

It has been raised consistently over the years in both developed and developing countries and is a central issue in the dialogue over the reform of MDB policies and aid effectiveness. It is a debate, however, in which each side can wrap the mantle of governance around its arguments. With rising concerns about corruption and declining confidence in public sector management, there are those that say we must continue to tighten the rules and limit discretion. There are others, however, who argue that the pendulum may have swung too far in response to 'zero tolerance'. They say that the proliferation of rules has stifled innovation and hampered a 'solutions-based' 'fit for purpose' approach to development challenges. This section presents the arguments on both sides of the scale and offers an approach to evaluating the trade-offs, one that starts from an outcomes-based perspective and assesses the corresponding integrity risks at each stage of the procurement cycle.

Turning again to the results of the World Bank's consultations with external stakeholders in 2010, one can see the tension in expectations. Figure 2 shows the relative weight that stakeholders place on key procurement issues. On the one hand, stakeholders most often bring up concerns about delays and the lack of responsiveness in MDB procurement processes (note that this is with regard to bid and award). On the other hand, fraud and corruption management is also among the top five concerns. Donors press for faster and more flexible processes in order to minimise time spent on procurement. At the same time, the donors hold the MDBs to a high fiduciary standard and demand more controls when issues of fraud and corruption arise.

Even the private sector offers mixed messages. Certainly the private sector wants a level playing field, along with clarity and predictability in the bid processes and transparency in the award decisions. More recently, however, many private companies from OECD countries are arguing for awards to be made on broader criteria than the seemingly straightforward price evaluation. 'Value for money', as discussed earlier, implies the incorporation of other variables including life-cycle costing and green procurement, which may be more difficult to quantify or monetise with wider scope for judgement calls.

B. The Case for More Discretion

The case for the application of greater discretion is made most forcefully by Steven Kelman (Administrator of the Office of Federal Procurement Policy in the Office of Management and Budget from 1993–97) in his 1990 book, *Procurement and Public Management: The Fear of Discretion and the Quality of Government Performance*. His basic premise is that cynicism about the behaviour of public officials has led to elaborate rules intended to rein them in. With each scandal, we typically add and tighten regulations.

His argument continues that such extensive rules do support good governance when government purchases are rather straightforward and standardised, such as the buying of office supplies. However, when public procurement begins to deal with complex transactions, such as the acquisition of information technology products, innovative approaches and adaptive solutions are required. In these cases, rules can be a serious constraint to development outcomes.

> The problem with the current system is that public officials cannot use common sense and good judgment in ways that would promote better vendor performance. I believe that the

> system should be significantly deregulated to allow public officials greater discretion. I believe that the ability to exercise discretion would allow government to gain greater value from procurement …
>
> In an environment too complex to be reducible to simple rules or in one that changes more rapidly than the rules can be changed, a decision-making system that depends on rules invites disaster.[40]

The book is focused on the purchase of computers and related technology and support by the US government in the 1980s, but is still relevant today. The excessive focus on the rules and related compliance distracts attention from the resulting performance or outcome of the acquisition. Kelman argues that various aspects of procurement bid and award regulations limit the government's ability to learn, adapt and ensure the best results. He contrasts this with the private sector, where long-term relationships with vendors are taken into account and open discussions on the overall value and probability of results are emphasised, rather than a single price indicator. Clearly, when we make significant purchases for ourselves (ie 'personal procurement' of homes, cars, etc), we apply substantial judgement beyond simply price. While public procurement must be held to a higher standard because it entails spending other people's money, do the rules lead to an acceptable outcome in terms of quality?

With regard to development aid, Andrew Natsios, former administrator of the US Agency for International Development describes the equivalent clash between the 'compliance' side of aid programmes and the 'technical programmatic' side in similar terms to Kelman.[41] He states, 'the essential balance between these two in development programs has now been skewed to such a degree in the U.S. aid system (and in the World Bank as well) that the imbalance threatens program integrity'.[42] He calls for reducing the layers of oversight and regulation and refers to it as a story of 'good intentions–accountability and transparency–gone bad'.[43]

This is not to say that Kelman and Natsios do not recognise the risks of corruption. But Kelman argues that such risks should be addressed by investing more in investigative capabilities and in harsher penalties for fraud and corruption, which would serve as effective deterrents.[44]

C. The Case for Stronger Compliance

Those who argue against discretion are proponents of compliance. The case for compliance is strong and gaining traction in developing countries. As indicated by the OECD, 'of all government activities, public procurement is also one of the most

[40] S Kelman, *Procurement and Public Management: The Fear of Discretion and the Quality of Government Performance* (Washington DC, American Enterprise Institute for Public Policy Research, 1990) 88, 11.

[41] A Natsios, 'The Clash of the Counter-bureaucracy and Development' (Center for Global Development Essay, 2010) available at www.cgdev.org/publication/clash-counter-bureaucracy-and-development.

[42] ibid.

[43] Natsios, 'The Clash of the Counter-bureaucracy and Development' (n 41) 5.

[44] Kelman, *Procurement and Public Management* (n 40).

vulnerable to fraud and corruption'. This is in part because of its complexity, the size of the financial flows it generates, and the close interaction between the public and private sectors it facilitates.[45] The Eurobarometer survey confirmed this cynicism for European countries.[46] The developing world, with weaker institutions, raises even greater cynicism.

Corruption is not a 'disease' specific to developing countries, as demonstrated by the recent roads case in Canada.[47] But in developing countries, the capacity to identify corruption issues, let alone investigate and prosecute, is seriously weak. The MDBs can only do so much through monitoring and review. The IEG evaluation of World Bank financed procurement hardly touched upon anti-corruption efforts. In response to comments over this gap in coverage, the IEG argued that much of the corruption evident in procurement was related to systemic corruption in the borrower countries or governments, and thus was not easily addressed through Bank transaction controls. The Integrity Department of the World Bank, which investigates complaints, seeks to collaborate with local officials and make case referrals for a country to follow up with investigative and legal proceedings. The track record, however, is poor in this regard. The relevant country agencies or institutions are overwhelmed and under-budgeted, and their legal systems are often inadequate.

Even the governments themselves are reluctant to allow discretion, even to ministers, in order to avoid any perception of corruption; bid processes follow the wording of the bidding documents to the letter, even when some variation could be justified without substantively harming the process. It is often the MDBs that press for more flexibility in differentiating between material versus minor deviations in supplier responses.

Thus, Kelman's call for a more effective deterrent through investigation and punishment in the United States seems a long way off for many developing countries. Without such a deterrent, then, it would seem that developing countries are left with the second-best option: the establishment of extensive rules. In their policy reform frameworks, the MDBs recognise this dilemma as do the relevant evaluations. Their response is to develop a more targeted approach to assessing risk. Rather than applying a blanket risk measure at a country level, the proposal is to look more specifically at the borrowing entity/agency in the country and its relative strengths and weaknesses in terms of procurement. The higher the risk rating of the agency, the greater would be the oversight and monitoring.

D. Reconciling the Arguments

It should be evident that both sides of the debate have strong arguments. The solution, then, is not so black and white. For those who argue for greater discretion, it is important

[45] OECD, 'Principles for Integrity in Public Procurement' (n 25) 9.

[46] European Commission, *Report from the Commission to the Council and the European Parliament: EU Anti-Corruption Report* (n 31).

[47] D LeBlanc and L Perreaux, 'Notes on a scandal: The story of the Charbonneau commission' *The Globe and Mail*, 17 October 2012, available at www.theglobeandmail.com/news/politics/notes-on-a-scandal-the-story-of-the-charbonneau-commission/article4619629.

to be specific about where greater discretion would contribute to better outcomes with limited risk and by whom it should be exercised. Similarly, for those who argue for stricter compliance, it is important to address the relative effectiveness of such rules and to consistently review the rules for continued relevance. Reconciling both sides requires a focus on outcomes and an assessment of benefits versus risks at each stage of the procurement process. As Herbert Kaufman once wrote, 'One person's "red tape" is another's treasured safeguard'.[48]

Consistent with the previous section, if one looks closely at the current approach of the MDBs for determining risks, the emphasis is singularly on the risks to the bid and award process. The level of complexity of the project, the relative cost and the capability of responsible institutions are seen in terms of what bidding approach should be applied and what *ex ante* clearance is required by the MDBs. This, however, ignores the relative risks at other stages of the process including upstream and, in particular, downstream. While the logic of assessing risk at each stage would seem evident, that is not reflected in current practice.

If one observes each stage of the procurement cycle, it is clear that, for all the rules, oversight and transparency applied to the bid and award stage, the contract management stage appears less constrained, with fewer rules, ineffective oversight and a lack of transparency. MDB policy is virtually silent on this fundamental discrepancy. Parallel efforts for enhanced transparency are being promoted, such as CoST and Open Contracting Partnership mentioned earlier, but these are outside formal policy and procedures. This 'blind spot' is evident in recent reviews of the lack of accessible information during project implementation beyond the bid and award of contracts.[49] Applying the lens of 'compliance versus discretion' to the contract management stage of the cycle, there appears to be a case for more compliance.

In the early design stage, extensive rules constrain the degree to which procurement staff can solicit the insight of potential suppliers as specifications are being prepared, for fear of a perception of conflict of interest and potential influences on the bidding documents. MDBs require client countries to hire consultants to prepare specifications who agree not to participate in the actual bidding process. This 'Chinese Wall' between procurement staff and potential supplier firms limits the ability of the procuring entity to take into account other ways of addressing its needs.

Most serious, then, is whether or not to allow for more discretion during the highly regulated bid and award stage. The new approaches to bid and award, beyond the straightforward lowest price determination, begin to open the door for some discretion as award criteria become more complex and less easily quantifiable.

E. Reform Response

The MDB policy reforms embrace a more extensive menu of tender options on the basis of the principle of 'fit for purpose'. This welcome modernisation of the policy is clearly

[48] H Kaufman, *Red Tape: Its Origins, Uses, and Abuses* (Washington DC, Brookings Institution Press, 1977) 19.

[49] J Gutman and C Horton, 'Accessibility and Effectiveness of Donor Disclosure Policies', Brookings Global Economy and Development Working Paper 85 (May 2015) available at www.brookings.edu/research/accessibility-and-effectiveness-of-donor-disclosure-policies-when-disclosure-clouds-transparency/.

aligned with ensuring that the selected mode of procurement is most appropriate for the type of investment. But it does raise concerns of fairness and clarity in terms of how various factors are taken into account in the final evaluation of bids. As discussed earlier, client countries are increasingly restricting discretion of executing agencies in order to avoid any perception of corruption or unfairness.

Ultimately it will come down to a question of what criteria will be applied in determining which country or agency will be allowed to apply alternative procurement methods. It also requires increasing the capability of procurement staff in the Bank and in the client countries. Lastly, it also underscores the need for the MDBs to clearly define their risk appetite. The debate around country systems at the World Bank became bogged down in arguing over how to define when a country passed the test.

While the new policy offers greater latitude in engaging with industry representatives upstream in the procurement cycle to help understand the markets and the alternative solutions and investment options when designing the investment and the procurement approach, there is no equivalent discussion of how to handle issues of discretion versus compliance downstream during contract implementation. As discussed earlier, it may be in the downstream stage of procurement that the balance between discretion versus compliance shifts towards greater compliance and fiduciary rule-making.

VI. Implications of an Outcomes-Based Approach: Determining the Roles of Stakeholders

A. Importance of Defining Roles

The previous two sections that call for broadening the focus to all stages of the procurement cycle and argue for a more analytical framework for balancing compliance versus discretion raise a third issue. What roles do the various stakeholders play during each stage of the cycle? Who has the power of discretion? What have been the effects of leaving these roles ill-defined and/or solely on the shoulders of the procurement staff? A policy that focuses only on the procurement professional is bound to fail. While the procurement agent's success is generally measured by a smooth and timely process, the success of the technical staff or programme manager is measured by the quality of the outcome. Thus, it is usually the technical staff that can provide judgement on what is and is not material in the process and what will contribute most to the quality of the outcome. Procurement policy cannot ignore the role of technical staff and the importance of their commitment and integration into the process. The weight of the roles of these two stakeholders will vary according to the stage of the procurement cycle with heavy inputs from technical experts during the design versus the heavy input by the procurement expert during the bid/award process. And the contract management stage represents the stage in which there is disagreement or lack of clarity over the relative roles.

Similarly, other stakeholders have substantive roles to play in ensuring the quality of outcomes such as the management of risks, particularly in the case of development aid. The MDBs as well as other donor agencies must define their roles and responsibilities in monitoring the use of funds and the outcomes. The client government has a critical role in ensuring systems, staff and institutional and legal frameworks to manage procurement. And clearly the private sector plays a critical role. Finally, it is crucial to provide space for civil society, especially the ultimate beneficiaries of the investment, to participate, contribute and monitor the process.

B. The Procurement Expert

There is recognition that procurement requires a professional stream and due accreditation. Presently there are various efforts to establish standards and provide such accreditation but these are far from taking hold worldwide, especially in developing countries. The MDBs have various modes of accreditation of staff for different types and different levels of procurement and these are continuously evolving. But there is recognition within the MDBs that staff skills in this area need to be upgraded to be able to handle the range of modes of procurement in the toolkit in order to properly advise countries. The profession is quickly changing, and staff preparation has fallen behind.

Besides the growing menu of procurement options, there has also been a tendency to add to the load of the procurement staff, placing more and more objectives onto the process and delegating responsibility for aspects well beyond the scope of that person's expertise. As social and environmental objectives are increasingly emphasised, the procurement expert is being asked to design a system that not only delivers the right outcome in terms of quality and price but also that it promotes targeted sources such as SMEs or historically disadvantaged populations or that considerations such as life-cycle costing or environmental factors are included in the bid criteria, well beyond the normal training of many procurement staff.

It is not surprising, then, that what has been called a 'risk-averse culture' has grown in procurement. This is a concern raised by the MDB evaluations but it is also highlighted in developed countries. Kelman identifies risk-averse behaviour as endemic to the procurement profession.[50] Similarly, Natsios calls the federal system in the United States 'overly risk averse'.[51] More recently, political scientist Darrell West opined about the US system: 'government bureaucrats know that a failure gets you on the front page of the newspaper; ten successes probably don't. And so there are kind of skewed incentives against risk-taking in the public sector'.[52] Applying judgement instead of following detailed rules leads to potential challenges from bidders as well as process delays. As timely conduct of procurement is often the key factor in a procurement agent's assessment, rather than procurement outcome, the incentive for procurement staff is to avoid the potential 'noise' of deviating from the rules. There is little to compensate the

[50] Kelman (n 40).
[51] Natsios (n 41) 57.
[52] The Brookings Institution, 'Social Physics: How Human Social Networks Spread Ideas', Panel Discussion at The Brookings Institution, Washington DC, 18 February 2014, available at www.brookings.edu/events/social-physics-how-human-social-networks-spread-ideas.

contracting officer for taking risks. Even if procurement policy allows for more discretion and the application of various modes of procurement, this risk-averse culture will still have to be faced.

Moreover, the procurement expert considers his or her job done when the contract is awarded. It is hard to believe, however, that such an expert would not be involved in ensuring that the contract is carried out according to what was agreed and to learn lessons from implementation to help guide future procurement. This is not to assign the primary burden for such implementation to the procurement expert (as some technical staff might argue), but rather to ensure they take a role and an interest in such oversight and evaluation.

C. The Technical Expert

A holistic perspective on the procurement cycle, including the design and setting of specifications and contract management, clearly indicates the important role that only the technical expert can play at key stages in the cycle. Procurement for information technology is different from procurement for pharmaceuticals, which is different from procurement for roads. The technical expert should understand the nature of the market and the important elements required to ensure the quality of the outcome. One would expect the technical expert to provide the professional judgement on what is material and what is not from a sectoral perspective. While the procurement expert is the virtual keeper of the rulebook, it is the technical expert who is key to applying effective discretion.

Moreover, the technical expert oversees project implementation, with a responsibility to ensure that contract management is consistent with expectations, that controls are in place to protect against corruption and that the terms continue to be relevant to quality outcomes. This refers to technical experts in the country as well as in the MDBs. In the earlier days of the MDBs, with most funding going towards infrastructure and a staff complement of engineers to match, the supervision function (now referred to as implementation support) was carried out by the MDB engineer who incorporated both technical and procurement expertise. In today's MDBs, with fewer engineers on board and a broader sectoral focus beyond infrastructure, a technical expert tends to steer clear of procurement.

The active engagement and commitment of the technical staff to the procurement function and cycle is absolutely essential. It is not that they need to be experts in procurement but that they are knowledgeable and engaged. It is unfortunate that most if not all university programmes for development practitioners and public policy-makers exclude any exposure to procurement, despite the fact that all of those who ultimately enter such fields will face this issue at some point in their careers.

D. The Government

The incentives that drive the procurement process are set by government. The government sets the rules and determines the accountability and related indices. If the focus is on turnaround time and minimum number of complaints, the procurement staff will focus accordingly. If the government focuses incentives and accountability on the outcomes and recognises the whole cycle, the results could be different. The World Bank's 2012 strategy for governance states the need for 'an operational policy framework that is less focused on transaction-based compliance and a corporate culture that provide incentives for both candor in the discussion of risks, and innovation and appropriate risk-taking for long-term development impact'.[53]

Most important is how the government actions contribute to the credibility of the process. Procurement needs to be seen as a core element in good governance. By encouraging and supporting transparency and the role of civil society, government can enhance credibility. By further supporting auditing, investigative functions and effective legal remedies, governments can deter fraud and corruption and permit greater discretion as indicated by Kelman.

E. The MDBs/Donor Community

Although MDB and donor funding for development represents a declining share of government expenditures, the impact of these institutions can still be significant in setting the standard, promoting credible approaches that balance fiduciary responsibility and the quality of the outcomes, and offering technical assistance and capacity-building. This requires adopting policies that represent the best practice in procurement adapted to the needs and context of the individual country and client institution. This also requires that the MDBs and donor community ensure the competency of their staff and the transparency of their mode of operation.

The MDBs and donors also must address the issue of risk aversion by staff. It seems evident that the efforts to promote accountability and fight corruption have had an effect on the ground. But it has also caused a reaction in avoiding decision-making and pushing issues 'up the chain of command'. While some of this can be addressed through better training and preparation and greater collaboration between technical and procurement staff, there is a need to clearly define the appetite for risk. Development aid is naturally risky business; otherwise, the private sector would have filled the void. But when management is unclear about what it means by 'informed' risk-taking and 'zero tolerance', it should not be surprised at the response of staff. Similarly, the aid community should be more strategic and targeted in its fights against corruption. Rules and procedures should be continuously reviewed to determine effectiveness and relevance.

Finally, the MDBs and the donor community need to move beyond simply disclosing information and look at the accessibility of the information they are disclosing. The true impact of their disclosure policies will be determined by the accessibility of the information by all types of stakeholders. Transparency in procurement is meaningless without attention to this issue.

[53] World Bank, 'Strengthening Governance: Tackling Corruption – The World Bank Group's Updated Strategy and Implementation Plan' (Washington DC, The World Bank Group, 2012) 47–48.

F. The Private Sector

The private sector worldwide has largely benefited from the procurement policies of the MDBs. The opening and maturing of markets and the expansion of participants have been the greatest contribution of these policies. There will be further benefits to upgrading the systems and practices of the developing countries beyond the transactions of the MDBs. While there is support for moving beyond price to incorporate more 'value for money' variables in the award equation, there is also a reluctance to lose the comfort of MDB presence to monitor processes.

The private sector can do more to explore ways to encourage innovation through procurement. It can also help to define industry standards that would normalise approaches to life-cycle costing and green procurement for various sectors. This assumes that views of developing countries are adequately represented. Both the MDBs and the private sector must encourage more interaction to address the challenges of applying a VfM approach.

Lastly, the private sector can do more to promote transparency and integrity. Active involvement of the private sector in initiatives such as CoST and Open Contracting Partnership can be the key ingredient to enhancing credibility and reducing cynicism surrounding public procurement.

G. Civil Society

Over the last 10 years, there have been an increasing number of initiatives to engage civil society and related organisations in the monitoring of procurement. A major focus has been on watching over the bid and award process. But where there is more opportunity for effective monitoring is with regard to contract implementation and management. Earlier in this chapter, it is discussed that the traditional model in which MDB project teams undertake such monitoring is no longer feasible to a sufficient scale and this would only affect a limited number of investments in any case as donor funding declines as a percentage of public investment. Government supervision is similarly inadequate on its own. This underscores the potential role for civil society. As more information is made available and more accessible, civil society organisations will have greater opportunities to fill an important oversight gap during this crucial stage of procurement. Such organisations have a particular incentive to look beyond simple compliance with rules but to the ultimate quality of the outcome. There are extensive examples underway with regard to small-scale infrastructure investments for community development. There is less experience with larger-scale investments but the potential benefits should be high.

To take advantage of the potential role of civil society, there are three issues that need to be addressed: formal recognition of civil society organisations; sustainable source of funding of such efforts; and capacity-building. The first issue of formal recognition is clearly necessary. Without government recognition, such organisations have limited ability to channel their findings through the system and have concerns addressed. It is important that there is a feedback loop with government to ensure that actions are taken.

The funding issue is complex as there is a need to avoid actual or perceived conflicts of interest as well as to ensure sufficient and sustainable funds. Will a civil society organisation be willing to take on the government if the funding comes from the government? In the past, there were concerns that government financing would lead to conflicts of interest or at least the perception of conflicts. Another option is financing by the MDBs, but conflict of interest concerns affect the credibility of such funding as well. A good option is donor funding such as a multi- or single-donor trust fund. But this is generally unsustainable for extended periods as such budgets cannot be guaranteed from year to year. The best option would seem to be a category for funding under a project for which financing is made for the duration of the project via a trust fund of donors not directly involved in the project. Yet, this will not solve the problem of serving the non-donor funded investments. A second best option would be a fund financed by government but independently managed.

The third issue, though, is equally fundamental. If civil society organisations do not have the capability to understand and monitor procurement, the credibility and effectiveness of these organisations will be undermined. As the MDBs and the donor community place more emphasis on capacity-building and local skill development under the procurement reform agenda, it is important that this includes a component for the appropriate capacity-building of local civil society organisations. And this capacity-building should focus not just on bid and award but address the other stages of the cycle as well, especially contract monitoring.

H. Reform Response

In the end it comes down to people and whether the roles are clear and their capability commensurate to the task. This has been recognised all across the MDBs. There is a particularly heavy emphasis on training procurement staff both in the MDBs as well as in the client countries themselves. Indeed, one notable element of the reform is the focus on capacity-building over and beyond the fiduciary focus on specific transactions. The broadening of the menu of procurement options and the attention to systems goes beyond the traditional role of an MDB procurement staff. The World Bank estimates that only 10 per cent of their over 200 procurement staff are prepared at such a level.[54]

To respond to the challenges required to make procurement reform affect outcomes, however, requires the inputs of a range of stakeholders and not just procurement specialists. It requires technical staff to be able to define clearly what is required, to understand the particular industry involved, assess criteria for evaluation and to ensure the monitoring of implementation. It requires policy-makers to understand the basics of procurement and its potential as a strategic instrument and the risks at each stage of the process. And it requires civil society to understand what is to be provided so that they can help to monitor and adapt during implementation. This all leads to the need

[54] Available at https://wbnpf.procurementinet.org/sites/default/files/Board-Paper-phase-ii-the-new-procurement-framework.pdf.

to clarify the roles of the different stakeholders at each stage of the cycle. It is not about simply applying discretion but rather who is the most appropriate stakeholder to apply discretion and who is responsible for monitoring that such discretion is appropriately applied. The World Bank policy[55] is not clear about the role of stakeholders other than procurement specialists, and especially about the role of technical staff in the Bank or in the client country.

As a result, its training efforts do not capture the scope and scale that is required to reach this larger audience. The implementation paper does recognise the need for such training across stakeholders but its programme, at least in the short-term, is directed at procurement staff.[56]

VII. Conclusion

As we enter the era of the Sustainable Development Goals (SDGs), it is very timely that it coincides with the MDBs pursuing a major overhaul of their procurement policies and practices governing development aid and investment. Recognising procurement as a strategic instrument for reaching development goals raises the challenge for all stakeholders to become engaged in the reform dialogue.

While MDB policy reform is framed with an emphasis on the impact of on investment outcomes, the question remains whether the practices and procedures of the MDBs will change sufficiently to achieve that objective. Writing a policy is easy, or at least easier, than implementing reforms that require a change in practice and culture. It is thus important to assess how the policy and related practices and procedures are adapted to address the three implications/challenges of applying an outcomes-based approach.

Ultimately, the best clue to whether the reforms are truly directed at improving outcomes is the method of evaluation and monitoring that the MDBs propose to measure progress. Historically MDBs have measured procurement effectiveness and efficiency against easily quantifiable indicators such as processing time of bid and award or number of bidders as a sign of the level of competition. All of these are directed at the bid and award stage of procurement and do not provide an indication of development impact.

The World Bank's implementation strategy includes a discussion of monitoring and evaluation. While the system is still to be prepared and indicators developed, the Bank states: 'M&E will assess the key areas of the implementation … focusing on their development impact'.[57] The discussion of what this might mean, however, quickly turns to measurable indicators including loan disbursements.

[55] Available at www.worldbank.org/en/projects-operations/products-and-services/brief/procurement-new-framework, Annex K.

[56] ibid.

[57] Available at https://wbnpf.procurementinet.org/sites/default/files/Board-Paper-phase-ii-the-new-procurement-framework.pdf, Annex K.

What is needed is a wholesale re-thinking of how to evaluate procurement beyond these traditional indicators. The question needs to be asked in terms of how did the design, process and actual implementation along the whole procurement cycle affect the project outcomes. One must look at the project outcome and then assess how the procurement process contributed to that outcome. If there were failures or suboptimal results, are they attributable to any particular stage of the procurement cycle? This is not easily reduced to a set of cross-cutting indicators. It is also not an evaluation that can be left only to procurement experts. Other stakeholders should be involved, especially the sectoral technical experts. The failure of previous evaluations is that they did not do this and thus did not focus on development outcome.

There are great expectations given the recent policy discussions but the nature of the reforms and the impact on the existing culture of procurement underscore the challenges for implementation and evaluation.

16

Concluding Remarks: 'Are We There Yet'?

ANNAMARIA LA CHIMIA AND PETER TREPTE

I. Introduction

Alice's conundrum is one that is becoming ever more pertinent to the subject matter of this book, namely the role of procurement in aid effectiveness. Having floundered for a number of years in the general approach to aid delivery, mostly seen as a purely technical issue of efficient delivery, procurement found a place as part of the overall governance agenda of the 1980s and beyond which addressed both institutions and processes before falling squarely within the aid effectiveness objectives conceived during the Monterrey Consensus and further articulated in the Paris Declaration and subsequent High-Level Fora. The roads to these objectives, in particular, to harmonisation, alignment, use of country systems and ownership, appear to have been both circuitous and potentially misconceived. Refining the objectives under the guise of development effectiveness (to include partnerships for development, a focus on results together with transparency and shared responsibility), and thus the routes to attaining them, appears not to have brought us any closer to reaching them. The emergence of new destinations (performance/outcomes-based procurement and sustainability) fundamentally alters the road so far trodden and sets us on some new paths.

II. False Starts and Dead Ends

The harmonisation road which began life as a desire to provide homogeneity and reduce capacity erosion in borrower countries has been perhaps the longest road. Great strides were made before the Paris Declaration through the efforts of the multilateral development banks (MDBs) which succeeded in largely standardising their own procurement guidelines and bidding documents (chapter 13). As a measure of harmonisation, this may now be seen as something of a high point, although as a measure for promoting aid effectiveness, its success is surely open to doubt. In the 1980s, harmonisation came to be seen as part of the governance agenda which led to a strong emphasis on improved governance structures and processes as the only way to promote aid success. More than just an issue of technical efficiency in the delivery of aid, procurement became part of the move to ensure robust institutions pursuing appropriate processes guaranteeing probity and integrity. As such, harmonisation, viewed as a step towards creating an ideal benchmark against which national systems could be measured, was imposed on beneficiary countries by way of conditionalities as part of the loan process (chapter 3). This was strengthened later by MDB efforts to create internationally acceptable benchmark tools to measure and assess national procurement systems in a way which allowed for little departure from the accepted norms (chapter 3 and chapter 9).

As recognised by the World Bank (chapter 13), the result of almost two decades of harmonisation was to create a 'model' procurement system which was heavily standardised, prescriptive and compliance based. Whilst this was driven in part by a desire to achieve technical efficiency in the implementation of donor projects through improved delivery and fiduciary compliance, it did not allow context to be taken into account and prevented the customisation of the procurement approach that came to be seen as an essential feature of country ownership. That lack of ownership and, more practically, the inability of the borrowers and donors properly to take into account the relevant context in determining the most effective procurement approach (whether that is country context, relevant market conditions, levels of capacity or the scope and management of risk), is now seen as an impediment to the success of procurement itself and thus, by implication, of the effectiveness of the aid that underpins it. It is perhaps no surprise that the World Bank and some of the other MDBs are moving away from this harmonised ideal (chapters 12 and 13) at a rapid pace. Whilst the MDBs continue to preach harmonisation, their actions speak clearly of new directions.

The disillusion with harmonisation spreads further (chapter 4) and takes in far-reaching procurement initiatives and systems (such as the UNCITRAL Model Law on Procurement and the World Trade Organization's Government Procurement Agreement) and is impacted by world events. Similarly, the coordinated and benign approach to development procurement which had seen some reduction in political and economic motivations to development assistance, has also disintegrated in the face of economic woes and crises in globalisation. Tied aid is re-emerging as an economic and political tool (chapter 6) putting into question the purity of the altruism of donors and laying bare the weaknesses of a system based on soft-law commitments and goodwill endeavours. Such a statement applies equally to the broader aid effectiveness agenda which, though framed as high level, has been little more than a series of 'soft' (unenforceable) political commitments which have been mostly honoured in the breach. Despite the grandstanding, the various promised paths to greater aid effectiveness have each crumbled in turn.

The harmonisation effort had also rallied behind the anti-corruption agenda creating a common front against corruption in procurement through the establishment of a largely standardised approach. Such standardisation has also, seemingly, failed to produce any significant results, at least none that can be supported by evidence, which again suggests the inadequacy of the chosen route (chapter 7). Harmonisation is clearly not the panacea it was hailed to be.

The journey to the other side of the harmonisation coin, namely alignment, has fared little better. Ostensibly a method of bringing together national procurement systems with donor systems, this was conceived as a means, ultimately, of creating national ownership through the ability of donors to rely on country procurement systems in the implementation of funded projects. The march towards the objectives of alignment (chapter 5) and the use of country systems (chapter 10) has led perhaps to the most spectacular, albeit unacknowledged, failures. There were many roadblocks to this destination, including the reliance placed on the harmonised model which, as we have seen, has also led to failure. Alignment was maybe never destined to succeed and was always an unachievable and inappropriate goal given the conflicting objectives of donors and beneficiary countries (chapter 5). It may be that this was always a destination which could never have been reached and the continuing failure of the donor community to make any significant gains in this direction makes their constant refrain to rely on country systems sound hollow and disingenuous at best.

III. Alternative Routes

It is perhaps noteworthy that when the group of stakeholders that began the highly visible campaign for improved aid effectiveness, notably in Monterey and Paris, placing reliance on, *inter alia*, harmonisation, alignment, use of country systems and ownership, met in their last High-Level Forum in Busan, the objective of their efforts mutated from achieving aid effectiveness to seeking development effectiveness. The articulation of the objectives also changed (chapter 3) and, although familiar, clearly led to a change of emphasis, bringing in a much wider range of goals. It is inevitable, therefore, that the role of procurement and the expression of what it might be able to achieve in the context of development effectiveness should also change. That is what has been seen on the ground.

The World Bank has led the way (chapter 12 and 13) in reforming MDB objectives by choosing, rather independently, to abandon the standardisation which emerged from the harmonisation process and focus instead on improving performance and the outcomes of the procurement process, basing itself much more on market and risk analyses with a view to adapting the procurement approach to one which is more relevant to the context (fit for purpose) and achieving better value for money. This is a modern approach which implies not technical efficiency but technical competence and a broader understanding of how procurement can be used to achieve more valuable outcomes (chapter 15).

Some other MDBs, but not all, have followed a similar but not identical path (chapter 13). The African Development Bank, for example, has also amended its rules to place greater emphasis on value for money (based on expanded objectives) whilst ensuring fiduciary compliance. The Asian Development Bank also seeks value for money and looks at the relevant markets and underlying risks but its objectives are primarily to improve timeliness, quality and delivery. The Asian Infrastructure and Investment Bank has partly followed the World Bank's lead but has not increased the flexibility inherent in a greater choice of procurement methods. Whilst the direction is similar, the paths taken are quite different. Other MDBs appear to be maintaining their current trajectories or envisage changes relevant to their own regions.

Whatever the public statements and whatever the future holds, the current road to harmonisation has come to an abrupt end and has been replaced by alternative routes to improved performance and better outcomes. This approach takes us beyond the incrementalism of the past, characterised as it was by the constant refinement of specific rules and clauses (chapter 3 and chapter 13) to satisfy one or other donor, and leads us to a much more productive discussion about the purpose of the procurement function and its articulation through the entire procurement cycle to allow for quality outcomes to be planned, procured, implemented and managed effectively.

Similarly, other donors have been focusing on practical measures to assess and improve procurement performance and outcomes. This might include improving means of relying on country systems (chapter 10), supporting the efforts of developing countries to reform their procurement systems (chapter 14) or building professional agency capacity as a means of enabling improved procurement outcomes (chapter 11).

Contemporaneously with the promotion of the aid effectiveness agenda and informing it, the development world witnessed the evolution of the UN's Millennium Development Goals to the Sustainable Development Goals which now feature prominently in any development programme and which have had a significant impact in the design and implementation of procurement reform (chapter 8). At the same time, the MAPS tool which appears to have been misused in the context of alignment has now been revised to offer a more aspirational assessment tool enabling countries to determine their own path to improved procurement outcomes (chapter 9) which includes sustainability.

IV. An Open Road

Notwithstanding the benefits of the road travelled thus far, including a better appreciation of the role of procurement in aid effectiveness, the aid effectiveness agenda of the last two decades based on harmonisation, alignment, use of country systems and ownership has, at the very least, run out of steam. Harmonisation has led to a more consistent approach to procurement and better understanding of what we might call good procurement rules (in terms of processes, methods and practices); the alignment effort has supported the development of countries' own procurement systems and had a positive effect on country ownership, even if the use of those country systems has been something of an unattainable goal. At the same time, it is clear that this was not enough. These approaches have brought us to a roadblock. Harmonisation has led to a level of standardisation and prescription which yields an inflexible stalemate where countries and donors cannot move to the next level. What that next level might be remains to be tested.

One possibility is to place greater emphasis on the destination in terms of better defining the outcomes of procurement. Rather than rely on the blind application of a set of standardised procurement rules to achieve the best results in terms of technical efficiency (though improved performance also requires timeliness, quality and efficient delivery), new approaches focus on improving performance and value for money by analysing and recognising the desired development outcomes, the market context and the inherent risks as a means of adopting the most appropriate procurement method. This requires customisation rather than harmonisation, flexibility rather than standardisation but the earlier achievements (for there is no reinventing of the wheel) provide a foundation on which to build. Such an approach also implies greater emphasis on borrower country capacity (institutional and personal) but for improved competence rather than greater compliance.

Sustainable procurement has also become important and allows borrowers to decide what outcomes are desirable or what needs to be taken into account in delivering the desired outcomes. This may include a broader range of development outcomes and will include the application of environmental requirements and social development objectives. This is seen as improving development targets rather than merely making aid effective.

Whatever lays in store, the new directions for development effectiveness as seen through the prism of public procurement and its reform promise to provide ample scope for further debate and controversy and the enduring need of donors to account for the expenditure of aid money will ensure that it will continue to be a vibrant area for research and reflection.

We started this chapter with Alice; we will end it with the Cheshire Cat. The false starts and dead ends of the journey so far do not mean the end of the journey. What has been achieved so far, lays the foundation for what is to come and the purpose of this publication was simply to create a forum within which that discussion can take place. Despite the opening up of some exciting new directions, these appear to be a reaction to the current status rather than an settled statement of where we need to be; the ultimate destination has yet to be articulated. Since we are still not clear on where we are going, the Cheshire Cat's answer to Alice is probably just as apposite as her question; it does not seem to matter which way we go. For sure, though, we still have a long journey before we 'get to somewhere'. We are not there yet.

INDEX

NB–page locators given in **bold** denote information in tables and those in *italics* denote information in figures.